Winner of the Fletcher Pratt Lit...
Presented by The Civil War Round Table of New York

"If asked to list my dozen favorite Civil War books, *The Class of 1846* would be included. . . . John C. Waugh, a distinguished journalist, gives to his story of the class a special and very human dimension that is missing from their standard biographies and autobiographies."

—Edwin C. Bearss
Author of *Vicksburg Campaign*

"First-rate and moving . . . A grand account . . . Waugh has vividly reconstructed the stirring, and often tragic, account of perhaps the most illustrious class ever to emerge from the military academy. . . . Thanks to Waugh, the legacy of that class—its sense of duty and honor—rings as clearly now as then. . . . This is history, but in the form of drama based on a broad array of background materials, including letters and memoirs. . . . Waugh's account of the West Point class of 1846 seems likely to become a minor classic."

—*The Christian Science Monitor*

"Penetrating . . . [A] fine book . . . There are as many ways to tell the story of the Civil War as there are writers to tell it, but some are more imaginative than others. John C. Waugh must be given high points for originality."

—*The Washington Post Book World*

"[Waugh] writes with a fine sense of irony and understated humor, yet misses none of the emotional drama of friends facing one another on the battlefield."

—*The Seattle Times*

"First class work . . . Waugh has catapulted himself into the first circle of those writers who concentrate on the Civil War. His first foray into the field is poignant and exciting, top notch in every way. Scrupulous in its research, enormous in breadth and scope, this is a highly readable history on the same level as the best of Catton or Foote. This is history as it should be told, powerful and sweeping, evocative to the very core."

—*The Tampa Tribune and Times*

"[A] wonderful saga . . . Of epic proportions equal to that of Michael Shaara's *The Killer Angels* . . . With wit and anecdote John C. Waugh has masterfully written this story of 'a brothers war.'"

—*BookPage*

Please turn the page for more reviews. . . .

"A COMPELLING WORK

which entertains was well as informs the general reader. . . . Waugh breathes life into the people he writes about . . . the men of '46 are well worth knowing, and John Waugh is to be commended for affording us the opportunity to make their acquaintance."

—James L. Morrison, Jr., Ph.D., Col. U.S.A. (Ret.)
Professor Emeritus,
York College of Pennsylvania
Author of *The Best School in the World:*
West Point, the Pre-Civil War Years, 1833-1860

"While written accounts of most of these soldiers already exist, Waugh presents his sketches in a way that makes them fresh again. . . . In some works, historical figures are as cold and lifeless as the statues that commemorate their victories: this is definitely not true of John C. Waugh and *The Class of 1846*. Waugh's writing style breathes life into his subjects and gives his readers a view of Jackson, McClellan, and their classmates as they have rarely been seen before. This touching story would be an attractive addition to many personal and scholarly libraries."

—*The Journal of Southern History*

"Waugh's description of [Jackson's] death is splendidly done, as is Waugh's retelling of Gettysburg, particularly of Pickett's charge, and of Lee's surrender. . . . Despite its massive subject, it is filled with the kind of incidents, quotations and anecdotes that make the Civil War book endlessly fascinating. It's a first-rate book that is highly recommended."

—*Gazette-Mail Sunday Life* (Charleston, W.V.)

"Every year, dozens of new books are published, many by first-rate scholar-writers. Only a handful of those touch our hearts and minds. John C. Waugh's book does more than that—it will haunt you. After reading it, a visit to a Civil War battlefield will take on a whole new meaning. Bring lots of tissues."

—*Martinsburgh Journal* (W.V.)

"Boasting a vigorous narrative that appeals to lay readers, *The Class of 1846* also merits the attention of scholars. . . . Better than any previous author, Waugh fleshes out these generalizations and conveys how profoundly the West Point experience influenced the lives of graduates. . . . Waugh captures the rhythms and traditions of life at the Academy, explores the bonding effect of service in Mexico and on the United States frontier, and touches on other factors that forged a close fraternity among the officers."

—*Reviews in American History*

"An exceedingly well-written narrative . . . Wonderful, poignant stories, often alluded to but rarely told, and even more rarely told well."

—*Kirkus Reviews*

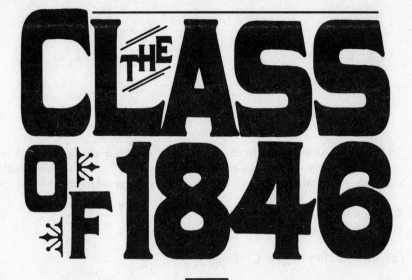

THE CLASS OF 1846

FROM WEST POINT TO APPOMATTOX: STONEWALL JACKSON, GEORGE McCLELLAN AND THEIR BROTHERS

JOHN C. WAUGH

Ballantine Books • New York

A Ballantine Book
Published by The Ballantine Publishing Group

Copyright © 1994 by John C. Waugh

All rights reserved under International and Pan-American Copyright Conventions. Published in the United States by The Ballantine Publishing Group, a division of Random House, Inc., New York, and distributed in Canada by Random House of Canada Limited, Toronto. Originally published by Warner Books, Inc., in 1994.

Ballantine and colophon are registered trademarks of Random House, Inc.

http://www.randomhouse.com/BB/

Library of Congress Catalog Card Number: 99-90081

ISBN: 0-345-43403-X

Manufactured in the United States of America

Cover design by David Stevenson
Cover illustration courtesy of The West Point Museum Collection United States Military Academy
Book design by L. McRee

First Ballantine Books Edition: May 1999

10 9 8 7 6 5 4 3 2

For Kathleen, my own companion in exile as I went off to war with the Class of 1846.

Contents

Contents

Contents

PART 3   AND THE WAR CAME

PART 4   DOWN IN THE VALLEY

PART 5   BROTHER AGAINST BROTHER

PART 6   CLOSING OUT THE WAR

Foreword
by
JAMES M. MCPHERSON

The description of the American Civil War as a war of brothers is more than a cliché. The war did divide families, especially in the border states. In hundreds of cases brother and brother, uncle and nephew, even father and son or son-in-law chose different sides. More than once they faced each other on the battlefield. Senator John J. Crittenden of Kentucky, whose ill-fated compromise proposal of 1861 failed to avert war, had one son who became a Union general and another who became a Confederate general. Seven brothers and brothers-in-law of Mary Todd Lincoln fought against the army whose commander in chief was her husband.

In a metaphorical as well as a literal sense it was a brothers' war. Americans often likened themselves to a family formed by the common heritage of a revolution that forged the nation and launched it on a perilous experiment of republican government. The quarrels that led to the falling out of 1861 threatened the survival not only of that experiment but also of the family itself.

These two themes of the brothers' war—literal and metaphorical—have received thorough treatment in the vast literature on the Civil War. This book treats a third aspect of the phenomenon. The United States Military Academy at West Point created a band of brothers more tightly bonded by mutual hardship and danger in war than biological brothers. Officers who fought shoulder to shoulder against a common enemy in Mexico from 1846 to 1848 fought against each other in the war of 1861 to 1865. Serving together on the staff of General-in-Chief Winfield Scott in Mexico were George B. McClellan and Pierre G. T. Beauregard. Captain Robert E. Lee's daring reconnaissances behind Mexican lines prepared the way for two crucial American victories in 1847; after one of those battles Captain Lee officially commended Lieutenant Ulysses S. Grant. The latter received official thanks for his role in the attack on Mexico City; those thanks were conveyed to him by Lieutenant John Pemberton, who sixteen years later would surrender to Grant at Vicksburg. Lieutenants James Longstreet and Winfield Scott Hancock fought side by side in the battle of Churubusco; sixteen years later Longstreet commanded the attack on Hancock's corps at Gettysburg, an attack led by George Pickett who doubtless recalled the day he picked up the colors of the Eighth Infantry in its assault at Chapultepec when Lieutenant Longstreet fell wounded while carrying those colors. Winning brevets for their performance in this battle, lieutenants Thomas J. Jackson and George Henry Gordon (both of the class of 1846) would fight against each other in the Shenandoah Valley fifteen years later. At Buena Fista in 1847, artillery officers George H. Thomas and Braxton Bragg fought alongside each other with the same spirit they would show as opposing commanders at Missionary Ridge a thousand miles and sixteen years distant.

And so it went. Most of the commanders of the Union and Confederate armies that slaughtered each other to the tune of 620,000 war dead from 1861 to 1865 had fought together as brothers in arms in Mexico—and in the Indian wars of the 1850s. Here, truly, was a brothers' war. And for no West Point class was this tragedy more poignant than for the class of 1846. Graduating just as the Mexican War began, fifty-three of the fifty-nine members of this class (the largest in the Academy's history to that time) fought in Mexico. Four of them lost their lives there. Two more were killed fighting Indians in the 1850s. Ten members of that class became Confederate generals; twelve became Union generals; three of the Confederates and one of the Unionists were killed or mortally wounded in action during the Civil War. *The Class of 1846* is their story.

And never has this story of a brothers' war been told so well. Jack Waugh takes these men from their first fearful day as plebes at West Point through their careers together and apart. He blends humor and anecdote with stirring narrative and incisive analysis. The reader learns how George McClellan and A. P. Hill, roommates at the Point and friends for life, courted the same woman. In that contest McClellan exhibited more determination and achieved greater success than he ever experienced on a Civil War battlefield.

The two most illustrious alumni of the class of 1846 were McClellan and Jackson. For the Civil War years this book becomes largely their story. In this interpretation of these two leaders, Jack Waugh does not challenge the orthodox portrait of McClellan as a disappointing failure and of Jackson as an eccentric genius. Indeed, this hard-hitting narrative sharpens and clarifies the portrait so that the reader comes away in full agreement with the author's conclusion that "McClellan had failed to fulfill the shining promise of greatness" while Jackson "turned out to be one of the best generals the world has ever produced."

But the two-thirds of this book that focuses on the Civil War is more than the story of McClellan and Jackson. The twenty other members of the class of 1846 who fought in that conflict play important supporting roles. At times, several of them appear on the stage together. "Indeed," Waugh writes, "there could have been a class reunion on the banks of the Antietam if the times had not been so troubled." McClellan of course commanded the Union army and Jackson commanded half of the Confederate army in that battle. Eight other members of the class, five Unionists and three Confederates, faced each other in the bloodiest single day of American history. And it was A. P. Hill's flank attack late in the day against his good friend Ambrose Burnside's (class of 1847) corps that prevented a complete victory for his former roommate and rival in love, George McClellan.

At Gettysburg, too, there occurred dramatic confrontations between former classmates and brothers in arms. Jackson and McClellan had been removed from the scene—one by death and the other by dismissal. But a half-dozen other members of the class of 1846 were there. The Union division commanded by John Gibbon (a North Carolinian whose three brothers fought for the Confederacy) bore the brunt of the assault commanded by his classmate George Pickett. The repulse of Pickett's charge by Gibbon's men was a microcosm of the Civil War—and of the part played in it by the class of 1846. Here is their story, told by a master craftsman, a saga of a band of brothers whose tragic separation was the nation's tragedy but whose reunification after Appomattox also became the nation's triumph.

Cast
of
Characters

The main characters in these true stories were at one time or another members of the West Point class of 1846, arguably the most illustrious of the academy's antebellum years. Thirty-four of them appear in this book in various roles, large and small. Of those, most started and graduated with the class. Some fell back into it from the class ahead; a few dropped out of it into the class behind and graduated a year later; a few didn't graduate at all. For purposes of this narrative all are considered members of the class of 1846.

A handful of the thirty-four listed here play starring roles, reappearing many times throughout the book. Some take featured parts and appear less frequently. Others are bit players, flashing for but a passing instant across a passing page, often on the way to their graves. A few in the class are merely mentioned, or not mentioned at all, and therefore are not listed in this cast of characters. Most, but not all, lived to fight in the Civil War. Many of them became generals. A few of them became immortal.

The following list of these thirty-four is offered as a thumbnail guide to their lives up through the rebellion, to help track them along the way. To learn what really happened to them, you must read on.

Name	Class Ranking	Highest Rank in Civil War	Union or Confederate
Adams, John	25	Brigadier General	Confederate—Killed at Franklin in 1864
Bacon, Rufus	23	Committed suicide in 1846	
Botts, Archibald	57	Died in Mexico in 1847	
Couch, Darius Nash	13	Major General	Union
Derby, George Horatio	7	Died as the war began, a celebrated American humorist	
Dutton, William	15	Colonel	Union—died in 1862
Easley, Thomas	48	Killed in the Mexican War in 1847	
Foster, John Gray	4	Major General	Union
Fry, Birkett Davenport	Dismissed	Brigadier General	Confederate
Gardner, William Montgomery	55	Brigadier General	Confederate
Gibbon, John	Graduated in 1847	Major General	Union
Gordon, George Henry	43	Major General	Union
Hardcastle, Edmund Lafayette	5	Resigned from the army in 1856	
Hill, Ambrose Powell	Graduated in 1847	Lieutenant General	Confederate—Killed at Petersburg in 1865
Jackson, Thomas Jonathan	17	Lieutenant General	Confederate—Mortally wounded at Chancellorsville in 1863

Name	Class Ranking	Highest Rank in Civil War	Union or Confederate
Jones, David Rumph	41	Major General	Confederate—Died in 1863
Lowe, Thomas J.	Dismissed for irrepressibly questionable conduct		
McClellan, George Brinton	2	Major General	Union
Maury, Dabney Herndon	37	Major General	Confederate
Maxey, Samuel Bell	58	Major General	Confederate
Oakes, James	34	Brigadier General	Union
Pickett, George Edward	59	Major General	Confederate
Raymond, Samuel H.	Died at West Point in 1845		
Reno, Jesse Lee	8	Major General	Union—Killed at South Mountain in 1862
Rodgers, Alexander Perry	30	Killed in the Mexican War in 1847	
Seymour, Truman	19	Major General	Union
Stewart, Charles Seaforth	1	Colonel	Union
Stoneman, George	33	Major General	Union
Stuart, James	39	Killed in the Indian Wars in 1851	
Sturgis, Samuel Davis	32	Major General	Union
Taylor, Oliver Hazard Perry	31	Killed in the Indian Wars in 1858	

Name	Class Ranking	Highest Rank in Civil War	Union or Confederate
Turnley, Parmenas Taylor	40	Captain	Union—Disabled and retired in 1863
Wilcox, Cadmus Marcellus	54	Major General	Confederate
Wilson, Clarendon J. L.	9	Died in New Mexico Territory in 1853	

PART 1
WEST
POINT

From
Every Degree of
Provincialism

Late spring had come at last to western Virginia in 1842, the trees were green again on the mountains, and Gibson Butcher was going to West Point. But Thomas J. Jackson couldn't generate much enthusiasm for his friend's good fortune. He wished he were going instead. He had wanted that appointment himself.

Earlier in the spring, four of them had taken an informal examination at the Bailey House in Weston. It had seemed the only fair way to see who was best qualified. Jackson had done all right, considering his education, but not good enough. Butcher was better at arithmetic, and everybody knew mathematics was the most important subject taught at West Point. So it was Butcher's name that Samuel L. Hays, the district's first-term Democratic congressman, sent to the secretary of war. It was Hays's first appointment to the military academy, and he wanted it to be right.

Butcher left in late May and arrived at the steamboat landing on the Hudson River on June 3. He was a young man of good character, well thought of and well connected in the district. He had a quick mind, and he was ambitious. It was believed he would do well at West Point.

But the academy wasn't what Butcher thought it would be—not

at all. When he saw what awaited him on the plain above the landing, he paled. When he learned of all of the duties, the discipline, the marching and studying he would have to do, he started back toward the landing. He was soon gone, telling nobody he was leaving.

At home again and glad to be back, he stopped at Jackson's Mill on the West Fork River between Weston and Clarksburg, where Tom lived with his uncle Cummins, one of the district's numerous and prominent Jacksons. Tom's father had died when he was only two years old, and he had come eventually under the care of this strapping, good-hearted uncle. Butcher knew how badly Tom had wanted that appointment. He could have it now if he still wanted it, because Butcher could never consent to live that kind of life.

Jackson's blue-gray eyes must have glowed as Butcher explained what had happened. Here was a second chance. He might not be as good as Butcher at arithmetic, but the examination at the Bailey House hadn't tested for doggedness. Nobody could outdo Tom Jackson for doggedness. In Butcher's place he never would have left West Point voluntarily once he arrived, no matter how much it distressed him. They would have had to throw him out. That's the way he was.[1]

Jackson was a constable in Lewis County, one of the youngest, at eighteen, in that part of the country. But his prospects were not promising. He was as ambitious as Butcher, perhaps more so. He wanted to make something of himself in the world, and that required a better education than he had or was likely to get there in the mountains. He didn't necessarily want to be a soldier. Soldiers were as rare in those parts as educations. Tom had perhaps never seen a soldier in his life.

But at the military academy educations were free, and the best you could get. Nearly twenty years before, President Andrew Jackson had called West Point "the best school in the world."[2] The academy still set the standard among institutions of higher learning in the country for engineering and science. West Point graduates were not only going on to become soldiers, but also engineers—among the finest in the world. Its graduates were designing and building the nation's most dramatic new internal improvements—its major roads, dams, canals, harbors, and railroads. An education like that was worth having, and now he might have it after all.[3]

The way seemed clear. Still, many of Jackson's friends and neigh-

4

bors were uneasy. There might be a problem in his obvious lack of academic preparation. He had virtually none. There was no doubt about his character, integrity, perseverance, or common sense. He had plenty of all that, and those who knew him were well disposed to his appointment. But he had little formal schooling. Could he stand up to the tough academic and disciplinary demands that had repelled Butcher?

Jackson answered this question in his abrupt, forthright manner. "I am very ignorant," he told one friend who asked it, "but I can make it up in study. I know I have the energy and I think I have the intellect."[4]

At least he was frank, as always. So with the blessings of his neighbors and friends, he packed his belongings and letters and petitions of support into two travel-stained saddlebags. Wearing his gray homespun, his wagoner's hat, and his outsized brogans, he mounted a borrowed horse and, with a young black slave as his companion, rode to Clarksburg to catch the stage on the first leg of the journey to Washington. Since time was short, he would have to present himself in person to Hays, win his support, and if appointed go on immediately from there to West Point.

When the two riders reached Clarksburg, they found that the Pioneer Stage Line's eastbound coach had already departed. They galloped on, overtaking it outside of Grafton, about twenty miles to the east. Jackson climbed aboard and his companion turned back toward home, riding one horse and leading the other. The stage lurched on into Maryland, where at the Green Valley depot east of Cumberland, Jackson caught a Baltimore and Ohio passenger train.

The cars pulled into the rail station in Washington on June 17. Just a few blocks away Jackson could see the shiny copper-sheathed dome of the capitol. He set out in that direction to find his congressman.[5]

Hays knew nothing of Butcher's defection from West Point, or that this rustic self-appointed replacement was about to stamp into his office. But the farmer-congressman from Lewis County, with his well-known flair for oratory, was a practical politician. He had been elected to his seat in the Twenty-seventh Congress only the year before, and he was heavily indebted to the political backing and good will of the Jacksons, so plentiful and powerful in his district—and

5

many of them related in one way or another to Tom. He was certain to go along with this unexpected last-minute switch of cadets. It was the secretary of war who would have to be convinced.

Still, Hays must have been surprised to see this particular Jackson walk into his office with the two saddlebags draped over his slim shoulders. It was not an unfamiliar sight. Cummins Jackson was Hays's neighbor in Lewis County, and the congressman knew Tom well. But he had never expected to see him striding into his office in Washington.[6]

Jackson began pulling papers and letters from the saddlebags and handing them to Hays.

"It is with deep regret," the letter from Butcher began, "that I have now to send you my resignation as 'Cadet' in the West Point Military Academy."

Hays must have scowled. His first appointment, and it had gone wrong.

"My friends here think it would have been a decided advantage for me to have remained at West Point," the letter said, "and I am of the same opinion if I could have remained there contented but this I could not do."

At the end of the letter Butcher endorsed Jackson as his replacement: "Mr. Jackson will deliver this letter to you, who is an applicant for the appointment."[7]

Jackson handed Hays a letter from Smith Gibson, a neighbor who had known him from childhood. "A meritorious young man . . ." Gibson said of Jackson, "quite a smart youth in every respect for his age and opportunity." Evan Carmack in another letter of endorsement saluted Jackson's "many noble facultys of soul and great moral worth." He assured his friend Hays that taking everything into consideration, "a better selection could not be made, west of the mountains. . . ."[8]

Two petitions pulled from the saddlebags praised the young man's "good demeanor and upright Deportment," his industry, perseverance, rectitude, and orphanhood. "Mr. Jacksons ancestry are mostly Dead . . . and he a destitute orphan," one of the petitions said.[9] Orphanhood was a trump card in a West Point application, to be played whenever possible.

Hays was convinced. He wrote Secretary of War John C. Spencer that same day.

After apologizing for Butcher's errant behavior, he assured Spencer that he had a replacement ready and waiting, one whom he was "personally and intimately acquainted with . . . about 19 years of age—fine athletic form and of manly appearance." Hays told Spencer how Jackson was "left an orphan at an early age—deprived of both father and mother and destitute of means," and how he had relied entirely on his own exertions ever since, "sustaining as he does a good moral character—and an improvable mind."[10]

Spencer had no problem with the new replacement. He endorsed the recommendation the next day, and John Tyler, Jr., son and private secretary to the president, took the appointment papers for the "poor young man" in for his father to sign.[11]

So it was done. Jackson had the appointment he had so much wanted and thought he couldn't have, in the class that would graduate from West Point in 1846.

Hays now suggested that he stop over in the capital a day or two to see the sights. Jackson, however, was anxious to push on. The deadline for reporting was now only two days away, and the appointment was still only conditional—all the appointments were. The academy hadn't admitted him yet, and he was not certain it ever would. Entrance examinations had to be passed. So he hurried on to New York City.

At the docks in New York he paid his fifty-cent fare and caught the steamboat up the Hudson, arriving at the landing below West Point on June 20. He threw the saddlebags over his shoulder one more time and started up the steep path that wound toward the flat dusty plain above.[12]

The Highlands that held the forty-acre plain in its rock cradle high over the Hudson hadn't changed in the forty years that cadets had been coming to West Point. It hadn't changed in human memory. Its western bank still ascended sharply from the water's edge; the same cliffs still overhung the river with a wild and awful sublimity. Everywhere the eye looked the aspect was high, rocky, savage, majestic, and somber. The sight of it had reminded one Revolutionary War officer many years before of "universal death." As the sun declined across it, the clouds gave the Highland a misty, shrouded appearance that darkened its face "with a melancholy sadness," and lent "a kind of funereal aspect" to every object within the horizon. The river itself, all brown and gloomy, rolled slowly past the cliffs below the plain, underscoring the sense of grandeur and tragedy.[13]

But it was also stunningly beautiful. The English writer and social critic Harriet Martineau had gazed down on the plain and river from the heights in the 1830s. She looked at the "woods climbing above woods, to the clouds and stretching to the horizon," and found the view from old Fort Putnam "really oppressive to the sense. . . . [an] awful radiance."[14]

About the time Jackson was arriving at the landing in 1842, another famous English writer, the celebrated novelist Charles Dickens, also visited the academy. Dickens was America's favorite author, touring the New World to wildly cheering acclaim. When he saw West Point for the first time he himself cheered, saying the academy "could not stand on more appropriate ground, and any ground more beautiful can hardly be."[15] There was no question about it, nature had worked on a grand scale there on the Hudson River.

But it might have been the lifeless Sahara for all George Brinton McClellan cared. That aspiring cadet, arriving earlier in the month, had never been more depressed in his young life. It was not the scenery that ruled his emotions at the moment; it was the dismal situation. He felt alone, homesick, and abandoned, "as much alone as if in a boat in the middle of the Atlantic." Not a soul here, he sadly wrote home to Philadelphia, "cares for, or thinks of me. Not one here would lift a finger to help me; I am entirely dependent on myself— must think for myself—direct myself, & take the blame of all my mistakes, without anyone to give me a word of advice."[16]

McClellan was an unusual conditional cadet, the kind that comes along only now and again. He was legally too young for West Point, so young that his fellow cadets would probably call him "Babe," the name they always gave the youngest man in the class. But the academic board waived the age requirement in his case. This gifted son of a prominent Philadelphia physician was precocious, bordering on genius. Despite his youth, he already had passed two years at the University of Pennsylvania, and had an impressive command of languages, the classics, and modern literature. He was even better at mathematics, and since the age of ten he had dreamed of going to

West Point and becoming a soldier. He hadn't counted on being homesick.[17]

Dabney Herndon Maury, a prospective classmate, arrived at West Point from Fredericksburg, Virginia, at about the same time. Look at that, Maury thought when he met McClellan, such a little born and bred gentleman. And only fifteen years and seven months old, while he, Maury—God save the mark—was twenty.[18]

Otherwise Maury was little impressed with what he saw. He believed that few men in the new class had either social or educational advantages out of the ordinary.[19] William Dutton, a newcomer from Connecticut, was more impressed. He was in fact awed by the competition, counting "about a dozen or 15 of splendid talent." There was even one graduate of Yale College. Dutton figured he would have to exert himself to the limit if he hoped to place anywhere near the head of this class.[20]

Whatever one believed about their intellect, they were a motley collection, coming from every part of the country and representing, as all new classes did, "every degree of provincialism."[21] The upperclassmen saw nothing impressive in any of them. They thought them a bunch of nobodies, mere plebes, and called them "things," "animals," "reptiles," and "beasts."[22] And still they kept coming, 122 of them by one count, the largest class to enter the academy in its forty-year history.[23]

Maury watched as they continued to arrive. He loitered about in the south barracks with three fellow Virginians and saw them come in from the steamboat landing, up the path into the receiving area. By the twentieth of June he and his three companions, Ambrose Powell Hill, George Edward Pickett, and Birkett Davenport Fry, had seen nearly everybody. It was now the last day for reporting, and the last of them were making the long winding climb from the landing to the plain.

The four boys stared as Tom Jackson arrived. Of all they had seen, there had not been another quite like this one.

Maury studied him carefully. He noted the odd apparition's sturdy step, cold blue-gray eyes, and thin, firm lips clamped resolutely shut.

"That fellow," he whispered to Hill, Pickett, and Fry, "looks as if he had come to stay."

Maury approached the cadet sergeant who had just escorted the newcomer to his quarters. "Who was that?" he asked.

"Cadet Jackson, of Virginia," the sergeant said.

Well now, thought Maury, what a coincidence. Then they must show some interest in him, welcome him properly—a fellow countryman after all. Maury climbed at once to Jackson's room and affably offered his hand.

Jackson glared back at him in frigid welcome, a rebuff of such chilling friendlessness that Maury regretted having made the effort. When someday they would call this dour character Stonewall, Maury would understand why. As he rejoined his three companions downstairs, he spoke sharply of the new cadet's intellectual shortcomings.[24]

There they were—122 of them, friendly and not so friendly, from Virginia and every other of the twenty-six states in the Union, representing every degree of provincialism, and wearing every mode of dress from rough country homespun to tailored city coats.

But where were they?

Captain Erasmus Keyes, who had been in their predicament more than a decade before and would one day be teaching them artillery and cavalry tactics, could have told them where they were. They were in "the only society of human beings that I have known in which the standing of an individual is dependent wholly on his own merits as far as they can be ascertained without influence. The son of the poorest and most obscure man, being admitted as cadet, has an equal chance to gain the honors of his class with the son of the most powerful and richest man in the country. All must submit to the same discipline, wear the same clothes, eat at the same table, come and go upon the same conditions. Birth, avarice, fashion and connections are without effect to determine promotion or punishment." In short, the military academy was a "model republic in all things saving respect to constituted authority and obedience to orders, without which an army is impossible."[25]

That is where they were.

George McClellan had it right, then. They were as alone as if in a boat in the middle of the Atlantic. They would have to sink or float on their own merits.

Sighing for
What We
Left Behind

Almost immediately there came the moment of truth—the examinations to see who in this big class would stay and who would leave.

In the last days of June, at about the summer solstice, the longest day of the year and perhaps one of the longest of their lives, the new plebes were marched to their first encounter with the blackboard. It was to be their baptism, their initial trial by recitation—the first of hundreds of such trials for those who would survive. There were few of them that day who didn't dread it.

Among the few who didn't was George Horatio Derby; he had it all figured out.

As he sat waiting his turn and watching others go "with trembling hearts" to the blackboard, Derby began to see a pattern. Those who hesitated or stopped as they tried to explain their solutions to the mathematics board were suspected of ignorance. He would remember that when his turn came.[1]

Derby was from Medfield, Massachusetts, the only member of the new class who owed his appointment to an ex-president. His congressman was John Quincy Adams, "Old Man Eloquent" himself, the nation's sixth president, a friend of the family. More than a hundred other friends from home had been recruited to sign petitions on Derby's behalf, and they had praised his talent, energy, dedication to knowledge, agreeable disposition, correct moral habits, peculiar talent for drawing, and providential lack of a father. However, they failed to warn the authorities of the young man's quirky sense of humor and addiction to pranks. That would become apparent soon enough.[2]

To reduce his chances of not being ready when the testing time came, Derby had gone to West Point early and enrolled in Z.J.D. Kinsley's classical and mathematical prep school adjacent to the academy grounds. There he had brushed up his algebra and French and heard Lieutenant Kinsley himself assure him that he had "an excellent mathematical head."[3]

The new plebes had taken their physical examinations two days before, in the hospital overlooking the river. They had been marched before a medical board of three doctors, who had probed their limbs for ringbone and spavin; thumped their chests for soundness of wind; examined their teeth for decay; inspected their feet for bunions; measured them; weighed them; and clucked over such apparent irregularities as badly knit, once-broken bones. To test cadet eyesight, a dime was held up at the far end of the room and they were asked if it was heads or tails.[4]

Some of them already had been sifted out and sent home then. Now Derby, safely past the physical—the doctors had greatly admired his chest—was waiting his turn in the recitation room, watching his classmates struggle with the dreaded academic examination. He knew that still others would surely be lost when this part of "the fiery ordeal to see who should be of the chosen" was over.[5] It was important to the academic board that the chosen be able to read and write and have enough knowledge of elementary arithmetic to do reduction, proportion, and fractions. Those lacking such rudimental skills would have no future at West Point.

Derby's classmates would soon learn that he had a quaint way of looking at things. As he sat waiting and watching in the recitation room, he mused that there were actually two boards up there, "the black board and the Board of 13 Army officers," with the hapless plebes trapped between.[6] As he considered this, he heard his own name called. He was about to go before the double boards himself.

He strode to the front, a picture of confidence. If they thought his chest had been fine, then wait until they saw his mathematics. He deftly worked his assigned problem, on proportion involving fractions, on the blackboard. There was no hesitating, no stopping. When finished, he turned resolutely to that second of the two boards and boldly rattled it all off as if it were a story—no mistakes, no uncertainty.

Albert Ensign Church, West Point's renowned professor of mathematics, who preferred things done with no mistakes, bowed and said, "That's sufficient, sir."[7]

Some of the cadets waiting their turn watched with fascination as Tom Jackson went between the two boards. There had been no Lieutenant Kinsley to tell him what a fine mathematical head he had. There had been no classical academies to speak of in the mountains where he came from that might have prepared him for this ordeal. Perhaps he had mastered a little grammar and could add up a column of figures, but as to vulgar or decimal fractions, it is doubtful if he had ever heard of them.[8]

Jackson was so single-mindedly bent on passing that it was painful to watch. Sweat streamed down his face. He swiped at the pouring perspiration with the cuffs of his coat, first the right sleeve then the left, as he labored at the blackboard. Tension gripped the room as he strove to come to terms with fractions. His anguish, and the examining board's, ended only when he was told at last that he could sit down. As he thankfully did so, every member of the panel turned aside to hide the smiles they could no longer suppress.[9]

On the following Friday afternoon, June 24, the academic board listed those it had found "duly qualified." The very last name on the list, hanging by a slim thread, narrowly escaping the scythe, was Tom Jackson.[10]

The class lost thirty members in the physical and mental examination rooms within the week and shrank to ninety-two survivors. Derby, one of the ninety-two, spoke with compassion of those who were not. "It is not thought a disgrace to be dismissed from here," he wrote his mother, "for the studies and discipline are very hard, and a man who succeeds should be thought uncommonly talented, and one found deficient should not be blamed, for I verily believe that not one half of those appointed can *possibly* graduate."[11]

George McClellan, whom the scythe never came near, was now

feeling better—even exuberant—about everything, particularly about his shoes. He had found a more comfortable pair of boots and had just had his first good outing on the plain. He was riding high.

In his joy he wrote his sister, Frederica: "You can't imagine how much more inspired I feel since I have acquitted myself handsomely at this morning's drill." He mused over how strange it was, "how some little circumstance like that can make so great a difference in our feelings. Before drill I felt low in spirits—homesick—& in doubt as to my competency to go through here with credit, but now, how different. I feel in high spirits. . . . I know I can do as well as anyone in both my studies & my military duties. If this state of mind continues I will be able to stay here for four years. . . ."[12]

That is more than Jackson was certain of. Not only had the academic entrance examination been a torment, but the drill McClellan was talking about was also for him a dubious experience. They were drilled twice a day now and marched everywhere besides. They were a shuffling mob, "as unused to marching as sheep," halting irregularly, bunching up, and tramping on one another's heels.[13] Jackson in his brogans must have been particularly stiff and memorable.

Their ragged line of march was no more appalling than their smell. Each of them had been issued two blankets, one to sleep on, the other to sleep under, and both reeked of the villainous odor of rancid lanolin left from the cleaning process. The aroma clung to every plebe, branding him for what he was. It would take weeks for it to work out of the blankets and out of themselves. Until then everybody would simply have to adjust and endure.[14]

The upperclassmen, many of them cadet officers and therefore superior beings in the academy hierarchy and bound to be obeyed, were now making life miserable for them. Deviling the plebes was as much a part of the process as the lanolin in the blankets and the ragged drill on the plain. However, William Montgomery Gardner, a wildly handsome plebe from Georgia, soon learned that a new cadet with a powerful pair of fists and the disposition to use them if provoked was generally left alone.

He could cite his own roommate as a case in point. Gardner arrived late at West Point and had drawn "a very rough Western specimen" named Thomas J. Lowe as a "bunkie." Quite early the rough-hewn Lowe had a two-fisted encounter with cadet authority. It happened in the mess hall.[15]

14

The dining hall was a zone of profound disquiet at best. Three times a day the new cadets were marched there in their ragged ranks and in rigid silence. Once there, the command "take seats" was followed by a scramble such as William Dutton, the plebe from Connecticut, had never experienced. "We have to eat as fast as we can," he explained in a letter home, "& before we get enough the command is given—'squad rise.' " He estimated that not more than two thirds of them managed under these circumstances to get a bite of any kind.[16]

"Such a 20 minutes of clawing jawing cursing calling masticating and hauling," another plebe from Connecticut, Samuel H. Raymond, agreed, "is rarely seen."[17]

William Gardner's bunkie, Thomas Lowe, was trying to get his bite when an upperclassman shouted down to him from the other end of the table.

"Plebe, pass up the bread."

Lowe neither replied nor passed the bread.

The upperclassman repeated the order, this time with qualifying adjectives.

"Did you address that remark to me, sir?" Lowe asked. There were some startled looks, for Lowe said it in an unhumble manner unbecoming a miserable fourth-classman. Oh, oh, they thought, a "rabid beast."[18]

"Yes, you d——d plebe!" said the upperclassman.

Lowe rose slowly, strode to the head of the table—without bringing the bread—and to the horror of every plebe in the room—and the stifled amusement of every upperclassman—sent his tormenter reeling from the bench with a blow from his powerful pair of fists.

He returned casually to his seat as if inwardly contemplating the philosophy of Thomas Moore, whom he admired and copiously quoted, and continued eating as placidly as if nothing had happened. A good deal had happened, however, and Lowe was marched to the guardhouse later with great pomp and indignation. But since he didn't scare at all and clearly had that powerful pair of fists, as well as the proven disposition to use them, he was little bothered after that.[19]

The food itself, when one did get some of it, was scarcely worth fighting for. "Trash," said Raymond, a farm boy who had been raised on tastier fare.[20]

It was bread and butter in the morning for breakfast, with a substance called hash—a mishmash of peeled potatoes cut and boiled in a large iron kettle with leathery chunks of meat left over from dinner the day before. To this combination was added something—Raymond knew not what—to make the gravy. The ingredients were stirred "with a kind of hoe" and when done, brought to the table with some "hard" coffee. For dinner it was roast beef with more boiled potatoes and sometimes boiled beef and rice. For supper it was bread, butter, and tea.

"It will stand chewing well," Raymond advised.[21]

He was soon writing home to West Hartford for his father to send him a barrel of apples.[22] Pleas were, in fact, going out wholesale through the mails for "a piece of cheese & some cake"—anything to augment, replace, offset, or counteract the daily disaster served at the mess hall.[23]

"I would like to see Mecklenburg," William Dutton wrote wistfully home to Connecticut, "& a field of corn—or wheat or some such thing & would above all things like to get into Aunt Dorcas's cupboard a *moment*."[24]

"I am thinking at this instant of my *hen yard*," George Derby wrote his mother, grandmother, and two maiden aunts, the four husbandless women who had raised him in Medfield. "How does that do," he asked plaintively, his hunger mixing with his homesickness, "and how is the garden, the grape vine, and all those things which keep fresh a remembrance of my performances in your minds."[25]

The longing to be anywhere but where they were and the yearning to hear from home were agonizing. "Answer immediately!" they demanded at the end of their letters or at the head or in the margins. They would be making such demands for the next four years. Letters would never come fast enough or often enough.

As A. P. Hill would complain in a letter home to Culpeper, Virginia, "I have been living on vain expectancy, which they say like love, is rather a poor sustenance." He viewed his letters from home as "somewhat like an Angel's visits, few and far between." He had no doubt that if King, the family dog, could write he would gladly do so. But those from home who were literate and should be writing, were not doing it.[26]

In these first weeks the plebes were therefore eagerly embracing anything and anybody that could solace them in their misery. The slightest suggestion of the familiar brought joy. A complete stranger only a month, a week, a day—even an hour—before, was clasped to the homesick breast if he hailed from anywhere near home.

"We even look on those from the same state as almost connected by the tie of consanguinity," Dutton said.[27]

One thing most of these new cadets had brought with them from home and would have liked to keep was their hair. Most of them came with more than they required or that West Point desired. Some of them wore their curls in the fashion of the times—long, in soaplocks, and reeking with bear's grease and Macassar oil. That would not do at West Point.[28]

"Have your hair cut, sir!" the frowning inspecting officer barked, giving the offending lock a sharp twitch as he passed along behind the file of stiff-standing plebes.

When the ranks broke, the "thing" with the hair stared about in bewilderment. What to do now? Where must he go to obey that order?[29] Maury knew. He had come to West Point early and could point the place out. It was in a tent where a barber named Joe "could cut hair quicker and shorter than any living man."[30]

The annual examinations ended for the upperclassmen in June, and the fact was celebrated by merrymaking and a spectacular display of fireworks on the plain. Horse-drawn cannon boomed, "& the way the . . . balls & bombs flew about was like hail," William Dutton marveled. "It seemed as if the earth would open. . . ."[31]

The graduating class left soon after, and its final parade put lumps in throats. The music, faint at first, gathered and swelled and throbbed as the band approached on the plain. The graduating cadets marched smartly in under the academy colors, and filed into their places in the ranks with clockwork cadence. They did not march at all in the disheveled lurching style of the gawky plebes. The band struck up "Old Lang Syne," and George Derby nearly burst with pent-up emotion. He knew what must be going through the minds of those fortunate cadets whose four-year trial was behind them and who were about to leave covered with honor. They were thinking of the miseries and hardships they had endured and the friendships they had made. As the band played that ultimate song of the heart, "Home, Sweet Home," they were remembering the homes they had left and would soon be seeing again. Derby believed there was not a dry eye among them.[32]

It was a feeling that four years from now they, too, might know.

* * *

So it had been a hectic beginning, a frazzling month of June. Most of those in the class had found it all new and very strange. Samuel Raymond thought it pleasant enough, but somewhat lacking in the necessary conveniences. Sometimes, he admitted, when they were feeling a little troubled and uncomfortable, "we sigh for what we left behind"—and lived in anticipation of what was to come.[33]

West Point's layout and lack of amenities didn't ease their anxieties or soothe their sense of abandonment. There was no such thing on the entire grounds as a paved walkway. There was no gas, and their crowded rooms were lit only by malodorous whale-oil lamps. Their quarters were innocent of furnaces and bathrooms. In the summer the roads were dusty, and in the winter muddy. When the arctic wind came howling down the Hudson, they would be cut off from the world entirely. The river would be frozen then and unnavigable. The railroad had not yet come to the Highlands, and there was no telegraph. The only communication was by boat in summer and by stage over the mountains to a station on the Erie Railroad in winter. And the plain itself wasn't really level. Water accumulated in its depressions in summer and froze into ice ponds in winter. They all had lived better in their short lifetimes.[34]

In early July they moved out of the barracks and onto the plain for their first summer encampment. They had been sleeping on floors in rooms in the north and south barracks buildings, scattered about as many as five to a room. Now for the next two months they would be lumped together three to a tent only ten feet square.

There they would find little rest.

Taps had just sounded on the first night of the encampment, and Derby had spread his blankets out on the tent floor, undressed, and blown out the candle.

Whap! Something pelted the sides of his tent. Pegs? Stones?

"Stop that noise in D Company!" a voice roared.

Someone struck the tent walls with a stick.

"Corporal of the Guard, Number Three!"

A patrol was heard arriving outside. Wang! The stick struck the canvas again.

"Halt!" a voice shouted.

An indignant head was thrust through the tent flap.

"Who is the orderly of this tent?" it demanded.

18

"DERBY!" Derby shouted.

"Turn out, Sir, we can't have this noise! Turn out, Sir!"

Derby looked wryly about the tent, which since taps had been as quiet as a street in Pompeii.[35] But it was useless to argue.

He was marched ignominiously to the guard tent, kept there a few minutes, and sent back. The patrol proceeded down the line to the next victim. Before the night was over every new cadet had been jerked out of his sleep and hustled away to make an accounting.

We shall do it next year to the next class of plebes, Derby vowed, if we are so lucky as to still be here.[36]

It was up every day now at 4:00 with the morning gun, on the drill field by 5:00, in the mess hall by 6:30, parade at 8:00, infantry or artillery drills through the rest of the morning, dinner at 1:00, more military exercises through the afternoon, parade at 6:00, stag dances without girls on the common until 9:00, in bed by 10:00.[37]

On the mornings of artillery drill, the plebes manned the bellowing guns for an hour and a half under a melting sun. Rays darted off the glittering barrels of the brass cannon, nearly blinding them. William Dutton, standing but eighteen inches from the muzzle of the piece, reeled and recoiled from the roar of it. It was an ear-blasting and dirty business.

Encampment was a dirty business all around. Each plebe had a two-foot-square box into which all his belongings were crammed. Repeatedly through the day they rummaged in them for clean changes of clothing. It was providential that their laundry was done for them, a bargain at fifty cents a week.

"I have changed my pants 4 times in one day & had my boots blacked as many times," Dutton complained. "If you step out of your tent with your coat not buttoned with *every* button & hooked in the neck, & with *clean* white gloves you are reported." They drilled with their immaculate white gloves on their hands, dirtying them wholesale.

And everywhere there were visitors thronging the plain, and the dances without ladies in the night. The scene, Dutton sighed, "never seems a reality to me."[38]

There was no study yet—that would begin in September—and the dancing was a rather dry business without ladies, as cadets had found through the years. But it was better than nothing.[39] Candles were lit in two rows, and the cadets, to the time of fife, violin, and drum, danced in the flickering light, assuming ludicrous positions and executing "all manner of out-landish steps." It satisfied George Derby's sense of the ridiculous. He intended to contribute some choreography of his own before the summer was over.[40]

West Point was a summertime showcase. The plain teemed with visitors and dignitaries, including ladies—whom regrettably the marching plebes could see only if they had remarkable peripheral vision. Their attention was fixed by rigid discipline and unrelenting supervision on a point fifteen paces in front of them. Many had yet to speak to a woman since they arrived, much less dance with one. Few had any immediate prospect of doing so.[41] Tom Jackson would not remember speaking to one during his entire four years at West Point.[42]

Early one evening that summer, Maury, Fry, and Hill—three Virginians—were stretched out on their lanolin-saturated camp bedding. Maury was reading a yellow-back novel.

As he casually glanced out the tent door, he saw Tom Jackson working about, a member of the day's police detail. The police detail was a miserable job that fell to plebes. It wasn't difficult work, but it was petty and disagreeable and took out of a cadet whatever conceit might still be left.

Ah, thought Maury, this would be an excellent time to make another attempt at being sociable with Cadet Jackson. He is a Virginian after all.

As Jackson passed by, bagging rubbish, Maury lifted the tent flap and, with a mock air of authority, commanded him to pay more attention to his work, pick up those cigar butts, and otherwise put a sharper show on things.

Too late Maury realized he had done the wrong thing again. Jackson stared back balefully, thin-lipped and without humor. Maury let the tent flap drop and became suddenly intensely interested again in his yellow-back novel.

When police was over, Maury miserably confessed to his tent mates that he had made Jackson angry and must at once humble himself and explain that he had not really been in command of that detail.

He found Jackson at the guard tent and called him out.

"Mr. Jackson," he confessed, "I find that I made a mistake just

20

now in speaking to you in a playful manner—not justified by our slight acquaintance. I regret that I did so."

Jackson gazed at him for a moment with his intent, humorless eyes.

"That is perfectly satisfactory, sir," he said finally in his rapid, jerky, stiff manner.

Maury returned to his tent and said to Fry and Hill, "Cadet Jackson, from Virginia, is a jackass."

His two tent mates emphatically agreed. None of them would try again soon to befriend such a humorless specimen.[43]

Jackson was stretched that summer as tight as the drums that beat the changes of the day. Unlike McClellan, who was confident now of staying at West Point the full four years and of doing well, Jackson was not confident of staying under any conditions. Not until after the first academic examinations in January, the next major weeding-out time, would he know if he was to stay or go. That cursed coming examination, widely and with good reason denounced as the "dreaded thing," the "agony," and the "inquisition," was in the back of everybody's mind.[44]

Jackson was depressed, as Gibson Butcher had been, by stories of the amount of study necessary to survive, and of the large number of cadets who would surely fail. He couldn't bear to think of the mortification of being sent home, which seemed a clear probability. He had rehearsed what he would say to his friends if that happened.

If *they* had been there, and found it as hard as he did, they would have failed too. He would tell them that.[45]

To escape from these mental agonies, Jackson began visiting Fort Putnam on Saturday afternoons. It was possible with the superintendent's permission to go out on the public lands adjacent to the academy grounds on Saturdays, and the hike up Mount Independence to the old fort was one of the first outings the plebes took. Jackson loved the ramshackle relic of a fort, as many before him had. To four decades of cadets it was "Old Put."

Of course, everything and everybody was "old" to these cadets, even the things they didn't love. Jackson himself was now called by his classmates "Old Jack."

Old Put was a haven to Old Jack. It was a wreck of a place, named for the high-ranking general officer of the revolutionary army who had played a key role in fortifying West Point against the British in the War for Independence. Now it was battered by passing time and the merciless elements. Its west side was built on a steep precipice and its stone walls all around jutted ten to thirty feet high. It was begun in 1778, partly rebuilt in 1794, and never completed. Since then it had progressively gone to ruin. But Jackson could still make out the ghosts of casemates that had held guns, supported chimneys, or served as storerooms.

The site soothed Jackson. He found peace of mind there that he couldn't find in the encampment below. The view, as Harriet Martineau had found a decade before, was breathtaking. Jackson could see below him the white tents that brightly dotted the plain, in sharp contrast to the gloomy savins standing like sentinels behind. He could see the flags snapping distantly in the breeze. Beyond and below curled the tranquil Hudson, flowing on past the Highlands to New York and the sea.

On the opposite bank of the river he could see the village of Cold Spring, and below it the busy West Point foundry pouring out clouds of smoke and supplying the entire northeast with "everything iron." He could see the graceful sloops that teemed on the Hudson's glassy surface. And looming over Fort Putnam, looming over everything, was that frowning cone, Crow's Nest, the highest point on the Highlands, casting its dark shadow on the opposite bank.[46]

It was perhaps from the heights of Old Put that Jackson first began putting down the list of maxims—rules he proposed to live by—which he entered that year into a personal notebook.

One of those maxims had special meaning for him now. It comforted him and buoyed his spirits. Perhaps it was in his thoughts, casting a beam of hope over an otherwise dreary prospect, as he returned late on a Saturday afternoon from the sanctity of Old Put. Perhaps he repeated it on his way down.

"You may be whatever you resolve to be," it said.[47]

As
Intelligible
as Sanskrit

On Sunday, the tenth of September, it looked like rain, and George McClellan was feeling the cold.

    The plebes were still wearing their lightweight summer trousers and there were no fires in their grates and no prospect of changing into winter uniforms until October. McClellan's room was in the south barracks on the second balcony, exposed to the north wind that whistled down the river. It was cold even though there was plenty of body heat in his quarters that day. Sunday morning inspection had just ended and his room was crowded with "visitors of all classes from the Lt. to the plebes."[1]

    The fact that reveille came every morning at 5:00, in a fanfare of throbbing drums when it was still dark, added to the lack of warmth the cadets were feeling. And the thought of the noon meal in the mess hall generated the wrong kind of heat. McClellan wrote his sister that he was planning to skip dinner altogether that day, as it was certain to be " 'bull-beef' & potatoes" again.[2]

    Summer encampment had been over for nearly two weeks. At 11:30 in the morning on the last day of August, the corps of cadets broke camp. The plain was swarming with spectators and the drums

23

were pounding. At the third beat the tents all collapsed in one grand concord, a last tribute to precision and a final farewell to summer.[3]

They had thought it would never end. Many of the new plebes felt as Sam Grant of Ohio, now a first-classman, had after his first summer encampment—sick of it, "as though I had been at West Point always."[4] They usually felt that way about their first one.[5]

Captain J. Addison Thomas, the commandant of cadets, took the plebes aside on the plain at the end of the encampment for a few words. Thomas, called "Ethical Tom" by the cadets, was a towering Tennessean whose credo was "Keep up the strut." He had been drilling that doctrine into them all summer long without letup.[6] His intention on this morning was to remind them of their obligations as officers and gentlemen now that they were leaving the drill field for the recitation rooms.

"You are not common soldiers!" he shouted at them. "You are Gentlemen—Gentlemen of manners, of politeness & of education. The U.S. looks to you! The Country looks to you! The Army looks to you and—and—ahemm! ahemmm!" It was a short list and it was already exhausted. So Thomas fell back on what he knew best— keeping up the strut.

"By company right wheel!" he barked. "Head of column to the left—guide right! Quick March!!!"[7]

So off they went. "The tug of war," as Derby put it, was about to begin.[8]

All the cadets who had been appointed to the new class had arrived, if they were coming at all. Even the "seps," the September arrivals,[9] were there by now. The class was scattered in rooms throughout the two barracks buildings and "living more like students than soldiers."[10]

However, the living was unlike anything most of them had ever known. Their quarters, even their belongings, were regimented. An order posted in each room read like a close-order drill on the plain. Everything must be in its place or risk the ever-present demerit: bedsteads against wall farthest from door; tables against same wall; trunks under bedsteads; lamps clean and on mantel; dress caps neatly arranged on shelf nearest door; shoes blacked and neatly arranged behind door; washstand clean and in corner nearest to door; looking glass between washstand and door; books neatly arranged on shelf farthest from door; broom stowed behind door; drawings and books under shelf farthest from door; muskets in gun rack with locks sprung; bayonets in scabbards; accouterments, sabers, cutlasses, and swords hanging over muskets; candle and box for scrubbing utensils against wall under shelf nearest door and fireplace; clothes hanging neatly on pegs over bedsteads (for the first time since they arrived they now had beds); mattress and blankets neatly folded; orderly board in position over mantel; chairs, when not in use, under tables; and all cadets—when not in use—presumably in bed with lights out.[11]

Since no curtains covered the shelves, their contents were equally exposed to dust and the critical eye of the inspecting officer—one more source of potential demerit, as if another were needed. The fish-oil lamps gave off a dim, yellow glow and a penetratingly offensive odor. The cadets sympathized with Jonah. This must have been the way it was in the belly of the whale.[12]

On the first day of class after encampment, they were marched to the long stone academic building that bulked on West Point's south end. This fine structure, the biggest on the plain, was 275 feet long, 75 feet wide, three stories high with a basement, and less than four years old. Its predecessor had burned to the ground in 1838. It was called the Academy, and it was the heart of West Point, its crucible of learning, its recitation emporium, a building they would come to know all too well.[13]

Dabney Maury found himself seated next to that precocious Philadelphia teenager, George McClellan. It was purely by the logic of the alphabet, and it would be for all too brief a time to suit Maury. "Next week he went up till he became head," Maury complained, "while I remained *tutisimus in medio*." He was very sorry to lose "Mac" from his side, "especially during recitations, for he used to tell me things, and was a great help."[14]

There would be only two subjects for the plebes to master this first year, mathematics and French. In each of these two subjects they were soon dividing into sections according to proficiency. They could all see that the first section would have "a glamor of sanctity shimmering about it," which would likely turn its members into a sort of intellectual aristocracy. There would be a shabbier section at the other end of the spectrum to balance it out—a depository for the so-called "Immortals," a dustbin for those hanging on the ragged edge of deficiency.[15]

After the first week, when Maury lost McClellan to the aristocracy, Tom Jackson left the alphabetical order to join the immortals at the other end. Maury and a host of others staked out the middle, where he already was situated alphabetically, "that easiest and safest of positions."[16]

Running with the shimmering aristocracy required keeping consistently to the high road in the academy's grading system—at a steady 2.6 to 3.0. That was the grade range for a "thorough" or "best" classroom recitation. A "perfect rag," as George Derby called it, was a 3.0, and he was soon getting enough perfect rags in the course he had a head for—mathematics—to make McClellan and him permanent section mates. From a perfect 3.0, the grading system fell away progressively downward. A 2.1 to 2.5 was a "good" recitation; a 2.0 was a "fair" one; a 1.1 to 1.9 was "tolerable"; a 0.1 to 1.0 was "bad" or "very incomplete"; a 0 was a "complete failure"—sub-immortal—the road to oblivion.[17]

Much of the mathematics promised to be about as intelligible as Sanskrit. When McClellan was feeling the cold in his room on that Sunday morning in early September, the plebes had been grappling with mathematics for over a week. It would be algebra, geometry, and trigonometry this first year, progressing to ever more hideous forms in the second.[18] Even a mind as mathematically fine-tuned as Derby's was finding a lot of Sanskrit there. The lesson today, he wrote home on October 3, dealt in equations of the second degree. He studied them all one day, found he couldn't do them, and gave up the idea altogether.[19]

There was no way around mathematics. It had to be taken head-on. It was the academic flywheel of West Point. It drove all the main pulleys. To not succeed in it was not to succeed at the academy. Seven of every ten hours of their curriculum time was now devoted to it. Seven of ten hours would be devoted to it or its offshoots, the sciences and engineering, for the entire four years. French was bunched into the mere three hours left over, and that would be so for every other nonmathematics, nonscience, nonengineering course still to come. Worse, mathematics would be the direct or the indirect cause of nearly nine of every ten dismissals; it was West Point's grim reaper.[20]

Some found it ironic, therefore, that Albert E. Church, the kindly professor of mathematics and an otherwise humane man, should be the cause of all this heartache. A short, stocky, brown-eyed, balding, broad-faced genius, Church walked about West Point with his head bowed, his eyes fixed on the ground, and his hands clasped behind him under the tails of his dress coat. It was as if he was constantly mulling some dim, elusive mathematical theorem.[21] What hair was left ringed the sides and back of his head in wild rebellion against the laws of mathematical order.

But in the classroom the plebes found him as precise as his mathematics. He was punctual to the minute, always in his seat to hear them recite. To those who had mastered the day's lesson, he was as friendly as a lap dog—all smiles—perhaps sharing with them his merry laugh. To the unprepared or the imprecise, however, woe betide. If the failure to master the material was owing to the complexity of the subject, not an unusual circumstance, Church spared no pains to clear things up, explaining without stint until he was convinced that the cadet either comprehended or was hopelessly obtuse, in which case he flunked him.

He regretted having to do that, but mathematics was a serious business. It had been a serious business with Church for all the years he had been teaching it at West Point—virtually since the day he graduated at the top of his class from the academy in 1828. By the fall of 1842, he was a giant in his discipline, one of the foremost mathematical minds in the world, the author of a seminal textbook on calculus, a full professor, and head of the department.[22]

To him, calculus was the "very poetry of mathematics," the only respectable way to solve a problem.[23] Nobody questioned his standing as a great man of numbers. As a teacher, however, some found him less than poetic. Dry as dust, grumped one cadet, "an old mathematical cinder, bereft of all natural feeling."[24] Others found him "ever-kind and considerate."[25] Captain Erasmus Keyes, the artillery instructor who thought West Point the perfect republic, believed him God-sent. "When the Omnipotent created 'all things for men's delightful use,' " Keyes said, "he made Albert E. Church to teach cadets algebra, geometry, trigonometry, conic sections, and calculus, and to find out all that candidates for admission know of vulgar and decimal fractions."[26]

When they didn't know these things, when they couldn't grasp conic sections or calculus, he had to flunk them, often at a fearful rate. There were members of this new class of plebes who would soon feel his relentless scythe. It saddened him. He was sorry so many cadets failed his beloved mathematics and had to be sent away. He wished it could be different. But that's the way it was.[27]

French was as unavoidable in its fashion as mathematics—not as important, but just as unavoidable. When Sylvanus Thayer, the superintendent of the academy from 1818 to 1833, set this math- and science-based curriculum in place at West Point, he found French an inescapable component. It was the language of the books he had bought for the academy library when he was in France. Indeed, it was the language of war, "the sole repository of Military science." Officers didn't necessarily need to know how to speak it, but they must know how to read it. Since Thayer believed it to have been inadequately taught at the academy before he arrived, one of the first things he did was add two new French instructors to the one already on the faculty.[28]

Some of the new plebes—Tom Jackson among them—were finding the French as much Sanskrit as the mathematics. But Claudius Berard, the head of the department, and his two Gallic associates were doing their best.

Berard was bland, detached, moderate, unobtrusive, and scholarly. Not even the French Revolution had stirred in him any passion for military glory. When he was drafted into Napoleon's army, his father hired a substitute. When the substitute was killed, making him eligible again for service, Berard simply migrated to America. With his excellent classical education, he got a job teaching Latin and Greek at Dickinson College, until he was appointed first teacher of French at West Point in 1815. He had been there ever since, teaching French with "invincible patience." No degree of dullness in a cadet seemed to disturb or discourage him. He was "always the kind and courteous Frenchman."[29]

Theophile D'Oremieulx, one of Berard's two associates, was his temperamental opposite. D'Oremieulx had enough passion for both of them, and most of it was for Bonaparte, whom he called "ze gr-r-rand Napoleon." The class soon learned that the way into D'Oremieulx's affections and to a high mark in his classes was to get in a favorable daily lick about Napoleon, in either French or English. Little of the stately decorum that obtained in Church's recitation rooms held in D'Oremieulx's. This was partly because, while fluent in his native tongue, the Frenchman made sad havoc of English.

Scarcely a day passed in his classroom without an absurd semantic incident of some kind.[30]

Neither did a day pass when these cadets were not reciting. It was West Point's teaching method, its modus operandi, and a frightening new fact of life. It penetrated cadet ignorance at the academy as incisively as Socrates had disrobed sloppy reasoning in Athens. The professor or one of his assistants explained the problem at hand. (Virtually every professor had at least one assistant instructor under him—academy graduates generally, who had returned for a tour of duty to teach a subject they knew particularly well.) The cadets went away at the end of the class with the explanation swarming in their heads. Overnight they "boned" it and reappeared the next day ready to recite it.

At that point it became a case of Russian roulette. The professor or the assistant called on victims at random. The designated cadet rose, armed himself with a piece of chalk and sponge, and went to the front. As he stood at attention, a problem was put to him, and he wheeled about to the blackboard and began to work it out. As he chalked and sponged, others worked and recited and came and went beside him. When he was finished he wheeled about to face the professor again, and when called on, explained what he had just done.[31]

Nobody was long overlooked, however much he might like to be. Each of the new plebes had an opportunity to recite every day. No matter how hard they sought "to bugle it" (to keep from reciting until the bugle blew),[32] there was nowhere to hide and it caught up with them sooner rather than later. They quickly found that recitations were very serious business, all sedate earnestness, to be conducted with the utmost precision and decorum. The work and the questions were clear-cut and definite. They must confine themselves directly to the point. There was no circumlocution or vagueness allowed, no back talk, disputation, buffoonery, or witticisms.[33]

Regrettably things did not always work out as hoped. With sometimes distressing regularity, some of them simply didn't know the material and had to admit it. That was called a "fess," which was followed by a "found" (delinquent), followed by serious ramifications. Happily, a lapse didn't necessarily mean dismissal. There was latitude for error. Tom Jackson was coming to class in these first weeks often still trying to puzzle out a lesson from the day or several days before.

Through no lack of diligence or hard work on his part, he was simply behind, and since he didn't like to get ahead of himself, he said so. The professors seemed willing to take this into account.[34]

In early October, the shivering corps was ordered at last into winter uniforms.[35] The Highlands also changed into something different as fall moved toward winter. The trees lost their greenery and became leafless and slate gray on the surrounding hills, and the river went to a dreary olive drab. With the changing season came a mid-October malaise. It was a vulnerable time, when most of the plebes were beginning to be disgusted with West Point. Some who now expected they would surely be dismissed in January became entirely disheartened and stopped trying.

Samuel Raymond, the farm boy from Connecticut, commiserated with them. "They feel keenly the disgrace of being obliged to leave any place on account of inferiority of talent and wish from the bottom of their heart that they had never seen the place."[36]

For those still in the running, life had become nonstop studying. "We are obliged to be in our rooms about ten hours each day as study hours," Raymond complained. "It is not the hum drum of a village academy which is here recited." William Dutton, Raymond's fellow plebe from Connecticut, found himself studying every spare moment from reveille to taps. He hadn't found time to do anything else. It couldn't be helped, he said, "if one thinks of staying."[37]

Everywhere there were drums to remind them of where they were, the "most startling beat of drums," pounding out changes in the daily schedule, beginning each morning before the sun was up. In cadence with cannon, fife, and bugle, the drumbeat hammered over the plain and through the barracks, to the mess hall, and the academic buildings. They rumbled everywhere; they were the heartbeat of West Point, always throbbing.

Only with tattoo at night, which called the cadets to their quarters and the day to an end, did the drums rattle to a stop. Even at that hour, 10:00 in the evening, they signaled anything but rest and repose. Up and down the beat resonated, in and around the barracks in a final farewell, "making the night sound . . . with soul-stirring strains."[38]

The plebes were also finding they had a magnetic attraction for demerits. The cursed things flew at them from every direction and stuck to them like lint. A code of regulations "more rigorous than

30

those of Deuteronomy" ruled West Point.[39] The don'ts were legion, six pages of them in the academy rule book under Article XII, titled: DISCIPLINE. Four more pages of them—afterthoughts, perhaps—followed later under a different heading, but which might just as well have read: MORE DISCIPLINE.[40]

The opportunities to transgress the rules were endless. Any one of the scores of offenses described in those ten pages of the rule book could bring down the demerit, and some of the more sinister could bring peremptory dismissal. At one time or another virtually every one of the don'ts was practiced or attempted by somebody. But there was a limit. Two hundred demerits in a year was all the system would tolerate from any one cadet, and some of the plebes who had given up hope were obeying no regulations at all, staying only long enough to amass their two hundred demerits and leave.[41]

The demerit was the great leveling agent of discipline and order, an ever-present force operating constantly.[42] The plebes were piling them up at every turn, having to bone conduct, in some cases, as hard as they boned mathematics and French.[43]

As 1842 ground toward a dismal end, one of the plebes, Sam Bell Maxey, the son of a Kentucky lawyer, defied paragraph 134 of the regulations forbidding physical assault. The defendant was another plebe, William Burns, who just before the attack had defied paragraph 133, the anti-defamation provision. Their resulting physical encounter bought both of them instant arrest and a prolonged public lecture in the Post Orders from Superintendent Richard Delafield. Even their later apologies and expressions of regret to one another couldn't save them from demerits and yet another lecture.[44]

When winter had fairly arrived and it became too cold to drill on the plain, the plebes did what forty classes of cadets had done before them. They took up hashmaking, a depravity profoundly frowned on in the regulations. "Hash" was defined as anything that could be smuggled out of the mess hall, mashed together, put in a pan with a slab of butter, seasoned to taste, cooked, and eaten surreptitiously.

These "Chinook orgies" were generally scheduled for Saturday nights when there were no lessons and no recitations pending the next day. Implicated cadets bootlegged forbidden food from the mess hall wrapped in paper and stuffed under their caps. It was not unique to see crowns of caps so far elevated from the tops of heads that they had to be strapped down.

The cooking was done sub rosa between inspection of rooms at call to quarters and taps, and it was a risky and complicated business. The sentinel on post had either to be duped or bought off with a helping of the hash. Even with his complicity the conspiracy had to be carried off with mouselike stealth. And often as not it came to grief in any case. An inspecting officer unexpectedly rapped at the door and the hash was quickly hustled out of sight. But since it continued to simmer loudly, nobody was deceived, the cooks were betrayed, and the tab paid all around was five demerits and two extra rounds of guard duty.[45]

Superintendent Richard Delafield grieved over such wanton disregard of the regulations and often used the day's Post Orders to lecture the cadets on good and evil. He knew the difference. When Sylvanus Thayer inaugurated order of merit numbers—a cadet's academic ranking in his class and consequently in the corps—the very first one went to Delafield, who graduated at the head of his class in 1818.

He had gone on to a distinguished career in the elite corps of engineers and become a specialist in the construction of permanent fortifications. For six years he was the superintending engineer in the construction of the Cumberland Road east of the Ohio River, and in 1838 he was named superintendent of the academy.

Delafield had his quirks. Among them was a penchant for reeling off sarcastic puns, which caused the cadets to call him Dicky the Punster.[46] But he was a superior administrator. Engineering Professor Dennis Hart Mahan admired him for his "clear sightedness, promptitude . . . and a determination to examine everything with his own eyes."[47]

Delafield examined everything through small steel-framed glasses set on "a pronounced eagle nose" that jutted out between sandy eyebrows under an abundant shock of sandy-gray hair.[48] He had a nervous temperament that propelled his pudgy frame perpetually about the post, where he took pride in "having everything different from what it used to be."[49]

He was an omnipresent being, an ironhanded disciplinarian, tirelessly on the lookout for petty infractions and the troublemakers responsible for them. The cadets considered him a tyrant. He punished every violation of the regulations, deprived the corps of amusements and recreation wherever possible, scheduled fire drills on free time, withdrew permission to attend officers' parties, and forced cadets to answer self-incriminating questions. The staff and faculty didn't like him any better than the cadets did. He never let up insisting that all faculty must attend Sunday services in the chapel, the same as the cadets.

However, Delafield was improving and upgrading the academy constantly with new roads and structures, and doing it on a shoestring. "He had the credit," Erasmus Keyes admitted, "of doing more with a dollar than any other man in the army."[50]

Despite their disapproval of him, the new cadets found Delafield approachable and accessible. He held regular audience hours between 7:00 A.M. and 8:00 A.M. daily, except Sundays, and any cadet who wished to see him then could.[51] He was open to reasonable suggestions, and willing to institute reforms where he saw a need, no matter how the need came to his attention or from whom.

One controversial need he had seen and acted on was a different way for cadets to button their trousers. The buttons ran up the side—always had. He ordered them changed to run up the front instead, fly-fashion. It was more practical and it pleased the cadets. However, it scandalized Mrs. Delafield and the other ladies of the post, who protested heatedly that the reform drew unseemly attention to a sensitive region of cadet anatomy. But buttons up the front was clearly having something different from what it was, and the reform stuck.[52]

But now it was January 1843, and where the buttons ran on the trousers mattered little to the plebes. There was a more pressing consideration at hand. George McClellan wrote home of "a continual state of excitement."[53] He meant panic. Their first semiannual examination, in mathematics and French, was to begin on January 3, at 8:00 A.M. in the library.[54]

The fearful thing was upon them, the hour of agony, the inquisition. Tom Jackson had come to another dangerous crossing.

Oh,
for the Sight
of Our Native Land

When Jackson marched rigidly to the library on January 3 to see if he could possibly survive, he was only a face in the crowd.

He was so modest and shy in his ways that he had been little noticed by his classmates in the first six months. Dabney Maury, in their two stiff unsuccessful social encounters, had probably gotten to know him as well as anybody. If there was any hail-fellow-well-met in Jackson at all, Maury had failed to find it.

In less than three weeks Jackson would turn nineteen. He was not unattractive. His features were strong, with a long thin nose and a broad, angular forehead. However, his face was round and red, Georgia's William Gardner remembered, "and without a single grace of manner or appearance." His blue-gray eyes were inset against a somewhat sallow complexion that colored deeply when he blushed, which was whenever he was spoken to. When he spoke to anybody, which was only when necessary, Gardner thought his voice soft and gentle. Others swore, however, that it was thin and reedy, almost squeaky. What he said came out in quick, jerky, stiff sentences, never to be repeated or amended in any form and framed in such a way as to discourage further conversation. He said only what he had to say

34

in the most economic way possible, and that was that. Take it or leave it.

Jackson was taller than average, at 5 feet 10 inches, but appeared shorter because of a habit of carrying his head downcast in thoughtful abstraction. There was a lot to think about at West Point. But he had a sweet smile, which he occasionally flashed on the world when something humorous or pleasing was said. He was never known, however, to say any such thing himself. It was believed that, when alone with one or two intimates, if indeed he had any, he was capable of animated conversation and intellectual combat. But in a larger circle he was always the silent interested listener, hanging on the edge of the conversation, rarely participating.[1]

A closer look at this nondescript cadet, however, yielded rewards for those with an appreciation for the slightly off-center. Jackson brought with him to West Point an obscure malady of the stomach and other internal organs that dictated the way he believed he must sit and stand. While studying, he never bent his body for fear of compressing some important inner organs and aggravating his condition. This produced an uncompromising bolt-upright posture, stiff as a stick. No chair he ever sat on appeared to need a back.[2]

His mental posture was just as rigid. When his section was caught in a drenching rainstorm and everybody else sensibly broke for cover, Jackson continued to march resolutely on at the prescribed pace and direction, veering neither left nor right, oblivious of the downpour and getting soaked. From the cover of the barracks the others looked back in wonder and said, "See old Jackson!" Some saw this and other eccentricities often enough to conclude that there must be some design to them. But nobody had the faintest notion what it might be.[3]

There was never a need for Jackson to bone concentration. "No one I have ever known," one of his roommates said, "could so perfectly withdraw his mind from surrounding objects or influences, and so thoroughly involve his whole being in the subject under consideration."[4]

His roommates were privy not only to this attribute, but to his nighttime study habits. Before taps he piled the grate high with anthracite coal. By the time the lamps went out, the coal was glowing, and Jackson was stretched out flat on the bare floor in front of the grate with his books—being careful not to compress the organs. There he boned the lesson for the next day late into the night, "until it was literally burned into his brain."[5]

Sam Grant, the first-classman from Ohio whose real first name wasn't Sam at all, but Ulysses, took Jackson for a fanatic. Grant looked at the awkward plebe from the west Virginia mountains and saw a manly but weird character who seemed to be in the clutches of some strange religious hypochondria. Despite appearances, however, Jackson came to command respect, including Grant's. "He had so much courage and energy, worked so hard, and governed his life by a discipline so stern," Grant admitted, that they all had to respect him. He lived by his maxims.[6]

He made no large impression otherwise. Grave, reticent, physically awkward, socially ungraceful, intense, unbending, disciplined, diffident, tenacious, and unnoticed. That was Jackson. Nobody saw in him any suggestion of genius or gift for command, nothing at all that promised a career out of the ordinary. It just wasn't there.[7] It might not even be in him to survive this first critical semiannual examination in the library.

Indeed, when it was all over, sixteen more of the class were "obliged to pack up and be off," as Samuel Raymond put it. "I pitied the poor fellows from the bottom of my heart—their hopes destroyed, their friends disappointed, themselves disgraced."[8] Jackson had survived, finishing sixty-second in mathematics and eighty-eighth in French.[9] He was still with them, hanging by his fingertips from the bottom ledge. But he was there.

George McClellan was still very much there, astride the uppermost rung, and full of himself. "They put me *head* of my class in mathematics!" he boasted in a letter to Frederica. "Are you contented with that, sister?"[10]

"Every day I am more pleased at my having come here—instead of doing nothing at home," he wrote his brother. "I am head of my class at West Point, a distinction well worth having—rather different from that of 'taking first honors' at college." The past, he boasted, had been child's play. This was the real thing. "I suppose those who stood above me at 'the infant school' I used to go to 'when I was a little boy' will say that they might easily do the same thing here." Hah! "No such thing," he said, "they could not do it to save their lives—I never studied at all at home, now I do study a little (not much I must confess). I am older too, my head is clearer & I take more pains than formerly."[11]

Dutton was closer to speaking for everybody when he groaned,

"Thought! thought!! thought!!! continual." It wears the flesh, he wrote Lucy Matthews, his cousin and the girl he planned to marry. "I do hope from the bottom of my heart that you will never touch another book to study. I have enough for both."[12]

On February 20 they at last became true cadets, although still fourth-classmen. In the cadet chapel that afternoon at 3:30 they took their oaths, signed their engagements, received their warrants, and the word "conditional" was dropped from their status.[13] The upper-classmen, however, would continue to call them beasts, animals, reptiles, and things.

The weather soared temporarily with their status, as weather will, passing from arctic cold at the beginning of the examinations to springlike at the end. The philosophical McClellan saw in this letup in the weather a lesson about life. "What a change in the appearance of the country two or three short weeks can make," he marvelled. "So it is with everything else on this earth—things which in one week are looked upon as extravagant, imaginary, & impossible may in the next, be common occurrences—someone who was poor & obscure may in as short a time take his place among the 'princes of the earth.' "[14]

But a different kind of attitude set in by the end of February, along with a change again in the weather. On Washington's birthday snow was on the ground and Raymond was writing home complaining of boredom: "Every day is so nearly alike to me that it has become rather dull business."[15]

There was no way around the weather, but there was a way around this last problem for those willing to take the risk, and many were. It was called Benny Havens.

Benny Havens was a man—indeed an institution—a lovable, good-hearted raconteur who ran a tavern in nearby Buttermilk Falls. There he had been selling spirits and viands to cadets, and thus corrupting them, for more than two decades. Getting caught at his establishment was a dismissal offense. But there were said to be three compelling reasons for taking the chance and going anyhow.

First was the character of the drinks Benny served, particularly a kicker called "hot flip," which he knew just when to flip for perfect flavor. Then there was the quality of the food he offered at his board, particularly the buckwheat flapjacks, which Benny could also flip to perfection. Sometimes when they had no money and their mouths watered for Benny's flapjacks, the cadets made out requisitions for Mackintosh blankets and smuggled them to the tavern as coin for supper. Benny knew just where to convert such contraband to currency.

The third reason for going to Benny's was Benny himself, a host of the old school, a friend and crony to cadets he favored, entertaining them with his ready smile, quick wit, and compelling stories. Though he had little formal schooling, he was inexplicably an able mathematician who also offered timely tutoring with his hot flip and flapjacks.

As a cadet who regularly and illegally patronized his establishment in the 1830s, poet-to-be Edgar Allan Poe considered Benny "the only congenial soul in the entire God-forsaken place."[16]

Benny was a native of the Hudson River valley, who had fallen into his congenial calling as a sideline. He had served as a first lieutenant in the volunteer army in the War of 1812 and afterward returned to enter the business of cutting "hoop poles," the young saplings from which barrel hoops were made. On the side he turned his cottage into a tavern of sorts and began filling and emptying a few barrels of his own.

The main source of spirituous and contraband drink at West Point at that early time was an off-limits but close-in establishment run by another congenial soul named Gridley. But Old Grid became such a nuisance that the authorities simply bought him out and turned his place into the post hospital.

"What was Gridley's loss was a great gain to 'Benny Havens, oh!' " said Professor Church, who occasionally noticed more than sines and cosines. To Benny's tavern, after Gridley was bought out, "there was at once a rush, and for years after he had a monopoly of the business."[17]

A fine business it was. Even the Marquis de Lafayette, in his triumphant hero's return to America in 1824, stopped in at Benny's for a hot flip, paying his tab with two gold gilt buttons bearing his image.

Benny's most valued and faithful clientele, however, were not the rich and famous, but the thirsty, hungry cadets who slipped out nights under threat of academic execution if caught. Many of these would one day become famous if not rich in their own right, and would always have a place in their hearts for Benny.

George Edward Pickett, a fellow-plebe whom William Gardner

thought "a jolly good fellow with fine natural gifts sadly neglected," was rapidly becoming devotedly addicted to Benny's enticements.[18] He was stealing away regularly now to lift his glass in good fellowship and his superb singing voice in Benny's anthem, set to the music of "Wearin' o' the Green":

> Come, fill your glasses fellows, and
>   stand up in a row
> To singing sentimentally, we're going
>   for to go;
> In the Army there's sobriety, promotion's
>   very slow,
> So we'll sing our reminiscences of
>   Benny Havens, oh!
> Oh, Benny Havens, oh! Oh, Benny Havens, oh!
> So we'll sing our reminiscences
>   of Benny Havens, oh![19]

Plebe A. P. Hill of Virginia was perhaps not debauching regularly at Benny Havens's tavern in the spring of 1843, but he was basking in the intoxicating weather. The season had "just begun to put forth its budding beauties," and the cloudless days and cool bracing air were sending the blood galloping through his veins.[20] There was much for them to be grateful for this spring. As Samuel Raymond said, "I have not had any fighting to do yet and am not therefore as yet either hurt or killed."[21]

But they were soon to experience the next worst thing. The annual June examination, bigger even than the semiannual ordeal in January, was at hand. The Post Orders on the last of May confirmed it, and when Winfield Scott arrived four days later, it became a grim certainty.

Major General Scott, the hero of wars past and wars yet to come, came every year as chairman of the board of visitors to bear witness to this apotheosis of cadet agony. The prestigious board, never less than five in number, men distinguished for their military and scientific knowledge, was appointed annually by the secretary of war. Its members came in June to attend the examination, judge cadet progress, review the state of the institution in general, and report to the secretary of war.[22] Scott loved doing it. West Point was one of his favorite places and the annual examination of cadets was one of his favorite diversions.

For these plebes this would be their first close-up exposure to the larger-than-life soldier who commanded the army to which they now belonged. Frightening in size, 6 feet 5 inches tall with the bulk to match, Scott was a giant in any age and by any standards. He was "magnificent in physical proportions and swelling with graceful hauteur."[23] He filled not just space, but every cadet with a reverential awe. He brought into their harried daily lives "some of the splendor that attaches to bravery and achievement."[24]

The day the examinations began, the plebes marched to the recitation hall where Scott and the other members of the board of visitors waited, with about twenty uniformed officers and a gathering of guests, including ladies. William Dutton thought the room was splendid. It was newly built at a cost of twelve thousand dollars, and the class filed into it with trembling fingers and fluttering hearts.[25]

Some of them, those who didn't survive the ordeal, were still being "found" and sent home by late June. Dutton was expecting as many as fifty casualties, some of them "talented fellows . . . & *all* would rather be shot!!"[26] When it was over, seventy-two were still left in the plebe class. A dozen had been lost. McClellan had slipped to third in the rankings. Thomas J. Lowe, William Gardner's rustic roommate, anchored the other end, with Gardner himself within hailing distance. Tom Jackson was still present, and surprisingly, sitting in fifty-first place. He was putting space between himself and the ledge. Dabney Maury as usual was situated almost precisely in the middle.[27]

A score of the plebes were promoted from private to corporal for the coming year, when they would all be third-classmen learning the duties of corporals. They were "yearlings" now, and as smug and contemptuous of the incoming class of plebes as the third-classmen had been of them the summer before. Promotion to corporal was a distinction going to the most admirable and soldierlike among them. McClellan was on the list, with Raymond and Derby. Maury would be added later in the summer. Jackson would remain a private. Not to be promoted was not a stain, however. Not everybody could be, and two-thirds of them were not. There would be other chances. In Jackson's case, promotion was too much to ask. Survival was still sufficient.[28]

So they all turned toward their second summer encampment, not remembering how dreary their first had been. In contrast to the ten-month study grind they had just been through, the encampment had been sublimated, at least in Raymond's mind, into "by far the pleasantest part of a cadet's life."[29] McClellan thought so too, for he was sitting pretty. He had become a permanent fixture in the firmament of class rankings, and one of only four picked to tutor the new plebe class in arithmetic—a bonus distinction.

He sat back in self-satisfaction and contemplated the coming months with pleasure. He would have a new roommate in this third-class year, his favorite Southerner, James Stuart of South Carolina. He liked the dashing Carolinian; they got on well. It was going to be a good year.

Somehow McClellan preferred Southerners generally. "I am sorry to say that the manners, feelings & opinions of the Southerners are far, far preferable to those of the majority of the Northerners at this place," he confessed to his brother, John. "I may be mistaken, but I like them better."[30] The slavery issue was not yet dividing the country as it one day would. Nor was it dividing the cadets in 1843; it was not yet a line drawn on the plain at West Point.

By mid August boredom had returned. Samuel Raymond as usual had no news to send home to Connecticut, "this being the last place in the world for anything of that kind." The weather had been rainy. In two more weeks the encampment would be over, "then for barracks study and the end of pleasure."[31]

At the end of pleasure, in that fall of 1843, waited the third-class curriculum and more mathematical Sanskrit—analytical geometry and calculus this year, "the most solid part."[32] But there would be some surveying fieldwork too, a diversion with romantic potential. As cadets before them had learned, survey instruments artfully fixed on nearby homes and buildings in Buttermilk Falls could often catch in the crosshairs members of the opposite sex—forms far more pleasing to the mind and eye than logarithms.[33] The second half of French, English grammar, rhetoric, geography, history, and the first parts of artillery and drawing also awaited them. The last subject in particular promised more trouble for Tom Jackson.

Perverse as it seemed, drawing, like French, had a purpose; an engineer must know how to draw, just as he must know how to read

French. So the class filed into the drawing studios on the Academy building's third floor in early September, and found there a distinguished American painter ready to teach them how to do it.

Robert Weir was the second faculty member they would meet of international reputation. There would be others. West Point attracted men of world class stature to its faculty, or often gave it to them later if they arrived without it.

When Weir produced his first painting at the age of nineteen, a rendering of *Paul Preaching at Athens*, friends saw raw talent there and arranged to send him to Europe to study. For four years he submerged himself in the masters—Michelangelo, Raphael, Titian, and others—and produced two notable works of his own, *Christ and Nicodemus*, and *The Angel Releasing Peter*. Back in New York his gifts brought him election as an associate of the National Academy, and in 1829, a member. The next year he became a professor of perspective there, a title full of honor, but with little pay. When President Jackson proposed to make him head of the department of drawing at West Point in 1834, much more gainful employment, he jumped at the offer.

Weir continued to paint as he taught, and had become by 1843 one of the luminaries of the Hudson River school of American art. During the past summer, he had completed his masterpiece, *The Embarkation of the Pilgrims*, which was to hang in the rotunda of the capitol building in Washington. Now, in the fall of the year, the class of 1846 was filing into his studios for the first time.[34]

Once again Weir's forbearance and artistic sensitivities would be severely taxed, as they always were. "It may well be imagined," said one cadet, "that the work of some was truly grotesque." To those "Old Bob" gave wide berth, only occasionally inquiring which splotch was the house, and which the cow.[35] Weir had introduced a decade of cadets to art and painting and had disciplined their hands to draw what their eyes could see.[36] There was no reason he couldn't do it with this class, Tom Jackson notwithstanding.

On the Saturday evening before Christmas, the class's second away from home, West Point celebrated the season with a yuletide soiree at the Academy building from 7:30 to taps. The fencing room was gaily lit and there was music for dancing. The band played, and the riding arena was set aside for athletic exercises and refreshments.

Superintendent Delafield tempered the festivities with unrelenting supervision. Perhaps with Benny Havens in mind, he cautioned the corps sternly that they could be absent from quarters to attend the party in the Academy building and for no other reason. No irregularity of any kind would be tolerated. No contraband was to be smuggled from the riding room into the barracks. All violators would be arrested and strictly dealt with. At seven o'clock and at other such times as the commandant saw fit, there would be an inspection of barracks. Merry Christmas, cadets.

A week later on the last day of the year, the superintendent announced that the semiannual examinations would begin the second day of the new year at 8:00 in the morning. The third class was to be prepared to recite mathematics, French, English grammar, and drawing. Happy New Year, cadets.[37]

The January examinations were a turning point in Tom Jackson's West Point experience. Not only did he survive another test of academic fire, but something gratifying happened. He climbed to the twenty-first ranking in mathematics, the subject that counted. He even improved in French, inching up from seventieth to sixty-first, and he was an acceptable fifty-eighth in English grammar. Only in drawing, now his biggest cross, did he still run with the immortals; he was ranked seventy-fourth.[38]

All in all it was a striking improvement. Not given to boasting, he nonetheless wrote his sister, Laura, that the examination had gone "rather to my advantage, as I rose considerably in mathematics, and a few files in the French language, though in the same time I fell a few files in ethics and in drawing."

He then said something truly revolutionary. "I passed in all my studies, and I bid fair to continue to do the same for the future." Jackson now believed he might get through this after all. Not only that, but he seemed to be reaching for the stars.

"I feel very confident that unless fortune frowns on me more than it has yet," he confided to the sister he adored, "I shall graduate in the upper half of my class. . . ."

His health was also better, "far better than it was when I parted with you, and indeed more flattering than it has been for the last two years; and I think by the time I graduate, if that should ever be, my health will be as good as ever."

43

He was content in other surprising ways this winter. "My friends here are numerous apparently," he confessed, "and all that I want to render myself happy on earth is the sight of you and my native land."[39]

Richard Delafield was far less sanguine this new year, in part because of the suspect behavior of some of Jackson's less well-adjusted classmates. The superintendent opened 1844 by evoking the name of General Washington in reprimanding the devilish Thomas Lowe and a plebe prankster named Henry Heth for taking the name of the Supreme Being in vain. He pointed out that Washington himself had issued direct strictures to his revolutionary army against such blasphemy sixty-five years ago when West Point was a fort in the War for Independence. The Founding Father would have been ashamed of Lowe and Heth—Delafield was certain of it. Henry Ehninger, a New Yorker and one of George Derby's roommates, was hit with twelve extra turns of Saturday guard duty and confined to limits for six months for some unspecified but apparently heinous offense. John Adams of Tennessee was awarded three extra turns of Saturday guard duty and confined to quarters for a week for violence against an unoffending servant and indecorous conduct at the mess table. Cadets Thomas Rush McConnell of Georgia and Clermont Livingston Best of New York, both Jackson's classmates, were ordered to pay for scrubbing the floor of the drawing academy in the aftermath of some undisclosed calamity.[40]

Derby, on the other hand, was having better luck. "You will be inexpressibly gratified to hear," he wrote his mother on Christmas Day, "that my good friend the commandant is making exertions to have the 2 demerits taken off, (there remaining some doubt of their legality and a great doubt of their necessity)."[41]

On Washington's birthday in 1844, it was Greenland cold when the band turned out on the plain to play the national airs. But not even the cold this winter dampened spirits as it might once have, for this was to be a benchmark year for the class of 1846; it was to be the summer of their midcourse furlough, two months at home away from West Point. Every class had its furlough in the summer following its second year. Members of this class had been aching for theirs since the day they arrived. Now, by the middle of May, it was less than two months away, glittering there just beyond the annual examinations in June.

But their plans were already hitting snags. The tailor the class had been counting on to come down from Boston to outfit them in furlough clothes had been forbidden to set foot on the landing.

"Dicky [Delafield] won't let our Tailor land," Derby complained, "as he says he deceived him once and he shall not appear again."[42]

Then the secretary of war interfered. He was a new man, "that old demented [William] Wilkins," who had replaced James Madison Porter in February, who had replaced John Spencer in March, the year before. Wilkins ordered their furlough delayed because he wanted personally to review the entire corps of cadets. Derby fumed, cursing Wilkins as that "vile old locofoco lawyer whom Tyler has cursed us with." He didn't believe Spencer would have acted so.[43]

The June examination came inexorably and Tom Jackson leaped another twenty-one files forward and now rested in thirtieth place in general merit, near the middle of the class. McClellan held fast to third place, unhappy about not being in first. Thomas Lowe smashed the demerit barrier with 280 for the year, putting him dead last in the entire corps of cadets for conduct and earning him a permanent return home to Kentucky.[44] Promotions to cadet sergeant also came through as the class awaited its furlough. Among those on the list were McClellan, Maury—and this time, Tom Jackson.[45]

At last, on Tuesday morning, June 25, the Post Orders told them what they had all been longing to hear. Their furloughs would begin immediately following parade that day, to last until two o'clock on August 28. There was only one thing. They could not stop in New York City on the way home, unless they lived there. Last year's furlough class had behaved shamefully in the city, and Delafield wasn't going to have it again. He announced he was sending Lieutenant Robert S. Granger, an assistant instructor of tactics, down the river with them to see that this edict was strictly enforced. Any cadet found lingering in the city or who was guilty of any other gross irregularity would be arrested and returned to West Point at once.[46]

It was a nuisance, but it failed to dim the joy of the day. Immediately after parade there was a happy clamoring of the furlough men to the steamboat landing. Tom Jackson was about to have all he wanted to be happy now on earth—the sight of Laura and his native land.

Death
in the
Family

In the fall of 1844 the roommate now watching Tom Jackson pile his grate with anthracite coal every night was doe-eyed George Stoneman of New York.

The two shared what may have been the most becalmed quarters in West Point history, a noiseless room on the first floor of the south barracks. Nobody ever heard from them. Their neighbor in the next room said he "scarcely knew they were there."[1]

They were much alike. Stoneman was the oldest of ten children, and nearly as taciturn as Jackson. Both were unobtrusive in the extreme, with meditative dispositions. Neither put himself forward in any way. Darius Couch, one of their classmates, thought them thinkers rather than talkers.

Stoneman wasn't as ascetic—"or, perhaps, puritanical"—as his roommate, and unlike Jackson he had social graces that endeared him to others. Jackson neither sought the solace of companionship nor got much of it. There was that ready, sweet smile of recognition that he occasionally flashed, which Couch thought most redeeming, so gracious "that one's heart went out to him." More hearts, however, went out on a regular basis to Stoneman, who was seen as a more "generous-hearted, whole-souled companion."[2]

46

They were all second-classmen now, an exalted status that was exposing them to new adventures in learning. Behind them, success-fully skirted, was the Scylla of mathematics; ahead lay the Charybdis of science, a treacherous academic whirlpool of natural philosophy (theoretical and experimental physics) and chemistry. They would continue with the second year of artillery and drawing as well, and they would learn the evolutions of the battalion and the duties of sergeants. But the sciences would now occupy seven of every ten of their academic hours, as mathematics had in their first two years. Now they were going to begin to learn to apply all the sines, cosines, conic sections, and calculus they had been learning.

Waiting in the new natural philosophy building next to the cadet chapel were four particularly unholy subjects: mechanics, optics, as-tronomy, and electricity. And perched among the telescopes waiting to teach them this dreaded quartet was William H. C. Bartlett, who probably knew more about those subjects than anybody in the world.

Bartlett was acknowledged as perhaps the most brilliant cadet to graduate from West Point in its forty-year history. He entered the academy in 1822 from Missouri with a backwoods background not unlike Tom Jackson's. Four years later, in 1826, he graduated first in his class.

By 1844 he was one of the world's great scientists. What the class of 1846 saw there among the telescopes in the natural philosophy building was an elflike creature with a mane of unmanageable hair, equally out-of-control beard, sharp nose, and constantly darting eyes. The great man also had a bizarre and unsettling nervous habit of violently jerking his head from side to side as if snapping at his collar.[3] It was said that his digestion was so temperamental that only the tenderest of birds would pass muster with his stomach.[4] Not for him was the bill of fare at the mess hall.

Some cadets found Bartlett a stimulating and unorthodox teacher as well as a great scientist, with a gift for making murky subjects understandable and interesting.[5] Some thought him luminous, exact, suggestive, and inspiring. He was apt to become impatient with slow or fat-witted minds, but he was fundamentally just, fair, and kind to all.[6]

Others, however, found him only a tolerable teacher, "more inclined to the dry mathematics of his subject than to the experimen-tal." One critic complained that he galloped through experiments with nervous impatience, often furnishing more amusement along the way than solid instruction: "If a cadet could only get his mathematical formulas correct, it mattered little whether he could tell . . . a telescope from a grindstone."[7]

The most dreaded of Bartlett's dispensations was a bugbear called "optics," particularly an inscrutable section of it called "optical images." The subject was all about light, but each year it left whole sections of cadets entirely in the dark. The course and the text Bartlett had written to go with it had been terrorizing second-classmen since he introduced them into the curriculum in 1839.

Dabney Maury, who in 1844 was feeling himself slipping from the middle of things toward the immortals, seized on this menacing and unlikely course as his potential ticket to salvation. If he could just master optics, the toughest course of all, his situation might yet be redeemed. He had always considered himself pretty good at a spurt. So he began boning optics, trying, like Jackson before the grate, to burn it into his brain.

When it mattered, Maury was ready. The day Professor Bartlett visited his section, Maury's instructor, Lieutenant George Deshon of the ordnance corps, said, "Mr. Maury will go to the board, and demonstrate the 'optical images.' "

Maury rose with a knowing smile, took up the chalk and sponge, and executed the problem as if he had been born understanding it. He "maxed" it with a perfect recitation, soared seventeen files in his standing, and saved himself from the immortals. Professor Bartlett was impressed, Lieutenant Deshon was gratified, and Maury's sectionmates were ecstatic.

"Peri," they cried after class, shouting his nickname and swarming joyously about him, "you are safe."[8]

It had been a curious winter, starting out cold in October, "a little of the coldest weather that ever I smelt at this season of the year," Derby thought. But by Christmas Eve they had not yet seen a snowflake,[9] and the superintendent in a warm gesture ordered up "as good a dinner as the nature of the case will permit" for Christmas Day.[10]

They had already had a gift of sorts. Captain J. Addison Thomas, the commandant of cadets, had gotten married. This was good news, because "Ethical Tom" had been getting on everybody's nerves. A wife might help. He could get on hers instead.

"Old Tom is getting worse & worse every day," John Adams of Tennessee had complained in September. "We have been expecting [him] to get married for some time, but so far we have been disappointed. I hope he will marry a woman who will whip him every day."[11]

What he finally did marry, a few weeks before Christmas, was what Derby described as "seventy thousand dollars, thirty-five years old, in New York. . . ." When the newlyweds returned to West Point from New York City, Derby was pleased to see that she had brought with her at the end of a leash, besides Thomas, "a little excessively ugly dog with a brass collar around his neck and a most abrupt termination to his tail."[12] Neither the bride nor her money nor her bobtail dog, however, had made Thomas any more ingratiating. He was as big a rascal as ever, Adams believed, but at least he no longer prowled about the barracks as he used to do.[13]

Derby also saw a change for the better in Thomas. "The Captain whose mind vacillates in different directions, with every 'creed of doctrine' has again turned the current of his affections towards me," Derby wrote home; "how long it will last however no one knows."[14]

Thomas was not life-threatening, no matter what the cadets might have thought. Not much was at West Point. It only seemed that way. Taking everything into account, the academy, while stressful in the extreme, was a safe place to be. A. P. Hill believed it might be "the healthiest institution in the world; there is generally about one death in two or three years, and even then proceeding from the bursting of a cannon, false stroke of a sword or some other casualty." A great many die away at the examinations, Hill admitted, but "revive again in some distant corner of the union where they live *ex-cadets*, something like *ex-presidents*."[15]

Therefore, Samuel Raymond wasn't worried, even though he wasn't feeling well. It was nothing serious, he assured his sister Mary back in West Hartford. He wasn't so sick he couldn't attend to his studies, but he felt ill enough to see the doctor. Don't give yourself any alarm, he reassured her, "for if I am more unwell I shall let you know it soon."[16]

Raymond was quiet, studious, melancholy, and well liked. Even the reclusive Tom Jackson liked him and considered him "a friend and fellow classmate in whom were combined both shining talents and the characteristics of a gentleman."[17] He was the oldest cadet in the class and that meant they could call him "Dad."[18]

By mid January, Dad had checked into the hospital with a bad cold and a severe cough. It had become so severe that he had to "Wheaton it"—get excused from duty by the post physician, Dr. W. V. Wheaton.[19] Wheaton diagnosed Raymond's trouble as inflammation of the lungs. George McClellan, who took a sympathetic interest in the case, called it "galloping consumption."[20]

Raymond was no stranger to the malady. He had been prone to it through the years, and it appeared to be within the control of medical skill. But then it took a turn for the worse. By January 20, Dr. Wheaton reported him "more alarmingly ill" and moved him into his own quarters where he and his family could give him around-the-clock attention.[21]

His worried classmates were standing vigil at his bedside, too, letting their classwork slide, doing all they could to comfort him. It may have been at about this time and on this occasion that some of them saw something they might not have noticed before about Tom Jackson. There was a tenderness beneath that abrupt, unsociable, unbending exterior that seemed to surface in situations such as this. Illness, bereavement, and misfortune to fellow cadets seemed to awaken the sympathetic Samaritan in him.[22]

William Gardner had noticed it. While confined to his quarters under arrest at another time, Gardner was surprised to see Jackson, who had never visited him before, appear suddenly at the door of his room. Jackson was not Gardner's intimate friend, but he wished to express his sympathy. It was the only visit Gardner ever had from him.[23] It was likely now that he was one of the classmates standing often at Raymond's bedside during these anxious days in late January.

By 7:40 in the evening of the twentieth, Raymond seemed to be resting more comfortably. Superintendent Delafield was still concerned, however—so concerned that he was writing at that moment to Raymond's brother, Josiah, in New York City, apprising him of his brother's condition.[24]

By the evening of the twenty-third, Raymond was suffering intensely, with his band of brothers rallying around him as best they could. His flesh and blood brothers were sent for and arrived later that night. At 2:10 P.M. the next day, he died.[25]

Only hours earlier West Point had been rocked by even more devastating news. Louisa Weir, Professor Weir's thirty-seven-year-old wife, was also dead. She had given birth ten days earlier to a baby girl and it had killed her.[26]

Classes were suspended on the twenty-fifth to permit the corps of cadets and the faculty to attend Mrs. Weir's funeral services in the cadet chapel at 11:00 A.M. Post Orders edged in black announced that Raymond would be buried in the cadet cemetery that coming Sunday morning.[27]

For George Derby it was a time of utter gloom and sorrow. Raymond had been in his section in mathematics and ethics and Derby thought him "a very fine, good hearted fellow, of superior talents, studious, and of much promise. . . ." McClellan, another of Raymond's section mates, called the two deaths "a melancholy thing," and Tom Jackson considered that in Raymond he had lost a friend.[28]

The Sunday of the funeral was bleak and cold, "cold as Greenland," Derby thought. The corps of cadets, grouped by class, marched through the bitter morning to the cadet chapel at half past ten. A boxy, white-steepled building seventy feet deep and not yet ten years old, the chapel stood beside the Academy building, dwarfed by it only in size. Its location was a quiet reminder that faith was coequal with academics and that this was a place not only for engineers and soldiers, but Christians. From any of its five hundred seats, cadets could look above the chancel and see yet another reminder of Robert Weir's preeminence as a painter: a work of his depicting war in the shape of a Roman soldier and peace as a female figure draped in creamy, flowing white. When the corps of cadets sat in chapel, as they must every Sunday, she was in all likelihood the only woman they had seen all week.

Drawn up somberly inside on this Sunday morning was the cadet escort under arms and at parade rest. The band waited in the aisle opposite. After the cadets filed in and were seated, the front door was opened and Raymond's coffin was carried in by his classmates. The band struck up "that wild and expressive melody," the "Dead March in Saul," and the chapel was plunged into "an inexpressibly sad and mournful" anguish.

The post chaplain and professor of ethics, the Reverend Martin P. Parks, met Raymond's casket at the door in his robes of office, and preceded it down the aisle past the mourners, intoning, "I am the resurrection and the life. . . ." The casket was placed at the front of the chapel under Professor Weir's painting and draped in the national colors as Reverend Park recounted Raymond's last agonizing hours of repentance, baptism, and hope of salvation.

After the service the cortege marched the mournful mile through the cold to the cadet cemetery. The coffin rocked gently on its caisson as the band played the dead march. The mourners followed in slow, swaying cadence to the bleak music and the beating drums. At the cemetery the coffin was lowered into its open grave, three sad volleys were fired into the cheerless January day, and Raymond was "left . . . to his long, last slumber."[29]

"We mourn him as a brother," a committee of classmates wrote Raymond's parents four days later, "a brother bound to us by strong ties, the severing of which makes our hearts bleed." His "many acts of kindness dictated by the warm impulses of a heart alive to every generous emotion," they wrote, "have endeared him to us, and will be ever referred to with deep feeling and registered in our hearts," though "we no longer grasp his hand and welcome him to our daily board."[30]

To these cadets death was still a novel and terrible thing. There was coming a day when it would be no less terrible, but no longer novel. More of them were yet to go prematurely and violently to open graves in the years of war and upheaval ahead, when they would be soldiers and death would be commonplace—even desirable, if the dead was the enemy.

Washington's birthday came a month after the funerals, bringing fair and welcomed weather. It hadn't looked for a while as if the weather would ever change. It had gone from bad to worse; the Greenland cold had turned even colder. February blew in so cold that the cadets on watch had to abandon their posts or freeze to death. The river had iced over rock hard.[31] On February 13 the cadets awoke to a temperature of ten degrees below zero; the thermometer had plunged thirty-eight degrees overnight.[32]

But on the morning of Washington's birthday the warm strains of martial music drifted in from the plain. The dreary cold had broken and given way to a fine springlike day. After promenades in the afternoon there was a dress parade in the evening. That night twenty-six guns bellowed salute to the Founding Father, reverberating through the Highlands. The band played and rockets streamed across the night sky. Heaps of brushwood and tar barrels piled against the ramparts of Old Put were put to the torch. It was "the grandest appearance of the kind" that William Dutton had ever seen.[33] They had needed that to help lift the darkness of death that had lain like a blanket on their spirits.

Life and study had to go on. There were daily demonstrations now in optics and magnetism, and the marvels of the magic lantern, camera obscura, and the solar microscope, which most of them were experiencing for the first time. They were seeing phenomena they had never seen before or dreamed existed—fleas under microscope "magnified to the size of a horse, and lice and other interesting creations on the same preposterous scale."[34]

They were also being exposed to the man who was opening many of the wonders of this new world to their vision, Jacob W. Bailey, the professor of chemistry, mineralogy, and geology. This kindly, warmhearted magician was showing them a miniature world that lived beyond their ordinary sight, and they were peering into it with awe and pleasure.

Little things mattered a great deal to Professor Bailey. A graduate of the West Point class of 1832, he was on his way to becoming what a fellow scientist would one day describe as "the father, in this country, of those branches of Natural History which relate to the *world of atoms*."[35] He was pioneering the development of the microscope in the field of botany, and winning international acclaim for his original studies of freshwater algae. Scientists the world over were going out of their way to consult him on the most difficult points of analysis and general physics.[36]

The professor was particularly well thought of by the cadets because he hated so to flunk them, not believing any boy otherwise qualified should be denied a commission simply because he could not comprehend the finer points of chemistry, mineralogy, or geology.[37] William Dutton thought him "a perfect love of a man."[38] He was of fragile frame and nervous organization—"as sensitive as an Aeolian harp, which pulsated with every harmony of nature and was jarred by all its discords." He had a passion for poetry, particularly for the old

English bards, and indulged a delicate fancy of writing rhyming letters to friends.[39] Like the kindly Duke Senior in Shakespeare's *As You Like It*, he found "tongues in trees, books in the running brooks, sermons in stones, and good in everything."[40]

Despite being the son of a minister—or perhaps because of it— he rejected organized religion and refused to attend Sunday chapel in stubborn defiance of Superintendent Delafield's standing edict. One can imagine the two discussing it, angrily staring at one another over the rims of their Ben Franklin eyeglasses. For Bailey, nature and not the chapel was "the mighty cathedral for his worship. . . ."[41]

"Oh! I wish you could just hear Prof. Bailey," Dutton wrote Lucy. "Ask him what question you will, he is fully prepared to answer you & you would think he had examined the very subject but a short time since."[42] They loved him for who he was and for the magical world he was showing them through his microscopes.

They were also discovering arresting new worlds far away through the long eyes of Professor Bartlett's telescopes. The class could now calculate eclipses and the phases of the moon and the transits of Mercury. It wasn't easy work. Derby found it "about the hardest stuff I have studied." And the still harder stuff, optics, magnetism, and galvanism, were still ahead.[43]

Even McClellan was finding the going stiff. He studied so hard before the semiannual examination in January that he could "scarcely see."[44] It was galling to him after all that work that he still stood only second in the class. He couldn't seem to overtake Charles Seaforth Stewart, who had come literally from the sea, having been born on a ship in the middle of the Pacific Ocean. A crack preparatory school in New Jersey had prepared Stewart, the only son of a navy chaplain and missionary, to excel at West Point, and he was leading everybody.

McClellan complained about this to his mother. "Toiling up hill is not what it is cracked up to be!" he wrote her. "I do not get marked as well for as good (or a better) recitation, as the man above me. . . . if I were already above him, I could distance him, I think." Getting above him is what he vowed to do by next June.[45]

Tom Jackson, unceasingly toiling to be what he resolved to be, was also bent on moving up. When he wrote Laura the results of the January examinations he said modestly that he had risen in each department of his studies.[46]

In truth, he was on a roll. Gardner noticed it, for "in his upward flight [he] landed in the section to which I belonged and tarried a while with us." In this brief stopover, the cometlike Jackson sat on Gardner's left in the recitation room. Called to the blackboard one day, he rose in his abrupt manner and shambled to the front, and the class had to repress a snicker. "General Jackson"—one of his nicknames, after General Andrew Jackson—was chalked across his back in large letters. Gardner was mistakenly believed to have done it and was ordered to brush it off. It didn't matter much to Jackson who had done it or that it had been done at all. Whatever was scrawled on his back, the section would get but a brief view of it, for he was soon on his way up to the next stop.[47] He had finally gotten the hang of West Point.

West Point, however, had entirely failed to get the hang of his classmate, George Derby, who marched to a drum nobody else seemed to hear and had a nickname that didn't seem to make any sense either—Squibob. Derby was a brilliant student, in the first section in everything, and considered one of the best draftsmen ever to step into the academy drawing rooms.[48] It was what he chose to do with his pen and pencil that was causing the uproar. His quirky behavior was making him a legend at West Point. Not only was John Quincy Adams's cadet the best draftsman the academy had ever seen, he was the most outrageous prankster and hoaxer anybody could remember.

Theophile D'Oremieulx knew this perhaps better than anybody. The French instructor had already started the lesson for the day when he stopped suddenly, remembering.

"Ah! it is the first of the month, I see. Gentlemen, hand me your textbooks."

All of the cadets passed their textbooks willingly to the front except Derby, who was intent on slipping his into his desk drawer instead.

"Mr. Derby," said D'Oremieulx sternly, "hand me your textbook, sir."

"Could I be excused just this once, sir?" said Derby falteringly.

"Certainly not, sir," said the Frenchman severely. "Do you not remember that you are the principal cause of this regulation? It is your textbook I particularly want to see, Mr. Derby. Bring it to me at once, Sir."

It was true, of course. All this was because of Derby. There was a stern prohibition against disfiguring textbooks, punishable by demerit or worse. So Derby had transformed all the pictures of the bones and fossils from primeval ages in his geology text into strange and grotesque monsters. The evidence was seized one day and placed indignantly before the academic board, who stared at it for as long as they could stand it, before breaking into delighted whoops. It had been worth the laugh, so there was no punishment—Derby's pranks were never dismissal offenses. But since then, on the first of each month, textbooks had to be called to the front and inspected, particularly Derby's.

"But I had rather not, sir," he protested to D'Oremieulx, all the color draining from his face.

"Perhaps so, sir," replied D'Oremieulx, "but you must."

Derby slowly, grudging every step, walked to the front through the profound silence now filling the room. With elaborate reluctance he handed D'Oremieulx his textbook.

The Frenchman flipped through it rapidly, expecting the worst— French verbs with fanciful faces, perhaps. Maybe even ze gr-r-rand Napoleon, God forbid, with a moustache or worse. But what is this? Nothing? Everything in the text in order? No desecration of any kind? Then he found the two words in the blank space above the opening chapter. They said simply, APRIL FOOL.

D'Oremieulx then remembered what first day of which month it was.[49]

Derby's trips to the blackboard always held potential for uproar, given his drafting skill. Ordered to the front to draw the model of a pump, Derby drew it flawlessly. But he also managed to make of it an unmistakable caricature of the professor, putting an almost unbearable strain on the class decorum.[50]

He is remembered also for this exchange in artillery class:

"Yes, Mr. Derby?" Captain Keyes asked. "Do you have a question?"

"Yes, sir," Derby said gravely—all of his outrages were delivered poker-faced. "What would be the effect," he asked solemnly, "of confining a single grain of gunpowder in the centre of the earth and setting fire to it?"

Keyes, equally grave—he had learned by experience to give like-for-like with Derby—confessed that he did not know, but would requisition the ordnance sergeant for a grain of powder and authorize the experiment.[51]

And for this conversation:

Professor: "Given: that a thousand men are besieging a fortress whose equipment of men, provisions, etc., are so and so—it is a military axiom that at the end of forty-five days the fort will surrender. Now, young men, if any of you were in command of such a fortress, how would you proceed? Yes, Mr. Derby, your hand is up?"

Derby, triumphantly: "I would march out, let the enemy in, and at the end of forty-five days I would change places with him."[52]

So it went with Derby. These were not really demerit offenses. Nobody knew how to classify them. But neither did everybody laugh.

Ambrose Burnside, a hellion in his own right from the class just behind, was arrested, courtmartialed, and nearly thrown out of West Point for one day aiding Thomas Lowe in a physical assault on Derby.[53] Cadet William L. Crittenden also took violent exception to him.

"What do you mean, Sir?" demanded Crittenden one Sunday morning as Derby was entering the north barracks following divine services.

"Mean by what, Sir?" Derby asked.

"By looking at me, Sir."

"Do you consider yourself too good to be looked at, Sir?"

Crittenden drew back, his hand on his sword hilt. "Yes, Sir. I do. And if you give me any more of your words G——d d——n you, I'll run you through."

"You must be a miserable coward, to threaten an unarmed man with a sword," retorted Derby.

Crittenden drew his weapon and thrust at Derby three times, cutting gashes in his chin, his right arm, and shoulder. Derby charged, but since Crittenden was now being restrained by other cadets, he pulled up. It would be cowardly now to retaliate. So instead, he "Wheatoned it" to the hospital and emerged three weeks later with a warlike scar along his chin and throat. Crittenden was courtmartialed and reduced in ranks, but to Derby's utter disgust permitted to remain at West Point.

Crittenden was a nephew of Senator John J. Crittenden of Kentucky. How else could he have gotten away with "clipping down a poor woman's boy from Massachusetts without any provocation?" Derby demanded of his sympathetic mother.[54]

Derby wrote his mother regularly. She was his main audience, his support in times of insult, injury, and depression, his cheering section, and his chief advisor on the subject of "spoons." A spoon was a ladylove, a sweetheart, a girl.[55] Like all young men much away from their company, the West Pointers thought often and favorably about spoons, and needed all the help they could get with them.

Mrs. Derby had tried some abortive matchmaking on her son's behalf in his first summer at West Point, sending him as a visitor the daughter of a friend, touting her to him as both pretty and genteel. She turned out to be neither. Derby was on his best behavior for the event—"have not made use of a cigar or a profane expression since I was here," he assured his mother. But the young lady was a letdown. "I never saw such a savage, grim looking woman," he reported later, "and she spoke to me as though she was speaking to some Irishman."[56]

Since then Derby had been in love many times, with little to show for it. "I am thinking I rather did the ridiculous while at home by Lizzy Jewall," he confessed to his mother around Washington's birthday in 1845. He would be more general in his attentions if he ever saw that spoon again. But, "Kate is too old, Mother," he protested in the same letter. "If I wanted a wife as old as myself I would go and pick up Mary Olmstead again (if I *could*) as I believe she is one of the best girls afloat except Miss Whiting, who wouldn't have me, or little Lizzy Allen who I believe I wouldn't have."[57]

The year before, another prospect, if she ever was that, also went aglimmering, lost to what appeared a hasty wedlock. "You have written to me two or three times about Mary Ann Grant's marriage, maternity etc," Derby complained to his mother, "and yet it is a singular fact, you have never told me who on earth she took. . . . Isn't 4 months and 19 days after marriage a very short time for children?"[58]

But never mind, he would assure Mrs. Derby early in the coming fall, he had found the right spoon at last and was desperately in love. Her name was Elizabeth Orr of Bridgewater, the daughter of old Dr. Orr. She was seventeen and as lovely as an angel. No, he hadn't met her yet, or even seen her. "But that's a trifle. My roommate knows her very well and is going to introduce me next July."[59]

The juices were even rising in Tom Jackson by early 1845. His sister Laura had just written him of her marriage in September to Jonathan Arnold in Beverly, Virginia. "I think that if happiness exists in this world," he wrote back wistfully, "matrimony is one of its principal factors."[60] Not exactly the words of a passionate romantic, but Jackson approached everything in stiff moderation, especially spoons.

There were not only girls to think about in this season, there were horses. They had begun riding.

"Jounce, jounce, jounce," moaned William Dutton. "Some of the horses are the hardest I ever rode."[61] The "hardest of all possible saddles, strapped on the backs of the hardest of all possible horses, and *without any stirrups*," Derby complained.[62] In fact they were the post artillery horses doing double duty, and some of their riders were pitching from their backs into the thick layer of tanbark that covered the riding hall.

Many in the class, particularly the southerners, had been raised in the saddle. Yet even one of these, Clarendon J. L. (Dominie) Wilson, of Virginia, was flung heavily from the same horse that had nearly unseated Dutton a few days before.[63] The New Yorker Darius Couch, "one of the very noblest fellows" Dutton had ever met,[64] was thrown from a horse named Pink, dashed violently against an iron pillar, and knocked insensible. For several days he hovered in a delirium at the hospital.[65]

Tom Jackson made as lasting an impression in the riding hall as he did at the blackboard and on the drill field. Maury thought him singularly awkward and uncomfortable to look at on a horse. "We were painfully anxious as we watched him leaping the bar and cutting at heads," Maury said. Although he had ridden much at Jackson's mill, even racing some of Uncle Cummins's horses, Jackson had a rough hand with the bridle and kept an ungainly seat. When he cut at a head on the ground with his sword, he tottered unsteadily, appearing about to plunge headlong. It was a mystery what kept him in the saddle—probably the same resolve that kept him in West Point.[66]

The annual examinations came again in June 1845, and when they were done sixty of the original class were left. Only nineteen of them now stood ahead of Jackson in general merit. He had lapped the other forty. He now ranked twentieth overall, eleventh in natural philosophy and twenty-fifth in chemistry. If it had not been for drawing, in which he was next to last, he would have stood several files higher still.[67]

The next level of promotions were announced, and many in the class became captains and lieutenants, the highest order of cadet officers. Jackson was not among them; he had reverted to a high private.[68]

But more important than anybody's rank or order of merit as the summer of their last year began was the fact that it was their last year. They were first-classmen, finally. Ahead lay 1846. Beyond a final summer encampment and a final year of engineering study, glimmered the finish line. Nothing else really mattered.[69] When a cadet got to be a first-classman, when he had gone this far, it was unlikely he would be found deficient in his studies. If he behaved himself and stayed out of serious trouble, he was bound to graduate.[70]

The worst was over. The hardest three years were behind them now and nothing much had changed. Every day was still depressingly like every other day. "There 'ain't no news' and I can't make any," Derby wrote home. The food in the mess hall hadn't improved. "India rubber boiled in Aqua forte could give no idea of the toughness of our roast beef," he said, "and we are so accustomed to stale bread that the sight of a hot biscuit might occasion hysterics."[71]

But it would soon be 1846, the finest set of numbers they had seen in three years of nothing but numbers. They could make it now. The rest should be easy.

Gone Are
the Days
of Our Youth

William Dutton had tried to explain it to his fiancée in Connecticut. The whole idea of this place, he told her, was "to make efficient officers who are capable of performing any scientific task that may be imposed upon them."[1]

That is why they were grappling this summer—their last—with pyrotechny. It was believed that as army officers they might someday command artillery in battle, and they would need to know then how explosives work. Indeed, it might happen sooner rather than later if the continuing tension between the United States and Mexico erupted into war.

So they were making cartridges, rockets, "& every species of infernal work" this last summer, covered from head to foot with perspiration and grime, working in pitch, paste, and brimstone "like so many Guy Fawkeses." The work was as hard as digging a ditch and made them black as charcoal.[2]

Two heart-warming departures marked the last months of 1845—one in the late summer, the other in the early fall, both morale boosters. Richard Delafield left in August. He decided that eight years of improving West Point, pinching pennies, and making things different, were enough. The corps saw him off and wished him well, but as West Point's Irish janitor said, "When the Major went down to the wharf to leave the Pint he was followed by many a dhry eye."[3]

When at parade two months later it was announced that Commandant of Cadets J. Addison Thomas was also leaving, it was nearly more than the cadets could do to contain their gratitude. As soon as the ranks broke they took off their caps as a body and gave three tremendous cheers, then three more, and again three, retiring to their quarters brimming with good cheer. Every cadet that evening set a light in the window to "show old Tom how glad we are he is going." The barracks "shone like a plebe's waist plate."[4] When Thomas actually left around Christmas time, it was another case of many a dry eye at the landing.

It turned numbingly cold in November. The wind whistled around the old barracks buildings, and Derby reported that his ink was "congealing (almost) in my shivering pen." With the pen he wrote his mother:

> Cold Winter's icy days have come
> And bleak the northern snow storm pelts.
> We want good fires to keep us warm
> And we *don't want anything else.*[5]

Only the week before, the old pump that serviced the academy broke down and was replaced by a new one. Since then the water had carried such a strong component of tar that Derby thought it did not require much poetic license to say that "we have to chew it before it can be swallowed."[6]

But nothing was as cold, nothing so hard to swallow, as what they now were encountering daily in the recitation rooms on the Academy building's second floor. There, in the long 75 feet by 22 feet alleyway called the engineering room,[7] they had finally come face-to-face with Dennis Hart Mahan.

This was the year they were to put it all together. Now they would combine all of the mathematics and science and drawing and French they had learned, with Professor Mahan's doctrines of engineering, fortifications, and military tactics. Here is where they would become what it was intended they become when they entered West Point three years before. There would be other things to learn this last year—more artillery, mineralogy and geology, rhetoric, moral philosophy, and political science. They must master the evolutions of the line and the duties of commissioned officers, and learn the uses of the saber. But Mahan and the engineering, fortifications, and the science of war that he taught were what this last year was all about. Mahan was what West Point was all about. The hardest part might not be behind them after all.

Mahan was a unique presence. The academic board ran the academy, and Mahan, with Bartlett and Church to a lesser extent, ran the board. Consisting mainly of the professors and heads of departments, this omnipotent body designed the curriculum, selected and—in many cases—wrote the textbooks, examined the cadets, decided order of merit standings, dictated who was to stay and who was to leave, and recommended branches of service for the cadets who graduated.[8]

If Mahan dominated the academic board, it is not difficult to imagine how thoroughly he ruled his classroom. When cadets entered his state-of-the-art recitation hall they knew they were in the presence of authority. All about him stood the reminders of his calling. There was a model of a perfect military fortification and a full representation of a perfect attack on a fortification. There were plaster models of the great engineering and architectural masterpieces of the ancient world—the Propylaea, the Parthenon, the Hypaethral Temple, and the "Lantern of Demosthenes." There were models of modern-day bridges, canal locks, steam engines, water wheels, and arches. And there was Mahan, more formidable than any of these creations.[9]

Aloof and relentlessly demanding, he detested sloppy thinking, sloppy posture, and a sloppy attitude toward duty. No cadet slouched in a Mahan classroom, for he would be bitingly rasped to attention by the professor's high, reedy, nasally congested voice. The moment they entered his recitation room cadets involuntarily snapped to and sharpened every sense and faculty, for they would need them all. All backs went ramrod straight. (His entry in the room therefore probably had very little effect on Tom Jackson, who seemed fixed in that physical attitude at all times.) Never from the moment they entered was there any doubt who was inferior to whom. All the rigid requirements of military subordination were enforced, all points of etiquette and every demand of the regulations strictly followed. Mahan would demand that they not only learn engineering and tactics, but that every manner and habit that characterizes an officer—gentlemanly deportment, strict integrity, devotion to duty, chivalric honor, and genuine loyalty—be pounded into them. His aim was to "rear soldiers worthy of the Republic."[10]

He was a merciless cross-examiner with an eerie talent for finding the one unprepared cadet in the section and publicly exposing him. He had an almost intuitive feel for the exact amount of information in a cadet's brain about the lesson at hand, and could quickly separate that kernel of knowledge from the chaff of unpreparedness. The ultimate horror at West Point was being caught unready by Professor Mahan.[11]

This irritable, erudite, captious soldier-professor had never seen a battle—and it was said never went for a walk without an umbrella.[12] Yet he was America's foremost military mind. Nearly all of the text-books in his engineering and science of war classes he wrote himself. And "woe betide the unfortunate who misunderstood any paragraph" in any one of them.[13]

Mahan believed with Theophile D'Oremieulx that there was nothing new to be learned after Napoleon, that "the task of the present . . . has been to systematize, and imbody in the form of doctrine, what was then largely traced out."[14] Mahan's interpretation of Napoleon was based mainly on the theories of Baron Henri Jomini, the Swiss military historian who had served under Bonaparte and was the leading interpreter of his campaigns.

None of Mahan's admiration for Napoleon, however, was ever meant to preclude an officer from thinking for himself on the battle-field. No two things in his military credo were more important than speed of movement—celerity, that secret of success—or the use of reason.[15] Mahan preached these twin virtues so vehemently and so often through his chronic nasal infection that the cadets called him "Old Cobbon Sense."[16]

One of Professor Mahan's most remarkable and feared weapons was his biting sarcasm, which Dabney Maury was to experience first-hand. On a good tall day Maury stood 5 feet 3 inches in his stocking feet. On one of those days, while the class was pondering the construc-tion of fortifications, Mahan asked:

"Mr. Maury, what is the height of the breast-height slope?"

"Five feet, sir," Maury replied.

Mahan turned that exceedingly cold eye on him and said, "If it were five feet, Mr. Maury, you could not shoot over it."[17]

Old Cobbon Sense was the son of Irish immigrants, born in New

York City and raised in Norfolk, Virginia. It was from Virginia that he came to the military academy as a cadet in 1820. It was not out of any martial fervor, or even for engineering, that he came. He was studying medicine in Richmond when he heard that drawing was taught at West Point; he loved drawing. He came, graduated at the top of his class in 1824, and went to the engineers. He was so brilliant that he was appointed an acting assistant professor of mathematics while only a third-classman. The army was so impressed with his mind that it sent him to Europe to study engineering and tactics in France. There Lafayette himself took the young officer into his own family and introduced him everywhere. When Mahan returned home in early September 1832 it was to take charge of the department of civil and military engineering at West Point.[18]

Now, fourteen Septembers later, he was subjecting the cadets of the class of 1846 to his unparalleled knowledge and acid disposition. He put them to work on permanent fortifications with recitations every day. It was hard, grinding duty. "But 'Nihil Desperandum' is my motto," said George Derby; "there is an end to everything and if I live I do believe I shall graduate one of these days."[19]

Mild weather heralded the entry of the year 1846. But it lasted only until the middle of January, when it turned around and gave them "a little taste of Spitzenbergen." By February everybody seemed to be down with either a cold, influenza, sore throats, stiff necks, aching faces, or rheumatism. "I think there is more coughing, sneezing, expectorating and flourishing of handkerchiefs on this post than I ever had the pleasure of witnessing before," Derby said.[20]

But who cared. It was 1846, and they were being molded into engineers and officers by Professor Mahan. They now knew the trip hammer theory of the steam engine and were learning all about field fortifications. Soon there was to be the week of military tactics, which would seem all too short considering that this was a military academy. In only nine hours of class time they would learn all that West Point intended to teach them about army organization, order of battle, laying out a military camp, reconnaissance, outpost duties, attack and defense, and the principles of strategy.[21] If they were to learn anything else it would have to be somewhere else some other time, very likely on the battlefield. But they had to remember that they were being trained not primarily as warriors, but as engineers.

By the middle of March, the snow had very nearly disappeared and McClellan was hoping he had seen the last of it. He ached to see the last of everything. "I have become pretty well tired of my four years slavery, & long to be free once more," he wrote home.[22]

Then it was May and the end at last came shimmering into view. "You have no idea in what a state of excitement we have been here," McClellan now wrote home. "Everything is topsy-turvy in our heads."[23]

A final improbable sign that the "long agony" was about over came on May 23, when Professor Mahan, he of the cold eye and unsympathetic ways, told them they would recite for him no more. He told them that they had done well, the first section in particular, and that "he returned us thanks for the very handsome manner in which we had uniformly conducted ourselves toward him." Their conduct, he said, "had been all that an instructor could wish for or expect from his pupils." He had made them into soldiers worthy of the Republic. Derby noticed that the great professor seemed "very much affected and could hardly speak as he bade us goodbye for-ever—as a section."[24]

So they were about through, the largest class in West Point's forty-four-year history. Fifty-nine of them had survived to see the end, bracketed on the final merit roll by Charles Seaforth Stewart at the top and demerit-ridden George Edward Pickett at the bottom.

McClellan had wanted to finish first, as he had vowed he would, but he fell short one file. He would have to settle for second. George Derby had finished seventh, despite his legendary pranks. Dabney Maury had finished in the back side of the middle in thirty-seventh place. William Gardner had finished within sight of George Pickett in fifty-fifth. William Dutton had placed fifteenth, a finish that would make his fiancée proud. George Stoneman, Jackson's quiet roommate, had finished thirty-third.[25]

There was no doubt in this class's mind who their real star had been. It had not been Stewart, despite the final rankings. It had been the born and bred little gentleman from Philadelphia. Gardner spoke for most of them when he said that McClellan was thought to be "the ablest man in the class. . . . We expected him to make a great record in the army, and if opportunity presented, we predicted real military fame for him."[26]

McClellan's shining potential was universally recognized, not only by his classmates, but among all the cadets of his time.[27] "Prepossessing," was how they described him.[28] Yet with all his personal prepossession, he "bore every evidence of gentle nature and high culture, and his countenance was as charming as his demeanor was modest and winning."[29] "A pleasanter pupil," said one of his instructors, "was never called to the blackboard."[30]

Tom Jackson, thought by his classmates to be as unprepossessing as McClellan was prepossessing,[31] was still marching straight ahead in the end, just as if he had been caught again in the rain. He finished in seventeenth place and it was said by his classmates, only half in jest, that "if we stay here another year, old Jack will be head of the class."[32]

Jackson had earned their respect, if not their love. "Cold and undemonstrative as he was," said Dabney Maury, who should know, "he was absolutely honest and kindly, intensely attending to his own business."[33] Parmenas Taylor Turnley, another of Jackson's roommates, a fellow country boy from Tennessee, believed that "while there were many who seemed to surpass him in intellect, in geniality, and in good-fellowship, there was no one of our class who more absolutely possessed the respect and confidence of all." In the end Old Jack with his desperate earnestness, his unflinching straightforwardness, and his high sense of honor came to be regarded by his classmates, almost despite himself, with something akin to affection.[34]

It might have surprised them had they known that he had come to look upon them in the same way. "It grieves me," he wrote his sister, "to think that in a short time I must be separated from amiable & meritorious friends whom an acquaintance of years has endeared to me by many ties."[35] Wistfully he had written in an earlier letter that gone "were the days of my youth; they have been succeeded by days of quite a different aspect; manhood with all its cares."[36]

The men of 1846 would now take their manhood and all its cares out into the United States Army—as brevet second lieutenants until openings in the regular service gave them real rank. In the old army promotion came only when someone above left the service, died, or was killed. Things, therefore, looked more promising, for Mexico was a powder keg. War was surely just ahead. Promotions might start coming more rapidly now.

There was the matter of where they would next be assigned. That was why their final class standings were so important; they dictated where they could and could not go and would likely set the compass for the rest of their army careers. Most of them would have preferred the engineers, for prestige's sake. But few were called, for engineers were "species of gods." So rarified was that branch of the service that even top-ranked cadets in some classes were not recommended for it after graduation. But this class had been outstanding. The first four finishers had been recommended—Stewart, McClellan, Charles E. Blunt, and John G. Foster. Just below this sanctified quartet in the hierarchal order stood four more good enough to qualify as topographical engineers. The "topogs" were but "demigods" in the order of things, but they were god enough. Finishers ranked five (Edmund Lafayette Hardcastle) to eight (Jesse L. Reno) qualified. They included George Derby.

In the order of rankings below these divines came ordnance, the "connecting link between the deities and ordinary mortals." And behind ordnance came the ordinary mortals themselves, the graduates who by their final rankings qualified for the artillery, infantry, mounted rifles, or dragoons. All of the class ranked between numbers nine (Clarendon J. L. Wilson) and twenty-seven (Henry N. Ehninger) theoretically qualified for any of those branches from ordnance down if they could wrangle the assignment. They included Jackson. Everybody below them, from number twenty-eight (Thomas F. Castor) to Pickett had only three branches to choose from—the mounted rifles, infantry, or dragoons. It was said of the dragoons, that bottom-most peg in the hierarchy, that "a good, square seat in the saddle was deemed of more importance than brains."[37]

Jackson preferred the artillery, but first, he would go dancing. Maury would go home to see a famous uncle. And Rufus Bacon would die.

Jackson would go home the way he had come, through Washington. Traveling with him would be the popular Cadmus Wilcox of Tennessee, who before the end of their plebe year had made friends of every member of the class. It was said that no cadet of his time had so many friends and was so universally esteemed.[38] Also in the party would be Archibald Blair Botts, called Archie, a Virginian who had finished third from the bottom of the class and nearly matched George Pickett demerit for demerit. The fourth member of the quartet would be Clarendon J. L. (Dominie) Wilson, a bright but liquor-loving Virginian who had finished ninth, but who would choose a square seat in the saddle with the dragoons.

In Washington the four would take a room together at Brown's Hotel, right under the roof where the hot air collected on warm summer nights. On reaching the capital Wilcox would go out for the evening and not return until about one o'clock in the morning. When he did return he would find the door locked and the sounds of a boisterous revelry roaring within. Pounding on the door for several futile moments and admitted at last, he would see an astonishing sight. Botts, deadened to the revelry and still dressed in his fine new uniform, would be asleep on the bed. But very much up and about would be Dominie and Old Jack arm-in-arm, dressed in but one garment apiece and singing with stunning effect the Benny Havens drinking song, blasting out original verses of their own composition and executing a barefoot back-step. The racket would spill out into the street and the innkeeper would be obliged to send up his compliments with a request that they hold it down.[39]

Dabney Maury would go home to Fredericksburg, happy to be free at last from his "four years of incarceration," those "four weary, profitless years," made livable only by the fast friendships and "the love of the truest people," which he had found there.[40]

Maury issued from naval stock. His father, John Minor Maury, had been a flag captain in Commodore David Porter's fleet and had died of yellow fever on the long voyage home from the West Indies, where the fleet had been fighting pirates. Fatherless at the age of two, young Dabney had become the ward of his father's brother, Matthew Fontaine Maury, a celebrated oceanic scientist who was charting the oceans and would one day win worldwide acclaim as the "Pathfinder of the Seas." Uncle Matt was a gentle man whom the ocean, despite his great knowledge of it, always made seasick.[41]

"Well, Dab, how did you come out?" the kindly uncle would ask.

"Very poorly, Uncle Matt. I graduated thirty-fifth [an exaggeration—he finished thirty-seventh]."

The great man would consider his nephew sadly for a moment, then brighten.

"How many were in the class?" he would ask.

"There were sixty of us."

"That was first rate. You beat me all hollow," the gracious uncle would say. "I was twenty-seventh and there were only forty in my class."[42]

Rufus Bacon, of Maine, had finished fourteen files ahead of Maury at West Point. He had been a leader in the class, a cadet lieutenant in his final year. He would be granted an authorized leave of absence on the first of July and return home. On August 12 he would be found dead. On the last day of that month his classmate Truman Seymour, of Vermont, would write a letter to William Dutton, home at last in Connecticut with his sweetheart, Lucy Matthews.

"*Bacon* is *dead*," Seymour would write. "Cut his throat in a fit of derangement—brought on by brain fever." The first of the class of 1846 had entered the bivouac of the dead. "Whose time will it [be] to go next," Seymour would wonder. "Heaven help us all—for we all sadly need help!"[43]

But all of that was yet to come. First they had to shut the door on their past four years.

Their last annual examination came and went, raising little of the terror in their hearts that the first one had three summers before. The board of surgeons saw them one more time, and suddenly it was over. There was nothing more to do, no more books to read, no more lessons to recite. They marched in their final dress parade—smartly now, no longer the clumsy plebes they had once been—before the throng of officials and summer visitors.

The Post Orders on June 18 directed that they be relieved from military duty with the battalion of cadets, to be carried on the rolls pending further orders. Two days later the orders came. They were relieved from duty at the military academy and directed to repair to their homes, there to await their assignments.[44]

Thousands of miles away war had erupted with Mexico. When they said their last farewells at the steamboat landing they were certain they would be summoned together soon again to the seat of war and to the wellspring of glory. There would be plenty of laurels for everybody if they could just get there in time.

PART 2
GONE
FOR A
SOLDIER

War
at
Last

When George McClellan heard the news, he was exultant.
Graduation had come with a gratifying bonus. Relations with
Mexico had gone completely to pot. "Hip! Hip! Hurrah!"
he wrote home. "War at last sure enough! Aint it glorious!"

McClellan had yearned for this to happen. He had had his heart
set on graduating and going directly to the halls of the Montezumas
to fight "the crowd—musquitoes & Mexicans &c." Now the government in Washington had just obliged him by declaring war on Mexico.
It didn't get much better than this.[1]

A war with Mexico, which they could all go to, and star in,
had been their true heart's longing all spring, as ardently desired as
graduating. "Nothing is heard but promotion, glory and laurels,"
George Derby wrote his mother.[2]

The likelihood of war between the two countries had been present for months, even years; but it had been heating up in earnest
since final U.S. annexation of Texas in December. Clashes of arms
had broken out along the Rio Grande in the spring without benefit of
a declaration of war. Things hadn't been right between the two nations
for some time. There had been long-standing claims by U.S. citizens
against Mexico, and an itchy desire to possess not only Texas but all

73

of the California and New Mexico territories—the entire southwest, if possible. James Polk, the Democrat elected president in 1844, had sent John Slidell, a Louisiana politician, to the City of Mexico to negotiate a purchase of the region.

When the Mexicans refused to sell, or even to receive Slidell, Polk prepared to acquire the property by other means. In March he ordered General Zachary Taylor's Army of Observation to occupy Point Isabel on the Rio Grande. Mexico, which considered the Nueces River, not the Rio Grande, as the proper boundary between it and Texas, took an uncharitable view of this move. In Mexican eyes it was aggression, pure and simple.

When a force of eighty U.S. dragoons sent out by Taylor to reconnoiter near Matamoras was ambushed in late April, and eleven of his soldiers killed, six wounded, and most of the others captured, the fat was in the fire. When the Mexicans cannonaded Fort Texas across the river from Matamoras on May 3, that did it. Polk condemned these acts as shameful violations of American soil and indignantly called on Congress for a declaration of war.

As far as folksy, homespun Zachary Taylor was concerned, hostilities had already begun and he acted accordingly, not bothering to wait for Congress to make it official. On successive days he fought and won two battles against the Mexicans, at Palo Alto on May 8 and Resaca de la Palma on May 9. On the thirteenth the Congress caught up with the general, declared war, and made George McClellan a happy cadet.[3]

On the day war was declared the United States Army was far from being a juggernaut. Americans were not in the habit of keeping large standing armies. There were 6,562 regulars available for duty army-wide—counting all of the noncommissioned officers, musicians (war was essentially unwageable without music), and privates. There were but fourteen regiments—two dragoon, four artillery, and eight infantry.[4] The president proposed to beef up this slim force dramatically, more than doubling the size of the regular army to fifteen thousand, and complementing it—or hamstringing it, depending on the point of view—with fifty thousand volunteers.

McClellan and his classmates were delighted with the plans to double the size of the regular army. That meant they were likely to be quickly promoted from their lowly graduate status as brevet second lieutenants. In peacetime they could stagnate in that rank waiting for the second lieutenants above them to be promoted, resign, or die. There was room only for so many second lieutenants in the army. In wartime, promotions came faster. Armies expanded and fought and people got killed. The war therefore seemed promising. It was very popular at West Point.

Members of the class were less thrilled with the idea of the fifty thousand volunteers. To the army regulars, and particularly to haughty young West Pointers such as these, volunteers were scum. McClellan viewed them so. It appeared to him that the government had placed General Taylor in a very dangerous situation, "from which, may the Lord deliver him, for it is pretty certain that the volunteers wont."[5]

McClellan didn't go to Mexico immediately after graduation as he had hoped he would. He was ordered instead across campus—an indirect route at best. Two days after Congress declared war on Mexico, it passed legislation creating a company of sappers, miners, and pontoners in the regular army—an engineering outfit. Such a company had long been needed. Up to then the army's elite engineering corps had consisted solely of officers and was all chiefs and no Indians. The new legislation called for a one-hundred-man company of enlisted engineer soldiers to be trained and stationed at West Point, capable of going anywhere to construct military roads, build bridges, erect fortifications, place batteries, lay siege lines, and, if necessary, fight. They would be recruited from scratch: ten sergeants, ten corporals, thirty-nine artificers or privates first class, thirty-nine laborers or privates second class, and two musicians to play the essential music.

Three officers would command the company. One of them, a captain, Alexander J. Swift, had already been selected months before and had simply been waiting for the necessary legislation. Now he was in business; he could name his two other officers and recruit his men. Swift was a brilliant engineer, a West Point graduate fresh from study in the French school of engineering in Metz where he had learned all the latest advanced practices. While waiting for the legislation to pass he continued to teach practical engineering at West Point. There he had found the man he wanted as his first lieutenant, Gustavus W. Smith, also a brilliant young engineer and an assistant professor of civil and military engineering. And Smith, known as "Legs," for his tall, spare, angular frame, had just the man in mind for the company's second lieutenant: his good friend, brand new graduate, and star of the class of 1846—George McClellan. And so it was.

While Swift knew all there was to know about the latest French engineering practices, he knew little about the latest techniques for handling troops. A new set of drill procedures had been adopted by the army since his cadet days at West Point. But Smith, and particularly McClellan, knew all about that. So while Swift supervised the engineering instruction and collected the necessary tools and equipment, Smith and McClellan would whip the new troops into shape.

It took time just to get the troops. Although the pay scale for the new company was higher than ordinary, so were the standards, and the officers had to be more particular whom they recruited. The prospective engineer soldier had to be American-born, single, active and sound in body, able to read and write, and have a "mechanical trade." It took about four months to find and attract enough men of such attributes to bring the company to three-quarter strength. Only four of the new recruits had ever served a prior enlistment. Three of those were immediately made sergeants and the fourth became the bugler. A dumpy Dutchman from Long Island, accustomed perhaps to eating his own cooking, became the company chef. Smith and McClellan soon had the seventy-one rank and file, called Company A, well fed, well led, well tuned, and ready for war.[6]

It hadn't been easy. McClellan put in long hours—every day until about 10:00 at night. "The men are all raw recruits," he wrote home, "& the whole affair is a new thing, both to officers & men, & we have not only to work but also to study." But it was getting done and McClellan predicted they would " 'astonish the natives' if they will only give us half a chance."[7]

Company A sailed from New York City for Mexico on September 26, 1846, arriving at Brazos de Santiago fourteen days later. McClellan believed it was "probably the very worst port that could be found on the whole American coast." They camped on a sandbar six miles long and half a mile wide, where "whenever a strong breeze blows the sand flies along in perfect clouds, filling your tent, eyes and every thing else."[8] But at least he was there. Mosquitoes and Mexicans beware.

Tom Jackson was at home on leave in western Virginia on July 22 when he was ordered to report to Fort Columbus on Governor's

Island in New York City. He left the next day, and on August 19 he and his commanding officer, Captain Francis Taylor, with their thirty artillerymen and forty horses, were on their way to Pittsburgh. There they caught a boat down the Ohio to the Mississippi to the Gulf of Mexico. About the time George McClellan and his company of sappers, miners, and pontoners were shipping from New York, Jackson and his artillery company were leaving New Orleans.[9]

Dabney Maury was in Virginia visiting his mother and explaining his class standing to the Pathfinder of the Seas when his orders arrived. He was directed to report to Captain Stevens T. Mason commanding a squadron of Mounted Riflemen. The regiment of Mounted Rifles was mint-new, created by Congress in May to patrol the Oregon Trail. But the trail would have to wait. There was a war going on. Four other members of the class were assigned to this crack new cavalry outfit as well: Innis Palmer, Alfred Gibbs, George Gordon, and McClellan's old roommate Jimmy Stuart. They were also ordered to the Rio Grande.

Maury's squadron shipped from Baltimore on a brig, the *Soldana*, an unseaworthy craft of about two hundred tons. With Maury, seven other officers, and 160 men ricocheting about inside, the *Soldana* rolled wretchedly in a gale, snapped a mast—a new one was hurriedly pieced together at sea—endured several other storms, was reported lost with all hands, and finally arrived at Point Isabel thirty-two days later. The news awaiting them as they swayed drunkenly down the gangplank was even worse than the trip. General Taylor had just wrested another city, Monterey, from the Mexicans—without any help at all from them.[10] McClellan had missed it too, "a piece of bad luck, which I shall regret as long as I live."[11] They all had.

William Montgomery Gardner, relegated by his final class standing to the infantry, received his orders about the same time as the others. As he was steaming up the Rio Grande, he caught the measles, and when he arrived at Camargo, General Taylor's base on the river, he was "in a pretty bad fix."[12] It was sad enough that he had landed at what a fellow officer described as "certainly the most filthy and disgusting place on this dirty earth,"[13] but Gardner had to be carried unheroically ashore ridden with the measles, and dumped in an abandoned abode house. There, or so it seemed to him, he was forgotten.

He was soon rediscovered, however, and moved to the post quartermaster's quarters where he continued to convalesce, but with an easier mind. No sooner had he recovered and reached his regiment, on the noon following the battle of Monterey, than he caught something else. This time he was put in a common private's tent, with a soldier detailed to wait on him, and began all over again the recuperating process. War was not a healthy thing for William Gardner. It wasn't at all what he expected. There was no glory in this.[14]

Whatever they expected, McClellan, Jackson, Maury, Gardner, and some thirty classmates had arrived at one place or another near the seat of war by the end of 1846.

Soon after Maury staggered ashore from the *Soldana*, he discovered that it was a very small world indeed and that nothing in it had changed very much. His squadron's first assignment was to escort some siege pieces being hauled to Monterey under the charge of that stern and unsociable cadet from his West Point days, Tom Jackson. Maury noted that Old Jack was working those siege pieces down the road as he used to work everything at West Point: they "had to move along."[15]

The company of sappers, miners, and pontoners was also working its way along, from Point Isabel to Camargo. McClellan, riding at its head with Captain Swift and "Legs" Smith, was the picture of military preparedness. He carried a double-barreled shotgun, two revolvers, a saber, a rapier, and a bowie knife. He was expecting trouble.[16]

Trouble soon came, not from the Mexicans, but from the mosquitoes. At Matamoras he began feeling no better than William Gardner. Racked with malaria and dysentery, he checked into the hospital and was there for nearly a month, nursed by his old West Point roommate, Jimmy Stuart, who had arrived with the Mounted Rifles.[17]

As it worked out, he missed very little. There was no transportation available to take the engineer train from Camargo to Taylor's headquarters at Monterey, so as he recuperated the company settled in and resumed engineer and infantry instruction. The amused army watched, and was soon calling it "the pick and shovel brigade."[18] There was little fighting at the time and not much else to keep a restless army amused. It was now simply a matter of waiting for the next battle.

The army had changed its job description. It was no longer an army of observation, but an army of invasion, and General Scott himself was on his way to Mexico to give new meaning to the concept. The canny Scott, a thinking man's general, was coming with a different idea about how to get to Mexico City. He planned to go by way of Vera Cruz, capturing that principal seaport first, then battering his way the 260 miles from there up the national road to the capital.

It wasn't an original idea. Hernando Cortez, the first non-Indian conqueror of Mexico some three centuries before, had done the same thing. The strategy worked then and ought to work again. The route was direct, and the road—the great national highway that the Aztecs had built—was ready-made for an invading army. To undertake this feat of arms, Scott simply appropriated most of Taylor's army, his right as general in chief, including virtually all of the young officers of the class of 1846.

Its objective thus refocused, the army began collecting at Tampico in the winter of 1846–1847 to await the general in chief's arrival.

Winfield Scott was certain of one thing. He needed West Pointers. All of his years of chairing the board of visitors at the June examinations had taught him something—that the talent of the army was embodied in the officers who had been graduating from the academy over the last few decades. He had heard enough recitations to be convinced of that. None of his generals, himself included, had that kind of engineering training. And he clearly saw that the conquest of Mexico would require it.

So he started surrounding himself with West Pointers, beginning with Colonel Ethan Allen Hitchcock, who had graduated from the academy in 1817 and served a tour of duty as its commandant of cadets. He installed Hitchcock as his inspector general, then brought in an elite group of West Point–trained engineers, all of them high graduates of their classes—the gods and demigods.

Chief among them was a gracious, exceedingly competent captain of engineers from the class of 1829, Robert E. Lee of Virginia. Another was a Creole lieutenant from Louisiana and from the class of 1838 with a fiery disposition and a Gallic name, Pierre Gustave Toutant Beauregard. Also among them, newly minted from the class of 1846, were young brevet second lieutenants George McClellan with the pick and shovel brigade, and two new topographical engineers, Edmund Lafayette Hardcastle and George Derby.

The wait for the invasion gave the members of the class of 1846 time to look around and register their disgust with those not as favored as they—the Mexicans and the volunteers. McClellan decided Mexico was "altogether the queerest place I ever came across—it is chaparal, chaparal, nothing but chaparal, so far." He concluded it was "very romantic perhaps at a distance, but there's a great deal of plain reality in it down here."[19] As for the Mexicans, "they are content to roll in the mud, eat their horrible beef and tortillas and dance all night at their fandangos."[20]

McClellan was even harsher in his judgment of the volunteers, now that he had seen them firsthand. The "confounded Voluntario," he raged, "a miserable thing with buttons on it, that knows nothing whatever."[21] Some "don't know the butt from the muzzle of a musket," another regular officer agreed. "They are useless, useless, useless,—expensive, wasteful—good for nothing."[22] The regulars were dismayed by the uncivilized conduct of many of the volunteers in Mexico. A. P. Hill, still at West Point, complained that some of them "have committed outrages . . . which would call the blush of shame to the cheek of a Goth."[23]

The one good-for-nothing thing with buttons on it that disgusted the class members and virtually every other West Pointer more than any other was Brigadier General Gideon Pillow. If there was ever an officer elevated undeservedly to high rank by political pull, they figured he was it. A former law partner of President Polk with no discernible military talents, Pillow offended the West Pointers with virtually everything he did. At Camargo he was credited in the press with having fortified the city by digging the ditch on the inside instead of the outside of the stronghold, thus raising a work to protect the attackers rather than the defenders. Even the lowest "immortal" at West Point knew that wasn't right. To underscore their scorn, Jimmy Stuart hilariously mounted a Texas mustang, galloped at the fortification and leaped the parapet and ditch in a single bound.[24]

George McClellan was out of bed and fit again. But now Captain Swift was sick. When the engineer company filed out of Matamoras four days before Christmas, there were only two officers, McClellan and Smith, and forty-five men still on their feet. The captain and twenty of the company were left behind in the hospital with their Mexican diarrhea and fevers.[25]

The company had been ordered to proceed overland with a column of volunteers under the command of Irish-born Major General

Robert Patterson. The company's job was to move in front of the column and make the road passable for the artillery and wagon trains that followed. On the 350 miles to Tampico, the sappers and miners hewed roads out of what had been little more than mule paths over which no wagon had ever rolled. The little company learned to build bridges over streams with no other material than the wretchedly stumpy crooked chaparral growing by the side of the trail.[26]

But the life suited McClellan. He wrote home that he could live this way for years without becoming tired of it. Around the campfires at night, he wrote his mother, "you never saw such a merry set as we are—no care, no trouble—we criticize the Generals—laugh & swear at the mustangs & volunteers. . . ." A regular officer, he assured her, has no habits—"it is immaterial to him whether he gets up at 2 A.M., or 9—or whether he don't go to bed at all. When on a march we get up at 2 or 3, when we halt, we *snooze* it, till 8 or 9—when we have cigars we smoke them, when we have none, we go without—when we have brandy, we drink it, when we have not, we make it up by laughing at our predicament—that is the way we live."[27]

That was all well and good for a social animal such as McClellan. But stiff, unsociable, nondrinking, nonsmoking Tom Jackson wanted a little warfare. Moving artillery pieces about the country was a duty, and he respected that, but it wasn't war.

One evening as he waited with the rest of Scott's gathering army at Point Isabel on the Gulf, he walked to Captain George Taylor's tent to find he already had a visitor, another West Pointer, Lieutenant Daniel Harvey Hill.

As Jackson approached, Taylor nodded in his direction and asked Hill, "Do you know Lieutenant Jackson?"

Hill looked up curiously.

"He will make his mark in this war," Taylor said. "I taught him at West Point; he came there badly prepared, but was rising all the time, and if the course had been four years longer, he would have been graduated at the head of his class."

Hill's interest was aroused. He had graduated from West Point the summer Jackson arrived.

"He never gave up anything," Taylor said, "and never passed over anything without understanding it."

Hill found Jackson reserved and reticent at first, but the two soon

81

warmed to one another, and Jackson proposed a walk on the beach. As they sauntered along, he became more sociable.

"I really envy you men who have been in action," Jackson confessed to Hill. "We who have just arrived look upon you as veterans."

Then he said: "I should like to be in one battle."

Hill, who would one day be Jackson's brother-in-law, noticed that as he said this his face lit up, his eyes sparkled, and "the shy hesitating manner gave way to the frank enthusiasm of the soldier."[28]

Old Jack was ready. All he lacked was the battle.

Battle was something Clarendon J. L. (Dominie) Wilson, Jackson's postgraduation dancing partner at Brown's Hotel, had plenty of at the moment. Wilson was more than a thousand miles from the beach where Jackson and Hill walked together. It was the middle of the afternoon in early February and Dominie was in New Mexico Territory sighting down the barrel of a six-pounder. His aim was fixed on the western wall of the large church in the Taos Pueblo. From a range of two hundred yards he was pounding the house of God with grapeshot.

Wilson was there because the acquisition of the New Mexico and California territories was the main goal of the war with Mexico. Polk had therefore taken steps to seize them, even as he sent the main army of invasion marching toward Mexico City. As soon as war was formally declared, the president ordered Colonel Stephen Watts Kearny to proceed to those territories with an Army of the West, occupy them, and force Mexico to hand them over. It would be a massive acquisition of land, second only to the Louisiana Purchase, because the California Territory then included all of that present-day state, and New Mexico Territory embraced all of what would one day become New Mexico, Arizona, Utah, Nevada, and parts of Colorado and Wyoming. In June 1846, Kearny set out across country with eighteen hundred troops. Making good time—about a hundred miles a week—he reached New Mexico in August, and occupied Santa Fe without firing a shot.[29]

By the end of September, Brigadier General Kearny—his promotion had caught up with him on the march—felt that he had adequately conquered New Mexico and could safely get on with subduing California. Mexican political and business leaders in Santa Fe had assured him that the people of New Mexico would become reconciled to the American occupation in good time and accept it without resentment. They assured him there would be no retaliation and no overt acts of insurrection.[30]

Since he believed them, Kearny divided his little army into three parts. One was to remain in New Mexico under the command of Colonel Sterling Price, a volunteer, politician, tobacco planter, and former legislator and congressman from Missouri. The second part led by Colonel Alexander W. Doniphan, another volunteer and lawyer from Missouri, was to march south and occupy Chihuahua across the Rio Grande. Kearny would take the third part to California.[31]

Kearny didn't know it at the time, but he had left Sterling Price with a problem. By December, talk of rebellion was rife around Santa Fe, despite the assurances that the Mexicans would become reconciled to the occupation. Open insurrection was in the air. On December 5, a reporter from the St. Louis *Daily Missouri Republican*, in New Mexico to cover the Missouri volunteers, told of treasonable letters that had been seized by the army. The letters described the province as ripe for revolt, needing only some military display from below to set it off. "It is clear," the reporter wrote, "that the Mexicans here are very much discontented. . . ." The clergy "are our enemies . . . the wealthier classes dislike our government . . . the patriotic . . . feel mortification and pain . . . and the lower classes lived too long in a state of abject slavery, dependence, and ignorance, to be at once capable of appreciating the benefits conferred on them by the change of government. All are dissatisfied—the rich, the poor, the high and the low." Even so, the reporter didn't believe the people were so foolhardy that they would attempt a revolt. He wrote it all off as Mexican braggadocio.[32]

Even as he wrote, Mexican insurrectionists were laying plans to make him a false prophet. One company of insurgents was preparing to strike from a church in Santa Fe. Another was to assemble in the valley of the Tesuque north of town. In the dead of night, at a signal from the bells on the church towers, the conspirators were to swarm into the streets, seize the guns, and massacre the Americans. The governor, Charles Bent, and Colonel Price were to be captured. This unchristian and murderous stroke, planned for the week before Christmas, was postponed to Christmas Eve. Then three days before it was to come off, the wife of one of the conspirators, dreading the inevitable bloodshed, informed Price. Some of the leaders were apprehended, and the rebellion appeared suppressed. When Lieutenant J. W. Abert of the army's topographical engineers arrived in Santa Fe two days before Christmas, the plot was the talk of the town. Sentinels had been posted in every direction. Field pieces and heavy guns were parked in the plaza, everything was in a state of preparation, and everybody was nervous.[33]

Among the American officers spending this unsettling yuletide in New Mexico were Brevet Second Lieutenants Wilson and Oliver Hazard Perry Taylor, both of the class of 1846 and now with the First Dragoons. They watched as the New Year came in and the situation went from bad to worse. On January 14, Governor Bent left Santa Fe for Taos, and in the early morning of the nineteenth, when snow covered the ground, the town was asleep, and it was as cold as Iceland, a cabal of Pueblo Indians and Mexicans forced their way into the governor's house and massacred him and five others, including Taos Sheriff Stephen Luis Lee and circuit attorney James W. Leal. That same day the bloodshed spread to Mora, Arroyo Honda, and the Rio Colorado.[34]

News of the massacres reached Colonel Price in Santa Fe the next day, and with it word that an insurgent army was approaching the capital, gathering adherents along its line of march. Price sent to Albuquerque for a company of First Dragoons and a regiment of Missouri mounted volunteers. Without waiting for them to arrive, he marched out on January 23 to meet the enemy, joined by a company of mounted volunteer "avengers" led by Governor Bent's law partner, Felix St. Vrain. Price's little force of 353 men was accompanied by four mountain howitzers.

They found the insurgents in force early in the afternoon the next day near the town of Cañada, and in the fight dislodged and scattered them. Four days later the dragoons and the regiment of Missouri mounted volunteers from Albuquerque caught up with Price at Luceros on the Rio del Norte. With them were Wilson, trailing the six-pounder, and Taylor. Now Price's force was at full strength, nearly five hundred rank and file.

They knew the insurgents were dug in on the steep slopes of the mountains that rose on each side of the cañon entrance to the town of Embudo. Since the road to Embudo wouldn't support artillery or wagons, Price detached dragoon Captain John H. K. Burgwin with about 180 men to handle the matter. Wilson, unable to take his six-pounder, but just as unable to stay behind, volunteered to go as a private soldier in St. Vrain's company of avengers. Taylor, in his accustomed rank, commanded one of the Dragoon units. At the pass, Burgwin threw out flanking parties on either side of the mountain pass where some six hundred to seven hundred insurgents waited. The fight didn't last long; soon the enemy were in full retreat, bounding along the steep and rugged sides of the mountains for Embudo "with a speed that defied pursuit." When Burgwin reached the town he was met only by a handful of city officials with a white flag.

When the detachment finished its work and rejoined the main force at Trampas, Price set out over the mountain through the deep winter snow and entered Taos on February 3. There the soldiers found the enemy holed up in the nearby Pueblo, and immediately opened on them with their batteries. Since his ammunition wagons had not yet arrived, and since all hands were nearly frozen by the cold and paralyzed by fatigue, Price ordered the firing stopped after about two and a half hours and called it a day.

Next morning the army was up and at it again, this time bringing the Pueblo and its church under a cross fire. When Price saw that neither Wilson's six-pounder nor the howitzers were making any kind of impression, he ordered the church stormed. That didn't work either. A few small holes were opened with axes in the western wall of the church and the roof was set afire, but that was all, and it cost Captain Burgwin his life.

Price then ordered Wilson to bring his gun around to the west wall. And that is where he now stood, cannonading the church with his six-pounder.

At about 3:30 in the afternoon, Wilson was ordered to run his gun up closer, to within sixty yards of the church. From there he fired ten more rounds, pounding away at the holes Burgwin had opened in the walls. His point-blank fire soon widened a practicable breach, and he ran the gun up to within ten yards and poured in three more rounds of grape. At his side all the way and gazing with him into the mouth of the breach was Taylor, his Yankee classmate from Rhode Island. Wilson lit a shell and hurled it into the gaping breach, and the two classmates, together with Lieutenant Alexander B. Dyer of ordnance and a small storming party, instantly followed it in. Through the thick smoke inside, they caught a fleeting glimpse of the enemy beating a retreat through the gallery without firing a backward shot.[35]

The fight was over. The class of 1846's two representatives in New Mexico had just put down the Taos Rebellion.

That City
Shall Soon
Be Ours

George McClellan stood before Vera Cruz, but his fight was not yet either with the mosquitoes or the Mexicans. It was with the fleas. The sand hills before the ancient walled city were alive with fleas. Dabney Maury had never seen so many. "If one were to stand ten minutes in the sand," he marveled, "the fleas would fall upon him in hundreds. How they live in that dry sand no one knows."[1]

McClellan and Legs Smith, the two officers of the pick and shovel brigade, had erected a telling fortification against this irritating army. They greased themselves all over nightly before bedtime with salt pork, and climbed into canvas bags drawn tight about their necks. They looked like men ready for a sack race and probably smelled worse, but they slept flea-free and were the envy of the less well equipped. Perhaps the fleas did not eat McClellan and Smith in the night, but they compensated for it by devouring Maury and everybody else who had no canvas bag.[2]

The fleas were penance, after a fashion, for the unexpected lack of Mexican opposition to the American landing at Vera Cruz. The armada carrying Scott's army had rendezvoused in the roadstead at the Lobos Islands 120 miles north of the fortified city in late February 1847. From there, on the second of March, it had sailed for Antón

Lizardo a dozen miles below Vera Cruz. Arriving three days later, the transports dropped anchor to shouts and cheers. On March 9, off Los Sacrificios, the island in the bay at Vera Cruz where Cortez had landed in 1520, wave after wave of surf boats packed with soldiers and rowed by sailors bobbed toward the beach. And from the city there was only silence.

The setting for the invasion was majestic. Mount Orizaba, the great sleeping volcano, the "mountain of the star," broke from its veil of haze and stood in magisterial relief against the cloudless March sky. Everything that day stood in bold relief. There was no stealth to this landing, no effort to creep in unseen and unheard. National airs blared across the bay, regimental colors snapped in the breeze, and boat after boat landed to exultant huzzahs.[3] Tom Jackson was bowled over. It was one of the most thrilling sights he had ever seen.[4]

Winfield Scott, who had seen other military extravaganzas in his time, was more worried than thrilled. An uglier coming invasion was tugging at the edge of his concern. He was running late and the yellow fever season, the time of the dreaded "el vomito," which always hit Vera Cruz with a vengeance in the spring, couldn't be far behind. It, not the Mexicans, was the most powerful potential defender of Vera Cruz.

He must therefore hurry. He must seize the fortress city as soon as possible and be on his way into the healthier interior. But he mustn't try to go too fast. Despite the need to hurry and despite the urgent insistence by some of his generals that he storm the city immediately, Scott decided to lay siege instead. It would take precious time, but it would save lives and he was going to need all the men he could muster for battles yet to come.

By midnight on the ninth, the 13,500-man army was ashore, and still there had been little opposition—only the fleas. It was not until that night that the Mexicans opened a steady drumfire on the invading force, which was by then rapidly deploying over the sand hills behind the city. Scott's forces quickly straddled the national road leading in from the interior and sealed off all communications, food, and water from the outside. By the thirteenth the city was thoroughly invested, and the mortars had begun coming ashore. The engineers worked around the clock as the army waited.

The pick and shovel brigade was in demand everywhere, opening roads through the hills of sand and chaparral, destroying aqueducts that gave Vera Cruz its water, making general reconnaissances, erecting batteries, trenches, and camouflaged approaches. It was work that had to be done for the most part under fire.[5]

But George McClellan was having the time of his life. On the sixteenth he returned to headquarters with his clothes ripped and torn, a grin on his face, and an exuberant account of the workday on his lips. He and his party had been under Mexican musket fire most of the day. Thank God they couldn't shoot straight.[6]

The engineers had to watch for bullets from both directions. They were in greater danger now of being shot by their own advance sentinels as they returned to their lines in the night than by the Mexicans. As they approached they shouted, "Don't shoot, we are American officers."[7]

If Mexican bullets were not felling the sappers and miners of Company A, Mexican fever was. Its main victim was Captain Swift. He had rejoined the company at Vera Cruz, but he was still unwell, and after a few hours in the merciless sun, he was finished. Passing permanent command of the company to Lieutenant Smith, he sailed sick and dying for home. About the time his little company entered Vera Cruz in triumph later in the month, he arrived in New Orleans and twenty-four hours later was dead.

But war goes on. Even before Swift left, a fourth officer had joined the company, another figure familiar to McClellan—the large frame, the ungainly walk, the genial disposition, the well-organized mind, the New Hampshire accent. His classmate John Gray Foster, separated from him on the final merit role by only two files, was now one of them.[8]

By 2:00 in the afternoon on March 22, seven mortars were in place and frowning on Vera Cruz. Three more would be on line the next day.[9] It was enough firepower to start the siege. As his army stared expectantly at the sixteen domes within the whitewashed walls of Vera Cruz and on the massive castle of San Juan de Ullúa bristling in the bay beyond, Scott sent a summons for the city to surrender. For thirteen days the Americans had not fired a shot, while the city had "belched forth its sulphurous contents in almost continual discharges of heavy mortars and paixhans."[10] It had been a drain on their nerves and a tax on their patience.

At 4:00 P.M. the city sent back word that it would defend itself to the last extremity. At 4:15, therefore, the American batteries opened fire, the shouts of approval from the army drowning the roar of the guns. The bark of those "faithful bulldogs" was sweet music to their ears. Like "hungry lions in search of prey," one soldier wrote, the mortar shells went "howling" to their mark. The batteries in the city answered in a blazing sheet of fire.[11] Lieutenant Edmund Lafayette Hardcastle, of the class of 1846, watched in awe, stunned by the "one continual thunder of artillery."[12] His classmate, Parmenas Taylor Turnley, saw it by night and called it "one of the grandest scenes in warfare."[13]

Artillery wasn't Edmund Hardcastle's job. He had arrived in Mexico with George Derby, his longtime section mate at the academy, and both had been assigned to General Scott's staff as topographical engineers. But he had nothing to do at the moment, the army was short of artillery officers, and he knew how to command mortars—he had learned it at West Point. So at 4:00 the next morning he and Derby reported to the batteries and were soon commanding guns aimed at Vera Cruz.

In the night, the Mexicans slackened their cannonade. But as the sun rose over the sand hills, they opened up once more with a "terrible fire." At about 10:00 in the morning their bombardment fell off again, but not its American counterpart. Peering through the smoke over his two mortars, Hardcastle saw that the shells from the American guns were bursting with ruinous effect in the city—tumbling steeples, shattering roofs, setting houses afire, and hurling immense fragments in the air.

By afternoon the enemy shot was coming down on the trenches as heavily as ever. Hardcastle's battery was barricaded behind a breastwork erected by Captain Robert E. Lee and the ever-present engineers, but it was not shot-proof. Between firings, Hardcastle counted the cannon balls that had penetrated the embankment in front of him and were either visible or about to fall through. There were more than he cared to think about. He remembered uneasily that on the first afternoon of the cannonade an officer and a soldier had been killed at this same battery. As if to remind him, a cannonball hurtled through the narrow three feet of space that separated him from the captain of the battery. Both men, bending over at the time attending their duties, straightened and looked at one another, grateful for small favors.

By now Hardcastle's ear was attuned to the subtle variations in the shrieks of the incoming shot. The shrill cry of a cannonball passing close enough to take off his head and the scream of more distant shot were different. Both sounds were unpleasant enough, but the former excruciatingly so.

At 4:00 the next morning Hardcastle was relieved after twenty-four straight hours at the battery, feeling "pretty well broke down." But he was still alive. A few hours later, a large shell from Vera Cruz crashed into the battery and exploded, hurling one of the mortars more than thirty feet, wounding six men and blanketing others with a mantle of powder and dust.[14]

Tom Jackson's eyes glinted with pleasure. Here was a battle at last. He was also commanding guns and attracting warm acclaim for his coolness and judgment. William Gardner, who was present and finally in good health, noticed that, although under fire for the first time, Old Jack was "as calm in the midst of a hurricane of bullets as though he were on dress parade at West Point."[15] Like Hardcastle, Jackson had watched a cannonball come within five steps of sweeping him into oblivion.[16]

By March 27, after Scott had borrowed a battery of heavier, more powerful guns from the navy, installed them in the sand hills, and turned them on the city, Vera Cruz decided it had had enough. With the surrender of the city that day, Scott had his foothold in Mexico, el vomito had still not come, and Tom Jackson had tasted battle. The Americans had thrown three thousand ten-inch shells, two hundred howitzer shells, a thousand Paixhan shot, and twenty-five hundred round shot into Vera Cruz—a total weight of metal of 250 tons. Two officers, two seamen, three soldiers, and one musician had been killed.[17]

Everybody in the army was now anxious to be on the road to Mexico City. Hardcastle was living high at Vera Cruz—garrisoned with Scott's staff in the palace itself—but the city depressed him. Not only was it badly battered, but it was filthy. It is no wonder, he thought, that yellow fever rages here with such virulence. The streets were so disgusting they were painful to behold. The repellent odors rising from "the green putrid matter with which the gutters are full" was enough to drive them into the Mexican interior.[18]

A garrison of buzzards, *les zopilotes*, patrolled and policed the city streets and tried to tidy up, but to little avail. Protected by the authorities, the ghoulish fowl roamed about town at will picking impurities from the streets. Although sanctioned by the civic power, they couldn't pick enough to quell the stench—and probably added to it.[19]

Two divisions of Scott's army left finally for Jalapa on April 8 and 9. A third left on the eleventh, and the fourth on the thirteenth. Scott and his staff departed on the twelfth.

The company of sappers, miners, and pontoners was scheduled to leave with the general in chief. But nobody thought to tell this to the mules. When General Scott and his staff left at 4:00 in the afternoon, transportation for Company A had not yet arrived. When it finally did, about dark, it turned out to be a troop of recalcitrant reject mules lassoed from the water as they swam ashore off a ship from Texas. Not only were the beasts seasick and wild, they were offended. Their teamsters were Mexicans who spoke English no better than they did, and who had never harnessed an animal in their lives. They were the least promising teams, men and beasts, McClellan had ever seen.[20]

A violent clash of wills consumed the entire night. The company and the intransigent mules, both on the edge of exhaustion, didn't get underway for Jalapa until half an hour before daylight on the thirteenth.[21] Progress up the road was managed only by continued irreverent haranguing and hard cussing. As General William J. Worth and his staff overtook and passed the company, they were embarrassed to hear the engineers indelicately swearing the teams slowly up yet another hill.[22]

When all the units of the army had departed Vera Cruz, William Gardner was unwillingly left behind in the path of el vomito. To his disgust, his battalion had been detailed to garrison the fallen city.[23] Considering his wobbly medical history so far in Mexico, Gardner is probably the last man who should have been left behind. He had been catching everything.

The march to Jalapa gave the rest of the army time to contemplate what lay ahead and to become acquainted with the Mexican country-side along the national road. To Tom Jackson there appeared to be but two seasons in Mexico—"wet and dry." It was now dry and sterile, the countryside through which they were passing was caught up in a drought, and there was but little vegetation.[24]

The soldiers could not only savor their conquest of Vera Cruz, but could also take satisfaction in the news from the north. General

Taylor and his much-depleted army had repulsed the Mexicans at Buena Vista on February 22 and 23. It had been the hardest battle of the war so far, and it had nearly been lost. The Mexican president and general in chief, Antonio Lopéz de Santa Anna, had hurled wave after wave of his army against Taylor's little force and the American line had quavered several times. But it didn't break, and under a withering counterfire from the roving American artillery, Santa Anna had simply claimed victory, given it up, and withdrawn.

And now there was trouble ahead on the high road to Jalapa. In a place called Cerro Gordo, dug in on a conical thousand-feet-high hill called "El Telegrafo," was the ubiquitous Santa Anna himself. The fiery one-legged president was back from Buena Vista and about as happy with the turn of events as the sapper and miner company's mules.

General David Emanuel Twiggs was the first to stumble onto this impediment in the road, since his was the lead American division. It could have been disastrous, for Twiggs's usual strategy in such cases was to attack anything in his path, no questions asked. Twiggs was a bluff bear of a man, 6 feet 2 inches tall with long flowing white hair and a beard, which hung to his chest. He looked like the prophet Aaron, and spoke like the volcano Vesuvius—in an erupting hellfire of curses and oratory. Indeed, the army called him "Old Orizaba."[25]

When Twiggs reached Cerro Gordo and saw what was ahead of him, he uncharacteristically drew up and waited for General Scott to arrive. The Mexican position appeared too strong to attack from the front. Santa Anna was well dug in across the main road. There had to be a better way, and Scott sent his West Point engineers to find it. As they fanned out to the left and right, Scott sat back to wait.

After three days of the "boldest examinations," Lee returned to confirm that Santa Anna was indeed unassailable from the front, but that a plan to turn him on his left might work.[26]

Lee's counterpart scouting the other side of the Mexican position was the irrepressible, prank-playing George Derby. He had reconnoitered up the Rio Del Plan about four and a half miles on the Mexican right flank while Lee was assessing the left. Accompanied by one man, Derby went all the way around into the rear of the enemy and made a report accompanied by a sketch detailing positions and numbers. He presented his findings at the same high level conference of general officers and engineers where Lee presented his. Scott decided to attack the Mexican left on the basis of these reconnaissances. [27]

Next to El Telegrafo was a smaller hill called La Atalaya, and a path leading to it over which, if improved, light batteries might approach without detection. Indeed, Santa Anna himself had briefly considered this possibility, but had dismissed it. He didn't believe in his heart that a goat could successfully approach his army from that direction.[28] Scott's intention based on Lee's assurances was to take advantage of this assumption. He would send Twiggs on a looping sweep around Santa Anna's left flank. The rest of the army would make a diversionary movement against his center and right in hopes the Mexican president would mistake that for the real thing and continue to believe in the impossibility of an attack from the left.

The plan was set in motion on April 17. Dabney Maury had a front row seat in this epic moment in history, but he wasn't at all certain it was the seat he wanted. He had marched with the Mounted Rifles earlier in the day at the front of Twiggs's division, and they had gotten around on the flank in good order. Twiggs was not yet ready to begin the major assault, but he made the mistake of telling one small American column during some preliminary skirmishing to "Charge 'em to hell!" and they had taken him literally. Over La Atalaya the column swept, down the slope, and part way up El Telegrafo, where it was quickly and unhappily pinned down under heavy Mexican cannon fire.[29]

As this was happening, Maury and the other Mounted Rifles were resting by the side of the road behind La Atalaya. The first he knew of the situation on the other side of the mountain was when somebody shouted, "Send up the Rifles!" The Rifles immediately rushed to the relief of the beleaguered little force and was soon sharing its predicament.

That is where Maury was at the moment, pinned down on the gun-swept side of Atalaya Hill. From his vantage point he could see clearly all that was happening. The Mexicans were keeping up a dropping fire on any Americans who inadvisedly showed themselves. He could see Santa Anna himself on the field in citizen's dress, mounted on a superb gray horse and personally in command. Several of Maury's men fired at him, but he was too far away.

Maury's little command hunched uneasily behind a clump of

undergrowth that crowned a hill, and from there he could see another small group of Rifles under the command of his classmate, Alfred Gibbs. They appeared to be better situated, in a sheltered spot nearer to the enemy, yet in little danger of being cut off. Maury wanted to be there too. So rising, he shouted, "Follow me!" and charged down the slope toward them. As he ran, the Mexicans opened up on him and before he had gone a hundred yards a ball shattered his left arm. He turned to see that he was entirely alone on that bare hillside; not one of his men had followed him. Understandably so.

He managed to drag himself and his shattered arm to the cover of a bush, where he slumped faint with pain. As he reached the cover, a rifleman sprang from behind the only available tree and ran to the rear for help. When the help arrived directly in the form of Sergeant Robert Coleman, it proved to Maury once again what a small world it was, even in the heat of battle on a barren Mexican hillside. Coleman was an old friend, one of the immortals of Maury's class at West Point who had been found deficient and sent away. But here he was again, and never a more welcome presence.

Coleman began carrying his wounded former classmate from the field, and was well on his way when they encountered Major Edwin Vose Sumner, who was temporarily in command of the Mounted Rifles in the absence of their permanent commander, Persifor F. Smith. Maury briefed Sumner as best he could through his pain, and the major, a man with the voice of a bugle and nicknamed "Bull of the Woods," hurried forward impetuously. Almost immediately he was bowled over himself by a glancing shot to the head. There were those in the army who would argue strongly that this was the safest possible place for Sumner to take a bullet and have it do the least harm. He too was carried to the rear, and as soon as he could walk he staggered over to Maury. The hit must have had a pacifying effect on the rough old dragoon's mind, for he spoke very kindly now to the wounded lieutenant whom he had often spoken so sharply to in times past, and called him "my brave boy."

In the rear, a surgeon inspected Maury's wound and shook his head sympathetically.

"You've a very bad arm," he said cheerfully. "I shall have to cut it off."

Maury blanched and began to stall for time. "There's a man over there whose leg is worse than my arm," he told the surgeon. "When you are ready for me you will find me behind that big rock down the hill."

When the surgeon went off, Maury made for the rock and there found yet further sign that this was a war being waged by old friends, classmates, and associates. Waiting there was Tom, Jimmy Stuart's slave, unhappily holding his master's horse, listening to the pounding gunfire and wishing himself elsewhere. Maury immediately mounted Stuart's horse and set out for Plan del Rio, the army's staging ground, where he knew there were proper accommodations for the wounded and perhaps surgeons less inclined to lop off limbs.

By now Maury was a sorry sight, pale and faint and covered with blood. A soldier led his horse while Tom, glad enough to be leaving the battle area, walked close by with a flask of Stuart's brandy ready in his hand. When he saw Maury about to faint he set him up with another pull.

In the medical tent at Plan del Rio, a doctor named Cuyler fixed Maury as comfortably as he could and inspected his wound.

"We can save that arm, Maury," he said.

That was what Maury longed to hear. "Do it at all risks," he said. "I will die before I will lose it, and I assume all responsibility."

Back on Atalaya Hill the small beleaguered American force that had charged 'em to hell and the Mounted Rifles who had rushed to their relief were eventually extracted under the protective fire of a howitzer manned by another of Maury's classmates, Jesse Lee Reno. But it was a little late for Maury. The battle of Cerro Gordo was over for him.[30]

When night fell on Saturday the seventeenth, the Americans were in possession of Atalaya Hill. Still Santa Anna couldn't believe, or would not admit, that Scott's main attack would come from that direction.[31]

But that was the fact, and the plan for Saturday night made Brevet Second Lieutenant Truman Seymour and every other soldier present swallow hard. The strategy called for them to drag three guns—a twenty-four-pounder siege piece and two twenty-four-pounder howitzers—up Atalaya Hill, plant them, and be ready to open fire on El Telegrafo first thing Sunday morning.[32]

To Seymour, of the class of 1846 and now in the First Artillery, the magnitude of the task seemed daunting. All that iron and brass had to be dragged up that steep, rocky mountainside without a road, path, or even a landmark to indicate the direction. It was as dark as Erebus and it was raining. At about 9:00 that night, a team of five hundred soldiers, hungry and already on the ragged edge of exhaustion, picked up the draglines attached to the twenty-four-pounders and began hauling. Relief teams of another five hundred followed, to take up the lines when their strength played out.

"Such a time of hard, grinding toil and persevering labor as then followed for six successive hours I hope never again to look upon, much less take part in," moaned one artillery officer. "Many of our strongest men gave out from utter exhaustion. . . ." While fresh parties were coming up, the wheels of the heavy gun carriages were chocked, braced, and chained—every precaution taken to prevent the guns from running backward down the mountain, crushing everything in their path. Water was carried from small muddy pools half a mile away to relieve the fainting and thirsty men. Many, unable to stand, simply fell out. When the last of the three guns was dragged to the crest at about three in the morning, the track over which they had toiled was strewn with spent, sleeping men from the top to the base of the mountain.[33]

Legs Smith had never been so tired in his life. His little company of sappers, miners, and pontoners had already been on the march for twenty-four hours. At about 3:00 A.M., he was so spent that he fell asleep on his feet and tumbled into a quarry hole. There he found himself staring into the glazed, glassy, open eyes of a dead Mexican soldier but inches away. He was suddenly wide awake.[34]

Smith's night, unlike the Mexican soldier's, was not yet over. The last gun had been dragged up the hill. But now it was his company's job to plant them. By dawn they had shoveled together enough earth from the barren soil to make a breastwork for the twenty-four-pounder. The two howitzers were left with no protection, wholly exposed to the Mexican artillery on El Telegrafo.[35]

Sunday morning broke clear and beautiful, with a gentle breeze from the Gulf fluttering the Mexican ensigns across the way. Into the exhausted senses of the sleeping soldiers strewn up and down the slopes of Atalaya Hill floated the sweet, plaintive, melancholy strain of music. From El Telegrafo the Mexican reveille drifted in, gliding gently over the intervening distance from one summit to the other. Those soldiers able to rouse themselves and look saw across the way the enemy just turning out in the rosy morning light.

The cream of the Mexican army was there: the lancers—the chivalry of Mexico—with their spikes and streaming pennons; the Zapadores (sappers); the artillerists drawn up beside their guns; and down the mountain slope, the Mexican infantry. Far below to the left stretched the road to Jalapa and the batteries that guarded it. There too, the Mexican reveille was floating on the soft morning air and the soldiers were turning out of their grass-thatched huts. Beyond them farther still were unmasked and exposed to view all of the remaining lines of the Mexican defenses. It was a breathtaking sight.[36]

None of those thousands of awakening Mexicans suspected that at that moment Truman Seymour waited on the neighboring hill with his hand gripping the lanyard of a newly planted artillery piece. None dreamed that a gun could ever be placed there. Even the weary Americans would never have believed it if they hadn't put it there themselves. When the three guns began to roar at about 7:00 in the morning in an unwelcome counterpoint to the sweet sound of their reveille, it came as a complete and hideous surprise to the Mexicans.[37]

As the cannons roared, Colonel William S. Harney rose and motioned to his attacking force, which embraced virtually everybody then on the Mexican left, including the small contingent of sappers, miners, and pontoners—and George Derby.

Derby had been ordered to report to Twiggs on the morning of the seventeenth, and Old Orizaba had assigned him to Harney. Early in the morning on the eighteenth he had reconnoitered the enemy position, and when Harney ordered the charge, he rose with the rest. This is how he described what happened next:

> Down we went through the whistling balls and crashing grape, men dropping here and there, the wounded groaning, but nobody scared, and with a tremendous yell we gained the ravine and commenced the ascent of Sierra Guarda [El Telegrafo].
>
> A fire, close, heavy and continued, from 1800 muskets was opened on us, but the ascent was so extremely precipitous that it afforded us protection, for most of the balls passed over our heads. The whistling was terrific, the air seemed alive with balls, but we went on cheering and returning the fire now and then, when we stopped for an instant to rest. At last we came to the

highest crest within ten rods of their first breastwork. We gave
one fire, then Col. Harney shouted with a voice like a trumpet,
"Forward, boys! Forward! Remember the dead! And give it to
'em." Away we went.

The Mexicans saw us coming. Nothing could withstand such
a charge, they gave one fire and ran. We followed, clambered up
over the breastwork, chased them from the tower, over the hill,
turned their own pieces on them, and the Sierra Guarda was ours.
Up went the American flag and down came the Mexican.

It was at this moment that a retreating party going down
turned and fired. I had discharged both pistols and was standing
on a little knoll directing a cannon at this same party, when I felt
myself struck—I fell in the arms of a kind fellow, named Buttrick
of the rifle regt. who has been with me night and day ever since.
The victory was complete, seeing us in the rear the whole army
surrendered and Santa Anna ran away. We took 5 Generals, 30
Cols., 5000 men, 30 pieces of Artillery and thus ended the greatest fight of the age, probably.

I had my wounds dressed and at 5 o'clock was brought down
to this place in a litter.[38]

The ball struck Derby in the left hip, turned on the bone, and
careened around the thigh. There it took up permanent lodging, the
surgeon deciding that any attempt to remove it would be dangerous.[39]

By 10:00 in the morning the Mexicans were in full flight up the
Jalapa road, and General Scott was on the battlefield congratulating
Colonel Harney and grieving over the killed and wounded. It is believed apocryphal, but nonetheless in character, that the following
exchange took place when the great general saw his stricken young
staff topographer lying on the field among the fallen:

Scott: My God, *Darby*, you're wounded!

Derby: Yes, General *Scatt*.

Scott, bristling: My name is *Scott*, not *Scatt*.

Derby: And my name is *Derby*, not *Darby*![40]

What really happened when Scott found him lying wounded on
the field, by Derby's own account, was this:

The general took his two hands warmly in his own large ones and
said: "Why, my poor boy, have they hit you too?"

Colonel Harney, standing by Scott's side, recounted the circumstances, and the general after staying with him five or ten minutes, left, saying, "Mr. Derby, I'm *proud* of you, Sir."[41]

The general was proud of many of his brave boys that day and he mentioned them in his official report to Washington. Four members of the class of 1846 were singled out for particular praise for courageous service under fire: Derby (twice, once for being "actively employed" and once for being wounded), Seymour, McClellan, and Hardcastle.[42]

Early that morning from his convalescent tent at Plan del Rio, Maury heard the sound of the battle raging. Then he heard the cheerful strains of "Yankee Doodle" drifting in from the passing band escorting Mexican prisoners to the rear. He knew the battle had been won.

Later in the morning he was transferred from the hospital tent to a spacious reed house in the village. It was airy and comfortable there and he still had his arm. His roommate was Joseph E. Johnston, one of the topographical engineers, who had been badly shot in a daring reconnaissance on the national road in front of Cerro Gordo six days earlier. Johnston was celebrating, somewhat painfully, his battlefield promotion to lieutenant colonel. Later in the day, Maury's captain, Stevens Mason, was also brought in, his leg carried away by a cannon ball. In terrible pain, he would soon die of blood poisoning.

Despite this, the days passed in relative serenity at the reed house until one day Dr. Cuyler approached Maury and said confidentially: "Maury, there's a young fellow, Derby, across the street, lying wounded among the volunteers, who says he is a classmate of yours and wishes to come over here."

Cuyler hesitated. "I would not agree to it without consulting you, for he is a coarse fellow; but I don't like him to be among the volunteers."

Maury smiled knowingly and cheerfully agreed that Squibob must be brought over at once. A cot was laid in the hall next to his own, and that was the last peaceful moment he and Johnston were to know in that reed house. The serenity was soon in tatters. Derby kept up an incessant torrent of coarse wit that utterly disgusted Johnston. The sober-minded lieutenant colonel suffered it in stoic silence for as long as he could. When one day a herd of goats passed by outside and he heard Derby order his servant to capture a kid from the flock and bring it on in, his patience snapped.

"If you dare to do that," he hissed through clenched teeth, "I'll have you court-martialed and cashiered or shot!"[43]

With the road now cleared, the army resumed its march on up the national highway toward Jalapa, carrying with it the wounded on litters. As they approached that beautiful city, about forty-five hundred feet above the Gulf, a rapid and magical change came over the landscape. Raphael Semmes, a young naval lieutenant traveling with the army on a mission for the navy, compared it to the effect of a scene change in a theater. The lifeless cactus and chaparral landscape gave way abruptly to a lush Eden. For two miles leading into the city the road was flanked by dense continuous hedges of shrubs and wild vines heavy with flowers and alive with the song of birds. The air was scented with the exquisite aroma of "the most delicious of perfumes." The city itself, embowered among the hills, seemed to Semmes "a delicate mosaic set in a massive frame of emerald."[44]

When a friend of George Derby's from home heard that the wounded lieutenant was being carried there, he wrote Mrs. Derby reassuringly that Jalapa was "one of the most delightful, & healthy places in the western world." There was no better place for George to convalesce.[45]

That, then, was also the place for William Gardner, who had finally been ordered out of Vera Cruz. In company with his black slave, Moses, he set out unescorted through the seventy-five guerrilla-infested miles between the fortress city and Jalapa. It was not a healthy thing to do, but healthier than waiting in Vera Cruz for el vomito. The two lone riders, master and the slave he had brought with him from home, arrived miraculously unmolested after two days' hard riding. Again with the army, Gardner rejoined his company in the Second Infantry Regiment.[46]

The army's stay in Jalapa was to be regrettably short. Scott was now forced by circumstances to suspend the war temporarily. The enlistments of four thousand of his volunteers—nearly half of his small army—had expired; he must send them home and await reinforcements. He decided that the waiting should be done at Puebla, closer to the ultimate target than Jalapa. So the army was soon on the move again.

Not leaving with it, however, and mortified by that fact, was Tom Jackson. His artillery company was being left behind to garrison

Jalapa. For anybody else, duty in that paradise might have been a welcome thing, with its happy climate and stunning señoritas. For Jackson, however, it was a ghastly setback. "I throw myself into the hands of an all wise God," he wrote disconsolately to his sister Laura, "and hope that it may yet be for the better." He told her he suspected it may have been the all-wise Providence's way of "diminishing my excessive ambition; and after having accomplished His purpose, whatever it may be, He then in His infinite wisdom may gratify my desire."[47]

Jackson intended to help the process along. His desire was to be where the fighting was, and since it wasn't to be at Jalapa, he had to get out of there. Looking for any way to return to the main army, he heard of a vacancy in Captain John B. Magruder's battery. For the average young artillerist this was an assignment from hell. Magruder was the devil to get along with. He kept his men in a constant state of turmoil with a trigger temper. But wherever there was a fight Magruder was generally there. Jackson liked that about him and therefore applied at once, bending all of his energies to win the assignment.

He was soon rewarded. However, it meant that he, like Gardner, must now make his way to the army through the guerrilla-plagued countryside. He was not far out on the road to Puebla with his small escort when he was set upon by an unsuspecting band of Mexican bandits. It was a gratifying development. Here Providence from His infinite bounty was rewarding Jackson with another battle. In a short hand-to-hand fight, he and his detachment routed the attackers, killing four of them and capturing three.[48]

Puebla, "that ancient and beautiful city of the angels," sat on the national road 150 miles from Vera Cruz, 75 miles from the city of Mexico, seven thousand feet above the Gulf. It was a handsome city of churches, domes, and spires that "seemed to sleep in silent but princely grandeur upon the soft velvet bosom" of a valley of uncommon fertility and beauty.[49] Washed by a fine flowing stream, it was, with its eighty thousand inhabitants, Mexico's second largest city. The army of invasion occupied it on May 15 and settled in to await the reinforcements and for the war to resume. For three months they waited, and the government sent down a special envoy, Nicholas P. Trist, to attempt to work out an accommodation that would avoid further fighting altogether.

The wait was wearing and tedious, and most of the young subalterns from the class of 1846 were broke. George Pickett was more fortunate than some. He had fifty cents in his pocket when one day he met his classmate William Gardner on the street.

"Gardner," Pickett said, "would you like a julep?"

It was a preposterous question. Of course Gardner would like a julep.

So they adjourned to a popular fonda and found it crowded with other "subs" as thirsty as and poorer than they, and all of them willing to be invited to the bar. Pickett and Gardner looked about for a time, conscience-stricken, not wanting to order drinks for themselves in front of the others, but perishing from thirst and prevented by poverty from treating the crowd. Finally Pickett rapped for attention and addressed the room of hopeful and faintly expectant faces.

"Fellows, I have asked Gardner to take a drink, and I am simply bound to have one myself. Now, if anyone can squeeze any more liquor out of that coin," throwing it on the table, "let him step up and imbibe!"

But juleps were twenty-five cents each, and nobody knew how to squeeze another drink from Pickett's coin. So the two drank in peace, free of a condemning conscience.[50]

By August 7 the reinforcements had arrived, Scott's army was again ten thousand strong, and the peace negotiations had broken down. That morning the army began to file out of Puebla up the national road through the mountains toward the city of Mexico. The long wait was over. The four divisions left Puebla a day apart, with the little company of sappers, miners, and pontoners in the van. The long column was supported by four field batteries, a brigade of cavalry, and a siege train.

They marched on toward the city of Mexico, through clear, cold mornings and under the hot midafternoon sun, past cultivated fields of corn on every side. Beyond the fields, in panoramic view, loomed "the sublime mountains, their white shining summits buried for thousands of feet in eternal snow and ice."[51] From that high elevation the soldiers could look, as Jackson had on the road from Jalapa, and see "the clouds below me and the rain descending from them, and above them all clear and calm."[52]

Beyond the pass at Rio Frio on the fourth day of the march, more than ten thousand feet into the clouds, they began to catch their first glimpses of the ancient city of the Aztecs through openings in the trees. As they descended the long western slope, the valley of Mexico, the magnificent basin that was once Montezuma's seat of empire and was now the capital of the Mexican people, broke full upon their enchanted view. Scott stood with his army, riveted as his soldiers were by the beauty of what he saw. The valley's majestic lakes, sparkling under a brilliant sun, seemed to him from the distance like pendant diamonds. The beautiful steeples of the city, with Popocatepetl looming ten thousand feet above them in the background and seeming near enough to touch, filled his mind with reverential awe. He was entranced.

"That splendid city," Scott thought to himself, "soon shall be ours!"[53]

The
Seventeen-Minute
Victory

It was a cold night in the little Mexican village of Cordova, much colder than it had been down in the lower elevations, although it was the middle of August. The three classmates had but one blanket each, so they pooled the three they had and were soon snuggled under them together, warm and comfortable.

Cordova was a long way from West Point, but these three had been close friends for a long time, and had shared a lot more than blankets. They had been section mates in many of their classes at the academy and had graduated only a few files apart in the bottom twenty. All three were Southerners. William Gardner was a Georgian, David Rumph ("Neighbor") Jones was a South Carolinian, and Tom Easley was a Virginian.

"Well, fellows," said Gardner cheerfully, "here are three of us together, and according to the law of chance, one of us will get knocked over in the impending fight. I wonder which one of us is destined to make a permanent settlement in Mexico?"

It was evident to everybody that serious fighting was at hand. The Mexicans had yet to challenge the American advance since it had entered the valley, even though it was now approaching the gates of the city of Mexico. But the Mexicans were there in force, outnum-

105

bering the small invading army by three to one. There was bound to be bloodshed soon.

Gardner's question made Tom Easley uncomfortable.

"Shut up, Gardner!" he snapped. "You and Jones may enjoy such speculations on future events, but I'll be dogged if I do!"[1]

A few nights later, on August 18, William Gardner's sleeping arrangements were less desirable and congenial. He was in a church in Xochomilco in the valley of Mexico and his bedmates were fleas, more fleas than he cared to think about. He was more pestered by them than he had ever been in his life, and that was saying something, for he had been in the sand dunes at Vera Cruz just like everybody else. It was a relief the next morning to leave them behind.[2]

The expected battle was near, and it had all come down to Contreras, a little town beside a twisted no-man's-land called the Pedregal. The army had come up on Ayotla on the national road approaching Mexico City and found Santa Anna again, strongly entrenched just as he had been at Cerro Gordo. And just as at Cerro Gordo, a frontal attack simply wouldn't do. So Scott veered south. The Mexicans swung around to meet him, and when he reached San Agustín he found them still blocking the road. Seeing that Scott did not intend to attack up the causeways leading to the city—not just yet anyhow—Santa Anna began to fortify the bridge and church at another little village called Churubusco, north of Contreras.

By now Santa Anna knew that Scott had a preference and a talent for flanking movements. But standing in the way of any such a movement now, like a malignant growth, was the Pedregal. If anything, it was less passable than the terrain Scott had somehow negotiated at Cerro Gordo. The Pedregal was as pure an unpassable piece of land that an army was ever likely to see. It was a barren stretch of terrain that looked as if a tumbling sea of molten rock had instantly congealed. It was fissured, pocked with caves, and bristling with jagged outcroppings. Only occasional stunted trees and clumps of bushes clung to life in an otherwise lifeless piece of desert.[3]

There was a jagged mule path wending through the Pedregal, but nothing over which an army could hope to pass. Nevertheless, Santa Anna was leery. He had been once burned. He sent one of his generals, Gabriel Valencia, down to San Angel toward Contreras, just in case the Americans did find some way through that twisted region and tried to advance on Churubusco up the road on its other side.

Something like that was just what Scott had in mind. But how to get around the Pedregal—or through it? It was another job for his West Point engineers. Robert E. Lee, who seemed to have a knack for finding passages through impossible places, was soon deep in the Pedregal looking thoughtfully at the mule path. As was generally the case, he saw opportunity there, and returned to tell Scott that with a great effort a road good enough to let the army through might indeed be scratched out. The engineer company with its picks and shovels was called up.

Valencia, meanwhile, had not only gone to San Angel, but beyond it, and then beyond San Geronimo along the outer edge of the Pedregal to a point just above Contreras. There he dug in. That was where the Americans found him in the midafternoon on August 19 when they emerged from the Pedregal. Valencia was beyond where Santa Anna really wanted him to be, but he was strongly entrenched in the foothills with six thousand troops and more than twenty pieces of heavy artillery. To get on to the city of Mexico, therefore, required first getting around Valencia. All progress abruptly halted. There was nothing to do but attack.

That was easier said than done. Tom Jackson learned that truth very early. His artillery battery caught the full wrath of Valencia's guns, and Lieutenant John Prestone Johnstone, in command of the battery, was mortally wounded, his leg torn away by a shot from an eighteen-pounder. Jackson assumed command of the three guns, but there was little he could do with them. He was thoroughly and completely pinned down. Nevertheless, with his limbers and caissons sheltered in the rocks behind, he worked his guns furiously from a hollow as best he could. It was futile; he was too far away for his guns to do damage, and Mexican metal was flying thick and fast. Its immense superiority in weight would simply overwhelm him if he attempted to venture from his cover.[4]

Still, this was where Jackson wanted to be. It was far better than being back in Jalapa boning Spanish, which is what he had been doing before he caught on with Magruder's battery.[5] This was more like it. This was action. It wasn't that Jackson loved war. Indeed, he deplored it. But if there had to be war and he had to be in it, then he wanted to be in the middle of it. He thirsted for distinction and distinction was to be won only in the thick of the fighting.[6]

It was also where George McClellan was. His thirst for honor and distinction ran as deep as Jackson's. But this was one of those days. The engineering company had been busy since dawn, hewing out the passage across the Pedregal under Lee's supervision. When Lee sent for Magruder's guns to support the attack on Valencia, it had been McClellan's job to place Old Jack's battery in position. When the job was done and the troops began to move on Valencia's entrenchments, the engineers dropped their tools, tethered their pack mules, and joined the fighting.[7] Two horses had already been shot from under McClellan that afternoon, and he had been knocked down once by canister, which had struck the hilt of his sword.[8]

Despite all this effort and peril, the assault was going nowhere, and word had come down that the Mexicans were bringing up reinforcements in strength. By nightfall the Americans were stalled before Valencia, who was so surprised and pleased not to have been driven off that he mistook it for a victory. As the guns fell silent he ordered up music and champagne and began awarding brevet promotions all around.[9]

The Americans shrugged and said maybe tomorrow would be better. As Valencia celebrated, a brigade under Colonel Bennett Riley filed quietly into San Geronimo, on the road behind Valencia's entrenched position, between him and San Angel. In the night Riley was joined by a second column under Persifor F. Smith. Valencia didn't know it, but his rear was in jeopardy.

Smith wanted to attack immediately. But night had closed in now with total and impenetrable darkness, and it had started to rain. The assault was therefore put off until three o'clock the next morning, and in the rain and blackness the Americans began laying the groundwork. Although Valencia was aware of none of this, Santa Anna was uneasy. He sent word for his lieutenant to pull out of his exposed position. But Valencia, who detested Santa Anna, scorned the order. Hadn't he just won a magnificent victory against the hated gringos? Santa Anna shrugged and pulled back into his own entrenchments at Churubusco, leaving Valencia to drink his champagne, make his toasts, and award his brevets.[10]

The Americans listened as the celebrating Mexicans reveled and sang the night away, their musicians striking up drunkenly, playing halfway through "Hail Columbia," then stopping and starting again.[11]

The rain began to fall about seven or eight o'clock that night, a torrential, drenching downpour. But William Gardner hadn't been this comfortable in days. His little company was assigned picket duty, and he and his captain had found a deserted house, which they had converted into headquarters for the guard. It apparently belonged to a priest and its charm included a well-stocked pantry. The two officers had just dined on stewed chicken, honey, chocolate, brandy and water, and hard bread. The departed padre had thoughtfully left a soft mattress with pillows and blankets, which the two officers could alternate sleeping on. There was nothing to complain about in point of lodgings—no three classmates huddled together for warmth, no fleas. This was soldiering in style.

Gardner might have known it was too good to last. He had scarcely begun his turn on the mattress when one of the engineering officers and General Twiggs's adjutant general arrived in search of an escort to protect a reconnaissance. Gardner turned out of his warm, dry quarters with a small command and plunged into "the most unpleasant night I almost ever saw." As he and his men plodded along through the rain, he learned of the plans to storm Valencia's position in the morning before daylight. Riley's infantry brigade, in which Gardner was an officer, was to lead the assault.

Gardner welcomed the news. He knew the storming party was in for a bloody morning, but he still felt relieved. The idea of being cannonaded all the next day without being able to return a shot was "rather too much for my equanimity." If he was to be killed he wanted it to be at close quarters, and not have his head knocked off by an unseen enemy half a mile away.

At about 3:00 in the morning—it was now the twentieth—the three regiments of Riley's command started for their position on Valencia's left flank, and Gardner was with them. A dense early morning fog had drifted in overnight,[12] and it was close to daylight when they reached a position about five hundred yards behind the Mexican camp. The Mexicans were still unaware of their presence. Indeed, many of them, newly promoted, were also hung over. As day broke, the storming party—some nine hundred men, artillery and infantry—formed into two columns.

It all seemed a little incongruous to Gardner. Those nine hundred troops, he mused, were about to attack this entrenched army with its twenty-seven pieces of ordnance and at least six thousand infantry, to say nothing of the unnumbered lancers with their pointed spikes. It seemed certain to him that two-thirds of the attacking force would be mowed down before they could get close enough to use their bayonets.

As the Americans crossed a deep barranca filled with two feet of water, the Mexicans finally saw them. It had an immediately sobering effect. Things began to happen. Gardner noted "a devil of a hubbub in their camp" and a frantic rush to arms and horses.

Near the top of the hill behind the Mexican position the attacking party halted for a moment to close up. At the top they halted again to catch their breath. Then it came, the first volley of fire from enemy infantry hastily thrown out to meet them. The storming column didn't return the fire, but stood up in the face of it—"as if they were throwing apples instead of lead at us," Gardner marveled—and marched forward for some twenty or thirty yards. There they halted again to deploy. During all this time not an American soldier had fired a shot. Gardner wondered at the coolness of the men, for they were dropping all about him and none of them lifting a musket.[13]

Two field pieces that the Mexicans had hurriedly run out on the left front suddenly opened fire. A hail of grape flew uncomfortably close over Gardner's head. He could see that if the Mexican gunners got the range there would be trouble. The guns had to be silenced.

He interrupted his captain, who was occupied deploying his troops, to suggest that he charge the guns immediately. But the captain didn't have time, so Gardner offered to take part of the company and lead the charge himself. As he and his little force rushed forward, the guns bellowed again, and again the grape flew just over their heads. They broke into a sprint; they might not be so lucky if the guns got off a third shot.

Gardner found himself immediately in a fierce hand-to-hand struggle with the gunners and a small squad of Mexican infantry, and was instantly in trouble. A Mexican soldier parried a blow with his musket and swept the sword from Gardner's hand. As his attacker lunged forward with his bayonet, a musket roared at Gardner's ear and the Mexican dropped, shot by one of Gardner's men—not an instant too soon.

Now Gardner saw that the Mexican gunners were attempting to reload to fire again. But abruptly, instead of firing, they fled. Gardner leaped to the guns and swung them around intending to hurl grape at their retreating backs, when the truth dawned on him. What the soldiers had been doing was driving spikes into the vents of the guns; the cannon were useless.

Gardner stopped to rest. He badly needed a breather. He saw now that the American line had been deployed and the assault was under way.

"Hurrah for the class of 1846!" a voice shouted, and a hand slapped him on the back.

George McClellan was grinning at him through the chaos. The engineers again were omnipresent. Another officer was with McClellan—a small swarthy lieutenant whom Gardner had never seen before.

"Mac, who's your friend?" the stranger asked.

There on the field amid the chaos McClellan did the honors: Beauregard, this is Gardner, a classmate from West Point. Gardner, this is Beauregard of the engineers.[14]

The Mexicans had had enough. They and their general, whose new-won glory had faded so suddenly with the dawn, were fleeing up the road toward San Angel. As they ran, Persifor Smith, who had wanted to do all this the night before, drew out his watch, consulted it, and said: "It has taken just seventeen minutes."[15] Valencia's army had been as utterly destroyed in those seventeen short minutes, Lieutenant Richard Ewell thought, "as though each man had been summoned to the other world."[16]

The happiest men on the field were from the Fourth Artillery. They recognized among the abandoned Mexican artillery two guns that belonged to them, but had been captured by the Mexicans at Buena Vista. Hardcastle found it affecting, "to see the officers & men of this reg't . . . embracing these engines of destruction, as they would an old friend."[17]

Hardcastle had little time to savor this touching scene, for Scott was pushing the pursuit. Elements of the army were at that moment on the road to Churubusco, hard on the heels of the retreating Mexicans.

But there was trouble ahead. A force under General Twiggs found it first, at the convent at Churubusco. From that house of the Lord, nothing godlike was coming, only sheets of deadly fire. This was indeed a strange convent in every way. Santa Anna had converted it to a very worldly purpose, surrounding it with a fieldwork, pocking it with embrasures and platforms for cannon, and crenelating it to accommodate musketry. Only 350 yards away he had created a tête-du-pont, a fortified bridge solidly and scientifically constructed with wet ditches, embrasures, and platforms for large armament. The river running past this fortification was straight, deep, and wide, and lined with Mexican troops for several hundred yards.

It was this bridge and convent, abristle with firepower, that Twiggs ran into as he hurried up the road to cut off the Mexican retreat. For the first time in the campaign, Scott decided on a frontal assault. He was eager to keep up the momentum from the seventeen-minute victory at Contreras. But very soon his army had its hands full, for Santa Anna was making a fierce stand.

Hardcastle by now had come up from Contreras, and he and Captain Henry Wayne were riding through a cornfield on the right of the Mexican position. Their job was to reconnoiter the ground over which one of the brigades was proposing to attack. Lifting his glass to his eyes for a better look, Hardcastle saw a foreign object coming directly for them at high speed through the cornfield. He spurred his horse quickly to the right as the cannonball whistled past, not more than three feet from his head. Close-flying shot was getting to be an occupational hazard with Hardcastle.

He and Wayne looked at one another, and Wayne shrugged and said, "A miss is as good as a mile."

By now grape, canister, and musketry were showering in on the Americans from the convent and the tête-du-pont. Churubusco was shrouded in smoke. The din was ear-shattering, "one continual deafening thunder."[18]

William Gardner's regiment was there, and he was with it. They had come up from Contreras, and Gardner now stood before Churubusco in a tall field of corn in full tassel and roasting ears.

Leading about thirty men of his company, he emerged cautiously from the corn into an open space. There were no other American troops in sight. But he soon saw that there were Mexicans. Just ahead beyond a ditch bordered by a thick row of native maguey plants was a long line of Mexican infantry within musket range. Conceding that he could do nothing against such odds, Gardner ordered his men to make for the ditch. As they ran, the Mexican soldiers opened up on them, felling a few of Gardner's men and riddling the tough maguey leaves with bullets. In the ditch Gardner caught his breath and braced himself for the attack he knew was surely to follow.

When it didn't come, Gardner began to consider what he must do next. He knew that if nothing else, they must get out of that ditch. Ordering his men to stoop low and keep the maguey plants between them and the Mexicans, they bolted toward another clump of trees some distance to the right, reaching them without a loss.

They had not been there long when Captain Louis Craig of the Third Infantry came up from another direction with his company, exultation shining in his eyes.

Gardner jumped up in alarm. "Where are you going, Craig?" he asked.

"I am going to advance through that clump of woodland to the front," Craig replied.

"How strong are you?" Gardner asked.

"One company," said Craig.

Now just hold on, Gardner told him, pointing to where he had just been, and telling him of the strong line of Mexican infantry waiting beyond the wood. Even if they joined forces, Gardner argued, they would be altogether too weak to effect anything. He suggested instead that they wait for Craig's regiment, or Gardner's, or both. But Craig was either too intoxicated with the success of the morning, had lost his head, or didn't believe Gardner. At any rate, he refused to listen and ordered his company forward.

As little as Gardner's judgment sanctioned the movement, he couldn't permit Craig to march alone to be massacred, so he immediately ordered his own men to fall in with the crazed captain's. The two officers led their men forward, rushing through the woods and emerging in the presence of the Mexican troops—very much to Craig's surprise, but not at all to Gardner's.

Then Craig said something even more surprising than anything he had said so far:

"Don't fire! The Mexicans are about to surrender."

The next thing Gardner felt, after astonishment, was the bullet. As it struck, he staggered backward and toppled into the corn. His first sergeant rushed to his side, picked him up, and began to carry him off. The pain of being lifted was so intense that Gardner ordered the sergeant to leave him and rejoin the command.

As Gardner lay bleeding in the corn, the fighting raged on. The stalks above his head were soon shredded by musket fire, as the maguey leaves had been. The Mexicans overwhelmed the small detachment, as Gardner knew they would, and began murdering all of the Americans lying wounded on the field. However, they failed to see him lying in the corn.[19]

The fighting around the convent and the tête-du-pont continued to roar on. Escopet balls whistled over the heads of the army and cannonballs continued to sing through the corn.[20] When the breakthrough came, it was at the tête-du-pont. In a final rush it was stormed and seized, and its defenders broke and fled. Artillery was then brought to bear on the convent, which surrendered before it also had to be taken by storm.

It had been triumphant, but terrible, thought Hardcastle. He had been everywhere on the field. The engineer officers had been used as extensions of the major commanders throughout the battle—Scott and the other generals frequently dispatching them to points in the field beyond their personal control. There the engineers found themselves handling emergencies in the name of the commanding general himself. Such was the regard in which the West Point engineers were now held that the second-level commanders cheerfully obeyed their orders, no questions asked, no matter how junior they were.[21]

How Hardcastle escaped without taking a bullet was a mystery to him. "Men were shot down on all sides of me," he wrote his uncle, "& the messengers of death flew about me in all directions." He had a great horror of being wounded, but he thought that he would willingly have taken a musket ball just to get out of the scrape honorably. But here he was out of it, and unscratched as well. But his heart was sickened by what he had seen.[22]

Perhaps one of the things that had sickened him was that brief moment when soldiers of the Second Infantry Regiment emerged from the cornfield and his classmate, Tom Easley, and a dozen soldiers under his command were gunned down by a volley of musketry. It had been Easley, under the warm covers at Cordova a few nights before, who hadn't wanted to hear William Gardner's morbid speculations on future events. Now Easley was dead—the one among the three after all who was destined to make a permanent settlement in Mexico.[23]

The loss of this member of the class of 1846 caused sadness as high up in the army as the general in chief himself. Scott in his official report spoke of Easley as that officer "of great merit," who fell "gallantly" before the convent. Scott also officially noted that

Lieutenants McClellan, Foster, Reno, and Hardcastle, the two engineers, ordnance officer, and topographer from the class, had "shared in the glory of this action." But they, unlike Easley, still lived to tell about it.[24]

After the firing stopped, Gardner continued to lie in the cornfield, until in the eerie quiet his sergeant and three men from his company came looking for him. They placed him gently on a blanket and using it as a stretcher, carried him to a small nearby house and laid him on the floor. Already there, not surprisingly, was a severely wounded Captain Craig. Gardner's wound was severe in the extreme. The musket ball had penetrated his body near the medial line at the edge of the chest bone, followed an upward and oblique course, passed near the heart, and stopped "the Lord only knows where." The surgeon considered his case so hopeless he decided not to probe for the ball. There was little likelihood that Gardner would survive the night.[25]

It was 5:00 in the afternoon when the battle ended, and the Americans were now within five miles of the city of Mexico, its spires and steeples in full view. The prize was within their grasp. But the army was also exhausted. It had fought and won two major battles that day. It needed rest. So Scott called a halt. During the night a flag of truce came out of the city, and two more the next day, and Scott entered into an armistice to permit the Mexican government to negotiate a peace.

Hardcastle hoped with all his heart that the negotiations would succeed. "I have seen fighting enough," he said. "I have seen blood enough spilt."[26]

It became apparent after two weeks of negotiations by President Polk's peacemaker, Nicholas Trist, that Santa Anna didn't really share Hardcastle's longing for peace. The embattled president used the cease-fire as a breather to beef up his defenses. If Santa Anna was outgeneraled by Winfield Scott in battle, which was clearly the case, it was the other way around in an armistice. After Trist tried fruitlessly for two weeks to make peace, Scott prepared in early September to get back to doing what he did best—make war.

To
the Halls of
the Montezumas

Scott's immediate problem was a castle called Chapultepec. In days long gone it had been a summer residence of the Aztec emperors. Now it blocked Scott's way to the city of Mexico, guarding the causeways that led to the capital. It had to be either seized or skirted, and Scott didn't yet know which.

If an army had ever encountered a roadblock, this was it. Looking up at Chapultepec's towering walls the Americans saw only trouble. It hulked there, a forbidding eminence jutting 150 feet upward on a massive outcropping of phosphoritic rock, so situated as to command every entrance to the city. Before Cortez's time, it had been both the burying place and the palace of the Aztec monarchs, and was called the "mount of the grasshopper." Now it was the National Military School, the West Point of Mexico, and was alive with difficulties. It bristled with dangerous approaches, protected by outworks both at its base and on its acclivities. It was the strongest fort on the American continent. Its inner walls were four feet thick and twenty feet high, mounting thirty-five pieces of artillery commanding the approaches on all sides. It was regarded as virtually impregnable.[1]

But it had to be taken. And it had to be taken by an army three hundred miles from its base of supply, without hope of reinforcement, without rations, short of ammunition, surrounded by a hostile population, confronted by strong works on every side, and facing an army many times its size.

Again Scott sent out his West Point reconnoitering teams; he would wait to see what they suggested.

Meanwhile there was the Molino. On the western edge of the compound that held Chapultepec was a low-lying row of strong stone buildings, huddling within a thousand yards of the castle itself. The complex, styled the Molino del Rey, had once housed a flour mill. But the Mexicans had converted it to a foundry, and reports had reached Scott at his headquarters at Tacubaya that steeple and church bells were being hammered into cannon barrels there. While he waited for his engineers to complete their assessments of Chapultepec, he would shut down this nuisance. He sent General William Worth to take the Molino and destroy the foundry and everything in it.

At about 3:00 in the morning on September 8, Worth put his command of three thousand men in motion toward the Molino across rough and rocky ground, through maguey hedges and over the embankments approaching the foundry. Five hundred of his men comprising a storming party would attack down the gentle slope leading immediately to the works. It could be dangerous for his men, a hell-hole, for the terrain was "without so much as a twig to shelter them."[2]

For John Gray Foster it was another day to do double duty. He was an engineer, one of the three officers of the little company of sappers, miners, and pontoners. His standing in the West Point class of 1846—fourth, just ahead of Edmund Hardcastle and only two files behind George McClellan—had won this son of a New Hampshire widow a place among the army's elite. But West Point had made these men jacks of all the military trades. The night before, as an engineering officer, he had reconnoitered the ground and therefore knew as much about it as any man in the army. This morning, however, he was an infantry officer for the day, waiting in the vanguard of the storming party and peering through the predawn darkness at a strangely silent foundry.[3]

It was still dark when the first American gun bellowed, announcing callers and demanding entrance. But there was still no stirring at the Molino. The works appeared abandoned. The storming party approached cautiously, to within point-blank range. Still nothing. Then suddenly a sheet of flame burst from the Molino and a hail of bullets broke from a thousand Mexican muskets. A battery roared, raining down grape and round shot everywhere, the Mexicans themselves pouring out after it. As Foster's classmate George Gordon was to describe the chaos, "The living, not wounded, were beaten backward into flight; the wounded, not killed, were slaughtered by lance or bayonet thrust where they fell."[4]

The first volley shattered the bones in Foster's leg below the knee, and several of his men dragged him to an obscure angle in the wall and left him there. On the strewn field the exultant Mexicans hacked and butchered until a second wave of Worth's column rolled in past the shattered storming party and hit them full on, driving them back again into the foundry. Foster lay within the angle of the wall in pain but alive; the Mexicans had not found him.[5]

Outnumbered three to one and paying a terrible price in dead and wounded, the Americans eventually beat the Mexicans back for good and stormed into the Molino at about 10:00 in the morning. There they found virtually nothing—no steeple or church bells being shaped into cannon. The only thing there had been death. To the ubiquitous and slightly squeamish Hardcastle the battle had been "the most horrid sight I ever witnessed, to see the dead, the dying & the wounded stretched on every side & presenting all the ghastly images the imagination can conceive of."[6] It had been the bloodiest day of the war, and none of it had been necessary.

When it was over the Americans withdrew to Tacubaya and in effect handed the empty Molino back to the Mexicans. An angry General Worth wanted to storm the accursed castle itself, on the spot. But Scott wasn't ready; his engineers weren't finished.[7]

The war ended for Foster at the Molino. After the battle he was found and rescued, but his wound was so severe that further service was out of the question. He hadn't counted on this. A violated calendar didn't square with his well-ordered engineering mind. Being shot, he said, had not been "foreseen in my calendar of futurities."[8] The wound, teamed with debilitating attacks of dysentery, everybody's enemy, compelled him to leave Mexico. He was borne home an emaciated and feeble shell of a son to his widowed mother's plain little one-storied cottage overlooking the mills and the river at Nashua, New Hampshire. He wouldn't be going on after all to the halls of the Montezumas with Legs Smith, George McClellan, and Company A.[9]

Death continued to hover about him for weeks. Only months

later could he write McClellan that it appeared he would live after all. His friend and classmate was relieved. "The last news we had heard from you, through Stewart, S.S.," McClellan answered happily from Mexico City, "were that your physicians had given you up as a gone coon."[10]

Four days after the bloodletting at the Molino, Scott was ready for Chapultepec. The engineers had reported, he had met with his generals, and he was convinced the castle must be attacked head on. His artillery therefore began shelling it in preparation on the morning of September 12. The engineer company, now without Foster, constructed the siege batteries the night before, and made reconnaissances on the San Cosme causeway over which General Worth's division was expected to enter the city when the castle fell.

The night before the cannonading began was an anxious one—"more like the Noche Triste[11] that the Spanish invaders under Cortes had passed in the Aztec capital than we had ever before known," thought George Gordon. It was a relief to him when with the first light of dawn the batteries opened up on the castle.[12]

The plan was for a column under General John A. Quitman to assault the castle's southeastern front, as General Gideon Pillow attacked from the western side. Quitman, a politician-general from Mississippi, was to approach up the Tacubaya road to the strong batteries at the base of the rock, over the exterior walls, and up the declivity to the castle. Pillow was to approach through Molino del Rey across an open field, over a line of ditches and entrenchments, through the cypress grove to the base of the rock, then over a redan halfway up the declivity to the castle. Two scaling parties of two hundred picked men each—one of whom was Jimmy Stuart, who volunteered for everything—were to swarm up the castle walls on ladders.

The main attack was to be on the castle's western wall under Pillow. The Voltigeurs, a crack unit commanded by Lieutenant Colonel Joseph E. Johnston, now fully recovered from his wound and from George Derby's coarse wit, was to lead the advance through the cypress grove to the base of the rock. As it halted and re-formed there, the storming party was to pass through to the front and scale the walls. To prevent the Mexicans from being reinforced from the city, and to hold the Mexican cavalry at bay on the left, Scott deployed two regiments of infantry under Colonel William Trousdale.[13]

On the morning of the thirteenth shortly after eight o'clock, the American cannonade ended and the assault began.

Tom Jackson was with Trousdale on the left, in very public trouble. He was stuck in a ditch with his guns, in full view of the American army and under fire by the Mexicans. Magruder had sent him forward to support one of Trousdale's infantry divisions, and from the moment he arrived he had problems. A Mexican field piece protected by a breastwork was raking the road from end to end. Heavy cannon fire from the heights was raining down on him. Nearly all of the horses in his battery had been killed or wounded. His men, understandably discouraged, had taken cover. The infantry, except for a small escort which continued to try to hold its ground, had disappeared.

Jackson could not disappear, nor did he want to: Providence willing, he intended to return the enemy fire. However, it meant getting a gun over the deep ditch that cut across the road, and he was having to do it alone. He had lifted one of the guns over, but he needed help to take it any farther. He strode up and down the shot-swept road in front of the army, prodding and exhorting his cowering command.

"There is no danger!" he pleaded as a cannonball caromed between his legs, "See! I am not hit!"

His men stared at him with skepticism. Even General Worth could hardly bear to watch. He sent an order to Jackson to retire and Jackson sent word back out of the smoke that it would be more dangerous now to withdraw than to stand fast. If the general would give him fifty veterans he would attempt to capture the breastwork instead.

The help came in the person of John Magruder himself, who lost his horse on the way but reached the road unhurt. There he found that Jackson had wheeled the gun in position with the help of a sergeant who had been moved by his example, and was already loading and firing at the enemy battery in a muzzle-to-muzzle shootout. Magruder helped hoist a second gun over the ditch, and Jackson's men, taking heart, rallied. In time, and by Jackson's sheer will, the Mexican gun was overpowered and the breastwork stormed.[14]

As Jackson was putting on this show, Colonel Johnston and his

Voltigeurs were sweeping through the cypress grove toward the castle, and it was hard going. Every tree hid an enemy. Every gun on the castle wall showered down grape and canister. An incessant storm of musketry erupted from behind every rock and breastwork. Through all this the Voltigeurs and the other regiments supporting the assault converged over ramp and lunette until they were at the ditch at the base of the castle's inner wall.

Even in an undertaking as well planned as this one, there was bound to be a glitch. When the members of the scaling party arrived as planned, they discovered that the ladders had been left behind. After a brief moment of consternation, they were sent for and brought up and all hands from all commands then at the wall leaped into the ditch and struggled to plant and mount them.

Lieutenant Lewis A. Armistead, first into the ditch, was immediately wounded. A step behind him, bearing the colors of the Eighth Infantry, bounded Lieutenant James Longstreet. And beside him, last in his class at West Point but first at Chapultepec, was George E. Pickett. A musket ball struck Longstreet, and as he fell Pickett caught the falling colors and carried them on over the wall into the castle. General Scott watched appreciatively as "streams of heroes" followed.[15]

Within the walls the storming party met the fierce will of the Mexican defenders, including cadets of the National Military Academy who had vowed to fight to the death. But the momentum of the assault was overwhelming. A foothold was quickly won, doors were battered down, and cadet vows were fulfilled. As the hand-to-hand fighting raged below, Pickett carried the colors on to the top of the castle.

On the field below, between Molino del Rey and the castle, Pickett's classmate, George Gordon of the Mounted Rifles, looked up and saw the Mexican flag fall from the heights.

"There goes the flag!" he shouted.

"Huh?" said his commander, Major Edwin Vose Sumner.

"There goes the flag!" Gordon repeated.

"Shot down, I suppose!" Sumner growled.

Then, before their eyes, the stars and stripes slowly rose and snapped free in the breeze over the castle.

"There goes the flag!" shouted Gordon again. Beside him he

became aware of a grunting cheer rumbling up from within the battle-beaten major. Officers and men all around broke into a shouting, sword-waving, cap-throwing mob.[16]

General Scott also watched and saw and listened and heard. One after another, regimental colors were flung from the upper ramparts with long-continued shouts and cheers. Scott thought how this must send a shudder of dismay all the way into the city of Mexico. No scene, be believed, could have been more animating or glorious.[17]

It was glorious, but it wasn't over. The morning was only half done and Scott's intention was to make that splendid city his before the day was finished. The army immediately started up the causeways toward the gates of the city.

As George Gordon galloped with the Rifles down the road along the northern wall of the castle, he passed Tom Jackson. His classmate was staring dejectedly through the smoking debris at the corpses of six of his horses, dead in harness. Gordon had never seen such woebegone sorrow on a human face.

"Well! Old Jack," he shouted as he galloped by, "it seems to me you are in a bad way."

Gordon caught his classmate's laconic reply over the clanging sabers and pounding hoofs.

" 'Pears I am!" he said.[18]

Jackson's depression was anchored in his frustrated desire to be off down the causeway himself, to the San Cosme gate, Scott's intended main line of assault on the city. But he wasn't going to get there this way. To replace his dead horses with others would take time, too much time. The war would be over. He knew that most of the horses hauling his ammunition caissons, which had been sequestered in the rear, had escaped unhurt. So he put an idea to Captain Magruder. To save time could he hitch his guns to the limbers of those caissons instead? Magruder quickly agreed and in an instant Jackson made the switch and he and his two guns were careening toward the San Cosme gate.[19]

He soon came up on two other young West Pointers as eager for military glory as he—D. H. Hill, with whom he had walked on the beach at Point Isabel, and Barnard Bee. When Magruder pulled up with more men, but no other guns, he found these three hotheads clamoring to continue the pursuit. This was a little pushy even for Magruder, whose own hotheadedness was legendary. Worth's division, which Scott had assigned to storm the San Cosme gate, was still far behind, and the chance of losing the two guns under such exposed circumstances was too much to risk. The three officers lobbied hard and Magruder soon gave in; it was not in his makeup to dodge danger. Jackson, who had already had a morning of mornings, thundered on and was soon throwing metal at a brigade of Mexican cavalry at the gates of the city.[20]

Not far away was George McClellan, taking a different route to the same place. Legs Smith's plan was to bore a corridor through the walls of the houses that ran along the left side of the causeway, making a continuous covered approach to the Mexican position. The engineer company, with McClellan in the lead, was attacking wall after wall in house after house with picks and crowbars. By late afternoon the corridor had reached a three-story building within forty yards of the Mexican works. An hour before sunset American soldiers, "as if by magic," appeared on the roof and began pouring a deadly musket fire into the enemy garrison.[21]

Two gates to the city lay beyond Chapultepec, the San Cosme gate on the left and the Belen gate on the right, and the route to both was over elevated causeways. Scott's intention was to concentrate his main attack on the most vulnerable of these gates—the San Cosme—and the assignment had fallen to Worth.

General Quitman was to approach the Belen gate warily and only in a threatening manner. He failed to do either, and was soon in an unexpected pitched battle for control of the gate. Lieutenant Beauregard, who was there, found it to be "emphatically a hot place," from which few who were present escaped without some kind of wound or another, including himself.

The most original hit of the day, perhaps of the war, was taken there by Cadmus Wilcox. The genial third-to-last finisher in the class of 1846 had landed a position on Quitman's staff and now found himself in the middle of that emphatically hot place. A Mexican musket ball hammered into the side of the Colt's revolver hanging from his left hip and spun him around. Dazed and bruised, but otherwise unhurt, he picked up the musket ball and looked at it. It was flattened to the thickness of a dollar by the impact. Clearly stamped on one side of this bullet-turned-wafer was the name of the maker of Wilcox's pistol and the place where it was made.[22]

By nightfall, the two gates had fallen after hard fighting. The only thing now standing between the American army and the city of Mexico was the citadel, where the Mexicans had taken refuge. Scott pulled up. There had been fighting enough for a day; the final attack must wait until tomorrow.

But the fight had gone out of Santa Anna. At daybreak a flag of surrender came over the American lines, and Scott was told by a delegation from the city that the Mexican army had left in the night. What Scott called "the second conquest of Mexico" was over. The city was his. At 7:00 in the morning the U.S. colors were hoisted over the halls of the Montezumas. Later that morning Scott entered the city under a brilliant sun at the head of the cavalry, the bands blaring. "Hail Columbia," "Washington's March," "Yankee Doodle," and "Hail to the Chief" proclaimed his coming.[23]

Lifting his eyes to the balcony of the National Palace, Scott saw the flag of the Mounted Riflemen unfurled to the breeze. A smile of pride broke across his broad face. Removing his hat and bowing low, he shouted, *"Brave Rifles! Veterans! You have been baptized in fire and blood and have come out steel."*[24]

There had been enough fire, blood, and steel to go around. Now there was only relief. McClellan sighed and said, "Here we are—the deed is done—I am glad no one can say 'poor Mac' over me."[25] Hardcastle, reviewing the battles that had brought Scott to the gates of the National Palace—Vera Cruz, Cerro Gordo, Contreras and Churubusco, Molino del Rey and Chapultepec—was also glad they were over, and that nobody could say poor Hardcastle over him. But he believed many a widow and orphan would remember these battles with deep and everlasting sorrow.[26]

Hardcastle had been lucky. A ball through his forage cap had been his closest call. But two in the class had not been so fortunate. Alexander Perry Rodgers had joined Tom Easley on the other side. Rodgers had been the scion of military nobility; Commodore Oliver Hazard Perry, the naval hero of the battle of Lake Erie, was his uncle. He had graduated thirtieth in the class, and now he was dead, gunned down at the storming of Chapultepec. Easley, now Rodgers, both dead.

For Hardcastle and his other surviving classmates, the lines of a poetic tribute written to the memory of the fallen Rodgers, if they could have read it, would have been more to the point than the victories:

Oh War! What is thy glory now!
Unwreath, unwreath the victor's brow,
And twine the mournful cypress leaf,
Fitting a widowed mother's grief:
Grief for her young and gallant son—
Grief for the lost, her martyr'd one—
Amid a band of brothers brave,
He rests within a hero's grave.
Who nobly fought—who nobly fell—
Let yon red field of carnage tell:
Laid by the fiery death-shot low,
In the fierce fight of Mexico.[27]

Those classmates who were lead-free, or could walk and ride, entered the city in triumph with Scott. Those who had been wounded were carried in. One who entered neither lead-free nor walking was William Gardner. Against all medical probability he had survived the terrible wound at Churubusco. His accomplished slave, Moses, whom Gardner had brought from home for just such a contingency, had taken up his case and nursed him back to life. After the final surrender of the city, Gardner was carried in on a litter by four soldiers, a very different and deflated mode of entry from the one he had envisioned for himself. His litter-bearers bore him to the National Palace, where his regiment was quartered, and left him there.[28]

The war was not yet entirely over, for trouble had erupted in the rear. The irrepressible Santa Anna, who had been fighting gringos since the days of the Alamo and San Jacinto—for over a decade now— was bloody, but not bowed. When he fled Mexico City and abandoned it to the Americans, he turned back on Puebla and put the small American garrison there under siege, in hopes of marooning Scott. The fall rains had softened the roads from Mexico City to Puebla and they could no longer support heavy wagons. There was no hope of relief therefore from the main army at Mexico City. Help, if it was to come, must come from Vera Cruz.

A brigade commanded by Brigadier General Joseph Lane was already on the march from the Gulf. But it was still a long way off, and Thomas Childs was edgy. The brevet lieutenant colonel commanding at Puebla was a skilled and seasoned veteran. He was cold of manner, clear in judgment, and inflexible in courage. But he was also under the gun.[29] Word had just come to him that Santa Anna's legions were at that moment advancing on the threatened city. Childs hurried to the ramparts to consult with H. L. Kendrick.

There was not a man in the class of 1846 who didn't know Kendrick. He had taught them chemistry, mineralogy, and geology at West Point. As Jacob W. Bailey's assistant, he had shared his mentor's merciful view of cadet academic shortcomings, and added a dimension of his own. With his easygoing blend of compassion and humor, theater and perspective, he had been the favorite of the corps. He had none of the worldwide academic acclaim of the academy's great professors. He had only graduated in the upper third of his West Point class in 1835, not first, but the cadets loved him for his quaint manner of speech and his appreciation of the ridiculous. Now he was commanding one of Childs's batteries at Puebla, as easygoing as ever, but a man to be relied on. Scott described him as the "the highly accomplished Captain Kendrick."[30]

He was at his battery on the walls at Puebla when Childs ran up shouting, "The crisis is coming—the crisis is coming! Why don't you fire?"

Kendrick turned to his lieutenant and said quietly, "Mr. Selden, commence firing."

Selden was mystified. He looked out beyond the parapets and saw nothing. "What am I to fire at?" he asked.

"Oh, fire at the crisis," Kendrick said.

Selden shrugged and canted the guns in the general direction of nowhere and commenced firing.[31]

Riding with Lane in the rescue brigade was another familiar face. Ambrose P. Hill, the Virginian who had fallen ill in his third-class year and been sent to the class behind, had finally graduated. He was a year late getting to Mexico, but now he was there on the road to Puebla, sent to fill the vacancy left in Magruder's battery when his former classmate, Tom Jackson, moved up to replace the fallen Lieutenant Johnstone.

Hill projected a colorful profile in Mexico from the start. On the national road to Puebla he wore a flaming red flannel shirt and a pair of coarse soldier's trousers tucked into red-topped boots. An outsized pair of Mexican spurs clinked at his heels and his head was shaded by a broad-brimmed sombrero. Packed together at his slim waist were a long artillery saber, a pair of large horse pistols stuffed into leather holsters, two revolvers crammed into one belt, and a large butcher knife jammed into another. "As villainous a looking rascal as ever threw a lasso," he said of himself. "You would never have recognized us for civilized Americans . . . a more brigandish looking a motley was never seen."[32] No Mexican was safe.

Lane's brigade had set out from Vera Cruz on September 19 to relieve the garrison at Puebla. It was wholly unaware of what it might encounter along the way, other than the heat, which was stifling. Water was selling on the road at five dollars a drink and men were dropping from dehydration and fatigue.[33]

Hill at any moment expected an ambush. He had never seen a country more favorable for one in his life. The road on each side was edged by an impenetrable chaparral so dense that an enemy could lie in wait wholly concealed. A twenty-power magnifying microscope couldn't have picked them out. Why they were not attacked baffled Hill; he expected it around every bend in the road.[34]

In truth, Santa Anna was waiting in ambush at a precipitous mountain pass on the national highway near a town called Huamantla. The Americans, dodging the ambush, pushed into the town where they fought a fierce engagement, defeated the Mexicans, and rolled on toward Puebla. They arrived in sight of the spires of the city on October 12, and that afternoon lifted the siege. Hill, the well-armed West Pointer, was among those commanding the guns that convinced the Mexicans the war was really over.[35]

It had been a most satisfactory war, meeting all of George McClellan's and Tom Jackson's expectations. It hadn't met all of William Gardner's or Dabney Maury's or George Derby's or John Foster's, since they had nearly been killed and either carried through it on a litter or sent home. But Gardner spoke for them all when he said: "The idea of 10,000 men marching through a hostile country upon a capital containing upwards of 200,000 inhabitants, defended by 30,000 troops equipped with 100 pieces of cannon, and fortified by both nature and art! The capture of the city of Mexico under such conditions was a feat of arms to astound the world."[36] Maury agreed. The war, he said, was "a fine experience for our troops. It was actively pressed . . . and was a series of victories without check, until the capital was captured and peace was made."[37]

127

From the beginning of the war to the end some one hundred thousand men, regulars and volunteers, had gone into the American army, but at no time did more than fourteen thousand fight in any one battle. Scott entered the valley of Mexico with only nine thousand men and was not reinforced until after the city fell. Taylor and Scott in Mexico—and Kearny in New Mexico and California—had worked a military masterpiece. Cortez hadn't done it any better.

In every battle fought the Mexicans were superior—often overwhelmingly so—in numbers of troops, in numbers of artillery, in weight of metal thrown, and in numbers of small arms. They had a superior cavalry and they fought gallantly. So why had it been so easy, so quickly won against such heavy odds, so successful?

There had simply been an overwhelming superiority on the American side in the numbers and weight of military skill. The Mexicans were outgeneraled and outmaneuvered from the top and outfought from the bottom. But it may have been in the middle that the war was so easily and effortlessly won—by the solid core of West Pointers who formed the backbone of the army's officer corps.

Scott said as much. "I give it as my fixed opinion," he said, "that but for our graduated cadets the war between the United States and Mexico might, and probably would, have lasted some four or five years, with, in its first half, more defeats than victories falling to our share; whereas in less than two campaigns we conquered a great country and a peace without the loss of a single battle or skirmish."[38]

Scott struck this theme repeatedly. At a dinner in Mexico City in December he said that but for the science of the military academy, "this army, multiplied by four, could not have entered the capital of Mexico."[39]

At Contreras, Scott had been so exalted by yet another act of military prestidigitation by his engineers that he had exclaimed: "If West Point had only produced the Corps of Engineers, the Country ought to be proud of that institution."[40]

It wasn't just the engineers. The regular army was for the most part officered by West Pointers at all levels below the rank of general—none of them as yet wore stars. It was the first conflict in which academy graduates had the opportunity to prove themselves. Five hundred twenty-three West Pointers fought in the war; 452 of them won brevet promotions, 49 were killed and 92 wounded. They made the war the most efficient in U.S. history—thirty encounters fought and all of them won in less than a year and a half, forty thousand Mexicans taken prisoner, a thousand cannon captured, ten fortified strongholds and a capital city vanquished.[41]

The most newly minted of these West Pointers, the class of 1846, had shone. Fifty-three of them, virtually the entire class, went to the war. Thirty-seven, well over half, were breveted for gallantry, several of them more than once. Two of them were killed. Two others died. Eleven were wounded. One was captured. A handful were conspicuous in battle. Jimmy Stuart, who was gaining an army-wide reputation as a hell-for-leather dragoon, volunteered five times to serve on five separate attacking parties in five of the six battles he was engaged in. He was breveted twice—to captain.[42]

Nor was he atypical. Atypical had been Tom Jackson. It appeared as if the dogged, persevering Jackson, who had toiled so hard on his march through the files at West Point, hadn't yet stopped trying to rise to the top of the class. It was as though nobody had told him they had graduated. Jackson was breveted three times in Mexico: to first lieutenant at Vera Cruz, to captain at Contreras and Churubusco, and to major at Chapultepec. Nobody in the war was breveted more. Hold a battle and Jackson would win a brevet. Battle, it seemed, gave him no anxieties. His only worry as so many were falling about him was a fear that he wouldn't adequately perform under the danger, and that his conduct would not be as conspicuous as he desired. The crucible of fire seemed to exalt him. The hotter it got the better he liked it. He became conscious that in the midst of the chaos of battle all of his faculties sharpened and became picture clear, and that he had perfect command of them all. The country boy from Jackson's Mill appeared to be a born fighter.[43]

General Pillow twice called him the "brave Lieutenant Jackson." General Worth called him "gallant" at Chapultepec. His captain, John Magruder, said of him that "if devotion, industry, talent, and gallantry are the highest qualities of a soldier, then he is entitled to the distinction which their possession confers."[44]

In Mexico City Scott held a celebratory levee. As Jackson approached in line and his name was called, the general drew himself up to his full formidable height and thrust his hands behind his back.

"I don't know that I shall shake hands with Mr. Jackson," he roared sternly.

An embarrassing hush fell on the room.

"If you can forgive yourself for the way in which you slaughtered those poor Mexicans with your guns, I am not sure that I can," Scott said.

He then held out his giant hand to the blushing and confused young brevet major.

Jackson's former classmate John Gibbon said: "No greater compliment could have been paid a young officer, and Jackson apparently did not know he had done anything remarkable till his general told him so."[45]

If what Jackson had done did not seem remarkable to him, the things he had seen in the war did seem so. "I have since my entry into this land," he wrote his sister Laura, "seen sights that would melt the heart of the most inhuman of beings: my friends dying around me and my brave soldiers breathing their last on the bloody fields of battle, deprived of every human comfort, and even now I can hardly open my eyes after entering a hospital, the atmosphere of which is generally so vitiated as to make the healthy sick."[46] Jackson had found that while battle exalted him, war did not.

In May 1848, when a treaty of peace was ratified in which Mexico at last handed over the California and New Mexico territories to the Americans, the victorious army returned down the national road to Vera Cruz and home. The little company of sappers, miners, and pontoners returned to West Point on June 22, wearing long beards and marching in triumph on the plain behind George McClellan—brevet Captain McClellan now. The band played a Mexican march, and in the path before the superintendent's quarters they were halted and hailed as heroes. That night the old north and south barracks were lit in celebration, the lights forming the word "Victory" and shining, as George Derby would have said, "like a plebe's waist plate."[47]

It had indeed been a perfect war. The class would not see another like it again.

Indian
Country

It was deadly, this pas de deux on horseback that Clarendon J. L. (Dominie) Wilson was stepping off with the Navajo Indian chief. Better the stag dances on the plain or the barefoot back-step with Old Jack at Brown's Hotel. Better a few bars of the Benny Havens drinking song than the dreaded slap of the bowstring and the keening of the arrow he was now hearing. Better a quadrille in 2/4 time than this lurching dance of death.

For twenty jumps of their horses Wilson and his fierce, painted enemy were locked in their high-stepping embrace. Wilson pointed his muzzle-loading single-shot pistol at his tormentor and fired. His horse plunged just as he pulled the trigger, and the powder in the pan of his flintlock scattered to the wind. The arrow shot at the same instant by the Indian grazed Dominie's chest and carried away the button of his fatigue jacket.[1]

This is what it had come down to after that perfect war in Mexico. There was nothing of the poetry of that other conflict in this one, none of the romance, none of the brilliant strategy and creative reconnaissances, none of the flawless execution, none of the triumphant stormings and endless string of victories. There was nothing clear-cut about this war Wilson and some of his classmates were now waging.

It was just a series of death-dealing pas de deux on the prairies, deserts, and mountains of the West and the everglades of the South, against an unchivalrous enemy who fought by no rules ever taught at West Point. These were the Indian Wars, in which "the front is all around, and the rear nowhere."[2]

This is where many members of the class of 1846, more than a score of them, had now gone—to fight in this frontless, rearless war in the West. Not all of them went this time, as nearly all had gone to Mexico. A handful had left the army, or would leave it before the end of the 1850s. George McClellan would leave, to become a railroad president. Tom Jackson would leave to become a professor of natural and experimental philosophy and artillery tactics at the Virginia Military Institute. Who of his classmates would have predicted that?

A handful would stay in the army in the East to practice the profession they had been trained for—engineering. A few would go to join the Great Reconnaissance, the exploration of that 960,000 largely trackless square miles of new territory they had all helped win in the Mexican War.

But a score or more of them would climb into the saddle, and to the quick-stepping strains of "The Girl I Left Behind Me" and "The Bold Soldier Boy,"[3] ride off with Dominie Wilson to fight the Indians who still believed all that land was theirs.

Before the Mexican War, white settlement in the United States ended at a line that ran from Texas in the south to Minnesota in the north. The territory west of that line was peopled by 160,000 Indians, and little else. Half of those Indians were of the Five Civilized Tribes, benign as their title implied, and confined to what was then known as the Indian Territory and is now the state of Oklahoma. They were generally what many Indians weren't—settled, peaceful, agricultural, and slaveholding. In the remaining Louisiana Purchase territory lived another seventy-five thousand Indians, mostly nomadic and not so peaceful, warring with whites and with one another.[4]

Overnight the treaty of Guadalupe Hidalgo ending the Mexican war ceded the United States nearly a million new square miles of territory. And it more than doubled the number of Indians in the equation. Four hundred thousand Indians capable of putting forty thousand highly skilled fighters in the field now stood in the way of any plans the white man might have to pacify, plunder, or settle this new-won land.[5]

The white man had plans—big plans, big dreams, big profits—in mind. The ink was hardly dry on the treaty when gold was discovered in the sand of the American River near Sacramento, complicating everything. The trickle of settlers trekking west swelled instantly to a torrent. Armies of gold seekers swarmed out onto the transcontinental trails to answer the siren call. They stampeded across what had been the Permanent Indian Frontier, demanding that the Indians who still believed it to be their country by treaty, step aside and let them through. They demanded, where necessary, that the government protect their aspirations by force.

So the score of officers from the class of 1846 went west with an army of protection that was little more than a skeleton force. This slim reed of strength, less than ten thousand in number, would be undermanned, ill-equipped, and lost in the vastness of the land they must now protect. The dangers, privations, and hardships would be death-dealing. The geography and climate would be unforgiving. The distances would be unimaginable. The seaboard and the foreign frontiers that bounded this vastness stretched for ten thousand miles, an Indian frontier for another eight thousand.[6] Most of the miles within these measureless borders were empty and uninhabited. In the twenty-five hundred miles from Fort Leavenworth in Kansas to the Columbia River in Oregon, which the Mounted Rifles would cross in 1849, there were but two existing forts—Laramie and Kearny—and not a single house otherwise.[7]

The soldiers sent to this wilderness would be garrisoned in seventy-nine lonely frontier forts, most of which did not exist when they arrived and had to be built. They were in effect going into exile, where they were to be far-flung, isolated, ignored, infrequently promoted, and thrown against one of the shrewdest, most elusive and frustrating enemies ever to sit a saddle.

It was said of the Indian warrior that he was perhaps the best guerrilla partisan in history, "the finest light horseman that the world has ever seen, with tactics that have never been equalled by Bedouin, Cossack, Numidian, or Tartar at his best."[8] He was an unfixed target, next to impossible to pin down, and taught from childhood to ride and fight and run. He was aggressive, warlike, courageous, strong, mentally alert, stealthy, and cunning. He knew the country and how to use it in a fight. He was highly motivated and highly skilled. In effect, he was the perfect soldier.[9]

Most of the army's battles with these hit-and-run fighters would be accidental, small skirmishes lasting no longer than it took the Indians to break contact. No Indians, if they could avoid it, would ever present a solid front for very long against the army's superior fire power. Nor would all Indians fight equally well. None would fight at all except on horseback. And of these, the officers of the class of 1846 would soon learn to expect the hardest fight from the Utes and Shoshones on the high plains, the Comanches and Kiowas in Texas, and the Navajos and Apaches in the deserts.

The only edge the horse soldiers seemed to have at first against this skillful, nebulous enemy were superior discipline and arms. Even the edge in arms, at first, was questionable. Artillery was essentially useless against this shadow adversary, although on large-scale sorties lightweight mountain howitzers were pulled along.

This was a war the soldiers would fight for a long time with pistols and a hybrid sidekick called the musketoon. A blunderbuss of sorts (some called it a "brevet musket"), the musketoon was a musket sawed off to two-thirds of its original length. Its rammer was fastened to the barrel by a swivel to prevent its being lost or dropped while being loaded at a full gallop. It fired the same cartridge as the musket, but had neither its range nor accuracy; yet it kicked like a mule. It was nearly as useless as the artillery, but it was convenient to carry on horseback.[10] One day it would give way to the rifled carbine, but many an Indian would survive its blast and many a trooper would be swept from his saddle by its wallop before that day came.

So the pistol was left as the weapon of choice against the Indian. At first it was the single-shot, muzzle-loading horse pistol, the kind that misfired for Dominie Wilson in his close encounter with the Navajo chief. That soon gave way to the Colt's cap-and-ball six-shooter that had become the rage in the Mexican War, and was the only sensible weapon for these close-in fights that lasted only moments or seconds.[11]

There would be no fighting this war as armies, or as divisions or brigades or even as regiments. On rare occasions companies from several forts might combine to fight Indians on a major warpath. But any such combinations of five hundred to six hundred troops was as rare as buffalo were plentiful. The Indian wars were fought by single companies from isolated forts making long, galloping sweeps against hit-and-run Indian bands. Many companies would fight through an entire decade without ever taking the field with another company.[12] Richard S. Ewell, one of the best of the Indian fighters, would one day say that he learned everything about commanding a company of fifty dragoons on the western plains and nothing about anything else.[13]

Not good sense, but government policy, required that the army fight the Indians mainly with infantry. It was too expensive to mount and maintain cavalry-only regiments throughout the remote Indian country. "Walk-a-heaps," the Indians called these foot soldiers, and it wasn't meant as a compliment. "As well might we send boys into a cornfield to catch marauding crows with hopes of success as to start foot-soldiers in pursuit of Indians," complained the *Daily Missouri Republican*. "The government had as well place its soldiery on crutches and to command them to capture the wild antelope, as to send them, on foot, in the war path of the well-mounted warriors of the plains," said the Brownsville (Texas) *American Flag*. "Infantry in the Indian country . . . are about the same use as so many stumps would be," said John W. Whitfield, an Indian agent on the upper Platte.[14] But that is the way it had to be.

The longer they fought the Indian, however, the more like him these soldiers became and the more like him they fought. The best of the Indian fighters learned to think like this enemy, and dress for the occasion.

Captain Edmund Kirby Smith described himself, "mounted on my mule . . . [;] courduroy pants; a hickory or blue flannel shirt, cut down in front, studded with pockets and worn outside; a slouched hat and long beard, cavalry boots worn over the pants, knife and revolver belted to the side and a double barrel gun across the pommel, complete the costume as truly serviceable as it is unmilitary."[15]

So there they were, exiles in their own land, fighting an untidy, exhausting war against a skilled and phantom enemy, "living the best years of their lives in remote frontier posts with rare glimpses of the refinements of civilization, having little reward in sight but a sense of duty done, growing gray in junior grades under the slow promotions of peace conditions, kept poor by the necessities of frequent changes of stations."[16]

For them, as one of their wives said, it was "days of weary marching, nights of sleepless watching." Whether in the sierras of the North, the prairies of the West, or the savannahs of the South, "their lives are always the same. Like a chain of sentinels, their insufficient garrisons are stretched from the south-east to the extreme north-west; the reveille waking loud echoes on the rock-bound shores of Oregon, while the tattoo softly murmurs through the orange groves of Florida." The reward? Lives "too often yielded in some ignoble border skirmish, sacrificed ingloriously to their country, leaving a nameless grave on some distant, unfrequented spot."[17]

Death was no stranger to James Stuart, but the nameless grave was anathema to him. He had seen too much of death, been near it too many times. He had faced it in battle after battle in Mexico and survived.

He had faced it as a boy in Beaufort, South Carolina, when he was only twelve years old. He had been sick then and believed dying.

"Mamma," he asked his mother, "the doctor has told you that I cannot live, has he not?"

"Yes—he has," his sobbing mother said.

"I thought so," said the dying boy, "but Mamma, don't cry for me. I am not afraid to die. And there is something I wish to beg you to do for me: Stop crying, and listen to me."

"Well, go on, my son," his mother said, trying to be brave, for "Jamie" was her first-born. "What is it?"

"When I am dead I wish you to carry me to Beaufort and bury me in the Beaufort church-yard by the side of grandmother, where the birds will sing over me. Promise me that you will do it."

The mother had promised through her tears.

But Jamie didn't die. He recovered and lived to be a handsome, dashing, sensitive young man who could quote the poetry of Robert Burns by heart. He had gone on to West Point and there became George McClellan's roommate and dearest friend.[18]

In Mexico there was no danger Jimmy Stuart wouldn't face, no storming party he wouldn't volunteer for, and no brevet he didn't win—two for gallantry under fire. He was "a soldier of winning though of modest and reserved address," his brother wrote of him, "of great beauty of person and of romantic and interesting character."[19] He was "handsome, and gentle as a woman," his classmate Dabney Maury said, yet "no soldier of our army surpassed him in courage and daring."[20]

After Mexico, Brevet Captain Stuart went with the Mounted Rifle Regiment to fulfill the mission it had been organized for—to police the Oregon Trail. He was with it when they rode the length of the trail from Fort Leavenworth to the Columbia River in 1849. Now it was the middle of June 1851, and he was camped in the Rogue River valley with a small detachment of Rifles driving army horses to California. The regiment was going to Texas and the horses were being transferred to its replacement regiment, the First Dragoons. Captain Philip Kearny was in command of this horse-driving detachment and his two officers were Stuart and John G. Walker.

The weather was fine and the line of march was taking them through one of the most beautiful river valleys in the Oregon Territory. There were Indians around; this was Rogue River Indian country. But they were known to be friendly. The hardest part of the journey was behind them, and Stuart was afire with anticipation. When they reached California he was going home to Beaufort on leave. The girl he left behind was waiting there; the soft murmur of the dove was calling these West Pointers now.

But on this night in June Stuart's mind was not full of love, but of trouble. There was no reality he couldn't bravely face. But what do you do about dreams? He shook Walker awake and told him he had a premonition that he was going to die. Nonsense, Walker protested. Maybe, Stuart said, but Walker must see to it that his last wishes were carried out. It is just a nightmare, Walker said, forget it.

In the morning the news was unexpected and ominous. The Rogue River Indians were unaccountably on the warpath. The Rifle column proceeded cautiously through the morning and later in the day came upon their trail. So it had come to this. Kearny made plans to follow the Indian war party the next morning, and Stuart passed another fitful night full of fatal premonitions. Over breakfast he told Walker of a dream: an Indian warrior had appeared at the door of their tent, drawn his bow on Walker, then changed his aim at the last moment and killed Stuart instead.

The column caught up to the Indian war party later that morning and there was a fierce fight. The Indians were beaten when Stuart rode up behind one brave so intent on what was passing in front that he didn't see him coming. Stuart could have killed him instantly with a shot through the head or back, but that wasn't his way. Chivalry for a defeated enemy was his code, even when the enemy were savages. Instead he would capture him. Uncocking his pistol, he took hold of the barrel and lightly tapped the Indian on the shoulder with the butt end. The startled brave leaped back and drove an arrow deep into Stuart's side, before being killed by the captain's troopers.

"Oh, to think that I should have passed through six battles in Mexico, to die at last by the hand of an Indian!" Stuart cried as Walker knelt beside him.

He lingered on, clinging to life until the next afternoon beside the road where he fell. Then he died, and Walker buried him under a live oak tree and carved his initials in the bark. He was but twenty-six years old.[21]

South Carolina mourned for him, as a family would for its son. The state's General Assembly ordered a sword inscribed to his courage, sheathed it in a scabbard of gold, and presented it to his grieving parents. "Among the sons of South Carolina who by their distinguished valor and military skill in the Mexican War, acquired renown for themselves, and adorned her annals," the proclamation read, "she cherishes with particular pride and affection the memory of Brevet Capt. Stuart."[22]

When word of Stuart's death reached George McClellan, he opened the journal he had kept in Mexico and wrote on a blank page at the end: "On the 18th of June, 1851, at five in the afternoon died Jimmie Stuart, my best and oldest friend."[23]

But Stuart did not die to be buried in a nameless grave under trees in a valley so far from home. Some of his classmates—McClellan, Maury, A. P. Hill—and other officers who loved him, sent Walker back for his remains.

In Charleston, Walker asked Stuart's mother for permission to bear the body on to West Point, there to bury it with military honors under a monument to his memory. But the mother remembered a promise she had made at another unhappy time so many years before, and she said no.

She buried him instead in the Beaufort churchyard beside his grandmother, where the birds in the big trees would sing over his grave. It was what he had wanted.[24]

Stuart's classmate Dominie Wilson survived his dance of death with the Navajo chief. But an even more deadly enemy had hold of him now. It was a foe that was present even in the room at Brown's Hotel when he and Tom Jackson had drunkenly danced the barefoot back-step and roared their rollicking tributes to Benny Havens. It had been stalking him ever since.

In the summer of 1852 Wilson was in Las Lunas, New Mexico Territory, serving under Richard Ewell. An excellent officer when sober, Ewell said of him, "but unfortunately is a confirmed sot and sets such an example to my men that my trouble is doubled when he is present."[25]

By early the next year Wilson was in Albuquerque and slipping away. On February 21, 1853, he died at twenty-eight, killed by hard liquor, and only two years older than Stuart had been.

"Poor Dominie," Dabney Maury mourned, "his long pent craving was never slaked . . . until his enfeebled frame was laid to rest in a soldier's grave away off in the shadow of the Rockies."[26]

Another mourner, Oliver H. P. Taylor, the classmate who had stormed the church at Taos by his side in the Mexican War and had become his closest friend, remembered something nobler. "I have never known any one," Taylor said, "so apparently unconscious of danger under all circumstances."[27]

That was the Dominie Wilson the Navajo chief would also have remembered.

India-Rubber Women
and
Buffalo Men

Well, here I am soldiering," Eliza Johnston told her diary on October 29, 1855.[1] Indian summer had come to Missouri, interceding with the coming winter, and Eliza was marching to Texas with the Second Cavalry. The weather was perfect for soldiering.

It was a common thing in the Indian wars for wives to march with their soldier-husbands to some frontier outpost to be their companions in exile. The colonel of this crack new regiment, Albert Sidney Johnston, was Eliza's husband. But the young subalterns of the class of 1846 had been falling in love and taking wives, too. Two of those young wives were marching with Eliza and the Second Cavalry to Texas. One of them had married James Oakes, thirty-fourth in the class; the other had wed Innis Newton Palmer, thirty-eighth. Their husbands were both captains and company commanders now, among the most promising young officers in the service.

Teresa Griffin Viele had also married an officer who for a while had been a member of the class. She would also one day be soldiering to Texas, to engage the Comanches, and would blame it all on West Point. "That mammoth trap," she called the academy, that source of their predicament, "where the coleur de rose of army-life serves as a bait for the unsophisticated, where reality wears the gloss of romance, and military glory appears in its brightest holiday dress, accompanied by all the poetry of war. Most delusive spot, where even the atmosphere seems heavily freighted with martial music and martial association."[2]

She had fallen for it; she had taken the bait. They all had. Captivated by the gloss of romance and lulled by the poetry of war, Teresa had met, fallen in love with, and married West Point and Egbert Louis Viele. Her husband, a New Yorker, had entered the academy with the class of 1846, but had been "found" and held back a year instead of dismissed, to graduate thirtieth of thirty-eight in the class of 1847.

"No recruit," Teresa Viele would say after her marriage to the army, "ever entered the service with more enthusiasm than I did, or felt more eager to prove himself a soldier."

In her fantasy's eye she beheld a beau-ideal heroine of the frontier, "a kind of tough, weather proof, India-rubber woman, 'six feet high—grand, epic, homicidal,' who could travel over hundreds of miles of prairie on horseback, or follow the train for months on top of a baggage-waggon."

Familiar fraternization with the most savage Indian tribes in the West would be de rigueur for this amazon-Teresa. Human sympathy, food, or rest would be "mere frivolous weaknesses, necessities of our fallen nature." These she would banish from her high-strung mind. A mighty energy of character would sustain her through the direst emergencies; nothing would unstring her dauntless nerves. The allurements of dress, petty artifices, tears—any of the little feminine failings—would have no place in her frontier psyche. Teresa's India-rubber woman would scorn them all, and the regiment, of course, would adore her. Her children, if she had any, would be "embryo soldiers arrayed in military baby clothes, cradled in a disabled drum, tucked in with a piece of 'star-spangled banner,' and teething on a drumstick." Marching away to war, this archetypal warrior-wife would be "the witness of many a thrilling and gory scene, with the din of battle in her ear, and stern endurance on her brow."[3]

And when the boys sang that stanza of the Benny Havens anthem they had written for her and those like her, her lusty soprano would soar proudly above their deep baritones:

141

To the ladies of the Army, our cups shall ever flow,
Companions of our exile, and our shields 'gainst every woe.
May they see their husbands generals, with double pay also,
And join us in our choruses of Benny Havens O!![4]

The Mesdames Johnston, Oakes, Palmer, and Johnson—the latter the wife of Lieutenant Richard W. Johnson—were all marching with the Second Cavalry now to Texas, living embodiments of Teresa Viele's heroine. They were a quartet of rubber-tough companions, up in the morning at 4:00 and soldiering in their ambulance-wagons from 6:00 to 6:00, making twenty more miles toward Texas on a good day. At the end of those days they were women again and their four tents, staked among the hundreds in the encircling encampment, became magnets, reminders to the horse soldiers of a softer world left behind.[5]

The Second Calvary was little more than half a year old. In early March 1855, the Congress had authorized four new regiments for the army, to answer the clamor on the frontier for a larger armed presence—two new cavalry regiments and two infantry. The Second Cavalry was one of these, and favored above all the others. Secretary of War Jefferson Davis had taken a particular personal interest in its composition, handpicking its colonel and lieutenant colonel—Johnston and Robert E. Lee—and all of its officers. It had therefore come to be known in the army as "Jeff Davis' Own."[6]

Through the spring and early summer the regiment's young company commanders, among them newly promoted Captains Oakes, Palmer, and Stoneman of the class of 1846, fanned out into the country to recruit the best fighting men they could find. Ohio, Kentucky, and Indiana were canvassed for the best cavalry horses money could buy. For an average price of $150 a head, grays were purchased for Company A; sorrels for Companies B and E; bays for Companies C, D, F, and I; browns for Companies G and H; and roans for Company K.[7] Six of the regiment's ten companies threw new brass-mounted Campbell saddles with wooden stirrups over the backs of these horses. The troopers carried state-of-the-art breech-loading carbines across their pommels and Colt's navy revolvers on their hips. The latest in dragoon sabers hung from the belts of their officers. There was nothing too good for the Second Cavalry.[8]

In late summer and early fall the regiment trained and drilled at Jefferson Barracks, and by October it was ready to march. They had been ordered to Texas because that state needed them most; it had an Indian problem bigger than any other region, a headache to match its size. Since the Mexican War, Indians had had their way in Texas, ransacking and raiding into the state from three directions—from Mexico to the south, New Mexico Territory to the west, and Indian Territory to the north. In 1850 the army had added five thousand more troops, scaling up from eight thousand to thirteen thousand men, in part to deal with the Indian trouble in Texas. But the higher numbers had hardly made a dent. And by 1855 the violent clash of the pro-slavery and anti-slavery interests in Kansas was pulling troops from Texas to an even more urgent crisis. Comanches, Kiowas, and Lupins were raiding at will across the state. Texas was said to be in a "defenceless condition." If a cavalry was ever needed to gallop to the rescue of beleaguered settlers, pennants flying and bugles blaring, it was needed there. The Second Cavalry was marching to answer the trumpet call.[9]

On October 27 the regiment left Jefferson Barracks. Its 750 men, 800 horses, twenty-nine wagons, one ambulance, and assorted private conveyances covered the trail for miles. The line of march from Jefferson Barracks to Fort Belknap was to take them from St. Louis southwest over the Ozarks, down the boundary line of Missouri to Maysville, Arkansas, then southwest through the Indian Territory into Texas.[10] The Indian summer foretold a benign march. It was balmy and mild through all those early first days, and Eliza Johnston was cheered. It made up for the ague that had kept her for a day in St. Louis and forced the regiment to leave on Saturday without her. But she had caught up on Sunday, and on Monday she was soldiering.[11]

"Especially pleasant," she told her diary, "were scenes at night with hundreds of campfires blazing before as many tents, and soldiers seated on blankets, swapping stories, or tending kettles of boiling food."[12]

But winter was encroaching on the fall, and by December 4 when they crossed the North Fork of the Canadian River into the Indian Territory, wolves were howling around the tents, venturing as close as they dared to the blazing campfires.[13] By Saturday, December 22, they were but fifty miles from Fort Belknap and the weather all day had been springlike. They should be at their destination easily by Christmas Day.

But at about 8:00 that evening the weather took an unbelievable turn. None in that long military train had ever seen anything like it. None would ever forget it. The coldest blue norther Eliza Johnston had ever felt, one of the coldest Texas had ever seen, came out of nowhere, howling across the prairie highland. The shrieking wind blew out the fires in their tents. The thermometer plunged to four degrees below zero. It became impossible to keep warm.[14]

"I do not believe that any of the hyperborean explorers felt the cold more intensely," Colonel Johnston wrote his son. "Think of a northern blast, sixty miles an hour, unceasing, unrelenting (the Mercury below zero, ice six inches thick), coming suddenly down on the highest table-lands of Texas, 2,000 feet above the sea, upon a regiment only a few moments before luxuriously enjoying the balmy, bland south breeze."[15]

All the next day the wind screamed across the tableland. On Christmas Day, when they thought they would be at the end of a happy march, they were still thirty-five miserable miles from Fort Belknap. It was clear and beautiful, but so cold they couldn't march at all. The next day Eliza Johnston celebrated her birthday, the coldest of her life. It was not until December 27, two months to the day after they left Jefferson Barracks, that the shivering regiment filed into its destination. The thermometer still held rigidly fixed below zero and they were colder than they had ever been or ever thought they could be.[16]

When the cold weather waned, as it finally did after a succession of freezing northers one after another, the regiment began to scatter to outposts throughout Texas. All along the border Indian war parties were raiding and terrorizing white settlements. Into their midst on February 22 rode James Oakes, class of 1846, tempered in the fires of Mexico, where he had won two brevets for gallantry, and seasoned in past Indian combats. His company launched the regiment's first countermeasures that day when he surprised and hammered a band of marauding Wacos. On the first day of May, at the end of a march of 450 miles, he also defeated a party of Comanches near the headwaters of the Concho.[17]

The Indian wars were on in earnest in Texas, and Captain Oakes had fired the first shots. For the next five years the horse soldiers of the Second Cavalry would ride out in sorties south of the Red River under Oakes, Palmer, Stoneman, and other West Pointers, to pound the Indians wherever they could find them. They would patrol endlessly, pursue relentlessly, and bring as many of the marauders to battle as they could catch and corner. They would fight forty engagements, ride out on scores of patrols, scouting assignments, and escort missions.

It would be a star-studded regiment. Out of it and the crucible of the Indian wars it would fight in Texas would come sixteen Civil War generals, eleven for the Confederacy and five—including Oakes, Palmer, and Stoneman—for the Union. The Second Cavalry would furnish the Confederacy with half of its eight four-star generals, Albert Sidney Johnston, Robert E. Lee, Edmund Kirby Smith, and John B. Hood. It was an elite fighting force, and Texas was a stern proving ground.[18]

In the regiment's first year in Texas, as the winter freeze thawed and spring wore on into summer, the terrorism abated. It would flare again; the quiet was only illusory and the Texas frontier was long, and "as open as the oceans." But the Second Cavalry, with its stars-to-be and its companions in exile, had arrived and the Indians knew it and soon felt it. It was not a regiment many of them cared to stand and fight face-to-face. Such lethal head-to-head warfare against such military talent paid diminishing returns; they would continue to raid and evade, scalp and steal and run.[19]

The problem Captain Samuel Davis Sturgis now saw thundering down on him across the prairie in Kansas was not something he cared to face either. Better, he thought, to run. But it was too late for that.

Sturgis had been making a name for himself on the frontier. The stout, curly-headed captain of cavalry had fighting in his genes. He was the nephew of Brevet Captain William Sturgis, who had died a hero's death at Lundy's Lane in the War of 1812. All of his letters of recommendation to the academy had mentioned the uncle, "as brave a man who ever drew a sword." It had been thought the connection would give Sturgis an inside track; it was an asset more potent even than orphanhood.[20]

Sturgis had married a companion for his exile, a yellow-haired Ohio girl named Jerusha, who had won him with her beautiful smile.[21] But she was not with him now on this march across the prairie in the spring of 1857, and the sight before him was an unhappy one. Even for his seasoned eyes, which had seen nearly everything there was to see in the decade he had passed in Indian country, it was frightening.

In those ten years Sturgis, like Oakes, Palmer, and Stoneman, had become one of the army's premier Indian fighters. In that decade the nephew of the hero of Lundy's Lane had come into his own with the reputation as a straight-ahead sort of soldier who dealt swiftly and directly with whatever was in his front. This trait had made him a prisoner of war for eight days in Mexico before the battle of Buena Vista. It had likewise made him into a fearless and implacable Indian fighter.[22]

His marathon pursuit of a band of Mescalero Apaches in New Mexico Territory in 1855 was already legendary in the army. Sturgis had been with the Department of New Mexico then, headquartered in Santa Fe, the town his commanding officer, Edwin Vose Sumner, called "that sink of vice and extravagance."[23]

The Mescaleros had raided the Eaton ranch near Galisteo, raped the women, shot two herders, and made off with seventy-five horses and mules. That night Sturgis took up the chase with eighteen dragoons and six civilians, including Eaton himself. For three bone-jamming days they rode, covering nearly sixty miles a day before stopping for a few hours' rest. They overtook the marauders 175 miles from Santa Fe on January 16, 1855, standing before their stolen stock shouting peace overtures in Apache. One thing Sturgis hadn't learned about Apaches over the years was their language.

"Well men," he said after trying to puzzle it out for a moment, "I do not understand a word they are saying, haul off and let them have it."

Pistols barked and musketoons roared. But the day was bitter cold, too cold for human hands on naked steel, and they could not reload. It mattered little to Sturgis how the job was accomplished as long as it got done.

"Charge!" he shouted, and three Indians were soon dead, four wounded, and the livestock recovered.[24]

That had been in the winter of 1855. It was now spring of 1857. Sturgis was a captain in the First Cavalry Regiment, another crack outfit, and the problem before him was entirely different.

The column had seen its first buffalo at Cottonwood Creek, about fifty miles west of Council Grove. There had been only small scattered herds at first. But they had gradually multiplied, until they covered the prairie in every direction. The sight of a great buffalo herd was something no soldier who saw one ever forgot.

Dabney Maury remembered marching through one herd for three days, thirty miles a day, without ever being out of its midst, the air around filled day and night with their ceaseless bellowing.[25] One soldier found them "as numerous as the stars in the heavens."[26] Richard Ewell said there were times they were so thick on the land that "the bare prairie could not be seen. Hill after hill covered with buffaloe ad infinitum."[27]

Now, two miles away and closing, buffalo ad infinitum were thundering directly down on the little column from the First Cavalry Regiment.

Its commander, Major John Sedgwick, stared at them in paralyzed disbelief. Sedgwick was an able officer, a quarter of a century in the service. He had graduated from West Point in 1837, nine years before Sturgis, the young officer from the class of 1846 who now sat on the horse beside him. Sedgwick had been an artillery officer for most of his twenty years in the army, not a horse soldier. Besides, he was from Cornwall Hollow, Connecticut, and what did they know of buffalo stampedes in Cornwall Hollow?[28]

Sedgwick knew, staring at this one, that he could see no end to it in any direction. He knew it was surging toward them in "an irresistible torrent." He knew that buffalo, set on a course, rarely turned from it unless forcefully persuaded otherwise; they just ran over anything in their way. What he did not know was what to do about it. His expertise was artillery, but he couldn't cannonade them all.

"Sturgis," he said, turning to his second in command, "what'll we do?"

Sturgis had been staring at the onrushing torrent, too. Perhaps he had closed one eye as he watched it coming, as was his fashion when he was very much interested in something.[29] He saw it a little differently from Sedgwick. To him it was another problem, not unlike many such problems he had dealt with in his decade on the frontier—a little more tricky perhaps, and maneuvering room was rapidly running out.

"Time is too precious for explanations now, Major," Sturgis said to Sedgwick; "better turn the command over to me for a little while—I'll steer you through it."

"Take command, Captain," Sedgwick said gratefully; "take command, and give your orders."

"Orderly bugler," said Sturgis to a soldier beside him. "Give my compliments to company commanders and say that Captain Sturgis is in command.

"Hurry on back to the train as fast as you can go," he then told him, "and give my compliments to the quartermaster and tell him to corral his wagons quickly, in as small a space as possible, teams heading south, with the beef cattle inside the corral."

The stampeding buffalo were now a hundred yards closer than they had been, and closing. In seconds Sturgis had the column turned about and in full galloping retreat toward the supply train in the rear. As they pulled abreast of it, the train was already forming in corral, with the beef herd on the inside as ordered.

"Dismount, to fight on foot!" Sturgis bellowed as he reined in.

Three troopers of every four, all now afoot, feverishly gripped their rifles. The fourth grasped the reins of their four horses and stood by. Quickly they formed ranks, and to their horror, Sturgis turned them about and ordered them to march "double quick" a hundred yards back toward the oncharging herd. The flanks of the column were now thrown back in a V-shaped line with the tip pointing like an arrow at the oncoming buffalo and the open end enclosing the horses, the beef herd, and the train. The earth trembled and shook.

My God, thought trooper R. M. Peck, staring at the brown wall bearing down on them, what will be left when that avalanche of horns and hoofs sweeps over us all? Sturgis had told them what they must do; they must try to split the herd by firing into it. Peck did not see how it could possibly work. Where could the beasts find room to divide?

"Commence firing!" Sturgis roared.

A sheet of fire slammed into the thundering herd from the Sharps rifles. To Peck's astonishment and relief the buffalo began doing the impossible—splitting, crowding savagely to the right and left of the tip of the V, trampling one another in their passion to escape the withering fire.

Down either flank of the V the heaving brown torrent surged without any discernible slackening of speed. The soldiers, their hearts in their throats, furiously pumped bullets into the herd as fast as they could load and fire. Boxes of cartridges were dragged from the ammunition wagons, and those not squeezing triggers reloaded guns. There must be no letup in the hail of fire raining on the herd.

It seemed to Peck that in spite of all this, they were about to be overwhelmed and trampled to death at any moment, "by that living tornado." The dust was blinding, and the wedge was slowly being bent back, foot by foot, until the soldiers were now tightly packed together about their horses and wagons in the ever-narrowing V. There was nowhere left to go. The slim line that separated them from being crushed to death seemed about to snap.

For half an hour the river of buffalo poured past without stint. Then just as suddenly as it had come, it began to thin and recede.

"Cease firing," Sturgis said at last.

The troopers lowered their rifles and tried to still their trembling fingers and quiet their screaming nerves. All about them lay dead and dying buffalo. Other beasts, wounded and straggling but still on their feet, staggered on in the aftertow of the disappearing herd.

Sturgis watched them go. It had been just another day's work on the frontier for the nephew of the hero of Lundy's Lane. Today it had been buffalo, tomorrow it might be Indians—probably would be—for that is what they were there for.

Turning to Sedgwick and undoubtedly giving him his compliments, he relinquished command of the column.[30]

149

The
Bloody
Saddle

Captain Oliver Hazard Perry Taylor turned in his saddle as the column rode out of Fort Walla Walla, and waved one more time in wordless farewell to his wife Kate and their little son and daughter.

These absences were hard on them all, but especially on Kate and the children. There was always the possibility he might not return. Like any other frontier wife, Kate lived in dread of that. There was also the possibility he might return and find them dead—that had also happened. On the frontier, death, disease, and violence were shadow companions—always waiting.

Since the class graduated from West Point in 1846, since he and Dominie Wilson had stormed the church together at the Taos Pueblo, Taylor had been in the West, a continent removed from his native Rhode Island. Now in the spring of 1858, after twelve years on the frontier, he was a battle-seasoned veteran of the Indian wars. His toughness showed in his bearing, in his lithe, saddle-hardened frame, his sharp angular face, his piercing eyes, and his fierce black moustache peaking like a low tent over his strong mouth.[1]

Eastern Washington had been generally peaceful up to then. Indians and whites had lived together in relative calm. The Spokanes and Coeur d'Alenes boasted that they had never shed the blood of a white man. But there were always tribes that could easily become angry and make trouble. The Palouses were that kind.

Two white men had been killed near the Palouse River on the road to Colville recently, and forty white settlers there, believing their lives and property in danger, had petitioned the army to send troops. Only a few nights before, a party of Palouses had raided the Walla Walla Valley and carried off livestock, including thirteen head of army beef cattle. The Palouses were on a tear and the territory was uneasy.

Lieutenant Colonel Edward J. Steptoe, commanding at Fort Walla Walla, was concerned. He wrote the department's commanding officer in San Francisco that he would ride out and take a look. If possible he would bring the murderers of the two men to justice.

Steptoe led the column out of Fort Walla Walla on May 6, and Taylor waved his last good-bye to his little family. Their line of march would take them northeast toward Red Wolf's crossing on the Snake River. The detachment numbered 158 horsemen in all—mainly three companies of dragoons under the command of Captain Taylor—and a few Nez Perce Indian guides. The troopers were armed with musketoons, revolvers, ten Sharps rifles, a light supply of ammunition—about forty rounds per man—and two mountain howitzers. A detachment of twenty-five mounted infantrymen under Lieutenant Charles S. Winder rode along to serve the guns.[2]

Reports reaching the advancing column from north of the river were mildly disturbing. Palouses were said to be gathered in force near the crossing at the mouth of the Alpowa Creek. However, when the troopers reached the crossing they were nowhere to be seen. As friendly Nez Perces ferried the column across the river in their fleet of canoes, swimming its horses after, the Palouses fled northward into Coeur d'Alene and Spokane country to try to incite those peaceable tribes against the approaching soldiers. They would succeed.

By Friday morning, May 14, eight days out of Fort Walla Walla, the column was camped on the banks of the Palouse River. As his soldiers swung into their saddles that morning, Steptoe was told that the Spokanes intended to resist his entry into their country. That was odd; the Spokanes had never been hostile before. Steptoe had heard there was some bad feeling, but he didn't seriously expect them to oppose his march. He had no grievance against them. He shrugged it off and set his column in motion.

Soon he began to see them—only scattered parties of Indians at first, in the distance. They grew in numbers that day and the next, some of them entering his lines to speak with the horse soldiers. Reports of the command's progress, equipment, size, and manner of march and discipline began flying northward to other war parties now moving toward the column.

Saturday night, May 15, passed quietly. But as the troopers mounted next morning there was another disturbing report. Hostile Spokanes were ahead of them in force. Steptoe shrugged again, but pulled his ranks in tighter than usual for the morning's march—just in case. There was no sign of trouble until about 11:00 in the morning, when suddenly the surrounding hills came alive with Indians: Spokanes, Palouses, Coeur d'Alenes, Yakimas, and a scattering from other tribes. Steptoe counted more than a thousand braves—"all armed, painted, and defiant."[3]

He halted his column about a hundred yards from the bristling line of warriors and signaled them that he wished to talk. Several Spokanes rode forward. Why were they opposing his advance? Steptoe asked. They heard the soldiers had come to annihilate them, the Spokanes answered. If that was so, they would fight. Steptoe, who was ready to believe the last part of this argument, vigorously denied the first part. He was merely passing through, he protested, on his way to Colville to mediate the trouble between the whites and the Indians there. His passing through Spokane country was peaceful.

After a while the Indians appeared mollified, but not enough to permit him to proceed. He could have no canoes to cross the Spokane River, and without canoes there would be no crossing. Steptoe looked beyond the Indian spokesmen to the angry, milling line of painted braves. He might be making some uncertain headway with the former, he thought, but he was apparently making no impression at all on the latter. They were seething with excitement. The Indian leaders broke off the conference, and Steptoe turned to his officers. Be ready to fight, he told them.

The column began moving with deliberate speed toward a stronger position, word passing quietly down the line from the officers to the men to expect an attack. As the Indians swarmed angrily at their rear and flanks, the soldiers assessed their situation. The prospect was not promising. Not only did the Indians outnumber them at least six to one, but they were better armed and better mounted. They carried rifles and they rode cayuses, tough, wiry little ponies capable of great endurance in battle.

The column of soldiers moved on deliberately, hectored by taunts and jeers, to the edge of a small lake. There Steptoe ordered a stop, but told his troopers to stay in their saddles.

The Indian leaders wanted to talk again. Why, if his mission was peaceful, they demanded, was he hauling two howitzers? Why, if he was bound for Colville, had he come so far east of a direct course from Fort Walla Walla? Not only would the soldiers not be permitted to cross the Spokane, they said, but the Indians threatened to seize the Nez Perce canoes on the Snake as well, cutting off their line of retreat.

The afternoon wore on. The air was thick with tension and threats, and the soldiers continued to sit in their saddles. At length the Indians said that since it was Sunday, they would not fight that day; but they would give battle tomorrow. The soldiers looked at one another. It was going to be another one of those Mondays.

For three hours they sat on their horses, not moving, not daring to dismount, taking an unrelenting stream of verbal threats and abuse, and saying nothing. But now the sun was setting, and the Indians were withdrawing toward the east. By dark they had vanished, and the soldiers dismounted at last, to pass the uneasy night sleeping on their guns.

Steptoe mulled his alternatives. They were all too few. He was fatally outnumbered if it came to a fight. His ammunition supply was marginal—the soldiers were wishing now they had brought more, but they hadn't expected this kind of trouble. The Indians were armed, painted, defiant, and promising a battle in the morning. Wisdom told him to get out of there without delay, avoiding a fight if possible. He would backtrack to the Snake River ninety miles to the rear, and try to get safely across.

Before daylight the next morning, the seventeenth, he sent one of the Nez Perce scouts out in the night to try to get through to the garrison at Fort Walla Walla. The message he carried was for a reinforcing column from the fort to meet them at the Snake crossing. Steptoe followed almost immediately with his entire command—riding into what? None of them knew.

The Indians began to appear again on the hills and in angry clusters at the rear of the column. Galloping out of their ranks toward the soldiers was the last thing any of them expected to see—a Catholic priest. Father Joset, missionary to the Coeur d'Alenes, had ridden all night from ninety miles north, summoned by Chief Vincent to intercede with the horse soldiers. Steptoe greeted the priest warmly; anybody was more welcome at that moment than an unhappy Indian. Father Joset's news was not comforting, but neither was it really news. He told Steptoe that Indian opposition to an advance in force by the soldiers to the north of the Snake River was growing, and that an attack by the Indians was imminent. Steptoe already knew that.

The priest urged him to meet again with the chiefs in a final effort to avert a fight. He would be pleased to do so, Steptoe said, but his packhorses were too badly spooked to risk stopping. Father Joset suggested he talk to them as he rode; the priest himself would round up the chiefs. Steptoe agreed, and Father Joset galloped away, returning with Vincent, the only chief he could find.

Steptoe told Vincent as they rode along that he was calling off his trip to Colville and returning to Fort Walla Walla. Vincent listened intently and sympathetically. He didn't like what was happening any better than Steptoe did. Confrontation was not the Coeur d'Alene way. His hands had never been tainted with the white man's blood and he didn't wish it to be so now.

At a critical moment in the discussion one of Steptoe's Nez Perce scouts, who had no compunction against tainting his hands with Coeur d'Alene blood, angrily accused Chief Vincent of speaking with a "forked tongue."

"Proud man," the Nez Perce shouted, "why do you not fire?" and struck Vincent across the shoulders with his whip.[4]

The Coeur D'Alene chief reeled in his saddle and was nearly unhorsed, but he ignored his attacker and continued to hear Steptoe out. He appeared satisfied that the colonel's intentions were honorable and was about to say so when another Coeur D'Alene galloped up and told him that the Palouses were preparing to open fire. Vincent wheeled and galloped away. It was all getting out of hand.

As the column crossed a small stream and headed for higher ground, a rifle shot rang out and a bullet whistled through the column's rear guard. The soldiers ignored it. The Indians weaving back and forth in the rear of the column started up an irregular pattern of rifle fire. When the soldiers still did not respond in kind, the emboldened

Indians began to ride recklessly along the flanks toward the head of the column, firing steadily and rapidly.

No soldier had yet fired a shot and nobody had been hit. But all hope of avoiding a fight now seemed lost, and there began a frantic two-mile rush by both sides for what high ground there was in the broken, uneven terrain. Seeing the Indians making for a hill in front of him, from which a devastating fire could be poured down on the passing column, Steptoe ordered Lieutenant David McM. Gregg to cut them off. In a breakneck race, Gregg and his dragoons reached the hill first, and the Indians immediately veered off toward another even more advantageous position nearby, which Gregg also quickly preempted.

The soldiers were now fighting back and the battle had become general. The high-pitched war whoops of the Indians rose above the continuous clatter of arms. The packhorses, now thoroughly spooked, tried repeatedly to bolt and were kept in line only with a mighty effort. Taylor's troopers and another company of dragoons under Lieutenant William Gaston charged the Indian lines, not once, but again and again. Coyote-like, the Indians fled when pursued, but surged back in returning waves as soon as the soldiers gave up the chase. Time and again they swarmed and fled, hit and ran. For the soldiers it was like swatting at an army of hornets, only far more deadly.

The line of march became ragged and irregular. The three companies of dragoons, still separated from one another by some hundreds of yards, were desperately trying to get together. But when Taylor and Gaston attempted to move toward Gregg to higher ground, the Indians pressed in to prevent it, fighting more fiercely and at closer range. At about eleven o'clock in the morning—the fighting had begun at 8:00—Lieutenant Winder reached Gregg's side with his mountain howitzers and was firing steadily at the galloping Indians, scaring them all, but hitting few.

Gaston reined up and considered his situation. He had pushed about as far toward Gregg as he could. Indians now blocked his way in front and behind. He was locked in from both directions and clearly in trouble. It was apparent what the young lieutenant must now do; he must try to batter his way through. Gregg saw this and readied his own company to charge the moment Gaston began to move. When Gaston's soldiers broke into a galloping charge, Gregg stormed off the hill to meet them.

The two companies hit the Indians at the same instant, and together they gradually beat their way back up the hill. Two of the three dragoon companies were now united. Only Taylor was still out.

Showing spectacular courage, he also beat his way to higher ground toward noon, and Steptoe's command was again fully combined. Some distance away the colonel could see the Tohotonimme River flowing in plain view to the south and west. He must get there. His greatest need now was for water, and the river seemed to be his answer.

The Indians, infuriated by the loss of a dozen of their warriors, were in no mood to let the soldiers reach the river. They had been steadily increasing in numbers all morning; signals had been going out all through the early fighting, calling to more tribes, and they had come. The Indians were ready for the decisive attack that would annihilate the horse soldiers.

A little before noon, Steptoe made his move. Throwing Taylor and Gaston out on either flank, the positions of greatest danger, he started for the river. The Indians hurled themselves screaming on the moving column, and the battlefield became pandemonium.

Lieutenant Gaston took a shot through the body and fell dying. The Indians attacked with renewed fury, slamming into his dispirited men, who gave way and began falling back on Winder and Gregg. Gregg swung his dragoons around to meet the charge, and Winder lashed out with his howitzers. Steptoe rode in among Gaston's leaderless troopers and attempted to rally them. Together they stalled the Indian attack and, for a brief moment, threw it back. On the other flank Taylor was fighting with all of the conspicuous ferocity and fire that he had always shown, and was a constantly inviting target.

It happened about 12:30. The column had moved half a mile toward the river, and Taylor suddenly tumbled from his horse, shot through the neck.

Seeing him fall, the Indians rushed forward to seize his body. Here was a prize they must have, the ultimate coup—the hard-fighting soldier-chief. Several of Taylor's dragoons leaped from their horses and thrust themselves between the Indians and their fallen captain. There they fought hand to hand, swinging their guns like clubs. The most desperate fighting on the field was now the struggle for possession of Taylor's body. Private Victor Charles DeMoy, who had been trained in the French army, swung his gun barrel viciously at the heads of the converging Indians, crying "My God, for a saber!"[5] He was soon lying by Taylor's side, himself desperately wounded.

Several soldiers lifted Taylor in their arms and fled away with him to safer ground, and the frustrated Indians seized on the only trophy left to them, Taylor's streaked and bloody saddle.[6]

Steptoe led his exhausted troops, two of his commanders now fallen, toward a nearby hill and halted. There he would make a last stand. The Indians converged on them from every direction; they were completely encircled.

Wearily the soldiers dismounted, picketed their horses close together in the center of the circle, placed the wounded in the most shielded spot, and threw themselves to the ground under cover of the rank growth of grass. Taylor lay among the wounded, plainly dying.

The Indians showered the circle of soldiers with bullets and arrows. Several braves, attempting to crawl closer through the grass, were picked off. The soldiers expected any instant to be massacred in a final screaming charge. The Indian war cries were now ear-splitting and hideous. But the charge didn't come; storming a strong position in broad daylight was an alien tactic for Indians. As the afternoon wore on, the angry whooping began to subside. By nightfall the Indians stopped firing. Suddenly, after a long day of sound and fury, all was eerie silence.

But the prospect for the soldiers was hopeless. It was the lull before disaster. Steptoe painfully counted the rounds of ammunition—no more than three left per man. There was nothing for them now but to await the inevitable assault, which was certain to come, and to die a soldier's death. He did not expect to have to wait long. It could come at any moment.

Steptoe's officers, however, were not content with that. They pressed him urgently. They must make a run for it under the cover of night. What did they have to lose? To remain there was certain death—or worse, capture and torture—before the night was over, and if not then, surely by the early morning light.

The will was gradually rekindled in Steptoe. All of the dead whose bodies could be reached were hastily buried in shallow graves—Taylor was now dead. The two howitzers were dismounted and buried. The fifteen wounded troopers were made ready to leave. Those who could ride sat their horses; those who couldn't were lashed to their saddles. The spare horses were tethered. At about ten o'clock, the column began to move in silence off the hill down into the narrow valley of the Tohotonimme and into the dark night. At about midnight the Indians stormed the position. All they found were the tethered riderless horses and the fresh-filled graves.

The column of exhausted soldiers galloped southward, ghostly and spectral against the ridges one moment, dropping unseen into the black ravines the next. Victor DeMoy, the gun-wielding Frenchman who had fallen with Taylor, was so grievously wounded and in such pain that the soldiers were compelled to leave him by the side of the trail. He was never seen again.

By dawn the next day, May 18, the stricken column reached the Palouse River. By ten o'clock that night, twenty-four sleepless hours after leaving the bloody hill on the Tohotonimme, they reached the Snake. There, on the north bank, they slumped to the ground exhausted and slept for the first time in two days. The sun was well up over the eastern hills the next morning when they began to recross the river in the Nez Perce canoes. Later in the day they met the relief column from Fort Walla Walla, galloping to meet them at the river crossing; the Nez Perce scout had made it through.

On Saturday, May 22, the exhausted and riddled column filed into Fort Walla Walla, to do the duty they all dreaded—telling Kate Taylor and her children that their husband and father was never coming home.

But the story doesn't end there.

On August 25 an avenging column of troopers under Colonel George Wright, a West Pointer from Vermont with retribution flaming in his eye, began crossing the Snake where Steptoe had crossed little more than three months before. The force filed out of a new temporary fort named after Taylor, and rode north, not looking this time to quiet Indian unrest, but to cause some.

Little more than a month later, Colonel Wright wrote to San Francisco from the heart of the Indian country. "The war is closed," he said. "Peace is restored with the Spokanes, Coeur d'Alenes and Pelouses."[7] He meant, of course, that the Indians had been crushed.

On September 24 a small detachment rode out with Spokane and Coeur d'Alene guides to the Steptoe battlefield, arriving about noon. They found it "as silent and deserted as a city of the dead." The bleached bones of the soldiers who could not be recovered and buried before the night retreat still lay scattered on the field. Two of Steptoe's surviving officers rode slowly through the grass describing the battle, all the sound and fury of that terrible day sweeping back through their memories.

The graves of Taylor and Gaston were found, the scattered bones of the dead were gathered up, and the two howitzers were unearthed. The soldiers fashioned a rude cross from a pair of shafts from one of the guns and planted it in the middle of the battlefield.[8]

Colonel Wright clapped the Palouse chief and two of his braves in irons and told the others to bring in the rest of the tribe—men, women, and children. If they didn't come he would hang the three he had.

They came. And on September 30 at 10:00 in the morning, Wright emerged from his tent and spoke to them plainly.

"Tell them they are a set of rascals," he told his interpreter, "and deserve to be hung; that if I should hang them all, I should not do wrong. Tell them I have made a written treaty with the Coeur d'Alenes and the Spokanes, but I will not make a written treaty with them; and if I catch one of them on the other side of Snake River, I will hang him. Tell them they shall not go into the Coeur d'Alene country, nor into the Spokane country, nor shall they allow the Walla Walla Indians to come into their country. If they behave themselves and do all that I direct them, I will make a written treaty with them next spring. If I do, there will be no more war between us. If they do not submit to these terms, I will make war on them; and if I come here again to war, I will hang them all, men, women, and children."[9]

In the report Wright sent to the adjutant of the Department of the Pacific later that day, he said, "I have treated these Indians severely, but they justly deserved it all. They will remember it."[10]

The avenging command returned to Fort Walla Walla on October 5. On October 7, all of the thirty-nine officers and eight hundred men on the post followed the caissons bearing the remains of Taylor and Gaston to the burial ground half a mile away. The horses of the dead, draped in black, their saddles empty but for swords and boots, followed the coffins. Three volleys were fired over the officers' remains and they were lowered into their graves.[11]

Nor does the story end there.

It ends where it all began for Oliver H. P. Taylor—at West Point.

A year later his body was disinterred once again, with Gaston's, and their remains were returned to the banks of the Hudson. It was autumn, the leaves of the chestnut trees were falling, and the haze of October was full on the Highlands. The caisson carrying the two coffins, covered with the stars of the flag, rolled slowly toward the cemetery, "that peaceful, silent spot, so pathetic with the names of the dead."[12] The drums beat a muffled cadence, the music wailed, and the corps with reversed arms marched slowly in columns of platoons to the graveside.

"Ready! Aim!" The command pierced the silent air. A nervous plebe, anticipating "Fire!" shot off his piece before the word could be uttered, and a general ragged discharge of shots followed.

"Report that man in B Company for gross carelessness!" the commandant of cadets barked.

Taylor would have smiled. It was business as usual at West Point. The next two rounds were perfect. Crow's Nest echoed each volley, smoke from the rifle barrels rose and dissipated without further censure, and the corps marched away in quick step to cheering music.[13]

Taylor once said of Dominie Wilson, that he had never known anyone so apparently unconscious of danger under all circumstances.[14] The same could have been said of Dominie's classmate and friend now left lying in that new-dug grave by the Hudson.

He had died living his own words.

The
Courtship
of Miss Nelly

Mary Ellen Marcy was a stunner. She had blue eyes and blonde hair and a gentle sweet smile. She was sprightly, intelligent, and tender. But she had strength of character, and when she said no, hearts were broken.

The boys called her Miss Nelly, and they loved her, or wished they could. More than one officer in the U.S. Army who was not in exile on the frontier in the 1850s was losing his heart to her on the eastern seaboard.[1]

She was just turning eleven the summer the class of 1846 graduated from West Point. And her father, an army officer, already saw in her the potential for widespread devastation. "You can make almost any one love you if you choose," he wrote her on May 20, 1846, three days after her birthday. "With your high and honorable sense of morality and right combined with your powers of pleasing . . . you will always have a host of friends."[2] It was an understatement.

Nelly was Captain and Mrs. Randolph B. Marcy's first-born and her father's pride, his "precious child." He doted on her, and as she was growing up he wrote her long letters of fatherly advice from frontier posts around the West. Marcy had ambitious plans for his daughter. When the time came he wished her to marry well—happily,

161

of course, if that could be arranged, but more to the point, as high up as possible on the social scale. He wanted for her a high station worthy of her charms.[3]

Marcy was himself a considerable presence in the U.S. Army, a nationally acclaimed soldier-explorer who occupied a place in the public eye only a notch below the romantic Colonel John C. Frémont, the famed Pathfinder. Like Frémont, Marcy led pathfinding expeditions on the unexplored frontier. But no matter where he was or what he was doing, he regularly wrote his young daughter, striving without stint to shape and mold and prepare her from half a continent away.

There was only one trait of character which he found lacking in his daughter, and that was sufficient ambition. Ambition, he wrote her, is all right, "perfectly in accordance with Christianity and we find it among the best people." He wanted his beautiful little daughter, who tended to devoutness, to understand that ambition was not only all right, but a duty. We have a duty to ourselves and our friends, he told her, to maintain a position in society as exalted as possible.[4]

It was also a duty, to Marcy's way of thinking, for a daughter to consult her parents in the important business of picking a husband. Indeed, he would go farther than that. He intended, if it ever became necessary, to exercise a veto.

By the time Ellen was fourteen going on fifteen and nearing the danger point, Marcy was shoveling advice of every sort her way, expecting it to be followed. Few details were overlooked, down to not neglecting exercise in the open air, learning to walk like a lady, and improving her penmanship.[5]

Thus relentlessly counseled through the years, Miss Nelly came of age—and eligible—in the mid 1850s. She had matured by then into a most desirable and delectable prize, to be seized by the suitor who could not only win her heart, but her old man's approval. The first requirement might be easier met than the second.

George McClellan was twenty-seven when this young thing first came into his line of vision. He was a first lieutenant of engineers and one of the brightest young subalterns in the army. When he saw her, rockets went off. He wrote her mother immediately, vowing that he intended "to win her if I can."[6]

Ambrose Powell Hill, McClellan's dear friend and one-time West Point roommate, was twenty-nine and a first lieutenant in the artillery when he saw her for the first time. He experienced generally the same emotion, ending in the same vow, although he had the good sense not to put his intentions in writing to the girl's mother.

Ellen's courtships tended naturally to rouse very strong reactions in Randolph Marcy. In the welter of advice he had given her over the years were repeated specific warnings against marrying an army officer of any kind, but especially an officer of the line, such as himself, who would wed her and be gone to the frontier for months—perhaps years—on end. Or worse, who would marry her and take her with him. In Marcy's view there were few army officers who could give his Ellen the high social position and comfortable life he so desperately coveted for her. None of them could give it to her on the frontier.

It happened that George McClellan was one of those few exceptions on Marcy's very short list. McClellan had served under Marcy in an expedition on the Red River in the early 1850s and the older officer had been impressed, not only with his abilities and his promise, but even more with his lofty station in Philadelphia society. Here was a young man worthy of his daughter, even though he was in the army. Marcy had even gone so far as to tout her to his young subaltern. It could be a match made in heaven. He believed McClellan ought to meet her.

McClellan's mother in Philadelphia thought so too. She wrote her son a note, which was in his stack of correspondence when he returned from a railroad survey in the Pacific Northwest in the spring of 1854. Mrs. McClellan had met Ellen Marcy, who was then eighteen, several times.

"She is beautiful," she wrote McClellan, and she has heard so much about you from her father that "she was just ready to fall in love with you."[7]

McClellan was very much open to the idea, and in the first week in April 1854, he finally met her. He was instantly deranged. But then, who wasn't? The difference in McClellan's case was that he had an inside track, and knew it. But he also knew protocol. The first thing he did was to write Mary Marcy and state his intentions.

He told the mother that he had decided to "make a bold plunge, & relieve my conscience by a *confidential* & candid confession of my sins." His sins were that though he hadn't seen a great deal of the little lady, that little had been sufficient. He would win her if he could, and he believed, surely, that he could. Up to then he had been only a soldier who thought of nothing but his career, who entertained no aspirations but to excel in his profession. The "little Presbyterian"—as he called his dazzling intended—had changed all that.

He forewarned Mrs. Marcy that he was about to storm the redoubt. If the mother had any objections, she should state them now in perfect candor. His desire was to "avoid sailing under false colours," particularly since Captain Marcy was away on the frontier. Now that he had confessed and shown his flag, it remained only for her to give him permission to "carry on the war as best I may." He had no doubt he would win this skirmish and that Miss Nelly would soon be his. But in closing he playfully asked the mother if she could tell him, confidentially, what her opinion was of his chances. "I hope there is no rascally interloper in advance of me that I'll have to poison or shoot!"[8]

Mary Marcy, who shared her husband's high opinion of McClellan, hoped not, too. Captain Marcy, away on the frontier, believed there had better not be. He wrote his wife that he was gratified McClellan had been so pleased "with my dear Nelly." He hoped she would like him as much, for he was talented, good-looking, agreeable, and in every respect preferable to another officer whom he didn't care to mention.

Marcy could not conceive that Ellen would not fall instantly in love with McClellan. As he assured his wife, "he is generally regarded as one of the most brilliant men of his rank in the Army and one that any young lady might justly be proud of. His family connections are unexceptionable and his staff position is such that his wife would always have a good and comfortable home."[9]

He was everything the Marcys had always hoped for. They loved him very much.

Unfortunately, their daughter didn't. To their horror and to McClellan's utter astonishment and chagrin, Nelly turned him down when, soon afterward—much too soon—he proposed. McClellan was unaccustomed to failing at anything. That he should fail at something so important in his life as this, was—well—unthinkable.

He was still reeling when he wrote Mrs. Marcy from Pensacola, Florida, where he had been sent on temporary duty. "I succeeded in making a very great blunder & doing a very foolish thing in the way of pushing too far & too quickly a certain little affair that you know of," he confessed. He feared he had blown his chances and, if so, would regret it forever. But he intended to make the best of a bad situation. He would not give up, but try now to undo the unfavorable impression he believed he had made. As Shakespeare so long ago had said, "hope is a lover's staff." He implored Mrs. Marcy to write him if she knew anything of the matter or thought anything, anything at all. He was desperate. "Give Miss Nelly my warmest regards," he wrote in anguished closing, "or anything warmer you please. You can't make it too strong."[10]

McClellan now shifted to the only strategy left to him. He began courting Mrs. Marcy. At least here was a sympathetic backdoor to the intended target, a willing co-mourner with whom he could share his secret anguish, sorrow, and shame. Besides, it was the only way he knew to keep a spark of contact alive, however dead it seemed to be.

In the many letters to Mrs. Marcy that followed, he kicked himself again and again, tending in his self-recrimination to be melodramatic. He said he wished not to remain in civilization under the circumstances. And, of course, in the army that could be arranged. But he didn't really mean it. He would willingly rather devote "the rest of my life to making Nellie happy & contented (if she will ever entrust her happiness to me)." He told the mother he would "wait as long as there is the shadow of a hope."[11]

It promised to be a long and fruitless wait. Miss Nelly was not giving McClellan the time of day—no encouragement of any kind, no letters, none of her soft, sweet, gentle, devastating smiles. It wasn't that she didn't like him. It was just that despite his handsome face, charming manner, brilliant mind, promising future, and high social elevation, she simply didn't love him. No matter how much Daddy liked him, she wasn't going to marry him.

By the spring of 1855 McClellan himself seems to have despaired of all hope. He had been promoted to captain and company commander in the newly formed First Cavalry Regiment and was no longer an engineer—a fact that further creased Marcy's already furrowed brow. This made him a line officer, and line officers tended to get sent to frontiers.

"After carefully & coolly thinking over all that has passed," McClellan wrote Mrs. Marcy in March, "I could only come to the conclusion that there is no hope of a successful termination, & that it would be extreme folly to sacrifice my professional prospects to a contingency so remote as to be next to impossible." He confessed sadly that he could not look back upon the winter just passed with any satisfaction—"would that that chapter in my history could be erased." As that was impossible, he must bear up and try not to make the same mistake again. It has had one good effect, he told his sympathetic correspondent, "in giving my vanity so good a lesson." He intended now to leave for faraway places. "It will, I doubt not," he mused, "be a relief to the young lady to know that I will soon be out of the way—& not persecute her any more."[12]

Very soon he was out of the way—but not to the frontier as he expected. Secretary of War Jefferson Davis had taken a liking to this brilliant young officer and had named him to a special commission to study European military systems. The senior member of the three-officer panel was to be Major Richard Delafield, Dicky the Punster of palmier days. It was a plum assignment, and McClellan, lucky in life, unlucky in love, sailed to the Crimea and out of Ellen Marcy's picture on April 11, 1855.

A. P. Hill loved his younger sister, Lucy. He called her Lute, and they had been close since childhood. But then, Hill loved women generally. He had loved them when they were Latin beauties cannon-ading him with those angry flashing eyes from the balconies in Puebla. He loved them when they were Washington girls casting coquettish glances across the crowded public rooms at Willard's Hotel. He loved them under all circumstances.

He had once written Lute: "You know I am so constituted that to be in love with some one is as necessary to me as my dinner."[13] From Mexico City he had written his father, " 'Tis a fact that the ladies of Mexico are beautiful,—and, oh, how beautiful—but very few of them have ever read Wayland's *'Moral Science.'* " That only endeared them the more to Hill. "You know my failing," he wrote his father. "'Tis an inheritance of the family, this partiality for the women."[14] "How would you relish a Mexican daughter-in-law?" he had queried his parents from Puebla.[15]

This partiality for the women had gotten him in deep trouble in his furlough summer at West Point. Contrary to Superintendent Delafield's warnings against stopping in New York City, he had done so on his way back through. His reward was a dose of gonorrhea, followed by complications, which were followed by lingering prostati-tis that finally took him out of the class of 1846 and put him into the class of 1847. His brief night of passion would dog him for the rest of his life.[16]

But it had done nothing to bank the fires of his desire to be in love. By the fall of 1848, Lute was at the Patapsco Female Academy at Ellicott City, Maryland, and Hill was back from Mexico and stationed in nearby Washington City. One of Lute's classmates was a dazzling brunette named Emma Wilson, just the thing for his constitution, and Hill began courting her. At first Emma's parents didn't mind their daughter being escorted by the dashing young army officer, as long as it went no farther than that. But Hill was too dashing. Their daughter fell in love with him, and when that happened the Wilsons, who considered Hill below them socially, cut it off.[17]

Six winters later, in November 1855, Hill was again in Washington City assigned to the coast survey. Also in Washington, in from Hartford and staying with her mother at Willard's Hotel, was Ellen Marcy. Her father, as usual, was away in Texas. It was a particularly gay winter socially in the capital city, and it was inevitable that Hill should meet Miss Nelly. McClellan was now nine months in Europe and suitors were swarming about the Marcys like moths to the flame.

It was not long before Nelly was seeing a lot of Lieutenant Hill. Captain Marcy, home on a temporary assignment early in the winter, noted this with an uneasy eye. Rather like the Wilsons, he didn't object to his daughter going about on the arm of the handsome young officer, but this wasn't going to get serious was it? Oh, no, Daddy, Ellen assured him, you mustn't worry. But Marcy returned to Laredo not fully convinced.[18]

Soon Hill was the officer in charge of Miss Nelly's heart. The quality that citizens of Culpeper County had particularly noted in recommending him for West Point—his "amiability of heart" and "amenity of manners that endeared him to all his acquaintances"— also endeared him to her.[19]

In the spring of 1856 he proposed and she immediately accepted—without first clearing it with her father. Hill gave her a ring in which were etched the words "Je t'aime." As Sylvanus Thayer, the father of West Point, had said so long ago, all the important things are written in French.

Captain Marcy in hot, dusty Laredo received the engagement announcement in a letter from Ellen, which hit his desk on May 28. Only six days before, Marcy had written her; their letters had crossed. In his letter, partly out of the nagging worry about Hill whom he didn't particularly like, he had rung some familiar themes. He painted for her once again as lurid a picture of garrison life on the frontier as he could. He reviewed the deplorable accommodations, the lack of vegetables, the nonexistence of the basic amenities of a civilized life.

"How in the world any girl of ordinary sense can think of marrying a line officer I cannot imagine," he wrote pointedly, "for they must make up their minds to spend a life of exile, deprivation and poverty." He concluded: "So my dearest Nelly I love you too well to see your happiness sacrificed in this way and I hope you will never entertain the idea."[20]

Marcy therefore could scarcely believe what he was reading in the letter from her now open on his desk at Fort McIntosh.

"Astonished," was the first adjective to burst from his angry pen as he sat down immediately to answer her. A marathon eleven pages of heated words tumbled out. In essence they said, How could you do this to us?

It was a document of mounting recrimination and rage. Gone was the velvet glove with which he had always handled his beloved daughter: "I could never have supposed after the repeated conversations I have had with you upon the subject of marriage, and your knowledge of my opposition to your uniting yourself to a profession which has caused so many privations and separations in families that you would desire to do the very act of all others that is the most objectionable to me."

As for Hill, "he seemed to be a gentlemanly man," Marcy conceded, "and if he was not in the army but engaged in some business that would insure you a comfortable home I should not have so much objection, but I should suppose you would have more ambition." He wrote this girl who knew only that she was in love, that "there are plenty of men who have wealth and position in society, who are equally agreeable as Mr. Hill, and would make you fully as good a husband. You do not think these things of any moment now, but you will see that it is stubborn truth in a few years."

In a coda to the letter as chilling as any that a father could write a daughter, he said: "I thought I could confide in you and that I had nothing to fear but I find instead of that, you must have been holding out encouragement to him from the time I left. Did my affection for you merit such a breach of confidence? . . . I forgive you, but I shall expect that you at once abandon all communication with Mr. Hill. If you do not comply with my wishes in this respect, I cannot tell what my feelings toward you would become. I fear that my ardent affection would turn to hate. Do nothing therefore my dear child without choosing between me and him. If I cannot trust you who can I trust?"[21]

A week later Marcy wrote her a more conciliatory letter, addressing it to "My Dear Sweet Child." Regretting that he may have caused her pain, he suggested that she postpone making up her mind on the subject for six months or a year. This would permit her to consider the subject "in all its bearings," and come to "a more just and reasonable conclusion," one more in line with his view of the matter.

He told her he needed more information about Hill. If the lieutenant had sufficient means to support her without his pay, he might look on him more favorably. He would make enquiries, but he would make no promises, "except that if I find he has not enough to make you independent in the event of his death, I shall refuse my consent."[22]

In his next letter, Marcy told Ellen he had heard from Hill. He was worth about ten thousand dollars. "This is something," the father conceded, "but not much." Ellen by now was fighting back. She reminded her father that McClellan was also in the army, but he had no objections to her marrying him. McClellan was a different case, Marcy argued. "Although I should not have objected to your marrying Capt. McClellan yet I had no great desire for it after he went into the line of the Army, as the same hard fare would have awaited you as with other officers. His talents and well known high character, with the warm friendship which exists between us would have caused me to disregard all other considerations and given you to him."[23]

In Washington meanwhile, Hill was feeling a strong sense of déjà-vu. This was Emma Wilson and her snooty parents all over again. But the worst was yet to come. While Marcy was playing hardball with his daughter, Mrs. Marcy was about to unload on Hill directly. She had somehow learned of his indiscretions at West Point and of the gonorrhea, and she would see that the word got out and about.[24]

Into this caldron, fresh from studying warfare in the Crimea, stepped the unsuspecting George McClellan. He had continued corresponding with Mrs. Marcy from Europe, for despite himself he couldn't give up entirely the possibility, no matter how unlikely, that her daughter might someday be his. Early in January, after not having heard from the mother since August, and fearing the worst, he wrote her a long unhappy letter from Venice. It was a letter forlorn of hope, every dejected word falling like notes from the Dead March of Saul.

"I have had ample time & opportunity to think over the past," he wrote her, "& to convince myself that, in certain matters, it would have been better long, long ago to have abandoned all hope—as I have done of late, & do fully now. It is idle to chase a phantom through life. . . . Silence is often eloquent. Yours is to me. I accept the omen."

If he was reaching the wrong conclusions he wished to know it frankly, for now he was writing from his heart. "What I have said is the result of long reflection and deep conviction—what it has cost me to arrive at this conclusion I need not say. . . . You understand that in all this I go upon the supposition that Miss Nelly's feelings are what I had every reason to believe them to be when I left—the most perfect indifference, if not actual dislike, to me; if by any miracle a change had come over the spirit of her dream it would I know bring back all my former hope & feelings. But such a change is not to be looked for, & I am sadly convinced that it were idle to think of it."[25]

Back in the United States, McClellan soon learned of Hill's courtship of Miss Nelly, and went directly to his old classmate for confirmation. McClellan was a gentlemen. When he learned that Hill loved Ellen, too, that settled it if nothing else did. He immediately withdrew from the competition—not that he was, realistically, still in it.

Hill was now seething. Rumors of his youthful indiscretions—the gonorrhea from West Point days and its ramifications—were out. Indeed, Mrs. Marcy was the suspected source. Now playing hardball herself, she had written disparagingly of Hill in two letters to McClellan. And now McClellan was also seething—upset that she would so defame his dear friend, former roommate, and now rival in love. He wrote her a stiff reply: "As a matter of course I transmitted to Hill *none* of the remarks you made; I thought that you would regret what you had written before the letter reached me—that reflection would convince you that you had been unjust to him, & that you had said unpleasant & bitter things to me in reference to one of my oldest & best friends."

Under no circumstance, he told her, would he have repeated

such things. "If a gentleman had made use of such expressions to me about Hill, I should have insulted him, & made the quarrel my own— as a personal insult to myself; had any lady, merely an ordinary acquaintance, done the same, I should have regarded it as sufficient ground to discontinue the acquaintance. . . ." But McClellan wouldn't risk alienating the mother entirely—an alienated daughter was more than enough. "In your case," he reassured her, "it is different. I know how much you felt, how deeply you have been distressed—& was confident that what you wrote was when under the influence of deep feeling, which for the moment overcame the natural kind impulses of your heart & judgment. So I shall destroy your letter & never allude to its contents to any human being."[26]

But he had had it. He was through once and for all with this entire depressing business. If there had ever been hope, it was now clearly dead. McClellan returned to writing his Crimea report and spending his days and nights in Philadelphia "pretty much in the old way—a vast number of cigars, a good deal of reading & not a little working."[27] If a loveless life was to be his lot, then pass the cigars.

About the time McClellan was beating this final retreat, Ellen was also writing her father a letter of surrender. She had also had enough. She would bow to his wishes and call off her engagement to Hill. Marcy had won, and he was expansive in victory. "My dear daughter," he wrote her, "I always had the most unbounded confidence in your integrity and purity of purpose." Her act of sacrifice fully confirmed his opinion that "you are a noble generous girl and I long to take you in my arms again. You are the pride of my heart and a dear good girl."[28]

Mrs. Marcy had mixed emotions. She too had won—and lost. Her hope had always been that Ellen would marry McClellan. That hope had been blasted in the Hill affair. She wrote her daughter: "Oh, Nell, such a treasure as you have lost forever. You can't realize it now, but the time is coming sooner or later just as sure as you live when you will regret it—if ever a woman did. Mark my word, I see it, I know it! Yet your perverseness will in the end make you miserable. I have done all that is in the power of a mother to do, and now whatever your fate may be hereafter, I cannot reproach myself. The more I dwell upon that affair in Washington, the more I am convinced that I am right and you will be convinced of it by and bye. You are laboring under a delusion that perfectly astonishes me. I cannot account for it.

You certainly have shown less good sense in this matter than I ever knew you to before."[29]

However, if McClellan was through, if Ellen and Marcy and Mrs. Marcy were through, Hill wasn't. He had been rejected, that was plain. Miss Nelly had reluctantly returned his ring with "Je t'aime" etched within, which he then gave to that other girl he loved, his sister Lute. But there was still the matter of his honor to settle. In the spring of 1857 he wrote Marcy demanding justice.

He charged Mrs. Marcy as the source of the affront to his character and good name. "I have ever thought her a woman of good feeling and judgment, though somewhat warped against me," Hill wrote Marcy. Her objection to his suit, he wrote, was apparently on grounds that from "certain early imprudences, (youthful indiscretions I suppose), my health and constitution had become so impaired, so weakened, that no mother could yield her daughter to me, unless to certain unhappiness." This was outrageous. The innuendo was "fatally blighting." He demanded that Marcy set it right and that Mrs. Marcy "correct this false impression with whomever she may have had any agency in hearing it." He demanded that "in justice both to herself and myself she should make known the name of her informant to be used by me as I may see fit."[30]

A man of honor, Marcy wrote his wife demanding to know if this were so. If Hill's charges were true, "I should insist upon Ellen's marrying Mr. Hill at once as a just reparation." But Mrs. Marcy was able to explain it away to her husband's satisfaction. Nothing more came of it and Hill didn't press the matter further. He too had finally had enough.[31]

But the result wasn't doing much for that quirk in his constitution that made being in love with someone as necessary as his dinner. He returned to the social circuit, threading his way through the round of Washington parties. One evening a year after he had hopelessly lost Ellen Marcy, he found what he was looking for across another crowded room. She was young, petite, blue-eyed, vivacious, and beautiful with a head of cascading chestnut hair.

This find, Kitty Grosh Morgan McClung, was even more than met the eye. She was, at twenty-three, a high-born Kentucky girl and already the widow of a wealthy young St. Louis merchant who had unexpectedly and tragically died. Her family were the Morgans of

Lexington. God willing, they wouldn't be like the Wilsons and the Marcys.

As a baby, Kitty had been virtually picture perfect, resembling a life-size china doll, so her black mammy had nicknamed her Dolly. She hadn't changed much over the years, adding to her arsenal of charms a soft, lovely talking voice, which when raised in song brought to mind the heavenly choir. Hill called her Dolly and fell in love with her. They courted through 1858, and on June 18, the next year, Hill wrote McClellan a letter.[32]

He wished he could tell his old friend this news over a cigar, he said, but a letter will have to do. "I'm afraid there is no mistake about it this time, old fellow," he wrote, "and please God, and Kentucky blue-grass, my bachelor life is about to end." He was about to swell the ranks of those other "blessed martyrs" who have been undone by "crinoline and blue eyes." He was about to marry a Kentucky " 'widder' . . . young, 24 years y no mas, gentle and amiable, yet lively, sufficiently good looking for me." What is more, Mac, "I know you will like her, and when you come to know her, say that I have done well." He said that he expected to assume his martyrdom in a ceremony in Lexington in July, and could Mac come down from Chicago for it? "You know that there is [none] whose presence would delight me more."

In the same letter Hill blew final taps over his affair with Ellen Marcy: "I have heard a report lately which has amazed me a good deal, that the Marcys had given their consent to my marrying Miss Nelly, and that I had declined." McClellan "would of course know this was untrue, but others might believe it. If you should ever hear it, please contradict it for me." In the last communication he had had with Miss Nelly, about two years ago, "she positively and without leaving a ray of hope, rejected me—and that's the truth."[33] McClellan knew how that felt.

Hill was married on July 18, 1859, at Hopemont, the Morgan home in Lexington, where Kitty's mammy had first called her Dolly. The bride wore net-covered taffeta and Hill wore his full-dress uniform, a flowing red moustache, and a satisfied smile.[34]

George McClellan finished his Crimea report in 1856 to the general acclaim of all who read it. It was outstanding, as everybody expected it would be. Then he had done what he had been threatening to do for a long time. He left the army, to take a job as chief engineer of the Illinois Central Railroad. By 1858, when many of his classmates were still on the frontier fighting Indians, he was in Chicago beginning his rise in the corporate world.

In March that year he was reading in the papers, as the rest of an enthralled nation was, of a daring army relief expedition from Wyoming to New Mexico. It was an incredible story of courage and endurance that had saved the snowbound U.S. Army command that had been sent to quell the Mormon rebellion in Utah Territory. Forty army volunteers, twenty-five mountain men, and sixty-five mules with rations for thirty days had set out across the bleak snow-mantled wilderness for Fort Massachusetts over six hundred miles away. The success or failure of the Mormon campaign depended on the mission succeeding. The redoubtable mountain man Jim Bridger warned that it could not be done. And it nearly couldn't. The journey took fifty-two days against inhuman hardships, an odyssey seldom matched for privation and suffering. It was making big headlines in newspapers in every city, and its leader had been Randolph Marcy.[35]

When McClellan read of it in Chicago, he set the papers aside and took up his pen. He saw this as more than the heroic epic of the century. He saw it as an opportunity. Slipping out a piece of official stationery impressively embossed with his title, Vice President of the Illinois Central Railroad Company, he wrote the date, March 17, 1858.

"My dear Nelly," he began.

McClellan had made a miraculous breakthrough not long before. He had managed to start up a tentative correspondence directly with Ellen Marcy herself. He had just received a letter from her with an extract of a letter from Marcy following his ordeal. Suitors were still jostling and panting all about Miss Nelly, but she had unbent enough toward McClellan to begin writing him after her years-long silence. After all his many letters to her mother, McClellan was now in direct contact with the real thing. Hope was alive again. The patient had come back from the dead.

In the letter he was writing her now he praised the father's heroism and soothed the daughter's fears. It was "the most difficult journey ever made by an Army officer," he wrote her of her father's heroics. He told her he felt "very keenly for you & your mother in the anxiety you have felt—but hope that you will now look upon the bright side of things—& not invent difficulties which do not exist." He promised her that the worst was over, that her father was now in no further danger. This coming from a man who ought to know must have been comforting to Ellen Marcy.

Having taken care of the father, McClellan now subtly turned down another avenue. "So you are as much of a Presbyterian as ever?" he asked playfully. From this he worked the letter around to his own lot in life. While things are going well with him, he said, they could be better. "I hate to think of the future now—it seems so blank—no goal to reach, no object to strive for! Yet, foolish fellow that I am, there are many much worse off than I am in this 'world, & who no doubt envy me my position! Was mortal man, *or* woman, ever contented? So life passes—we wish, and dream—build castles in the air—struggle for the unattainable." Yes, he told her, "fate does not throw roses alone in our path," and at last, when it is often too late, we awake to the fact that we have been "grasping at shadows all our lives! Is that not true—little lady?"

As for that "splendid young lady" Nelly had suggested he must be showering with his attentions, she did not exist. He reminded her that he had already had one bad experience along that line—perhaps she would remember it. "A burned child dreads the fire," he wrote, and "it is difficult to catch an old bird with chaff." Keep writing, he urged her. He had a foot in the door after all these years and he didn't want it slamming shut again.[36]

She did keep writing. After four long heart-lonely years, McClellan was back in business with the beautiful Ellen Marcy. It was still a brother-sister relationship, but he was getting in some subtle hits. All she need do was read between the lines. Even in Chicago, half a continent away, he remained after all these years her most faithful and persistent admirer. Surely she could see that.

Another major window of opportunity opened for McClellan in the fall of 1859. Major Marcy had been promoted and reassigned to St. Paul, in the new state of Minnesota. Ellen and Mrs. Marcy had decided to travel with him and spend the winter with him there. McClellan immediately fired off an invitation for them to stop over in Chicago on the way—as his guests. He had recently moved into a large house at No. 1 Park Row on the lake, where he was living congenially with Ambrose Burnside, Benny Havens's one-time best customer, and his wife. There was plenty of room. He sent the invitation to both Marcy and Ellen, to make certain at least one of them got it.[37]

Marcy hadn't seen McClellan in years, but they had kept up a warm correspondence and Marcy had been pleased when McClellan had left the army. He made a point of telling Ellen so.[38] Now he wrote McClellan that they would accept his hospitality. They intended to leave for St. Paul about October 10. They would stop a day or two with him on the way.[39]

As Ellen stepped down from the train in Chicago on October 20 she saw a new McClellan, but with that same desire for her still burning in his eyes. It had incredibly survived five long years forlorn of hope, but there it was, as undimmed as ever. Ellen had always liked him—there were few who didn't—but had never loved him. But he had changed somehow. He was more mature, impressively prominent in the business world, with a home on the lake. And he obviously loved her with a doglike fidelity. There was no indication that he had ever loved anyone else.

She was wavering. Could she be in love with him after all?

When the Marcys left for St. Paul on October 24, McClellan put his private rail car at their disposal, and climbed aboard himself. A day out of Chicago on the way to St. Paul he risked it all again. He proposed. This time Miss Nelly said yes. A change had come over the spirit of her dream after all. It was a miracle.[40]

By some calculations it was Ellen's ninth proposal of marriage, two of them from this one persistent suitor. And there were still others out there dreaming dreams. The field, therefore, required some tidying up. Ellen urged that they keep their engagement secret until after Christmas.

Only days before she left Washington, she had received a letter from one of her suitors telling her "how very dear you are to me, how much I love you." For the past two years she had been his only thought, and the hope of being with her this winter had supported him during all that dreary time in Utah. Now he had arrived home to find her departing for the West. Disappointed, he asked if there was any hope for him.

"Please give me an answer soon," he begged, "for I shall know no peace till I hear from you."[41]

He was to know none after hearing from her, either. Even as she was stepping from the train in Chicago on McClellan's arm, this latest reject was writing her from New York with a broken heart.

On the day McClellan was proposing to her on his private rail car to La Crosse, still another suitor was writing from the frontier. He had been expecting a letter from her for weeks, something "to cheer me on my lonely way." But nothing had come and he had imagined a thousand reasons why she had not written. Perhaps she had been sick, perhaps she had forgotten how much he loved her. Could it be she couldn't love him? Of all the disappointments in life, he wrote her, blighted friendship and unrequited love were the most fatal.[42]

He, and who knows how many others, had to be confronted now and their hopes dashed. It would take some time. It might be messy.

McClellan would have preferred to marry immediately, now that his dream was so wondrously close to coming true. He wrote her urging an early wedding; six years had been long enough to wait. How about February? "Now there is a programme that is feasible," he argued, "sensible & all that sort of thing. Don't talk to me about going East to 'prepare to be married.' As I've told you before I don't want any preparation. I want *you* & *you alone*. I want you just as you are, in the clear blue dress or any other . . . we don't need any trousseau. I want Nelly Marcy just as she is."[43]

He wrote her unceasingly now, pouring out all of the love and thoughts he had held inside for all those years. He wrote of how his love for her had changed him: "My idea of happiness used to be *rank & name*! Now it is domestic happiness with my wife." "Do you know that every letter of yours I receive, every thought I bestow upon you," he wrote, "makes me respect you more & more? I can't tell you how happy & *proud* I am that you are mine & all mine, *mine forever*." The enthusiastic fiancé confessed that "we can't tell what *may* be in store for us. . . . I *may* yet play my part on the stage of the world's affairs and leave a name in history, but Nelly whatever the future may have in store for me *you* will be the chief actor in the play. . . . Why darling the wealth of India in its most fabulous times of yore the glory of the first Napoleon at the apogee of his career would be nothing absolutely nothing to me in comparison with what I feel now when I know & realize that I have gained your love. A heart so pure as yours, a mind so bright as yours—to gain these is better than to gain an empire. *You* are my empire."[44]

By Christmas the field had been swept clean and Ellen was ready to announce their engagement. McClellan went to St. Paul for the holidays and with her at his elbow, he wrote his mother first. Elizabeth McClellan surely must have smiled as she read his joyous letter. For she wrote her future daughter-in-law immediately, for herself and McClellan's sister Mary, speaking of the pleasure "the Captain's most acceptable intelligence" had given them. It was the "best of news— not a *surprise* by any means . . . my surprise has been, that it should have not occurred before. From the unusually excited style of George's letters a few weeks since, Mary & I put our heads together, & whispered to each other, what we hoped would most probably happen, provided always, the young lady 'was willing.' "

To this gracious beginning, Mrs. McClellan wrote this gracious ending: "Dear Miss Nelly, I know Mary & I need not now, offer great protestations of affection, for, from the earliest times of our acquaintance, our hearts warmed to you, & you have ever since been thought & spoken of by us both, as one to be dearly loved."[45]

Most of McClellan's classmates were already married. But it is unlikely that any of them had loved the same woman another classmate had loved. Few had probably found it necessary to court the mother to win the daughter.

Even Old Jack had married, not once, but twice. Uttering words of tender endearment in Spanish, which he had picked up in Mexico and which he considered a loving tongue, Jackson had won the heart first of the daughter of a Presbyterian minister and president of Washington College. He was by then teaching artillery and natural philosophy at neighboring VMI in Lexington. When his bride died not long after they married he mourned for a time and then courted and won Mary Anna Morrison, the daughter of another Presbyterian minister and university president. Jackson, as always, was consistent.

But in the matter of love, McClellan had demonstrated a Jackson-like doggedness unmatched by any of his classmates. He had laid an endless, apparently hopeless, but in the end successful, siege on the only woman he ever loved. And at last she had surrendered.

The wedding was in New York City on May 22, 1860, in the Cavalry Protestant Episcopal Church at the corner of 21st Street and 4th Avenue, the Reverend Francis H. Hawks officiating. The *New York Herald* the next day reported the "fashionable commotion" under the heading, "Personal Intelligence. Marriage among the Elite."

Many of the elite attended. General Scott was there. Ex-Governor Thomas H. Seymour of Connecticut was there. Colonels Delafield and Joseph E. Johnston were there. Legs Smith was there. George Granger, one of the rejected rivals for Miss Nelly's hand, was there. Cadmus Wilcox was there. A. P. Hill was even there.[46]

And McClellan was very much there. He made only one trumpet-call of an entry in his diary that day. "!!May 22!!" he wrote. "Le jour de ma vie." Few could have begrudged him that in any language. He had earned the right to say it—the hard way.[47]

PART 3

AND THE WAR CAME

Our Men
at
Sumter

The army had been good to Truman Seymour. But as he stared at the angry crowd facing him on the dock at the U.S. arsenal in Charleston, South Carolina, on November 7, 1860, he must have wondered if his luck had run out.

In the fourteen and a half years since the class of 1846 had graduated from West Point, Seymour had won two brevet promotions for gallantry in Mexico, fought the Seminoles for two years in Florida, become an accomplished artillerist, and married the boss's daughter. He had experienced none of the hard, lonely, isolated garrison life of the western frontier. Indeed, he was now in his second tour of duty at one of the poshest posts in the army, old Fort Moultrie in Charleston Harbor.[1]

Seymour had always been a man who enjoyed himself with his pencils and paints. His skill along that line had won him a return to West Point in 1850 as an assistant professor of drawing under Robert Weir. By 1852, he had won the heart of the professor's daughter, Louisa, and they had married that year in the little Gothic Revival church of the Holy Innocents in Highland Falls.[2]

It is understandable that this daughter of the great artist would have been attracted to this sensitive young officer. They were well matched. Seymour was from Vermont, the son of a Methodist preacher. Letters of endorsement in his application papers to West Point had praised him as a young man "destined for eminence." He was gifted, they said, with "literary and scientific acquirements . . . quite superior to his years."[3]

In the years since, he had become what his fellow company commander at Fort Moultrie, Abner Doubleday, considered "an excellent artillery officer, full of invention and resource, a lover of poetry, and an adept at music and painting."[4]

But at the moment he was in a tight spot. It wasn't entirely unexpected, since Charleston had been losing much of its charm as a duty assignment over the past few months, with angry talk of secession turning the air ugly from one end of the harbor to the other. His being there on the dock, and in this particular fix, had been mostly of his own making. He had convinced his commander at Fort Moultrie, Lieutenant Colonel John L. Gardner, that given the hostile mood in the city, something must be done. The thirty thousand rounds of musket ammunition and cartridges housed at the arsenal in Charleston ought to be reclaimed and carried to Fort Moultrie, to prevent it from falling into unfriendly hands and turned against the garrison. Gardner had taken Seymour's advice and ordered his adjutant, Lieutenant Norman J. Hall, to see to it the next morning. But when Hall overslept, Gardner ordered Seymour to go instead.

At about nine o'clock on November 7, Seymour and his detachment boarded the little schooner in civilian dress, to avoid agitating the public mind any more than it already was. Arriving at the arsenal about 3:00 in the afternoon, they tied up at the wharf on the Ashley River and Seymour went to explain his mission to the ordnance storekeeper, A. A. Humphreys, who cheerfully agreed to release the ammunition. But as soon as Seymour's men began carrying boxes out to the schooner, they were stopped by an indignant committee of Charlestonians. The townsfolk told Seymour flatly that he was to take nothing from that arsenal; they would prevent it by force if necessary.

These were very tense and touchy times. The troubled nation had just voted for a new president the day before, and had elected the Republican candidate, Abraham Lincoln. South Carolina had vowed that if that happened it would secede from the Union and demand that the forts in Charleston Harbor be surrendered to the new nation. Meanwhile, they didn't want any Yankee soldiers taking out any guns and ammunition. If it wasn't their arsenal and their ammunition yet, it soon would be.

Seymour was a stubborn Yankee with strict views in the opposite direction. We will see about that, he told the angry crowd. He demanded a carriage to take him to the mayor, a neighbor of his and Louisa's on Sullivan's Island. But no carriage was available, it was too far to walk, it was already near sunset, and the tide was dropping so fast that the schooner would soon be aground. So Seymour decided to give it up temporarily. He ordered the ammunition boxes carried back into the arsenal, and set sail again for Fort Moultrie, arriving about 9:00 that night.

The next morning Seymour convinced Gardner to let him return to Charleston. In town he found the mayor to be genial, sympathetic, and neighborly. Removing the ammunition seemed perfectly proper; after all, both it and the arsenal still belonged to the U.S. government. The mayor said he would advise the police to that effect and the ammunition and cartridges could be removed whenever Gardner wished.

When Seymour returned to Fort Moultrie with this good news, he found that Gardner was now waffling. The colonel feared that if Seymour returned for the ammunition now the mob might get out of hand despite the mayor's orders. The mood in town was just too ugly.[5]

The mood in the town was one of the first things John Gray Foster noticed three days later when he arrived in Charleston. The army had also been good to Seymour's big, strapping classmate. After he recovered from the shattered leg wound sustained at Molino del Rey in Mexico—it had taken two years—Foster limped away from his mother's home above the river in Nashua and picked up his career again. By November 1860 he was thirty-seven years old, of commanding presence, with a reputation in the army as a gifted administrator and one of its best engineers. He was also prized as a raconteur of talent with a vast and ready store of anecdote and story, and widely admired for his genial, sympathetic, and cordial nature. Moreover he sported one of the army's most splendidly cultivated beards, silky and flowing. In Doubleday's opinion, he was "one of the most fearless and reliable men in the service."[6]

Foster arrived at Charleston on November 11, sent there by the Corps of Engineers to oversee repairs at Fort Moultrie and to complete work on Fort Sumter, which had been under construction since the late 1820s. He had been assigned the job in September, but unfinished projects in the north had delayed him. The day after the presidential election, however, he was ordered to give the forts at Charleston Harbor his immediate personal attention.[7]

Foster was no stranger to Charleston. He had been one of the engineers employed in Sumter's construction. Now the fort at the mouth of the harbor was nearly finished—a pentagon-shaped shell of masonry needing more than anything else to have its guns mounted and ready to fire. When finished and fully manned it would be a perfect Gibraltar, with 146 guns and a garrison of 650 men.

Of the other two forts in the harbor, Moultrie on Sullivan's Island was only minimally garrisoned. Castle Pinckney, the third fort and the one nearest the city, was manned only by an ordnance sergeant and his family. The undermanned, unfinished condition of these forts was, in fact, an embarrassment. The three together were built to house over a thousand soldiers and command enormous fire power. However, Sumter was unoccupied, Castle Pinckney virtually so, and Moultrie, ordinarily defended by a complement of three hundred men, was manned by but two understaffed artillery companies commanded by Seymour and Doubleday, and eight musicians—"sixty-four soldiers and a brass band," grumped Doubleday.[8]

As Foster was opening up a little office in Charleston to begin hiring local help, he was appalled by the city's angry mood. Its agitated condition seemed unbecoming to such a beautiful and serene setting. But there it was, in an "unsettled state of the public mind . . . the temper of which seems not to be improving."[9]

Fort Moultrie was a particular headache—for everybody. The South Carolinians didn't like it the way it was; now that Lincoln had been elected and they were about to secede, they wanted the army to hand it over and get out. The garrison didn't like it the way it was, because under the circumstances it was almost impossible to defend.

Moultrie was an old Revolutionary War fort, a creaky relic of cracked masonry built to defend against invaders from the sea; never in anybody's wildest fancy was it ever believed it might have to defend itself against Charleston. Its walls were hardly higher than an ordinary room—about twelve feet. Sand from the surrounding hills had drifted up against it almost to its parapets. Anything from a cud-chewing cow to a drunken derelict could just walk over the top and into the place.

"A child ten years old can easily come into the fort over the sand-banks," an officer had said of it, "and the wall offers little or no obstacle."[10] Some of the officers and men of the garrison wouldn't live in it, but had taken houses in nearby Moultrieville. Even the hospital had moved out.[11]

Foster began immediately correcting its more glaring drawbacks. He removed the sand that had overtopped the scarp wall and repaired the walls all around. He threw up some temporary obstructions and defenses, and built a glacis—a gentle slope down which attackers could be swept with fire. Then he dug a wet ditch fifteen feet wide around the perimeter. There wasn't much he could do about the range of sand hills that commanded the approach, or the houses beyond, whose roofs overlooked the parapets and could conceal riflemen.[12]

For the seventy-five soldiers whose duty it was to defend Charleston Harbor—from any quarter—the real threat to their well-being came neither from the sea nor from Charleston, but from Washington. Abner Doubleday believed this emphatically. Another outspoken Yankee, Doubleday had been at Fort Moultrie for nearly two years and had watched with alarm what he considered the treasonous behavior of the Buchanan administration in Washington. He was not alone. The president appeared to many in this troubled time as a weak and vacillating figurehead, clearly under the sway of a cabal of perfidious southerners who dominated his cabinet. Treasury Secretary Howell Cobb, a Georgian, believed it was the duty of the South to dissolve the Union. His hope was that each southern state would secede separately on March 4, the day Lincoln was to be inaugurated. Interior Secretary Jacob Thompson was ready to follow any secessionist course his state, Mississippi, might chose to take. The assistant Secretary of State, W. H. Trescot, a South Carolinian, was openly abetting secession, and in Secretary of State Lewis Cass's absence from June to October—a critical five months—had been acting secretary. These men packed weight with the president, who was from Pennsylvania, and was not only indecisive and easily manipulated, but sympathetic to the southern cause.[13] There was a word for his kind; he was a "doughface." As one critic had put it, "Old Dr. Buchanan does not certainly know yet whether he wants to see his patient perish, or be cured by remedies alien to his school." It seemed to many in the north at that moment that the government was in the malignant hands of a gang of southern traitors working openly for its destruction.[14]

The most malignant of these ingrates, in the view of Doubleday and the other loyal officers in the Moultrie garrison, the one best positioned to do them dirt, was Secretary of War John B. Floyd. Floyd was an ex-governor of Virginia, who had started out an avowed Union man who thought secession unnecessary. However, he also believed secession was only a little less sacred than a divine right for any state wishing to exercise it. He therefore sympathized with the South in whatever action it might see fit to take, and absolutely opposed any move on the part of the federal government to stop it. These views by November 1860 had translated into what looked to Doubleday like barefaced complicity with South Carolina. Floyd seemed intent on thwarting any effort to keep and strengthen the forts in Charleston Harbor—unless to prepare them for a southern takeover. As far as Doubleday was concerned, having a man with those sentiments running the war department was having the wolf watching the sheep.[15]

The wolf in this troubled November was not happy with the aged and gouty colonel who was commanding in Charleston harbor. Colonel Gardner had seen better days. He went all the way back to the War of 1812, had fought the Seminoles in Florida, been breveted twice in the Mexican War, and was now creaky in the joints. Major Fitz John Porter, sent that fall by Floyd to make a thorough examination of the garrison, had recommended he be replaced. He just wasn't right for this very sensitive and demanding post at this delicate and trying hour. Gardner was quite southern in politics—an agreeable fact as far as Floyd was concerned. But the secretary wanted someone commanding in Charleston who was younger and better able to cope with the sensitive situation there—somebody with special qualities. He thought he had just the man.[16]

On November 12, Major Robert Anderson in New York received an urgent message from Washington: "The Secretary of War desires to see you, and directs that you proceed to this city and report to him without unnecessary delay." On November 15, Anderson had his orders to proceed immediately to Fort Moultrie to relieve Colonel Gardner.[17]

Floyd believed he had in Anderson, a Kentuckian by birth who had married a Georgia girl, a man who could be relied on to carry out the southern program. In the army Anderson had a reputation as a gentleman—courteous, honest, intelligent, and one of the most thoroughly knowledgeable artillerists in the entire service. As an artillery instructor at West Point he had written the standard textbook on the subject. His friends knew him to be a strong pro-slavery man who was nevertheless opposed to secession and to southern extremism.[18]

They all knew, from the secretary down, that he could be counted on to use the utmost restraint, courtesy, and discretion in dealing with the inflamed mood in Charleston. "Of all my acquaintances among men," a friend said of him, "Anderson had the fewest vices of any one of them." No "wine, women and play" were in him.[19] However, a relative of Anderson's, who knew him perhaps better than most, could have told Floyd he might be fundamentally wrong about the major's allegiances. "The Ten Commandments, the Constitution of the United States, and the Army Regulations were his guides in life," that relative wrote.[20] It might be very difficult to persuade a man of such beliefs not to faithfully serve his country and his flag.

Anderson arrived in Charleston on November 21, and on the twenty-third toured the forts in the harbor accompanied by Foster. It wasn't as if the major needed a guide. Anderson had a mystical kinship with this city and its harbor. Indeed, he felt he had an hereditary right to be there to defend it. His father had defended Fort Moultrie before him, against the British in the Revolutionary War, and been imprisoned there.[21]

At Molino del Rey Foster and Anderson had lain within yards of one another, both with bloody wounds. However, Foster knew the new commander only by reputation. Anderson had graduated from West Point in 1825, served on General Scott's staff in the Mexican War, fought in the Indian wars in Florida, and in the Black Hawk War in Illinois. Foster sized him up as they toured the harbor together. He saw a slight, slender man, three or four inches shorter than himself. He would be about fifty-five years old now, nearly twenty years Foster's senior, a handsome man with short-cropped hair turning iron gray. He was slim and soldierly with sloping shoulders—it was said a tailor found him easy to fit. His complexion was swarthy, his forehead high and narrow, his eyes hazel, his nose well formed, and his face clean-shaven. He spoke with a rich, melodious voice and abundant gestures. Foster was very likely struck, as everybody was, by his agreeable and gentlemanly manner. One got the impression that here was a quiet, dignified, but firm and decisive man.[22]

Anderson was not happy with what he saw in the harbor. Moultrie was in a dilapidated condition, the garrison was absurdly undermanned, all the munitions were in a state of chaos, Charlestonians were hysterical, and the authority of the U.S. government was likely to be assailed at any moment.

That night he wrote the war department. The garrison is so weak, he reported, as to invite an attack, which is "openly and publicly threatened." He urged that Sumter, now empty but for workmen, and Castle Pinckney, now manned only by the ordnance sergeant, be garrisoned immediately if the government intends to keep command of the harbor. The clouds, he wrote, "are threatening, and the storm may break upon us at any moment." He warned that "if we neglect . . . to strengthen ourselves, she [South Carolina] will, unless these works are surrendered on their first demand, most assuredly immediately attack us." He sought special instructions, for this was more than just a military problem.[23]

Secretary of War Floyd, of course, preferred things as they were. Anderson was not to be reinforced. While work on Sumter and Pinckney were to continue, neither fort was to be garrisoned. Floyd believed that to send more soldiers to Charleston would unnecessarily irritate the South Carolinians. In December, the secretary sent Major Don Carlos Buell from the war department with these verbal instructions: Anderson was to hold the forts in the harbor without any more garrison and if attacked, to defend them to the last extremity.[24]

But Floyd didn't really mean for Anderson to take these instructions literally. In a confidential letter delivered a few days later he said, in effect, that if attacked Anderson should give up the forts. You might infer from the verbal instructions, the secretary figuratively whispered in Anderson's ear, "that you are required to make a vain and useless sacrifice of your own life and the lives of the men under your command, upon a mere point of honor. This is far from the President's intentions. You are to exercise a sound military discretion on this subject."

It was neither expected nor desired, Floyd whispered, "that you should expose your own life or that of your men in a hopeless conflict in defense of these forts. If they are invested or attacked by a force so superior that resistance would, in your judgment, be a useless waste of life, it will be your duty to yield to necessity, and make the best terms in your power." This, he assured Anderson, "will be the conduct of an honorable, brave, and humane officer, and you will be fully justified in such action."[25]

So that was it. Anderson was to avoid every act that would need-lessly upset and provoke the South Carolinians, and to take no position that could be construed as hostile unless absolutely necessary. At the same time he was to hold the forts in the harbor and if attacked defend himself to the last extremity—but not really.

None of this, of course, was any help at all. "If I had been here before the commencement of expenditures on this work [Fort Moultrie], and supposed that this garrison would not be increased," Anderson grumbled, "I should have advised its withdrawal, with the exception of a small guard, and its removal to Fort Sumter, which so perfectly commands the harbor and this fort." But he began to make do with what he had.[26]

It was clear to Anderson that there was "a romantic desire urging the South Carolinians to *have possession of* this work. . . ."[27] Therefore, besides ordering all the sand removed from about the walls of Fort Moultrie, he had heavy gates erected to keep out the romantics, and a small manhole cut for people to crawl in and out through. It was rumored in Charleston that two thousand riflemen had been detailed to occupy the roofs of the houses that crowded about the fort. This troubled Anderson and outraged Captain Doubleday, his second in command, who was for burning every house around to the ground.[28]

Anderson wasn't prepared to go that far. But he wanted to do something. He wrote Washington again. The sand hills commanding the fort to the east must be leveled, he told the war department. Would doing this be construed as initiating a collision? Under what circumstances would he be justified in setting fire to or destroying the houses near the fort that "afford dangerous shelter to an enemy?" Would he be justified in firing on an armed body approaching the fort? The answers that came back were no, don't level the dunes, and no, don't destroy the houses. As for an approaching enemy, ask them what they intend, warn them to keep off, and if they don't respond, then it is their own fault what happens next.[29]

OK, said Anderson grudgingly, he wouldn't level the dunes or destroy the houses until convinced an attack was underway. But he warned the war department that both the hills with their sparse, stunted vegetation and the houses were lethal havens for sharpshoot-ers who might in a few hours, "with ordinary good luck, pick off the major part of my little band, if we stand to our guns."[30]

Anderson told his superiors that the government must decide, the sooner the better, what he should do when South Carolina secedes, as now appeared inevitable. Was he to surrender the forts or not? If not, then they had better send him reinforcements now, or vessels of war. The South Carolinians, he said "are making every preparation (drilling nightly, &c) for the fight which they say must take place, and insist on our not doing anything." Conceding in advance that he probably couldn't expect much help from Washington, he would "go steadily on, preparing for the worst, trusting hopefully in the God of Battles to guard and guide me in my course."[31]

That was also all the guidance Foster was getting at the moment. He was peppering his superiors at the Corps of Engineers in Washington with as many questions as Anderson was putting to the war department. There were things he also needed to know: If Fort Sumter was to be risked against the chances of attack, he needed to know that so he could adjust his program against its possible loss. If not, he had to prepare to defend it until help arrived. If the garrison at Moultrie was to be transferred, he needed to know that too, so he could stop spending all that money to make it defensible.[32]

Foster tended not to be as politically sensitive as he might be. He was intent only on getting the job done. When he first arrived he had hired laborers locally, all of them secessionists to the core. He sent to Baltimore for 150 stonemasons, many of whom had worked for him there. They were excellent workmen, but in some cases questionable Unionists. So all of the Charleston laborers and much of the imported help from Baltimore were sympathetic with the southern cause; many of them came wearing secessionist badges. This disgusted Doubleday. In his view Foster was unwittingly infesting the garrison with a gang of Judases.[33]

Foster was also experiencing an even worse embarrassment at the Charleston arsenal than Seymour had a few weeks earlier. Soon after arriving, Foster ordered forty muskets from the arsenal, with which to arm his workmen. He believed that given the overheated situation, both the workmen and the valuable public property at Fort Sumter and Castle Pinckney needed protecting.

Several weeks passed and Foster heard nothing more of his requisition. On December 17, he went to the arsenal to pick up two other muskets he had been authorized to draw. The storekeeper argued that he had no authority to issue the two muskets, but there was that old order for forty guns, which were now there and available for delivery. Would Foster like them?

Foster hauled them away, not stopped this time by angry townspeople as Seymour had been. He issued two of the muskets to the ordnance sergeants at Sumter and Pinckney and stored the remainder in the magazines at the two forts. Shortly after, he received an urgent note from the storekeeper at the arsenal. The weapons he had just issued Foster were causing such great excitement in the city, the storekeeper said, that he felt obliged to pledge his word that they would be back in the arsenal by the next night. Would Foster please return them immediately?

Foster objected. "To give them up on a demand of this kind seems to me as an act not expected of me by the Government, and as almost suicidal under the circumstances," he wrote to the chief of engineers in Washington. "It would place the two forts under my charge at the mercy of a mob. . . . I am not disposed to surrender these arms under a threat of this kind, especially when I know that I am only doing my duty to the Government."

It appeared that nobody had acquainted Foster with John Floyd, who was the government. On December 20, at 2:00 in the morning, a telegram arrived from the secretary. "I have just received a telegraphic dispatch informing me that you have removed forty muskets from Charleston Arsenal to Fort Moultrie," the telegram said curtly. "If you have removed any arms, return them instantly."

Foster returned them that morning, but was still steaming when he wrote the chief of engineers later that day. "The order of the Secretary of War of last night I must consider as decisive upon the question of any efforts on my part to defend Fort Sumter and Castle Pinckney," he fumed. "The defense now can only extend to keeping the gates closed and shutters fastened, and must cease when these are forced."[34]

Anderson meanwhile was about to make a move that would upset the secretary far more than Foster's forty muskets.

The situation at Fort Moultrie was making Anderson exceedingly nervous. "When I inform you that my garrison consists of only sixty effective men," he wrote a friend on Christmas Eve, "that we are in a very indefensible work . . . you will at once see that if attacked in force, headed by any one not a simpleton, there is scarcely a probability of our being able to hold out long enough to enable our friends to come to our succor."[35]

The old fort was under the constant, suspicious, and watchful eyes of hostile Charleston. Bands of secessionists roamed nearby day and night. The garrison was so worn out watching them, that Louisa Seymour and Mary Doubleday had on one occasion relieved their husbands on guard duty so they could get some rest.[36]

All of this was more than Anderson could stand, and it had only gotten worse since South Carolina had seceded on December 20, as threatened. Since then steamers from Charleston had stood constantly off Fort Sumter to prevent any troops, other than workmen, from being landed. A clash of some kind seemed imminent. Anderson wished to God he "only had men enough here to man fully my guns."[37]

Even before South Carolina seceded, Anderson had made up his mind to abandon Moultrie and move his little garrison to Fort Sumter. Foster nearly had the place ready for occupancy, and could soon make it fit for defense. It was infinitely safer for his command than Moultrie. He could defend himself there indefinitely, even with his pathetically small command.[38]

It had to be carefully and cautiously done. Anderson therefore told nobody of his plans, not even his officers. He had hoped to do it on Christmas Day, when Charleston would be celebrating and its guard would be down. But it rained hard all that day; the move would have to wait.[39] On Christmas night he joined his fellow officers— and several Charlestonian secessionists—at a party at John and Mary Foster's house in Moultrieville. Nobody present had any idea of the bombshell he planned to drop the next day.[40]

In the morning he told his engineering officers to ready their boats—he was moving the command that evening. He ordered his adjutant, Lieutenant Hall, to pack the camp baggage and the wives and children of the soldiers in three chartered schooners on the pretext of removing them from the path of a possible conflict. This would excite no suspicions. Hall was to lay off old Fort Johnson across the harbor with his cargo and wait for a signal to land at Sumter.[41]

Seymour had been suspecting something like this. He had packed up his personal property, and sent Louisa off only that afternoon to stay with friends in Charleston.[42] Doubleday, the other company commander, however, suspected nothing. Earlier that day Anderson had given up his own mess and come to live with him. That should have told Doubleday something. But he still suspected nothing until that evening when he went to the parapet to tell Anderson tea was ready. The major turned to him and said, "Captain, in twenty minutes you will leave this fort with your company for Fort Sumter."[43]

Surprised, but delighted, Doubleday rushed to rouse his men. He then ran to his house to tell his wife that there might be fighting and that she must get out of the fort as soon as possible and take refuge behind the sand hills. Twenty minutes later Doubleday and his men joined Seymour and his company for the short quarter-mile march from the fort to the landing at Moultrieville. It was near sunset and the siesta hour, and the Charleston militia were taking their late afternoon naps. The command slipped through without being noticed. Waiting for them at the wharf with two boats were Foster's two young engineering officers, Lieutenants G. W. Snyder and R. K. Meade. "Captain," Snyder said to Doubleday, "those boats are for your men."[44]

Foster stared nervously out into the harbor through the gathering dusk where a guard vessel was approaching Doubleday's boat. The captain was doing double duty again, being an artillery officer this time, standing on the ramparts of Moultrie beside five loaded cannon. With him were a crew of gunners, his brother-in-law and clerk Edward Moall, and Surgeon Samuel Crawford, the post physician. He had orders from Anderson to fire on any vessel that attempted to interfere with the transfer.[45] As the guard boat, the *General Clinch*—named for Major Anderson's father-in-law—approached, Doubleday ordered his thirty men to take off their coats and cover their muskets. He hurriedly stripped off his own coat and threw it down in the bottom of the boat to conceal his army insignia.

Foster and his little band of gunners watched, held their breaths, and fingered their lanyards as the *General Clinch* stopped dead in the water near the boat. After a moment, however, it started up again and passed on, persuaded that the boat only carried workmen. The gunners relaxed their grip on the lanyards, and the little boat continued on its way.

Doubleday was the first to arrive at Sumter. At the wharf the workmen, most of them secessionists and some of them armed with pistols, swarmed down to the water's edge.

"What are these soldiers doing here?" they demanded. "What is the meaning of this?"

Doubleday answered with pointed bayonets, driving the workers back into the center of the fort. After taking over the guardroom commanding the main entrance and placing his sentinels, Doubleday sent the boat back for Seymour and his company. Anderson, who had meanwhile arrived in the other engineer boat, fired a cannon twice and Lieutenant Hall set out immediately from Fort Johnson with his cargo of wives, children, and stores. The entire operation took less than two hours. Everybody was safely within the fort now except the rear guard left at Moultrie under Captain Foster.[46]

The little garrison at Sumter listened intently for any sign that their move had been discovered. When none came, Anderson began sending boats back and forth to tie up loose ends. One of the loose ends was the soldier's wife who was in charge of the officer's mess. So well had Anderson kept his move secret that she, knowing nothing of it, had cooked the evening meal as usual, and was perplexed and a little more than out of sorts when nobody showed up to eat it. When Lieutenant Jefferson C. Davis, who had been left with the rear guard at Moultrie, walked to the mess later, he found her waiting, a good deal hotter by this time than the meal was. He bundled her and her pots and pans and the stone-cold meal into a boat and transferred them all to Sumter.[47]

When Mary Doubleday fled Fort Moultrie over the sand hills earlier in the afternoon she hurried first to the home of the post sutler, then to the bosom of the family of the post chaplain, Matthias Harris. That evening as she paced the beach with the Reverend Harris and his family, peering anxiously toward Fort Sumter a mile across the water, Major Anderson was composing a wire to Washington. "I have just completed, by the blessing of God," he said in his own pious way, "the removal to this fort of all of my garrison, except the surgeon, four non-commissioned officers, and seven men. We have one year's supply of hospital stores and about four months' supply of provisions for my command."[48]

He might as well have reported casually that he had just leveled Charleston and taken no prisoners.

The next morning, having spiked the guns at Moultrie, destroyed the gun carriages facing the harbor, cut down the flagstaff, and sent the last lighter-load of ammunition and supplies to Sumter, Foster rowed to Charleston to close his bank accounts and his engineer office. He was therefore on hand to see the city react to this covert move it had so utterly failed to notice the night before.[49]

The reaction was hysterical. Charleston thought what the commissioners sent to Washington to negotiate the delivery of the U.S. forts and other property to the new nation of South Carolina thought: that Anderson had as good as waged war on them. "No other words will describe his action," the commissioners protested in writing to President Buchanan. "It was not a peaceful change from one fort to another; it was a hostile act in the highest sense—one only justified in the presence of a superior enemy, and in imminent peril. He abandoned his position, spiked his guns, burned his gun carriages, made preparations for the destruction of his post, and withdrew, under cover of the night, to a safer position. This was war . . . and without the slightest provocation."[50]

Louisa Seymour was out in her host's garden in Charleston at about 9:00 on the morning after, picking roses, when the bells in the city began to ring frantically. When she discovered what it meant she couldn't believe it, and ran down to the steamboat landing to ask if it were true. It was, and word was spreading that Moultrie had been mined and would soon be blown to heaven.[51]

South Carolina Governor Francis W. Pickens was outraged. He rushed a note to Anderson demanding that he return his command to Moultrie immediately. Anderson replied that he could not and would not do so, that as commander of the harbor he had a right to move his command anywhere he saw fit.[52] Pickens in his frustration seized Castle Pinckney and occupied Fort Moultrie that afternoon.

The news flew to Washington faster even than Anderson's telegram, and Secretary Floyd was as upset as Governor Pickens. He wired Anderson, demanding to know if it was true. "It is not believed," the secretary said, "because there is no order for any such movement. Explain the meaning of this report."[53] Floyd had forgotten that the verbal instructions he had sent to Anderson earlier that month had given him permission to move to any fort in the harbor he wished if he felt his command in peril.[54]

Anderson answered frankly: "It was my solemn duty to move my command from a fort which we could not probably have held longer than forty-eight or sixty hours, to this one, where my power of resistance is increased to a very great degree."[55] Floyd must have wondered if this was the officer with the southern sympathies, the husband of a Georgia girl, that he had sent to Charleston because he thought he could be counted on to do what was right.

Lieutenant Theodore Talbot, one of Anderson's officers, put it as well as anybody. Anderson's move, he said, "has cut the Gordian Knot. It is now in the power of the authorities to maintain the supremacy of the Genl. Govt if they choose to do so and it seems to me that they can no longer evade the question."[56] That is probably what upset Floyd so. He didn't want to maintain that supremacy, but now the pressure was on to do something. Damn that Anderson.

Emotions continued to seethe and churn like a hurricane in the harbor as the two West Point classmates, Foster and Seymour, rowed over the troubled waters to Moultrie together the following Saturday, the twenty-ninth—Foster on private and Seymour on official business. They were met at the fort with the announcement that they were now prisoners and would be taken to Charleston. Foster replied that he weighed two hundred pounds and wouldn't go unless he was carried. Seymour said he was not quite that heavy, but that he also would resist to the best of his weight and ability. The Carolinians thought about this, probably giving particularly serious consideration to Foster's impressive bulk, and permitted them to return unarrested to Sumter.[57]

Later that day Seymour was sent to Charleston on orders from Anderson. Arriving at the landing about 3:00 in the afternoon in civilian dress, he went as soon as he could to look for his wife. He found her suffering for his sins. In the hysterical backlash of the garrison's overnight move, her hosts had grown so cool and distant that a continued stay seemed impractical. Seymour could linger only long enough to advise her to find a boardinghouse in the city as soon as possible and move there. He had to return to Sumter, and he couldn't take her with him.[58]

On his way to the landing he stopped at an apothecary shop to buy chemicals to make fuses for mines and other exploding machines, with which he had successfully experimented at Fort Moultrie. Walking on down Broad Street toward his boat he turned into a newspaper office where telegrams were posted. As he stepped in he found a crowd clustered around an announcement that Secretary Floyd, under the gun of a financial scandal in Washington, had resigned.

"I'm glad of it," Seymour said.

The crowd turned to stare at him. "Why?"

"He's better out of Washington," said Seymour.

Nobody openly challenged this, so Seymour sauntered on to find another crowd clustered about his boat at the landing and his crew gone. The crowd explained that the soldiers had been taken to the city guardhouse. This meant Seymour had to make another trip to see his old neighbor, the mayor of the city, whom he found in his office. Seymour stated his case and the mayor, as genial as ever, ordered the crew released and escorted back to the boat. As they pushed off for Sumter without further interference, Seymour could have mused how much easier it was to get men out of Charleston than ammunition. But that might not long be the case, given the present mood in the city.[59]

If the garrison's odyssey was over, Louisa Seymour's ordeal and that of the other officers' wives were just beginning. Mary Doubleday had been the only one of them still at Moultrie when the peremptory transfer began. Louisa had been packed off to Charleston earlier in the day. Mary Foster and her sister, each with a young daughter, had also gone to Charleston. The wives of the soldiers, who had a different status, were already with their men at Sumter. Left behind in the move, the officers' wives wanted to be there too.

Mary Foster and Mary Doubleday got there the easy way. Mrs. Foster and her sister managed after some time to wrangle a permit to visit the fort from Governor Pickens. Mrs. Doubleday on January 3 discovered a boatload of workmen going to Sumter, took a seat in the stern, and told them she was going with them.

Louisa Seymour's arrival at Fort Sumter was in the black of night and a bit more complicated.

On January 4, after half a morning of negotiating for a room, she had returned to Sullivan's Island. There she appealed to the South Carolina general in command at Fort Moultrie for permission to visit Sumter, and was turned down. She then appealed to the post sutler, Dan Sinclair. Sinclair had three boys, one of whom was present, and who when asked to take her to Sumter said he would not dare do so. But later that evening after dark as Louisa sat dejectedly in front of the fire in Chaplain Harris's living room, Sinclair tapped at the window and called her out. He and his two other boys were there to row her across.

It was only a small boat, but the night was still and the water perfectly placid. Coming up to the wharf in the rear of the fort, the boat was hailed by the sentinel on duty, who fired his musket. Sinclair shouted that the captain's wife was aboard.

Inside the fort, Louisa found the wives of Doubleday and Foster already there. The next question, now that they were there, was what to do with them. Louisa Seymour begged Anderson to let them stay, saying she would make herself useful in any way she could. But Anderson decided it was impractical; the officers' wives had to leave. Reluctantly they embarked for Charleston, Louisa Seymour and Mary Doubleday returning in the small rowboat that night with Sinclair and his two boys.[60]

Two days later, to everybody's surprise, particularly Major Anderson's, his own wife appeared at the wharf with reinforcements. Eba Anderson was not well—indeed, she was an invalid—and the major had left her in New York when he had come to Charleston in November. When she read in the papers that her husband was now caged at Fort Sumter, she vowed that he should not be there without Peter Hart. Hart, an Irishman, had been Anderson's orderly sergeant in Mexico and was devoted to him. She would find this faithful and resourceful man wherever he was and get him to her husband's side even if it killed her. After a long and hurried search she found Hart on the New York City police force, and called him to her.

When he came and brought his wife, Mrs. Anderson said, "I have sent for you to ask you to do me a favor."

"Anything Mrs. Anderson wishes, I will do." Hart replied.

"But it may be more than you imagine."

"Anything Mrs. Anderson wishes."

"I want you to go with me to Fort Sumter."

Hart looked for a fleeting moment at Mrs. Hart.

"I will go, Madame."

"But, Hart, I want you to *stay* with the major," Mrs. Anderson said. "You will leave your family, and give up a good situation."

Hart again looked inquiringly at his wife, and seeing there what he sought, said: "I will go, Madame."

"But Margaret," Mrs. Anderson said, turning now to Hart's wife, "what do you say?"

"Indade, Ma'am," Margaret said, "and it's Margaret's sorry she can't do as much for you as Pater can."

Twenty-four hours later, against the advice of her doctors, Eba Anderson was on the cars with Hart headed for Charleston. There they wrung permission to visit Sumter from Governor Pickens and when they put in at the wharf and her arrival was announced, Anderson rushed out exclaiming, "My glorious wife!"

"I have brought you Peter Hart," she replied cryptically. "The children are well; I return to-night."[61]

The other officers' wives left Charleston about the same time, in a body on January 8 on the midnight train. They hated to leave their husbands in these straits, but they could no longer endure the hostile atmosphere in the angry city. Like Eba Anderson, they would have to do what they could from New York.

Waiting
for the
Ball to Begin

A little after dawn on the day after his wife left for New York, Abner Doubleday mounted the parapets at Fort Sumter and frowned unhappily out into the harbor.

He was depressed. The fort itself was bleak—a dark, gloomy, unfinished hollow of an amphitheater encased in high walls that only grudgingly let in the sun. And when he ascended to the parapet he saw everywhere the accursed South Carolina flags, representing palmettos, pelicans, and other strange devices, and hanging from flagstaffs about the harbor where Old Glory used to fly. It was an affront to this steadfast New York unionist.

For God's sake where was his country? Not an echo had come back from the loyal North to hearten and encourage the tiny garrison since its dramatic move from Moultrie two weeks before—only the outraged telegram from Floyd and all this grief from the South Carolina secessionists. He couldn't count the times his glasses had swept the horizon in vain for a sign of the one flag he longed to see.

This morning he looked again, out to the open sea. This time there was something. A ship passing the bar, moving swiftly. Could this be the answer from the North? But that was impossible; this was no man-of-war steaming boldly in. It was only a merchant ship, a sidewheeler churning up the channel.

But as it steamed on, a cannon shot skittered across the water—a salvo from the new masked battery on Morris Island at the harbor entrance.[1]

So here it was at last, the impatiently awaited echo from the North. The Buchanan administration, now minus Floyd, who had been superseded by Postmaster General Joseph Holt, was sending reinforcements. To avoid something—suspicion, war, chaos, embarrassment?—help was coming down the channel in the guise of a lowly unarmed merchant ship.

Inside the sidewheeler, called the *Star of the West*, 250 armed soldiers waited tensely. The first shot from the Morris Island battery came as a complete surprise to Captain John McGowan on the bridge of his ship. There wasn't supposed to be a battery there, not that close to the harbor entrance. But it was undeniably a shot ricocheting over the water from that direction, plunging and skipping along and falling short. It was, of course, an invitation to stop, but the captain was disinclined to accept it. Instead, he defiantly ran up a garrison-size national ensign, which was answered by another shot from the masked battery—this one bounding over the vessel at head level, between the smokestack and the walking-beam of the engine.

"Booh!" McGowan shouted. "You must give us bigger guns than that, boys, or you can not hurt us!"

The next shot ripped into the ship just abaft the forerigging and stove in the planking. Another followed that the captain saw come "within an ace" of carrying away the rudder. Now a steamer with a cutter in tow was speeding toward them from Charleston. The man on the *Star of the West* wondered why the guns on Fort Sumter didn't answer those infernal batteries.[2]

At Fort Moultrie farther up the channel, H. M. Clarkson, a newly promoted corporal in the service of South Carolina, nervously sighted down the barrel of Gun No. 13, a ten-inch columbiad lovingly called "Edith." He peered toward the merchant ship drawing now within range. Clarkson's battery commander, Major R. S. Ripley, standing on the parapet with his glass glued to the vessel, barked an order: "Gunner No. 13, prepare to fire."

A short pause followed, then Ripley shouted, "Fire!"

In a burst of smoke and a boom like thunder, Edith hurled her 128-pound ball across the bow of the *Star of the West*. The shattering boom shook the masonry where Edith crouched, but it shook Captain McGowan even more.[3]

"Helm out of port!" he screamed to his helmsman, and the *Star of the West* churned about in the water and steamed back down the channel toward the mouth of the harbor.[4]

With the first shot from the masked battery, Captain Doubleday sprinted below to wake Major Anderson, who ordered him to beat the long roll and post the men immediately at the newly emplaced barbette guns. By the time the two reached the parapet, Edith and the guns on Morris Island were all barking at the vessel.[5] Anderson took in the scene and hesitated. This called for a conference. He and several of his officers repaired to the laundry room.

In a few moments Captain Foster emerged, bounded angrily up the two or three steps that led to the terreplein, smashing his hat in his fist. He was clearly upset and it apparently had nothing to do with the laundry service. He was heard muttering something about the flag and "trample on it."[6]

The indignant soldiers and their wives and children—everybody was on the parapets now—watched as the *Star of the West* turned and steamed back toward the open sea. They were outraged, wild with impatience to avenge the affront to the flag, yet Anderson apparently was not going to do anything.

It was more than the tall young wife of Private John H. Davis could stand. Baring her slim white arm and with a friction tube in her fingers, she sprang to one of the guns exclaiming that she would fire it herself. Captain Doubleday gently pulled her back.

"You have a great deal of courage," he said.

"Courage!" she stamped impatiently. "I should think, Sir, a soldier's wife *ought* to have courage!"[7]

It was no good. The vessel had recrossed the bar. As quickly as it had begun it was over, and the guns of Sumter had remained silent throughout. Anderson had been unwilling to start a war over a merchant vessel.

But he was willing to protest to South Carolina. Was the firing on the vessel flying a United States flag done with his sanction or authority? he angrily enquired of Governor Pickens. If it was, he would henceforth permit no vessels to pass peaceably within range of

Sumter's guns. When Pickens answered that he had authorized the firing and that it was perfectly justified, Anderson hurried to consult Washington. He dispatched Lieutenant Theodore Talbot to the war department in person to ask about the *Star of the West*, to explain Anderson's actions, and to request instructions.[8]

So this was the answer from the North, fumed Abner Doubleday. This was the craven manner in which the flag had come, "in a timid, apologetic way, and not as a representative of the war power of the Government."[9]

Foster was also upset. He wrote his superiors at the Corps of Engineers in Washington saying he feared the incident had "opened the war." He reported three days later that "the temper of the people of this state is becoming every day more bitter, and I do not see how we can avoid a bloody conflict."[10]

From the public in the North there was an angry outcry. The incident was "a calm dishonorable, vile submission," wrote one New Yorker in his diary. "I fear we are a decomposing nation."[11]

However, few in the country blamed Anderson personally for not answering the batteries. Secretary Holt apologized to him for not forewarning the garrison that the vessel was coming. It was understandable under the circumstances, the secretary admitted, that Anderson didn't "feel the force of the obligation to protect her approach." He wrote the major that the government had no further plans to try to reinforce the garrison, since any attempt was likely now to bring a collision of arms, a calamity the president was most anxious to avoid.[12]

Harper's Weekly saluted Anderson with a limn of Columbia herself and a stanza of bad doggerel:

> Bob Anderson, my beau, Bob, when we were first acquent,
> You were in Mex-i-co, Bob, because by order sent;
> But now you are in Sumter, Bob, because you chose to go;
> And blessings on you, any how, Bob Anderson, my beau![13]

But something now had to be done about the soldiers' wives and children. "We have one another yet, though, thank God," one of the wives had said when so many things were found lost or missing in the hasty move from Fort Moultrie.[14] Now they weren't even to have each other. Major Anderson had decided that they, like the officers' wives, must leave. By the time Lieutenant Talbot returned from Washington on January 17 with the news that there would be no further attempt to reinforce or resupply the fort, the want of fuel had become a hardship. On the nineteenth the trips to the markets in Charleston had stopped. The *Star of the West* incident had ratcheted the tension up another turn. That an attack was forthcoming was evident. The wives and children had to leave. It just wouldn't do to have them there.

This distressed the wives. They had left Moultrie with their husbands, now they were leaving Sumter without them. But they were good soldiers. "With smothered sighs and suppressed tears," they prepared to say their last good-byes and depart. God knew when, or if ever, they would see one another again.[15]

"We have been seven years married, and I never had reason to find fault with you," one wife told her husband as she turned to leave. "Now, whatever may happen, I *know* I shall never have cause to blush for you." Another told the man she loved, her wet tears betraying her bold words, "And I don't want you to think of *us*, Ben; the children and myself will get along, and you'll have enough to think of here." Private Thomas Carroll's Irish wife issued these parting orders to her husband: "May God bless, and take care o' you, Thomas,—I'll never cease to pray for you; but do you juty, darlint;—God forbid that my love should interfere with that."[16]

The forty-two women and children boarded the steamer in a high wind on February 1, and the storm that followed kept them in the harbor for two more days. But at noon on Sunday, February 3, they stood out toward the bar and the open sea, bound for New York. As the steamer passed under the guns of Fort Sumter the men crowded the parapets, firing a single shot in a final farewell, answered by the steamer. Three cheers rose from the parapets; answering handkerchiefs fluttered on the deck of the ship. The men continued to stand and stare after the steamer until it was lost to view on the far horizon.[17]

Now they were alone, surrounded by hostile neighbors who coveted their last four acres of land in the harbor. An attack was a foregone conclusion—it was only a question of time. It seemed that too much was being made over a half-finished slab of masonry erected on an artificial island built on imported chips of Yankee granite. But such

1. West Point on the Hudson River—as it looked to the members of the class of 1846.

2. The plain and the academy buildings in the 1840s.

3. The academy grounds with the old West Point Hotel in the distance.

4. (*Top, left*) The West Point cadet
of the 1840s in full-dress uniform—
a rendering by George Horatio Derby
of the class of 1846.

5. (*Top, right*) A cadet at study—also
by George Derby.

6. As they really looked—a photograph of Derby
himself in his cadet uniform; probably taken in
1844, the summer of the class furlough.

7. The stag dance, common at West Point's summer encampment—
"a rather dry business without ladies."

The West Point Faculty in the 1840s

8. West Point Superintendent Richard Delafield—the cadets called him "Dicky the Punster."

9. Dennis Hart Mahan, the greatly feared Professor of Civil and Military Engineering and the Art of War—alias "Old Cobbon Sense."

10. Albert Ensign Church, Professor of Mathematics—one cadet thought him "an old mathematical cinder," dry as dust.

11. William H. C. Bartlett, Professor of Natural and Experimental Philosophy—a world-respected scientist and arguably the academy's most brilliant graduate.

12. Jacob W. Bailey, Professor of Chemistry, Mineralogy and Geology—one in the class called him "a perfect love of a man."

13. Robert W. Weir, Teacher of Drawing—"he disciplined their hands to draw what their eyes could see."

14. Henry L. Kendrick, Assistant Professor of Chemistry, Mineralogy and Geology—a cadet favorite. At Puebla in Mexico he ordered his lieutenant to "fire at the crisis."

15

16

17

18

15. Thomas J. Jackson as a young officer. The face is genuine; the uniform was painted on later.

16. George B. McClellan as a new lieutenant—with his father and younger brother, Arthur.

17. George Derby of the topographical engineers—he would become a famous American humorist.

18. William Montgomery Gardner, the wildly handsome young Georgian, desperately wounded at Churubusco.

19. (*Inset*) General Winfield Scott, commanding the Army of Invasion in Mexico—he brought into their lives "some of the splendor that attaches to bravery and achievement."

20. (*Top*) The landing of the army at Vera Cruz—Jackson thought it the most thrilling sight he had ever seen.

21. (*Bottom*) The battle of Cerro Gordo, where the war ended abruptly for George Derby and Dabney Maury.

22. The storming of Chapultepec castle, where Thomas Jackson dodged cannonballs, distinguished himself, and won his third brevet promotion.

23. General Scott entering the City of Mexico in triumph—to the class of 1846 it had been "a perfect war."

24. The not-so-perfect war in the American West—fighting Indians where "the front is all around, and the rear nowhere."

25. The young A. P. Hill—he won the beautiful Mary Ellen Marcy's heart . . .

26. . . . but his West Point roommate, George McClellan, won her hand.

27. The Union officers at Fort Sumter. Seated left to right: Abner Doubleday, Robert Anderson, Samuel Wylie Crawford, John Gray Foster.
Standing: Truman Seymour, George W. Snyder, Jefferson C. Davis, and R. K. Meade.
Not pictured: Theodore Talbot and Norman C. Hall.

28. Truman Seymour's drawing of Fort Moultrie as seen from Fort Sumter.

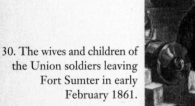

29. Fort Sumter before the bombardment.

30. The wives and children of the Union soldiers leaving Fort Sumter in early February 1861.

31. Truman Seymour of the class of 1846, a hero of Sumter—he married the boss's daughter and drew elegant sketches of the Confederate positions.

32. John Gray Foster of the class of 1846, another hero of Sumter—he counted the Confederate guns ringing the fort and erected the defenses.

as it was, it was now the only home they had, and they were bound to defend it.

Foster set to work with Yankee efficiency making it ready for a vigorous defense. He erected galleries, traverses, and splinter-proof shelters; plugged embrasures with brick, stone, earth, iron, lead, and concrete; mined the wharf and the gorge; cleared the parade; opened communications throughout the fort and its quarters; and finished mounting the guns.[18]

Positioning the necessary guns on the lower tier and the eight-inch columbiads on the upper tier was comparatively easy work and went rapidly. Placing two of the heavier ten-inch columbiads on the upper tier was something else again. It involved a big-time hoisting operation, lifting eight-ton monsters fifty feet above the parade. It required a jury-rigged derrick and lusty choruses of "On the Plains of Mexico." Even so, the second columbiad had only risen as high as the level of the terreplein, when it let loose and hurtled back down breech first, burying itself trunnion-deep in the sand. The second try after the derrick was repaired succeeded, but there was no attempt to hoist the third gun. It was mounted instead as a mortar on the parade and pointed toward Charleston. It became a ritual after retreat each evening to see who was man enough to carry a 128-pound shot up the three flights of stairs.[19]

As Foster armed the fort, the inventive Seymour, using the chemicals he had purchased from the apothecary in Charleston, improvised a "flying fougasse," or what the men called a bursting barrel. This diabolical machine was an ordinary cask filled with broken stones—Yankee granite doubtless—and rigged with a fuse connecting the powder in the canister with a friction primer in the bung. It was designed to be rolled off the parapet at the appropriate moment like a shell grenade, and when the lanyard attached to the eye of the primer was pulled, to explode at invader level, spewing stones in every direction at bullet velocity. In a test firing, the stones lashed the surface of the water well out in the harbor. The boiling foam was observed with alarm in Charleston, and stories of an "infernal machine" made the papers the next day. Seymour was so pleased he built three of them.[20]

For men in their situation, morale at the fort remained unaccountably high. The soldiers—many of them but recent immigrants from Europe and in the army because it was the best job they could get—

were eager to "strike a blow for 'Uncle Sam.' "[21] Even Foster's forty loyal workmen still on the job caught the spirit. No grumbling was heard until the soldiers ran out of tobacco and were forced to gratify their cravings on spun yarn. The tobacco gave out long before the rations did, and raised a far louder outcry.[22]

Anderson seemed satisfied with his officers. Besides himself, there were Doubleday and the two West Pointers from the class of 1846, Foster and Seymour—all captains. First Lieutenant Theodore Talbot, a cultivated Kentuckian, had served in the Frémont expeditions in the West in his younger days. Doubleday described him as "equally ready to meet his friend at the festive board, or his enemy at ten paces." But Talbot was sick—dying of tuberculosis.

The post physician, Surgeon Samuel Wylie Crawford, was a doctor who wanted to be a soldier and who would one day be a general, and whom Doubleday found to be "a genial companion, studious, and full of varied information." Crawford had seen service on the frontier and had been with the garrison since September. The frail, bearded first lieutenant of artillery with the ironic name of Jefferson C. Davis had won both his commission in the regular army and his nickname, the "boy-sergeant of Buena Vista," with his heroism in Mexico. As the nickname implied, he was "brave, generous, and impetuous." Three young recent graduates from West Point rounded out the officers' corps. Lieutenant Norman J. Hall was Anderson's adjutant. Lieutenants G. W. Snyder and R. K. Meade were Foster's assistant engineers. All three were, in Doubleday's opinion, "full of zeal, intelligence, and energy."[23]

And there were the two civilians who were part of the family: Foster's brother-in-law and clerk, Edward Moale; and Anderson's resourceful former New York policeman and orderly sergeant, Peter Hart, who was a jack of all trades.

When Foster wasn't making Sumter ready, he was squinting through his binoculars, watching what was happening in the harbor. Nearly every day now he was identifying a new gun in place that hadn't been there the day before. He methodically noted them all, assessing their firepower, adding it all up, and reporting daily to Washington. Batteries were going up all around them, a ring of potential fire growing more awesome day by day. Foster was so familiar with them by now that he had taken to criticizing their engineering. While the work appeared to Anderson to be well devised and well executed, to Foster's discerning engineer's eye the new floating battery the rebels had built "does not meet expectations. . . . I do not think [it] . . . will prove very formidable."[24]

But the work in general was good enough. Guns were either turned now directly on them or pointed down the channel to welcome any help Washington might think of sending. It was awesome enough for one of Doubleday's artillerymen to write home, "When once the ball is commenced, God only knows where or when it will end."[25]

As Foster peered intently in three directions of the compass, ticking off the batteries as they grew, Seymour sketched, making drawings of what his classmate was seeing through his glasses. They were artful sketches representing, Anderson thought, "very prettily and accurately the batteries within our view"—pretty enough to hang in a gallery. Anderson was enclosing them in the daily reports he was sending in the mails to the war department in Washington.[26]

Foster was now also writing his daily report to the chief of engineers, "if only a line, so that you may know if there is any interruption of the communication."[27] Between the reports of the two officers and Seymour's sketches, Washington was being kept current on what was happening daily inside and outside the fort—as far as it could be seen and interpreted.

As Anderson studied the shoreline through his glasses, he felt more and more like "a sheep tied watching the butcher sharpening a knife to cut his throat."[28] There wasn't much he could do but watch. His latest instructions from Secretary Holt were still the same: to act strictly on the defensive, and to avoid if possible a collision with the angry forces surrounding him.[29]

Given those orders, Anderson did not ask for reinforcements—didn't want them—fearing that from the moment it was known they were coming he would be immediately attacked and a civil war would be under way. Anderson was like many of his peers, a military man who detested war because he knew how horrible it was. "An appeal to arms and to brute force is unbecoming the age in which we live," Anderson wrote his South Carolina friend Robert N. Gourdin in December. "Would to God that the time had come when there should be no more war, and that religion and peace should reign throughout the world." He was secure for the present in his stronghold, and his intention was to keep still, preserve peace if possible, buy time for the excitement to die down, and hope to avoid bloodshed. He had asked for reinforcements when he first arrived in Charleston. But the time when they might have been safely sent had passed weeks ago.[30]

Anderson and his garrison were not heartened by what they read in the Charleston newspapers arriving on the daily mail boat. Anderson complained to the war department of "the animus of these people." There was no escaping it, even in the obituary columns. Young Thaddeus S. Strawinski, only eighteen, a volunteer with the Columbia Artillery at Fort Moultrie, had been mortally wounded by an accidental shot from a revolver. His obituary in the *Charleston Mercury* reported that while being carried by his comrades to the hospital he had said, "Friends, O, how sorry I am you are to attack Fort Sumter without me!"[31]

Now the batteries ringing the harbor were taking regular target practice, lobbing shells out into the ship channel. The garrison watched and noted that the range and accuracy were both improving. Anderson calculated all this with his keen artilleryman's eye, and admitted it was "pretty good." He regretted he had no ammunition to spare, to "show them our proficiency."[32]

Only Lieutenant Talbot, ill with his consumption, had seen any harbinger of good will. As he was alone in his room reading, a little bird "came gently tapping at the window pane having halted on his way to some more favored spot." Talbot confessed in a letter to his mother that he was not particularly superstitious, "but I chose to consider this a kindly omen without pretending to its exact interpretation."[33]

In the middle of February the Provisional Congress of the Confederate States in Montgomery took over in Charleston. Anderson's enemy was now the Confederacy, led by Jefferson Davis, a fellow West Pointer and one-time secretary of war. Davis had assigned a newly appointed brigadier to run the show in Charleston, and when Anderson heard who it was, he must have smiled ruefully. It was ironic. Anderson knew the man well; he had taught him all he knew about artillery.

The new commander and old friend, Pierre Gustave Toutant Beauregard, one of the young engineering wizards of the Mexican War, arrived on March 1. He was forty-two now and graying slightly, but he still had that compact figure and that same quick intelligence and practiced engineer's eye. Until a few weeks ago when Louisiana had seceded, he had been the new superintendent of the military academy. Now he was in Charleston in rebellion against the flag he had served all those years, ordered to seize Fort Sumter at the first opportunity, and until then to prevent it from being reinforced.[34]

Nobody knew Fort Sumter better than Beauregard. As an army engineer he had helped build it. He knew its strengths and weaknesses and its interior arrangements in detail. He understood well what firepower Anderson could and couldn't bring to bear against his batteries in the harbor. He knew if properly garrisoned and armed, it would be "a perfect Gibralter," impregnable to anything but endless shelling, night and day, from the four points of the compass. He knew that his principal asset was the small size of the garrison now manning it. It must be kept small.[35]

He also knew the officers in the garrison. As he gazed across the harbor at the unfinished fort, he must have thought of Robert Anderson, his dear friend and mentor, with mixed emotions. When Beauregard was a cadet, Anderson had been his instructor of artillery, and after he graduated Beauregard had stayed on for a while as his assistant. It would be no picnic exchanging cannonades with so skillful a cannoneer. Beauregard hoped it would not come to that.

Another officer in the new Confederate provisional army, Major David Rumph Jones, Beauregard's chief of staff, was also looking across the water at Sumter with mixed emotions. He also had friends in the garrison—friends and classmates—Foster and Seymour, as dear to him as Anderson was to Beauregard. Jones was the same agreeable man they had all known as "Neighbor" at West Point. He was more stately and mature now, and he had married into the upper echelons of Confederate society. His wife, Rebecca, a niece of Zachary Taylor, was also a cousin of Jefferson Davis's first wife.[36]

The three officers in Sumter, who had such binding ties to their enemy, knew that in Beauregard they faced a dangerous and resourceful foe. There was no question in their minds that his presence insured that whatever the rebels now did would be done with skill and sound judgment. On March 4 Anderson saw through his binoculars a flurry of movement around the harbor and knew that his old friend and protégé had assumed command and was making an inspection. They could now expect the noose to tighten.[37]

The changes began to come immediately. A system of detached batteries went up along the shores of both Morris and Sullivan's islands. Foster observed mortar batteries appearing just beyond the range of Sumter's guns at every available point on the bay. It was clear that Sumter was to be the center of a circle of fire. Beauregard was correcting some of the faults Foster had criticized when the engineering was in South Carolina's hands. The rebel commander was making no attempt to disguise anything he was doing. He was hiding nothing from them. There was no need to.[38]

Bending over maps and plans in his office in Charleston, flanked on either side of his table by two vases filled with freshly cut flowers,[39] Beauregard worked quickly. He was having to change some misconceptions, and he was trying to do it with tact and sensitivity. By March 8 he was able to report some progress. "Every one here," he wrote Confederate Secretary of War Leroy P. Walker, "seems to be gradually becoming aware, through my cautious representations, that we are not yet prepared for the contest." He agreed with Walker that the first priority was to keep reinforcements from Fort Sumter by strengthening the channel defenses. He hoped to accomplish that "in about a week or ten days." In the meantime, he assured the secretary, "I will go on organizing everything around me." By mid March he was telling Walker: "I am straining every nerve. . . . I believe in a very few days I will be ready at all points."[40]

There was also a new government in Washington. Abraham Lincoln had been sworn in on March 4. Buchanan, visibly relieved, had passed the brutal problem of secession and civil war on to his successor and returned to his peaceful estate in Pennsylvania. It had all been more than he could handle.

In his inaugural address, Lincoln had said something very pertinent to the situation in Charleston Harbor. He said that he intended to "hold, occupy, and possess the property, and places belonging to the government."[41]

Estimates by all of the officers at Fort Sumter of how large a force it would take to hold, occupy, and possess their place were already on hand in Washington. They had written down their opinions in late February, at Anderson's request. Their calculations ranged from Lieutenant Davis's optimistic reckoning that it would take only 3,000 troops and six ships of war, to the more pessimistic and realistic predictions of the senior officers of the garrison that it would take 10,000 to 20,000 regulars, more than the nation possessed.[42]

Anderson believed it couldn't be done now with less than 20,000 good and well-disciplined troops. Seymour argued that it would take at least that. He considered it highly unlikely that Sumter could be provisioned at all now by ruse or by a few men with a few provisions. To supply it openly by vessels alone, unless they were shot-proof, was now virtually impossible. The numerous batteries frowning on them from every direction were simply too formidable. An all-out attack would bring help flying to Charleston from as many directions as there were guns. At least 20,000 secessionist marksmen from neighboring states, trained for months past, would swarm into South Carolina before an attacking force could set sail from northern ports. The harbor would be closed, and would become a Sebastopol. It struck Seymour that unlimited means would be necessary to break through, and by then the garrison would be starved out anyhow.[43]

Being starved out was now a probability no matter what happened. Anderson had just told Washington, to Lincoln's great dismay, that provisions were dangerously low and that he could not hold out much longer. Since Anderson had not been clamoring to be resupplied, everybody had assumed he was well-enough stocked to hold out for some time yet. But that wasn't so; Anderson hadn't asked to be resupplied simply because he hadn't wanted to risk a war. When he was told within hours after his inaugural that the garrison was running out of everything, Lincoln was stunned. He had to decide what to do about it, and he had to decide soon.

Lincoln and Anderson were acquainted. Anderson had been the inspector general of the Illinois Volunteers in the Black Hawk War in 1832 and had sworn young Captain Lincoln into the service with his Clary Grove boys and mustered him out again when the war ended. Now, nearly thirty years later, Lincoln wanted to do what he could for him.

On March 15 the president asked his secretary of war, Simon Cameron, if he thought it wise under the circumstances to attempt to provision the fort, assuming it was still possible. The answer was an emphatic no. No lesser authority than the general in chief of the army himself, the tottering but still unquenchable Winfield Scott, said no. In the first days of the crisis in November and December, Scott had insistently urged it. Now he was saying no because "as a practical military question the time for succoring Fort Sumter with any means at hand had passed away nearly a month ago. Since then a surrender under assault or from starvation has been merely a question of time."[44]

Indeed, despite what Lincoln had said at his inaugural, it was generally assumed now that Fort Sumter was not to be provisioned, but evacuated—and soon. The highest officials in Washington—notably Secretary of State William H. Seward—were promising as much to South Carolina on a daily basis. By late March everybody seemed to believe it. Anderson and his little garrison also believed it, and when Lincoln's friend Ward Hill Lamon visited Sumter on March 25 what he said made them certain of it. South Carolinians believed it, because their emissaries in Washington were assuring them that evacuation would occur at any moment. All those batteries Beauregard was building around Sumter might not be necessary after all.

But everybody seemed to be forgetting what Lincoln had said in his inaugural, everybody but him. The president hadn't given up the idea of holding, occupying, and possessing the government property. While the army hadn't given him any encouragement, the navy had. There were those in the navy who not only believed Sumter could be provisioned, but that it ought to be, and that they could do it—and Lincoln was listening. .

The last days of March came and went and there was still no evacuation. Secessionists in Charleston and Montgomery were growing daily more uneasy. Associate Supreme Court Justice John A. Campbell, their chief inside source with a direct line to Seward, had assured them on March 15 that he was confident Sumter would be evacuated in five days. At the end of the five days he wired that he was confident that the decision still held. Then on All Fools' Day he telegraphed Governor Pickens in Charleston that "I am authorized to say this Government will not undertake to supply Sumter without notice to you."[45]

Whoa! cried every secessionist from Charleston to Montgomery. That didn't sound like evacuation to them. In fact, Lincoln had decided to adopt the navy's plan and had set the wheels in motion.

Anderson and his beleaguered little garrison knew nothing of this. They had been led to believe they would be evacuated, and were as anxious to be gone as the Confederates were to have them gone. Their last barrel of flour had been issued on March 29, and Anderson was sick of the whole business. "The truth is," he wrote the war department, "the sooner we are out of this harbor the better. Our flag runs an hourly risk of being insulted, and my hands are tied by my orders, and if that was not the case, I have not the power to protect it. God grant that neither I nor any other officer of our Army may be again placed in a position of such mortification and humiliation."[46]

On April 7, the day after he wrote that, a message arrived from Washington pressing him to hold out if he could until the eleventh or twelfth, for flour was on its way. An expedition was to arrive at Charleston harbor, and if his flag was still flying it would "attempt to provision you, and, in case the effort is resisted, will endeavor also to re-enforce you."[47]

This news took Anderson's breath away. He replied shakily that he would do his duty as a soldier, "though I frankly say that my heart is not in the war which I see is to be thus commenced."[48]

The next day the secessionists, who had been in an angry sweat since Campbell had told them Sumter would not be resupplied without advance word, got the advance word—with help from Lieutenant Talbot. In the midst of all the turmoil, Talbot had been transferred to Washington—something he had been expecting—and had barely arrived when the secretary of war sent him back to Charleston with a message for Pickens from the president. Talbot and Robert S. Chew of the state department arrived in Charleston on April 8 and Chew formally presented the bad news to the governor and Beauregard.

Allowing a moment for Beauregard to digest the notice of the resupply operation, Talbot then asked to be permitted to return to Sumter, to be with the garrison. Certainly not, snapped Beauregard. Then could he go there, speak with Anderson, and return? Absolutely not, Beauregard said icily, there would be no further communication whatever with Anderson now except to convey an order to evacuate the fort.[49]

In a few quick strokes, Beauregard then cut Sumter off entirely from the outside world. He seized all of its mail—including Anderson's sad-hearted letter to Washington acknowledging the coming attempt to provision him—and stopped all supplies to the fort. He wired the news to the Confederate secretary of war in Montgomery and sat back to await further orders.

On April 1, a month after he arrived at Charleston, Beauregard had telegraphed Secretary Walker that all of his batteries were in place and ready to open on Sumter. "What instructions?" he had asked then.[50] Now the instructions came—emphatic and tight-lipped. Lincoln wanted to send groceries to starving men, but as far as the Confederate leadership at Montgomery was concerned war was coming with the groceries.

"Under no circumstances," the Confederate war department now wired Beauregard, "are you to allow provisions to be sent to Fort Sumter." Two days later, on April 10, the provisional government went a step further. If Beauregard thought that the intention was to supply Fort Sumter by force, he was to "at once demand its evacuation and if this is refused proceed, in such manner as you may determine, to reduce it." Beauregard replied that the demand would be delivered the next day at noon.[51]

The next day, April 11, broke bright and clear in Charleston, and Dr. Crawford was clearly impressed by what was happening in the harbor. From the first break of dawn the waters swarmed with activity. The harbor was covered with the sails of ships putting hastily to sea. The guard boats were running busily between the harbor and the bar, signaling incessantly. "Nothing," Crawford marveled, "could exceed the activity everywhere manifested."[52]

Anderson could have explained it all to Crawford. As he gazed on the scene it was clear to him that the Confederates were expecting the arrival of a hostile force, and were making ready to receive it. They were obviously aiming their guns where provisions would have to be landed. "Had they been in possession of the information contained in your letter," he wrote the war department with no hope that the message would ever be posted, "they could not have made better arrangements than those they have made, and are making, to thwart the contemplated scheme."[53]

They were, of course, in possession of the information, having confiscated all the mail, and were acting accordingly. Beauregard had stopped every other courtesy as well, and the surveillance of Sumter had become implacable. The noose had been hitched up several notches.

For Foster, life had been more hectic than normal for the past several days. The four-gun battery on Sullivan's Island had been unmasked on April 8. The battery could enfilade the terrepleins on both flanks of the works at Sumter and sweep the outside of the scarp wall where a provisioning vessel would be likely to tie up. Foster rushed to throw up a traverse to intercept the fire and to shield the guns that would have to reply to such an attack. At dawn on the eleventh the floating Confederate battery on the upper end of Sullivan's Island had been run up and anchored on the shore where it could sweep the left flank of the fort. This was particularly frustrating, since the breakwater would protect the battery from any of Sumter's ricocheting shots.[54]

Foster cut an opening large enough to receive a barrel at the only embrasure that could possibly be used under the circumstances. The reprovisioning plan seemed madness, and the sense of doom and foreboding continued to grow in Anderson's mind. He felt he ought to have been informed earlier and allowed to counsel against the scheme. He had told the war department in one of the letters the Confederates had confiscated that he feared "its result cannot fail to be disastrous to all concerned." It was going to be particularly suicidal for the men who would attempt to reprovision them. Anderson and his officers and men felt more fear for their fate than for the garrison's.[55]

This meant war. But it was too late now. The ships of the expedition force had already sailed from New York. They would soon be standing outside the bar, ready to blast their way in. There was nothing to do but get ready to receive them. Anderson moved the garrison out of quarters under the cover of the casemates. Foster and his engineers readied water pipes and faucets to fight the inevitable fires the bombardment was certain to start. The men distributed shot and shell to the guns. Cartridge bags—the cloth containers for the cannon charges—were going to be a problem. There were only about seven hundred on hand, not nearly enough. More would have to be stitched out of whatever cloth they could find—blankets, sheets, shirts, socks, anything—and there were but half a dozen needles in the entire fort; there would have to be sewing around the clock.[56]

Even as they worked, their cupboard was becoming alarmingly bare. Foster had tried to get his forty sympathetic workmen still at Sumter evacuated, but the Confederates wouldn't hear of it. So they had to continue to be fed with the rest of the garrison. Bread, like cartridge bags, had been in scarce supply for days. Now it was gone. So was firewood; they had dismantled the last of the temporary buildings on the parade and burned the wood days ago.

If food and firewood were more plentiful on the Confederate

side, the mood was hardly more upbeat. Martin J. Crawford had wired Beauregard grimly from Washington on April 9 that "diplomacy has failed. The sword must now preserve our independence."[57]

That about summed it up. The Confederate provisional government was unsheathing the sword, and while most South Carolinians favored it, they weren't necessarily happy about it. Mary Chesnut had begun keeping a diary while her husband, James Chesnut, Jr., the former U.S. senator from South Carolina and now an aide to General Beauregard, was away in the harbor doing mysterious things.

"Why did that green goose Anderson go into Fort Sumter?" Mary agonized in her diary. "Then everything began to go wrong."[58]

Another errant U.S. senator, Louis Trezevant Wigfall of Texas, a stormy hothead whom Horace Greeley of the *New York Tribune* described as "a Carolinian by birth, a Nullifier by training, and a duelist by vocation,"[59] had come down to Charleston, still on the Senate payroll, to be in the middle of things. Mary Chesnut judged him to be "the only thoroughly happy person I see."[60]

Young Roger Atkinson Pryor, another firebrand and ex-U.S. congressman, had come down to Charleston to be in the middle of things, too—and if possible to help get something started. Unlike Wigfall, he had resigned his seat in Congress, to attach himself to Beauregard's staff and to agitate openly. He was disgusted that his state, Virginia, hadn't yet seceded, but he knew exactly what needed to be done to make that happen.

Speaking in a hotel in Charleston on April 10 he said: "I thank you especially that you have at last annihilated this accursed Union, reeking with corruption and insolent with excess of tyranny. Not only is it gone, but gone forever. As sure as tomorrow's sun will rise upon us, just so sure will old Virginia be a member of the Southern Confederacy; and I will tell your Governor what will put her in the Southern Confederacy in less than an hour by a Shrewsbury clock. Strike a blow! The very moment that blood is shed, old Virginia will make common cause with her sisters of the South."[61]

The ball was about to commence.

The
First
Shot

General Beauregard's three staff officers stepped into a boat in Charleston at about 2:30 in the afternoon on April 11. They rowed across the harbor toward Fort Sumter under the muzzles of forty-seven Confederate guns, aimed and ready.

John Gray Foster knew there were forty-seven. He had counted them all several times. There were thirty cannon and seventeen mortars. He had watched them go up through his binoculars. He had estimated their caliber and range, pinpointed their positions, and noted their ever-improving accuracy in practice rounds or when they fired salutes to visiting Confederate dignitaries. He thought he had a handle now on what the garrison was in for when the ball began.[1]

Fort Sumter could theoretically reply with equal firepower. The garrison had twenty-seven guns on the barbette tier and twenty-one in the casemates below; forty-eight in all, plus five columbiads on the parade serving as makeshift mortars, one of them tilted toward Charleston, the other four toward Cummings Point only 1,325 yards away. But when all that metal started flying in from around the harbor it was doubtful if any but the twenty-one round-shotted guns in the casemates could be fired. It was doubtful if any living thing could survive on the open-aired barbette tier or on the parade. It was doubt-

219

ful if any of these guns, protected or unprotected, could be fired for long given the limited supply of ammunition and the scarcity of cartridge bags and needles to stitch them with.[2]

The little boat from Charleston, flying a white flag and carrying Beauregard's three aides-de-camp, Colonel James Chesnut, Jr.—Mary's husband—Lieutenant Colonel A. R. Chisolm, and Captain Stephen D. Lee, reached Sumter's wharf at 3:45 in the afternoon. Lieutenant Jefferson Davis, the officer of the day, went out to meet them, and Major Anderson received them in the guardroom.[3]

The three emissaries handed Anderson his eviction notice. "The Confederate States," it read, "can no longer delay assuming actual possession of a fortification commanding the entrance of one of their harbors, and necessary to its defense and security." Beauregard assured Anderson that "all proper facilities will be afforded for the removal of yourself and command, together with company arms and property, and all private property, to any post in the United States which you may select. The flag which you have upheld so long and with so much fortitude, under the most trying circumstances, may be saluted by you on taking it down."[4]

Anderson read Beauregard's dispatch, excused himself, and called his officers to a conference in his private quarters. There he laid out the facts: A relief expedition was on the way, might be standing in the harbor at any moment, and here is the formal demand to evacuate. What did they think? A long earnest discussion followed, and Anderson emerged half an hour later with a written reply.[5] "It is a demand with which I regret that my sense of honor, and of my obligations to my Government, prevent my compliance," it said.[6]

Anderson and Dr. Crawford walked the three Confederates back to their boat, and as they were climbing in with the written refusal in their hands, Anderson said offhandedly, "Gentlemen, if you do not batter the fort to pieces about us, we shall be starved out in a few days."

Chesnut paused, half-in and half-out of the boat. What was that he said? He wasn't sure he had heard right. Would Anderson care to repeat it?

"If you do not batter the fort to pieces about us," Anderson repeated obligingly, "we shall be starved out in a few days."[7]

Well now, this put an entirely different coloration on the matter.

The three aides-de-camp rowed quickly back to Charleston and handed Beauregard the written refusal to evacuate and told him what Anderson had just said. Beauregard immediately wired Montgomery. Then everybody settled in to wait.

The Confederates manning the guns ringing the harbor had expected the order to open fire at 8:00 P.M. Everybody in Charleston had checked their watches. But eight o'clock came and went and nothing happened. The night wore on toward midnight and there was still no gunfire. The scores of Charlestonians who had lined the Battery all evening to see the show began drifting away to bed.[8]

Yet everyone knew they were but a command away from a great, perhaps a tragic, event.

The answer to Beauregard's dispatch arrived from Montgomery at about 11:00 in the evening, and Beauregard penned another message to Anderson. The three aides-de-camp, joined this time by ex-Congressman Roger Pryor, got back in the boat and rowed once more for Fort Sumter. At 12:45 in the morning they put in at the wharf and handed Anderson a revised eviction notice. If Anderson would state precisely when he would evacuate, Beauregard wrote this time, he would abstain from battering the place down.

Anderson stalled as long as he could, meeting at length with his officers, leaving the three emissaries to cool their heels in the guardroom. Finally by 3:15, when they were unwilling to wait any longer, Anderson wrote out his reply. He would evacuate the fort by April 15, three days hence, if—here was the rub—if not ordered otherwise by Washington or if not resupplied before then.

They had waited around for two and a half hours in the middle of the night to hear Anderson tell them that? At 3:20 Chesnut dictated, as Lee wrote and Chisolm copied, a courteous but terse response, and handed it to the major: The batteries in the harbor will open fire on him in precisely one hour.

Anderson read the note gravely and answered solemnly: "Gentlemen, I will await your fire."

He and Foster, the polite hosts always, escorted them to the wharf. As the Confederates climbed into the boat where Pryor waited—he had not come in—Anderson pressed each of their hands sadly, cordially, and said: "If we never meet in this world again, God grant that we may meet in the next."[9]

Imagine that, the firebrand Louis Wigfall chuckled when he heard about it later, Anderson "giving Chesnut a rendez in the other world."[10]

The little boat cast out on the water, all glassy and calm, and made immediately for old Fort Johnson, 2,400 yards away. They arrived at four o'clock, and were met at the wharf by Captain George S. James, commanding the Johnson batteries. On Beauregard's authority, the officers in the boat ordered James to fire the signal gun at the designated time.

James, recognizing the fire-eating Roger Pryor in the boat, said: "Mr. Pryor, I have always been a great admirer of yours, and now offer you the honor of firing the first shot at Fort Sumter."[11]

Pryor drew back in dismay. In a husky voice he said, "I could not fire the first gun of the war."[12]

Pryor welcomed the notion of striking a blow—he had boldly urged it—but his state hadn't yet seceded. It would be unseemly. That is why he had waited in the boat at Fort Sumter and not gone in with the rest of them.[13]

Another officer stepped forward to take up the offer, but James demurred. "No!" he said, "I will fire it myself."[14]

Fifteen minutes later, Beauregard's boatload of aides-de-camp stopped a moment in the harbor and lay on their oars. As they watched, a 10-inch mortar on Fort Johnson boomed and a shell "sped aloft, describing its peculiar arc of fire and, bursting over Fort Sumter, fell, with crashing noise, in the very center of the parade."[15]

More than a mile away old Edmund Ruffin stood gripping the lanyard of a cannon in the Iron Battery on Morris Island. Ruffin, another Virginian, was as disgusted as Roger Pryor that his state had not yet seceded, and had also come to Charleston to help get things moving. The old man, a noted authority on agriculture and a hot-headed firebrand, had been in the city since November—longer even than Major Anderson. He had started for South Carolina on Election Day, just after going to the polls to vote emphatically for the states' rights ticket of Breckenridge and Lane. He had been in Charleston ever since, preaching secession and looking forward to the first shot of the holy war. Now that moment had come and there he was, being asked by the boys in the Palmetto Guard to fire the first shot from the Iron Battery. He was bothered by none of Pryor's compunctions.

When he heard the signal shot from Fort Johnson he yanked the lanyard and sent his own cannonball streaking toward Sumter.[16]

Inside the fort, Abner Doubleday lay on his cot trying to get some sleep. Anderson had awakened him only half an hour before to inform him they would be fired upon within the hour. The shot from Ruffin's cannon rumbled in, struck the magazine where Doubleday was lying, penetrated the masonry, and burst near his right ear.[17] After that it became harder than ever to sleep. Within fifteen minutes the cannonading from the batteries encircling the harbor was general, the guns pounding away alternately, raining fire down on the unhappy fort. It was the reveille of a lifetime.

It roused more than just the 128 men and workers at Fort Sumter. It "woke the echoes from every nook and corner of the harbor," as Stephen Lee put it, "and in this dead hour of night, before dawn, that shot was a sound of alarm that brought every soldier in the harbor to his feet, and every man, woman, and child in the city of Charleston from their beds."[18]

Charleston's fifty thousand residents, many of them having retired in disgust from the first fruitless vigil only hours before, rushed to the waterfront, to their piazzas and housetops, throwing on clothes as they ran. Hurrahing wildly, they flocked to the Battery, "men without coats, women without crinoline and children in their night gowns."[19]

Mary Chesnut sprang from her bed and fell beside it to her knees. Prostrate, she "prayed as I never prayed before. . . . The regular roar of cannon—there it was. And who could tell what each volley accomplished of death and destruction."[20]

Mary knew that her colonel husband was out in that dark harbor somewhere in a rowboat. He and his three companions, after watching the first shot arch heavenward toward the fort and explode overhead, had rowed the three miles back to Charleston to report to Beauregard.

Three miles in the other direction, out to sea, another group of men saw the same arching shot and could do nothing about it. The U.S. Navy's Gustavus Fox had arrived outside the bar with part of his provisioning expedition at three in the morning. His flagship, the *Baltic*, had been in a gale the whole way from New York. And when he arrived, Fox had found only the revenue cutter, *Harriet Lane*, waiting. The plan called for two tugs and three ships of the line, the

Pawnee, *Powhatan*, and *Pocahantas*, to rendezvous there as well. But they had not yet arrived, and nothing could be done without them; they were the muscle of the expedition. All Fox could do was watch helplessly as the guns in the harbor rained their shot on Sumter.[21]

Francis Lejau Parker, a young Confederate gunner on Morris Island, gazed at the exploding ring of fire from the rebel batteries and marveled. "And now shell answers shell," he wrote, "and batteries from the various points send back to each other their warlike sounds until the whole circle plays on Sumter, lighting up momentarily her guns' outlines, scarcely visible in the morning light."

Through it all stood Sumter, "bold defiant . . . as quiet as death." The ball had fairly begun. But as one, two, nearly three hours, passed the fort still did not answer. Why? The question was on everybody's lips. Why doesn't Anderson return this terrible fire? A wave of admiration swept over the men in the batteries as dawn broke and they saw the Union flag still floating defiantly over the fort, heedless of the shot and shell whistling and exploding around it. What is Anderson doing?[22]

Anderson was having a leisurely breakfast. It wasn't much. The cupboard was nearly bare. Fat-pork and water—that's all that was left to eat. The men formed as usual, under the bomb proofs, and the roll was called as if nothing unusual was happening. Then they went to breakfast too, worried down a little of the fat-pork, and waited for assembly to beat on the drums. As they waited, they stared beyond the casemates at the shot and shell screeching and pounding without. By 7:30 in the morning when the drums beat assembly, they had been under fire for three hours. They were again paraded, and the orders of the day announced.[23]

Doubleday, the senior captain, would take the first tour at the guns, assisted by the engineering officer, Lieutenant Snyder, and the doctor, Surgeon Crawford. He would be relieved after the first four hours by Captain Seymour, assisted by Lieutenant Hall. Lieutenant Davis, with Lieutenant Meade, the other engineering officer, would take the third shift. The forty-three loyal workmen, volunteering to help, would carry shot, stitch cartridge bags, and assist the gunners.[24]

When all appeared ready, Major Anderson made a final inspection tour. "Be careful of your lives," he cautioned them all; "make no imprudent exposure of your persons to the enemy's fire; do your duty coolly, determinedly and *cautiously*. Indiscretion is not valor; reckless disregard of life is not bravery." With his brow anxious and his voice breaking, he said: "Manifest your loyalty and zeal by preserving yourselves from injury for the continued service of our cause; *and show your love to me by guarding all your powers to aid me through this important duty.*"[25]

Doubleday's first shot screeched toward the ironclad battery at Cummings Point. As he watched, it struck the sloping roof, caromed off, and skittered away into the marsh and creek beyond, scattering herons as it went. The feeling of relief in the batteries ringing the fort was palpable. At last Sumter had opened. The sound of a gun not their own had been heard; Major Anderson was not dead or asleep. Soon shot was succeeding shot. The guns of the fort also began answering Moultrie and pounding away at the floating battery.[26]

A reporter from the *Charleston Courier* described it. "The curling, white smoke," he wrote, "hung above the angry pieces of friend and foe, and the jarring boom rolled at regular intervals upon the anxious ear. The atmosphere was charged with the smell of villainous saltpetre, and, as if in sympathy with the melancholy scene, the sky was covered with heavy clouds and everything wore a sober aspect."[27]

Inside Fort Sumter it was pandemonium.

An Irish gunner took a breather for a moment behind a column. "Aye!" he exclaimed, "there's a great crowd o' them against us, but it's the Republic they're fightin'—not us—and, in the name of the Republic, we're able for them."[28]

Captain Doubleday was disgusted. Through the morning he had watched the shot from his guns bounce off the sloping iron rails of the battery across the way "like peas upon a trencher, utterly failing to make any impression."[29]

He was glad to see Seymour coming to relieve him.

"Doubleday," Seymour said with mock sternness, "what in the world is the matter here, and what is all this uproar about?"

"There is a trifling difference of opinion between us and our neighbors opposite," Doubleday answered straight-faced, "and we are trying to settle it."

"Very well; do you wish me to take a hand?"

"Yes, I would like to have you go in."

"All right. What is your elevation and range?"

"Five degrees, and twelve hundred yards."

"Well, here goes!" Taking up where Doubleday left off, Seymour went to work with a will. But he could also only watch his shot carom off the roof of the iron battery and bound into the marsh beyond.[30]

There was not much that could be done about it. The fort could deliver only solid shot and horizontal fire. The only mortars were in the parade and they were unreachable under the heavy Confederate cannonade. Nor were the guns on the barbette tier of any use. They were the most powerful in the fort, but might as well not exist; they were simply too exposed. Not even the traverses Foster had built would protect a man's life up there.

Anderson decided early that only the guns in the casemate would be employed. That immediately cut the fort's firepower by more than half—down to twenty-one guns—and those the least powerful in his repertoire, lacking sufficient caliber to take any serious toll on the enemy batteries. And even those must be husbanded very carefully. As fast as the six needles were flying, there was a painfully finite number of cartridges. Every spare piece of cloth in the fort was being transfigured into cartridge bags. But the six needles couldn't possibly keep up. At this rate the gunners would soon run out.

At midday Anderson scaled back his response. He was now firing only six of his guns—two against the batteries on Morris Island, two against Moultrie, and two others aimed at the west end of Sullivan's Island.[31]

As darkness fell, Sumter stopped firing entirely and the Confederates settled into a pace of a shell every ten or fifteen minutes. The night was impenetrable, dark and stormy with lightning and thunder, a rain that fell in torrents, and a wind that howled drearily among the sand hills. To light the darkness the Confederates burned night fires all along the harbor shoreline.

In Sumter the rain came as a blessing. It, together with the leaking cisterns, banked the fires started during the day. The needles continued to fly until midnight. Every scrap of clothing, extra hospital sheets, any coarse paper that could be found—all of it was falling under the scissors to make cartridge bags for tomorrow.[32] Several dozen pairs of Major Anderson's woolen socks had already been hurled at the Confederates.[33]

The reprovisioning fleet, or as much of it as was coming—part of it never arrived—stood helplessly outside the harbor. The Confederates had waited all day with nervous trigger fingers for men-of-war to begin knifing up the main ship channel. They continued to worry it through the night. But there was no movement, and it was difficult to tell who was more offended—the federal garrison or the Confederate gunners.

The Confederates considered the fleet's failure to come to the aid of their men at Sumter unchivalrous, not worthy of the courageous stand Anderson was making inside, even though an attack from them now would complicate their own lives. "Miserable cowards," the Confederates grumbled.[34]

The sun the next day, April 13, rose gloriously and chased away everything—the darkness, the gloom, and the lingering clouds. "Everything looks bright and cheerful," Francis Parker, the Confederate gunner on Morris Island, exulted; "our men are in fine spirits and the firing is steady, continuous and determined. Sumter shows no signs of yielding." Anderson this morning seemed to be concentrating his fire on Fort Moultrie and the floating battery, which was not floating at all, but fixed hard to the shore. He seemed to be ignoring the Cummings Point and the Morris Island batteries entirely, and this fact didn't escape the Confederate gunners' notice.[35]

Hot-shot began streaming into Sumter from the rebel batteries, bringing fire with it. Quickly this new shot began to tell on the garrison. By 8:30 the fires had started again in the officers' quarters and the casemates, and was threatening the magazines. The fort was becoming an inferno of exploding shells, crashing masonry, and acrid smoke. The buildings, riddled and broken, and wet with the rain and the water from the smashed cisterns, now burned with a terrible hissing, sending out dense billowing clouds of vapor and smoke. These soon filled the casemates, making it difficult to breathe. The men now had to stop often and lie on the floor with wet cloths—those that hadn't been fired away as cartridge bags—covering their faces.[36]

Nor were those faces any longer a pretty sight. The defenders of Fort Sumter, from Major Anderson on down, were blackened and begrimed by smoke and cinders, and their bodies were exhausted from the unrelieved strain of the bombardment.

The sight of Sumter afire, however, was a very pretty sight to the Confederates. "Fort Sumter is on fire, hurrah," exulted Parker; "thousands stand on sand hills, embankments and traverses, the cheering is deafening. It goes on from hill to hill till it reaches the farthest end of the island. Now we have him—but no, there wave the Stars and Stripes towering above the flames and smoke, cries of what a gallant fellow Anderson is, he is all pluck, pluck to the backbone. And now the shot and shell fall like hail on Sumter. Every battery redoubles its fire. Shells burst amongst the flames and shot after shot in quick succession, pound the front walls; brick and mortar fly."[37]

The situation inside Sumter was now desperate. The enemy's aim had become more exact since yesterday, and with the hot-shot it was now impossible to contain the fires. They had reached the magazines, the stair towers, and the implement rooms on the gorge. Ammunition had to be dumped into the harbor to keep the fort from blowing sky high. Moreover, Sumter's own firepower was now severely restricted. The stock of cartridges had continued to dwindle despite the night of stitching, and there was no staying ahead. Because of it the guns were down to firing at ten-minute intervals.[38]

At about 12:30 the flagstaff, which had been grazed by shot several times, finally took one shot too many. It splintered, broke in half and fell heavily to the parade. Lieutenant Hall leaped out of the sanctuary of the casemate through the fire, smoke, and ruin, flinging obstacles aside, to seize the colors. Everybody surged forward, straining their eyes to see through the smoke. After an agonizing moment, Hall emerged more begrimed than ever with soot, choking and about to faint, his face and hair singed, his clothes scorched, but holding aloft the rescued flag. A heartfelt cheer went up from parched throats. Peter Hart snatched the ensign from Hall's blistered hands as the heroic lieutenant slumped to the floor exhausted, and swiftly fashioned a jury-rigged substitute flagstaff. Within minutes, under Seymour's supervision, the colors were again flying defiantly over the fort.[39]

It had come the turn of one of the guns on Sumter's left face to hurl its shot. As its cannoneer, Private John Thompson, approached to load, a sight as stirring in its way as the flag flying again over the ramparts met his eye. There at the embrasure, staring in at him with blazing eyes, was Louis Trezevant Wigfall holding a saber with a white handkerchief tied to its tip.

Wigfall was a formidable sight under any circumstances. His friend Mary Chesnut thought him "the very spirit of war."[40] He was tall and powerfully built with a wild mass of black hair tinged with gray. His straight broad brow, from which hair shot up like the vegetation on a river bank, shrouded beetling black eyebrows. His mouth was coarse and grim, his jaw square, his nose thick and argumentative. The eyes staring in at Thompson were of wonderful depth and lit, as somebody had suggested, by a light found only in the head of a wild beast, fierce yet calm. One got the feeling he would as soon kill you as look at you. He is said to have slain more than half a dozen men in duels. On the Senate floor he was venomous and taunting, indiscriminately insulting to his fellow senators and always eager for a personal confrontation. But one of his virtues, suggested by Horace Greeley, was his repugnance for conflicts between parties so palpably ill-matched, as in this case. Perhaps his greatest social failing, suggested by another admirer, was his desire to be always where he could be as rude as he pleased. And here he was at the embrasure at Fort Sumter staring rudely in at Private Thompson.[41]

A brief argument followed, for Thompson was no pushover either.

"I wish to see the commandant—my name is Wigfall and I come from General Beauregard," the impostor announced. As he was hauled in he relinquished his sword to Thompson and turned to confront Captain Foster and Lieutenant Davis, who had stepped forward to meet him.

"Let us stop this firing," Wigfall demanded. "You are on fire, and your flag is down—let us quit."

"No, Sir," Davis said, "our flag is not down. Step out here and you will see it waving over the ramparts."

Wigfall ran out and looked up and was blinded by the smoke. Anderson, meanwhile, had arrived.

"To what am I indebted for this visit?" he asked Wigfall.

"I am Colonel Wigfall, of General Beauregard's staff," Wigfall replied. "For God's sake, Major, let this thing stop. There has been enough bloodshed already."

"There has been none on my side," Anderson reported, "and besides, your batteries are still firing on me."

"I'll soon stop that." Wigfall turned to Thompson, who still held his sword, and pointed to the handkerchief. "Wave that out there."

Thompson said something that boiled down to "Wave it yourself," and Wigfall snatched the sword and took a few steps toward the embrasure.

Anderson called him back. "If you desire that to be seen you had better send it to the parapet."

A white hospital sheet was soon produced and waved by one of the gunners, and Wigfall got down to business. "You have defended your flag nobly, Sir. You have done all that is possible for man to do, and General Beauregard wishes to stop the fight. On what terms, Major Anderson, will you evacuate this fort?"

"Terms? *I shall evacuate on the most honorable terms—or die here.*"

Would he evacuate on the terms proposed by Beauregard on April 11?

"On the terms *last proposed* I will," Anderson replied.

"Then, Sir," Wigfall said expectantly, "I understand that the fort is to be ours?"

"On those conditions *only*, I repeat."

"Well, Sir," said Wigfall, "I will return to General Beauregard." Bowing low he left by the way he had come.[42]

Beauregard knew nothing of this, of course. Wigfall was on the general's staff as he claimed, but he had been on Morris Island and hadn't seen the general in two days. The commander at Morris Island had sent Wigfall over, on his own authority after the flag had fallen, to ask Anderson if he was ready to call it quits.[43]

When Beauregard in Charleston saw the flag fall, he acted under the same impulse. He ordered Stephen Lee, Roger Pryor, and William Porcher Miles into a rowboat with directions to proceed to Sumter, inform Anderson that his flag was down, that his quarters were in flames, and ask if he needed help. Halfway there, the delegation saw that the U.S. flag had been hoisted again over the fort—Peter Hart's work. So they turned around and started back toward Charleston. They had not gone far when they saw a white flag now floating over the ramparts instead—Louis Wigfall's work.

They swung the boat about again and continued to bob along toward Sumter, arriving shortly after Wigfall left. On landing and being conducted to Anderson they asked if he needed help.

"Present my compliments to General Beauregard," Anderson replied, "and say to him I thank him for his kindness, but need no assistance."

All this wasn't looking quite right to Anderson. "Gentlemen," he continued in a worried voice, "do I understand you have come direct from General Beauregard?"

They assured him they had.

"Why," Anderson said, his alarm rising, "Colonel Wigfall has just been here as an aide to and by authority of General Beauregard, and proposed the same terms of evacuation offered on the 11th instant."

The three said they knew nothing of Wigfall's visit, but assured Anderson again that they had just left the general in Charleston. Would Anderson care to reduce to writing the terms proposed by Wigfall?

Anderson was mortified. Well, no, he didn't mind. But he was going to run his flag up again, regretting now that he had ever taken it down. He would not have done so if he had known Wigfall had not come directly from Beauregard—that he had not been the general's official emissary.

The three urged him not to raise the flag again until they could return to Beauregard with the terms of evacuation. Anderson agreed, and they hurried back to the boat and began rowing toward Charleston.[44]

It was midafternoon when Major David Rumph Jones and Colonel Charles Allston, Jr., climbed into a boat and headed for Sumter as Beauregard's second wave of emissaries. As they approached the fort at about three o'clock, Jones saw Truman Seymour standing at the wharf waiting for them. Even though Seymour needed a bath, Jones would have recognized his old classmate anywhere. Seymour must have seen the irony in all of this. Neighbor Jones had come calling—and on the most absurd bit of unneighborly business. Wait until Foster saw this.

Jones and Allston told Anderson, who was still trying to explain his Wigfall mistake, that they were authorized to offer the terms of April 11, minus the right to salute the flag. Anderson deplored this omission, and urged that it be reconsidered. The two Confederate peacemakers left, saying they would see what they could do.[45]

At about seven that evening Jones returned, this time with three others and the good news that the garrison would be permitted to salute the flag on leaving after all. Anderson read the final terms aloud to his officers and told them he was pleased—Beauregard was being most generous. It was agreed that the garrison would evacuate the fort at 9:00 the next morning.[46]

The issue had never been in doubt. Anderson's had been a token defense, but far more of a fight than what former Secretary of War

Floyd would have expected and hoped of a Kentucky soldier with a Georgia wife. Floyd had expected he would be more reasonable in handing over the fort. Even so it had been far less than what Anderson might have done. He had held out for thirty-four hours, but Foster believed the men would have cheerfully held out one or two more days, perhaps longer, on pork alone. He overheard one of the men say, "I would rather live on pork for two weeks than see *that flag* come down."[47]

It wasn't will that gave out; it was everything else. Nevertheless Anderson's dedication to his duty had left Sumter in ruins. The Confederates had poured four thousand cannonballs into the fort. Some six hundred shot marks pocked the face of the scarp wall. The living quarters had been demolished, the main gates destroyed, the gorge walls grievously damaged, the magazine doors sealed by the heat. Just about everything that could be burned was burned.[48] When the Confederates finally raised their flags the next morning it was over a wreck. As a reporter said, "it were as if the Genius of Destruction had tasked its energies to make the thing complete, brooded over by the desolation of ages."[49]

The next morning, Sunday April 14, was clear and warm. With the war had come the spring. The harbor teemed with vessels of every description filled with anxious spectators. Inside the fort a salute of one hundred guns began a long, cadenced booming; but at the fiftieth shot it abruptly stopped. What thirty-four hours of cannonading had not done—killed a man on either side—the salute had. A cartridge gun exploded, killing Private Daniel Hough instantly and mortally wounding Edward Gallway. The new war had claimed its first victims. Anderson wrapped black crepe around his arm, folded up the shot-torn colors to take as the winding sheet for his own burial day, and marched out of Fort Sumter at the head of his little garrison. The drums throbbed. The band played "Yankee Doodle" as the soldiers marched across the parade, then broke into "Hail to the Chief" as Anderson emerged from the gate.[50]

Beauregard wired Montgomery: "I have possession of Sumter."[51]

The evicted defenders boarded the Confederate steamer *Isabel*, and early the next morning with the rising tide sailed slowly out of the harbor. Confederate artillerymen on Cummings Point lined the beach to watch them leave, heads uncovered in a final silent salute to the commander who was "pluck, pluck to the backbone," and his soot-covered artillerymen. The *Isabel* took them to the *Baltic* waiting in the harbor. The expedition that had come to help them stay and could only watch them endure, would now take them home.[52]

Later that day—the fifteenth—Abraham Lincoln called for 75,000 volunteers to put down the rebellion, and four more states, including Roger Pryor's and Edmund Ruffin's Virginia, seceded.

So that was it. They didn't take it all that seriously in England. "Many a 'difficulty' at the bar has cost more bloodshed," editorialized the *London Times*. Virtually everybody in America knew it immediately for what it was, however—a national catastrophe. "The heather is on fire," George Ticknor wrote his friend Sir Edmund Head. "The Rubicon was passed," said Stephen Lee, who had seen it all firsthand and close up. "Oh to think that I should have lived to see the day when Brother should rise against Brother," cried a grandmother in Indiana.[53]

In late April Truman Seymour went home to West Point, and on a clear moonlit night fifty cadets marched to Professor Robert Weir's quarters to serenade him. Seymour came to the window after a while and responded with a patriotic speech. "We could see his features well," said one of the serenaders, "and he looked as if he had had a hard time at Fort Sumter. When he made his appearance at the window the cadets applauded everything that he said, from beginning to end. But he would have been applauded if he had not said a word, for actions speak louder than words, and his actions at Fort Sumter had preceded him and endeared him to every true American heart."[54]

The news of Sumter reached Seymour's old classmate John Gibbon at a fort in Utah Territory ironically named for John B. Floyd. The word had come by Pony Express from Fort Kearney. As spring had advanced and the threat of impending war had become more real, the anxiety in the garrisons on the frontier had become almost unbearable.

On "pony day" when the rider galloped into Camp Floyd and left a copy of the news at the post trader's store, Gibbon and all the other officers were waiting for him. Some had been waiting on the roof, peering anxiously out across the broad, dusty sagebrush plain toward the east.

"Here he comes!" someone shouted, and the cry, "The Pony is

coming," raced through the camp. Those not already at the store hurried there. And a reader read it all aloud: Beauregard's summons to surrender and Anderson's reply; the threat to open fire; the first shot; the harbor of Charleston trembling under the roar of cannon manned on both sides by officers they knew—lifelong friends trying to kill one another. All of them clustered about the store fell quiet, and eventually began to drift away with their broken hearts, all hopes of peace blasted.

"Our once happy and prosperous country was plunged into the horrors of civil war, the end of which no man could foretell," Gibbon thought sadly.

More news followed on successive pony days—the failure to relieve the fort, the final surrender, the excitement sweeping the country, Washington in peril, the marshaling of forces, Lincoln's call for volunteers, more states preparing to secede, and the general preparations everywhere for the struggle all now saw coming. Southern officers at the garrison began resigning and starting for home. Soon orders came down to break up, abandon the post, forget the rebellious Mormons and the Indians, and march to Fort Leavenworth in Kansas. There was more urgent business at hand.[55]

Dabney Maury—the adjutant for the Department of New Mexico—was in Santa Fe when he heard. He had been watching for the weekly arrival of the mail with the same suspense and anxiety as his old classmate at Camp Floyd. The days dragged between one mail delivery and the next. The mail came only once a week, and if the Indians chose to interfere, not that often. Officers at the post gathered on those days in Maury's parlor to wait for the mail to be sorted. Usually the letters from home were seized first. But not this time. They were pushed aside and everybody turned expectantly toward the reader.

One after another they took the sheet and tried to read aloud, and each voice broke with emotion and could not continue. When finally they had gotten through it, it was some time before they could grasp what they had just read. For several minutes they sat staring at one another in disbelieving silence.

Maury realized after a time that only the handful of officers in the room knew, and he seized the papers and ran out into the street to the officers' quarters shouting the news as he ran.[56]

At Camp Floyd, now renamed Fort Crittenden, the garrison be-

234

gan to dismantle. Most of its stores were sold at auction, the arms and ammunition were destroyed, and the soldiers started the slow, sad march to Leavenworth. Gibbon arrived there on October 8, seventy-four days after he left Fort Crittenden, and learned that his state, North Carolina, had seceded. He had been cut off for months from any communication with his family, and at Leavenworth he learned that his three brothers had joined the Confederate army. His heart was heavy when he went to reaffirm his loyalty to the Union.[57]

Maury, in Santa Fe, immediately sent his resignation to the war department and prepared to go home to fight for Virginia. He waited until Colonel E.R.S. Canby, who was out leading a large expedition against the Navajos, returned. The Canbys had been staying with Maury and his wife in Santa Fe. Maury carefully explained to Canby how and where he had distributed the troops of the department. When that final duty was done, he turned both his office and his house over to the colonel, and left with his wife for Leavenworth. He would go from there to Richmond to offer his services to his state.[58]

And so it was to be brother against brother, classmate against classmate, dear friend against dear friend. Whatever their choice, it was made with sad and wounded hearts.

Stonewall's
Great Locomotive
Heist

Whe n the Virginia Constitutional Convention voted to secede from the Union after the fall of Fort Sumter, Tom Jackson was a plain, "big-footed, taciturn, fearless, prayerful, tender-hearted and punctiliously polite" professor of artillery and natural philosophy at the Virginia Military Institute.[1] And he elected to fight for his state against his country, even though he deplored slavery, regretted the rebellion, and decried war.

He had seen enough of war to cause him to consider it "the sum of all evils."[2] But if your state was bound to fight a war, for whatever unfortunate reason against whatever enemy, then he believed that was the time to "draw your swords and throw away the scabbards."[3]

So when the governor of Virginia asked for a battalion of VMI cadets to help drill the state's new tangle-footed volunteers, Major Jackson took the cadet drillmasters to Staunton on Sunday, April 21, to catch the Monday morning train to Richmond. And when his name came up in connection with the important command at Harpers Ferry later that week, a member of the convention demanded:

"Who is this Major Jackson, that we are asked to commit to him so responsible a post?"

A delegate from Rockbridge acquainted with the resolute over-achiever from the class of 1846 answered:

"He is one who, if you order him to hold a post, will never leave it alive to be occupied by the enemy."[4]

The state's governor, John Letcher, already knew that. He was Jackson's neighbor in Lexington; he knew what kind of man Jackson was. He commissioned him a colonel of volunteers and gave him the Harpers Ferry command on Saturday, April 27. Harpers Ferry on the Baltimore and Ohio Railroad, with its armory and arsenal, was considered critical to the state's security.

Jackson's eyes must have blazed. It was perfect: an independent command where the next shot was most likely to be fired.

"The post I prefer above all others . . . ," he wrote his wife, Anna. "Little one, you must not expect to hear from me very often, as I expect to have more work than I ever had in the same length of time before."[5]

Jackson reported for work at Harpers Ferry two days later. The arms-making machinery at the arsenal was thought particularly important to the Confederacy, and Jackson's job was either to hold the arsenal and/or get the machinery out and sent south.

On the day he arrived, his command numbered two thousand volunteers and militia and was augmenting hourly. They were like all volunteers that early in the war—unorganized, undrilled, untrained, and ill-armed. Jackson began immediately moving out the machinery and whipping this green and growing army into shape.

One of the first distractions to stir his ire, disrupt his sleep, and aggravate his dyspepsia was the Baltimore and Ohio Railroad. The peacetime professor of artillery and natural philosophy found the war-time activity on the B&O's main stem insufferable. Whistling locomotives pounded up and down the line relentlessly. Heavy freights loaded with coal for the Union cause swayed and thundered eastbound by day. Empty cars rocked and banged and clattered westbound back up the main stem by night.

Permitting all those trains to pass unchallenged and untouched was hard on Jackson. Not only was the steam coal they hauled helping the enemy, but he knew the Confederacy was desperate for rolling stock, particularly locomotives. It could use some of those big engines thundering by. But since he was under orders from Richmond to leave the railroad alone for the present, he suffered and endured.[6]

By late May, however, he was through doing both. "The noise of your trains is intolerable," he had complained to B&O President John W. Garrett earlier in the month. "My men find their repose disturbed by them each night. You will have to work out some other method of operating them."[7]

The forty-one-year-old Garrett was not one to complain to lightly, or as a regular thing. Although his intimate letters revealed him as kindly and affectionate, his public persona was brawny, broad-shouldered, ironhanded, blunt-spoken, and given to working the road in rough clothes with his construction gangs.[8]

But Jackson, as his West Point classmates knew, conceded nothing to any man for blunt speaking. And he was at that moment in military command of the area through which Garrett's trains must pass. The president of the line was at the Confederacy's mercy and prey to Jackson's will. Jackson's will was that the B&O confine the nighttime traffic on its main stem to regularly scheduled passenger and express trains only.

Garrett's sidewhiskers must have quivered with impatience and displeasure. But he didn't have much choice. Jackson not only held the whip hand, but Garrett must have suspected that he had the temperament, and very likely the inclination, to shut down his line altogether.

Garrett no sooner had his nighttime traffic painfully rearranged to suit Jackson's taste than the infuriating Confederate commander took exception to his daytime schedule as well. He believed it interfered with necessary military routine. So the railroad president had to work out yet another arrangement: The B&O was now to funnel *all* of its freight traffic, eastbound and westbound, through a daily two-hour window—11:00 A.M. to 1:00 P.M.[9]

"We then had, for two hours every day," said Confederate Captain John D. Imboden, one of Jackson's officers, "the liveliest railroad in America."[10] It was a train dispatcher's nightmare.

Virginians awoke on May 23 to the palpable feel of history in the making. Great events hung like smoke on the morning air; it was the day of the state's secession referendum. The convention's decision to leave the Union was before the people for a vote. Virginians were going to the polls, and Jackson that day had scheduled major trouble for the B&O. While the electorate was at the ballot box endorsing

238

secession by three to one, he dramatically ended the hands-off policy toward the railroad. He had never liked it in the first place.

With the line's traffic patterns now constricted to his liking, he ordered Captain John Imboden at Point of Rocks on the Maryland side of the Potomac, to permit all westbound trains to pass as usual until 12:00 noon on that day, but let none go east. At noon Imboden was to disrupt the line so that it would take several days to repair. At the same time Colonel Kenton Harper in Martinsburg was to let all trains pass east, but let none go west. At noon Harper was to foul the line on his end. At that moment the B&O's main stem between Point of Rocks and Martinsburg slammed shut, bottling up fifty-six locomotives and more than three hundred cars in the thirty-one-mile pocket between the two points.

It was a train robbery to write home about. Jackson's earlier demands on Garrett for changes in the schedule were now seen for what they really were—a setup.[11]

Jackson's cache of confiscated locomotives and cars was for the benefit of the Confederate quartermasters in Richmond. The loot now collected in the yards at Martinsburg was ready for hijacking south.

It wouldn't be easy. There was a set of flimsy flat-bar rails running to Winchester that could handle light locomotives—and Jackson had bagged at least four engines of acceptable size. They could be put on tracks at the Manassas Gap Railway in Strasburg, if they could just get there. But between Winchester and Strasburg lay twenty miles without tracks of any gauge. It was a sizable hitch, one not generally covered in the West Point curriculum.

The way the war and everything else was moving from Winchester to Strasburg was down the Valley Turnpike, the "Great Wagon Road" that bisected the Shenandoah Valley. Why not the locomotives? Hitched to teams of horses, why couldn't they go that way too? It might appear bizarre, but the turnpike could handle it. It was one of America's premier highways, twenty-two feet wide, eighteen feet of its width covered by a foot-thick layer of macadam.

The four light locomotives were soon moving southward, dragged along by teams of horses through the turnpike traffic. It was cumbersome, unnatural, and comment-provoking, but it worked. All four of the engines made the gap to Strasburg and were soon on the rails to Richmond.[12]

By mid-June the Union army was seriously crowding the Confederates around Harpers Ferry. Brigadier General Joseph E. Johnston, now in overall command of rebel forces in the region, ordered the town evacuated. Jackson pulled out as ordered, leaving behind a chaotic legacy of blown-up and burning railway bridges and buildings. Jackson also put the torch to the captured locomotives and railroad cars at Martinsburg. He obeyed this last command with regret. He was not happy burning the rolling stock he had so cleverly liberated. But orders were orders.

"It was your husband that did so much mischief at Martinsburg," he confessed in a letter to Anna. "To destroy so many fine locomotives, cars, and railroad property was a sad work. . . ."[13]

The B&O's John Garrett doubtless agreed. He emphatically did not agree with what happened next. Iron doesn't burn all that well, and many of the locomotives were still salvageable. The Confederacy still needed engines. So the hijacking operation came back on line, big time.

The Confederacy had just the man to handle the job: Pennsylvania-born Captain Thomas R. Sharp, an acting Confederate quartermaster general. At twenty-seven, Sharp was already a seasoned manager of southern rail lines. He was a hard-nosed autocrat with the mind of a martinet, who had learned railroading in the old school. He wouldn't blink from enforcing discipline with his fists if his tongue wasn't getting the job done. He lacked nothing in imagination, originality, or brashness. The project required all three attributes. The locomotives to be sent south this time were far larger and heavier than the little rattletrap branch line to Winchester could handle. So the distance without tracks would be eighteen miles longer. But never mind. Richmond would send up Hugh Longust, another veteran railroader, to help out. Together Sharp and Longust organized a crew of thirty-five men headed by a twenty-one-year-old engineer named John O'Brien.[14]

Forty strong horses were requisitioned from farmers in the Valley. With this horsepower standing by, Longust pointed to a begrimed fifty-ton wood-burner sitting on a side track near the gutted Martinsburg roundhouse.

"That's the fellow we've got to begin on," he announced. "Go in, boys!"[15]

The boys—six machinists to deal with the engine, ten teamsters to drive the horses, and a dozen laborers to do the dirty work—went in. They swarmed over the big engine, an army of Lilliputians binding Gulliver. They uncoupled and drew away the tender. They jacked up the engine and stripped off everything that was detachable—side rods, piston rods, valves, levers, pumps, lamps, bell, whistle, and sand box—to lighten the load and lessen the chance of damage. They removed every wheel but the flanged drivers at the very rear. And they propped the front of the locomotive on a crudely built emergency truck fitted with thick wooden wheels. An iron bolt attached to the engine's bumper served as a linchpin.

A chain connected the beast to single, double, and "fou'ble" whiffletrees. They in turn were connected to the forty horses. The ten teamsters, at Longust's signal, cracked their whips. The horses, four abreast and ten deep and stretching a hundred feet ahead of their load, strained at the traces. The chain straightened and creaked. The iron horse lurched toward the Manassas Gap Railway thirty-eight miles to the south—three days away on the turnpike road.

The operation incorporated none of the stealth generally associated with big-time corporate theft. This making off with the goods was to the high-decibel, air-polluting accompaniment of cracking whips, groaning iron, jangling harnesses, stamping hooves, and snorts and whinnies and shouts and curses of horses and humans in unholy league. It was an operation calling for collective body English and mouths held just right.

Not infrequently a giant engine became simply too much for the turnpike's thick macadam crust. Then the locomotive sank axle-deep into the soft underdirt and had to be pried out with jacks and timbers. At times the thirty to forty horses were not enough; manpower had to be added. On the steeper uphill grades as many as two hundred men manned draglines in collusion with the horses, filling the air with shouts, curses, neighings, and wild singing. "On to Strasburg!" was the cry.[16]

Since this was war, the engines and their attendants were obliged now and again to stop and defend themselves or their cause. In such cases the locomotive's escort unhitched the horses, left the load wherever it happened to rest at the moment, and went off to answer the more urgent summons. The hulks waited there by the side of the road, silhouetted and solitary against the night sky. In at least two cases the escorts and the horses never returned and the engines, like beached whales, languished in abandoned solitude by the turnpike until the war's end.

Jackson's hijackers were still ransacking the B&O as winter turned to spring in 1862. In truth, Sharp was preparing his masterpiece. The candidate for heisting this time was Engine 199, a monster Ross Winans camelback cursed with a peculiar high-shrieking whistle and an engine house that looked like a sun porch. It was one of the biggest locomotives that Jackson's trainmen ever elected to send to the Confederacy. It awaited them on a side track at Mount Jackson south of Strasburg.

By this time the Union army had closed off the Manassas Gap Railway. If this behemoth was to make the tracks to Richmond it had to be dragged all the way to Staunton, seventy miles on the high and trackless road. And the Yankees by now were in a better position to dispute such highway robbery.

Engine 199 was stripped in the usual manner, hitched to its horses, and hauled the first few hundred yards to a sharp dropoff just south of Mount Jackson. The locomotive lurched down the decline and shuddered to a stop at the bottom, still headed south. Plunging on to Rude's Hill, it halted at the foot of yet another problem. Only with the help of a small augmenting army of soldiers and civilians did the balky leviathan make the hill.

The engine and its retinue toiled southward for four frenetic days, carpenters going out ahead of the caravan to shore up the bridges. As the load groaned on through the Valley, children ran out to point and holler, dogs to protest, and old-timers to nod sagely and agree that it was a hell of a way to run a railroad.

At the end of the four days, early in the morning, Old 199 is said to have lumbered into Staunton for a theatrical curtain call. As most of the town looked on, it is reputed—although the story may have been artistically exaggerated over the years—to have broken loose two blocks from its destination, careened down German Street, and toppled over in a thundering climax. If true, it was a showy denouement to what was the longest and most hectic journey of any of Jackson's appropriated locomotives.

The mastodon's indulgent escort soon had it up again and on the tracks to Richmond. From there it went to the repair shops of the Raleigh and Gaston Railroad in North Carolina, where all the other locomotives had gone to be refitted. Leaving the roundhouse in Raleigh with a new persona, Engine 199 went on to enjoy a distinguished high-shrieking career in the Confederate service throughout the rest of the war.[17]

The pageantry of the B&O's rolling stock swaying trackless down the Valley Pike had become a common sight by the spring of 1862, and it never lost its power to evoke wonder, comment, and alarm.

In Southern eyes the looting of the Yankee railroad was both justified and romantic. But to John Garrett it was simple grand larceny. Jackson, Sharp, and associates had not limited their practice to locomotives and cars. They had also helped themselves to assorted machinery, engine parts, rails, and even a roundhouse turntable. W. P. Smith, Garrett's master of transportation, viewed these depredations, together with the other affronts to Garrett's line in 1861 and 1862, with mingled disbelief, amazement, and disgust. "Remarkable events of a political and military character," he called them, events that "had a very peculiar influence upon . . . operations, deranging them to an extraordinary degree."[18]

Although he was indignant, Garrett couldn't help in hindsight but appreciate the inventiveness and know-how it took to heist his company's property. He was never able to accord Jackson a grudging acknowledgment personally. But he was able much later to pay his compliments to Sharp. When the war was over, Garrett tracked Sharp down in the defeated South and summoned him to Baltimore.

It is said that as Sharp entered the great man's office, Garrett growled: "Well, Colonel, your name is pretty familiar to us. A man who can steal a section of railroad, not to mention several million dollars worth of rolling stock, move the plunder across the country on a dirt road and place it on another fellow's line ought to be pretty well up in the transportation business."

If that had to be, Garrett this time wanted him on his side. "We have a vacancy in that department," he told Sharp, "and I have sent for you to offer you the position of master of transportation, not doubting your ability to fill it after the demonstration you gave at Martinsburg."[19]

So Sharp, Jackson's chief accomplice, became the right-hand man to the president of the line he had so skillfully plundered.

The
Shirttail
Skedaddle

By 2:00 in the morning on July 22, 1861, heavy clouds were rolling in over Washington, "forming a most fantastic mass of shapes in the sky." The full moon, which had so brilliantly lit the roads to the city earlier in the evening, had disappeared.[1]

At that moment an operator in the telegraph office on the war department's mezzanine floor tapped out an urgent twenty-one-word message to a member of the West Point class of 1846.

"Circumstances make your presence here necessary," the message said. "Charge Rosecrans or some other general with your present department and come hither without delay."[2]

By 6:00 in the morning the rain was falling in torrents and the "circumstances" were depressingly visible in the streets. The day before, Washington had seen the Civil War firsthand for the first time on the banks of Bull Run, a little stream near the plains of Manassas. Now despite the early hour the city was wide awake, staring in stunned disbelief at the straggling, rain-soaked remnants of a disaster.

The day before had been a Sunday, and Washington had greeted it with more than prayer and humble supplication. Politicians and prominent citizens and their ladies packed picnic lunches and rode gaily out the twenty-six miles to Bull Run to watch the battle that was expected to end the rebellion. Instead, a green Union army had thrown itself against a green Confederate army on the other side of the stream and been hurled back. The reeling, battered, and beaten army stumbled into Washington all through the evening and night, carrying with it the panicked spectators. Hundreds of picnics had been ruined.

The disaster confirmed Brigadier General Irvin McDowell's worst fears. For weeks the country had clamored for him to strike a blow. "On to Richmond!" had become the national mantra.

McDowell, the Union army's teetotalling commander, was as short on combat experience as most of his troops. He had never commanded so much as a company in battle. But he was one of the best military scholars and theoretical soldiers in the service. The members of the class of 1846 remembered him well. He had been the adjutant at West Point during most of their four years there.[3]

He knew his army wasn't ready. He also knew that his own classmate, Confederate Brigadier General P.G.T. Beauregard, fresh from reducing Fort Sumter, was out near Manassas Junction massing an opposing force of uncertain size.

McDowell had very little other hard information. William Howard Russell of the *London Times* ran into him repeatedly in the days before the battle. Russell reported that the general "did not hesitate to speak with great openness of the difficulties he had to contend with, and the imperfection of all the arrangements of the Army." Russell found that McDowell knew little or nothing of the country before him, more than the general direction of the main roads, which were bad at best. Nor could he get any information, with the enemy confronting him in full force all along his front. He lacked a decent map of Virginia and had not a cavalry officer capable of conducting a reconnaissance.[4]

McDowell had done the best he could with his lack of information, but he had been unlucky. By late Sunday afternoon his bid for laurels lay with the dead at Bull Run. So the telegram went out at 2:00 in the morning from the war department mezzanine to the benighted hamlet of Beverly in western Virginia. For out there in the dark was hope. Out there in the mountains was George Brinton McClellan, the star of the West Point class of 1846. The war department and the nation at that desperate hour so early in the morning and so early in the war believed that he was the one man who could now save the Union.

They believed this because of what had just happened in those laurel-knotted mountains two hundred miles from Washington. It was an improbable place to find an aristocratic Philadelphia physician's son in mid 1861. But it now appeared as if it had been written in the stars.

The past three months had been fast-moving for George McClellan. The bombardment of Fort Sumter and President Lincoln's call for seventy-five thousand state militia to put down the rebellion had turned West Pointers overnight into hot national commodities. The states of the North urgently needed experienced military talent to train and command the raw volunteers streaming to their standards.

No West Pointer was hotter than McClellan. Three states—Pennsylvania, Ohio, and New York—all sought the confident, talented young former captain, who seemed to know all about how war worked. It was McClellan who had written the exemplary study of the Crimean War in the mid-fifties. It was McClellan who knew as much as anybody in the country about strategy on a grand scale, and who had since become a happily married man and a railroad president in Cincinnati.

McClellan wanted to fight for his native state. He wrote his friend Major Fitz John Porter on April 18 that he would take the Pennsylvania command if it was offered. He wrote his wife, Nelly: "I feel that I owe much to my state. I am proud of it & would like to make it proud of me."[5]

But by April 23, the expected call had not yet arrived from Pennsylvania. So McClellan boarded a train in Cincinnati and headed for Harrisburg to speak personally with Governor Andrew G. Curtin. However, since Ohio's governor had asked him for an assessment of the military situation in the Ohio Valley, he agreed to stop over in Columbus on the way to Harrisburg.

Ohio Governor William Dennison was a Republican lawyer-businessman who lacked the politician's charisma and was therefore not very popular with the electorate. But he knew how to run large operations, and he was skillful and persuasive.[6] He sent Jacob D. Cox, a fellow lawyer-politician and new brigadier general of the Ohio militia, out to meet McClellan at the station.

The railroad executive who stepped down from the train to greet

Cox still had his boyish looks, although his waistline was beginning to crowd his belt. Cox found him "muscularly formed, with broad shoulders and a well-poised head"—"a good head firmly planted by a neck of bovine force upon ample shoulders," as a reporter from the *Washington Evening Star* put it. He moved quickly and gracefully on slightly bowed legs. His brow was small, contracted, and furrowed, suggesting some distant disquietude. His hair was dark auburn and his moustache short, thick, and reddish. He wore plain traveling attire and a narrow-brimmed soft felt hat. He seemed to Cox to be what he was, "a railway superintendent in his business clothes."[7]

However, as Cox listened to McClellan and the governor talk, he was impressed. The West Pointer's appearance was quiet and modest, but when drawn out he showed no lack of confidence in himself. Dennison outlined the problems that the new war presented. The state was expected to raise thirteen regiments, about ten thousand troops, one of every seven called for by the president. Organizing that rabble would require extraordinary leadership. Having carefully explained the setup, the governor offered McClellan the job on the spot, and he accepted. Pennsylvania was too late. New York was out of the running. McClellan's employers at the Ohio and Mississippi Railroad would simply have to understand. Even Nelly, "*you*, who share all my thoughts," would have to be told later.[8]

Dennison rammed a special bill through the Ohio legislature that same day. By evening McClellan had rocketed from a retired captain in the regular army to major general of volunteers and commander of all Ohio troops. The next day the offer of the Pennsylvania command arrived, twenty-four hours too late. It had preceded Ohio's bid, but had been sent by mistake to Chicago.[9]

Out at the armory in Columbus the next morning, McClellan began to see the dimensions of his problem. He and Cox found only a few cases of smooth-bore muskets, without belts, cartridge boxes, or other essentials. There were two or three worn-out smooth-bore six-pounder field pieces, and a tangled heap of mildewed harnesses. That was all.

"A fine stock of munitions on which to begin a great war," McClellan muttered.[10]

He immediately shot off requisitions to Washington for arms and equipment and issued his first general order to his undrilled troops.

"Discipline and instruction," he lectured them, "are of as much importance in war as mere courage." Indeed, he said, discipline and efficiency were "the surest guarantees of success."[11]

William S. Rosecrans, a volunteer colonel from the West Point class of 1842 who had left the presidency of an unsuccessful kerosene refinery in Cincinnati to answer the call, laid out a training camp seventeen miles east of Cincinnati on the Little Miami Railroad. They called it Camp Dennison and McClellan took his raw volunteers there and began hammering them into an army on his anvil of discipline.

The war department in Washington watched McClellan with a smile of satisfaction. Within the month it elevated him to command of the entire Department of the Ohio, including Indiana, Illinois, western Pennsylvania, western Virginia, and Missouri. It then promoted him to major general in the regular army—an instant catapult through five permanent ranks. A month into the war and not yet thirty-five years old, McClellan commanded all of the region west of the Alleghenies. He outranked everybody in the army except Winfield Scott, the general in chief himself, who antedated him by four decades.

The caldron in the new major general's expanding command was already seething. To the east across the Ohio River, western Virginia was in turmoil. The government in Richmond had taken the state out of the Union. But mountain Virginia, the two-fifths west of the Alleghenies, was balking. It was pro-Union, wanting nothing to do with secession.

This troubled Major General Robert E. Lee, the brilliant former captain of engineers and lieutenant colonel of the Second Cavalry, who now commanded Virginia's armed forces. In late April Lee had sent McClellan's classmate, Tom Jackson, to Harpers Ferry to harass the Baltimore and Ohio Railroad's top management. Now Lee ordered Colonel George A. Porterfield, another Mexican War veteran, to the western Virginia rail town of Grafton. Porterfield's orders were to "select a position . . . for the protection and defense of that part of the country." Lee told him he must hold both branches of the B&O to the Ohio River.[12]

When Porterfield reached Grafton in mid-May, he found himself a man without much of an army; recruits to the Confederate cause were hard to come by. And in Wheeling, a hundred miles to the northwest, a B&O freight agent named Benjamin Franklin Kelley had already cobbled together an opposing regiment. Kelley was a transplanted Yankee, who had migrated to Virginia from New Hampshire as a youth and brought his pro-Union convictions with him. He began organizing the first Union regiment south of the Mason-Dixon Line after the fall of Fort Sumter.[13]

McClellan was at Camp Dennison on Sunday afternoon, May 26, when word came in from over the river that Porterfield had just burned two rail bridges near Grafton. McClellan hurried back to Cincinnati and began sending telegrams. One went to Kelley with orders to set his First Virginia Volunteers in motion toward the destroyed bridges. Another launched supporting regiments out of Ohio and Indiana over the river and into the mountains.

From his dining room, in the utmost haste, with the ladies of his family conversing all about him, and without consulting anyone, McClellan sent messages of inspiration and reassurance to his army and to the people of western Virginia. His army was coming, he told the Virginians. But they shouldn't be alarmed. It meant them no harm; it was coming only to rid them of "armed traitors."[14]

As Kelley hurried toward the burned bridges, Porterfield backed out of Grafton. He moved his modest force of 600 Confederate infantry and 175 cavalry fifteen miles south, to Philippi on the Tygart Valley River. Clattering over a new covered toll bridge called the Monarch of the River, the Confederates filed into the sleepy little Barbour County seat and bivouacked. Philippi, where the only thing exciting that ever happened was a minor stir over a lawsuit at the courthouse, snapped awake. Suddenly it was occupied by one army and threatened by yet another.[15]

McClellan's advance under Colonel Kelley pulled into Grafton on Porterfield's trail Thursday, May 30. Big "Ben" Kelley wore a goatee, and a brocaded vest under a semimilitary coat, the coat being the only genuine piece of military clothing in the entire regiment. His men had come to the war wearing an irregular assortment of jeans and work clothes, and armed with knives and clubs of their own devising and rifles imported from Massachusetts. What ammunition they had they carried in their pockets.[16] But they were ready for a fight even if they didn't look it, and were being augmented hourly by the better-dressed, better-armed Ohioans and Indianans that McClellan was sending from over the river. With this force Kelley proposed to attack the Confederates at Philippi on Sunday, June 2.

The Confederate troops waiting there were even less prepared for war than their Union counterparts. Arms that Porterfield requested hadn't arrived. Such firepower as his small command possessed came down to assorted pistols, shotguns, and old flintlock muskets for which there were no cartridges, only loose powder and shot.[17]

Before Kelley could hurl his growing command against Porterfield's inadequate one, Brigadier General Thomas A. Morris of the Indiana volunteers arrived in Grafton. Morris was Indiana's first brigadier, a no-small-talk professional, another of those West Point engineers, class of 1834, who had planned and built the new Union rail depot at Indianapolis. A fellow Indianan saw him as "a man so quiet, so grave, so almost stolid in countenance and demeanor, with features so blunt, and coloring so dark and dead."[18]

Whatever he may have looked like, he outranked Kelley. Assuming command, he postponed the attack on Philippi by one day—from Sunday to Monday. Then he complicated it with a plan calling for pinpoint coordination. Two columns were to loop toward Philippi during the night. At precisely 4:00 in the morning on June 3 they were to arrive together from separate directions, cannonade, seize, and occupy the town.

Ebenezer Dumont, an Indiana colonel, would lead the first column. Dumont was a politician-soldier, a former two-term U.S. congressman and veteran of the Mexican War. He was said to be sallow, lean, irascible, and given to occasional attacks of devoutness.[19] He was to arrive in Philippi at 4:00 A.M., occupy the heights above the town, and at a prearranged signal bombard the Confederates with his two six-pounders.

Kelley would lead the second column. He was to feint a move against Harpers Ferry and then make for Philippi from the east. His orders were to attack in consort with Dumont's cannonade and cut off any attempted Confederate retreat down the turnpike. The plan looked good on paper; it all depended on the timing.

Porterfield waited at Philippi with a troubled mind. Reports were arriving hourly warning of an imminent attack. Two comely young Confederate sympathizers from Fairmont, the Misses Mary McLeod and Abbie Kerr, rode half the day on Sunday to warn him that five thousand Yankees had passed through their town with plans to attack him either that night or the next morning. Porterfield ordered his little army to be ready to march.

Then it began to rain, a pitiless, pounding rain, a downpour that drenched everything—Morris's two columns now on the march, the Confederate pickets on watch, and everybody's spirits generally. As the night wore on and the rain poured down, the pickets came to believe that nobody, least of all Yankees, would be out on such a night. They therefore headed for cover, and the rest of the Confederate encampment went to bed. Porterfield's plan was to get out of town early the next morning.[20]

On through the pitch of night, through the driving rain, through mud "deep in the ravines, slippery on the hill-sides," the Union columns slogged toward Philippi. At 3:00 in the morning Dumont found himself still five miles out and ordered his troops into double time, cajoling them as they ran: "Close up, boys! Close up! If the enemy were to fire now, they couldn't hit one of you."[21]

Out ahead of Dumont's column ranged a thoroughgoing extrovert named Frederick West Lander, a volunteer colonel and aide-de-camp to McClellan. Staying closed up behind the athletic Lander was not easy for any army. At age thirty-nine, Lander was already a nationally acclaimed transcontinental explorer. He had played a hand in five major pathfinding surveys on the western frontier in the 1850s, including one in the Pacific Northwest in 1853 with then Lieutenant George McClellan. Lander was born in Salem, Massachusetts, with the middle name of William, but had since changed it legally to West, more appropriate to his calling. Lander was of commanding stature and great physical strength, who in his spare time wrote stirringly patriotic poetry and lectured women's groups on the fine arts. Only eighteen months before in San Francisco he had topped even himself by marrying Jean Margaret Davenport, the Shirley Temple of her time. A famous and beautiful stage actress whose small voice chimed like a silver bell, Miss Davenport, now thirty-two, had dazzled audiences on two continents since her days as a child prodigy in England. On this wet, early summer night, her dashing new husband was hurrying toward Philippi to dazzle the rebels in western Virginia.[22]

With this restless romantic reconnoitering in front and Dumont shouting for his men to close up behind, the column arrived on Talbott Hill above the town miraculously on time. But Kelley had not yet arrived, and nobody had taken Mrs. Thomas Humphreys into account.

The sound of tramping feet outside her house on Talbott Hill in the early predawn had awakened Mrs. Humphreys, a Philippi housewife, mother, and Confederate sympathizer. She watched with ascending indignation as Dumont's troops deployed outside, and the two brass six-pounders were rolled into place under Lander's supervision and pointed toward the town. Everything was soon ready. They had only to await Colonel Kelley's arrival and the pistol shot that was to signal the six-pounders to open fire. As the moments ticked by and Kelley still didn't arrive, Lander's cannoneers grew ever more itchy-fingered.

Into this tense tableau Mrs. Humphreys unexpectedly injected herself, her strong Confederate sympathies, and her young son Oliver. She put Oliver on a horse with directions to hie into town and warn Colonel Porterfield. He got only as far as the first Union soldiers, who dragged him from his mount. Mrs. Humphreys rushed from the house, beat off the soldiers, and put Oliver back in the saddle. The soldiers pulled him down again. Then Mrs. Humphreys drew a pistol from her bodice and fired.[23]

It wasn't the signal Lander's light-fingered cannoneers had been waiting for, but it would do. They opened up with their two field pieces. A cannonball shrieked into town, jolting Porterfield's sleeping Confederates awake, making Oliver's trip unnecessary, and persuading them that their contemplated departure had been delayed long enough.

What followed has come down to us as the "Philippi Races," a genuine shirttail skedaddle. The Confederates leaped from their bedrolls and "pell-mell, helter-skelter, without boots, without hats, without coats, without pantaloons, through the town, up the southern road, over the wall of hills, away they fled, incontinently, ingloriously, ignominiously." They were soon well ahead of Porterfield's more orderly anticipated withdrawal scheduled for later that morning.[24]

Some eyewitnesses believed that the rebels were "in too great a hurry about taking to their heels to wait for any such perilous ceremony as putting on their clothes." Colonel Dumont reined up to watch the departure and muttered that they were "great on a run, if not much for a fight."[25]

As this juncture Kelley arrived, fifteen minutes late. Seeing the Confederates leaving without his input, he plunged into town in headlong pursuit. Careening into the streets about the same time was the unsinkable Colonel Lander, no longer able to restrain himself on

Talbott Hill. Mounted on his "gallant gray," and looking "more like a demon than a man," he exploded off the hill at a breakneck gallop, leaped a fence, thundered through the bridge hard on the heels of the charging infantry, and dashed through the streets in advance of the column.[26]

While Lander was rocketing down the hill, over the bridge, and through the town, Kelley was getting shot. Who shot him is a matter of some debate. The hyperactive Colonel Lander, easily the busiest man on the battlefield, is said in one account to have captured the suspect. In this version Kelley was shot in the right breast with an old-fashioned horse pistol by an eastern Virginian named Simms from down around Richmond.[27]

A second version had him shot in the right breast by a green mountain boy named John W. Sheffee. Young Sheffee, this account has it, "took dead aim at Colonel Kelly, and when the gun cracked he, with great glee, came jumping forward to his companions, and exclaimed, 'Sergeant, I have done it!' 'Done what?' 'I flopped that big fellow from his horse that was coming after us so savage.' "[28]

Whoever shot him, the big fellow thought himself done for. "I expect I shall have to die," he murmured. "I would be glad to live, if it might be, that I might do something for my country; but if it cannot be, I shall have at least the consolation of knowing that I fell in a just cause."[29]

McClellan, monitoring the action closely from Cincinnati, wired condolences through General Morris: "Say to Colonel Kelley that I cannot believe it possible that one who has opened his course so brilliantly can be mortally wounded. . . . If it can cheer him in his last moments tell him I cannot repair his loss and I only regret that I cannot be by his side to thank him in person. God bless him"[30]

For McClellan, Kelley's anticipated death was the only stain on an otherwise perfect morning. For the next two days the Confederates continued to put distance between themselves and the Monarch of the River. They didn't finally stop until they reached Huttonsville thirty miles to the south with absolutely nobody still in pursuit, not even Lander. They were not to be blamed for running, one critic said. That was understandable under the circumstances. What he blamed them for was that they hadn't stopped running when the Yankees stopped, which had been two days earlier.[31]

As the rebels fled south they gradually became more presentable.

Farmers living a half-dozen miles or more from Philippi testified "that the brave cavaliers came up to their doors begging for pairs of breeches to cover their nakedness."[32]

Philippi was the first land engagement of the Civil War and George McClellan's first victory. Although he was in Cincinnati 250 miles away, he was getting the credit. It had been relatively bloodless. Only five Union soldiers were wounded. Even Kelley, who was thought surely dying, lived to be thanked personally by McClellan, to be promoted to brigadier general, and to fight throughout the war. Owing perhaps to the nimbleness of the retreat, only two Confederates were shot at all. Each lost a leg, one of them to a random cannonball. Nobody died.

William Rosecrans, who had been sent to Washington by Governor Dennison to acquire pay and outfitting for the Ohio troops, wrote McClellan from there two days after the battle. The news from Philippi, he reported, "created a lively sensation of pleasure here." It was welcome solace for a city then draped in mourning for McClellan's old friend and Abraham Lincoln's old rival, Senator Stephen A. Douglas of Illinois, who had died on the day of the Philippi Races.[33]

It was not, however, welcome news in Richmond. It gave General Lee no lively sensation of pleasure. Control of western Virginia was too important, losing it more than he cared to concede. So he set in motion another attempt to hold it. This time he sent his own adjutant, forty-two-year-old Brigadier General Robert S. Garnett, into the mountains.

Garnett was an officer of great skill and reputation, another of those scions of the southern aristocracy with a West Point education, class of 1841. His father had been a five-term U.S. congressman from Virginia and his mother was the daughter of a French general. In the war with Mexico Garnett had been Major General Zachary Taylor's aide-de-camp. In the early 1850s he had returned to West Point as commandant of cadets and instructor of infantry tactics. Then tragedy struck. On the Northwestern frontier in 1857 he was away from his garrison on an expedition when bilious fever swept away his young wife and infant son.[34]

He had been "proud, reserved, and morose" even before that, "cold as an icicle to all." Now he became "more frozen and stern and isolated than ever"—and more single-minded.[35] "In every one else," a fellow Confederate officer wrote, "I have seen some mere human traits, but in Garnett every trait was purely military."[36]

This "dreary-hearted man" arrived in Huttonsville on June 14 to take over from the luckless Porterfield. By the next evening he had his inherited army on the move northward. His small force was being beefed up daily by volunteers from eastern Virginia, Georgia, and Tennessee. But it still looked inadequate for the job at hand.

Two turnpikes ran through the mountains in north central western Virginia. One curled out of Philippi south through Belington. The other swung through Buckhannon over the rugged pass at Rich Mountain. The two roads met at Beverly on the floor of the Tygart River valley and continued on as one into eastern Virginia. Garnett detached about a thousand of his troops to the western foot of Rich Mountain, and took the rest—about four thousand men—to Laurel Hill outside of Belington to face the federal army encamped at Philippi. At those two "gates to the northwestern country," fifteen miles apart, he dug in.[37]

The country he hoped to hold was stunningly scenic. It had been impressing people long before Garnett ever saw it. The earliest explorers who had to beat their roadless way over its rolling ranks of humped mountains, had grudgingly conceded its dramatic beauty. Robert Fallam, a member of the first expedition into the country in 1671, wrote of mountains so steep "that we could scarse keep ourselves from sliding down again." From one such elevation he saw only other "very high mountains lying to the north and south as far as we could discern." It was, he wrote, "a pleasing tho' dreadful sight to see the mountains and hills as if piled one upon another."[38]

For Garnett there was nothing pleasing in it. It was all dreadful, alien, and hostile, an uncongenial land in which he could attract but a handful of local recruits against a well-endowed enemy. The roads on which to move an army were few, narrow, and difficult. The mountainsides, of which there were far too many, were blanketed by laurel brakes stretching "like inland seas, and with never-fading leaves and snake-like branches interlaced."[39] Its terrain was difficult even for skirmishers to penetrate, and positions suitable for placing and handling artillery were rare.[40]

Garnett appealed to Lee for more men and arms, and Lee did his best. But as he moved into position at Laurel Hill, bountifully fragrant with the "cologne" of the western Virginia summer, Garnett felt doomed. The night before leaving Richmond he had said: "They have not given me an adequate force. I can do nothing. They have sent me to my death."[41]

Watching the joyless Garnett from Ohio, McClellan decided it was time for him to go personally to the front. On June 20 at about 11:30 in the morning he left Nelly, now six months pregnant, and caught a train into the mountains.

The first thing the young general met on the way was adulation, a "continual ovation all along the road." "At every station where we stopped," he wrote Nelly, "crowds had assembled to see the 'Young Napoleon.' Gray-headed old men & women; mothers holding up their children to take my hand, girls, boys, all sorts, cheering and crying, God bless you! I never went thro' such a scene in my life & never expect to go thro' such another one."[42]

To this applause he passed over the Ohio River and into Virginia at Parkersburg. On June 23 he was in Grafton. From there he hailed his troops: "Soldiers! I have heard that there was danger here. I have come to place myself at your head and to share it with you. I fear now but one thing—that you will not find foemen worthy of your steel."[43]

McClellan had come into the mountains with more than neo-Napoleonic pronouncements. He also had a plan. He would move Morris down from Philippi to Laurel Hill to keep Garnett "amused." He would place himself at the head of the larger force and personally lead the main attack at Rich Mountain. He would crush the rebel encampment there and sweep on into Beverly. Cut off and compromised in his rear, Garnett could only surrender, retreat, or be destroyed. The spine of Confederate strength in western Virginia would be snapped once and for all.

McClellan expected "to thrash the infamous scamps before a week is over—all I fear is that I can't catch them." However, he was having some trouble fixing on the number of scamps this might involve. "It is very difficult to learn anything definite about our friends in front of us," he confessed in his daily letter to Nelly. "Sometimes I am half inclined to doubt whether there are many of them; then again it looks as if there were a good many." Before leaving Grafton at the end of June he was estimating enemy strength at six to seven thousand, most of it with Garnett at Laurel Hill.[44]

Against this enemy, whatever its true size, McClellan could count on "some 18 rgts, 2 batteries, 2 co's of cavalry at my disposal—enough to thrash anything I find. I think the danger has been greatly exaggerated & anticipate little or no chance of winning laurels." He had a few organizational wrinkles to iron out. "Everything here needs the hand of the master," he explained to Nelly, "& is getting it fast."[45]

By July 2 the master was camped fourteen miles south of Clarksburg en route to Buckhannon and writing home that "I doubt whether the rebels will fight—it is possible they may, but I begin to think that my successes will be due to manoeuvers, & that I shall have no brilliant victories to record."[46]

On Independence Day, one of the hottest in memory, McClellan was in Buckhannon, still glorying in "perfect ovations" and being looked on wherever he and his army went as the "deliverer from tyranny."[47] He stood bareheaded in the blazing sun on July 4 and watched his delivering army pass in review, eight thousand strong; he had left four thousand more with Morris on Garnett's front. One western Virginian watched the soldiers march by and said, "Lordy, I didn't know there were so many folkses in the world."[48]

On July 5 McClellan wrote Nelly that the enemy was in his front and that he would probably move forward the next day, and come in contact with them the day after. He promised her that "I shall feel my way & be very cautious, for I recognize the fact that everything requires success in my first operations. You need not be at all alarmed as to the result—God is on our side." He confided to her that "I realize now the dreadful responsibility on me—the lives of my men—the reputation of the country & the success of our cause."[49]

On July 7 his army brushed aside a small Confederate detachment at the Middle Fork Bridge midway between Buckhannon and the rebel stronghold at the foot of Rich Mountain, now called Camp Garnett. Two days later his force pulled up warily at Roaring Creek two miles from the Confederate position. From that distance McClellan could not tell if the enemy had steel enough for his soldiers. But he believed there were more of them than he had originally thought. He now put the total Confederate force at 10,000—8,000 at Laurel Hill and 2,000 before him at Rich Mountain. That was about twice their actual numbers, in both cases.[50]

Dug in at his front were but thirteen hundred Confederates, positioned there on June 14 by Garnett. They were now under the command of Lieutenant Colonel John Pegram, a haughty West Pointer from the class of 1854, who had just arrived and whose familiarity with his surroundings was absolutely zero. Pegram had been among those who had first heard of this war in Dabney Maury's living room in Santa Fe only three months before.[51]

McClellan, whose acquaintance with the terrain was not much better than Pegram's, lowered his binoculars and ordered an armed reconnaissance. He hoped to stage a brilliant turning movement at Rich Mountain patterned on General Scott's much admired maneuver at Cerro Gordo in the Mexican War. But his reconnaissance soon told him it wouldn't work. The thick laurel-studded wilderness on both sides of the road seemed impenetrable. There was no one at hand who knew the way through that maze to the Confederate rear. What he needed was what Scott had—Robert E. Lee to find a way. McClellan hated to do it, but he decided that a direct attack on the Confederate front was unavoidable. William Rosecrans, now a brigadier general and back from Washington, would lead the assault.

On the eve of his first battle in the field McClellan was not happy with any of his top commanders. He complained to Nelly that he had "not a Brig Genl worth his salt." He considered Morris a "timid old woman." Newton Schleich "knows nothing." Rosecrans was "a silly fussy goose." McClellan had wanted an entirely different, personally hand-picked set of brigadiers. He hadn't gotten them, so he was making do. He did have with him, however, one hand-picked officer he trusted implicitly: his father-in-law, Randolph B. Marcy, the legendary explorer, who was his inspector general.[52]

Rosecrans, his leading brigadier, was forty-two, nearly six feet tall, lean and compact. He had an ample brow, a hawk nose, a well-trimmed beard, and penetrating, restless eyes. He had been converted to Catholicism at West Point, and was now an impassioned student of the Bible who loved to argue theology. He was also a workaholic, rarely retiring earlier than 2:00 in the morning, often not until 4:00, and sometimes not at all. He seemed to his bleary-eyed staff to have no need of sleep whatever.[53]

He was sleepless as usual the night before the proposed assault at Rich Mountain—up fussing, as McClellan might have described it—when one of his lieutenants brought in David Hart. Rosecrans had been looking all over for Hart, a young twenty-three-year-old with Union sympathies and an intimate knowledge of the tangled terrain around them. His father lived in a house in the saddle of the mountain two miles in the Confederate rear. The young Hart had herded cattle all over the region. Now on the eve of the scheduled frontal attack, he told Rosecrans he could show him a trail through the laurel brakes around the Confederate left to the Hart house. Here was Cerro Gordo on a plate.

Rosecrans took Hart to see McClellan. Presented unexpectedly at that late hour with the prospect of a turning movement after all, McClellan hesitated. For an hour they had to argue the plan's merits before he would give it his blessing. It was finally agreed that the march would get under way the next morning before dawn. Rosecrans would lead it, keeping in touch hourly with his commander. When McClellan heard the sound of battle in the rebel rear, he would storm its front at Camp Garnett. The march to the Hart farm was expected to take three hours.

Rosecrans set out before daybreak on July 11 with 1,917 Indianans and Ohioans. They filed into the underbrush in silence, under arms, without knapsacks, with one's day's rations, and their canteens filled with water.[54]

They had no artillery; there was no way to get a cannon through the thick laurel brakes, over the hanging cliffs, and up and down the steep ravines. At the head of the column was Hart and, as had become virtually obligatory there in the mountains, Colonel Frederick West Lander. Also present was a pounding rain.

About midmorning Pegram's Confederates intercepted a Union courier and learned that a federal flanking movement was under way. Pegram, misreading the information, assumed the movement was going around his right, rather than his left. So he sent Captain Julius A. De Lagnel, Garnett's chief of artillery, up the turnpike to the Hart house with 310 men. There De Lagnel hurriedly dug in on the road across from the two-story frame farmhouse. His men and their single cannon took up a position facing north, the expected direction of attack, and waited for it to come.

Rosecrans was running dramatically behind schedule. The three hours had already stretched into ten. It wasn't until 3:00 in the afternoon that Confederate pickets encountered his column approaching through the woods from the south. De Lagnel's startled command scrambled to the other side of the road and swung its cannon around. As the Union troops swarmed out of the trees above the Hart house,

De Lagnel opened fire. Rosecrans fell back under the cannon blast, regrouped and attacked again, fell back once more, and attacked a third time. It was not until about 6:00 in the evening and on the third try that the Union force finally overran the small rebel detachment and its one overworked gun.

Aleck Hart, a civilian in Beverly five miles away, kept a running tally of the number of times he heard the cannon roar and counted 165. By then only one cannoneer was still manning the cannon—Captain De Lagnel himself. After firing the 165th round, just before the Yankees overran his position, he crawled away wounded and bleeding into a nearby thicket and hid himself.[55]

Down the road to the east the little town of Beverly listened to the distant rattle of musketry, counted the cannon booms, and wondered what was happening. Two miles in the other direction, George McClellan wondered the same thing. It was obvious that a fight was going on. But what did it mean? Why was it all happening so late in the day? Why hadn't he heard anything from Rosecrans? Why did it all seem so distant and stationary? Why wasn't it approaching down the mountain as it ought to be?

"With indecision stamped on every line of his countenance," one soldier said, McClellan did nothing. He didn't attack Camp Garnett as agreed, or make any attempt to divert the enemy in his front. At one point, he watched as a Confederate officer galloped into the enemy works and delivered a speech. The prolonged cheering that followed persuaded McClellan that Rosecrans had run into bad luck on the mountain and had been defeated.[56]

Having worried the problem through all those uncertain hours, McClellan decided it was now too late and too dark to do anything. So he called it a day and withdrew to Roaring Creek for the night.

At the top of the mountain, Rosecrans was in his own quandary. McClellan had not attacked from the front as agreed, so he assumed that the enemy, whose strength had been reported to him by this time as "probably from 5,000 to 8,000 men," still lay in force between the two Union commands. Having endured since before dawn a pounding rain, an unkind mountain trail, a pitched battle with three charges, and no sleep, he also decided to call it a day. But it promised to be another long night. He expected a counterattack in force at any moment.[57]

An attack, however, was the last thing on John Pegram's mind.

With Yankees in his front, in his rear, and for all he knew on his left, his only thought was to clear out through the forest to his right. After dark his small detachment began snaking up the steep hill to the north of the encampment. The head of the column was led by a mapmaker named Jedediah Hotchkiss, who knew where he was going. Hotchkiss steadily pulled away from that part of the column led by Pegram, who had no idea at all where he was going.

Pushing on, Hotchkiss skirted Rosecrans at the summit of the mountain with about fifty men, slipped through Beverly, and escaped down the turnpike toward Huttonsville. Pegram, with 560 men and twenty-five officers, wandered to within sight of the turnpike north of Beverly, spotted troops on the road, and incorrectly assumed they belonged to McClellan. Disgusted, disheartened, and still hurting from a recent fall from his horse, he turned back into the Stygian woods.

McClellan awoke on the morning of July 12 and prepared to attack an enemy who was no longer there. Before he could order the assault, however, a messenger arrived from Rosecrans with news of yesterday's victory. The fussy old goose had won the battle after all. And the enemy at Camp Garnett, lacking sufficient steel, had fled in the night. Surprised but delighted, McClellan started triumphantly, but still cautiously, up and over the mountain toward Beverly.

By nightfall, with his men exhausted and hungry, Pegram called a conference of his officers at the Kittle house near the river. What should they do? His officers advised surrender, so Pegram sent a messenger to find McClellan, who was by now in Beverly. Happy to accommodate, McClellan sent a cavalry escort of twenty men and two officers to the Kittle house. In one of the war's more bizarre surrenders, Pegram and his twenty-five officers and 560 men, still armed to the teeth, plodded in with McClellan's twenty-two-man escort to give themselves up. Anything was better than another night and day in the western Virginia underbrush.

Garnett, unlike McClellan, knew Rosecrans had won the battle of Rich Mountain soon after it was fought. There was nothing left for him to do, with a big army at his front and an even bigger one now occupying his rear, but to clear out. After dark he set his command in motion, leaving his tents standing, his campfires burning, and his guard posts mounted to deceive Morris. Only with daylight on the twelfth did Morris discover that the enemy, whom he thought he was keeping amused, had ungratefully walked out on him. He took up a belated pursuit. And as he did, it began to rain again.

Like Pegram, Garnett incorrectly assumed that McClellan was already in Beverly. Instead of successfully retreating south through the town, as he could have, he turned and headed northeast up a rough muddy road into a quagmire.

The reporter for the *Cincinnati Commercial* traveling with Morris's troops was soon cursing on paper the road which the retreating and the pursuing armies were using in common. It was "of the worst description," he wrote. "At every step the mud grew deeper and the way more difficult, and one felt as though somebody were tugging at his heels to pull off his shoes. Now slipping down in the mud, now plunging into a pool knee deep, staggering about in the mire like drunken men. . . ." By the time they reached the little village of New Interest [present-day Kerens, ten miles north of Beverly], "there was not a dry thread in our clothing."[58]

If it was misery for the pursuers, it was disaster for the pursued. The fleeing Confederates were pounded by the rain, swamped by the swelling creeks they repeatedly had to cross, and mired in muck. They began to jettison their baggage, littering the road with it, marking the way for Morris's army.

That army splashed up on the Confederate rear on Saturday, July 13. At a desolate, rain-clogged crossing at Corricks Ford on the Cheat River the two sides fought a short, angry skirmish. During the engagement a straight-shooting Methodist preacher with the Indiana troops was particularly conspicuous for his zeal and his steady fire. "He fired carefully, with perfect coolness, and always after a steady aim," the *Cincinnati Gazette*'s Whitelaw Reid reported, "and the boys declare that every time, as he took down his gun, after firing, he said, 'And may the Lord have mercy on your soul!' "[59]

The aroma in Garnett's nostrils on this day was no longer Laurel Hill's sweet cologne of summer, but the fatal fragrance of gunpowder. Marksmen from the Seventh Indiana found him at a small crossing above Corricks Ford astride a yellow horse. He was wearing a black overcoat and deploying a knot of sharpshooters behind a small stand of driftwood. An Indiana sergeant named Burlingame drew a bead from across the ford and fired. The ball struck Garnett as he was turning to rally his riflemen, and he tumbled backward to the creek bank.

Reid studied the Confederate commander's dead body later as it lay there, the first general of either side to fall in the war. He noted the slight build, the "small head, finely cut and intelligent features, delicate hands and feet, black hair, and . . . full beard and moustache, kept closely trimmed, and just beginning to be grizzled with white hairs." It was the sad end of a still young career that had held such promise. The doom Garnett had so greatly feared had found him.[60]

His death beside the bleak, rain-choked Cheat River ended the three encounters in western Virginia. The shattered remnants of Garnett's army hurried on without him, only just eluding a final effort by McClellan to slam the door shut.

Contrary to his earlier pessimistic expectations, the sensational young West Pointer of the class of 1846 had earned laurels. He had won three Union victories in succession, the first and only in the war so far. He had shown a gift for command. Now he was about to show an equal gift for hype.

All through the campaign McClellan had trailed a telegraph line into every encampment. Many superstitious mountaineers saw this new technology stringing along behind the army as a supernatural agency.[61] The Confederates weren't happy with it either. "My God, Jim," exclaimed one of them as he marched in custody past McClellan's headquarters, "no wonder they whipped us; they have the telegraph with them."[62]

Some of McClellan's own officers viewed the new technology as a nuisance. Many of them thought that the telegraph could not be useful in war, and decried all efforts to introduce it.[63]

Anson Stager, the general superintendent of the Western Union Telegraph Company from Cleveland, had been brought in by McClellan to link the line to his army in the field. McClellan had seen the telegraph used in a limited way in the Crimean War and made note of it. In early July as the army moved from Clarksburg through Buckhannon to Roaring Creek and on to Beverly, Stager followed behind laying his wire. For the first time in history the telegraph accompanied an American army into battle.

McClellan used it with skill. It suited his personality. His code name, Mecca, crackled over the lines from command to command. Besides keeping him in nearly instant touch with his commanders—with the notable exception of Rosecrans on Rich Mountain—it had another stimulating potential that hadn't escaped the Young Napoleon of the West, as he was now being called. It could also put him in instant touch with the entire North wanting word of a victory—any victory.[64]

McClellan put bold and stirring words on the line. To the war department in Washington he wired in his crisp staccato style: "Garnett and forces routed; his baggage and one gun taken; his army demoralized; Garnett killed. We have annihilated the enemy in Western Virginia. . . . The troops defeated are the crack regiments of Eastern Virginia, aided by Georgians, Tennesseeans, and Carolinians. Our success is complete, and secession is killed in this country."[65]

He addressed his soldiers with a similar trumpet blast: "I am more than satisfied with you. You have annihilated two armies, commanded by educated and experienced soldiers, intrenched in mountain fastnesses fortified at their leisure. . . . I am proud to say that you have gained the highest reward that American troops can receive—the thanks of Congress and the applause of your fellow-citizens."[66]

The war department, the administration, and the Congress were more than impressed. From Washington, General Scott, McClellan's old mentor from Cerro Gordo, wired that he "and what is more, the Cabinet, including the President, are charmed with your activity, valor, and consequent successes." In a follow-up letter Scott wrote: "You have the applause of all who are high in authority here."[67]

Congress sent a unanimous joint resolution of thanks to him and his army "for the series of brilliant and decisive victories."[68]

The nation was electrified. Here at last was the military genius the agonized times so desperately sought. Sophia Hawthorne, wife of New England's celebrated man of letters, read one of McClellan's stirring pronouncements and exclaimed: "How like the sound of the silver trumpets of Judah. . . . I conceive an adoring army following the lead of such a ringing of true steel."[69]

"Glorious, isn't it!" the *New York Times* editorialized. "We feel very proud of our wise and brave young Major-General. There is a future before him, if his life be spared, which he will make illustrious." "It is a thing completely done," the *Louisville Journal* intoned from Kentucky. "It is a finished piece of work. It stands before us perfect and entire, wanting nothing; like a statue or picture just leaving the creative hand of the artist, and embodying the whole idea." The *Journal* coined a new word for what had just happened to the enemy in the mountains: they had been "McClellanized."[70]

From Cincinnati came the most welcomed praise of all, a telegram from Nelly: "Am more happy than I can express. Do come home and receive my congratulations."[71]

But her young hero-husband, now the most acclaimed name in the war, was headed in the other direction. He had been called to Washington. He was to write her a few days later: "Who would have thought when we were married, that I should so soon be called upon to save my country?"[72]

There was irony in these three little mountain victories. The new savior of the Republic had won three engagements, but had not been present at any of them. He hadn't been in the same state for the first—the races at Philippi. He had only heard the thunder of the second, two miles away on Rich Mountain, and had misread it. And he was twenty-six miles from the third and final skirmish at Corricks Ford. Yet on the strength of these mud-spattered encounters, none of which he had personally commanded, he was being called out of the West to save the Union. Closely scrutinized, the credentials were somewhat suspect. But who else had done as much?

The rain-soaked little victories did much more than just catapult George McClellan into the big time. They also unclasped for good the Confederate hold on the western two-fifths of Virginia soil. The rebels would continue to raid through the mountains until the end of the war. But the Union, in effect, now held the ground and the railroad at Cheat River, which Lee had believed it "would be worth to us an army" to rupture.[73] In late July 1861, Lee himself would set out for western Virginia in a last effort to redeem Confederate fortunes. But he too would fail, and Virginia would lose its western two-fifths forever.

Because of these victories, Union-minded western Virginia would make its own counter-secession from Virginia stick. Just one month short of two years after McClellan was called to Washington to save the country, West Virginia would become that nation's thirty-fifth state.

McClellan had done well in the mountains, but that hardly surprised his classmates. He was expected to do well anywhere. He was bound for glory, if any one of them was. They had known it all along.

PART 4
DOWN
IN THE
VALLEY

The
Valley Man

In the war's first big battle at Manassas in July 1861, Tom Jackson had attracted attention to himself simply by being himself— unreasonably adamant.

As the wave of Union troops rolled toward his position on Henry Hill, he vowed that he and his brigade would stand and give them the bayonet if necessary. Confederate Brigadier General Barnard Bee, whether in admiration or disgust, had remarked before dying that there stood Jackson like a stone wall. This stirring image captured imaginations everywhere. Jackson was known after that, even in the North, as Stonewall and his brigade as the Stonewall Brigade.

After Manassas, Jackson remained with his now famous command near Centreville until late October, when a letter came from Confederate Secretary of War Judah Benjamin. The rebel high command had just reorganized its eastern army into a Department of Northern Virginia under the command of Joseph E. Johnston and had split it into three wings—a Potomac District, Aquia District, and Valley District.

Benjamin's letter told Jackson he had been picked to command the Valley District. The secretary explained that the exposed condition of the Shenandoah Valley between the Blue Ridge and the Allegheny mountains worried Richmond. The war department was buried

269

in appeals from the people in the Valley to send "a perfectly reliable officer" to protect them from the Yankees. By that they meant Jackson. The choice, Benjamin said, had been dictated in part by an appreciation of Jackson's qualities as a commander, his knowledge of the country, its population, and its resources. But the clincher had been popular demand. "The people of that district, with one voice," Benjamin told Jackson, "have made constant and urgent appeals that to you, in whom they have confidence, should their defense be assigned." His command would be necessarily small to begin with, Benjamin admitted, but it would be beefed up as rapidly as Richmond could manage to do it.[1]

It was all true what the people of the Valley said about Jackson. This West Pointer of few words and stonewall determination was a Valley man. He was one of them. They felt safe in his resolute hands. The women of the Valley seemed ready to send their husbands, sons, and lovers to battle "as cheerfully as to marriage feasts"—if it meant they would fight under Jackson's command.[2] One of these women said of him, "He is such an idol with me, that I devour every line about him."[3]

To take the Valley command Jackson had to leave his brigade behind, and neither he nor his soldiers welcomed this. The idea of waging war without him leading them was unthinkable. They were his; he was theirs.[4] Like the people of the valley, the soldiers of the Stonewall Brigade—Valley men themselves for the most part—had come to love this unlovable man, and he them in his own peculiar fashion. Jackson told Secretary Benjamin he regretted having to leave his brigade, which "I had hoped to command through the war."[5]

In early November, when his final orders came and he had to go, he undertook to tell them good-bye. But speechmaking was not his forte.

"I am not here to make a speech," he began, "but simply to say farewell. I first met you at Harper's Ferry in the commencement of the war, and I cannot take leave of you without giving expression to my admiration of your conduct from that day to this,—whether on the march, in the bivouac, the tented field, or on the bloody plains of Manassas, where you gained the well-deserved reputation of having decided the fate of the battle."

He went on, saying among other things: "You have already gained a brilliant and deservedly high reputation, throughout the army and the whole Confederacy, and I trust in the future by your own deeds on the field, and by the assistance of the same Kind Providence who has heretofore favored our cause, that you will gain more victories, and add additional lustre to the reputation you now enjoy. . . . I shall look with great anxiety to your future movements, and I trust whenever I shall hear of the First Brigade on the field of battle it will be of still nobler deeds achieved and higher reputation won."

He paused, then stood in his stirrups, raised his right arm in an electric gesture, and shouted: "In the army of the Shenandoah you were the First Brigade; in the army of the Potomac you were the First Brigade; in the second corps of this army you are the First Brigade; you are the First Brigade in the affections of your General; and I hope by your future deeds and bearing, you will be handed down to posterity as the First Brigade in our Second War of Independence. Farewell!"[6]

Then he caught the first train to the Valley that night vowing, "I shall never forget them. In battle I shall always want them. I shall not be satisfied until I get them."[7]

Within the month he had them. When he arrived in Winchester, where he was to make his headquarters, he found the Valley basically undefended but for a small ineffectual force of Virginia militia. So he asked immediately for his old brigade and it came. Richmond also sent a command from western Virginia, and by the end of the year Jackson's little army had grown to about 8,500 troops. With this force he went to work.

His orders were to stay in touch with General Johnston at Centerville and to drive the Federals from the Valley if possible. As Dabney Maury had said of him in another context, things "had to move along."[8] By late December he had damaged a principal dam on the Potomac River that fed the Chesapeake and Ohio Canal.

"That will give the enemy abundance of trouble," a clerk in the war department in Richmond noted appreciatively. "This Gen. Jackson is always doing something to vex the enemy; and I think he is destined to annoy them more."[9] By January 14 he had harassed and annoyed them right out of the Valley. "Through the blessing of God," he wrote Judah Benjamin that day, "I regard this district as essentially in our possession." He had done all he felt the circumstances would justify. He had left the Federals in possession of the Confederate frontier; but the Valley was his.[10]

Jackson believed that having the valley of Virginia in his possession was mandatory, and in line with the designs and intentions of almighty Providence. This is "our valley," he told his soldiers flatly, and if it is lost, Virginia is lost.[11]

It was one of the most beautiful river valleys in America. Bounded by the Blue Ridge on the east and the Alleghenies on the west, it was an amphitheater that stretched for 120 miles from Staunton in the south to the Potomac in the north. Its average width was twenty-five miles and its surface was unlike a valley, swelling gracefully from rise to rise and flaring occasionally into abrupt hills.

Down its center, rising suddenly from the plain near Harrisonburg in the south and running parallel to the Blue Ridge to Strasburg, humped Massanutton Mountain. The Massanutton was more than a mountain. It was a series of interlocking ridges bonded together into one great whole, a giant backbone that split the Valley into two valleys. Up its Allegheny side, giving the Valley its name, ran the North Fork of the Shenandoah River. On the other side, between this tangled green wall and the Blue Ridge, lay the Luray Valley.

To an astute strategist, the Massanutton could be "the glory of the Valley," a shield and a comfort, an opaque curtain behind which to mobilize, march, strike, and disappear. For a victim it could be a maddening blind, blocking off all vision, hiding every movement and intention, screening an attack, and bringing bitter disaster.[12]

Jackson knew the Valley. Its geography and the distances between its towns were burned into his brain like his lessons at West Point. He seemed to know every hole and corner of it, someone said, every cow path and goat track, "as if he had made it, or, at least, as if it had been designed for his own use."[13]

But he had to know it better; he had to have it laid out before him on paper in detail. And he knew how to get that done. He called for Jedediah Hotchkiss.

Hotchkiss had led the small breakaway party of fifty beaten rebels safely from the disaster at Rich Mountain the year before. He had since joined Jackson's little army in the Shenandoah. This was his valley, too. He was a schoolteacher by profession, the owner and headmaster of the Loch Willow Academy at Churchville, Virginia, and a self-taught topographer and mapmaker. Like Jackson, he was an ardent Presbyterian. In late March 1862 Jackson called him to his headquarters and told him, "I want you to make me a map of the Valley, from Harpers Ferry to Lexington."[14]

It was too much to expect that the Union army would not want to reclaim this wondrous valley, so strategic in the war. George McClellan, now the general in chief of that army, agreed with his West Point classmate that to hold Virginia one must hold the Shenandoah. Northern opinion at the moment was demanding that he hold Virginia as soon as possible, beginning with Richmond. McClellan knew, however, that first things must come first. If he was to invade the living room, then he must first secure the back door. Winchester, where Jackson was now wintered, was but a scant sixty miles from Washington. And it did not make those miles seem any safer to know that sitting out there at the end of them was that unpredictable classmate, whom McClellan well knew to be "a man of vigor & nerve, as well as a good soldier."[15]

The Shenandoah had to be under federal control to make the march on Richmond work. So in late February McClellan launched an invasion of the Valley as a prelude to the larger event. A force under Major General Nathaniel Banks, a Massachusetts politician inexperienced in war, entered the Valley on February 22 to try to wrest back what Jackson had taken earlier in the winter.

By February 24 Banks had occupied Harpers Ferry. Two days later he was in Charles Town with more than thirty thousand soldiers. As the month ended he was cautiously advancing toward Winchester twenty-two miles up the Valley, where Jackson waited with little more than five thousand men.

On the first day of March, Joseph E. Johnston wired orders to Jackson. Since Johnston was confronted with McClellan's huge army, twice the size of his own, preparing to take Richmond, he didn't want that army to be any bigger than it already was. Now that Banks was in the Valley, Johnston wanted him to stay there. His orders therefore were for Jackson to employ Banks's invading force in such a way as to keep it in the Valley. Jackson must stay near enough to Banks to keep him from reinforcing McClellan, yet not so near as to be compelled to fight and to risk defeat.[16]

Jackson would obey, of course, but with one important mental reservation. He didn't intend to avoid provoking a fight if the opportunity arose.[17] Jackson's young staff officer, Sandie Pendleton, would go even further than that. "If we do not drive Banks discomfited from the Valley, if the men will only rally as they should to the rescue . . . I am no true prophet."[18]

So on March 6 when Banks's advance appeared four miles from Winchester, Jackson formed a line in front of his fortifications and offered battle. Banks, wanting none of it, paused and stepped back. On March 11 Banks inched his left cautiously to Berryville ten miles east of Winchester and Jackson again drew up his little army and waited all day for an attack. None came. This was maddening to Jackson. If Banks wouldn't attack him then he would attack Banks— he preferred it that way anyhow. At a council of war with his commanders that evening, Jackson proposed an attack on Banks before daylight the next morning. His commanders voted against it.

So much for councils of war. Jackson would never hold another one. He would attack anyhow. But then he found that his army had already retired without orders and was five miles from Winchester on a slow withdrawal—too far to recall for a night march and attack.

Sometime after midnight Jackson was seen by one of his soldiers, alone by the side of the road bending over a dying campfire. Jackson stood there for a while warming his hands, apparently in deep meditation and as silent as the glow that played over the embers. Finally he drew his faded cap closer over his brow, mounted his horse, and rode slowly away toward the south.[19]

Banks occupied Winchester the next day, March 12; Jackson was then in Strasburg. As Banks followed, Jackson backed down the Valley farther still to Woodstock and then to Mount Jackson. All of this pleased McClellan, who was about to take his legions to the Peninsula. Jackson was apparently not going to fight, and McClellan was satisfied that the Valley could be held with a token force. He ordered Banks to cross the Blue Ridge and entrench part of his army at Manassas, part near Front Royal, and part near Strasburg, with a detachment at Winchester to keep an eye on things. This should handily protect both Washington and that part of his army now moving toward Fredericksburg, and take care of Jackson at the same time.

McClellan either had not observed Jackson carefully enough at West Point or had forgotten how dogged he was. He had never taken his classmate for clever. But Old Jack did not follow scripts, particularly federal scripts. He was biding his time, keeping his cavalry commander, Turner Ashby, in perpetual contact with the federal advance—flushing out its pickets, peering into its camps, and reporting what it was up to. When Ashby advised Jackson on the evening of March 21 that Banks had evacuated Strasburg and was pulling troops out of the Valley wholesale, Jackson wheeled and began marching his little army rapidly back toward Winchester. Banks must not be allowed to leave the Valley.[20]

Banks was, in fact, anxious to entrain for Washington. He now believed he could safely leave matters in the hands of Brigadier General James Shields in Winchester long enough to go there and come back. Nothing important seemed to be happening. The withdrawal east of the Blue Ridge was under way and reconnaissance had told them Jackson would retire from the Valley without a fight. This made sense. That is what they would have done in his place. Banks had no idea, as he prepared to leave for Washington, that Jackson was at that moment doing the unexpected—rolling toward Winchester looking to make trouble.[21]

In Winchester, Shields was having some mild misgivings. Ashby was causing him fits and they had even had some hard skirmishing that evening. Shields had taken a shell fragment in the shoulder and was now in bed with a broken arm. But even so, it looked to him like the Confederates had only a small cavalry force in the field. It was unlikely Jackson would be venturing so far from his base of support. But still . . .[22]

The tenacious Ashby had concluded that the Union army was withdrawing in a big way. All his looking and prying had convinced him of it. So he had sent word to Jackson on the twenty-first that all but four of the Union regiments had left for the north and the rest seemed about to follow.

Jackson arrived at Kernstown three miles south of Winchester at about 1:00 P.M. on March 23, his troops weary-legged from the twenty-five miles he had driven them over the past day and a half. He planned to bivouac for the night. It was Sunday and he hated to fight on the Lord's Day, and his troops could use the rest. On further examination, however, he found that the position he had taken south of Kernstown could be seen by the enemy and that it would be dangerous to wait. The Federals now knew he was there and they could be reinforced overnight. He decided to attack immediately, even though it was Sunday and late in the day.

Lying in bed in Winchester, Shields knew one thing Jackson didn't. Ashby, who wasn't often wrong about such things, was wrong about the number of troops Shields still had. Although the withdrawal across the Blue Ridge was under way, Shields could still muster some seven thousand men at Winchester, far more than the four regiments Ashby thought he had.[23]

Jackson disliked hitting any enemy square on if he could avoid it, so he feinted toward Shields's right center, then hit him on the right flank. But something didn't seem quite right; it wasn't turning out to be so easy. It all became clear when Sandie Pendleton, who had been out reconnoitering, returned to report the terrible truth: there were at least ten thousand Yankees out there, not just four regiments.

Jackson was painfully aware that about the best he could muster was 3,500 men. "Say nothing about it," he told Pendleton, "we are in for it."[24]

It got hot and heavy in a hurry. Jackson couldn't remember ever having heard such a roar of musketry.[25] Many of his soldiers were hearing this same musketry, and worse, the thunder of cannon, for the first time in their lives. One of them described the first shell he ever heard four months earlier as a "hark from the tomb." When it had all ended at Kernstown and the battle was done and he was still alive, the same soldier thought gratefully: "Mother, Home, Heaven are all sweet words, but the grandest sentence I ever heard from mortal lips was uttered this evening . . . 'Boys, the battle is over.' "[26]

Before it was over, about dusk, Jackson had fought gamely and lost. But he thought he ought to have won. Indeed, he thought he was on the verge of winning until Brigadier General Richard Garnett, commanding his old Stonewall Brigade, abruptly withdrew without orders. Garnett's men had run out of ammunition and he had—wisely, everybody but Jackson thought—decided his position was untenable. That did it; Jackson was beaten. He could do nothing then but pull back.

Flush with rage, he clapped Garnett under arrest and relieved him of command. Jackson was convinced that if the Stonewall Brigade had just held on another ten minutes—giving them the bayonet, throwing rocks, anything—the Union army would have given it up and retired.

Despite his anger and frustration, Jackson could take some satisfaction from events as he bedded down that night. He had lost the battle, but won the day. Banks, hearing the uproar behind him, had turned around at Harpers Ferry and come back. The troops that were being withdrawn were also returned. McClellan wasn't going to get the reinforcements he had been counting on.

In his report of the battle Jackson wrote: "Though Winchester was not recovered, yet the more important object for the present, that of calling back troops that were leaving the valley, and thus preventing a junction of Banks' command with other forces, was accomplished. . . . though the field is in possession of the enemy, yet the most essential fruits of the battle are ours."[27]

Jackson not only felt that way; he acted that way. His pullback from Kernstown was sullen but unhurried. When he reached Mount Jackson he halted on the other side of the North Fork of the Shenandoah and set up headquarters in the front parlor of the hospitable home of the Reverend Anders Rudolph Rude, and acted as if he planned to stay awhile. He stayed three weeks.

Banks was in no hurry to pursue this pest; he had swatted it, but it still might have sting left. He didn't begin following Jackson until April Fools' Day, a week after the battle at Kernstown. On that day he put his army out on the turnpike with bayonets glinting in the early spring sun to see what he could see. What he saw was Turner Ashby again.

Ashby was a first-rate nuisance. Being the rear guard was his thing. He was at his best when operating in that no-man's-land between the friend's rear and the enemy's advance, at the head of his raucous and undisciplined cavalry. He was like a deranged boxer, dancing in and out and about, jabbing and pulling back, weaving and dodging. He was taunting and insolent, thrusting his chin forward to invite his adversary's best shot, then whirling away just before the blow landed. The contour of the Valley lent itself to such antics. There was an excellent artillery position around every bend in the road. Ashby would set up his highly mobile battery of guns on one of these and open fire on the head of the federal column as it marched into view. The column would halt and bring up a battery of its own. After exchanging a few shots, Ashby's guns would limber up and gallop to the next convenient position and repeat the exercise.[28]

This was ludicrous, because at any time Banks with his superior force could have plowed at will over Ashby, battery and all. Working this way in the enemy's immediate front was nerve-racking for Ashby's artillerymen, "service both active and arduous," said one of them, "full of alarms, hardships, and excitement."[29] For every other Confederate, however, it was reassuring. "I never slept more soundly in my life than when in sight of the enemy's camp-fires, with Ashby between us," said the adjutant of the Second Virginia, "for I knew that it was wellnigh impossible for them to surprise him."[30]

For Colonel George H. Gordon of the West Point class of 1846, now in command of Banks's advance, swatting Ashby was a little like trying to pin down the Scarlet Pimpernel. Catch them, he ordered, pointing to Ashby's illusive cavalry.

"I can't catch them, sir," his own cavalry commander would explain, "they leap the fences and walls like deer: neither our men nor our horses are so trained."[31]

This whirligig of artillery brawling and picket-stalking continued until Banks reached Mount Jackson and pulled into view of Jackson's main army at Rude's Hill. On April 17, when Banks began to crowd him, Jackson thanked the Reverend Doctor Rude and his daughters for their hospitality, indicated he would be moving on, and set his army in motion toward Harrisonburg. He arrived the next evening, and there at about dusk in a driving rain he called for Henry Kyd Douglas.

Not yet twenty-four, Douglas was by his own description a "boy soldier," with hair as black as his coat.[32] He had been raised around Harpers Ferry and Shepherdstown in western Virginia. When the war came in 1861 he became a private in Colonel Jackson's brigade at Harpers Ferry. In July when Jackson, promoted to a brigadier, had stood like a stonewall at Manassas, Douglas, promoted to a company orderly sergeant, stood with him. By August, Douglas, a lawyer by education, was a junior lieutenant, and by April 1862 he was a captain on Jackson's staff—"one of your wide awake, smart young men," Jed Hotchkiss called him.[33]

What Jackson now wanted Douglas to do was to take a night ride over the Massanutton to the vicinity of Culpeper on the Rappahannock River line, sixty miles away, with a message for Major General Richard S. Ewell. So young Douglas, having no clear idea how to get there, galloped away into a stormy night as dark as Erebus.[34]

Jackson had had a lot of time to think at Rude's Hill. He would think some more over the next few days as he took his little army around the base of Massanutton Mountain to Conrad's Store in front of Swift Run Gap on the Blue Ridge.

Why Jackson went there was not immediately clear to the casual observer. It was true that from there he held Banks in check; any aggressive move the Union general might make now could bring Jackson in an instant across the Massanutton and onto his rear. But at the same time Jackson had taken himself out of the Valley he had been assigned to protect—an unsettling strategy, it seemed, to the people of the Valley. Sandie Pendleton attempted to explain it in a letter to his mother. "Leaving the Valley in order to protect it is singular," he confessed, "but bids fare to be efficacious."[35] Not even Pendleton, however, knew exactly what his chief had in mind or whether it would work. Nobody did.

Jackson's immediate task had been to press Banks as closely as circumstances would justify, and he had settled in at Rude's Hill with that in mind. When Banks had marched into Ashby's view across Stony Creek, Jackson had fallen back, hoping to draw him up the Valley after him. But he was not convinced he could lure Banks much beyond Mount Jackson. Jackson believed that if Banks could be attacked and defeated at some point, that would even more emphatically retard McClellan's movements on the Peninsula. One thought he had, which he shared with Robert E. Lee in Richmond, was the possibility of getting behind Banks's rear at either New Market or Harrisonburg. Jackson wrote Lee that he intended to lie quietly at Swift Run Gap for a few days to see if Banks might make a move in some direction that would permit him, with the blessing of Providence, to attack his advance and drive back his entire force. If that failed perhaps Banks could at least be induced "to follow me through this gap, where our forces would have greatly the advantage."[36]

But the circumspect Banks gave him neither opportunity, and by the end of April Jackson's thinking had turned toward more active alternatives. He saw three possibilities, all three involving Ewell, whose division on the Rappahannock had been put at Jackson's disposal. Jackson summarized these three alternatives to Lee on April 29: He could leave Ewell at Swift Run Gap to watch Banks, while he moved rapidly back into the Valley to attack the Union force then threatening Confederate Brigadier General Edward ("Allegheny Ed") Johnson near Staunton. Then he could deal with Banks. Or in consort with Ewell he could hit Banks's detached force between New Market and the North Fork of the Shenandoah, and if successful drive him back down the Valley. Or he could pass down the South Fork of the Shenandoah by another route and threaten Winchester via Front Royal. With any of these plans or a combination of them he intended, particularly if Lee could spare some reinforcements, to make life miserable for Banks. Of the three plans he preferred the first, after which he could turn on Banks without having to contend with anybody else.[37]

Whatever he decided to do, Ewell was the key. Without Ewell's eight-thousand-man division none of the plans would work. Ewell was to be his accomplice. That is why he had sent Douglas out into the dark and stormy night. He had to have Ewell.

The
Odd Couple

O nly a Providence with a lively imagination could have con-
cocted any such partnership as Stonewall Jackson and Richard
Ewell. No odder couple existed in the Confederate army, or
any army.

Jackson in the spring of 1862 was thirty-eight years old, and
looking as little like a general as the day he entered West Point
wearing his homespun. A young lady who saw him at a prayer meeting
in Winchester admitted he was "right nice looking—though not much
like a general in appearance." She had supposed, therefore, that what
he looked like didn't matter, but "it's the head that makes all."[1]
When one of his foot soldiers first saw him, he thought it hardly
possible that it was the general; he looked more like a "crank."[2]
"Such a dry old stick too!" said another.[3]

The Jackson that met the eye was a near six-footer topped with
a rust-colored head of wavy or curly hair, and a full beard. He had a
small sharp nose and thin pallid lips that were generally clamped
relentlessly shut. The eyes that looked out from this face were kindly,
but unflinching and steely blue-gray, and troubling him now when he
tried to read under artificial light. The lower part of his face was
leathery and tanned from exposure. Although usually wooden in ex-

pression, his face, under certain circumstances, could be highly animated and the mouth very mobile. It could also light up with that same sweet smile his classmates at West Point remembered. His voice, in giving commands, was either low and drawling, or high, piping, and querulous, depending upon the situation. His forehead was high, broad, and white under his cap. However, the cap, given him by his wife, was generally on and was sunburnt yellow—worn with its visor pulled down so far over the eyes that Jackson had to keep his chin upthrust to see both friend and foe.

He was well put together, although he tended to be somewhat sway-backed and sprung in the knees. The angular body was clothed in a uniform of a style to match the cap—dingy, faded, and "sun-embrowned."[4] Like the cap, it had begun life in a brighter hue, but had been transmuted by time and hard use. The coat was seasoned in the soil of his beloved Valley and nearly out at the elbows. He had worn it in rain and under scorching sun, slept in it, ridden in it, and fought in it. On his legs he wore big cavalry boots reaching to the knees.

He carried himself in the accustomed ramrod configuration that made people account him stiff. He still thought it best for his health to keep his alimentary canal straight. Both afoot and on horseback he was awkward in his movements, as always. His sole objective in either case was to cover the ground and it didn't matter much to him how he looked doing it. The truth was, as someone said, Jackson was "not educated in Mr. Turveydrop's school of politeness, nor versed in the poetry of motion."[5] In an age when stylish uniforms and fine horses were the rule, he was clearly marching to a different and more ragged drum.[6]

His horse matched him perfectly in appearance. His name was Little Sorrel, which was also his description. He was, Henry Kyd Douglas observed, "as little like a Pegasus as his master was like an Apollo."[7] Jackson purchased him as a gift for his wife when he was at Harpers Ferry hijacking locomotives. He had at first named him Fancy, which was a barefaced misnomer, for he was the plainest of horses. But Jackson preferred him for his easy gait—"as easy," he said, "as the rocking of a cradle."[8] Little Sorrel was like his master in many ways. He could readily doze between pauses in the fighting and he moved calmly about in the passion of battle as if nothing was happening. Jackson's men swore that Little Sorrel "could not run except toward the enemy."[9] But in time the horse came to recognize an ovation for Jackson by these same men as worse than war and a signal to hightail it out of there. Because the horse had intelligent eyes "as soft as a gazelle's,"[10] Jackson loved him and would hand-feed him apples along the side of the road.

On this war horse, Jackson sat stiffly with arms akimbo, legs straightened rigidly before him, and toes pointed zenithward. When Little Sorrel started off on his inevitable lope, the general's body swayed in accompaniment with an awkward jerking motion, as though a stiff spring had been inserted in the back of the saddle. The bearing of neither could be considered martial. Indeed, it could have been said of them together, as it had been said of the man alone since his West Point days: strange looking, and quite unprepossessing.[11]

The ovations that invariably greeted his passage through his army were an embarrassment to him. His appearance created the same uproar generally caused by a rabbit, which the soldiers loved to run down with raucous shouts and cries. When distant cheering was heard the army would assume, "That's Jackson or a rabbit."[12] Jackson tried to get these visitations over with as quickly as possible. He loped up the line as fast as he could on Little Sorrel, his body bent forward, his hat snatched off his head and held out stiffly before him by way of a salute. On he rocketed in this manner, looking "like a rusty-jointed collector of contributions at a protracted meeting."[13]

Mounted or afoot Jackson was a complicated combination of characteristics and eccentricities.

He was different. "Nobody ever understood him," a soldier said, "and nobody has ever been quite able to account for him."[14] He "knew the country, the people, and himself," a Richmond insider said. "The last was not known to any other in the country."[15] One of his officers said: "No one could love the man for himself. He seems to be cut off from his fellow men and to commune with his own spirit only, or with spirits of which we know not."[16]

He was likened, under normal circumstances, to a country schoolmaster, unaccustomed to the saddle but inexplicably sitting in one anyhow, and engaged in some difficult and absorbing mathematical calculation as he jogged along his way. In battle, however, when cannon thundered, small arms fire rattled, and sabers flashed, all that changed. He was transfigured into something else entirely. Out went the schoolmaster, in came the fighter; out went tranquility, in came devouring excitement; out went the ice, in came the fire. In this mode, the possibility of losing the battle he was engaged in at the moment never crossed his mind.[17]

He was devout. One of the reasons losing never entered his mind was that he considered the whole affair to be out of his hands entirely and in those of an all-kind Providence. "We know that all things work together for good to them that love God," was the way he felt about life in general and battle in particular.[18] Victories were God's doing, and to Him went the credit. Out of guns or bullets? Then under Divine blessing "we must rely upon the bayonet," he said.[19]

When Jackson decided to take up religion as his way of life here and hereafter, it was like everything else he ever took up: he took it up entirely. When he decided to become a Presbyterian, he became one heart and soul. When he married, he married the daughter of a Presbyterian divine. When she died after a short time, he married the daughter of another Presbyterian divine. When he came to believe that one should sanctify Sundays, he sanctified them wholly and without stint. He would not travel on the Sabbath, or let anything that had to do with him travel on that day—including his mail. Nor would he even read a letter on Sunday. When he learned that a railroad in which he owned stock engaged in a large amount of Sunday trafficking, he sold the stock.[20]

None of this meant, however, that he wouldn't fight on Sunday. The battle at Bull Run was fought on Sunday. So was the clash at Kernstown. He hated to do it, but that was the way he was. The one thing that outranked Providence was duty. In any conflict between the two, duty won every time. Providence said thou shalt not kill. But if duty said it was necessary, he did it without hesitation, wholesale if possible. Indeed there were those who believed that Providence and duty were one and the same with Jackson. His first wife, Elinor Junkin, believed that. She told him in their short time together that duty was the goddess of his worship. He did everything from a sense of duty. His sister-in-law insisted he even ate from a sense of duty.[21]

He was rigidly abstemious. But this also had to do with duty. His brother-in-law, Confederate General Daniel Harvey Hill, who had walked with him on the beach in Mexico, said that like Paul, Jackson "kept his body under." He would not let any appetite control him or any weakness overcome him. He therefore used neither tobacco, coffee, nor spirits. He would go all winter without a cloak or overcoat, for no other reason than he "did not wish to give way to cold."[22]

This would explain why he never left ranks to run from the rain at West Point. It would also explain why loving strong drink, he never touched it. When Dominie Wilson danced the inebriated two-step with him at Brown's Hotel, it was a once-in-a-lifetime thing. He told a brother officer that he was more afraid of drink than he was of federal bullets.[23] He therefore considered it part of his duty to protect his soldiers from the first if not from the second. At Harpers Ferry in the first year of the war he issued an order forbidding any shopkeeper in town to sell ardent spirits to his soldiers, on penalty of being shut down and the liquor confiscated.[24] Since the soldiers managed to get the spirits anyhow, he had to order all the whiskey in town poured from barrels into the gutters. The men dipped it up in buckets. He ordered it poured into the Potomac; the soldiers came with buckets tied to the ends of ropes and caught it as it cascaded to the waters below. At least that was what cavalryman John N. Opie swears happened, although he may have been drunk at the time.[25] It was with men of such tenacity, ingenuity, and dedication that Jackson fashioned the Stonewall Brigade.

He was taciturn and modest. "If silence is golden, then Jackson was rich indeed," a soldier said of him.[26] He talked like he came and went: suddenly, and it didn't take him long to say what he had to say. He blushed like a schoolgirl at a compliment and was easily confused in the presence of strangers. If the strangers were pretty young women threatening him with smiles and embraces, he was utterly paralyzed and stampeded.[27] If ambition was in him, self-aggrandizement wasn't. Not until he had asked the hand of Elinor Junkin in marriage and the records of his army career were placed before her father, did the family have any idea that he had so distinguished himself in the Mexican War.[28]

He was tender—in his fashion; and domesticated—to a degree. D. H. Hill spoke of his "tenderness of conscience."[29] He addressed his second wife, Anna, as "my precious little darling" and my "little pet," and by other endearing terms that would have scandalized his West Point classmates.[30] He lavished Spanish love-words on his loved ones, and in the privacy of his own living room at Lexington he danced the polka.[31] This would have astonished Dabney Maury who had believed that the idea of Jackson dancing the german was a self-evident absurdity. It would not have surprised Dominie Wilson, however, who had danced the two-step with him.[32]

He was dyspeptic. Anna called this malady his "arch-enemy,"[33] and it added to the aura of eccentricity that encased him. He had other real and imagined ailments that contributed to this aura as well. He told Maury and McClellan before the war that one arm and one leg were heavier than the others and that he therefore occasionally raised his arm straight up to let the blood run back into his body and relieve the excessive weight. Given his reputation as a praying man, this procedure was often mistaken on the battlefield as a form of supplication to the Almighty.[34] A severe inflammation of his ear and throat coupled with an attack of neuralgia in his early years at VMI had left him hard of hearing in his right ear.[35]

But dyspepsia was the main problem, and it made Jackson prone to the common dyspeptic tendency to nod off sometimes when he ought not to. This beset him most sorely in church, where he always sat as usual in a perfectly bolt-upright position, disdaining to lean against the back of the pew. D. H. Hill had seen him often in church sitting like a ramrod, but with his head bowed down to his knees, sound asleep. He was awake for the text and a few opening words of the sermon, but not for much else. His chief ecclesiastical victim over the years had been the Reverend Dr. William S. White, his pastor in Lexington. The story was told that one evening the faculty of the two institutions of higher learning in Lexington, VMI and Washington College, were invited to attend a special lecture of a celebrated mesmerist, at which many citizens of the town were also present. After some impressive feats of hypnotism, the mesmerist wished to try his hand on one of the professors in the audience, and Jackson went forward. He was the last one in the audience the mesmerist should have selected. Jackson's will was too strong and the spell had no effect—to everyone's amusement. But the fun ran over when a female voice from the audience said in a stage whisper: "No one can put Major Jackson to sleep but the Rev. Dr. White!"[36]

Ironically, the Union generals came to believe he never slept. Henry Kyd Douglas could have told them he slept a great deal, and not just from dyspepsia. Give him five minutes to rest and he could sleep for three of it. When nothing important was happening he slept—in any position and anywhere, in a chair, under fire, on horse-back. Time other men gave to conversation Jackson gave to sleep.[37]

He was fearless. One of his soldiers described him in battle: With his "war-look" on he "rode about the battlefield regardless of shot and shell, looking as if nothing was going on."[38] Although he was partially deaf in one ear, with weak eyes and a fragile nervous system, none of these were to be confused with a weak will. The nervous system caused the muscles of his face to twitch convulsively when a battle was about to begin. His hand would tremble so that he could not write, and his soldiers would say, "Old Jack is making mouths at the Yankees."[39] One of Jackson's favorite maxims was, "Never take counsel of your fears."[40] He practiced it and recommended it to others, generals and couriers alike.

He was a workaholic. It was early to rise and late to bed with Jackson—or better yet, never to bed at all. He always moved his army at daybreak or else started the night before.[41] He was a "second day man," his soldiers said—beginning early and fighting late and beginning again early the next day. His basic work ethic was to ad-vance and fight and to go on doing it until the enemy was whipped.[42]

And in all things but one he was a stonewall. To those who knew him, the nickname he won at Manassas fit perfectly, not so much because of his heroic stand there, but for his unyielding stand about everything everywhere. He was a stonewall before he was ever chris-tened that in fire and blood at Manassas. Fifty-eight West Point class-mates had found that out about him years before. The one exception was in moving his army. When Dennis Hart Mahan talked of the importance of celerity at West Point now, he could point to this former cadet as an example of what he meant. As on the frontier, so in Jackson's battles: The front was all around and the rear was nowhere. And in Jackson's army there was little sympathy with human infirmity. The idea was getting around among his troops that he was a relent-lessly "one idea'd man," who looked upon broken-down soldiers and stragglers as the same odious thing—weak creatures wanting in patriotism.[43]

His men nonetheless laughed when they saw him on his sorrel with the rim of his cap resting on his nose and his chin upthrust seeking the light. But their cheers as he rode by said the laughter was the laughter of respect. It was hard not to laugh at this strange man with his oddities, eccentricities, and one-idea'dness, but it was just as hard not to respect him. Beneath the oddness was a fighter—and, although it was tough to see sometimes, a general.

The soldier he was calling from the Rappahannock to be with him in the Valley was a fighter and a general too. And it was as difficult to believe it of him as it was of Jackson.

Richard Ewell was already convinced of his new commander's lunacy. How could a man who wouldn't eat pepper, as Jackson wouldn't because he believed it produced a weakness in his left leg, be anything but over the edge? But just about everybody agreed that when it came to being over the edge, Ewell left Jackson well back from the cliff. Dick Taylor, one of Ewell's brigadiers, believed that Virginia probably never produced a truer gentleman, braver soldier, more lovable—or odder—man.[44]

Ewell's eccentricity began with his appearance. He was nearly bald—one of his nicknames was "Old Bald Head"—and had been since his twenties when his hair had started to fall out and he had written home to his sister Rebecca that he was now shaving his head "to keep what little I have left from following suit."[45] This gave his head a bomb-shaped configuration. He had bright prominent eyes and an aquiline nose, which the literate and well-read Taylor compared to that of Francis of Valois, and the disposition of a nervous bird. All in all, Taylor thought he bore a striking resemblance to a woodcock. This was confirmed by a birdlike habit of cocking his head to one side and making quaint utterances delivered in a lisp.[46]

Although Ewell may have looked like a woodcock, he swore like a screech owl. "His profanity," one officer noted, "did not consist of single or even double oaths, but was ingeniously wrought into whole sentences. It was profanity which might be parsed, and seemed the result of careful study and long practice."[47] It was a talent that would cause the pious Jackson to say at one point in their relationship: "Ewell, that was well done, and I don't see how a man of your habits and who uses language like yours can do his work so well."[48]

It was a talent that may have been cultivated on the Indian frontier, where Ewell had spent most of his army career after graduating from West Point in 1840. There was no accounting for it in his background, for he came from one of the most genteel and prominent of Virginia families. His father had been a distinguished physician in Washington City and his mother had been the daughter of the first secretary of the navy. His grandfather had been a classmate of Thomas Jefferson at William and Mary College.[49]

In many ways his heart was not in this war. It had come much to his bitter regret. Like many others who had been in the old army, he now fought for his state out of "a painful sense of duty." He was to write of the war, after the war, "It was like death to me."[50]

On the frontier Ewell had been without equal as a cavalry captain. It was a measure of the regard in which he was held that a fort was named for him in Texas and a county named for him in Arizona Territory—Ewell County, later changed to Pima.[51] When there had been a need recently to go foraging for the division, Ewell had gone out personally, returning late in the day in triumph leading a single bull. Taylor told him it was truly impressive, but that it would hardly feed eight thousand men. "Ah!" said the general, "I was thinking of my fifty dragoons."[52] This tendency to think only company-size may have been one of the reasons he believed "the road to glory cannot be followed with much baggage."[53]

Ewell, like Jackson, fancied himself a victim of mysterious internal maladies. Jackson wouldn't eat pepper because of it, but Ewell would confine his diet to frumenty, a preparation made from wheat. His nervousness often prevented him from sleeping in the normal fashion and he would pass nights curled up around a camp stool in positions that would dislocate the joints of an ordinary human body and, as Taylor said, drive the "caoutchouc man" to despair.[54]

When cross about something, Ewell could be difficult to deal with, brusque and abrupt, sparing nobody with his profane lisping rebuke. But this masked a true nature that was chivalric in the extreme, tender, and humane, "as generous a heart as ever beat in human bosom," one of his kin said of him.[55] Listening in on a Ewell conversation could be an experience. He was given to inexplicable comments that came from nobody knew where. "General Taylor!" he asked his brigadier suddenly one day, "What do you suppose President Davis made me a major-general for?"[56]

At Bull Run in the first year of the war, an expected order from General P.G.T. Beauregard directing Ewell to begin an assault on the Union left hadn't arrived. One of his lieutenants, John B. Gordon, found Ewell in an agony of suspense, chafing like a caged lion, mounting his horse one moment, dismounting it the next, walking to and fro muttering to himself, "No orders, no orders."

Ewell's own written orders were full, accurate, and lucid. His verbal orders, however, especially when he was under intense excitement, were direct from Babel, understandable by no man in any tongue. At such times his eyes glittered with a peculiar brilliancy and his brain far outpaced his speech. His thoughts leaped across great chasms which his words could never hope to cross. He was given to wildly improbable combinations of words and ideas, such as this invitation to Gordon to join him in breakfast before the battle of Bull Run:

"Come and eat a cracker with me; we will breakfast together here and dine together in hell."

When the order from Beauregard at Manassas still hadn't come—it would never arrive, a casualty of the war—Ewell, now in a frenzy, interrupted his mounting and dismounting long enough to demand that Gordon at once send him a man on a horse "with sense enough to go and find out what was the matter." Gordon hurried off to get one of the brightest of the governor's Horse Guard, a crack volunteer outfit peopled by some of the best young blood of the Virginia aristocracy. When the bright young trooper arrived, Ewell hit him with some of the most rapid-fire, incomprehensible, and incomplete instructions ever uttered on a battlefield.

"Do you understand, Sir?" Ewell demanded when he was finished.

When the dazed subaltern asked for—uh—more explicit information, Ewell waved him away impatiently. "Go away from here," he snapped, "and send me a man who has some sense!"

It was also at Manassas that a comely young Virginian, seventeen or eighteen years old, who had been caught between the lines and seen some things, rode up to Ewell in a flutter of martial excitement. At that moment Ewell was directing the placement of a battery to fire on federal forces on the opposite hill. The girl began to pour out the intelligence she had collected, believing it of first importance to the Confederate cause. Ewell listened for a few moments, then pointed to the Union batteries going up on the opposite hill.

"Look there, look there, miss!" he said in his quick, quaint manner. "Don't you see those men with the blue clothes on, in the edge of the woods? Look at those men loading those big guns. They are going to fire, and fire quick, and fire right here. You'll get killed. You'll be a *dead damsel* in less than a minute. *Get away from here! Get away!*"

The intense young woman glanced absently at the blue coats and the big guns, paying not the slightest attention to either, intent only on continuing to tell of all she had seen. Ewell, a longtime bachelor who knew far more about renegade Indians and dragoons than he knew about women, was astonished. He stared at her in mute wonder for a few moments, then turned abruptly to Gordon and said: "Women—I tell you, sir, women would make a grand brigade—if it was not for snakes and spiders." Then thoughtfully he added: "They don't mind bullets—women are not afraid of bullets; but one big black-snake would put a whole army to flight."[57]

In about a year he would marry one of these amazing creatures, his cousin Lizinka, a widow whom he had loved since childhood, but who had spurned him to marry a man named Brown, now deceased. She would give Ewell religion and moderate his language—some would insist she ruined him—and he would, among other things, introduce her to his friends as: "My wife, Mrs. Brown, sir."[58]

But in the early spring of 1862 this quaint man, still a bachelor, and every bit Jackson's match for fearlessness, fighting, and idiosyncracy, was coming to join him in the Valley. He was riding as usual in advance of his division—just as he used to do at the head of his fifty dragoons.

Ewell's division was a crack outfit, three infantry brigades under three able brigadiers—Arnold Elzey, Isaac Trimble, and Richard Taylor—two regiments of cavalry, and field artillery to go with it: 7,529 men in all, and in an admirable state of efficiency.[59] They reached Conrad's Store at Swift Run Gap on the evening of April 30. In front of them the South Fork of the Shenandoah shimmered and to their rear the Blue Ridge loomed, and Jackson was just leaving.

Where was he going? He wasn't saying, but he would be in touch. Jackson ordered his mapmaker, Jed Hotchkiss, to brief Ewell on the federal position around Harrisonburg. Then he was gone, and Ewell would not hear from him for days.[60]

Ewell was being exposed to yet another of Jackson's maddening idiosyncracies—his passion for not telling anybody anything. Ewell need not have been offended; Jackson wouldn't have told his wife, whom he called his dearest pet, where he was going or how he intended to get there. "If my coat knew what I intended to do," he had been known to say, "I'd take it off and throw it away."[61] If he was not going to tell his coat where he was going or what he was going to do, he was not going to tell anything that could talk and tell somebody else. And there were no exceptions. Jackson kept his own friends, staff, fellow generals, soldiers, and wife as deeply in the dark as his enemies. It was his maxim always to mystify, mislead, and surprise—and that meant everybody. "I had learned never to ask him questions about his plans," said one of his officers, "for he would never answer such to any one."[62]

He asked no advice, particularly after his one and only war council in front of Winchester. He shaped his own plans and told them to nobody. And when he set out on a march neither his soldiers nor his staff had any idea whether they were going north, south, east, or west, or why they were going there at all. Perhaps the only man who could predict in a general way what might be up was Jackson's personal slave, Jim Lewis. He got his insight from the general's prayer patterns. When Jackson got up in the night to pray, Jim said, "then I begin to cook rations and pack up for there will be hell to pay in the morning."[63]

It was as if Jackson believed that the day anybody, friend or foe, knew what he was about, that would be the day he would lose a battle. "Charlie," explained an officer trying to help artillery Captain Charles Squires find Jackson before the battle at Bull Run, "this Gen. Jackson is the hardest man to find in all the army."[64] Union generals thought so too, except when he suddenly appeared before them, and when they didn't particularly want to find him. But as Jackson said, "if I can deceive my own people, I shall have no trouble in deceiving the enemy."[65] It was to become a common thing for his soldiers to say, "If the Yankees are as ignorant of this move as we are old Jack has them."[66]

Ewell, a friend and ally, now knew nothing of Jackson's plans, except some vague mention of Staunton. As he took Jackson's place at Conrad's Store and watched him march away toward somewhere, a lack of specific information was all that Ewell had left. Naturally nervous to begin with, he became apoplectic.

Where had Jackson gone? When was he coming back? Would he

be back at all? Colonel James A. Walker of the Thirteenth Virginia came to see Ewell on business and Ewell demanded as he walked in his tent: "Colonel Walker, did it ever occur to you that General Jackson is crazy?"

"I don't know, General," Walker replied, "we used to call him 'Fool Tom Jackson' at the Virginia Military Institute, but I don't suppose he is really crazy."

"I tell you, sir," Ewell protested, "he is as crazy as a March hare. He has gone away, I don't know where, and left me here with some instructions to stay until he returns, but Banks' whole army is advancing on me and I haven't the most remote idea where to communicate with General Jackson. I tell you, sir, he is crazy and I will just march my division away from here. I do not mean to have it cut to pieces at the behest of a crazy man."[67]

It looked like the beginning of a warm relationship based on a common lunacy.

From
under the
Little Faded Cap

Jackson left Conrad's Store with his little army on the last day of April 1862 and headed south down the western edge of the Blue Ridge.

Not a soldier in the army had any more idea where they were going "than the buttons on their coats." Some thought Richmond; most didn't know what to think. It was typical Jackson, as one soldier said, "just a little piece of pure strategy fresh from under the little faded cap."[1]

It soon appeared to most of them that what was under the little faded cap was tetched. The sixteen miles from Swift Run Gap to Port Republic, which was the way they found themselves going, was over an unpaved country road, which the heavy rains of the past ten days had turned into a multimile quagmire. It was the worst stretch of road for mud that Jed Hotchkiss had ever seen in the Valley, and he had seen plenty of them.[2]

It was bottomless. Horses, wagons, and guns sank nearly out of sight and had to be dragged out by the cursing soldiers, with Jackson often stopping to lend a hand. One infantryman was denouncing the general with stunning eloquence, when the object of his passion rode by and said, in his short way, "It's for your own good, sir!"[3]

It took them two and a half days to make the sixteen miles, and it hadn't made any sense to anybody but Jackson. Out of the mire, they marched rapidly, crossing to the east side of the Blue Ridge at Brown's Gap and on to the railway stop at Meechum's River Station on the Virginia Central Railroad, where the foot soldiers were put on a train. When the train then headed west, the artillery caissons and the wagon trains following, the soldiers felt a surge of astonishment and joy. They were headed back to the Valley!

"Our homes," one of them exulted, "might still be ours." It was a qualified joy, however. They still didn't know what Jackson had in mind or where they were going or why. Wild conjecture swept the ranks. But since nobody could figure it out, one of his soldiers said magnanimously, "we concluded to let him have his own way."[4]

When they began pulling into Staunton on Sunday, May 4, everybody in town was surprised, delighted, and grateful. The last they had heard, Jackson appeared to be marching from the Valley altogether. But suddenly, there he was in Staunton in time for church, and the town went with a happy heart to praise God.[5]

"So here we are, Gen. Jackson and the army," Sandie Pendleton wrote his mother from Staunton, "and the enemy have left Harrisonburg and gone back down the Valley."[6]

Banks, of course, was as mystified as anybody. He also had thought Jackson gone from the Valley, and now he pulled back under orders from Washington in some perplexity and bewilderment. Perhaps things would become clearer later.

He was no more perplexed and bewildered, however, than Jackson's new chief of staff. The Reverend R. L. Dabney was not only in doubt where they were headed; he was confounded why he was with the army at all. He was just a parson, a "soldier of the Prince of Peace," as he put it, "innocent, even in youth, of any tincture of military knowledge." He had only recently been ministering to the troops as a chaplain, and now here he was Jackson's adjutant general.

Only a month before he had been at home trying to shake off a fever, caught while doing the Lord's work among the troops, when a letter arrived from Jackson. The West Pointer whom some considered a little odd had written this man of the cloth that his regular chief of staff, James Armstrong, a member of the Virginia state senate, was unable to continue because of an extra session of the legislature. To Dabney's utter astonishment, Jackson offered him the job. He would have the rank of major and his duties "will require early rising and industry."

Dabney hurried to Conrad's Store to protest his unfitness. He argued eloquently that he was not only unqualified, but half broken by camp fevers.

"But Providence," Jackson countered, "will preserve your health, if he designs to use you."

"But I am unused to arms," Dabney protested, ignorant of all military art.

"You can learn," Jackson insisted.

"When would you have me assume my office," Dabney asked lamely.

"Rest to-day, and study the 'Articles of War' and begin tomorrow."

"But I have neither outfit, nor arms, nor horse, for immediate service," Dabney objected.

"My quartermaster shall lend them, until you procure your own," Jackson said.

"But I have a graver disqualification, which candor requires me to disclose to you. . . ." Dabney said, playing his ace. "I am not sanguine of success; our leaders and legislators do not seem to me to comprehend the crisis, nor our people to respond to it; and, in truth, the impulse which I feel to fly out of my sacred calling, to my country's succor, is chiefly the conviction that her need is so desperate. The effect on me is the reverse of that which the old saw ascribes to the rats when they believe the ship is sinking."

"But, if the rats will only run this way," Jackson said with a laugh, "the ship will not sink."

So Dabney became the unlikely adjutant general to this unlikely general and marched off with him through the mud on the roundabout road to Staunton. And he had had no more idea where they were going than the buttons on his coat.[7]

Jackson in fact didn't intend to stay long in Staunton. He stopped only long enough to get his hair cut and take off the old blue U.S. major's uniform he had been wearing and exchange it for a suit of Confederate gray.[8] He was about to leave the Valley again and go to McDowell, a small village nestled among sheer cliffs in the Alleghenies, to attack a Union force under the command of a former Indiana lawyer named Robert Huston Milroy.

Milroy had been moving toward Staunton from the direction of Monterey. Part of his command had already crossed to the east of the Shenandoah Mountain and was encamped near the Harrisonburg and Warm Springs turnpike. If he wasn't stopped, he might unite with Banks and cause serious trouble. Jackson intended to put a stop to it by uniting with somebody himself. The Confederate brigadier, Edward ("Allegheny Ed") Johnson, was standing in Milroy's path six miles west of Staunton with two thousand soldiers. Jackson's plan was to join Johnson and attack Milroy, and when he had whipped him, team with Johnson and Ewell for an assault on Banks in the Valley. Nobody, of course, had any idea he had this in mind, except Robert E. Lee in Richmond, who had been exposed to the plan in theory.

On Wednesday morning, May 7, with his hair cut and his clothes changed, Jackson broke camp and set out behind Allegheny Ed, "who knew the country almost as well as if he had made it."[9] Allegheny Ed had been wounded in the eye in the Mexican War, and when he was in the least startled or agitated the eye winked incessantly. Johnson meant nothing by it, indeed he didn't know it was happening. The eye vibrated independent of his will. It was probably twitching this morning as they marched along.[10]

With Jackson's column was a battalion of cadets from VMI, who had come to fight under their old professor. Bringing up the rear was the Stonewall Brigade, now under the iron hand of a new brigadier, Charles S. Winder. This harsh disciplinarian had fought side by side with a member of the class of 1846 before. He had commanded the mountain howitzers that terrible day four years before on the bloody battlefield in eastern Washington when the northwestern Indians killed Oliver Taylor.

As the army marched along, Sandie Pendleton looked about with disgust and disapproval. It was the meanest country he had ever seen. "It is up one mountain and up another and so on for the whole road," he wrote his mother. "But still it is old Virginia and we must have it."[11]

Johnson's advance found Milroy later that day at Shaw Ridge, and the next morning—May 8—Jackson wrote Ewell, whom he had left staring at Banks from Swift Run Gap, to tell him where he was. "This morning we move forward," he wrote, "and I pray that God will bless us with success."[12]

As they ascended Bull Pasture Mountain later in the morning,

297

Jed Hotchkiss, who knew the country as well as Allegheny Ed, went ahead with the skirmishers up the winding turnpike road. At each bend, finding the way clear, he waved his handkerchief and Jackson came on with the main column. In the afternoon, when they reached the summit, Hotchkiss and Jackson stood together on a spur and looked down on the town below. There in the valley lay the Union camp. Milroy had been reinforced that morning by Brigadier General Robert Schenck, who had hurried down from Franklin and taken command. Hotchkiss quickly sketched a map of the enemy position as Jackson looked over his shoulder.[13]

Whatever Jackson was thinking, Schenck and Milroy made it academic. They decided not to wait for the rebels to attack. About 4:00 in the afternoon, they launched an assault of their own. This surprised Jackson; he preferred it to be the other way around. A vicious four-hour fight followed. But it was a no-win situation for Milroy and Schenck from the beginning; they found that it was just another stonewall. Jackson and Johnson had seized the high ground and there was no taking it back. Fighting was hard in mean terrain such as this, and the Federals fought hard for four bloody hours with not much to show for it. But they shattered a bone in Johnson's ankle, and they about wore out the Confederate soldiers.

"It seemed to me we had been at it about a week," one rebel soldier sighed, when at last it ended.[14]

But not much else had been accomplished, and once was enough. The next morning the Union force, so much present and hard-fighting the afternoon and evening before, was just as suddenly gone. Schenck and Milroy were marching back to Franklin, where they could unite with a much larger force marching down from the north under their commanding general, John C. Frémont.

Jackson ordered an immediate pursuit, intending to follow as far as practicable. That wasn't very far, as it turned out. Pursuing up that narrow trench of a valley was not easy to begin with, and when the Federals set fire to the forest to mask their flight, it became nearly impossible. The valley and the sky above were soon choked with smoke and the middle of the day was like the middle of the night. Jackson called off the pursuit on May 12 and retraced his steps to McDowell. Now that Milroy was out of the way as scheduled, he had other matters to attend to.

But first things first. After the battle, before the pursuit, Jackson wrote a terse message to Richmond which he had sent out of the mountains with Captain John D. Imboden to be dispatched from Staunton. The message said the minimum and gave credit where Jackson thought credit was due. "God blessed our arms with victory at McDowell yesterday," was all it said.[15]

After he had called off the pursuit, Jackson in his short, curt way spoke a few words of congratulation to his soldiers for their gallantry in the battle. He appointed ten o'clock that morning as an occasion of prayer and thanksgiving to Providence and to implore His continued favor. Down on its knees and with Jackson standing motionless with his capless head bent, the little army prayed, glancing nervously up now and then as a few of Milroy's cannonballs screeched overhead. They prayed, one of them said, "with real devotion, by the book, 'from battle, murder, and sudden death, good Lord deliver us.' "[16]

To whomever properly went the credit, a union of Milroy and Banks had been prevented and Jackson, as one of his soldiers said, had taught Milroy "how magnificently Jack can be turned up in the laurel bushes on the mountain side."[17] He now intended to turn up in other laurel bushes on other mountainsides before other startled enemies back in his Valley.

On the other side of the Valley, the now nearly frenetic Richard Ewell had just received another enigmatic message from Jackson, which didn't materially change his view that his new commander was a looney.

"Your dispatch received," Jackson had written hurriedly from McDowell. "*Hold your position—don't move.* I have driven General Milroy from McDowell; through God's assistance, have captured most of his wagon train. . . ."[18]

What is the meaning of this? demanded Ewell. He had just learned from captured prisoners that Shields was about to depart the Luray Valley with eight thousand men to join Irvin McDowell, and he was wild to attack him before he could get away. But Jackson said *don't move* and had underlined it. His hands were tied. All he could do was stay, and send Colonel Thomas Munford with some cavalry to harass Shields on the road to Warrenton.

At about midnight Munford was ready to go and went to report to Ewell before leaving. He found the general in bed.

Hand me that map, Ewell said. Under the dim glow of the

miserable lard lamp, he attempted to show Munford where Jackson was. Before his cavalry officer could figure out what he was after, Ewell bounded out of bed in only his nightshirt and spread the map open on the carpetless floor. Ewell fell to his hands and knees before the map, his bones rattling, his bald head and long beard suggesting a witch rather than a Confederate major general. Growing every minute more exited and agitated, he jammed his finger first at Jackson's position on the map, then at Shields's, then at McDowell's.

After one of his wondrous parsed oaths, he shouted, "This *great wagon hunter* is after a *Dutchman*, an old fool! General Lee at Richmond will have little use for wagons if all *these people* close in around him; we are left out here in *the cold*."

Warming to the subject, he assured Munford that "this man Jackson is certainly a crazy fool, an idiot. Now look at this."

Ewell handed Munford the small piece of paper with Jackson's message on it, and leaped to his feet and ran all around the room, shouting: "What has Providence to do with Milroy's wagon train?" Then he stopped and said to Munford: "*I'll stay here*, but you go and do all you can to keep *these people* from *getting together*."

After Munford left, Ewell climbed back into bed again where he continued to simmer. Outside someone approached his quarters and began to climb the stairs, his saber banging on each ascending step. Rapping at the door, the unsuspecting innocent, a courier, asked for Colonel Munford.

Come in, Ewell beckoned, and light the lamp. With the lamp lit, he stared malevolently at the courier.

"*Look under the bed!*" he shouted. "Do you see him there? Do you know how many steps you came up?"

"No sir," stammered the courier.

"Well I do!" roared Ewell, "by every lick you gave them with that *thing* you have hanging about your feet, which should be *hooked* up when you come *to my quarters*. Do you know how many *ears you have*?"

With the courier growing wilder and wilder in his frantic discomfort, Ewell shouted, "You will go out of here less *one*, and *maybe both*, if you ever wake me up this time anight looking for your Colonel."

Rushing out, his saber now riding high on his hip and well off the floor, the courier found Munford and begged never to be sent to Ewell again.[19]

It had been a frustrating fortnight for Ewell all around—one of his worst. "I have spent two weeks of the most unhappy I ever remember. . . ." he wrote his favorite niece, Lizzie. "Jackson wants me to watch Banks. At Richmond, they want me elsewhere and call me off, when, at the same time, I am compelled to remain until that enthusiastic fanatic comes to some conclusion. . . . I have a bad headache, what with the bother and folly of things. I never suffered as much from dyspepsia in my life. As an Irishman would say, 'I'm kilt entirely.' "[20]

At New Market, Banks felt about the same way Ewell did at Conrad's Store. He had no idea what Jackson had in mind either. He didn't even know where he was. But he did have orders from Washington to fall back and fortify Strasburg.

"I cannot think that those who gave the order know why they gave it," David Strother fumed. Strother was himself a Valley man and a Virginian, and one of Banks's staff officers. He had been lobbying his commander for weeks to attack Jackson. He believed they ought to have cleared the valley of Confederates long before this.[21]

Banks started withdrawing according to orders on May 12, the day Jackson decided to give up chasing Milroy and Schenck. The weather was bright and mild in the Valley that day, but the mood was depressing. By the fourteenth it had begun to rain and there was that pesky Turner Ashby nipping at his heels again all the way to Strasburg. Shields had left to join McDowell, who was on his way to reinforce McClellan on the Peninsula, and Banks had only about eight thousand troops with him now. He had placed a thousand of them, mostly Marylanders, at Front Royal to guard the Manassas Gap Railroad and the roads to Winchester. He settled in with the rest of his dwindling command at Strasburg.[22]

For Jackson's troops, coming out of the mountains into the Valley was coming home again. Their march from Monterey to Mt. Solon was through a springtime paradise. The cherry and the peach trees were in full bloom, their petals all soft and white and pink, and the fields were rank with clover.[23]

They marched with a purpose, as they always did with Jackson. Their commander had a dispatch from Robert E. Lee that went along well with his own line of thinking. "Whatever may be Banks' intention," Lee had written, "it is very desirable to prevent him from going either to Fredericksburg or the Peninsula, and also to destroy the Manassas [Gap Rail]road." Lee had cautioned Jackson that he must also keep himself ready to come to Johnston's support on the Peninsula, at a moment's notice if necessary. But until then he was free to do what he would. Whatever he decided to do against Banks, however, he must "do it speedily, and if successful drive him back toward the Potomac, and create the impression, as far as practicable, that you design threatening that line."[24] These were the kind of orders Jackson liked.

His men, marching happily through the blossoming valley, had no idea, as usual, where they were going or why. "What we are to do next," Sandie Pendleton wrote home, "I cannot divine."[25]

This tore it as far as Richard Ewell was concerned. He held in his hands two conflicting sets of orders. Jackson was back in the Valley at Mossy Creek, and had ordered him to prepare to join him for an attack on Banks. But just now—it was May 17—contrary orders had come from Joseph E. Johnston to move toward Richmond.

Ordering up his horse, Ewell swung into the saddle and galloped off alone to the west. At about daylight the next day—a Sunday—he pulled into Jackson's camp at Mt. Solon.

Jackson greeted him affably. "General Ewell," he said, "I'm glad to see you. Get off!"

"You will not be so glad, when I tell you what brought me," Ewell grumbled.

"What—are the Yankees after you?" inquired Jackson.

"Worse than that. I am ordered to join General Johnston."

Jackson's face clouded. This wasn't what he wanted to hear at all. Without Ewell's division there would be no attack on Banks. Would Providence thus deny him the privilege of striking a blow? Must he be satisfied with the humble alternative of hiding his little army in the mountains and watching others wage war? Would Providence do that to him?

Ewell dismounted and the two generals walked apart to a nearby grove where Ewell produced Johnston's order. Jackson was shaken. But Ewell had an idea. If Jackson would take the responsibility, he would ignore Johnston's order long enough for them to attack Banks together. Johnston could be remonstrated with later.

Jackson bought it. He ordered Ewell to bring his command across the Massanutton as soon as possible, and Ewell remounted and galloped back to his command at Conrad's Store.[26]

Jackson was on the march the next morning when the sun rose. The day was bright and warm, the Valley looking tender and beautiful in its new spring colors.[27] As his army swung down the Valley Pike from Mossy Creek toward New Market, Jackson could count eight thousand men, recently increased by Allegheny Ed Johnson's two thousand. When Ewell joined them he would have sixteen thousand men and forty guns, enough to ruin the war for Banks.

Jackson camped on the Pike, and the next day—the twentieth—the first of Ewell's division arrived. Dick Taylor's brigade of Louisianans with its sprinkling of Irishmen had left Conrad's Store as soon as Ewell returned from Mt. Solon, and had swung around the foot of the Massanutton and down the Pike on the western side of the mountain. Jackson sat on a topmost fence rail and watched them come. Taylor's brigade would have turned anybody's head, marching in brisk and perfect cadence down the broad smooth turnpike in their fresh gray uniforms and white gaiters. They wheeled into camp, not a straggler in sight, every man in his place, the setting sun glinting from their gleaming bayonets, and their bands blaring.[28]

"A 'daisy' she was," said one of Jackson's admiring foot soldiers.[29]

Taylor swung down from his saddle and asked for Jackson, for they had never met. They hardly would have, except for this war. Taylor was a Louisiana planter and politician of wealth and prominence. He was the only son of Zachary Taylor, who was better at producing daughters—three of them—than he was sons. One of those daughters had married Jefferson Davis, but had soon died. However, Taylor had remained close to his ex-brother-in-law, now the President of the Confederacy. Taylor's own marriage had connected him quite as highly in the other direction, to the most respectable Creole families in Louisiana. Aside from being well connected, he was gifted, cultured, and competent.[30]

As Taylor and Jackson met and talked, the Acadian band of the Eighth Louisiana struck up a waltz and Taylor's Creoles, as they often did at the end of a day, began to dance in couples. Jackson stared, and after a contemplative suck at a lemon, muttered: "Thoughtless fellows for serious work."[31]

The Louisianans stared back at Jackson. It was their first sight of him, and what they saw was not reassuring. There was nothing in his appearance that suggested anything above average ability. There must be some mistake, they thought. If he was an able man he showed it less than any general they had ever seen. But there he was, such as he was, the commanding general of this expedition, whatever that was and wherever it was going.[32]

The next morning they started down the turnpike toward Strasburg, Taylor in the lead with Jackson riding at his side, that wooden look in his eyes, and saying scarcely a word. At New Market, Jackson abruptly took the army off the Pike and up the road that cut through the Massanutton eastward to the Luray Valley. Just as suddenly as he had appeared, he disappeared again. Now you see him, now you don't.

Jackson's men paid the sudden change of direction no heed. They were so accustomed by now to their general's whimsical departures from the road ahead that there was not the slightest ripple of surprise. They camped three miles north of Luray that night on the road to Front Royal instead of on the Pike to Strasburg. Richard Ewell filed in with the rest of his division and camped beside them. Everybody was present and accounted for.

Now what?

Since May 14 Banks in Strasburg had been reporting in his dispatches to the war department in Washington that all was quiet in the Valley. Quiet, except for Ashby who continued to dance about in his front, making it difficult to see anything up the Valley with any clarity. But on May 22, Banks felt something was not quite right. He reported to Washington that there could be no doubt Jackson was now back in the Valley. "Compelled to believe that he meditates attack here," Banks urged Secretary of War Edwin Stanton to send heavier artillery and more infantry. He correctly put Jackson's probable strength at not less than sixteen thousand men, against his own five thousand infantry, eighteen hundred cavalry, and sixteen pieces of artillery.[33] Banks's staff man from the Valley, David Strother, was even more uneasy. "The report is that Jackson is at New Market," Strother told his meticulously maintained diary. "If true we are liable to attack at any moment."[34]

As Banks and Strother were penning their respective apprehensions, Jackson on the twenty-second was marching north down the Luray Valley with Ewell in the lead. That night they bivouacked only ten miles from Front Royal. At dawn the next day they were on the road again, drawing ever nearer as the morning wore on. There was no sign of opposition, not the slightest indication that they had been seen. When Ewell learned that the Federal First Maryland was holding Front Royal, he halted his column and sent a courier galloping back down the line to find Bradley Johnson.

The First Maryland Yankees had been a longtime object of interest to Colonel Johnson and his boys in the Confederate First Maryland. They had heard often how their Yankee counterparts from home yearned to make their acquaintance, and the feeling was mutual. If there was anything they did desire, next to marching down Baltimore Street, it was to get as close to the bogus First Maryland as possible. And there they were at last, just up ahead. Johnson could hardly rein in his delight, which was heightened by Ewell's orders to bring his regiment to the front of the column. They were to open the fight, he told his boys, they were to be in the post of honor.

Ewell's division stood aside for them as the Marylanders moved up. It cheered as they passed and shouted affectionately, "There they go! look at them!" The Louisiana brigade presented arms. Not 250-strong, the overjoyed Marylanders hurried at quick time through column after column, seeming "to tread on air as they swung along."[35]

The morning had opened in beauty and serenity for the Federal First Maryland at Front Royal. The trees of the richest green were bathed by the morning sun. The fields around glistened with dew. They had no idea that their rebel neighbors from home were less than ten miles away and closing fast, with a meeting on their minds. In Strasburg, Union Colonel George Henry Gordon of Massachusetts thought that everything this morning seemed more in harmony with life and peace than with bloodshed and death. He also had an old friend—a West Point classmate named Jackson—in that Confederate column moving now toward the little garrison at Front Royal. But like everybody else in the Union camp he didn't know he was coming.[36]

A Union sentinel in a red shirt lay full length under a rail shelter at Front Royal taking his ease. It was a lazy Friday afternoon and all was quiet. At about one o'clock he looked out through hooded eyes toward the road leading south and saw a group of horsemen who hadn't been there a moment before. He looked again, as if he couldn't believe what he was seeing, and after a moment he lazily rose to his feet and reached slowly for his musket. Raising it quickly, he fired toward the horsemen, then bolted, running for his life. The terrible truth had dawned. Those were rebels, come from nowhere.[37]

Henry Kyd Douglas, who had a sure eye for the ladies, was the first to see her. She was just a solitary figure in a dark blue dress covered by a little fancy apron, and she was waving a white sunbonnet. She was approaching from town over a looping route to the eastward to avoid the Yankees. She was signaling urgently. For a moment she disappeared behind a rise, then reappeared again, seeming to heed neither weeds nor fences nor the cross fire now erupting between the two sides.

Douglas called Jackson's attention to this bizarre apparition as she disappeared into another depression. They all watched her come and wondered who she was, and why she was there. Ewell, who since Bull Run was rather accustomed to young women behaving in strange ways, suggested somebody go find out. Jackson sent Douglas, who had seen her first.

It was a task well suited to Douglas's romantic nature. The woman's tall, supple figure struck him most favorably as he drew near. There was something oddly familiar about her. Her speed slackened as he approached, and he was startled to hear her call his name.

"Good God, Belle, you here!" Douglas exclaimed in a burst of sudden recognition. "What is it?"

Douglas should have known. Who else would it be but Belle Boyd, whom he had known from earliest childhood? She had been spying on the Federals again.

Her hand pressed against her heart and nearly exhausted by her long run through the fields, Belle gasped, "Oh, Harry, give me time to recover my breath."

After a few seconds her words came in a rush. "I knew it must be Stonewall, when I heard the first gun. Go back quick and tell him that the Yankee force is very small—one regiment of Maryland infantry, several pieces of artillery and several companies of cavalry. Tell him I know, for I went through the camps and got it out of an officer. Tell him to charge right down and he will catch them all."

The flabbergasted Douglas nodded.

"I must hurry back," she exclaimed. "Good-bye. My love to all the dear boys—and remember if you meet me in town you haven't seen me today."

Douglas raised his cap in salute. Belle blew him a kiss, and was gone.

This was just the sort of information Jackson needed. He had not been certain of the Union strength at Front Royal until Belle had appeared. There was no reason now to hold back. He would do as she suggested and do it quickly. As the Confederate First Maryland rushed down the hill with Major Roberdeau Wheat's Louisianans by their side, Jackson turned to Douglas with a half smile and suggested he go along with them and see if he could get any more information from that young lady.[38]

None of this would have surprised Kate Sperry. Kate was an eighteen-year-old acquaintance of Belle's from Winchester. The last time she had seen her, in October, Kate was certain the budding Confederate spy had gone over the edge. "Of all the fools I ever saw of the womankind," Kate thought then, "she certainly beats all—perfectly insane on the subject of men." Belle had been wearing a dark green riding dress the day Kate last saw her, with brass buttons down the front, a pair of lieutenant colonel shoulder straps, a small riding hat with a row of brass buttons on the rim representing every state in the Confederacy, a gold palmetto breast pin, and a genuine palmetto sticking straight up atop her head. Put all this together with no brains, Kate told her diary, "and you have a full picture of the far-famed Belle Boyd. . . . Since the army has been around her senses are perfectly gone."[39]

In Front Royal, Bradley Johnson, commanding the Confederate First Maryland, stopped a prisoner being double-quicked to the rear by a rebel cavalryman.

"What regiment do you belong to?" he demanded.

"I pelongs to de First Maryland," the prisoner said.

It figures, from the accent, thought Johnson. While he knew there were a lot of bona fide Baltimore boys in the Federal First Maryland, there were also a lot of Dutch Yankees in it too, who really didn't belong. He had found his neighbors at last.

"There's the First Maryland!" he shouted to his men.

Away his regiment sprang with an exuberant cry. Johnson noted with pride and satisfaction that every man was "doing his prettiest with his legs" to go to greet their Maryland neighbors.[40] As one of Jackson's foot soldiers put it, it was a case of Greek meeting Greek.[41]

Jackson and Ewell galloped over the field, one of the foot soldiers noted, "like knights of the olden time, cheering on their men"[42] At one point before all of his guns were up, Jackson saw an opportunity that made his gunner's heart pound with anticipation, and which, to his grief, was fast slipping away.

"Oh, what an opportunity for artillery!" he moaned. "Oh, that my guns were here!"

He turned on the only aide with him at the moment and said fiercely, "Order up every rifled gun, and every brigade in the army."[43]

But Jackson's troops, with their overwhelming numbers and with the First Maryland and Wheat's Louisianans in the lead, made short work of it. The Federals had no time to burn the bridge over the South Fork after crossing, and were soon in full retreat with Jackson and the Sixth Virginia Cavalry in pursuit. Earlier, Ashby had swung over from in front of Banks at Strasburg to destroy the railroad and telegraph between the two federal positions and to stop any attempted reinforcements from Strasburg or a retreat of the enemy from Front Royal.

Darkness finally halted the pursuit, but the federal flank had been turned and the roads to Strasburg and Winchester were now wide open. It had all happened so swiftly. As one of Jackson's foot soldiers said, "no man, woman or child, all the way from Luray, knew we were coming until we had passed, except Belle Boyd."[44]

The Confederate First Maryland, with the Federal First Maryland in custody, could not have been happier. In town they bivouacked and watched the rest of the column march into camp, and heard them shout as they passed, "The real First Maryland has whipped the bogus." The regiment's brigade commander, Arnold Elzey, rode up, took off his hat, and said, "Boys, I knew you'd do it."[45]

My Friend,
My Enemy

F riday afternoon in Strasburg had been hot and languid, and particularly stifling under the canvas of Colonel George Gordon's tent. Gordon knew nothing of the trouble in Front Royal a dozen miles away until about 4:00 in the afternoon, when a mounted orderly reined up violently before his tent and asked for General Banks.[1]

Gordon commanded one of the best regiments in Banks's army, the Second Massachusetts. He had organized it, and marched it to war. In the luck of the draw he had been spending most of that war so far—since July 1861—in and out of the Shenandoah Valley. He had been a brigade commander under Banks in the cautious advance on Winchester in March and had jousted with Turner Ashby all way up the Valley in April.

Gordon remembered now, as the excited orderly told of Jackson's attack that afternoon at Front Royal, what he had told his troops earlier in the spring. They had complained about letting Jackson hightail it out of the Valley without a good fight. But Gordon knew Jackson—all too well. They were friends from a long way back. He remembered him as his awkward classmate at West Point. He remembered his heroic action before the walls at Chapultepec in the war with Mexico. He remembered a lot about Jackson. He had assured his unhappy troops that before the war was over they would probably get all the entertainment from him that they could reasonably stand. Now that prophecy was coming painfully true.[2]

Night fell, starry and clear, and the lights gleamed brightly from windows of the houses in town and shed a murky glow through the canvas tents of the camp. And Gordon began to worry. Nothing was happening. Banks was doing nothing, just sitting in his quarters. There was no sign that the general grasped what was about to happen to him if he didn't move. They still knew little of the strength of the Confederate force that had struck Front Royal that afternoon. Gordon had never thought it very smart to have concentrated their force in Strasburg in the first place. Washington had ordered Banks to fortify Strasburg and leave Front Royal an outpost. Gordon had believed the priorities were wrong, that it ought to have been the other way around. He had urged Banks to press for permission to move his main command to Front Royal, placing himself on his line of communications so he could not be surrounded by a larger force of the enemy. Banks had refused. There was nothing they could do about that now.

But there was a lot that could still be done, must be done. It wasn't happening. The excessive stores that had been collected at Strasburg ought to be sent to Winchester immediately, out of harm's way. They risked losing it all, if he read Jackson's intentions correctly, and he thought he did.

Gordon could stand it no longer. He knew Jackson was out there. And he had no doubt what he would do next. He would attack, and it could happen at any moment; Gordon would do the same in Jackson's place. Indeed, he would have attacked before now. He went to Banks and insisted it was the commanding general's duty to retreat immediately under darkness down the turnpike to Winchester. He urged him to carry his sick and all the supplies he could transport and to destroy the rest. But above all, get out. It would be better to fight from Winchester with the enemy in our front, Gordon argued, than at Strasburg with him in our rear.

But Banks had been assured by David Strother, his staff officer from Virginia who knew this country so well, that there was no possibility of an enemy attack in their rear, and he refused to listen to Gordon. Instead he repeated over and over, "I must develop the force of the enemy." Gordon left, more depressed than ever, with nothing accomplished.

Later in the evening Banks's chief of staff urged Gordon to try to persuade Banks one more time. This time Gordon put his case with warmth and indignation bordering on insubordination.

"It is not a retreat," he shouted at Banks, "but a true military movement to escape from being cut off; to prevent stores and sick from falling into the hands of the enemy."

Rising indignantly from his chair, Banks shouted back, "By God, sir, I will not retreat! We have more to fear, sir, from the opinions of our own friends than the bayonets of our enemies."

Ah, so that's it, thought Gordon. He is afraid of being thought afraid. In despair Gordon rose to leave.

"This, sir," he said as he did so, "is not a military ground for occupying a false position." He added stiffly: "General Banks, I shall now return to my brigade and prepare it for an instantaneous movement, for I am convinced that at last you will move suddenly. At a moment's notice you will find me ready. I shall strike my tents, pack my wagons, hitch up my artillery horses, and hold myself in readiness to form line of battle. I have to request that you will send me word if anything new transpires."

It was 11:00 at night when Gordon left Banks's quarters. As he walked back toward the tents of his command he saw no signs that anybody else was any more troubled about what tomorrow would surely bring than Banks himself. Well, Gordon knew. His relentless classmate was out there somewhere this side of Front Royal and Gordon was as certain as night was night and day was day that he was preparing a drama for them. What merriment, he thought ruefully, the morning would bring.[3]

Gordon worked through the night, and when morning dawned cool and misty he had his brigade and regimental wagon trains ready to move on the Pike toward Winchester. He learned that Banks had also sent off some ambulances with sick and disabled, but nothing else.

As Gordon knew he would be, Jackson was under way by mid-morning. Jackson knew he must move quickly to prevent Banks's escaping toward the Potomac, past Front Royal, or through Winchester. He sent Ewell directly from Front Royal on the road to Winchester, and started off himself across country toward the junction on the turnpike at Middletown, five miles from Strasburg and thirteen from Winchester. He then had all the escape routes covered.

At about 11:00 in the morning Banks became a believer. The peril of his position finally hit him, and he struck out for Winchester, sending the federal column straight down the Pike. It had suddenly become a matter of legs—whether or not he could outrun Jackson. Gordon rode at the head of his brigade, marveling as he went at the immensity of the train in front and behind, and hoping they were not too late. At about 1:00 in the afternoon, Gordon passed through Middletown, and there was still no sign of Jackson.

Shortly after he passed, however, Jackson arrived and stared at the long wagon train hurrying down the turnpike toward Winchester, and at the Union cavalry moving directly in his front. He had no idea how much of Banks's army had already passed, but he would strike what was there. The turnpike, which had been teeming with life moments before suddenly presented "a most appalling spectacle of carnage and destruction."[4] The road became clogged with struggling and dying horses and riders. R. L. Dabney, still reluctantly installed as Jackson's chief of staff, was horrified. "At every fierce volley," he wrote, "the troopers seemed to melt by scores from their saddles; while the frantic, riderless horses, rushed up and down, trampling the wounded wretches into the dust."[5]

As its shattered cavalry scattered, the federal artillery began shelling Jackson from the direction of Strasburg, in an effort to cut through. But it soon became apparent to Jackson that the main body of Banks's army had already passed on the way to Winchester. That was far larger game, and Jackson spun about and started after it.

Up ahead Gordon turned back and quickly formed a new rear guard with artillery from his own brigade. He would try to hold the rebels back and protect what train was left.

When Jackson struck, Banks's heart—and Strother's—sank. What Strother had told his general couldn't happen, just had.

"It seems we were mistaken in our calculation," Banks said simply.

The mortified Strother could manage only a bow. "It seems so," he replied.[6]

Banks galloped back toward Gordon with reinforcements, and the rear guard was quickly reconstituted. This done, he turned away and rode back toward the head of the column, leaving Gordon with no orders of any kind. He had simply ordered the Twenty-Eighth New York, which he had brought with him, to report to the cavalry commander, Brigadier General John Hatch. But Hatch was somewhere back in that chaos on the turnpike. So Gordon, with no authority to do so, shrugged and assumed command. It was to be war between him and his old classmate.

Gordon made his stand at Newtown five and a half miles from Winchester. At about twilight, in the middle of the fight, General Hatch appeared. Having escaped the carnage on the Pike, he had come by a circuitous road to his left. Gordon immediately tendered him command of the rear, but Hatch said he could do no better than Gordon was doing and rode on toward Winchester with his staff, leaving behind six companies of cavalry to help out. So Gordon picked up the fight again. For four hours he held Jackson at bay at Newtown, but it was all he could do. Threatened with being surrounded, he began to back away. He had at least bought Banks some precious time.[7]

Nothing, however, could buy back the wagons full of commissary stores abandoned by Banks along the turnpike to Newtown—the high cost of a hurried retreat. The wagons lined the road in such numbers that the Confederates found it reasonable to believe that if Banks reached Winchester it would be without a train, perhaps without an army. This gratified Jackson, who enjoyed confiscating enemy wagons only slightly less than he enjoyed destroying their owners.

He was not gratified, however, when Ashby's cavalry and infantry abandoned themselves to wholesale pillaging and the pursuit stalled because of it. He was pained and outraged. It was inconceivable to him that they could be so forgetful of their duty as the advance element of a pursuing army. But there was nothing to be done; troop discipline was not one of Turner Ashby's strong points.[8]

Jackson was nonetheless moving up the turnpike as night came, as rapidly as Gordon's stubborn defense would permit, and occasionally letting his mind dwell on more pleasant thoughts. Henry Kyd Douglas rode beside him, absently meditating on some social movements he intended to execute in Winchester when they got there.

Jackson's mind was on the ladies as well. Perhaps it was the recollection of Belle Boyd that triggered it. He had sent her a note the night before from Front Royal. "I thank you, for myself and for the army," he had written her, "for the immense service that you have rendered your country to-day." Belle was probably clutching it ecstatically to her bosom at that moment.[9]

"Mr. Douglas," came Jackson's voice from across the road, shattering Douglas's private meditations. "What do you think of the ladies of Winchester?"

The startled Douglas blushed.

"I mean the ladies generally," Jackson continued with a quiet smile. "Don't you think they are a noble set, worth fighting for?"

Douglas couldn't very well argue with that.

"I do," Jackson went on. "They are the truest people in the South."

He drew his cap down farther over his eyes, moved Little Sorrel into a better pace, and lapsed into his usual silence. Douglas assumed he expected no reply, and there was no disputing the point.[10]

It was past dark when they finally dislodged the stubborn Gordon and could push beyond Newtown. Jackson wanted to be on the heights above Winchester by morning; there was to be no rest for his little army already exhausted by lack of sleep.

"This is uncivilized," muttered Lieutenant Colonel Stapleton Crutchfield, Jackson's chief of artillery. Several staff officers fell asleep, as if in agreement, and were left by the roadside. Others dozed unsteadily in their saddles.[11]

But Gordon contrived to keep them all awake. Although he was withdrawing, he was not through resisting. There were still as many abandoned wagons lining the turnpike, but the Federals had put the torch to them and they lit the road all the way to Winchester. Gordon lit it ever more brightly with ambushes. A stitching of fire erupted immediately ahead of Jackson and danced along a wall. Bullets hissed up the road past him and his cavalry escort and staff.

It was more than his escort could stand. They drew rein and wavered.

"Charge them! Charge them!" Jackson cried.

The escort advanced tentatively and when a second volley hissed about them, they broke and streamed back past Jackson at a gallop.

Left alone on the road with his staff, Jackson was beside himself.

"Shameful!" he cried in a rage of passion.

He turned on the staff officer beside him. "Did you see anybody struck, sir?"

He sat among the humming bullets, continuing to grieve for his inconstant cavalry escort. "Surely they need not have run," he said, "at least until they were hurt!"[12]

May was one of Cornelia Peake McDonald's favorite months of the year in Winchester. When May came the trees began to show their young leaves, the lush lawns deepened to a bright, vivid green, and spring flowers filled the gardens.[13] That's the way it was in Cornelia's Winchester on Sunday morning, May 25, 1862. A bright sun was just rising as Jackson and his army stood in the outskirts and looked down on the town. The sun had never shone on a prettier country nor a lovelier May morning, one of his cannoneers thought as he gazed on the sleeping scene. The only blot on the beautiful day seemed to be the Yankee battle line stretching before them.[14]

But Jackson had the advantage and he knew it. He outnumbered this broken Union army nearly three to one. As he had ravaged the Pike in the day and slowly pushed Gordon back through the night, Ewell had marched up the back road from Front Royal to Winchester. His division had slept on their arms where they stopped that night, three miles from the city. He was on the high ground overlooking Abrams Creek the next morning as Jackson arrived, armed and ready. Regrettably it was another Sabbath. But there could be no help for that; Jackson had to strike.[15]

Gordon arrived at Winchester in the middle of the night, forty-eight hours without sleep, and had gone immediately to find Banks. Again he pressed the general to do something the general didn't want to do—get out of there, retire in proper order before Jackson ran him out with his overwhelming force. The odds were just too great. Gordon met the same stolid front he had in Strasburg. It seemed to the colonel that dark night that there were stonewalls everywhere—one in Winchester refusing to do the right thing and another just outside of town preparing a death blow. He walked from Banks's headquarters, found a bed, and threw himself across it fully clothed for as much sleep as Jackson would allow him.

It wouldn't be much. At 4:00 in the morning one of his staff officers, Major Wilder Dwight, galloped up.

"Colonel!" he shouted, "the pickets are falling back! the enemy is advancing."

Gordon leaped from the bed.

"Yes," he told Dwight. "I will be there instantly."

As Dwight galloped away, Gordon raced toward Banks's headquarters, and rushed into his bedroom.

"General Banks," he exclaimed, "the question of what is to be done has at last settled itself. The enemy, now moving in force, has almost reached the town. I shall put my brigade instantly in line of battle upon the heights I now occupy. If you have any orders to give, you will find me there to receive them."[16]

In the early dawn Jackson stood without a cloak to keep him from the chill and peered at the figures of Gordon's skirmishers silhouetted on the ridges against a lightening sky. The smoke of battle would soon cover the entire field and block out the bright May sun. Jackson and Ewell were everywhere, Jackson where he shouldn't be, Taylor thought, riding on the flank of his Louisiana brigade between it and the enemy line. It wasn't where the general of the army ought to be, and Taylor told him so. Jackson ignored him.[17]

Jackson ignored all such advice—he always did. "Be jabers," an Irish rebel cried out when he saw him, "have your eye on Auld Jack. I'll wager you he thinks them blatherin' bangs are singin' birds."[18]

Taylor was no less heedless of danger than his commander. Indeed, he was annoyed with his men. Enemy fire was whistling wildly about them, and to his disgust they were as "nervous as a lady, ducking like a mandarin."

"What the h—— are you dodging for?" he demanded. "If there is any more of it, you will be halted under this fire for an hour."

As Taylor spoke he felt a gentle hand on his shoulder. Jackson was there. "I am afraid you are a wicked fellow," he admonished softly.[19]

By now the clouds of murderous smoke were making deceptively beautiful spirals in the sky and the battle was going slowly but implacably against Gordon. For three hours he held out against Jackson's assaults, and finally he could do no more. His battery had but fifteen rounds left and there was no ammunition train from which to replenish either it or the spent cartridge boxes of his infantry. He was done.[20]

The Union line broke. And as it broke, Taylor saw Ewell cheering himself hoarse as he surged forward with frantic new energy.[21] Jackson leaned over to Douglas and said, "Order forward the whole line, the battle's won." As Taylor's troops and his old Stonewall Brigade swept past, Jackson shouted, "Very good! Now let's holler!"

And he snatched the faded old cap off his nose and waved it over his head. His staff took up the cheer and the whole line followed with a triumphant howl.[22] Jackson grasped Taylor's hand warmly, a gesture, Taylor thought, "worth a thousand words from another."[23]

They swept through downtown Winchester, the Federals now in full rout and the Confederates not three hundred yards behind. David Strother, the Valley man turned federal staff officer, bolted from the hotel in a rain of pistol shots, just ahead of the pursuing rebels. He saw the pursuers pouring in at every street. They came, he thought, "like a flood of dirty water . . . grey, ragged, and unwashed," screaming their "hideous yells and war whoops."[24]

The people of Winchester were Southern to the bone, and the horde of ragtag Confederates was beautiful in their sight and their yells were the music of redemption. They threw open their doors and windows and rushed into the streets—old men, women, and children dressed and undressed, in their Sunday clothes and in their nightshirts, hurrahing, crying, laughing, screaming, crazy with joy. Oblivious to the flying bullets, they ran in among the horses as if to embrace the knees of their deliverers. Many wildly waved their arms or their handkerchiefs, screaming their welcome in cheers and blessings, while a few of the less demonstrative simply stood on their doorsteps with their faces bathed in tears.[25] Jackson was so moved that he said of Winchester: "A noble old town. It and its people are worth fighting for."[26]

Many of the townspeople were doing some fighting of their own, demonstrating their joy by standing at their windows firing at the fleeing enemy. Some in one breath were blessing the rebels for coming and in the next blaspheming them for letting so many Yankees escape.[27] Those are the ones George Gordon noticed as he left town. Fired on not only by Jackson's men, but by the people at their windows hurling bullets, hot water, and missiles of every description, he left with an oath on his lips against a "merciless foe" and "the hellish spirit of murder."[28]

At least he got out. His staff officer, Major Wilder Dwight, wasn't so lucky. As he was racing through Winchester he stopped to help a wounded man and was himself instantly surrounded by Confederates. In captivity Dwight continued to work to comfort the Union wounded and to bury the dead. But because he required some help to do those things, he was at last compelled to appeal personally to Jackson.

Dwight figured he might have a lever there—an old friendship. He would mention Gordon, whom he had often heard speak of Jackson as a classmate at West Point and a companion in the Mexican War. Jackson's heart might be softened by this old friendship.

Dwight identified himself to Jackson as a major in the Second Massachusetts, commanded by Colonel Gordon, "who is, I believe, an old friend of yours."

"Friend of mine, sir?" said Jackson curtly. "He was, sir, once a friend."

Dwight retired. So much for connections. So much for friendships. Released later and reunited with his commander, Dwight told him the story.

When Gordon heard it he sighed for what used to be—that "boy companion," that "honest, dear 'old Jack,' " who as Stonewall Jackson remembered him no longer as a friend.[29]

Perhaps Jackson remembered him better now as an enemy. For if Jackson had demonstrated how to conduct a relentless attack, Gordon had shown how to conduct a creditable retreat. In the long bitter hours between the night of May 23 and the morning of May 25, Gordon had argued with one general, Banks, and fought another, Jackson. He had covered the eighteen miles from Strasburg to Winchester fighting a stubborn rear guard action most of the way. He had held Jackson at bay for four hours at Newtown, annoyed him on the road afterward, and then finished with a three-hour stand in Winchester, broken finally by overwhelming numbers.

He had proved a worthy foe for Jackson. And why not? The two enemy-friends had learned their craft in the same classroom.

In Winchester, Jackson saw he still had lessons to teach. He was in a passion to pursue and destroy the crushed enemy. Full of impatience, he exhorted his army as it paused to bask in the worshipping acclaim of a grateful Winchester. "Push on!" he cried. "Push on to the Potomac!"[30]

Jackson agreed with those impatient townspeople who believed they were letting too many Yankees get away alive. Among his battle axioms—right up there at the top with celerity and mystification— was pursuit. When you strike an enemy and overcome him, Jackson had lectured Captain John Imboden, "never let up in the pursuit so long as your men have strength to follow; for an army routed, if hotly pursued, becomes panic-stricken, and can then be destroyed by half their number."[31]

That was the preaching Jackson burned now to practice. All of the elements were there—the enemy had been struck and overcome and was now routed and panic-stricken. He must be pursued. What wasn't there, however, was Jackson's cavalry. In the battle it had become as scattered and disorganized as the Union army itself.

"Never was there such a chance for cavalry," he grieved as he saw the enemy footing it down the turnpike in such beaten disarray and so vulnerable to final destruction. "Oh that my cavalry were in place!"

Would artillery do? an aide asked.

"Yes," cried Jackson. "Go back and order up the nearest batteries you find."

To another he shouted, "Order every battery and every brigade forward to the Potomac."[32]

But artillery and infantry, particularly an infantry dead on its feet from what seemed hundreds of endless miles of sleepless marching and fighting, could not do it alone. When the pursuit continued for some time and cavalry still hadn't appeared, Jackson called for Sandie Pendleton. Pendleton must go find the cavalry.

Alexander Swift Pendleton had no idea where the cavalry was at that moment. But he was another of those wide awake, smart young men Jackson seemed to attract. He was the son of a soldier. His father, William Nelson Pendleton, was a West Point–trained artilleryman whom his son affectionately called "the stern warrior,"[33] and who not only dispensed fire, but brimstone, being an episcopal preacher by vocation. At the outbreak of the Civil War, the fifty-one-year-old father had taken command of the Rockbridge Artillery and had named his four cannon, small brass six-pounders from VMI, Matthew, Mark, Luke, and John.[34]

At about the time the father was baptizing his cannon, the twenty-one-year-old son was joining Jackson's staff at Harpers Ferry as brigade ordnance officer. They were a good match, this young University of Virginia graduate student and his commander. They had known one another in Lexington, where Pendleton had attended Washington College. They had belonged to the same literary society. Young Sandie also shared Jackson's religious fanaticism. He seemed destined, by birth and the luck of the draw, to be associated with stern warriors.[35]

319

Now, by the luck of another draw, he found himself in Winchester looking for Jackson's cavalry. Failing to find any there, he rode eastward toward Ewell's division, where he knew there was cavalry under the command of Brigadier General George Hume Steuart. He found Steuart's men, but not Steuart, on the Berryville Road about two and a half miles from Winchester, taking their ease with their horses grazing in a field of clover, as if there was no war. They told Pendleton they were not going anywhere without orders from Steuart. So Pendleton galloped on and found Steuart about half a mile down the road. But Steuart was not going anywhere without orders from Ewell.

For God's sake, Pendleton argued, this was a peremptory order direct from Jackson! That made no difference to Steuart. So Pendleton galloped on to find Ewell, perhaps mindful for the first time why Jackson preferred young, energetic staff men who were not easily discouraged. Two miles farther down the road he found Ewell, who seemed surprised that Steuart hadn't agreed to go at once. Pounding back up the road with this endorsement, Pendleton ran into Steuart again, who rather than rushing to get his cavalry in motion, had slowly followed Pendleton toward Ewell, wasting yet more precious time. But now he seemed satisfied. He galloped back to his command, ordered them mounted and formed, and thundered off at last to carry out Jackson's order. Pendleton hurried along after, probably thinking there were better ways to spend a Sunday morning.[36]

When Steuart arrived to take up the pursuit, Jackson called off his infantry to give them some rest—their first in days. They were utterly exhausted. "Nature," R. L. Dabney observed, "could do no more."[37]

None of these internal Confederate snarl-ups made any difference to Banks, who now needed no urging from Gordon to get out of there. On he ran, hounded past Martinsburg and through Charles Town, where, as one pursing Confederate noted with satisfaction, that damned insurrectionist, John Brown, had "obtained a permit to paddle his canoe across the Styx."[38]

At last, after racing sixty miles in thirty-six hours, Banks crossed his own Styx, the Potomac, never happier to see the other side of a river in his life. "There were never more grateful hearts in the same number of men," he wrote Washington, "than when at midday of the 26th we stood on the opposite shore."[39]

That same day Jackson sent Richmond another of his laconic announcements: "During the last three days God has blessed our arms with brilliant success." Then he ordered up another divine service to thank Providence and ask His continued favor.[40]

They were a convincing pair, this general and his God.

Delightful
Excitement

If General Banks saw salvation across the river and Stonewall Jackson saw the hand of Providence in victory, Abraham Lincoln saw opportunity still alive in the Valley.

The uppermost thought in the president's mind as Jackson chased Banks north across the Potomac, was to bag him before he could get back out. So he put John C. Frémont's Mountain Division in motion from the west and Irvin McDowell's division on the road from the east with orders to slam the gate shut on the troublesome rebel before he could escape.

The first thing Lincoln did was wire George McClellan, who was clamoring for reinforcements on the Peninsula and was expecting McDowell to arrive momentarily. Sorry, the president said, but "in consequence of Gen. Banks' critical position I have been compelled to suspend Gen. McDowell's movement to join you. The enemy are making a desperate push upon Harper's Ferry, and we are trying to throw Frémont's force & part of McDowell's in their rear."[1]

Lincoln then began barking orders over the telegraph to those two generals, exhorting them to hurry. If they could converge in Jackson's rear and prevent him from leaving the lower Valley, they would have him.

He ordered Frémont in the Alleghenies to move toward Harrison-burg. "Much—perhaps all—depends upon the celerity with which you can execute it," he told the Pathfinder. "Put the utmost speed into it. Do not lose a minute."[2]

This was not the way Frémont had hoped to spend the summer—chasing that fanatic Jackson up the Shenandoah. When he assumed command of the new Mountain Department late in March, he had something else in mind. Banks's defeat, and now this, were deranging his plans. But orders were orders. So he began the requested move-ment by heading in the wrong direction.

Lincoln was aghast. "I see that you are at Moorefield." he wired Frémont. "You were expressly ordered to march to Harrisonburg. What does this mean?"[3]

When Frémont looked toward Harrisonburg, he saw only futility. Jackson had obstructed all but one of the roads leading that way out of the mountains when he was at McDowell. The only route left open would take him on a long looping detour. Frémont believed that any movement now toward Harrisonburg would be fatal to his lines of supply, leaving them exposed to the very prey he was sup-posed to be hunting. There was no telling what Jackson might do with such an opportunity. Besides, it had been raining without letup for a week. The roads were ribbons of mud. So Frémont had marched toward Moorefield instead, obeying the spirit of the order rather than the letter, with the idea of cutting off Jackson's retreat at Strasburg. He assured Lincoln he could be in Strasburg by noon on Friday, May 30. So be it. Lincoln could adjust. McDowell was even then converging on Front Royal from the other direction. If they could get there in time, and at the same time, Jackson's way would be blocked.[4]

On the morning of the thirtieth, Frémont was thirty-eight miles from Strasburg, but his advance was ten miles closer. Shields's division of McDowell's command was twenty miles away, but his advance was already in Front Royal. McDowell was following with two other divisions.

Tom Jackson was asleep under a tree in front of Harpers Ferry fifty miles away. His mind was at peace. He was keeping thousands of federal troops tied up in the Valley and McDowell's entire army from reinforcing McClellan on the Peninsula. Washington was re-acting exactly as they had all hoped it would, following the Confederate script. Jackson had done his duty. And now he was getting a few winks.

A. R. Boteler watched Jackson for a few moments, then took out paper and pencil and began sketching him. Boteler was a Confederate congressman with a bent for art. And he was attached for a time, between sessions in Richmond, as a colonel on Jackson's staff. He sketched busily for a while, absorbed in his work. Glancing up, he saw Jackson's eyes wide open now and fixed on him.

The general smiled and extended his hand for the drawing. "Let me see what you have been doing there," he said.

Jackson studied the sketch. "My hardest tasks at West Point were the drawing lessons," he said, "and I never could do anything in that line to satisfy myself." He laughed. "Or indeed, anybody else."

The two men sat a moment in silence. Then Jackson said, "But, colonel, I have some harder work than this for you to do, and if you'll sit down here, now, I'll tell you what it is."

Jackson wanted the congressman to go to Richmond. "I must have reinforcements," he said. "You can explain to them down there what the situation is here. Get as many men as can be spared, and I'd like you, if you please, to go as soon as you can."

Boteler told Jackson that he would go willingly. "But you must first tell me, general, what is the situation here?"

Jackson explained how the federal armies even at that moment were closing in behind him up the Valley. He told Boteler to tell Richmond that he intended to send his prisoners and the captured stores through and to do what he could with his present force to frustrate Union plans. But if he could get his command up to forty thousand men, he would push beyond the Potomac into Maryland toward Washington, "raise the siege of Richmond, and transfer this campaign from the banks of the James to those of the Susquehanna."

Here was Jackson, with two armies closing in on his rear in overwhelming numbers with orders to crush or capture him. Yet he wanted to push on deeper still into enemy territory, farther still from safety.

That afternoon Jackson and Boteler caught the train together back to Winchester. As soon as they were aboard, Jackson put his arm on the back of the seat ahead and dozed. Near Summit Point a Confederate cavalryman approached at a gallop. Jackson stopped the train and the rider thrust a dispatch in through the window. The dispatch told Jackson that the Twelfth Georgia had been driven in at Front Royal and that the federal advance was within twelve miles of Strasburg. The door was closing.

Jackson glanced at the dispatch, tore it up, and dropped the fragments on the floor of the car. "Go on, sir, if you please," he told the conductor, and went back to sleep.

They reached Winchester at dusk in a heavy rainstorm. Boteler prepared to go on to Richmond as ordered. Jackson stepped down from the train to call in his army from Harpers Ferry. He had pushed his luck about as far as it could be pushed, farther than anybody else felt prudent. The race to slip through the closing gate at Strasburg was about to begin. It was to be a matter of legs again.[5]

Jackson summoned Jed Hotchkiss.

"I want you to go to Charles Town and bring up the First Brigade," he told his mapmaker. He would wait for them as long as he could, but if the gate swung shut on them at Strasburg, Hotchkiss must bring them around through the mountains.[6]

Hotchkiss started north down the Valley Pike and Jackson on May 31 started his main army south in a falling rain. First he sent the 2,300 federal prisoners under guard. It would be the swiftest these soldiers ever marched for any general. The wagon train, stretching for seven miles, pregnant with captured federal stores, rolled into the line of march behind them.

Jackson's soldiers believed he would stay rather than leave those wagons behind. Rather than give up a single wagon they reckoned he would fight a skirmish; rather than give up several he would fight a pitched battle. If a wheel came off a wagon he would stop the whole train and wait for it to be fixed, while the rear guard held off the baying enemy. "He would fight for a wheelbarrow in a retreat," one of his officer's said. Some called him the Wagon Hunter.[7]

Jackson's army, all of it but the Stonewall Brigade, the brigade's Second Virginia, and the First Maryland, which were still in Charles Town and Harpers Ferry, filed in behind the wagons. The army was still eighteen miles from the closing gate, farther from it than the advance troops of the two converging federal armies. Frémont was in Wardensville and closing. Shields was at Front Royal less than a dozen miles away.

But when Jackson reached Strasburg early that evening it was still unoccupied. Frémont had not arrived from the west when he told Lincoln he would, and there was no sign of Shields down the Front Royal road to the east. Jackson was in time. But would the Stonewall Brigade and the Maryland regiment also be in time? They were still miles behind. Could he hold the gate open long enough for them?

When Jed Hotchkiss reached Brigadier General Charles Winder with orders to wrap it up and hurry south, Winder's Stonewall Brigade and the First Maryland were still busy with the Federals around Charles Town, thirty miles from Strasburg. The Second Virginia was several miles farther down the road still, at Loudoun Heights above Harpers Ferry, shelling Yankee positions in the town. Winder immediately called everybody in and they started back.

For many of these foot soldiers it was a case of here we go again. They had no information. Jackson had told them nothing, as usual. But they must be in a tight place, because they were marching furiously.[8] That wasn't anything new either. It was Stonewall Jackson's way. "He forgets that one ever gets tired, hungry, or sleepy. . . ." one general was to say of him. "[He] would kill up any army the way he marches." He will never get his vote for president, the general vowed.[9]

Right then Jackson wasn't running for president, but a lot of these men marching for their lives might agree with the basic thesis. "Why is Old Jack a better general than Moses?" was the question they liked to ask. "Because it took Moses forty years to lead the Israelites through the wilderness," the answer went, "and Old Jack would have double-quicked them through in three days."[10]

"Man that is born of a woman, and enlisteth in Jackson's army," went another old saw, "is of few days and short rations."[11] Thinking of this probably reminded most of these men that they hadn't eaten all day, just marched in the rain and the mud. The men of Jackson's old Stonewall Brigade often felt that their general singled them out for this sort of particular misery because they had once been his. "I wish the Yankees were in Hell!" one of them said. "I don't," sighed another. "Old Jack would follow them there, with our brigade in front!"[12]

To all this banter Jackson would simply have said it was for their own good, that he was obliged to sweat them hard today that he might save their blood tomorrow.[13] But he did allow them to rest every hour for a few moments on all their marches no matter how hard and no matter in how much of a hurry. He insisted on it and preferred for them to do it lying flat down, since "a man rests all over when he lies down."[14] Everybody in his army tended to obey, even Little Sorrel.

For these soldiers who did it all with their feet, the cavalry, who did it all with another part of the anatomy, was a sore sticking point. As the two branches of the service passed on marches, the foot soldiers would shout derisions at the horse soldiers: "Come down out o' that hat, know yo're thar; see your legs a hanging down!" Or "Get from behin' them boots! Needn't say you aint thar; see your ears a workin'!"[15]

On they flew, these soldiers who did it with their feet, and when they marched into Winchester in the late evening, on the last day of May, they found it deserted except for stragglers. Still Winder drove them on, and they reached Newtown about 10:00 that night, and dropped exhausted into a "cheerless, rainy bivouac." Most of them had marched thirty miles, the Second Virginia even farther, and they had not eaten all day. They slept where they stopped and the next morning—June 1—broke bright and clear following the rain. Overnight Winder had procured barrels of crackers for them, and after eating they hurried out on the turnpike again. Strasburg was now but a morning's march away.[16]

As they marched toward it they heard a new sound replacing yesterday's pounding rain. Cannon were roaring on the right, ahead of them in the distance. Jackson must be in Strasburg still, waiting as he promised he would, holding the gate open for them. He was a hard man for a march, but he was a man of his word.

Jackson was there. He had sent the prisoners and the wagons on through Strasburg and up the Pike out of harm's way. But he and his army were still there, waiting between the two Union commands that had been sent to crush them.

It had now been two days since Lincoln had seen time and opportunity slipping away and wired Frémont.

"Where is your force?" he had demanded. "It ought this minute to be near Strasburg. Answer at once."[17]

Frémont assured him then that he would be there around five o'clock the next afternoon. But here it was the morning of June 1 and Jackson was in Strasburg, but Frémont wasn't.

It was another Sunday, and duty was calling Jackson again louder than Providence. He sent Ewell out on the west side of town to hold off Frémont's arriving army, and to keep the gate from slamming shut before Winder could squeeze through. Down the road to the east there was, incredibly, still no sign of Shields or McDowell.

Winder was coming as fast as he could through the morning, approaching Middletown. Captain McHenry Howard of his staff was riding about a hundred yards in front of the hurrying column when he saw ahead of him a group of horsemen waiting at the turnoff of the road to Front Royal. As he approached, one of the officers rode out to meet him, and Howard recognized Turner Ashby.

"Is that General Winder coming up?" Ashby asked Howard.

Howard told him it was.

Ashby's swarthy face relaxed in a smile. "Thank God for that!"

As Winder rode up, Ashby gripped his hand warmly and said, "General, I was never so relieved in my life. I thought that you would be cut off and had made up my mind to join you and advise you to make your escape over the mountain to Gordonsville."[18]

Ahead the soldiers saw the smoke from the guns they had been hearing. Their roar was now immediate, directly in their front. They had now only to squeeze through the still-open gate. And when they were safely past in the early afternoon, slipping "through the jaws of the closing vice like a greased rat,"[19] Jackson sent a message to Ewell, and Ewell pulled back. The trapdoor slammed shut, but the game, as Lincoln called Jackson, was gone.

When the two Union armies entered Strasburg that evening, Jackson was twelve miles up the turnpike, making his camp in Woodstock and calling it a day. The soldiers of the Stonewall Brigade bivouacked along fence rows on the turnpike well south of Strasburg. It is very likely that as they retired for the night, dog tired, they cursed Jackson one more time. And they probably smiled when they said it.

The next day was Monday, the beginning of a new week, and the whole business had now turned into a stern-chase and another footrace. Frémont, too slow in slamming the door, now had to throw his army after Jackson up the Valley on the western side of the Massanutton. McDowell sent Shields racing up the eastern side on a parallel track to try to cut him off.

Shields had been worrying Jackson. He had not showed up at Strasburg when the Confederates passed through the day before, although he had been in possession of Front Royal for more than forty-eight hours. This could only mean one thing; he must be moving up the Valley on the other side of the mountain to get in front of him or cross one of the bridges and hit him in the flank. Jackson knew he must foreclose this possibility, and above all he must prevent a union of Shields and Frémont anywhere along the track. The solution was simple enough: burn the bridges.

This happened to be one of Turner Ashby's specialties. Soon the White House Bridge over the South Fork of the Shenandoah and the Columbia Bridge upriver were in flames. As Jackson marched over the North Fork bridge at Mount Jackson, he burned it as well. Frémont arrived just in time to see it falling into the river, and wearily called for pontoons. The only bridge still spanning the Shenandoah was the one at Port Republic around the south end of the Massanutton.[20]

While Ashby was away burning bridges, the Stonewall Brigade was bringing up the rear doing his work, withdrawing before Frémont slowly, regiment by regiment, gun by gun—setting up, checking him, withdrawing, setting up again. It was the same maddening ritual that had frustrated Banks and Gordon in their pursuit of Jackson up the Valley a month and a half earlier.

When Ashby returned to take charge of the rear again, things settled down into a more leisurely routine. Jackson's retreats, unlike his advances, were never hurried—busy, but not hurried. At Mount Jackson on that Monday he paused long enough to write Anna. "I am again retiring before the enemy," he told her cheerfully. "They endeavored to get in my rear by moving on both flanks of my gallant army, but our God has been my guide and saved me from their grasp. You must not expect long letters from me in such busy times as these, but always believe that your husband never forgets his little darling."[21]

All through the day the army marched along to the constant thudding of artillery in their rear. But in the evening the guns grew quiet and the Sixteenth Mississippi's little cornet band ministered to the tired spirits of the footsore soldiers with a concert. "Bonnie Blue Flag," "Gentle Annie," "The Marseilles Hymn," "Maryland, My Maryland," and "Dixie" swelled on the quiet night air, ending wistfully with that ultimate song of the heart, "Home Sweet Home," and the rebel yell.[22]

Jackson was not looking for either quiet or home. He was thinking as he rode along where would be the best place to strike the Federals yet another blow. He had Frémont behind him and Shields blocked off on the other side of the mountain, and now his busy mind was pondering how he might turn first on one, crush him, then turn on the other. He believed he knew just the place. Twice on one day during the retreat he called in Jed Hotchkiss to ask him questions about the country around Port Republic, where he had left that one bridge standing.[23]

The little army moved along up the Valley, with Ashby badgering Frémont in the rear, for the next three days. The main column reached Harrisonburg before midday on June 5 and took the road leading southeast. For many of these soldiers this retreat was a replay of the earlier one. They had done it all before, only last April. They could only wonder now as they had wondered then: What is going on under that little faded cap?

Turner Ashby was much like the general he served. It was just as impossible to divine what was going on in his battle-crazed mind as it was to figure what was happening under Jackson's sun-browned cap. Ashby was slender, spare and graceful, of medium height and as dark as a Moor. "Nothing [was] light in his appearance," Captain McHenry Howard said, "but the whites of his eyes. I thought he looked more like an Arab, or the common idea of one, than any man I ever saw."[24]

Put him on the stunning milk-white horse he rode until it was inevitably shot out from under him, and you had the perfect picture of the dark avenger. He had jet-black hair and a long jetty beard that floated on the wind like wavy silk, so long that it often mingled with the mane of his galloping horse.[25] His eyes were piercing gray, and he had a magical way with a horse and an understanding that seemed to R. L. Dabney to have been "formed by nature for war."[26] His home was in the saddle, a friend said of him. He was a man who "looked like work," always spattered by whatever the earth at the moment was throwing up, mud or dust, with eyes that never blinked at peril. He seemed to dare his enemies to kill him and gave them constant opportunity. And how they tried.[27]

Ashby's men were another matter altogether. Most of them were from Virginia's northern and western border counties. They had never been in a camp of instruction in their lives and were never likely ever to be in one. Most of them had no idea how to perform the simplest evolutions of a company drill, and no sense of discipline. They were the despair of Stonewall Jackson. It was simply impossible for Ashby to do anything with them but lead them into a fight, armed as they were with such weapons as they could pick up, and totally without any regard for order. And he did that supremely well. Like another rough-hewn Confederate horseman named Bedford Forrest, who was winning a like reputation for courage and skill in the West, Ashby was a natural soldier. But don't ask him to organize anybody.[28]

J.E.B. Stuart, Ashby's counterpart in the Confederate Army of Northern Virginia, had a word for the life they led. It was the world of "the sleepless watch and the harassing daily *petite guerre*."[29]

On June 6 Ashby was between Harrisonburg and Port Republic waging one of those "little wars" in the rear of Jackson's slowly retreating army. He had set up on the road about sunset and was beating back an enemy cavalry charge. Expecting a major thrust, he had sent to Ewell for infantry support and Ewell had hurried to him with the First Maryland and Fifty-eighth Virginia. He found Ashby, as usual tempting fate beyond all reason, exposing himself beyond anything war called for. His horse, another one, had just been shot from under him. Extracting himself from beneath it, he rose to his feet one more time and shouted, "Charge men; for God's sake, charge!" As he said it a musket ball hit him full in the breast and he died instantly. The Yankees had finally caught him.[30]

Ashby's death paralyzed emotions throughout Jackson's army, from the general to the lowest private. There was probably nobody who doubted it would happen sometime and nobody who could believe it when it did. When Ashby's body was carried on to Port Republic to be prepared for the grave, Jackson came to where it lay and demanded to see it. There he stood for a time in sorrowful silence.[31]

Jackson had had his differences with Ashby; there was little love lost between them. Jackson disapproved of Ashby's lack of discipline. But right then Jackson was as close to unutterable grief as he had been at any time in the war. "As a partisan officer," he was to say of his fallen cavalry commander, "I never knew his superior; his daring was proverbial; his powers of endurance almost incredible; his tone of character heroic, and his sagacity almost intuitive in divining the purposes and movements of the enemy."[32]

An artilleryman in the ranks, who had fought beside Ashby in his many *petites guerres*, was more emotional: "Ashby is gone. He has passed the picket line that is posted along the silent river. . . . tenting to-night on the eternal camping-ground that lies beyond the mist that hangs over the River of Death, where no more harsh reveilles will disturb his peaceful rest nor sounding charge summon him to the deadly combat again."[33] He had passed by, a friend lamented, "like a dream of chivalry," devoted to death and to glory, "the bold rider, the brave partisan . . . the knight without fear."[34]

Ashby had been the young Confederacy's knight-errant, its dashing cavalier, its Galahad, and he had died in the morning of his glory. The army would miss him terribly.

James Shields, the only Union general yet to have beaten Jackson in a battle—at Kernstown—was out to catch the pest once and for all. Jackson had eluded them again at Strasburg, but it was going to be different this time. As Frémont pursued him up the Shenandoah side of the Massanutton, Shields was paralleling the chase up the Luray Valley, looking for a bridge to cross that would let him fall on Jackson's flank as Frémont hit him from the rear. Jackson had burned the bridge at the White House crossing. The one at Columbia was also gone. So Shields hurried on, hoping to find the bridge at Conrad's Store still standing. No luck. Jackson had burned that one, too. The rain wasn't helping. It had been coming down in torrents for three days; the Shenandoah was overflowing its banks and the mountain streams were turning into rivers. It looked to Shields like the showdown was to be at Port Republic. If he could get there first, Jackson would be caught in a vice between his army and Frémont's with an impassable river in his front and nowhere to go. It was a perfect plan. He had to get a message through to Frémont. Jackson was caught this time.[35]

Sunday morning, June 8, found Captain McHenry Howard of the Stonewall Brigade looking forward to a quiet day in camp. He had taken the little store of clothing from his carpetbag and had it lying about him, when he heard a cannon roar in the direction of Port Republic. He began immediately thrusting his things back in the bag.

"What are you doing?" someone asked him.

"Well," said Howard, "it's Sunday and you hear that shot."

They should have guessed. It was the Sabbath, so naturally there was going to be a fight. By now Jackson's soldiers believed he would rather fight on Sunday than on any other day. And in truth, Howard that morning had overheard Jackson whispering to Dabney in a confidential undertone, "Major, wouldn't it be a blessed thing if God would give us a glorious victory today?"[36]

All of the ingredients were there. Frémont was nearby, having come up on Jackson's heels from Harrisonburg. As one of the rebel soldiers said, "We were ready again for our usual Sabbath exercises, and Frémont was on hand with his congregation."[37] Shields was believed to be at Conrad's Store only fifteen miles away, and also of a mind to attend the services, with his advance already within hailing distance.

Shields's advance, in fact, was closer than that. Jackson was prepared to mount his horse early that morning to visit Ewell's command, which had camped a few miles back, across the river toward Harrisonburg at a place called Cross Keys. Jackson discovered that Shields was nearer than he thought when the small cavalry detachment he had sent out to fix the Union position came rushing back in what he thought to be disgraceful disorder, with Shields's cavalry pursuing.[38]

For a brief moment Shields's advance seized the south approach to the bridge over the river and Jackson narrowly missed becoming the war's most celebrated prisoner. As one Yankee soldier said, they had him "in a box with the lid on, but he kicked the bottom out and got away."[39]

Jackson's intent had been to hold off Frémont at Cross Keys and fight the main battle against Shields at Port Republic. But Frémont and his congregation had opened fire on Ewell at Cross Keys in earnest. The Fifteenth Alabama stepped forward to detain them until things were more nearly ready. Arnold Elzey had picked the defensive ground and Ewell had found it wisely done. Now with Brigadiers Trimble on the right, Elzey in the center, Steuart on the left, Taylor in reserve, and the First Maryland as usual thrown forward, the services commenced.

The First Marylanders could take pride in this fight at Cross Keys, because it was Maryland-made, Maryland-manned, and Maryland-led. All the brigadiers commanding were Marylanders, and Ewell was "more than half one."[40] All afternoon they fought, Ewell being pushed back for a time, but recovering all of his lost ground by evening. When at about sundown the First Maryland ran out of ammunition and was ordered to the rear to clean up and refit, it was about over.

Frémont had fought all afternoon and gotten nowhere. But when an optimistic message arrived from across the river from Shields that he thought "Jackson is caught this time," Frémont celebrated that prospect by suspending operations for the day, with plans to renew them tomorrow. Maybe Shields was right and tomorrow would be the first day of a better workweek.[41]

Jackson had spent most of the day at Port Republic waiting for Shields, and listening to Ewell working the Sabbath at Cross Keys. He had assumed that the assault on the bridge that morning was the precursor of a full-scale attack from Shields. But when it never came, Jackson decided to attack instead first thing the next morning.

At dawn on the ninth—another beautiful early summer day— Jackson called Ewell across the river, and Ewell came, bringing his entire command except Trimble's brigade and part of another, which he left in front of Frémont. The Pathfinder wasn't wanted at this party—at least not by Jackson, and at least not just then.

Shields would have preferred for Frémont to be present, but he would do his best without him. Neither was Shields personally present, but it became apparent by midmorning that his best, in the person of Brigadier General Erastus Tyler and his two brigades, was pretty good; he was turning out to be a handful. So Trimble was also called across the river and the last thing Frémont saw as the last Confederate crossed over was a sight he had seen too much of already—another bridge burning and falling into the river in front of him. For him it was to be a short workday.

For Jackson the day was to be as rewarding as all the others had been. "Delightful excitement," he told Taylor as that general approached with his Louisiana brigade.[42] Before the day ended, Jackson had hit Tyler often enough with such ferocity that the federal force had finally buckled and retreated. Jackson, who knew he had been in a fight, had won another one—or as he preferred, the Higher Power had.

"General," he said to Ewell, laying his hand on his chief lieutenant's arm, "he who does not see the hand of God in this is blind, Sir, blind![43]

Shields didn't see much there except a perfect plan for Jackson's destruction gone wrong. In Washington, a frustrated Abraham Lincoln saw the futility of any further effort to bag Jackson and called the whole thing off. Shields was ordered to withdraw to Luray, and Frémont started back down the Valley.[44] Jackson took his little army on up the road to Weyer's Cave where his men could praise God, see some stalactites, and wait for whatever strategy might next issue from under that little faded cap.[45]

* * *

Jackson's unlikely dash down the Valley and up again became an immediate military classic, and made him a legend in his time. North and South he was now looked at with either adulation or disgust, but in both cases with respect. Here was a magician "who could disappear and reappear so suddenly and unexpectedly, and while making such audacious marches right into the jaws of his powerful enemies, deliver such fearful blows and get out whole."[46]

John B. Jones, a rebel war clerk in Richmond, had exulted as he saw the Valley campaign beginning. "There is lightning in the northwest," he told his diary. "Jackson . . . is sweeping everything before him." Nor was he surprised. The year before, when Jackson had gone to Richmond with the VMI cadets, Jones had seen something unusual in their professor. "I hope he will take the field himself," he had written then in his diary, "and if he does, I predict for him a successful career."[47]

Not only was Jackson making a prophet of John Jones, he was making a believer of Mary Chesnut in Columbia, South Carolina. She wrote in her diary in early June: "Down here we sleep securely, with the serenest faith that Stonewall is to flank everybody and never to be flanked himself."[48]

This is what Jackson had done in this one busy month and a half in the Valley: By quick and strategic movements, forced marches, deceptive maneuvering, effectual fighting and, of course, mystification of both friend and enemy, he had covered 650 miles, taken 3,500 prisoners, and captured 10,000 muskets and nine rifled guns and so many of Banks's quartermaster stores that everybody was now calling that hapless general "Commissary Banks." With 17,000 troops Jackson had fought four pitched battles, six formal skirmishes, and numerous minor actions—all victories. The victories were a bonus; they had not been the primary goal. The goal had been to distract, confuse, check, discomfit, confound, and prevent. He knew he could not defeat the forty thousand Union troops that were eventually turned loose upon him. But he could keep them from combining, and he could detain them in the Valley while Johnston and Lee dealt with his classmate, McClellan, on the Peninsula in front of Richmond. That had been his duty. And he had done it, one of his soldiers said, "with the mathematical accuracy and resistless force of a Corliss engine in motion."[49] It is perhaps not too much to say that what he did in the Valley had saved Richmond 120 miles away.

Richmond was appropriately grateful. Jefferson Davis wired him on June 4 that "the army under your command encourages us to hope for all which men can achieve." Lee, whose opinion Jackson valued most highly—next to the opinion of Providence—told the Confederate secretary of war what Jackson would most likely have wanted to hear. Of a Jackson plan to attack Shields, Lee had said: "He is a good soldier, I expect him to do it." After Ashby was killed and Lee was considering names for a likely new cavalry commander to send Jackson, he told the secretary, "We must aid a gallant man if we perish." To Jackson himself Lee wrote on June 8, "I congratulate you upon defeating and then avoiding your enemy. Your march to Winchester has been of great advantage, and has been conducted with your accustomed skill and boldness."[50]

But from down the Valley another Virginian of a different stripe, the Union staff officer, David Strother, was disgusted with the whole thing: "From what I can learn here," he growled into his diary in early June, "Jackson is gone beyond pursuit. Thus culminates this disgraceful affair, the most disgraceful to the Federal armies that has occurred during the whole war. I am utterly humiliated to have been mixed up in it."[51]

Richard Ewell felt a lot different now about Jackson. The fanatic was as maddening as ever about never telling him anything of his plans. And Ewell never saw one of Jackson's couriers approach without expecting an order to storm the North Pole.[52] But what is eccentricity anyhow, if not common to all humanity? That is how Ewell's older brother, Benjamin, felt about it as he watched his younger brother's partnership with Jackson ripen in the Valley. The elder Ewell was himself a West Point graduate and a staff officer with Joseph Johnston. In his view, "most of us are in the estimation of our best friends more or less eccentric. So Taylor and Ewell thought Jackson, and so Taylor thought Ewell and so Ewell thought Taylor, and I have no doubt that if Jackson's mind hadn't been full of more important matters he would have thought so of Ewell and Taylor."[53]

So what if Jackson was an enthusiastic fanatic? What if Ewell looked like a woodcock, swore like a magpie, and said strange things? What did it matter? Loony or not they had worked a military miracle together in the Valley. Ewell had shone with nearly the radiance of Jackson himself. While he did not have to show it under Jackson, Ewell's tactical eye was thought to be nearly as keen as his commander's. But Ewell was a hands-on general; he couldn't shake all those years as a company commander on the Indian frontier. He longed to fight with the skirmish line. On two occasions in the Valley, when Jackson was temporarily absent from the front, Ewell had summoned Taylor to watch things while he rushed immediately out among the skirmishes where some sharp work was going on, as oblivious of the bullets as Jackson ever was.[54]

In many minds the campaign in the Valley was a Jackson-Ewell triumph. The rebel clerk John Jones in Richmond called Ewell Jackson's "coadjutor . . . worthy of his companionship."[55] Even Lincoln, in several impatient dispatches to his Union generals in the Valley, referred to the Confederate force they were vainly chasing as Jackson and Ewell.

The night following the final thunderbolt victory at Port Republic, Ewell was in an expansive mood. When the cavalryman, Colonel Thomas Munford, dropped by, Ewell invited him to stay for dinner. Afterward as they sat before the tent, Ewell turned to Munford and said in his quick, nervous way, "Look here, Munford, do you remember a conversation we had one day at Conrad's Store?"

Munford laughed and asked, "To what do you allude?"

"Why, to old Trimble, to General Jackson and that other fellow, Colonel Kirkland, of North Carolina." Ewell had in one way or another in the past slandered all three.

"I take it all back," Ewell said, "and will never prejudge another man. Old Jackson is no fool; he knows how to keep his own counsel, and does curious things; but he has a method in his madness; he has disappointed me entirely."

He went on to exonerate Trimble of overcautiousness, calling him as bold as any man at Cross Keys—a battle Trimble had largely won—and to praise Kirkland's handsome behavior near Winchester.[56]

Ewell had embarked on the Valley campaign thinking Jackson crazy; he had ended it thinking him inspired.[57]

Jackson, near Weyer's Cave, had yet another mission for Congressman A. R. Boteler. He wished him to return to Richmond and renew the request for the forty thousand troops with which to invade the North. He hadn't given up the idea. He asked Boteler this time to make formal application. Boteler left Friday evening, June 13, and this time took the appeal directly to General Lee in his tent before McClellan on the Peninsula. Lee listened to him with the same courtesy with which he listened to everybody, and then said quietly, "Colonel, don't you think General Jackson had better come down here first and help me drive these troublesome people away from before Richmond?"[58]

Orders to Jackson along that line had already gone out. Lee had sent a message on the day of the battle at Cross Keys, ordering Jackson to prepare to come to Richmond. "Make your arrangements accordingly," Lee told Jackson. Not a man to discourage creative improvisation, Lee had added: "But should an opportunity occur for striking the enemy a successful blow do not let it escape you."[59] And Jackson hadn't.

But now the time had come. The orders from Lee were imperative. Jackson had a clear duty. He must go. On June 17 he put his army on the road again, starting out, naturally, at night. And none of his soldiers knew any more about where they were going than the buttons on their coats.

PART 5

BROTHER AGAINST BROTHER

High Hopes
and
Paranoia

Ge>eorge McClellan arrived in Washington wearing his palms of
victory from western Virginia on Saturday, July 27, 1861.
Almost immediately the paranoia set in.

There were a few days before it started. At first there was nothing
but good will and high hopes. The Young Napoleon from the West
was the only proven winner the North had produced so far in this
young war, and he was borne into the capital on a triumphant tide of
national adulation.

It was difficult not to like McClellan. He was a man of extraordinary personal charm. His West Point classmates had been dazzled by
him. Strangers instantly liked him. Those thrown much in his company unavoidably grew fond of him. His troops idolized him. He
inspired deep personal affection and regard.[1]

From the moment he arrived nearly everybody felt things would
now be all right, that the army was in good hands, that the Union was
saved. He went to work immediately with an exhaustless energy,
wearing out aides, endearing himself to his soldiers, and doing what
he did best—bringing organization and order out of chaos. Nobody
whipped things into shape better than George McClellan. When he
arrived, the Division of the Potomac—soon to be renamed the Army

of the Potomac—was a beaten body of fifty thousand demoralized, disorganized troops still traumatized by their disaster at Bull Run. Within three months he would triple its size and hammer it into the most impressive and disciplined military machine ever assembled on the North American continent.

Not everybody in Washington liked the idea of George McClellan, even though they might be charmed by him. Irvin McDowell, the former commander of the Potomac division and the hard-luck victim of Bull Run, was hardly overjoyed to see him. McDowell had been the adjutant at West Point when McClellan was a precocious teenaged cadet. Now this upstart had not only replaced him as head of the army in the East, but outranked him. McDowell was relegated to commanding a division in the young hero's army. Joseph King Fenno Mansfield, with his shaggy white hair, beard, and timeless longevity, liked the arrangement even less. He commanded the District of Columbia troops and had been in the army since before McClellan was born. Now he was subordinate as well to this young comer from the West who was hardly half his age.[2]

Some believed that McClellan's triumphs in western Virginia, while laudable, were hardly worth all the hoopla and adulation. The three small skirmishes hadn't proved conclusively his qualifications for battlefield command.

The skeptical English journalist, William Howard Russell, called him " 'the little corporal' of unfought fields," but admitted that he was nevertheless " 'the man on horseback' just now." "Everyone," Russell said with a suggestion of disgust, "is willing to do as he bids: the President confides in him, and 'Georges' him; the press fawn upon him, the people trust him."[3]

There were those who saw an arrogant streak coursing beneath all that youthful McClellan charm and glamor. Some of his critics said he was the only man ever born who could strut while sitting down.[4]

But this was just nitpicking, little sinks of envy, discontent, and carping on the margins of McClellan's enormous national popularity. He was in that late summer of 1861 the man of the hour, the savior-elect of the Union.

He himself believed his press notices. He couldn't resist writing Nelly, still in Cincinnati and pregnant, that he found himself in a new and strange position in Washington: "Presdt, Cabinet, Genl Scott &

all deferring to me—by some strange operation of magic I seem to have become *the* power of the land. I almost think that were I to win some small success now I could become Dictator or anything else that might please me—but nothing of that kind would please me—*therefore* I *won't* be Dictator. Admirable self denial!"[5]

When he visited the Senate to lobby for a bill giving him power to appoint as many aides as he pleased from civil and army life, he was moved by the attention of all those famous names. "I suppose half a dozen of the oldest made the remark I am becoming so much used to," he wrote Nelly. " 'Why how young you look—& yet an old soldier!!' . . . They give me my way in everything, full swing & unbounded confidence. All tell me that I am held responsible for the fate of the Nation & that all its resources shall be placed at my disposal." Outside the Senate chamber the crowd stared at him with curiosity and awe: their new national idol. He learned with a surge of quiet pride what they were saying of him in Richmond—"that there was only one man they feared & that was McClellan."[6]

In the warm glow of this head-turning esteem, North and South, McClellan in early August sent Abraham Lincoln a list of the resources he would need to save the Union. If the president wanted him not simply to win a peace and make an advantageous treaty—the ordinary object of war—but to crush a well-backed well-run rebellion, he must have an army of 273,000 men. He broke this down for the president: 250 regiments of infantry—225,000 troops—100 field batteries of 600 guns and 15,000 men, twenty-eight regiments of cavalry with 25,500 men, five engineering regiments of 7,500 troops, and a strong supporting naval force. He envisioned a monstrous one-time offensive against the Confederates in Virginia and a merciless push in the West, with a strong movement on the Mississippi. His basic idea was to crush the enemy in one massive, rebellion-ending battle. That was going to take manpower and money—a lot of both. But in his view it was the only way to deal with the situation.[7] It must be done "En grand," he explained to Nelly. "I flatter myself," he told her, "that Beauregard has gained his last victory."[8] He didn't intend to have any Bull Runs on his record.

It was at about this time that the paranoia set in. Lincoln's two young secretaries, John Nicolay and John Hay, were to call it "a strange and permanent hallucination upon two points"—first that he was vastly outnumbered by the rebels, and second, that he was also outnumbered by his own government, and that both of these enemies were hostile and seeking his destruction.[9]

Just how and when the hallucination began that he was always astronomically outnumbered by the Confederates—as much as three to one, when the reverse was generally true—had to do with E. J. Allen. The tendency to overestimate enemy numbers was present with McClellan in western Virginia, where he also supposed the Confederate force to be far larger than it actually was. But it blossomed when Allen followed him to Washington.

One of the first things McClellan did—three days after arriving in the capital city—was to wire Allen in Cincinnati to come immediately and bring two or three of his best men. Allen was the nom de guerre of detective Allan Pinkerton, whose skills McClellan admired and whom he intended to put in charge of military intelligence-gathering for his Army of the Potomac.[10] Pinkerton-alias-Allen had come with his two or three best men as ordered, together with a talent for estimating enemy troops at two or three times their actual numbers. His inflated figures, and McClellan's desire to believe them, began dictating Union military policy from the start.

On August 8, McClellan wrote Winfield Scott, now decrepit, but still the commanding general of the Union armies, that he believed one hundred thousand Confederates were "in front of us." In scary contrast, McClellan could count only half that number of his own, entirely insufficient for the emergency and deficient in all the arms of the service—infantry, artillery, and cavalry. He petitioned the old general to strip other commands wholesale to bring the strength of his army in Washington up to parity with this huge Confederate juggernaut, and to do it "without one hour's delay."[11] In McClellan's mind nowhere else counted. Warfare in any other theater was "a mere bagatelle" compared with what was about to happen in his front.[12]

By August 19, McClellan and Pinkerton were estimating enemy strength before Washington at one hundred fifty thousand, and rising. He was still unable to count more than fifty-five thousand troops of his own to throw against those legions. Reinforcements were streaming in from the North and he was becoming stronger every day, but he was still not being reinforced fast enough to deal with the peril of the times. Not only were the Confederates terrifyingly superior in numbers, but far better organized and entrenched, and preparing at any moment to sweep his inadequate little army from the face of the earth. For days he had been expecting the blow to fall, not getting a minute's rest, sleeping with one eye open at night, "looking out sharply for Beauregard."[13]

Scott meanwhile was looking sharply at McClellan's apprehensions, and finding them nonsense. He didn't believe his young commander's estimate of enemy numbers, nor did he believe there was any imminent danger. "I am confident in the opposite opinion. . . ." he told Secretary of War Simon Cameron. "I have not the slightest apprehension for the safety of the Government here."[14]

It was at that point that McClellan's second hallucination began to set in—that the Lincoln administration north of the Potomac was as dangerous to his well-being as the Confederate army south of it. He was surrounded by enemies. This paranoia about a perfidious administration at his back centered first on Scott, but then spread rapidly. By mid-August it included the entire cabinet and the president himself. As he was to write his mother, " 'the Young General' has no bed of roses on which to recline."[15]

Scott had begun to aggravate the young general within a week after he arrived from western Virginia. On August 2 McClellan confided to Nelly that "the old man . . . is fast becoming very slow & very old." At a White House state dinner two days later Scott had hobbled in leaning on McClellan's arm. McClellan had found this tellingly significant—"the old veteran . . . & his young successor; I could see that many marked the contrast."[16]

But after August 8, when Scott wouldn't buy McClellan's assessment of enemy strength and the imminence of doomsday, it was plainly war between them. "I do not know whether he is a *dotard* or a *traitor*!" McClellan grumbled. "I can't tell which. He *cannot* or *will* not comprehend the condition in which we are placed & is entirely unequal to the emergency." He assured Nelly that he was "leaving nothing undone to increase our force—but that confounded old Genl always comes in the way—he is a perfect imbecile. He understands nothing, appreciates nothing & is ever in my way."[17]

By the next week McClellan was certain that the old general was his most dangerous antagonist, and that "either he or I must leave here—our ideas are so widely different that it is impossible for us to work together much longer—*tant pour cela* ['so much for that']!"[18]

They began to fight publicly—open rows, one of them in a

cabinet meeting. McClellan began making end runs around his general in chief, taking his differences with the old man to powerful cabinet members, telling them he must have a free hand if he was to save the Union. Disgusted, Scott told the secretary of war he was too old for such guerrilla operations and asked Lincoln to permit him to resign. While McClellan favored that, Lincoln refused to hear of it. But the signs of the times seemed clear. McClellan was confident the day would soon come when he would displace the old man, unless in the meantime he lost a battle, which he didn't intend to do.[19]

Indeed, McClellan did not intend to fight one at all—at least not soon—if he could help it. Not until he was perfectly ready and prepared, which meant not until there was not the slightest doubt that he would win. That was far from certain now, considering the enemy's imagined superiority.

By mid August he was still expecting to be attacked at any moment. It hadn't happened yet, but McClellan credited that to heaven-sent rains that had bloated the Potomac and made the roads impassable. If they remained impassable, then he believed "we are saved." "Give me two weeks," he wrote Nelly, "& I will defy Beauregard—in a week the chances will be at least even."[20]

In the scale of dangers, however, the threat within now more than equaled the threat without in McClellan's mind. He was not just menaced from abroad, but surrounded by imbeciles at home. "I am here in a terrible place—" he complained to Nelly, "the enemy have from 3 to 4 times my force—the Presdt is an idiot, the old General in his dotage—they cannot or will not see the true state of affairs." It wore on him. "I am weary of all this," he wrote her. "I have no ambition in the present affairs—only wish to save my country—& find the incapables around me will not permit it!"[21]

The president and Scott weren't the only two incapables. McClellan was beginning to lump the entire cabinet into that company. By October he was telling Nelly how disgusted he had become with the whole set of them. "Some of the greatest geese" he had ever seen, was the best he could say of them in a more charitable moment, "enough to tax the patience of Job." When he wrote her again the next day they had become "wretched politicians . . . a most despicable set of men." Secretary of State Seward was "the meanest of them all—a meddling, officious, incompetent little puppy," who has "done more than any other one man to bring all this misery upon the country &

is one of the least competent to get us out of the scrape." The President was little more than "a well-meaning baboon." Secretary of the Navy Gideon Welles was "weaker than the most garrulous old woman you were ever annoyed by." Attorney General Edward Bates was "a good inoffensive old man—so it goes." The only man of courage and sense in the cabinet as far as he could see was Postmaster General Montgomery Blair, "& I do not altogether fancy him!"[22]

McClellan was even convinced that his old Mexican War buddy, Beauregard, now his enemy across the Potomac, was also some kind of a fool, because, incredibly, with his overwhelming numbers, he had not yet attacked. The possibility that his old friend had never intended to attack in the first place did not seem to occur to McClellan. The fact that in truth, General Joseph E. Johnston, Beauregard's immediate superior, was himself too undermanned and unprepared to attack would have struck McClellan as preposterous. He could show them both Pinkerton's estimates that the rebel force under their command was approaching one hundred seventy thousand well-trained troops. But the Confederates on a good day could only count about forty-five thousand—and not all that well trained and entrenched.

By August 20, McClellan was telling Nelly that if Beauregard continued giving him time, "in a week I ought to be perfectly safe." Before the week was up, he was telling her that Beauregard had missed his chance and that he now had gained the time he had most desperately needed. He had sixty-five thousand effective men and would have seventy-five thousand by the end of the week. Even though he believed the rebels certainly had double that number, the threat had passed; the danger was over.[23]

He could breathe a little easier now, maybe stop merely existing. For days he had worked and worried himself half to death, enjoying no privacy, no leisure, and no relaxation, except writing and receiving letters from Nelly. Maybe he could now begin taking his meals more often at Wormley's, the old colored gentleman's restaurant around the corner on I Street. Often as not during the crisis he had been having breakfast sent over and letting dinner take its chances.[24]

His sole joy in the whole difficult few weeks had been the love he felt from the soldiers of his growing army. "You have no idea how the men brighten up now, when I go among them—" he told Nelly. "I can see every eye glisten." The scamps, he told her, had taken it into their heads to call him "our George." "I ought to take good care

347

of these men," he said, "for I believe they love me from the bottom of their hearts."[25]

Scott could have told our George that he might have been enjoying life and taking his meals at Wormley's all along, if it was the thought of the rebel threat that kept him from it. But it didn't matter anymore. Lincoln had finally agreed to let Scott retire. And on November 3 the old general went to catch the train that would take him to New York and away from all this. McClellan, at his most endearingly gracious now that the old pest was leaving, rode out with his escort in the predawn rain to see him off. Scott was polite, with kind messages for Ellen and little May, the baby girl born to the McClellans on October 12. The tender heart in McClellan was moved with sympathy for the old general. "I saw there," he wrote Nelly, "the end of a long, active & ambitious life—the end of the career of the first soldier of this nation—& it was a feeble old man scarce able to walk—hardly any one there to see him off but his successor."[26]

But McClellan could afford to be charitable; he now had what he wanted, command of the entire Union army, east and west, north—and such as it was—south. He had come a long way since 1846. Nobody was surprised, of course; his West Point classmates had all expected it. They hadn't thought it would happen so soon, in only fifteen years. But such are the fortunes of war.

Lincoln, whose rise to the top had also been cometlike, although far less expected, elevated McClellan to the sublime pinnacle of army ambition with some misgivings.

"I should be perfectly satisfied if I thought that this vast increase of responsibility would not embarrass you," the president told him.

"It is a great relief, Sir," McClellan answered. "I feel as if several tons were taken from my shoulders today. I am now in contact with you, and the Secretary. I am not embarrassed by intervention."

"Well, draw on me for all the sense I have, and all the information," Lincoln said. "In addition to your present command, the supreme command of the army will entail a vast labor upon you."

"I can do it all," said McClellan quietly.[27]

McClellan intended to do it all without drawing on any of Lincoln's sense or information, mainly because he didn't believe he had any. The only thing this haughty young general found to admire even remotely in the lanky backwoods lawyer who had inexplicably become president, was his ability to tell a story. "I never in my life met anyone so full of anecdote as our friend Abraham—" he wrote Nelly one day, "he is never at a loss for a story apropos of any known subject or incident." But if McClellan found Lincoln's stories ever apropos, he also found them "ever unworthy of one holding his high position."[28]

Indeed, McClellan found Lincoln unworthy of McClellan, and in every way his intellectual, social, and moral inferior. Soon after he arrived in Washington the general began calling Lincoln what Buchanan's acid-tongued attorney general, Edwin Stanton, had called him: "the *original gorilla*."[29]

"What a specimen to be at the head of our affairs now!" he told Nelly. He gave Lincoln credit for being honest and well-meaning, but for not much else. "I suppose our country has richly merited some great punishment," he wrote her, "else we should not now have such wretched triflers at the head of affairs." His contempt for Lincoln, of course, applied even more pointedly to that "poor little varlet Seward" and the rest of the cabinet. "It is perfectly sickening to have to work with such people," he told Nelly, "& to see the fate of the nation in such hands."[30]

Feeling this way about it, McClellan resented any kind of advice or interference from the president, and avoided him whenever he could. When he wanted to get some work done he concealed himself at his friend Stanton's, "to dodge all enemies in shape of 'browsing' Presdt etc."[31] He slighted the president without compunction. When Lincoln set up a conference in his office between McClellan, another general, and Ohio Governor William Dennison, McClellan didn't show up. Lincoln's two guests were outraged, but the president said, "Never mind; I will hold McClellan's horse if he will only bring us success."[32]

McClellan's most brazen snub of the long-suffering president was on an evening in mid November, not two weeks after Lincoln had elevated him to command of the Union armies. The president, Seward, and John Hay had come to the general's quarters to see him. McClellan's servant told them McClellan was at a wedding, but would return soon. So they waited. An hour passed and McClellan still hadn't returned. When finally he did, he appeared to pay no particular attention when told that the president was waiting. He simply went upstairs, passing the room where they sat, without saying a word. They waited another half hour, and sent again for the servant to tell the general they were there. But McClellan had gone to bed.

On the way home Hay fumed, denouncing through clenched teeth this "unparalleled insolence of epaulettes." But Lincoln appeared not to have taken any offense, telling his young secretary that it was better at this time not to be making points of etiquette and personal dignity. However it was the last time the president was ever to call on McClellan in his quarters; hereafter the general would be sent for.[33]

There were many times in the weeks to come that Lincoln itched to see McClellan under any circumstances—to talk with him, prod him, urge him, convince him, reason with him, anything to get him moving. A disturbing characteristic had surfaced in the new general in chief. He seemed not to want to fight. He now had this powerful army, trained and ready and huge, the biggest and best-equipped ever assembled on the continent. But there seemed to be no plans now to take it out and fight the Confederates with it. Many, particularly the impatient and ill-humored Republican Radicals in Congress, who had liked McClellan in the beginning, were outraged. They began to ask angrily when this great army planned to attack Richmond. Five months had now passed since the Young Napoleon had come out of the West on the wings of such hope and expectation. The only thing to show for it was organization, dress reviews, drills, one unfruitful reconnaissance, and a minor Union disaster at Ball's Bluff near Leesburg.

Everything had seemed perfect for a fall offensive. The weather had been splendid, the air clear, the roads dry. Even the Confederates looked northward and wondered why they hadn't been attacked. The Union army was twice the size of theirs and here was this long, lingering Indian summer, with roads firmer and skies more beautiful than Virginia had seen in years. The gods seemed to be inviting an enemy advance, but none had come.

The gods could not keep things beautiful and dry forever. The rains fell, the cold and the mud came, and the opportunity left. The Young Napoleon had seemed to have forgotten what the first Napoleon and Professor Dennis Hart Mahan had said about celerity.

McClellan blamed everything but the weather on the "incapables" who were thwarting and deceiving him at every turn. "It now

350

begins to look as if we are condemned to a winter of inactivity," he admitted. "If it is so the fault will not be mine."[34]

The Radicals, not conceiving who else's fault it might be, began to visit the White House on a regular basis to worry the president into action. Even Lincoln, manfully trying to defend and protect his general and to buy him time, began to wonder when McClellan planned to move.

McClellan had continued to resist—to ignore, rather—all of this insistent pressure to fight. He still wasn't ready. *"Festina lente,"* make haste slowly, was his policy,[35] and he wasn't going to be stampeded by a bunch of imbecile politicians. They were all incompetents as far as he was concerned.

"Don't let them hurry me, is all I ask," McClellan urged the president in October.

"You shall have your own way in the matter, I assure you," Lincoln had told him.[36]

But as the weeks wore on Lincoln grew more restless and uncomfortable. He deprecated the senseless popular impatience to storm Richmond. But at the same time the pressure from the country to do something had to be taken into account.

However, Lincoln continued to reassure McClellan that "you must not fight til you are ready."

"I have everything at stake," McClellan agreed. "If I fail, I will not see you again or anybody."

The idea of not seeing anybody again—particularly those pesky and humorless Radicals—appealed to Lincoln's antic fancy. "I have a notion to go out with you and stand or fall with the battle," he told McClellan.[37]

When McClellan came down with typhoid fever two days before Christmas and all hope of an early offensive went to bed with him, it was almost more than even Lincoln could endure. At just the time when the public howl for action was at its shrillest, the army simply rested, "almost with folded hands," waiting for its general to recover—or die.[38]

The Radicals, who had now established a joint committee of Congress to watchdog the conduct of the war—or lack of it—saw McClellan's illness as a subterfuge. Lincoln tried to reassure them, but they continued to find the inaction inexcusable, and demanded to confront the general himself.[39]

Lincoln had to confess that "delay is ruining us." He looked westward to see if he could get anything started there. But that was no good either. "As everywhere else," he concluded after consulting with his western generals, "nothing can be done."[40]

McClellan continued to lie in his sick bed through the early days of the new year, and Lincoln walked into Brigadier General Montgomery C. Meigs's office and sat down dejectedly before the open fire.

"General," he asked the army's able quartermaster general, "what shall I do?"

Meigs listened sympathetically.

"The people are impatient," Lincoln explained. "Chase [Treasury Secretary Salmon Portland Chase] has no money and he tells me he can raise no more; the General of the Army has typhoid fever. The bottom is out of the tub. What shall I do?"[41]

Meigs suggested that he consult some of the other generals in the army, since McClellan was indisposed, and see what they thought. Lincoln did so, calling a meeting on January 13. This act got McClellan out of bed. Not only did some generals and cabinet members show up, but so did he, still wobbly, but there nonetheless, and in black ill humor. It was a stiff meeting, spoiled by McClellan's refusal first to reveal his intentions, then by his refusal to say anything at all.

Meigs moved his chair next to McClellan's.

"The president evidently expects you to speak," Meigs whispered to him. "Can you not promise some movement towards Manassas? You are strong."

"I cannot move on them with as great a force as they have," McClellan snapped.

"Why, you have near 200,000 men, how many have they?"

"Not less than 175,000 according to my advices."

Meigs was taken aback. "Do you think so?"

Nevertheless, Meigs thought McClellan ought to say something. "The President expects something from you," he persisted.

"If I tell him my plans they will be in the New York Herald tomorrow morning," McClellan rasped. "He can't keep a secret, he will tell them to Tadd [Lincoln's nine-year-old son, Tad]."

"That is a pity," Meigs sympathized, "but he is the President— the commander in chief; he has a right to know; it is not respectful to sit mute when he so clearly requires you to speak. He is superior to all."[42]

The best Lincoln was able to get out of McClellan at the meeting was the notion that he did have some plans, although he wasn't going to tell anybody what they were. At least he was out of bed; that was something.

McClellan was not a complete brick wall. When Lincoln's young son, Willie, caught typhoid in February and died, the general's basic decency and compassion welled up in a letter of sympathy. McClellan now had Nelly and little May in Washington with him, at the house he had taken for them at H and 15th streets. His new little daughter delighted him. "The baby is splendid," he wrote his mother-in-law—"laughs inordinately & so loudly that it is almost a nuisance—converses intelligently in 3 languages."[43]

Now he was writing Lincoln, a fellow father, a grief-stricken note on the death of eleven-year-old Willie. The compassionate McClellan, the one everybody loved, sorrowed with the president over "the sad calamity that has befallen you & your family." He told Lincoln that "You have been a kind true friend to me in the midst of the great cares & difficulties by which we have been surrounded during the past few months—your confidence has upheld me when I should otherwise have felt weak. I wish now only to assure you & your family that I have felt the deepest sympathy in your affliction."[44]

But tragedy didn't serve to stir the general to action any more than anything else did. Early in the new year Lincoln had said, not joking, that if McClellan didn't want to use the army, he would like to borrow it, provided he could see how it could be made to do something.[45] The general seemed absolutely without initiative. He answered every suggestion of advance with a demand for reinforcements, met entreaties and reproaches with arguments showing how much stronger the enemy was and how insufficient his resources were in contrast. Yet he continued to enjoy to a spectacular degree the enthusiastic devotion of his friends and the absolute confidence of the rank and file of his army. Lincoln kept on hoping that if he could just get him started he was indeed capable of great things.[46]

By the end of January the president still hadn't been able to get him started and, at wit's end, he issued General Order No. 1, calling for a movement of all Union land and naval forces on February 22.[47]

This didn't stir McClellan either. The teeth-gnashings—electric perturbations, Lincoln's young secretaries called them—increased at the executive mansion and at the capitol, and didn't seem to register at all with McClellan. February 22 came and went and there was no general movement.[48]

McClellan had a better idea. He had been giving the whole thing a lot of thought, and had been hinting at a plan of campaign since early December that he didn't think either the enemy or his friends could anticipate. On February 3 he sprung it on Lincoln and Stanton. Incredibly, the original gorilla had named Stanton as his new secretary of war replacing Simon Cameron in January, "a most unexpected piece of good fortune" as far as McClellan was concerned. Stanton had been McClellan's sympathetic secret ally against the administration's politicians for months. Now he was a friend within the gates.[49]

McClellan's proposal to the president and the secretary was for an end-around. Instead of a direct assault on the Confederates dug in at Centerville, which he did not favor, he would debark his army to the lower Chesapeake at Urbana, and strike the rebels from there. This, he thought, had every virtue. It would give him the shortest possible land route to Richmond. It would put him on the Confederate flank and force them to abandon their entrenched position at Centerville to defend their capital. This one bold stroke would likely give him Richmond, all of the enemy communications and supplies, the city of Norfolk, all of the waters of the Chesapeake, and all of Virginia. It would probably force the Confederates to abandon east Tennessee and North Carolina, and it would not put Washington in jeopardy. It would be the one decisive stroke that could end the war. If circumstances made Urbana undesirable then he would sideslip down to Mob Jack Bay, or if worst came to worst, land at Fort Monroe and strike up the Peninsula. He figured to need 110,000 to 140,000 men for the job—the latter number preferred. "Nothing is *certain* in war—" he told the president and Stanton, "but all the chances are in favor of this movement." He would stake his life and reputation on it.[50]

The plan worried Lincoln, raising serious questions in his mind. Was not McClellan's proposal more costly in time and money than Lincoln's own—a direct attack on the Confederates in front? Was it more certain of victory? Would the victory be more valuable? If it met disaster, would it not make a safe retreat more difficult?[51] Lincoln finally gave reluctant approval despite his reservations, provided Washington was left amply protected.

Then the Confederates themselves threw the plan into confusion by pulling out of their entrenched position in front of Manassas. It had never been a tenable position in their minds in the first place. This forced McClellan to abandon both Urbana and Mob Jack Bay. Worst had come to worst, and in mid-March he began loading his great army on transports, and on April 1 climbed aboard the steamer *Commodore* and left for Fort Monroe and the Peninsula.

He was more than gratified to get away from Washington, "that sink of iniquity."[52] He believed the incapables had done their worst. The cabal in Washington had decided to take supreme command of all the armies from McClellan and leave him with only his Army of the Potomac—at least for the duration of the coming campaign. And they were withholding troops from him that he had been counting on. They had promised him Irvin McDowell's force of forty thousand men, without which he didn't think he could make the invasion a success. Lincoln and Stanton felt that contrary to his promises, McClellan hadn't left Washington adequately protected. Besides, McClellan's classmate in the Valley, Tom Jackson, was making everybody nervous. Nobody knew what he would do next. He was a loose and loaded cannon pointed at Washington.

McClellan had few friends left in Congress, and he knew it. A month earlier he had written Major General Henry Halleck in the West that "the abolitionists are doing their best to displace me & I shall be content if I can keep my head above water until I am ready to strike the final blow."[53]

The only thing he felt good about was his army. He wished it larger, far larger, although it was nearly double what the Confederates had. They were good men, these soldiers of his. He had organized and trained them well.

As he prepared to take them to the Peninsula, he addressed them: "I have held you back, that you might give the death-blow to the rebellion that has distracted our once happy country. . . . The Army of the Potomac is now a real Army,—magnificent in material, admirable in discipline and instruction, excellently equipped and armed;—your commanders are all that I could wish. The moment for action has arrived, and I know that I can trust in you to save our country." He had ridden among them many times and had seen "the sure presage of victory" in their faces and he knew "you will do whatever I ask of you."[54]

In the strength of that faith, he embarked at last to the seat of war.

Maryland,
My Maryland

Being at the seat of war did not necessarily inspire George McClellan to fight, and Abraham Lincoln was alarmed.

The first thing McClellan did on reaching the Peninsula was to organize a siege of Yorktown. That would take time, and time meant a great deal to Lincoln. "You now have over one hundred thousand troops. . . ." he wrote the general. "I think you better break the enemies' line from York-town to Warwick River, at once. They will probably use *time*, as advantageously as you can."[1]

"I was much tempted," McClellan snorted in a letter to Nelly, "to reply that he had better come & do it himself."[2]

Lincoln was now writing McClellan often. On April 9 he wrote him a long letter of fatherly advice, with a frank, heart-to-heart ending. Lincoln had always liked McClellan. He felt kindly toward him, had supported him and tried to protect him, but now the political heat was getting too much even for the patient president.

"And, once more let me tell you," he wrote McClellan on the ninth, "it is indispensible to *you* that you strike a blow. *I* am powerless to help this. . . . The country will not fail to note—is now noting—that the present hesitation to move upon an intrenched enemy, is but the story of Manassas repeated. I beg to assure you that I have never written you, or spoken to you, in greater kindness of feeling than now, nor with a fuller purpose to sustain you, so far as in my most anxious judgment, I consistently can. *But you must act.*"[3]

Theoretically, the Confederates in McClellan's front agreed with the president. Confederate Major General John B. Magruder, Tom Jackson's artillery commander from the Mexican War, was now blocking McClellan's way in Yorktown. He was astonished that McClellan didn't just roll over him. He had only five thousand available troops with which to hold back the federal juggernaut. Instead McClellan prepared for a siege, and permitted days to pass without opening hostilities.[4] Magruder was pleased to cooperate by staging theatrical march-abouts to make it appear he had far more men than he actually did.

General Joseph E. Johnston, in overall command of Confederate forces on the Peninsula, was puzzled by McClellan as well. He had to admit that his old friend "seems not to value time especially."[5]

McClellan did value sieges, however. He had admired them for years. He had seen two of the best ever staged—at Vera Cruz in Mexico and at Sebastapol in the Crimea. He came to the Peninsula inclined to mount one of his own, and Yorktown seemed the perfect time and place for it.

As he was installing his siege batteries, however, he learned that Lincoln and Stanton were not going to send him McDowell's corps of forty thousand men as they had promised. The administration feared for the safety of Washington, and believed McClellan hadn't adequately provided for it.

But what of the safety of this army? protested McClellan. He saw in his mind's eye the huge enemy force at his front and petitioned Lincoln to reconsider. He argued that depriving him of McDowell's forty thousand troops imperiled the success of his campaign. He expected to have to fight the entire Confederate army not far from Yorktown. "Do not force me to do so with diminished numbers," he begged the president.[6]

To Nelly he vented his true feelings: what the president had done was "the most infamous thing that history has recorded."[7]

It only confirmed his worst suspicions: they were out to get him. But "dont worry about the wretches—" he assured Nelly a few days later, "they have done nearly their worst & can't do much more. I am sure that I will win in the end, in spite of all their rascality. History will present a sad record of these traitors who are willing to sacrifice the country & its army for personal spite & personal aims. The people will soon understand the whole matter & then woe betide the guilty ones."[8]

McClellan continued to plead without ceasing for reinforcements. Stanton, now himself a Judas, the prince of traitors in McClellan's mind, "without exception the vilest man I ever knew or heard of," was disenchanted and disgusted.[9] McClellan already had well over one hundred thousand troops by Stanton's count, far more than the enemy. What else did he want? "If he had a million men," the secretary fumed, "he would swear the enemy had two millions, and then he would sit down in the mud and yell for three."[10]

May rolled around and McClellan had not yet fired on Yorktown—he was still setting up. When he telegraphed asking for Parrott guns, Lincoln blanched. "It argues indefinite procrastination," he wired McClellan.[11]

"All is being done that human labor can accomplish," McClellan assured the president.[12] He expected to be ready to open on Yorktown by May 5, the sixth at the latest.[13]

But on the fourth the Confederates pulled out; simply left. It was as if a raiding party with a huge battering ram had been pounding at full gallop toward a bolted door and at the last instant the door was flung open.

Not a shot had been fired, but McClellan was ecstatic. "The success is brilliant," he wired Stanton.[14]

Two days later the Confederates had pulled back beyond Williamsburg with McClellan cautiously following. Now he occupied both of the historic old towns where General George Washington had broken the back of the British and won American independence eighty years before. Surely the all-ending battle in this second American revolution, "a life-and-death contest," could not be far away. McClellan called again for reinforcements.[15]

As he wrote his daily letter to Nelly late on the night of May 12 he listened dreamily as the distant strains of tattoo drifted softly into his tent. "A grand sound this lovely moonlight night . . ." he mused to Nelly. "Are you satisfied now with my bloodless victories?" he asked her. He had saved the lives of many men by his maneuvers. That was an accomplishment, and it pleased him more than anything that had happened. But now there was to be a great battle, and unavoidable bloodshed. The rebels were concentrating all of their mighty force against him, and his government, alas, was giving him no aid.[16]

It was as it had been those first days at West Point so many years ago. He was as much alone as if in a boat in the middle of the Atlantic.

A battle finally came at Fair Oaks on the last day of May, and on the first day of June McClellan was within six miles of Richmond. His troops could hear the church bells tolling in the city. It hadn't been the great rebellion-ending battle McClellan had been expecting, but it had taken one Confederate commander, his old friend Joe Johnston, out of the picture severely wounded, and raised another, Robert E. Lee, to field command of the rebel army.

Lee was an old friend too, a fellow engineer, but he wasn't a commander the Young Napoleon feared. "*Too* cautious & weak under grave responsibility," he had told Lincoln in an earlier assessment. Lee was personally brave and energetic to a fault, no question about that, but McClellan found him "wanting in moral firmness when pressed by heavy responsibility & is likely to be timid & irresolute in action."[17] Lincoln might have mused—and perhaps he did—that McClellan was perfectly describing himself.

After Fair Oaks, McClellan believed the next leap would be the last one. But it had started to rain and all final leaps had to be postponed. For days he was checked by the weather. McClellan had what Lincoln thought was a one-sided view of weather. He seemed to regard it as exclusively hurtful to him and not the enemy. He seemed to think, the president said of him, that in defiance of Scripture, Heaven sent its rain only on the just and not on the unjust.[18]

As the rain continued to fall on both the just and unjust indiscriminately, McClellan's twin paranoias quickened. He continued to see folly in his rear and overwhelming numbers in his front. It all made him feel that the salvation of the country demanded he be prudent in the extreme, that he "must not run the slightest risk of disaster, for if anything happened to this army our cause would be lost." He wrote Nelly words a loving and worried wife likes to hear, that "I feel too that I must not unnecessarily risk my life—for the fate of the army depends on me & they all know it." He feared desperately for the lives of his men as well: "Every poor fellow that is killed or wounded almost haunts me!"[19]

Jackson had arrived from the Valley and the enemy in McClellan's front now numbered eighty-five thousand. It was the largest force the Confederates would ever assemble in one place in the entire war. But for every one rebel, McClellan counted at least two. He told Stanton that there were two hundred thousand Confederates between him and Richmond, a host twice the size of his own. He deplored his imagined inferiority in numbers, but it wasn't his fault. Hadn't he repeatedly asked for reinforcements, so often that there was no use asking for them again?[20]

A weary Lincoln wired him on June 26: "I give you all I can, and act on the presumption that you will do the best you can with what you have, while you continue, ungenerously I think, to assume that I could give you more if I would. I have omitted and shall omit no opportunity to send you re-enforcements whenever I possibly can."[21]

Even as Lincoln wrote, Lee attacked. For seven days the Confederate general whom McClellan thought too cautious, timid, and irresolute, struck for the jugular, unfazed by the Union army's superiority in numbers. Lee could not seem to land a knockout blow, however, and he suffered galling losses trying. But he harried the Young Napoleon without letup, driving him back from Richmond, all the way to Harrison's Landing twenty-six miles from Richmond, where McClellan ducked gratefully under the protective cannon of the navy's gunboats on the James River and stopped to catch his breath.

McClellan had waged a brilliant series of defensive battles and had parried some mighty blows. But since he had come to wage the great offensive battle that was to have won the war in a single massive stroke, it hadn't lived up to expectations.

"We have had a terrible time," he wrote Nelly from Harrison's Landing.[22]

He knew exactly how and why it had happened—no doubt of it in his mind. It had not been his fault. He had been beaten by an enemy crushingly superior in numbers and stabbed in the back by the "set of heartless villains" in Washington.[23]

Edwards S. Sanford, head of the war department's telegraphic office in Washington, had read many messages from McClellan since the campaign opened on the Peninsula. But the sentence on the tag end of the one coming in as the Seven Days battles raged, made him start violently. It was addressed to Stanton.

"If I save this Army now," it read, "I tell you plainly that I owe no thanks to you or any other persons in Washington. You have done your best to sacrifice this Army."[24]

My God, thought Sanford, he couldn't let the secretary see that. He ordered the rest of the message copied and given to Stanton, but with the venomous ending scissored out. It said everything McClellan believed about the administration in Washington, but if Stanton had seen it, it would likely have gotten him fired that day.[25]

Even Lincoln's bottomless reservoir of good will and patience was being stretched to the breaking point. When a few days later McClellan, on the run for Harrison's Landing, asked for at least fifty thousand more men that didn't exist, the president's forbearance nearly snapped. He had sent, altogether, one hundred sixty thousand men to McClellan on the Peninsula and he had no more to send.[26]

The president took up his tired pen one more time. "Allow me to reason with you a moment. . . ." he began. "The idea of sending you fifty thousand, or any other considerable force promptly, is simply absurd. . . . If you think you are not strong enough to take Richmond just now, I do not ask you to try just now. Save the Army, material and personnel; and I will strengthen it for the offensive again, as fast as I can."[27]

McClellan sat and simmered in the wilting heat at Harrison's Landing through the early days of July. Lee had pulled his own tired and battered army back, and was leaving him alone for the moment. But Lincoln wasn't. The president came down in the insufferable heat for a personal visit. But he seemed, as far as McClellan could see, "quite incapable of rising to the height of the merits of the question & the magnitude of the crisis."[28]

Nelly sympathized with her husband's outrage and anger. She wrote him that she thought Lincoln "an old stick"—"& of pretty poor timber at that," McClellan agreed.[29] Stick was perhaps not an inappropriate description of what the gaunt president looked like physically as he visited the army and inspected the troops. One soldier described the spindly chief executive on horseback as "nothing else than a pair of tongs on a chair back."[30]

There was now talk of withdrawing the army from the Peninsula altogether, and the idea chilled McClellan, despite the heat. He wished rather to be reinforced so that he might throw his army again upon Richmond and find redemption. But the administration was having none of it. As the prospects turned more and more sour, so did McClellan's rancor, most of it now centering on his erstwhile friend and ally, Stanton. If Lincoln was an old stick of poor timber, Stanton was "the most unmitigated scoundrel I ever knew, heard or read of." He told Nelly that had Stanton lived in Jesus' time he would have superseded Judas as the Savior's betrayer. "I hate to think that humanity *can* sink so low. . . . it makes me sick to think of him! Faugh!!"[31]

McClellan was now hearing through the grapevine that Major General Henry Halleck was about to be brought from the West and made general in chief of the armies. The post had been vacant since mid-March when McClellan was preparing to leave for the Peninsula. McClellan knew that the rumor was fact by July 20. He saw it as another terrible mistake by the incapables in Washington. In his view Halleck was just another incompetent, despite his nickname, "Old Brains." This would fix in concrete McClellan's displacement from overall command and leave him with only the Army of the Potomac. And considering his fall so far from grace, he didn't know how long he would have even that.

Not long, as it turned out. John Pope, another major general from the West, the hero of the Union victory at Island No. 10 on the Mississippi in early April, had just been put in command of a new Army of Virginia in front of Washington. McClellan was ordered in early August to close the book on the Peninsula, embark his army from Harrison's Landing, and take it to the relief of Pope, who was now facing a major fight at Manassas.

The order to leave the Peninsula caused McClellan "the greatest pain I ever experienced." He objected in a message to Halleck that it would prove "disastrous in the extreme to our cause—I fear it will be a fatal blow."[32]

If McClellan disdained Halleck, he despised Pope—another man inferior to himself in every way, who had said some grating things about the way the army in the East had been handled. But McClellan believed Pope was about to get his comeuppance. Stonewall Jackson was after him, and that probably meant that "the paltry young man who wanted to teach me the art of war will in less than a week either be in full retreat or badly whipped."[33]

McClellan tried to warn Halleck about Jackson. "I don't like Jackson's movements," he told the new general in chief as he was leaving the Peninsula. "He will suddenly appear when least expected." It would develop that McClellan was a prophet.[34]

In late August McClellan reluctantly brought his army back below Washington, and then watched it leave him to fight for Pope. This was almost more than he could bear. "I have a terrible task on my hands now—" he wrote Nelly who was away in New Jersey, "perfect imbecility to correct. . . . Two of my Corps will either save that fool Pope or be sacrificed for the country."[35]

Blue and disgusted, he lit up a cigar, listened to the distant thunder of artillery, and tried in vain to get into a better humor. "They have taken *all* my troops from me—" he moaned. "I have even sent off my personal escort & camp guard & am here with a few orderlies & the aides."[36]

Without an army, stripped of everything but his staff, he sat and listened and brooded and smoked his cigar as Jackson turned up where least expected as he had predicted—in the rear of the mystified Pope. For the second time in little more than a year, a Union army was retreating battered and beaten back into Washington from Manassas. For the North it was a depressing case of déjà vu.

McClellan could have said I told you so. What he said was even worse. As Pope was sinking deeper and deeper into trouble and defeat, McClellan suggested that the president leave that unfortunate general to get out of his scrape as best he could and bend every effort to make the capital safe instead.[37]

This uncaring proposal astonished Lincoln; he considered it mean-spirited. But he was now in a box. Pope had been soundly beaten and he had nowhere to turn but back to McClellan. The young general had dragged his feet shamefully before sending help to Pope, and had ungraciously suggested letting him shift for himself. He had acted badly, and the president was convinced he had the "slows" and was "good for nothing for an onward movement." But McClellan was a wizard for reordering disordered armies, and for defending the capital at that moment he was the best the president had. He must use what tools were at hand.[38]

Lincoln explained all that to his stunned cabinet, which wanted to cashier McClellan outright, not give him back his army. "Giving the command to him was equivalent to giving Washington to the rebels," bristled Treasury Secretary Salmon Chase, who had been circulating a petition to get rid of him.[39]

The president argued that there was no man in the army who could "lick these troops of ours into shape half as well as he." He said that although McClellan couldn't fight himself, he was a genius at getting others ready to fight. So he was going to give him back his army, and Pope's with it. Washington needed saving again.[40]

Ohio Senator Ben Wade, angrier than anybody in the cabinet, had taken up the subject of McClellan with Lincoln earlier in the summer.

Get somebody else, Wade demanded.

"Well, put yourself in my place for a moment," Lincoln said. "If I relieve McClellan, whom shall I put in command?"

"Why, anybody!" Wade suggested.

"Wade, *anybody* will do for you, but not for me," Lincoln answered wearily. "I must have *somebody*."[41]

McClellan could feel it coming. It has become a waiting game, he wrote Nelly. "Our affairs here now much tangled up & I opine that in a day or two your old husband will be called upon to unsnarl them."[42]

On September 2, as Pope fell back on Washington, McClellan was back in command of the army. It was an army a little worse for wear, but it was his again. "It makes my heart bleed," he wrote Nelly, "to see the poor shattered remnants of my noble Army of the Potomac, poor fellows! and to see how they love me even now. I hear them calling out to me as I ride among them—'George—don't leave us again!' 'They *shan't* take you away from us again. . . .' "[43]

McClellan's job was to defend Washington. But he found that to do that he must go to Maryland.

After its stunning victory at Second Manassas, Lee's army crossed the Potomac and began invading Maryland on September 4, Tom Jackson's corps in the lead. It had been one of those incomparably beautiful, warm fall days. The sun had risen in a cloudless sky, bathing the summit of the mountains to the west. The broad river, bordered to its banks by lofty trees in full foliage, flowed languidly beneath the passing army. Autumnal wildflowers were everywhere, down to the very margins of the stream. The scenery reminded many of Jackson's men of their own beautiful Shenandoah Valley.[44]

The mood of the tattered rebel army matched the weather. As they crossed the river at White's Ford above Leesburg, they laughed, shouted, and sang. "Maryland, My Maryland!" their voices roared out, booming across the river and fading into the trees. They were a spectral band, a scarecrow chorus, "coon-jawed" and "hollow-eyed."[45] At Leesburg as they passed through on the way to the ford, an old lady with upraised arms and brimming tears exclaimed, "The Lord bless your dirty ragged souls!"[46]

They were to get no less ragged and dirty as the days went by. A resident of Frederick, named Kate, looked at them in disgust and wrote her friend Minnie in Baltimore: "Oh! they are so dirty! I don't think the Potomac River could wash them clean; and ragged!—there is not a scarecrow in the corn-fields that would not scorn to exchange clothes with them; and so tattered!—there isn't a decently dressed soldier in their whole army."[47]

There wasn't a soldier in that whole army who would not have agreed with her. This was a threadbare, vermin-infested congregation of invaders, "as dirty as the ground itself and . . . nearly of the same color."[48] There was hardly a one of them without the "camp itch," brought to them by grayback vermin. The vermin "followed Johnny Reb everywhere," one of the inflicted moaned, "staid by him, refused to leave, resisted every effort of force, opposed every attempt at compromises. . . . where they came from and how they arrived were mysteries never solved." They "had more lives than a cat, and bred and propagated faster than a roe-herring." The problem had seemed worse than at any other time in the war, because most of them had not changed clothes in weeks.[49]

But tattered, ragged, dirty, and vermin-ridden, they were happy to be in Maryland. It was such a rich, lush land—a cornucopia. Many of them would one day agree with the Yankee poet John Greenleaf Whittier, who would write of it: "Fair as a garden of the Lord,/ To the eyes of the famished rebel horde."[50]

As the Confederate Army of Northern Virginia passed over the river onto northern soil, the Union Army of the Potomac began filing out of Washington City in wary pursuit. It was an army still reeling from the beatings on the Peninsula and at Second Manassas. But it was still a huge fighting machine, one hundred thousand strong, and with George McClellan once more in command. McClellan's object was "to feel the enemy—to compel him to develop his intentions . . . to cover Baltimore or Washington, to attack him should he hold the line of the Monocacy, or to follow him into Pennsylvania if necessary."[51]

McClellan believed he was still outnumbered by the Confederates by at least 25 percent—he put their strength at not less than one hundred twenty thousand. So as his army marched after Lee, McClellan wired urgently back for reinforcements.[52]

It was a wonderful march. If he had not believed himself so seriously outnumbered in front and behind he would have enjoyed it more. Even so, he reveled in the country they were passing through. He thought it one of the most lovely regions he had ever seen, "quite broken," he told Nelly, "with lovely valleys in all directions, & some fine mountains in the distance."[53]

After crossing the river at White's Ford, the Confederates moved on into Frederick City where Lee stopped to promulgate a strategy. He had supposed that his advance on Frederick would cause Martinsburg and Harpers Ferry to be evacuated. That hadn't happened. So he must forcibly dislodge them, for he couldn't afford to have them menacing his rear and flank.

He would send Stonewall Jackson to handle the matter—and with him Lafayette McLaws to seize Maryland Heights above Harpers Ferry and John G. Walker, who had buried Jimmy Stuart in the Rogue River Valley a decade before, to occupy Loudoun Heights. Then he would further divide his army—not large to begin with, not half the size of the army that McClellan was marching toward him out of Washington. He would position D. H. Hill's division at Boonsboro as the army's rear guard, and send James Longstreet temporarily to Hagerstown to investigate the rumor of an approaching federal force from that direction.

This dividing of an army in front of a far larger foe was against all the rules of sound military strategy. But Lee knew McClellan. He believed he could divide and reassemble his army well before that overcautious general was ready to bring him to battle. Lee did not intend to stop McClellan's coming through the passes at South Mountain. He wanted to lure him on as far as he could, fight him as far as possible from his base in Washington.

That was the plan. And McClellan, approaching cautiously, as Lee knew he would, was soon privy to it. On September 13, the day McClellan arrived in Frederick, a copy of the orders detailing all of Lee's dispositions was found by Union soldiers in a field, wrapped around three cigars. The found orders told McClellan that Lee's army was perilously, perhaps fatally divided. Rarely if ever in the history of war had a general known so clearly the disposition of the enemy in his front. McClellan assumed, as he always did, that Lee's army was twice the size of his own. Nevertheless, the plans wrapped around the three cigars were the key to the destruction of that army. If acted on it could end the war, and McClellan knew it.

Late that evening in his tent he shared his find with his ex–West Point classmate John Gibbon. "Here is a paper," he exulted, "with which if I can't whip 'Bobbie Lee,' I will be willing to go home."

He turned down one corner of the golden document for Gibbon, now a brigade commander in his army, to see. "I will not show you the document now," he told Gibbon. "But there is the signature."

Gibbon read it: "R. H. Chilton, Adjt. Gen." The orders were genuine, no doubt about that.

"It gives the movement of every division of Lee's army," McClellan said. "Tomorrow we will pitch into his centre and if you people will only do two good, hard days' marching I will put Lee in a position he will find hard to get out of."[54]

The next day McClellan did march, faster than Lee had ever known him to march, up the slopes toward South Mountain. It was not as fast as Tom Jackson or Lee himself might have marched had he had the same blueprint of enemy intentions, but it was fast for McClellan, and it puzzled Lee. This was not the McClellan he knew. And it was fast enough to hearten Lincoln. "God bless you, and all with you," the president wired McClellan. "Destroy the rebel army, if possible."[55]

That night Lee learned that McClellan had found the lost orders. It explained everything and it changed everything. It was trouble, "a shabby trick for fate to play us," said one of his officers.[56]

South Mountain was a long way from West Point in time and place for classmates Jesse Lee Reno and Samuel Davis Sturgis. They were a good deal alike in some ways—both short and stubby and brusque. But after their graduation in 1846 they had taken far different routes to get to where they were. They were now Union generals, but Reno, one of the stars of the class, had graduated eighth and gone on to become one of the army's outstanding ordnance officers. Sturgis, graduating thirty-second, had found his home in the saddle and made his reputation on the frontier as one of the army's premier Indian fighters.

Now both were serving under *the* star of the class, George

McClellan. And they were both hotly engaged on South Mountain, pushing against the force Lee had hurried there to stay McClellan's advance until he could make new arrangements. Both Reno and Sturgis were in the left wing of McClellan's advancing army, moving together toward Fox Gap. The center and right of the army was one mile north at Turner's Gap before Middletown, the point of McClellan's main attack.

Even though McClellan had had Lee's lost orders for twenty-four hours, and was moving more rapidly with them than he would have without them, he was still advancing with caution. There were still some uncertainties, and uncertainties made McClellan nervous and tentative. The lost orders had not been helpful in telling him Lee's actual present position or strength. Instead of moving immediately and at full speed, he had waited a day. It was now the fourteenth. Lee had had time to hurry D. H. Hill with his little division back to South Mountain to try to slow the northern juggernaut. And he had recalled Longstreet from Hagerstown to back up Hill. Lee now needed time more than he needed anything, time to pull his widely scattered army together again or face disaster. If the Union force broke through at South Mountain before he could do that, it could easily fall on the rear of Lafayette McLaws on Maryland Heights and in Pleasant Valley and imperil Jackson's Harpers Ferry expedition.

D. H. Hill, Tom Jackson's brother-in-law, was dug in on the South Mountain passes with but five thousand men painfully outmanned and outgunned. All morning and into the afternoon he had not been able to drive the Federals back. But neither had McClellan been able to force his way over the mountain, not until late afternoon, when the breakthrough came at Fox Gap. There Reno had been in the thick of it, leading the advance. As the rebel line was about to break, a musket ball found him and slammed into his stubby body.

Sturgis stepped to the side of his stretcher as Reno's soldiers carried him past.

"Hallo, Sam, I'm dead," Reno said, his voice firm and natural as always.

Sturgis could not believe him seriously hurt. "Oh, no, General, not as bad as all that, I hope."

"Yes, yes," Reno said. "I'm dead—good bye."

Within minutes the war was over forever for Jesse Reno.[57] He had been killed by Confederate rifle fire.

But the Union army had broken through, and Lee began backing down, pulling into an enclave around the little town of Sharpsburg. There he stopped, deploying that part of the army that was now with him—Longstreet and D. H. Hill—in a triangle of undulating land behind a little creek called the Antietam. At his back rolled the Potomac. From there he began calling all the scattered parts of his army to his side. There was going to be hell to pay now, and he would need everybody he could get.

McClellan came on, following slowly, pulling into view of Sharpsburg and the Confederate line at midafternoon on September 15. The Confederates were in battle array, so favorably positioned and strong, McClellan thought, that only desperate fighting could drive them out. A great and terrible battle was at hand; the situation must be studied. So all the rest of that day and the day following— the sixteenth—he reconnoitered, and Lee waited.[58]

Jackson had started from Frederick to execute Lee's plans for Harpers Ferry on September 10, driving his corps, including A. P. Hill's Light Division, at his accustomed breakneck pace. They re-crossed the Potomac into Virginia at Williamsport on the eleventh, less than a week after crossing it for the first time into Maryland. The band struck up, and the soldiers lustily broke into song again. "Carry me back to Ole Virginny, to the old Virginny shore," they sang as they swept over the river and wheeled toward Martinsburg.[59]

The scourge of the Valley was home again where he loved to be and doing what he loved to do—driving Yankees. The federal force at Martinsburg fled eastward in the face of his advance to seek ques-tionable sanctuary at Harpers Ferry. The Compte de Paris, attached to McClellan's army, called it "a kind of grand hunting-match through the lower valley of Virgina, driving all the federal detachments before him, and forcing them to crowd into the blind alley of Harper's Ferry."[60]

A. P. Hill's division pulled within sight of Bolivar Heights above Harpers Ferry on the morning of September 13. That same day John G. Walker occupied Loudoun Heights. Lafayette McLaws, with the tougher job, finally drove the Federals from Maryland Heights and on the fourteenth Harpers Ferry, with its eleven thousand trapped Union soldiers, was surrounded, their fate sealed.

It was another Sunday, and Hill began to move in. He marched his command along the left bank of the Shenandoah, around the federal flank, and there he deployed and waited. He would strike the Union line early the next morning. At daybreak, he opened a rapid enfilade fire, and in about an hour the federal guns slackened, then fell silent. Hill ordered his batteries to cease and signaled his soldiers to storm the works. Within moments a white flag went up and the Union garrison of eleven thousand surrendered themselves, seventy-three cannon, twelve thousand stand of arms, equipment, and numerous stores to the Confederate invaders.

Jackson rode into Harpers Ferry one more time, as the curious Union soldiers stared at him. So that was Stonewall Jackson? One of them looked at the faded old uniform and the sunburnt little hat and said, "Boys, he's not much for looks, but if we'd had him we wouldn't have been caught in this trap!"[61]

Jackson then exchanged messages with Lee. By the grace of Providence Harpers Ferry is ours, Jackson told him. Come immediately to Sharpsburg, ordered a gratified Lee. And Jackson set out that day, the fifteenth, to answer the summons. As he pushed out onto the road leading north along the river, he ordered Walker and McLaws to follow without delay. He left his ex-classmate A. P. Hill to continue processing the federal surrender at Harpers Ferry and to guard the public property.[62]

When Lee arrived in Sharpsburg he positioned the force that was with him—Longstreet and D. H. Hill—along the range of hills between the town and Antietam creek. His thin line ran for two miles roughly parallel to the creek, with Longstreet on the right of the Boonsboro road and Hill on the left. When Jackson arrived he would run him into the slot to the left of Hill and to the left of the command of John B. Hood. He would position Stuart's cavalry on the rise behind Jackson, and Walker on the extreme right to beef up the thin, tattered line held by Major General David Rumph (Neighbor) Jones. He would shift Walker and McLaws up and down the line as the demands of the battle dictated.

It promised to be an uneven match no matter what he did. All day the fifteenth and most of the sixteenth Lee waited there with but eighteen thousand men. The legions of McClellan's army were streaming in, eighty-five thousand strong, on the other side of the creek. Even when Jackson and Walker and McLaws arrived—and they were coming as fast as they could—Lee would have no more than forty thousand men to throw against those overwhelming numbers. Before him across the creek he could see rifled guns going into place, bringing into range the entire Confederate line, except for Stuart's cavalry on the left. Lee had no guns that could reach them. At his back flowed the Potomac with but a single avenue of escape, Boteler's Ford below Shepherdstown—and it was a bad one, rocky and deep. The best Lee could hope for seemed to be a drawn battle. Against it he risked utter destruction. But he waited calmly for what that day, or the next, would bring.[63]

By the evening of the sixteenth McClellan had decided what he must do. He would launch his main assault the next morning against Lee's left, at the same time striking his right. As soon as one or both of these flanking movements succeeded, he would hit Lee's center a crushing blow. It was a good plan, and he began late that day putting his army into position. His right wing under Joe Hooker, followed by Joseph Mansfield, crossed the creek and approached the Confederate left. His left wing under Ambrose Burnside filed into the hills overlooking a quiet bridge that spanned the Antietam down creek in front of the Confederate right.[64]

As the Union troops began to move, shifting in the night, the Confederates waited around their campfires and heard a faint cheering in their rear. From it gradually grew the unmistakable sound of mounted men, the distant strains of artillery bugles, and the tramp of heavy columns. It was a good sound, a reassuring sound, the sound of approaching reinforcements. The arrival of couriers and the jingle of artillery caissons soon left no doubt. Jackson's corps was arriving from Harpers Ferry and taking its place in the line. They came in such order, and made such a rustle among the deep layer of leaves that it seemed to doubly magnify their numbers and strength. Swiftly, as was Jackson's way, they passed through the woods and took their position on the left, facing Joe Hooker.[65]

All through the evening this shifting and placing went on. In the strange half-lights of earth and sky, the moving masses were dimly visible from across the creek. One of Burnside's soldiers watched and wrote, "There was something weirdly impressive yet unreal in the gradual drawing together of those whispering armies under cover of the night—something of awe and dread, as always in the secret preparation for momentous deeds."[66]

It was the prelude to something brilliant and terrible, and they all knew it.

In Hagerstown a dozen miles north of Sharpsburg, the townsfolk awoke to the cannonade at first light the next morning. It rolled and thundered through the valley, from cloud to mountain and from mountain to cloud. Charles Carleton Coffin, a newspaper correspondent, listened as it grew into "a continuous roar, like the unbroken roll of a thunder-storm." Soon he began to hear the puncturing rattle of musketry against the thunder-roar of the cannon—like pattering drops of rain on a roof at first, then "a roll, crash, roar, and rush, like a mighty ocean billow upon the shore . . . wave on wave."[67]

In Shepherdstown across the Potomac, Mary Bedinger Mitchell and the other women ministering to the Confederate wounded already pouring into the town, heard the clash of battle too. Every now and then they heard the echo of some charging cheer borne to them on the wind over the cannon's roar. As the human voices pierced the "demoniacal clangor," the women caught their breaths and tried not to sob.[68]

The fighting at Antietam began that morning, the seventeenth. It began, as McClellan had planned, against the Confederate left, against his old classmate, Tom Jackson. The troops of both armies had slept within earshot of one another the night before. Early in the morning Joe Hooker started the fight, hurling his First Corps at Jackson, setting his sights on the white Dunker church house beyond an intervening cornfield. There followed through that early morning a bloody pushing and shoving of two armies, such as the war had not seen. Striking through the cornfield in full cry, Hooker bent Jackson's line slowly back. But on the brink of a breakthrough, he was hit by Hood's troops, pouring into the breech. Hooker's drive slowed, stalled, and was thrown back.

Mansfield then pushed in with the Union Twelfth Corps, driving Hood. First Walker, who had hurried across the entire Confederate line all the way from the right, struck him. Then Lafayette McLaws, arriving from Maryland Heights, rushed to meet him. Hooker had been shot through the foot and Mansfield lay dying. The Union Second Corps under old Edwin Vose Sumner, still serving after all these years, came up and hurled itself upon the Confederate line. Sumner's attack, under John Sedgwick, the artillerist and cavalryman from Connecticut, penetrated deeper than any division so far, then also stalled, and was chewed to pieces.

By midmorning the fight on the Confederate left was over. Jackson's eight thousand hungry, shoeless, ragged Confederates, with help sent from Lee, had held off nearly thirty thousand fiercely attacking Union troops. The action now shifted to the right center. There, across a bloody sunken road, thousands of Confederate and Union soldiers collided, and under the sheer weight of the attack the Confederate line sagged and nearly snapped. But the Union attackers had suffered horribly and there was no follow-up. It was another standoff, a case of a battle won and the winner not knowing it.

By early afternoon it had all come down to Burnside on the Confederate right, waiting above the little arched bridge that spanned Antietam creek.

So far the battle had been fought by divisions, one after another. There had been no unity of action, no hammering all along the line at the same time, no follow-up of heavy concerted blows. It had been different from any fight in the war so far—a pitched battle in an open field. There had been no cover, no breastworks, no abatis, no intervening woodlands, no abrupt hills behind which to hide. There were no impassable streams. The space over which the assaulting federal army hurled itself upon the Confederate lines was a ground of gentle undulations covered by green grass and ripening corn.[69]

Walker, who had been from one end of the line to the other, described it as a battle in which more than a hundred thousand men armed with the latest weaponry had engaged in slaughtering one another at close quarters. It was a ghastly scene, "the constant booming of cannon, the ceaseless rattle and roar of musketry, the glimpses of galloping horsemen and marching infantry, now seen, now lost in the smoke, adding weirdness to terror."[70]

The sun had beat down without mercy all morning, as unrelenting as the fighting itself. The suspense had been racking, the anxiety intense. "Mars was striking with iron and fire," Henry Kyd Douglas thought, "time moving with leaden heel."[71] The artillery on both sides had been bellowing without letup from the start, heard in Hagerstown and Shepherdstown. The unceasing thunder of cannon had turned the peaceful Antietam valley into what Colonel Stephen D. Lee called an "Artillery Hell." Lee had seen and heard the terrible bombardment at Fort Sumter and this was far worse. He prayed that they might never see another like it.[72]

George Gordon of the class of 1846, now with Mansfield's Twelfth Corps, had also seen and heard it all. He had watched the battle ebb and flow, and the soldiers on both sides grapple with one another in lines of regiments, brigades, and divisions. He had watched whole regiments, brigades, and divisions melt away under a terrible fire, leaving long lines of piled dead to mark where the living had stood but a moment before. He had seen fields of corn trampled underfoot, woods shattered and splintered, huge limbs sent crashing to the earth, battered by shell and round shot. He had heard the hissing scream of shrapnel and canister. He had heard and seen it and called it a "hellish carnival."[73]

All through the battle George McClellan had been standing in a redan of fence rails at his headquarters overlooking the shifting scene. At his side, Major General Fitz John Porter studied the field below through a telescope resting on the top rail, and by nods, signs, or in words so low-toned and brief that few of the surrounding coterie of staff and aides could make them out, passed information to his chief. McClellan and Porter knew one another well; they were best of friends. There hardly had to be more than a nod or a sign between them.

When not engaged with Porter, McClellan stood in his soldierly, strutting way and intently watched the battle unfold. It was the first time he had ever seen his army fight. He had not personally seen the fighting at Rich Mountain, nor on the Peninsula. A commanding general often has other claims on his time than watching the battle he is masterminding.

As he watched now, he smoked a cigar and with the utmost apparent calmness, conversed with surrounding officers and issued orders in the most quiet of undertones. Close beside him at all times hovered the one man above all others he could trust without question—Nelly's father and his chief of staff, Brigadier General Marcy. Marcy was his right hand, and had been from the beginning. Now he was relaying his son-in-law's orders to waiting aides-de-camp, who galloped away with them to distant parts of the field below. Several officers of the French, Prussian, and Sardinian service clustered about trying to comprehend this bizarre fight between brothers and classmates and friends and enemies.

"Everything was as quiet and punctilious as a drawing room ceremony," marveled David Strother, the Virginian who had survived Nathaniel Banks's disastrous Valley campaign against Jackson and was now an aide to McClellan.

In the middle of the day the ferocious fighting at the sunken road riveted McClellan's attention. "By George," he exclaimed, "this is a magnificent field, and if we win this fight it will cover all our errors and misfortunes forever!"

Strother, standing near and always ready with advice, offered some now: "General, fortune favors the bold; hurl all our power upon them at once, and we will make a glorious finish of the campaign and the war."[74]

Unlike Banks who followed Strother's advice at Strasburg and shouldn't have, McClellan didn't follow it at Antietam and should have. He would not hurl his full power upon Lee at once. But at 1:45 in the afternoon he would take time out to wire Nelly. "We are in the midst of the most terrible battle of the age," he told her.[75]

The Man
in the
Red Battle Shirt

The message from Lee to A. P. Hill arrived at Harpers Ferry at 6:30 in the morning as the battle at Antietam was just beginning. By 7:30, Hill had his Light Division filing out of the town and marching rapidly northward.

Maxcy Gregg's brigade left first, followed immediately by James Archer's, its commander sick and riding in an ambulance. Three more of Hill's six brigades were soon in motion behind the first two. The sixth would remain at Harpers Ferry.

The day was already hot; it was going to be a scorcher, with another long, dusty, grueling march ahead of them. Nobody relished it. But Lee had called. "Those people" had the outmanned Army of Northern Virginia in a tight spot at Sharpsburg. The Union assault was already under way; Lee would need every man he could get. Hill must come up. He must get his division there as fast as legs could carry it.

Getting his Light Division there when it counted was what Hill did. It was his specialty. No division commander in the Confederate army did it better. It was twelve miles to Sharpsburg as the crow flies. But Hill would take his division up the road by the river and across

Boteler's Ford below Shepherdstown. By that route it would be seventeen hard-marching miles.

Hill's quondam West Point classmate Darius Couch hovered nearby with a Union division. In better times Hill would have been delighted to see his old friend again. But now Couch was an enemy who must be avoided at all costs. The fight was at Sharpsburg and nothing must be allowed to interfere with getting his division there.

As his soldiers marched they could hear the thunder of battle ahead—a discordant, distant rumbling, growing ever louder, drawing them on. Many of Hill's ragged soldiers were respectably attired now, for the first time in months, wearing pieces of blue Union uniforms seized in the captured stores at Harpers Ferry.

The pace was killing and the sun and the dust and the heat were merciless. Men were dropping out all along the line of march, spent and exhausted. But still the column moved on. The ten-minute rest stops every hour that Jackson demanded were ignored. To hell with Jackson. He was already in Sharpsburg and the roar of the guns was insistent and demanding. Hill ranged up and down the column, a long-bearded demon in his red battle shirt shorn of all insignia of rank—cursing, prodding, exhorting, sometimes with the point or the flat of his saber. Lee needed this division in Sharpsburg and, by God, Hill was going to get it there.[1]

The husband that Dolly Hill loved—and the lover who had once won the heart of Nelly Marcy—was gentle, genial, approachable, affectionate, and witty. But this Confederate major general in the red hunting shirt driving his division toward Sharpsburg was someone those two beautiful women might not have recognized—restless, relentless, impetuous, and cursing like a stable sergeant.

Hill, thirty-seven years old, had already won a reputation in the Army of Northern Virginia as a fearless and able fighter, without peer as a division commander and with an unquenchable thirst for battle. His natural bent for war had surfaced strongly on the Peninsula, where he had thrown his division impetuously against the army of his dear friend and West Point roommate, George McClellan. At Cedar Mountain in early August his timely arrival had saved the day for another classmate, Stonewall Jackson. He was a fighter who could be relied on to be there when battle called.

Hill stared at the world through cold, almost colorless and penetrating eyes, and with a mien of quiet cynicism. Beneath the calm smoldered a pride and a hair-trigger wrath worthy of Achilles, capable of reacting fiercely to any slight, real or imagined. He did not fear to differ with generals above him. He had been known to criticize Lee, and he had bickered openly and bitterly—nearly to the point of a duel—with James Longstreet, his wing commander before Jackson. Even now he was quarreling with Jackson. Hill scoffed at men, such as Jackson, who sought the favors of an intervening Providence. That wasn't for him. War to Hill was a calculating science, wholly manmade; Providence had nothing to do with it. Yet there was in him a streak of the superstitious. There was that red flannel hunting shirt he wore in battle—which he was wearing now—and the good-luck hambone from his mother that he always carried in his pocket.

Hill was a slender 5 feet 9 inches tall with a Grecian nose tapering from a high forehead. His hair, thick and auburn, tended to curl around his collar, and the tip of his full red beard nearly reached his breast. Normally he spoke in the soft low-pitched drawl of the southern cavalier, but his voice rose to a high feminine shrill when he became angry or excited, as in battle. He was quick with a wry jest, often teasing his couriers under fire. His laugh, when he was amused, came in a whisper ending with a quiet "key! key! key!" When not riding into battle he sometimes dressed the cavalier, in a close-fitting double-breasted gray tunic with dark trousers tucked into black polished leather boots almost to the hips, with a brass spur on the right heel. He often wore a large black campaign hat rimmed in gold and black cord, and carried white buckskin gauntlets. When reconnoitering he sometimes wore a long black cape, with a curved artillery saber jutting from beneath. (The saber was now unsheathed and he was using it to prod his army toward Sharpsburg.) Pistols, field glasses, and a tobacco pipe carved by one of his soldiers completed his ensemble. But whether dressed as the cavalier with the gold stars of his rank on the collar of his coat, or in the insignia-free red shirt that made him indistinguishable from the men he led, he was clearly a general.

He was not so much the general, however, that he wouldn't snatch up his pistol and join his men in a squirrel chase now and then. A squirrel in a tree invariably set up a hideous clamor, such as Jackson's men used to greet rabbits. Terminally unstrung, desperate, and bewildered, the little animal would leap toward the next tree, sometimes thirty feet or more away, with branches often far beyond its capacity and dreams. When it plummeted to the ground, the army in full cry picked up the pursuit. In a voice roaring above the others, Hill would shout, "Stand aside, boys, and let me get a crack at him!"[2]

What Hill wanted on September 17, 1862, was a crack at the Yankees in Sharpsburg. His fast-marching division was drawing closer by the moment. The din of battle, as morning passed into afternoon, could still be heard. There might still be time.

It was the nature of this supremely ironic war that Hill was marching to attack one of his best friends. McClellan was there and he had to be struck. And Hill would strike—as hard as he could, as he always did, as if Mac were the most hated of his enemies, rather than the dear roommate of his West Point years. How many cigars had these old friends shared down through two decades? How many warm moments of tender friendship, grounded on mutual trust? They had even loved and courted the same beautiful woman.

There was a story going around the Army of the Potomac about that. The soldiers knew that McClellan and Hill had both wooed the lovely Nelly Marcy, and that McClellan had won her hand. The talk, wholly fictional, was that Hill somehow held this against his old friend. The Union soldiers were sure of it. On the Peninsula and since, it seemed that every time the rebels attacked with such demon ferocity, it more often than not had been Hill's doing. Whether struck in the front, flank, or rear—especially in the early morning—it was by Hill's division. McClellan's soldiers began to tire of this harassment, laying it to Hill's spite and vengeance over the loss of Nelly Marcy. Early one dark morning, before either the sun or the federal army had risen, there came again the dull thud of artillery and the rattle of musketry, telling them Hill was again beating reveille. The long roll in the Union camp was followed by commotion and confusion everywhere and a rush to arms. One weary veteran rolled from his blanket in disgust and cried out, "My God, Nelly, why didn't you marry him!"[3]

That was the story they told about this happily married man in the red battle shirt, who adored the wife he finally did win, but who perhaps loved war as much, and was driving hellbent for Sharpsburg.

There were old friends and classmates other than McClellan waiting up the road. Hill knew that Burnside was there somewhere. If Hill had a closer friend than McClellan, it was Ambrose Burnside. After Hill had been put back a year into the class of 1847, his best friends had been Julian McAllister, Henry Heth, and Burnside. The four had been inseparable, the social lions of the class and dear friends. Hill's friendship with Burnside had deepened in the years since. Hill had loaned him $8,000 before the war, a debt still owed but very hard to collect in these divided times.[4]

Indeed, there could have been a class reunion on the banks of the Antietam if the times had not been so troubled. Sam Sturgis was there commanding a Union division in Burnside's corps. George Gordon, John Gibbon, and Truman Seymour were all there commanding federal brigades. Couch was with his division near Harpers Ferry. Reno had been there, but was now dead. Among the Confederates were Birkett Fry, a victim of mathematics at the end of their second year, now a colonel in D. H. Hill's division.

And there was Old Jack. The name was gall and wormwood to Hill. Jackson was now his corps commander and it was one of the unhappiest fits in the Confederate army. The outgoing Hill had never liked this strange, reclusive, and stubborn man. He had not liked him at West Point and he didn't like him now. Nor did Jackson, not celebrated for his affection, waste any of it on Hill. Indeed, even as Hill marched toward Sharpsburg on this September afternoon, he was technically under arrest, put there by Jackson but two weeks before. He was back in command of his division only because Jackson knew there was no better fighter in the army than Hill, and the moment demanded fighters.

Putting his commanders under arrest was not a personal thing with Jackson. He had put virtually every general who had ever served under him—Ewell was an exception—under arrest at one time or another in this war. But Jackson no longer had Ewell. Less than a month before, at the battle of Groveton on August 28, Ewell was irrepressibly being a company commander again, personally leading one of his regiments into the fight. As he was dismounted and kneeling to observe the direction of the Union cross fire, a fusillade shattered his right knee, and he had lost the leg.

Jackson's sense of duty was as stern as his sense of Jehovah. He had arrested the unfortunate Richard Garnett at Kernstown, and others after him. Brigadier General Alexander Lawton, commanding Ewell's division in this Maryland campaign, told his brother-in-law, Edward Porter Alexander, that he was the only division commander in Jackson's entire corps who was not at that moment in arrest.[5]

Hill had run into trouble, as they all did, for what Jackson perceived as a failure to obey orders—a failure to do his duty as Jackson saw it. Jackson had observed that Hill tended to be lax about marches that didn't matter, and had mildly reprimanded him for it earlier in August. Hill didn't seem to take Jackson's strict orders about marching seriously enough. He permitted altogether too much straggling, and he didn't conscientiously observe Jackson's hourly rest stops. It was exasperating. On the way to Maryland this character flaw had landed Hill in arrest.

Hill did not take reprimands or interferences with his division in good grace. So when Jackson personally halted one of his brigades on the way to Maryland, Hill galloped up and demanded, "Who halted my command?"

"I did, sir," said his brigadier.

"By whose orders?"

"By orders of General Jackson."

Hill swung from his saddle in a towering rage, strode up to Jackson, and presented his sword.

"If you take command of my troops in my presence, take my sword also," he thundered.

"Put up your sword," Jackson said coldly, "and consider yourself under arrest."

A short time later, orders came down the line for Lawrence O'Bryan Branch, Hill's ranking brigadier, to assume command of his division.[6]

For more than a week Hill had ridden at the rear of his division awaiting formal charges. One of his soldiers remembered him with "an old white hat slouched down over his eyes, his coat off and wearing an old flannel shirt, looking as mad as a bull."[7]

Marching with his division but having no authority to command it was more than Hill could long stand. After they crossed the Potomac on the way to Harpers Ferry he sent for Henry Kyd Douglas. It was evident, Hill told Douglas, that a battle was at hand and he didn't want anyone else to lead his division if there was to be a fight. He asked Douglas to say to Jackson that he wished to be restored to command until the fighting was over, when he would report himself again under arrest. Douglas galloped back and put this proposal to Jackson, arguing that no one could command Hill's division as well as Hill could. He didn't need to tell Jackson that. Besides, Jackson could never refuse a request to be permitted to fight. Hill was restored to command.[8]

The moment the order came down, Hill threw on his coat, fastened his sword about his slim waist, mounted his horse, and galloped up the line to the front of his troops, looking, one of his soldiers said, "like a young eagle in search of his prey."[9]

Throughout the rest of the march, through Martinsburg and the investment and capture of Harpers Ferry, Hill's division with him back in front had done the important work.

Now it was marching to Sharpsburg. The beckoning guns continued to thunder up ahead, louder than ever.

At 8:00 that morning McClellan had sent a message to Ambrose Burnside. Burnside had been waiting with his Ninth Corps in front of the bridge on the Confederate right since the night before. He knew that at a signal from McClellan he was to cross the bridge, roll the Confederate right back into Sharpsburg, and cut off the rebel army's only line of retreat across the Potomac. He knew that it was to be done in concert with a crushing blow against the Confederate left.

All through the early morning he had stood with Brigadier General Jacob Cox and watched the assault against the left. They had looked down between the opposing lines as they would have looked down an open street. They saw the federal assault slam into the Confederate line, then stall. They had watched anxiously, uncertain whether the Union line would now collapse or hold, charge or retreat. Then the message arrived from McClellan; Burnside's turn had come. He read the order and handed it to Cox, who would command the corps in the coming attack.[10]

Only David Rumph (Neighbor) Jones, commanding a thin Confederate line of two thousand troops, stood between Burnside and Sharpsburg. Lee had been diluting his right all morning to save his left. As each command came up from Harpers Ferry he shuttled it up and down the two-mile front to buttress Jackson and Longstreet and D. H. Hill. Jones had been left with his depleted division to defend a line a mile long, to keep the Federals out of Sharpsburg, to divert disaster, and hope A. P. Hill would come up in time. It was beginning to have the hopeless look of a last stand.

Cox was to open the Union assault on the bridge with the Second Brigade of his own Kanahwa Division—mainly Ohio troops—commanded by Colonel George Crook. But in the first of a chain of events frustrating Burnside almost beyond endurance, Crook couldn't find the bridge. He had come out on the Antietam at an awkward point north of the crossing and into a withering fire from across the creek. It was virtually impossible from his position to carry the bridge.

Sam Sturgis waited in reserve behind the Antietam with his Second Division as Crook groped for the bridge and couldn't find it. Now Cox turned to Sturgis, much as John Sedgwick at another moment four years before had turned to him to save the command from a buffalo stampede. Sturgis wasn't in the habit of failing, and he immediately threw his Second Maryland and his Sixth New Hampshire at the bridge. They found it, but it was at that moment on that day the most undesireable crossing of any creek in America. It was a starkly exposed bridge that had to be approached over a long stretch of road that ran for several hundred yards parallel to the creek. Those several hundred yards and the bridge itself were entirely exposed and unprotected from any weapons that might be trained on them from the heights on the other side of the creek.

And the weapons were there. Confederate Brigadier General Robert Toombs had been waiting to use them all morning. He had been waiting since the war began for just such a moment. Soldiering wasn't Toombs's natural occupation. He was a politician, a powerful one, who had represented Georgia in the U.S. Congress before his state had seceded, and had been one of the most eloquent voices raised in the South for secession. After secession, he was for a time the Confederate Secretary of State. Then he had gone for a soldier, and he wanted to be a successful one. Now he waited on the bluffs above the bridge with the Second, Twentieth, and Fiftieth Georgia, of Neighbor Jones's stripped-down division. It was fire he must now deal out, not oratory.

Toombs had only five hundred muskets. But he had the advantage of terrain. As Sturgis's Second Maryland and Sixth New Hampshire ran up the road toward the bridge, Toombs turned all five hundred of those muskets loose, virtually point-blank. The federal plan was for the two lead regiments to cross the bridge and fan out on the other side, as other regiments poured across behind them. The two lead regiments, however, never reached the other side. The rain of fire from Toombs's musketry drove them back. Again and again Sturgis threw men at the bridge and nobody crossed alive.

At Union headquarters as the morning wore on, McClellan grew more and more impatient and irritated. He sent another messenger to Burnside, then another. Still the bridge hadn't been crossed. The opportunity for the federal left and right to operate in concert was fast slipping away. All that had come back from "Old Burn" was vague word that he had not yet crossed the creek and couldn't carry the bridge.

"What is Burnside about?" McClellan snapped. "Why do we not hear from him?"[11]

He sent yet another messenger. Now harried and frustrated and nearly as nettled by the string of incessant messages from McClellan as he was by his inability to carry the bridge, Burnside sent Sturgis a virtual ultimatum: Take that bridge "at all hazards."[12]

Earlier in the morning Union Brigadier General Isaac Rodman had started down the creek with his reinforced Third Division to try to find Snavely's Ford and cross it on the Confederate flank. But the ford hadn't been where they had supposed it to be, and Rodman still wasn't across. The little creek was proving itself a Confederate ally. Every resident within miles of the Antietam knew that all around the bridge, above and below, there were fords closer than Snavely's that could have been easily crossed out of range of the rebel guns on the heights. But nobody in the single-minded fixation with getting across that damnable bridge had seemed to consider that.

By now it was getting on toward one o'clock in the afternoon. The fighting on the Confederate left and center had all but ceased. On the heights above the bridge, about half of Toombs's five hundred muskets had also been silenced, but he had not been driven out.

Now Sturgis called up his twin Fifty-firsts—the Fifty-first New York and the Fifty-first Pennsylvania—and ordered them to charge the bridge with the bayonet, but from a different angle this time. They started from behind a spur fronting the bridge instead of approaching up the deadly parallel road. The two regiments swept over the slope in front of the bridge and broke into a sprint, scrambling across and on to the other side. At about the same time, Rodman's troops finally crossed Snavely's Ford. Toombs, facing disaster now in front and on his flank, pulled back into Jones's main line of resistance before Sharpsburg. But the politician had risen to the occasion as a soldier. For half a day he had kept the left and right of the Union army from acting in concert. He had frustrated McClellan's central design.[13]

It was now 1:00. Although Sturgis was across the creek, he was spent and out of ammunition. Instead of pushing on, Burnside decided to regroup. He would bring up a fresh division under Orlando Willcox for the push into Sharpsburg. For the next two hours activity seemed to stop all along the line as Burnside made ready. Nothing appeared to be happening; there was no federal follow-up from the bridge and the heights. The Confederates waited, and wondered when the hammer would fall. All of the rebels knew A. P. Hill was coming. If the Union troops waited long enough, he might yet get there in time.

As the moments ticked on and nothing happened on his left, McClellan sent Burnside still another message. Burnside only sent word back that he thought he could hold the bridge.

McClellan exploded: "He should be able to do that with five thousand men; if he can do no more I must take the remainder of his troops and use them elsewhere in the field."[14] McClellan had never spoken so harshly of the friend who was dearer to him than any other on earth.

At 3:00 in the afternoon Burnside was finally ready, and his troops, united now with Rodman and outnumbering Jones's ragged division nearly five to one, drove toward Sharpsburg. On they drove, across the rolling terrain of cornfields and haystacks, over fences— many of them of stone with rebel riflemen crouched behind nearly every one. Artillery boomed across the littered field from both sides.

Of the oncoming federal tide Henry Douglas said: "The earth seemed to tremble beneath their tread. It was a splendid and fearful sight. . . . The artillery tore, but did not stay them."[15]

A charging Union soldier wrote that "the air was full of the hiss of bullets and the hurtle of grape-shot. The mental strain was so great that I saw at that moment . . . the whole landscape for an instant turned slightly red."[16]

Neighbor Jones's ragged rebel line ranged itself behind every cover capable of protecting life. "We had placed our guns through the board fence," a Confederate soldier wrote, "drawn back the hammers, and stood with fingers on triggers, ready to fire as soon as the enemy emerged from the corn."[17]

"Never did I feel . . . so much solicitude for the safety of our army," the soldier wrote, "for I knew that no help could be expected from our left, as our troops on that part of the field had been fought to exhaustion."[18] Tom Jackson, always thinking offensively, reconnoitered quickly on the Confederate left to see if he could mount a counterattack and take the pressure off the embattled right. But even this most willing of attackers could see it was no use.

The rebels on the right were now standing up against the heavy Union onslaught on heart alone—"more from a blind dogged obstinacy than anything else," one soldier said, giving them back "fire for fire, shot for shot, and death for death. But it was a pin's point against Pelides' spear."[19]

A. P. Hill's division—what was left of it; nearly half of his five thousand men had dropped out in the hard, hot march—plunged into the cool waters of the Potomac at Boteler's Ford at about 2:30 in the afternoon. The current in the river was swift and the ledges of rock, jutting out at sharp angles, made the passage difficult and painful. Wading it as rapidly as they could, Hill's men climbed dripping up the slippery bank on the other side and broke into a trot. Hill galloped ahead, looking for Lee.[20]

For Lee the afternoon had been anxious and fretful. He knew that everything now depended on A. P. Hill and whether he got there on time. But time was running out.

Suddenly a clump of riders on sweat-lathered horses appeared before him. At its head was the slender, red-bearded general in the red battle shirt. Lee had never seen a more welcome sight. He embraced Hill, in as much a show of emotion as he was ever likely to exhibit, and sent him immediately to confer with Neighbor Jones.[21]

Hill found Jones, who gave him information that his ignorance of the ground required. The two former classmates agreed on how Hill would place his brigades when they arrived—they were still an hour away. Until then it would be up to Jones and the artillery to hold back the federal wave.[22]

The federal army was now virtually at the doorsteps of Sharpsburg. A few federal flags appeared on the hill in the rear of the town nearly astraddle Lee's only avenue of escape. The town was all but enveloped in flames. Flocks of terrified pigeons flapped in confusion through the clouds of smoke, driven from the rooftops by the screaming and bursting shells.[23]

As Lee stared at the Union line plunging toward him under cover of the smoke, a battery of North Carolina artillery pounded past. It had just been resupplied with ammunition and was galloping again toward the front. Lee, seeing the telescope carried by its commander, Lieutenant John A. Ramsay, called out to him.

Pointing, he asked, "What troops are those?"

Ramsay drew his telescope from its case and offered it to Lee. The general held up two splinted and bandaged hands. The day after Second Manassas he had painfully injured them both in an accident with his horse.[24]

"Can't use it," he said to Ramsay. "What troops are those?"

Ramsay dismounted, adjusted the glass, and looked.

"They are flying the United States flag," he said.

Lee pointed at another body of troops nearly at right angles from the others and said, "What troops are those?"

Ramsay peered again through his glass and said, "They are flying the Virginia and Confederate flags."

"It is A. P. Hill, from Harpers Ferry," said Lee.

Help—perhaps salvation—was at hand.

Lee ordered Ramsay to unlimber his guns on a little knoll on the right of the road and to commence firing at the troops he had first identified.

Ramsay hesitated. "General Lee," he said, "as soon as we fire we will draw the enemy's fire."

"Never mind me," Lee replied.

Ramsay's first shell exploded in the middle of the Union line, the next a little to the right of the first, and after five shots the enemy had evaporated.

"Well done!" Lee exclaimed, and rode away with new hope. Hill had come, not a moment too soon.[25]

The Union signal officers on the summit of Red Hill had the best seat in the house. They could see for miles. The entire Confederate line lay before them in panoramic display from end to end. All afternoon they had been sending down messages about all they saw. They first noticed the heavy dust rising out of the south earlier in the day, and had alerted McClellan. At about 3:00 in the afternoon signal officer J. Gloskioski sent a message to Burnside.

"Look out well on your left," he warned, "the enemy are moving a strong force in that direction."[26]

This cryptic first federal notice of the arrival of A. P. Hill's division to the Antietam battlefield was sent about the time Burnside was hurling his corps at Neighbor Jones in a final lunge toward Sharpsburg. It was either not received, received but not looked at, or looked at and ignored in the chaos of the moment. At any rate, nobody took it to heart. Down on the battlefield itself a few of Burnside's troops noticed that there was a force approaching on their left flank. But it had a blue aura to it—our own boys, they thought.[27]

The blue aura advancing toward them was disaster, wearing captured Harpers Ferry uniforms. It was the resurrection of Lee's army arriving dead tired but battle-eager from seventeen miles of hard marching in the hot sun at the tip of Hill's prodding saber. It was another product of Robert E. Lee's prestidigitation, a rabbit pulled from the hat, arriving "as if summoned by the lamp of Aladdin,"[28] seeming to spring, as James Longstreet said, "from the earth."[29]

As his brigades stormed onto the battlefield, Hill hurled them into the flank of Burnside's corps. James Archer, dragging himself from his ambulance, led the assault, his men screaming their eerie rebel yell.

"Just then," said one of Jones's grateful soldiers, "we saw another and another Confederate brigade rise to their feet and advance in the same direction. . . . then there was a grand, a wild Confederate yell and charge along the whole line."[30]

What Hill's men saw as they threw themselves at the advancing federal force would have given them pause had they stopped a moment to think about it. In their front, one of them wrote, "we could see the blue lines of the Federals, moving to the attack over the smooth, round hills, marching in perfect order, with banners flying and guns and bayonets glittering in the sun." It was an awesome sight.[31]

Henry Douglas, who could at that moment claim some credit for Hill being a free man, watched as three of his brigades slammed into the exposed Union flank, "taking no note of their numbers." Douglas could hardly contain his awe: "The blue line staggered and hesitated, and hesitating, was lost. At the critical moment A. P. Hill was always at his strongest. . . . Again . . . as at Manassas, Harpers Ferry, and elsewhere, [he] had struck with the right hand of Mars."[32] The effect this right hand of Mars had on the left wing of Burnside's corps was to "roll it up like a scroll."[33]

A marvelous transformation took place before their eyes. "One moment," a Confederate high private wrote, "the lines of blue are steadily advancing everywhere and sweeping everything before them; another moment and all is altered. . . . Still forward came the wave of gray, still backward receded the billows of blue, heralded by warning hiss of the bullets, the sparkling of the rifle flashes, the purplish vapor settling like a veil over the lines, the mingled hurrahs and wild yells, and the bass accompaniment . . . of the hoarse cannonading."[34]

One Union general was later to call Hill's march and thunderbolt attack "a brilliant feat of arms."[35] The adjutant of one of the attacking North Carolina regiments was to put it more fundamentally. Burnside's corps, he said, "should have swept us off the earth, the mere handful that we were to them in numbers. How Hill's division stood before them was wonderful, but it had gone there to fight and was too tired to run."[36]

As Burnside's corps stumbled back to the banks of the Antietam, the Confederate pursuit stopped at the bluffs above the bridge that had been such an obstacle to the Union cause all that morning. The two armies were spent.

"Nature has its limits," said the Carolina adjutant, "and we had reached ours, with fearful sacrifice."[37] On the other end of the Confederate line, where the morning's fighting had left them exhausted, the sounds coming from the right told the whole story. They knew Hill had arrived. General Walker knew it instantly when the sound of musketry, which had almost ceased, roared out again louder than ever. "For thirty minutes," he wrote, "the sound of firing came steadily from the same direction; then it seemed to recede eastward, and finally to die away almost entirely. We knew then that Hill *was* up; that the Federals had been driven back, and that the Confederate army had narrowly escaped defeat."[38]

Darkness fell mercifully all along the bloody battle line. For the men on both sides who had fought it, the end came as a God-sent relief. "The sun seemed almost to go backwards," one of them said of the day, "and it appeared as if night would never come."[39] Yet it seemed to have settled nothing. It had been a bloody standoff. The two armies lay basically where they had lain twelve hours earlier, minus more than twenty-three thousand dead, wounded, captured, or missing between them—the bloodiest day of this bloody war.

Neighbor Jones put it this way: "Night had now come on, putting an end to the conflict, and leaving my command in possession of the ground we had held in the morning, with the exception of the mere bridge."[40] That "mere bridge" had been the key to the whole day. But for it, there might have been an altogether different ending. But for it, the man in the red battle shirt might never have come up in time. But for it, Lee might not that night have had an army.

That night, over the cries and moans of the thousands of Federals and Confederates who still lay wounded and dying on the field, some Union soldiers sang a wistful song:

> Do they miss me at home? Do they miss me?
>   'Twould be an assurance most dear
> To know that this moment some loved one
>   Were saying, "I wish he were here,"
> To feel that the group at the fireside
>   Were thinking of me as I roam;
> Oh, yes, 'twould be joy beyond measure
>   To know that they miss me at home.[41]

David Strother listened as messengers came and went to McClellan's headquarters through the night. Strother had watched all that day in mounting distress as McClellan threw his divisions at the enemy piecemeal instead of hurling all of his overwhelming might simultaneously on Lee's cornered army. McClellan had held a good part of his force in reserve on the battlefield. And he had left his classmate, Darius Couch, standing by with an unfought division near Harpers Ferry.

Strother despaired further when he heard McClellan tell an officer sometime between midnight and dawn that they were to hold the ground they occupied, but were not to attack without further orders. The day wore on and no further orders came and the opportunity to destroy Lee's army, as Lincoln had so ardently hoped, was lost.

"The empty name of victory," Strother wrote sadly in his diary—and it had hardly been victory—"is not sufficient; we needed a result crushing and conclusive, and have failed to obtain it."[42]

All the next day after the battle of Antietam, Lee waited defiantly for McClellan to resume the attack, too spent and wasted and too few in numbers to launch an assault of his own. When the day passed and no attack came, he resolved to wait no longer. McClellan could only get stronger and Lee could look for no increase in strength. All the day before he had fought an army twice his size and the odds were not going to get any better. So under the cover of night he took his army back over the Potomac and out of Maryland. McClellan did not try to stop him.

What McClellan had won was not the decisive victory he might have, but a standoff in which his chief claim to victory was possession of an abandoned field.[43]

But it satisfied him. He wrote Nelly the day after the fight that "those in whose judgment I rely tell me that I fought the battle splendidly & that it was a masterpiece of art." The first thing he did on the morning of the nineteenth when he found the field abandoned, was wire her again: "Our victory complete."[44]

That same afternoon he wired Halleck: "I have the honor to report that Maryland is entirely freed from the presence of the enemy, who have been driven across the Potomac. No fears need now be entertained for the safety of Pennsylvania."[45]

The more he thought about it, the more elated he became. As he explained it to Nelly the next day, "with a beaten and demoralized army" he had "defeated Lee so utterly, & saved the North so completely" that he would now demand that those two fools, Stanton and Halleck, be removed. "No success is possible with them. . . ." he said. "I have shown that I can fight battles & *win* them! I think my enemies [the ones behind him] are pretty effectively killed by this time! May they remain so!!"[46]

For A. P. Hill, some things had been settled satisfactorily and some hadn't. He had made an unbelievable march—the most dramatic of the war—and a brilliant attack. He had redeemed an old classmate, Neighbor Jones, in his hour of greatest peril. He had frustrated the grand strategy of a roommate he dearly loved, Little Mac, and denied him the clear-cut victory he had so desperately needed. He had ruined the afternoon of another classmate whom he also dearly loved, Burnside, and the $8,000 loan was still unpaid. And he was still technically under arrest by yet another classmate, Old Jack, whom he didn't love at all.

But as Hill now knew about life, you can't have everything. It was enough to have saved an army.

The Night
the General
Was Fired

It was that Confederate army, still in front of McClellan, that bothered Lincoln—the fact that it existed at all, that it had not been destroyed.

At Antietam, McClellan seemed content to have driven Lee from northern soil and saved Maryland and Pennsylvania. Lincoln wished his generals would get the idea out of their heads that this constituted victory. The president believed the whole country North and South to be Union soil.[1]

It was enough of a victory, however, to persuade Lincoln that he could now issue the preliminary Emancipation Proclamation, which he had been keeping in his desk awaiting a change of fortune on the battlefield. But he grieved for what might have been.

In the field, David Strother saw yet another opportunity to redeem what might have been. September 22 began in fog, which lifted to reveal a day fine and warm and clear. Lee's weakened army lay in front of them near Shepherdstown. It was an open invitation to attack, to do the job they had failed to do at Antietam. But alas, Strother had to write in his diary that night that it was not to be: "This magnificent army, thoroughly equipped and supplied, full of courage and confidence, is to stand on the defensive before its half-starved, defeated,

393

and disorganized adversary across the river. Adieu my budding hopes, which like Jonah's gourd, have withered in a night!"[2]

By now McClellan had noticed a disturbing fact. Nobody in Washington had praised him for his victory. "Not yet even have I a word from anyone in Washn about the battle of Antietam," he wrote Nelly on September 29. All he had from them was more faultfinding. It was just another bitter sign. And now there was the president's Emancipation Proclamation, "an accursed doctrine," in McClellan's view. Moreover, Stanton and Halleck were still in office. He was depressed and disgusted.[3]

He was also not moving. And this depressed and disgusted Lincoln, who looked at the missed opportunity somewhat as Strother looked at it. So on the first day of October the president drove up to Antietam to see the general.

McClellan had written Halleck late in September that he didn't believe his army was now in condition to undertake another campaign or bring on another battle; that he intended to hold it where it was now; that if Lee's army was considerably reinforced, and his own wasn't, "it is possible that I may have too much on my hands in the next battle."[4]

To Lincoln that looked like there would be no fighting and no rebel army destroyed. And he went to Antietam ostensibly to visit the Union army, but really to see if he could get McClellan to do something. McClellan wasn't fooled by the visit. The president's real purpose, he wrote Nelly, is "to push me into a premature advance into Virginia. . . . The real truth is that my army is not fit to advance."[5]

The president was affable as always. He sat in McClellan's field tent, surrounded by trophies of the battle, and they talked. A day and night into the visit, Lincoln took an early morning walk with his friend from Illinois Ozias M. Hatch, who had accompanied the presidential party to Antietam. They paused on an eminence that overlooked the Union army and the president spoke.

"Do you know what this is?" Lincoln asked, his gaze sweeping the vast encampment of white tents glistening in the morning sun.

Hatch was surprised by the question. "It is the army of the Potomac," he replied.

"So it is called," said the president sadly, "but that is a mistake; it is only McClellan's body-guard."[6]

But Lincoln left Antietam on October 4 thinking McClellan

would begin to move. When he got home and the general began to argue instead why he ought not do so, the president on the sixth sent him a peremptory order.[7] It directed him to cross the Potomac immediately and give battle to the enemy or drive him south. "Your army," the president told him, "must move now while the roads are good."[8]

Still McClellan did not move. For three weeks more he stayed where he was and argued instead for reinforcements and supplies. The army had suffered horribly at Antietam and was badly in need of rest and repair. It was without shoes and clothing—a situation the Confederates considered normal operating conditions. He wrote Washington that his cavalry horses were broken down with fatigue. Lincoln, in a rare outward show of his inward irritation, wired back curtly: "Will you pardon me for asking what the horses of your army have done since the battle of Antietam that fatigue anything?"[9] This hit a nerve. "It was one of those dirty little flings that I can't get used to when they are not merited," he wrote Nelly.[10]

But mostly the president continued to reason with his general. "You remember my speaking to you of what I called your overcautiousness," he wrote him on October 13. "Are you not overcautious when you assume that you cannot do what the enemy is constantly doing? Should you not claim to be at least his equal in prowess, and act upon the claim?"

The president thought again about McClellan's elation at having driven the enemy from northern soil. "We should not so operate as to merely drive him away," he continued. "As we must beat him somewhere or fail finally, we can do it, if at all, easier near to us than far away. If we cannot beat the enemy where he now is, we never can, he again being within the intrenchments of Richmond."

Lincoln told McClellan he favored pursuing Lee on an inside track: "I should think it preferable to take the route nearest the enemy, disabling him to make an important move without your knowledge, and compelling him to keep his forces together for dread of you."

As Lee moved, McClellan could strike him, if the time seemed right, through gaps in the Blue Ridge. "For a great part of the way," Lincoln wrote the general, "you would be practically between the enemy and both Washington and Richmond, enabling us to spare you the greatest number of troops from here. When at length running for

Richmond ahead of him enables him to move this way, if he does so, turn and attack him in the rear. But I think he should be engaged long before such point is reached. It is all easy if our troops march as well as the enemy, and it is unmanly to say they cannot do it."[11]

This unsolicited tactical advice from the president depressed McClellan. Darius Couch, his West Point classmate, now a corps commander in his army, was surprised to see McClellan rein up at his corps headquarters at Harpers Ferry at about 10:00 in the morning on the sixteenth. Spreading a map of Virginia before them, McClellan began showing Couch the strategic features of the Shenandoah Valley, indicating the movements he intended to make to compel Lee to concentrate around Gordonsville or Charlottesville, and there fight a great battle.

Then he turned to Couch. "But I may not have command of the army much longer. Lincoln is down on me."

He fished the president's letter from his pocket and began reading it aloud. Couch was taken aback. McClellan had never before especially confided in him. Now he was telling everything. When he finished reading the letter, Couch tried to reassure him. He said he saw no ill feeling in the tone of it.

McClellan believed there was. "Yes, Couch," he said, "I expect to be relieved from the Army of the Potomac, and to have a command in the West."[12]

But still he didn't act. Another ten days passed. Finally, on October 26, more than a month after Antietam, he began pushing his army across the Potomac on Lincoln's inside track.

But an unhappier general never crossed a river. As he passed over—it was November 1 before the movement was entirely complete—he wrote Nelly of "the mean & dirty character" of the dispatches from Washington. "When it is possible to misunderstand, & when it is not possible, whenever there is a chance of a wretched innuendo—there it comes." What rankled most was that it came "from men whom I know to be greatly my inferiors socially, intellectually & morally!" He was talking of Lincoln in particular: "There never was a truer epithet applied to a certain individual than that of the 'Gorilla.' "[13]

At least the epithet was something he could give Stanton credit for, although Stanton had by now probably changed his mind about that, too. McClellan's great hope for the campaign he was now undertaking was that if it succeeded he might yet drive Stanton from office. "If I can crush him I will," he wrote Nelly, "—relentlessly & without remorse."[14]

He would have to strike quickly, more quickly than he realized, more quickly than was his wont, for the Gorilla had by now decided on a final litmus test for the general. He had resolved that if McClellan permitted Lee to cross the Blue Ridge and place himself between Richmond and the Army of the Potomac, he would remove him from command.[15]

By November 5 McClellan had worked his way to Rectortown— "thus far down into rebeldom," he told Nelly.[16] But the rebels had also put themselves between him and Richmond. And that day Lincoln wrote out a final order to George McClellan.

Francis Preston Blair had been around Washington a long time. He had been one of Andrew Jackson's confidants and he had been advising presidents ever since. He was Washington's venerated old man of politics. He had a son, Francis, Jr., who was sometimes a general and sometimes a congressman; and another son, Montgomery, who was Lincoln's postmaster general. Lincoln liked the old man and always treated him with the respect his years and experience commanded.

Old man Blair liked McClellan, and he was worried about him. He knew Lincoln was considering sacking him, and he thought it would be a mistake. At Montgomery's urging, he drove out to the Soldiers' Home on the outskirts of Washington, where Lincoln was staying, to see what he could do.

Lincoln listened respectfully to the old man, as he always did. When Blair was finished, he stood and stretched his long arms almost to the ceiling, and said: "I said I would remove him if he let Lee's army get away from him, and I must do so. He has got the 'slows,' Mr. Blair."[17] He had tried long enough, he told the old man, "to bore with an auger too dull to take hold."[18]

Brigadier General Catharinus P. Buckingham was in his office adjoining Secretary Stanton's private room, and it was late—10:00 at night on September 6. Everybody knew the secretary was a workaholic and Buckingham was finding it out firsthand. He hadn't been at this desk job very long, but desk jobs were what he did in this war. That's what he had done in the volunteer army in Ohio before he had come to Washington, and it was what he was doing now on special assignment to the secretary's office.

Buckingham was white-bearded, fifty-five years old, smart, studious, and scholarly—a mathematics instructor at West Point for a time, then a professor at Kenyon College. But iron was his thing. Before the war he had owned and run the Kokosing Iron Works in Knox County, Ohio. Robert E. Lee was one of his best friends; they had graduated from West Point together.[19]

And here it was, two hours before midnight, and the secretary was sending for him. When Buckingham stepped into Stanton's office, Halleck was also there. The secretary said he wished Buckingham to undertake a special assignment; he was to go by train to McClellan's headquarters. Stanton told him in detail the route he should take, and handed him two unsealed envelopes. He was to take them to his office, read them, and seal them.[20]

In the quiet of his office, Buckingham opened the two envelopes and was thunderstruck. One of them contained an order from Lincoln relieving McClellan from command of the army, and another from Halleck ordering him to repair to New Jersey and report by letter to the war department. The contents of the second letter were no less surprising—two orders for Ambrose Burnside, one from the president appointing him to command of the army, and the other from Halleck directing him to report his plans.

Why me? Buckingham wondered. Why did he have to be the one to deliver these two explosive sets of orders? McClellan was his friend. Why did he have to be the one to do this to a friend? The next morning before leaving, the perplexed general saw Stanton at his house and the secretary explained. He was sending an officer of Buckingham's rank because he feared Burnside would not accept the command, and Buckingham if necessary must use the strongest arguments possible to induce him not to refuse. Second, Stanton explained, not only did he have no confidence in McClellan's military skill, but he very much doubted his patriotism, and even his loyalty. He was afraid that McClellan might not give up the command, and he wished, therefore, that the order should be delivered by an officer of high rank, direct from the war department, so it would carry the full weight of the president's authority.

Stanton's orders were for Buckingham to find Burnside first and get his decision. If he agreed to accept the command, whatever that might take, Buckingham was then to confront McClellan. However if Burnside would not accept, despite Buckingham's persuasions, then he was to return to Washington at once without seeing McClellan. This was a very delicate and precise assignment, even for a mathematician of Buckingham's talents. Better perhaps that he had been a diplomat before the war rather than an iron manufacturer.

The weather didn't make the trip any more pleasant. Northern Virginia was in the grip of one of the worst snowstorms for that time of year on record. Buckingham's special train chugged out toward Salem, where Burnside's corps headquarters was believed to be, through driving snow and bitter cold. Buckingham found Burnside camped about fifteen miles south of Salem.

Buckingham knew the universal feeling in the army about Burnside, and surely shared it. No sweeter, kinder, or truer-hearted man existed—loving, lovable, dashing, romantic, picturesque, with that spectacular growth of beard that circled his face like a halo. But he was not fit for the command of an army. Burnside himself knew he was not. He had publicly said he was not when offered high command earlier, and nobody had the least reason for believing otherwise, except perhaps Lincoln, Stanton, and Halleck, who were desperate.[21]

Lincoln had perhaps by now come around to Senator Wade's way of thinking: anybody would do.

Perhaps the most distasteful aspect of the whole matter for Burnside was the ghastly prospect of having to supersede his dearest friend. Buckingham was doubtless aware of all these ramifications as he entered Burnside's chambers, closed the door, and made his loathsome errand known. Burnside declined the promotion at once, as Buckingham expected he would. Whatever his own private opinion might be, Buckingham now must somehow persuade Burnside to change his mind.

Knowing Lincoln was set on removing McClellan at all events, Buckingham argued that Burnside must accept. Burnside cited his want of confidence in himself and his particularly close friendship with McClellan, to whom he felt under the strongest personal obligations. Buckingham countered that McClellan's removal was foregone, and that if Burnside didn't accept the command it would be given to Fighting Joe Hooker. Such a bleak prospect finally eroded Burnside's opposition, and at length, after much arguing by Buckingham, and with a heavy heart, he gave in. Buckingham then asked the new commander of the Army of the Potomac to go with him to deliver the news to the old one. So they rode together back through the snowstorm to Buckingham's train and took it on up the line to McClellan's camp near Rectortown.

At about 11:00 in the night they found McClellan's quarters and knocked on his tent-pole. The general was writing Nelly his nightly letter. He was not surprised to see them, despite the weather. He had heard that a special train carrying Buckingham from Washington had arrived near his camp earlier in the day. He also knew that Buckingham had left the car, and without coming to see him first had proceeded on horseback through the driving snowstorm to Burnside's camp on the Rappahannock. McClellan at once suspected the truth, but he had kept his own counsel. Now here they were, both looking very solemn.

McClellan was nothing if not gracious. He received them in his usual kind and cordial manner. Buckingham found this part of his task particularly painful and distasteful. He had always entertained, as almost everybody did, very friendly feelings for McClellan. But if the blow had to come, he was now persuaded, he was glad it was not to be delivered by an unsympathetic hand in a mortifying way.

The amiable McClellan began a conversation on general subjects, as if visitors in a heavy snowstorm in the middle of the night in the middle of nowhere was an everyday occurrence. After a few moments Buckingham turned to Burnside.

"Well, general," he said, "I think we had better tell General McClellan the object of our visit."

"I should be glad to learn it," McClellan said.

Buckingham handed him the envelope with the orders from Lincoln and Halleck.

As McClellan opened the envelope, he saw that both men, especially Buckingham, watched him intently. As he silently read, not a muscle quivered nor did his face show any expression. They shall not have that triumph, he thought.

After a moment he turned with a smile to the miserable and mortified Burnside.

"Well, Burnside," he said. "I turn the command over to you."[22]

"I then assumed command," the unhappy Burnside recounted later, "in the midst of a violent snow-storm, with the army in a position that I knew but little of. . . . I probably knew less than any other corps commander of the positions and relative strength of the several corps of the army."[23]

"They have made a great mistake," McClellan wrote, picking up his pen again when his visitors had left and continuing his letter to Nelly, "—alas for my poor country—I know in my innermost heart she never had a truer servant. . . . Our consolation must be that we have tried to do what was right—if we have failed it was not our fault."[24]

Darius Couch knew nothing of this as he dismounted at about dark the next evening to oversee camp arrangements for his corps. As he stood there in the snow McClellan rode up with his staff, accompanied by Burnside.

McClellan reined in and said immediately, "Couch, I am relieved from the command of the army, and Burnside is my successor."

Couch stepped up to him and took hold of his hand. "General McClellan," he said, "I am sorry for it."

He then strode around the head of McClellan's horse to Burnside. "General Burnside," he said, "I congratulate you."

Burnside made a dismissing gesture. "Couch, don't say a word about it." His manner told Couch he didn't wish to talk of it, that he thought it neither the time nor the place.[25]

By nightfall the entire army knew. McClellan had told them. "In parting from you," he wrote, "I cannot express the love and gratitude I bear to you. As an army, you have grown up under my care. In you I have never found doubt or coldness. The battles you have fought under my command will proudly live in our nation's history. The glory you have achieved, our mutual perils and fatigues, the graves of our comrades fallen in battle and by disease, the broken forms of those whom wounds and sickness have disabled—the strongest associations which can exist among men—unite us still by an indissoluble tie."[26]

The army was staggered and enraged. "Our George" was being taken from them again—this time apparently for good. A spasm of anger, outrage, chagrin, and gloom swept it from top to bottom. It was "all as cold as Charity & dark as Egypt. . . ." wrote Brigadier General Marsena R. Patrick in his diary that night. "The Army is in mourning & this is a blue day for us all." The next night, Sunday, November 9, he told his diary of "a feeling as deep as I have ever seen." He reported the regulars "uproarious," demanding that if McClellan be removed at all, it be to the command of all the armies.[27]

There was dark talk, particularly among McClellan's large staff, of defying the president's order and marching on Washington to take possession of the government. McClellan anticipated this and moved quickly to quash it. He tacked a precautionary word to the end of his message to his soldiers announcing the change in command. "We shall ever be comrades in supporting the Constitution of our country and the nationality of its people," he wrote.[28] On the day he left for good, the eleventh, he would tell them, "I wish you to stand by Burnside as you have stood by me, and all will be well."[29]

His soldiers demanded to see him one more time. So on the morning of November 10 he rode out to say good-bye. As he rode past Marsena Patrick's troops in this last farewell, they cheered him, but it was too irregular to suit Patrick. As they passed the front of his command, Patrick swung his cap over his head.

"Once More and All Together!" he shouted.

There was an explosion of cheers that Patrick found "magical." Shouts rose from thousands of throats as the departing McClellan continued to ride through the army, past division after division and corps after corps, past troops drawn up in ranks on either side of the road for miles. Patrick marveled: "Such waving of tattered banners & shouts of Soldiery!"[30]

"Such a sight I shall never see again," Colonel Charles Wainwright wrote in his journal. He saw tears; there was hardly a dry eye in the ranks. "Very many of the men wept like children, while others could be seen gazing after him in mute grief, one may almost say despair, as a mourner looks down into the grave of a dearly loved friend."[31]

At 2:00 in the afternoon McClellan paused to share this bittersweet good-bye with Nelly. "I am very well & taking leave of the men," he wrote her. "I did not know before how much they loved me nor how dear they were to me. Gray haired men came to me with tears streaming down their cheeks. I never before had to exercise so much self control. The scenes of today repay me for all that I have endured."[32]

Whatever they might have thought of McClellan as a general, Wainwright believed that no one who saw him on this day "could help pronouncing him a good and great man: great in soul if not in mind." And when McClellan rode past the Second Corps and galloped out of their sight for the last time, Francis Walker believed the romance of war was over for the Army of the Potomac.[33]

McClellan left the next day believing they had relieved him from command "when the game was in my hands."[34] His onetime West Point classmate, John Gibbon, believed the effect "was that of applying brakes to a lightning express."[35]

The Confederates, who knew him so well, were glad to see him go. "We seemed to understand his limitations and defects of military character," Henry Kyd Douglas said of him, "and yet we were invariably relieved when he was relieved, for we unquestionably always believed him to be a stronger and more dangerous man than anyone who might be his successor."[36] A Confederate soldier said, "We liked him because he made war like a gentleman: *and we loved him for the enemies he had made!*"[37] Lee worried that one day if they kept making these changes in commanders they might find someone whom he didn't understand.[38]

Lincoln had at last been forced to give up on the auger too dull to dig. It was a pity; he had tried. A friend of both men, who knew them well and liked them equally, believed McClellan was "one of the most excellent and lovable characters I have ever met . . . patriotic in everything that he did, however he may have erred."[39]

But the Young Napoleon had been a victim of his own paranoia. He had failed to understand the rebel commanders in his front, who were his enemies. Perhaps worse, he had failed to understand Lincoln in his rear, who had been ready to be his friend.

These failures brought him down, his hope of military glory forever blasted. If McClellan could fail, some of his classmates must have wondered, then who of them could succeed?

Caught
in the Rain

The rain had already been more than slightly overdone along the banks of the Rappahannock River by the early morning of April 15, 1863. It was a damned nuisance, for Major General George Stoneman desperately wished to cross the swollen river and couldn't.

When Stoneman went to bed the night before it had been a magnificent evening and his troopers were in high spirits, ready for tomorrow's grand adventure. Tomorrow was to have brought a crossing of the river and the biggest, most important Union cavalry movement of the war. Instead it had brought rain—torrents of rain. By midmorning, the Union cavalry was awash in water several inches deep. They slogged through it toward the crossings, but the river had risen as if a dam had burst. The fords were swimming. What Stoneman needed was Noah's ark. There would be no crossing that day, or for many days to come.[1]

Brigadier General John Buford gazed out into the pouring rain and thought the land had become a sea. He had never seen anything like it. Rations became waterlogged as soon as they were issued. It was as though nature or something or somebody was doing it to them on purpose, in monstrous combination against their epic advance.[2]

Within a few days the mud had become "oceanic," and the troopers were saying that April deserved "to be classed among the Weeping Sisters."[3] Every rivulet was swimming, the roads were next to impossible for horses or pack mules—forget the heavy stuff, such as artillery and wagons. The only direction of advance seemed to be straight down. The river was out of its banks, and the railroad bridge had been partly carried away. It was one of the most violent rainstorms Stoneman had ever experienced. And more was being carried away than just railroad bridges. His brilliant cavalry movement was awash in the flood.[4]

Nothing much surprised the quiet, stolid Stoneman anymore. He had seen just about everything in the way of weather in the nearly two decades since he had left West Point in 1846 and gone for a soldier. But he had a naturally sad-eyed look, and the rain was doing nothing to lighten that.

His career in the old army had been on the whole distinguished. There had been a glitch here and there, but nothing to permanently mar his record or dim his promise. Despite his quiet ways, he had been considered one of the best company commanders in the crack Second Cavalry Regiment, a highly accomplished officer with a knack for commanding men. Richard W. Johnson, a fellow officer, praised him as "a fine soldier, strict in discipline and exemplary in habits." Another officer remembered him from his earlier service in the First Dragoons: "Indeed I may say with truth, [he] was the most popular officer in it [the regiment]." He affected a brusque exterior and was a hard disciplinarian, but his soldiers had confidence in him.[5]

After Sumter, Stoneman courageously defied Major General David Twiggs when that old campaigner, then in command of U.S. forces in Texas, threw in with the Confederacy. Refusing to surrender his command, Stoneman led it north to fight for the Union. His classmate George McClellan thought well of him, and made him his chief of cavalry in the Peninsula campaign.

The Union cavalry hadn't amounted to much in those early days of the war. It was certainly no match for the skilled and hard-riding Confederate cavalry under J.E.B. Stuart. But all that had changed. When Major General Joe Hooker succeeded Ambrose Burnside following the Union calamity at Fredericksburg in the winter just ended, he had taken dramatic steps to make something of the cavalry. He reorganized it into a separate corps, beefed it up to twelve thousand men and thirteen thousand horses, and put Stoneman in command.[6] Now, in the spring of 1863, the Union cavalry outnumbered Stuart's horsemen three to one. No army had ever seen such an impressive array of men and horses. It had to be taken seriously, and so did its commander.

"Stoneman we believe in," one of his officers, Captain Charles Francis Adams, Jr., said. "We believe in his judgment, his courage and determination. We know he is ready to shoulder responsibility, that he will take good care of us and won't get us into places from which he can't get us out."[7]

Stoneman in 1863 looked much as he had when he and Tom Jackson were the two most reclusive roommates at West Point, except he was nearly two decades older. He was still lithe, severe, gristly, and sanguine—but for those sad, doelike eyes. Perhaps the sad eyes, which one reporter said "flashed even in repose,"[8] had to do in part with the painful fact that despite being the Union's number one cavalryman, he could never seem to sit comfortably in the saddle. It hurt when he rode; he had a devastating case of hemorrhoids.[9]

And right now he also had this endless rain.

Joe Hooker had big plans for Stoneman and his cavalry in the spring campaign he was about to launch against Robert E. Lee. Indeed Stoneman had the most critical role. He would be the first to move. Much was riding on his getting across the Rappahannock. Hooker's plan was to send the cavalry—virtually all of it—across the upper fords of the river on April 13, two weeks before the projected main offensive. Stoneman would swarm over Lee's lines of communication between Fredericksburg and Richmond, raiding and raising hell all across the Confederate rear and flank. This theoretically would force Lee to fall back on Richmond, at which point Hooker would pounce across the river on what would then be the rebel rear with the full might of what he called "the finest army on the planet."[10] Lee would be crushed in a vise.

It was an excellent plan, and its success was riding on Stoneman. The raid in Lee's rear had to succeed. Hooker sent Stoneman orders on April 12 full of stirring admonitions. Stoneman was to march at 7:00 A.M. the next day. He was to cross the river with his entire command, less one brigade, and throw his cavalry between Lee and Richmond, "isolating him from his supplies, checking his retreat, and inflicting on him every possible injury which will tend to his discomfiture and defeat." The raiders were to destroy railroad bridges, trains, cars, storage depots, and telegraph lines. They were to harass the retiring enemy "day and night on the march and in camp unceasingly. If you cannot cut off from his columns large slices . . . you will not fail to take small ones. Let your watchword be fight, and let all your orders be fight, fight, fight, bearing in mind that time is as valuable to the general as the rebel carcasses."[11] It was an order with "the ring of bright metal in it," one of Stoneman's troopers admitted.[12]

Stoneman ordered the march to begin the next day. One brigade would cross the night before at about midnight, to clear out enemy resistance across the river. The three divisions would then cross, two at one ford, the third at another.[13]

The corps began to move toward the fords as scheduled. It mustered that day 9,895 cavalry, and four batteries of horse artillery with 427 men and twenty-two three-inch rifled guns. The riders were stocked with six days' rations and five days' short forage, transported on the horses of the mounted men, on pack mules, and in wagon supply trains that were following the command to the fords. Another 275-wagon supply train was bringing up another three days' subsistence and three days' short forage. These were to be issued the night of the fourteenth, just before the crossing.[14]

Everything was ready. Stoneman on the afternoon of the fourteenth advised Hooker that his command would be across the river before daylight the next day.[15]

Then the rains came, and the advance ground to a waterlogged halt at the river's edge.

The waiting troopers knew little of the master strategy of the campaign, only that the crossing had been given up on account of the storm, that they were surrounded by water, that the rain was soaking everything and everybody, and nothing was done all day.

"What are we waiting for?" Henry Lee Higginson asked himself. For the river to fall, he fancied. But he wasn't sure; the details of the campaign had been kept secret.[16]

It rained the next day, the next, and the next, and the cavalry waited, the army waited, the campaign waited, and the enemy waited—the latter with a wry smile. By now Stoneman's role in whatever movement Hooker was planning was fully known to Lee as a matter of course. Even the rebel pickets seemed well informed. They sniggered and called over the river, asking what was the matter with the cavalry that it didn't cross.[17]

At first Hooker wasn't anxious. He still believed on the fifteenth that Stoneman had crossed the river before the deluge. He believed that, even though he could personally see nothing beyond his own doorstep because of the storm. The campaign would not be seriously set back as long as Stoneman had reached his position. But Stoneman hadn't reached his position, and Hooker soon learned that all the streams were swimming, the mud had halted the artillery, and his spring campaign was on indefinite hold.[18]

To Abraham Lincoln in Washington the situation had the ring of depressing familiarity. "The rain and mud, of course, were to be calculated upon," he wired Hooker. "General S. is not moving rapidly enough to make the expedition come to anything. He has now been out three days, two of which were unusually fair weather, and all three without hinderance from the enemy, and yet he is not 25 miles from where he started." The president knew what that portended. "I greatly fear," he said, "it is another failure already."[19]

Hooker was no longer sanguine either. He was upset, but not— at least not yet—with Stoneman. While his cavalry commander's failure to cross the river and move with the necessary celerity was regrettable, Hooker assured the president he could find nothing in Stoneman's conduct calling for censure. "We cannot control the elements," he shrugged.[20]

As Stoneman continued to hope for a letup in the weather and for a fordable ford, Hooker went back to the drawing board. The rain had ruined his original strategy, and in fact was ruining all plans. He would have to go ahead without Stoneman. As soon as possible he would march three of his infantry corps upstream beyond the Confederate left and start them across the river. If well masked, this movement would put him on Lee's flank. To help mask it, he would start one corps across the river at Fredericksburg to attack Lee's center. Properly executed, these two movements in tandem would catch the Confederates between two grinding forces of infantry, each as large as Lee's entire army.[21]

Despite the unfortunate rain delay, Hooker still planned for Stoneman to hurl his cavalry between Lee and Richmond in consort with the movement of the main army. He was not looking for a moment's delay. Just as soon as Stoneman was able to cross he wanted him to make his raid; he was still counting on it. He sent Stoneman revised orders: After crossing the Rappahannock and then the Rapidan, he was to subdivide his command and send them on different missions, to meet again later on the line of general operations. They were to "dash off to the right and left, and inflict a vast deal of mischief, and at the same time bewilder the enemy as to the course and intentions of the main body." He ordered Stoneman to move without artillery if necessary. The important thing was to take the rebels by surprise. "You have officers and men in your command," he reminded him, "who have been over much of the country in which you're operating; make use of them. You must move quickly and make long marches."[22]

But still the rain fell.

It wasn't until April 27 that it stopped at last, the sun came out, the flood began to recede, and the roads to harden.[23] It was about time, thought Charles Francis Adams, Jr. He was sick of running around looking for a ford. He had begun to doubt whether they would ever get across that miserable river.[24] On the twenty-eighth they finally did, two weeks late and no longer deluded that they were taking anybody by surprise.[25]

When they were across, Stoneman called a midnight meeting of his regimental commanders. He told them they had dropped in that region of country like a shell, and that he intended "to burst it in every direction, expecting each piece or fragment would do as much harm and create nearly as much terror as would result from sending the whole shell, and thus magnify our small force into overwhelming numbers."[26]

"Where then, General?" Lieutenant Colonel Hasbrouck Davis of the Twelfth Illinois Cavalry asked Stoneman at about 3:00 in the morning, seeking specifics.

"God only knows," answered Stoneman. "If you succeed in getting down the Peninsula, you had better continue on, if possible, and report to Gen. Rufus King at Yorktown. It will be a tough proposition at best, and I fear you won't make the trip without some pretty hard fighting."

Ten minutes later "boots and saddles" roused them all; Stoneman's raid was about to begin.[27]

Stoneman sent Brigadier General William W. Averell with his

division, one brigade, and six pieces of artillery toward Culpeper Court House. Stoneman, with his hemorrhoids, would ride with Brigadier General David McM. Gregg's division and Brigadier General John Buford's Reserve Brigade toward Raccoon Ford on the Rapidan. After the Rappahannock there was still one more river to cross.

At the Rapidan they stripped down to what they could carry on their horses—three days' subsistence, three days' short forage, and forty rounds of carbine and twenty rounds of pistol cartridges per trooper. The only things going along that had wheels were the artillery caissons.[28] By this time the waterlogged troopers were ready to attack the first thing they saw. David Gregg reported that "every officer and enlisted man of my command seemed to have but one single desire of inflicting the greatest amount of injury upon the enemy without violating any of the recognized rules of civilized warfare."[29]

The first thing they saw was the Virginia countryside. "A very beautiful country indeed . . ." Henry Lee Higginson noted as they rode along toward Culpeper. "The grass is wonderfully green, the slopes from hill to valley are beautiful. . . . The houses are quite fine and very stately."[30] Charles Francis Adams, Jr., who as one of the Massachusetts Adamses was accustomed to beautiful country and stately homes, was seeing the same thing his friend Higginson was seeing; but he was unimpressed. "The country looks old, war-worn and wasted. . . ." he sniffed. "Most of the houses along the road were deserted and apparently had been so for a long time. Some of them were evidently old Virginia plantation houses, and once had been aristocratic and lazy. Now they are pretty thoroughly out of doors."[31]

For the next nine days Stoneman's cavalry ranged more or less at will behind enemy lines raising havoc, blowing things up, felling trees, rolling logs, jamming fords, cutting transportation lines—ruining anything that might be useful to an enemy—and being themselves exceedingly uncomfortable.[32] There was a lot of dozing on the run— "stealing poor sleep," the troopers called it. They soon ran out of subsistence and had to forage for food, living on anything they could find in the country, cooking it when they had time, eating it raw when they didn't.[33] For most of the time there were no fires, no bugle calls, and all orders were delivered *sotto voce.*[34]

They marched night after night over paths that could hardly be called roads. And it was raining again, drenching them as they rode. It was so dark that Captain J. M. Robertson of the artillery couldn't see his horse's ears, and the mud was so deep that his mount could pull its hooves from the sucking muck only with difficulty.[35]

For Charles Francis Adams, Jr., being a cavalryman was boiling down to one fundamental thing. "I have but one rule," he wrote his mother, "a horse must go until he can't be spurred any further, and then the rider must get another horse as soon as he can seize on one."[36] Confederate Brigadier General W.H.F. (Rooney) Lee, commander of the Confederate cavalry that was trying to deal with this invasion, began to notice that Stoneman was "taking all the horses in his reach."[37]

The horses, in fact, were worn out, used up, and suffering more than the men. "The air of Virginia is literally burdened today with the stench of dead horses, federal and confederate," Adams wrote his mother. "You pass them on every road and find them in every field, while from their carrions you can follow the march of every army that moves." It wasn't just the Union cavalry that was wearing out horses. Adams found the roads on which they were riding "made pestilent by the dead horses of the vanished rebels."[38]

The raiders at one point reached the outskirts of Richmond, but their presence didn't seem to impress the city's beleaguered residents. The raid somehow was not getting its proper respect. John B. Jones, the rebel war clerk, sniffed disdainfully at the whole business. "They are like frightened quails when the hawks are after them," he said, "skurrying about the country in battalions and regiments." Nothing but wild cavalry as far as he was concerned, "the mad prank of a desperate commander."[39]

At last on May 8 it was over. Nothing had seemed to come of Hooker's invasion to the north. So Stoneman brought his raiders back over the Rapidan and the Rappahannock, and on the ninth Adams wrote his distinguished father, for whom he was named and who was the U.S. ambassador to England: "So ends today the four toughest weeks campaigning that I have ever felt—mud and rain, rain and mud, long marches and short forages." The curious thing about it all, as he wrote his mother a few days later, "we were in the field four weeks, and only once did I see the enemy, even at a distance." Such were "the *non*-fighting details of waste and suffering of war."[40]

The people of the North didn't seem to be any more impressed with the raid than the people of the South. Stoneman returned to less than a hero's welcome. But then, nobody in the North was happy about anything on May 8. On May 2 the raiders had heard the thunder of heavy fighting from the direction of Chancellorsville. As they were to learn later, it was another Union catastrophe in the making. Hooker, who had crossed the river on his two-pronged advance the day after Stoneman had launched his raid, first lost his nerve, and was then hit a numbing blow on his flank by that Confederate flanking specialist, Tom Jackson. He had limped back across the Rappahannock beaten and demoralized, and was in no mood to feel good about anything his cavalry might have accomplished.

As it turned out, his cavalry hadn't accomplished much. At first Secretary of War Stanton, ready to see any silver lining in the dismal clouds, acclaimed it "a brilliant success."[41] The *New York Times* published an inventory: 22 bridges, 7 culverts, and 5 ferries destroyed; 7 railroads and 3 canals cut or broken (in spots); 3 trains of rail cars, 4 supply trains, and 5 canal boats burned; 122 wagons destroyed; 200 horses and 104 mules rustled; 4 telegraph stations burned and 5 wires cut (in places); 3 depots burned; 25 towns visited; and 150 contrabands liberated. Every line of communication between the rebel army on the Rappahannock and Richmond, and the canal through which more than half the supplies floated, were disabled. Millions of dollars in commissary stores and supplies were destroyed. Travel on the main pikes was disrupted when the raiders destroyed all the bridges over large streams. It looked good in the paper.[42]

But Stanton's silver lining began to fade into dreary disillusionment almost immediately. Everybody learned that the rail communications between Fredericksburg and Richmond were disrupted for but one day, and the important bridges appeared to have been untouched. "My instructions appear to have been entirely disregarded by General Stoneman," Hooker growled.[43]

Hooker was perhaps beginning to see that he should have kept his cavalry with him at Chancellorsville, instead of sending it away on its pointless mission. A big, inquisitive cavalry corps might have saved him from Jackson's humiliating flank attack.

There were those critics who now believed that all the things Stoneman had burned or destroyed, captured or freed, had only exasperated without terrifying the enemy, giving color to accusations that the federal cavalry were merely mounted robbers. Better that Stoneman had destroyed Rooney Lee's rebel cavalry, which he could have done. Better that he had sacked Richmond, which he also could have done. He had been close enough and the Confederate capital was virtually unprotected, most of its able-bodied men being with Lee's army at Chancellorsville.[44]

A consensus was building in the North that the raid's pregnant promise, like Chancellorsville in general, had given birth to small fulfillment.[45] One critic was to say that instead of hurling his troopers like a thunderbolt on the rebels, Stoneman had divided and frittered away the strength of his command, detaching and scattering it into mere scouting parties to "raid on smoke-houses and capture hen-roosts."[46]

The more Hooker thought about it, the angrier he became. Stoneman had "almost destroyed one-half of my serviceable cavalry force," he told Stanton.[47] Hooker hadn't really wanted Stoneman in command of his cavalry to begin with. He would have preferred somebody else, but the seniority rule of the service had tied his hands. So he had been stuck with this "wooden man" instead.[48]

Within a few days the wooden man, ailing physically—perhaps the hemorrhoids again—relinquished his command. Within a few weeks, Hooker, who seemed to plan badly and fight well as an inferior and plan well and fight badly as a chief, was himself out of a job.[49] And Lee was again invading the North, already in Pennsylvania.

Hooker would eventually become more philosophical and less wrathful, although no less regretful, about what had happened at Chancellorsville. He would shift the blame to Stoneman's classmate, George McClellan. Over dinner with John Hay and others in Washington several months later, Hooker said that Stoneman was an instance of the "cankerous influence" of McClellan's staff. "I sent him out to destroy the bridges behind Lee," Hooker said of Stoneman. "He rode 150 miles and came back without seeing the bridges he should have destroyed. . . . His purposeless ride had all the result of a defeat."

But, without emphasizing that the ride had been his idea in the first place, Hooker was now inclined to be forgiving of his cavalry commander. "He is a brave good man," Hooker conceded, "but he is spoiled by McClellan and the piles." The finest army on the planet in Hooker's view lacked only vigor, and that was because in its early days it had fallen into evil hands, McClellan's hands—"the hands of a baby who knew something of drill, little of organization, and nothing of the *morale* of the army." Hooker believed the army had been "fashioned by the congenial spirit of this man into a mass of languid inertness destitute of either dash or cohesion." It was that, Hooker believed, that had "spoiled" Stoneman and ruined the raid.[50]

There were those who argued that Fighting Joe himself had shown a fatal lack of vigor at Chancellorsville. And there were many Union cavalrymen who conceded that while the raid was not a huge success, they were proud of it anyhow.

It had a galvanizing moral effect. "For the first time," one of them was to write, "the cavalry found themselves made useful by their general, and treated as something better than military watchmen for the army." They saw that the time had come when they would be permitted to win honor and reputation, when they would cease to be tied to the slow-moving infantry, when they would be permitted to strike a blow independently for the cause of the country and the credit of their commanders. The raid, one of them said, "gave our troopers self-respect, and obliged the enemy to respect them."[51]

It was "the first great achievement of the Union cavalry of the Army of the Potomac," a member of the First Maine would write. It had been enough that they had been "a part and parcel of this expedition, and shared its dangers, its hardships and its triumphs." He believed it was ever after a matter of pride with the boys that they were on Stoneman's raid.[52]

Years afterward, troopers were still saying it had been unrivaled in the annals of war for discomfort and hardship, considering the time it had taken. They had to admit that it had probably been more trouble than it had been worth.[53]

But perhaps the most trouble of all, as the raid ended and the troopers turned back toward the fords of the Rapidan and the Rappahannock, was being visited on a frightened woman in a living room in Richmond. There Mary Anna Jackson was distraught. She had just learned that her husband had been wounded in the flank attack at Chancellorsville. She didn't know how badly. She knew only that he had called her to his side and that she must go. But she couldn't, because her husband's soft-spoken West Point roommate had stopped the train traffic to the front.

It was not stopped long—she had to wait but a day or so. But to this distracted and loving wife, it would seem like a lifetime.

Shots
in the Night

The last days of April had been as happy and joyful for Tom and Anna Jackson as they were dismal and wet for George Stoneman. Jackson's corps was camped on the Rappahannock near Fredericksburg awaiting the spring campaign, and Anna came up from Richmond on Monday the twentieth to be with him. They had enjoyed but little time together since the war began. Jackson seemed always going from one battle to the next, and he never took leave.

Anna brought their little six-month-old daughter, Julia, for her doting daddy to dandle proudly on his knee. Henry Kyd Douglas called her "little Miss Stonewall," and she and her mother were the hit of the army. Anna's attractive looks, manners, and good sense made her popular with her husband's troops.[1] She could have ridden down the line and they would have shouted "Jackson or a rabbit!" for her, too.

Early Wednesday morning, the twenty-ninth—about breakfast time—Major Samuel Hale of Major General Jubal Early's staff galloped into camp to tell Jackson that Hooker's army was on the move and crossing the Rappahannock. Jackson told Anna that she and Julia must leave, and that afternoon he sent them "to the rear as extra baggage." The winter was over, the war was about to begin again, and Douglas could see that the general was in fine spirits. The light was glimmering again in those blue-gray eyes, as it always did when there was the prospect of a "scrimmage."[2]

Hooker had sent John Sedgwick's corps across Deep Run two miles below Fredericksburg that morning. It was a movement in force, and Jackson rode out to have a look. Later in the day J.E.B. Stuart's cavalry observed an even larger Union force crossing the Rappahannock at Kelley's Ford twenty miles above Fredericksburg, heading for Chancellorsville. So the crossing at Fredericksburg was only a feint. Hooker's big push was to get around on the Confederate left flank. It was very admirable, an excellent plan. Jackson could appreciate such thinking.

The situation was this: Hooker had put Sedgwick's thirty thousand men across the river in front of Lee's army. The main body of the Union army, another hundred thousand, minus Stoneman's cavalry, was moving in on the Confederate left with not less than four hundred guns. To counter this monstrous force, Lee could muster perhaps sixty thousand men of all arms, and less than half as many guns. Of the two corps that made up the Army of Northern Virginia, only Jackson's was present in force. Most of James Longstreet's corps—three divisions—was absent on a reforaging mission in southern Virginia and North Carolina.

When Hooker's flanking force reached the Rapidan, Richard H. (Fighting Dick) Anderson's division and Lafayette McLaws's division—what was left behind of Longstreet's corps—marched westward to meet the invasion. For the time being Jackson remained where he was in front of Sedgwick. The question puzzling Lee was which half of this divided Union army he ought to attack first.

At about midnight on April 30, Jackson left Jubal Early's seven thousand troops in place before Sedgwick, and began marching the rest of his corps out of the trenches at Fredericksburg under a brilliant moon. Before the mists of early morning had lifted on Friday, May 1, he was well on his way westward toward Anderson and McLaws. Reaching them at about 11:00 in the morning, he began pressing Hooker immediately, to learn more of his true strength, position, and intentions. This went on all afternoon.

That night Lee and Jackson met about a mile in front of Hooker's works, on the brow of a gentle hill among the pine trees, on ground carpeted with clean dry sedge and fallen leaves. Stuart, riding in from the left, joined them. They all knew that it was but a matter of time before Jackson's disappearance from Sedgwick's front would be noted. Hooker must be attacked soon.

The idea of a flanking movement of their own promptly surfaced; that was the way these men thought. Hooker was now stopped around the little villa of Chancellorsville, where the old turnpike and the plank road from Fredericksburg met the Ely's Ford road. The terrain was gently undulating, and where the roads joined was cleared farm-land. Immediately to the west of the cleared land was a thick wall of woods called the Wilderness. It was decided that Jackson, the forced-march and flanking specialist, would drive his entire command around Hooker's outthrust right flank and hit him in the rear through this forest wall. Stuart would cover the movement, and Lee would stay behind and entertain Hooker with Anderson's and McLaws's divisions until Jackson struck from the west.

This all involved yet another "grand detachment" of the army in the face of an active and overwhelming federal force—against all the rules of sensible warfare. But hadn't they already tempted fate by leaving Early at Fredericksburg? And that was working so far. Hooker was inviting a flank attack by having sent his cavalry on that mindless mission in the rear. If he was careful, Jackson might make the entire fifteen-mile march around the Union flank unobserved. Against Hooker, whom they seemed to know as well as they had known McClellan, the plan made sense. It would probably work.[3]

It had been a long day for Jackson's young staff officer, James Power Smith, and it wasn't until late in the night on May 1 that he finally wrapped himself in his saddle blanket and fell into a weary sleep. Sometime after midnight he awoke to the early morning chill. Turning over, he caught a glimpse of a little flame flickering on the slope above. Sitting up, he saw Lee and Jackson seated together on two captured Yankee cracker boxes, quietly talking.[4]

That talk meant trouble, and probably another long day in the morning. A little after sunrise on Saturday, May 2, Jackson had his corps up and on the move again. Lee stood by the side of the road to watch the head of the column march by and to exchange a final few words with Jackson.[5]

Not a soldier in Jackson's corps could imagine where they were going, but all of them knew that serious business was afoot, for they were marching hellbent.[6] On through the morning they moved, past Catharine Furnace, a regiment from McLaws's division guarding the entrance to the blind road to prevent a federal attack on the marching flank. Out in the country between the line of march and the enemy outposts rode Stuart's horsemen, screening the moving column from prying federal eyes. On into the early afternoon they marched, down the connecting backroads under a beating sun. It was another hot, oppressive, mystifying march with Stonewall Jackson. But his soldiers were used to that.

Hooker's scouts sighted the fast-moving column from the heights of the tall trees southeast of the Chancellor house, and reported it to Hooker. The Union commander, who didn't know Lee and Jackson as well as they knew him, smiled. A retreat, surely, he convinced himself; Lee was turning tail in the face of the finest army on the planet.[7]

By 3:00 in the afternoon Jackson had arrived six miles west of Chancellorsville on Hooker's right flank. He stopped his army there and hurriedly scribbled a note to Lee. "General," he wrote, "the enemy has made a stand at Chancellor's which is about 2 miles from Chancellorsville. I hope as soon as practicable to attack." He didn't forget to add: "I trust that an ever kind Providence will bless us with great success."[8]

There ahead, on the other side of that wilderness forest, its flank in the air and its arms stacked, as unsuspecting as if on a picnic, the troops of Hooker's Eleventh Corps were thinking about their Saturday night dinner.

Jack Haydon, a hunter of the region, who knew every turn in every dirt road for miles around, had guided Jackson's march from Catharine Furnace to the Orange turnpike. Now his job was finished, and he was about to leave. On his way out, he rode up and paused in front of Jackson.

General, he said, would you do me a favor?

"What is it, sir?" snapped Jackson, his mind now on more urgent matters.

"Take care of yourself," Haydon said.[9]

Taking care of himself was the last thing on Jackson's mind at that moment. He must now prepare his twenty-seven thousand troops for an attack. For the next two hours that's what he did, arraying his columns in two parallel lines of battle: Robert E. Rodes's division in front and Raleigh Colston's next. Four of A. P. Hill's six brigades closed up in the rear of Colston. Richard Ewell was not present; he was still recovering from his amputation at Groveton.

At about 5:15 in the afternoon, with his visor pulled low over his eyes, his lips compressed, and his watch in his hand, Jackson turned to Rodes, who was sitting on a horse beside him.

"Are you ready, General Rodes?" he asked.

"Yes, sir!" said Rodes.

"You can go forward, then."

The woods rang with answering bugle calls and Jackson's corps surged into the wilderness.[10]

The soldiers of the Union Eleventh Corps looked up from their cookpots into the late afternoon sun and saw deer, turkey, rabbits, and other wildlife running for their lives out of the dense, tangled woods, and wondered what it meant. It meant disaster. Immediately out of the wilderness behind the bounding animals, with a crazed cry, erupted Rodes's division followed closely by Colston's.

The Union soldiers hastily canceled dinner plans and joined the wildlife. Benjamin Leigh, a Confederate officer who had just that morning come on A. P. Hill's staff, watched as they ran "like sheep . . . throwing away their arms, knapsacks and everything of which they could divest themselves."[11] Jackson's soldiers surged after them, galloping through the enemy camp past tents, past kettles still bubbling over the fires. In one tent a huge Newfoundland dog continued to sit placidly as if nothing was going on—a change in masters, perhaps.[12]

For the next three miles it was a running fight, mostly running. Jackson drove the panicked Eleventh Corps before him relentlessly. Fugitives, armed men, ambulances, and artillery became mixed together in a scrambled mass, all reeling madly to the rear, trying to escape the screaming Confederates.

"General," a young Confederate officer cried out, "they are running too fast for us; we can't come up with them."

"They never run too fast for me, sir," Jackson replied.[13]

In the path of the onslaught Union artillerymen struggled to dig in and stem the tide if they could. First Lieutenant J. W. Martin, commanding a battery of federal horse artillery, worked frantically to set up his guns amid a tableau of "indescribable confusion." Carriages, wagons, horses without riders, and panic-stricken infantry stormed headlong through his battery, overturning his guns and limbers, smashing his caissons, and trampling his horse holders.[14]

Several forges, battery wagons, and ambulances that had been left in the plank road and were now being moved to safety smashed into the line and added to the confusion. Behind them in the wood rose the eerie rebel yell and the roar of musketry. The frightened horses in the batteries reared and plunged, and for an uncertain instant it appeared as if the batteries themselves would be swept away in the general panic. But as the torrent swept by, the artillerymen held on, and when the Confederates sprinted from the wood in front of them they let go with a volley of double-shotted canister. The surprised Confederate line shuddered, wavered, slowed, then stopped and ducked for cover. It was the first serious resistance they had encountered in three miles of ceaseless pursuit.[15]

A regiment of federal horse soldiers nearby was also doing its best, inadvertently, to stem the rebel tide. A brigade of Stoneman's cavalry had been left behind under Brigadier General Alfred Pleasonton, and the troopers of the Eighth Pennsylvania found themselves at about dusk blundering into the midst of Jackson's rampant assault.

One of the cavalry officers turned around and said, "I think this is the last of the Eighth Pennsylvania Cavalry."

The other replied, "I think so too, but let us go down with our colors flying."[16]

Their commander, Major Pennock Huey, did what any self-respecting cavalry commander would do in that situation, what anybody would do when bumbling into an ambush or other appalling adversity. He shouted, "Draw sabres! Charge!" and that is what they did. As Huey was to admit later, the charge was irregular and ineffective, and thirty troopers were killed; but it was something.[17]

Then darkness set in.

Stonewall Jackson hated to see the sun go down. He was at the apex of what was unquestionably his greatest victory. "Press forward!" was his urgent plea to every general, and his answer to every inquiry. "Never before," R. L. Dabney thought, "had his pre-occupation of mind, and his insensibility to danger been so great."[18]

But it was now 8:00 at night, the federal artillery was raising havoc, and the pursuit has lost its steam. Moreover there were several imponderables and a few incoveniences to be worked out. Rodes's line, the most advanced, had stopped within a mile of Chancellorsville and was still enveloped in the bushy woods surrounding the Union entrenchments. There was no way of knowing the ground or the nature of the defenses in their front. And there was unholy disorder within the Confederate lines. In the stampede, Jackson's two lead divisions had become hopelessly intertangled. Few soldiers knew where they were or where they were supposed to be. It had to be sorted out. Jackson moved quickly to relieve his front line, ordering up Hill's division, which had cruised along in the wake of the pursuit and was still fresh.[19]

In the scramble to sort out the divisions, the soldiers kept up "a terrible noise and confusion, hallooing for this regiment and that regiment."[20]

Jackson was by no means finished for the day, despite the darkness and the confusion. He was sending members of his staff in every direction—to Hill and to the other general officers—urging them on. He intended to storm the enemy's works at Chancellorsville as soon as he could re-form his lines and before the federal army had time to recover from the jolt he had just dealt it. He intended to insert the left wing of his corps between Hooker and the river. There was a lot yet to be done.[21]

Having sent virtually his entire staff away on an urgent errand of some kind, Jackson sat for a moment on Little Sorrel in front of the plank road and peered ahead into the night. Then he began to ride slowly forward, planning to go as far as the skirmish line to see what he could see.

This raised a red flag in Sandie Pendleton's worried mind. "General," he said, "don't you think this is the wrong place for you?"

Jackson waved the warning aside. "The danger is over," he replied, "the enemy is routed. Go back and tell A. P. Hill to press forward."[22]

He continued to ride slowly ahead. Captain Robert E. Wilbourn, his signal officer and the only staff aide still by his side, rode with him, followed by two signalmen and a handful of couriers. Not far behind in the darkness came A. P. Hill and his staff, with two of Jackson's own aides riding with him: James K. Boswell, the engineering officer, and Joseph G. Morrison, Anna's younger brother.

Jackson had moved some hundred yards forward and still had not encountered the Confederate skirmish line. It had to be out there somewhere; Jackson always required it in such situations.

Abruptly a volley of musketry erupted on their right and spread rapidly toward their front. Bullets whistled among them, striking several horses. This was enemy fire, the Union line assailing the barricade. That meant there was no skirmish line. Jackson spun Little Sorrel around and began to hurry back toward the Confederate position. To avoid fire now coming out of the darkness on the south side of the road, he turned quickly into the woods to the north.[23]

The Eighteenth North Carolina infantry regiment found itself, as it often did, at the front of things, at the very edge of a no-man's-land. There was nothing between them and the federal battle line now but the woods and the road. But there was an ever-present danger of a Union cavalry attack. To be prepared for that likelihood, the riflemen of the regiment had gone down on one knee with their rifles primed and ready.

From out of the darkness horses suddenly appeared, looming up in their line of sight. Enemy cavalry, they thought—just as they suspected. They reacted instantly.

The first thing Jackson and his party saw was the flash of their muskets, a sheet of fire coming from low to the ground, not thirty yards away. Then they heard Hill calling at the top of his voice to cease firing.[24]

Three rifle balls hit Jackson. One ripped into his left arm three inches below the shoulder joint, shattering the bone and severing the artery. A second passed through the same arm lower down, on his forearm below the elbow, blowing out through his wrist. The third entered the palm of his right hand and broke two bones.[25]

At the instant he was hit, he was holding his reins in his left hand and his right was upraised either in the singular gesture habitual to him at times of excitement, or to protect his face from the boughs in the thicket. His left hand immediately dropped the reins and fell useless to his side. Panic-stricken and no longer under control, Little Sorrel wheeled away from the fire and bolted toward the Union lines.

The horse plunged between two trees under a branch that ran at about the height of Jackson's head. The branch caught the general full in the face, ripping off his cap, throwing him violently back on Little Sorrel, and nearly jerking him from the saddle. Struggling to rise erect, he caught the bridle with his broken and bleeding right hand and jerked the horse painfully about. Untouched by the deadly volley, Wilbourn crowded alongside and caught Little Sorrel's reins as Jackson swayed and nearly tumbled off.

Confusion and chaos were everywhere. Horses mad with fright ran in every direction, some riderless, others defying control. All around in the thicket lay wounded and dying men. Jackson's entire party, except for Wilbourn and one of his signalmen, had been killed, wounded, or scattered. Hill's party, also caught in the volley, had been decimated. Boswell, shot through the heart, died instantly and his frightened horse galloped into enemy lines bearing his rider's dead body.

As the volley struck, Morrison leaped from his horse, which was also streaking for the Union lines, and ran toward the source of the firing.

"Cease firing!" he shouted. "You are firing into our own men!"

Major John D. Barry, commanding the Eighteenth North Carolina, didn't believe a word of it. "Who gave that order?" he cried. "It's a lie! Pour it into them."

Morrison ran into the middle of the kneeling riflemen and screamed at the major. That Morrison was telling the truth finally got through to Barry. After helping him stop the firing, Morrison turned and raced back toward the plank road. On his mind was his sister's husband, and in his heart was a sick sinking feeling.[26]

Standing by Jackson's horse, Wilbourn said to the general, "They certainly must be our troops."

Jackson gazed painfully up the road toward his lines in apparent astonishment. He simply nodded and continued to stare. The blood poured from his arm and streamed into his gauntlets.

Wilbourn asked him if he was much injured and could he move his fingers. The captain knew that if he could, it would mean his arm was not broken. Jackson looked down at his hand and tried, but the fingers wouldn't move. When Wilbourn attempted to straighten Jackson's arm, a terrific pain shot though the general's body.

"You had better take me down," he told Wilbourn, as he leaned forward and fell into his arms.

Jackson was so much exhausted by loss of blood that he was unable to take his feet from his stirrups without help. Wilbourn's one remaining signal officer, Lieutenant W. T. Wynn, quickly pulled them out. At that moment Wilbourn, Wynn, and Jackson were the only figures on an utterly deserted turnpike.

Out of the night, however, a mounted rider appeared abruptly in the thicket beside them and stopped, as if at a loss what to do next. He seemed to be cut off from his command, to have blundered across Jackson's party just as they were in the act of carrying the wounded general off the pike.

Wilbourn, assuming him a Confederate, spoke urgently: "Ride up there and see what troops those were."

The figure rode slowly away in that direction without a word. Wilbourn never saw him again. [27]

Together Wilbourn and Wynn carried Jackson to the side of the road and laid him under a small tree. As he supported the general's head, Wilbourn ordered Wynn to go for a surgeon—Hunter McGuire if possible—and an ambulance.

Wilbourn then began to examine Jackson's wounds. He removed the general's field glasses and his haversack, which he saw contained paper and envelopes for dispatches and two religious tracts. Wilbourn removed the tracts and slipped them into his own pocket for safekeeping. Cradling Jackson's head on his lap he began cutting away the sleeves of his India-rubber overall with his penknife, then the sleeves of the coat and the two shirts he was wearing. The mangled arm was now exposed, blood flowing from it in a stream down his wrist.

Jackson spoke. Get a skillful surgeon, he urged Wilbourn, don't permit any but a skilled doctor to attend him. Wilbourn told Jackson he had already sent for Dr. McGuire and an ambulance.

"Very good," Jackson said.

At about this moment Morrison arrived—and an instant later, A. P. Hill.

Hill had not in the seven months since Sharpsburg forgotten that Jackson had put him under arrest before the Maryland campaign. He had not forgiven, and he was not going to let anybody else forget. Jackson hadn't pressed the matter, but Hill had. The battle of Antietam was not two weeks over before Hill was sending letters to Lee challenging his ex-classmate's charges against him in full.

"I deny the truth of every allegation made," Hill wrote Lee. And he was ready to prove it.

"These charges made by General Jackson are of a serious character, involving my reputation and standing as an officer commanding a division of this army," Hill wrote, "and, if true, I should be deprived of the command." If untrue then the censure should be put where it belonged—on Jackson. He requested a court of inquiry.

Jackson would just as soon have let the matter drop. His purpose for arresting Hill had been to get stricter attention to orders. That had happened, and he didn't see any need for further action on his part. Besides, he respected Hill as a fighter. But Jackson stood second to no man for dogged stubbornness. If Hill insisted on keeping the matter alive, so be it. On the same day that he forwarded Hill's letter and request for an inquiry to Lee, he sent along his own charges and specifications of Hill's alleged neglect of duty.

The matter continued to simmer. Lee hated this sort of squabbling between two of his most valued lieutenants. But Hill wouldn't let it rest. He wrote J.E.B. Stuart in November, calling Jackson that "crazy old Presbyterian fool." "The Almighty," he said, "will get tired of helping Jackson after a while, and then he'll get the damndest thrashing—and the shoe pinches, for I shall get my share and probably all the blame, for the people will never blame Stonewall for any disaster."

In January, Hill was still asking that the charges be tried. He was worried that there would soon be no witnesses left alive. Two of his most important ones had already been killed; others had left. Lee was hating the whole thing, wishing it would go away. He told Hill he didn't think a trial by court-martial was necessary. The arrest might seem harsh to Hill, but Jackson had the right to make it as a commanding officer.

Hill said he didn't dispute that right; it was the public rebuke by Jackson without trial that rankled him. Moreover, he told Lee that as far as he was concerned Jackson was a "slumbering volcano," and that he intended to guard himself against any new eruptions by preserving every scrap of paper sent to him from that crazy Presbyterian's headquarters. He repeated his demand for a trial.

That is where the matter still stood as Hill arrived at the wounded Jackson's side at Chancellorsville.[28]

The volley that came so abruptly out of the night hit Hill's party as hard as it hit Jackson's. It was as if they had been struck by a bolt of lightning.[29]

Captain Murray Taylor's horse was hit and fell heavily to the ground. Pinned beneath the dying beast, Taylor struggled to free himself. As he struggled, he heard Hill's voice call out: Was any of his staff still alive? Taylor answered, and Hill sprang from his own horse and ran to his side. As Hill was pulling and hauling to help free Taylor, a courier hurried up and told him Jackson had been wounded.

Hill said to Taylor, "Help yourself; I must go to Gen. Jackson; don't tell the troops." He rose and hurried back to his horse.[30]

Captain Benjamin Leigh hadn't asked for any of this—yet in a way, he had. Only that morning he had been with the Irish Battalion, his regular unit, safely in the rear. The battalion was acting as the provost guard of Jackson's corps well behind the lines, out of the action. But Leigh hadn't been happy with that and had asked for an assignment at the front. He was pleased when word came down that morning that he had been assigned to A. P. Hill's staff as a volunteer aide-de-camp. Now it was night, and he was in a hellhole. But at least he was still alive, which was more than could be said of much the rest of Hill's staff.[31]

As Hill rode up to Jackson, Wilbourn was still ripping clothing from the stricken general's mangled arm. Hill swung down from his horse, motioning to Leigh as he hurried toward Jackson, ordering him to go immediately for a surgeon and an ambulance.

Hill dropped to the ground beside Jackson, telling him how sorry he was that he was hit.

Is the wound painful? he asked.

"Very painful," Jackson admitted. He told Hill his arm was broken.[32]

Hill took his old classmate in his own arms, pulled off his gauntlets, which were now full of blood, and removed his saber and belt.

Jackson then seemed to rest easier. Captain R.H.T. Adams, another survivor from Hill's staff, produced a flask of brandy, and Hill offered it to Jackson. Jackson hesitated, but Wilbourn urged it on him, telling him it was absolutely necessary; it would revive and sustain him until they could get him safely to the rear. Jackson relented, and drank a sip.

It seemed impossible to move him, but Hill knew they must. The enemy was no more than 150 yards away and might advance at any moment and capture them all. This fact became painfully apparent when two federal skirmishers with cocked muskets stepped from behind a cluster of bushes and stared at the small clump of men.

In an undertone Hill said, "Seize those men."

Captain Adams shouted, "Halt! Surrender! Fire on them if they don't surrender!"[33]

In the next moment the astonished federal skirmishers were prisoners of war.

Morrison stepped out into the road, suspecting that if two Union soldiers could be so close, other federal troops might also be nearby. About a hundred yards away in the moonlight he saw federal cannoneers unlimbering two pieces of artillery in the road. He hurriedly returned and told Hill.

James Power Smith, Jackson's young aide-de-camp, had been looking for his general. During the pursuit Jackson had left Smith as a center of communication between himself and the cavalry on the flanks and the artillery moving up from the rear. As night was falling Smith started forward with his couriers through the dusky twilight. The storm of the battle had swept to the east and he rode in that direction.

He found General Robert Rodes and his staff near an old cabin in an open field about a mile west of Chancellorsville.

"General Jackson is just ahead on the road, Captain," Rodes said. "Tell him I will be here at this cabin if I am wanted."[34]

Smith had not gone another hundred yards when he heard firing ahead of him, a shot or two, then a volley on the right of the road and another on the left. Moments later he met Murray Taylor, now out from under his fallen horse, who told him that Jackson had been wounded, shot by his own troops.

Smith's heart, like Morrison's, sank. He spurred his horse into a gallop, soon passed the Confederate line of battle, and some three or four rods beyond found Little Sorrel beside a pine sapling. A rod beyond that he saw men bending over a wounded officer. He reined up and dismounted.

Sandie Pendleton was also riding back through the night toward the battle line when he learned Jackson had been hit. He spun his horse around immediately and spurred furiously to the rear. He must find Dr. McGuire.[35]

The men in the thicket, now joined by Smith, worked quickly

over Jackson. They bound his wounds, tried to staunch the flow of blood, and wrapped his arm in a sling. An assistant surgeon of Dorsey Pender's brigade, Dr. Richard R. Barr, arrived in company with Benjamin Leigh. But he saw there was very little he could do that hadn't already been done. It was urgent now that they get Jackson out of there, back within Confederate lines.

Hill stood. He was in command of the corps now, and must see to business. As he prepared to leave, he spoke briefly once more with Jackson. He told him he would keep word of his wounding from the troops. Jackson thanked him. Hill ordered Leigh, who was now standing beside them with a stretcher, to stay and help move the wounded general to the rear. He then mounted and rode away.

To the stricken classmate whom he had never liked, Hill had given all the help and love he could. The deadly volley had shattered more than men's bodies; it had shattered the bitter differences between the two classmates—at least for a time. Now it was left to the four young staff officers, Morrison, Smith, Wilbourn, and Leigh.

"Let us take the General up in our arms and carry him off," Morrison suggested.

"No," Jackson objected, still in command, "if you can help me up I can walk."[36]

As they lifted him to his feet, the Union batteries on the road in front opened up. Slumped against Leigh's shoulder, Jackson began to drag himself down the plank road toward the Confederate lines.

The young campaign, but four days old, had been a series of close calls so far for Henry Kyd Douglas. He had not been with Jackson, as he so often was, when the volley struck. But two days earlier as he sat on his horse reading a letter from a young lady, a piece of shell had sliced through his horse's bridle and halter and snatched the letter rudely from his hands. Now he was riding with Hill, who had just left the wounded Jackson. From out of the night a smattering of shell rocketed between them, and a piece cut through Douglas's boot, severing his stirrup leather and dropping the stirrup to the ground. Federal fire was gradually sheering away all of his possessions. The next day a ball would enter his new cap just above the visor and cut off a lock of his abundant black hair on its way out the other side. Douglas was finding the war an enigma—life threatening on one hand, but on the other he seemed to be leading a charmed life.[37]

Hill was worse off. A fragment from that smattering of shell fire that had carried away Douglas's stirrup had also cut painfully into the calf of Hill's leg. The Second Corps of the Army of Northern Virginia had just lost its second commander in the space of half an hour.

Making his own way back toward the front, Captain Murray Taylor found Hill riding with his foot out of the stirrup and his horse being led by the artillery officer, Major William Pegram. Hill quickly explained to Taylor that since there was now no major general left in the corps to take command, he had sent for Stuart, the nearest one he knew of. Hill ordered Taylor to find Lee and report what had happened—both he and Jackson wounded, and Stuart now in command of the corps.[38]

Jackson meanwhile was being Jackson, taking his wound as he would any other duty, doggedly and without complaint. His young staff aides had yet to hear him groan. But he was bleeding all over the new coat Leigh's wife had recently stitched and given to her husband. Leigh suggested that they place the general on the litter. A combination of men and the officers lay Jackson gently on it, lifted him to their shoulders, and hurried on.[39]

Now the fire raking the road was coming uncomfortably close, and one of the litter-bearers was hit in both arms. As the litter fell to the ground, Leigh leaped forward and caught it. As it was gingerly lowered the rest of the way, a hurricane of fire swept the road. Having endured all they could, several of the men fled into the woods, leaving Jackson alone on the pike with his staff officers.

It seemed as if nothing could survive the storm of shot now sweeping over them. Leigh, Smith, and Morrison lay down with Jackson in the middle of the road to shield his body with theirs.

All about them shot and shell tore at the road, hissing and raising sparkling flashes from the flinty gravel. Jackson started violently and attempted to get up.

Smith threw an arm over him and held him down. "Sir, you must lie still; it will cost you your life if you rise."[40]

Jackson lay quiet. In truth none of them expected to escape alive no matter what they did. But after a few moments the federal fire moved on. They sprang to their feet and helped Jackson to his and continued to hobble down the road, proceeding along the margin of the traffic. The plank road was again filling with soldiers, Hill's men moving up.

As the troops passed the little party, many of them looked curiously through the shield of horses Wilbourn was pulling along to hide Jackson from view.

The questions began to come. "Who is that—who have you there?"

The answers were lame and unconvincing. "Oh, it's only a friend of ours who is wounded."

The enquiries became more frequent and insistent—the soldiers weren't fooled; they sensed that there must be more there than met the eye.

"Just say it is a Confederate officer," Jackson murmured.

Some of the soldiers began going around the horses, straining to see. One of them caught a glimpse of the bareheaded general in the moonlight.

"Great God," he said, "that is General Jackson!"

There was another evasive reply. The soldier looked from them to Jackson in bewilderment, and passed on down the road without another word. He was surely unconvinced.[41]

By then they had reached the Confederate line of battle, and Dorsey Pender, one of Hill's brigadiers, reined up before them. He was curious too.

Who was wounded? he asked.

"A Confederate officer," said Smith.

Pender wasn't deceived. Recognizing Jackson, he sprang from his horse.

"Oh, General," he said hurriedly, "I hope you are not seriously wounded." Then he said: "I will have to retire my troops to re-form them, they are so much broken by this fire."

The scene was fearful, alive with shrieking shells and whistling bullets. It seemed to justify what Pender was telling him. Horses without riders and mad with fright galloped mindlessly. Men were leaving the ranks and bolting for the rear. The groans of the wounded and dying were intermingled with wild shouts.

Now nearly faint from loss of blood, Jackson shook off Morrison and Smith and turned to Pender.

"You must hold your ground, General Pender," he said feebly, but distinctly, loud enough to be heard over the chaos, "you must hold your ground, sir!"[42]

Exhausted and in intense pain, Jackson then asked to be permitted to lie down for a few moments. Leigh frantically tried to recruit litter bearers, but with little luck. So he violated Jackson's orders and told them who it was for. Immediately he had more hands than he needed.

With Jackson again on a litter, the party headed out through the brush, still under a rain of fire. They had gone about half a mile toward the rear when one of the litter bearers caught his foot in a grapevine and fell. Jackson tumbled heavily to the ground, and for the first time they heard him groan.

Smith sprang to his side. "General, are you much hurt?"

Jackson quickly composed himself. "Never mind me, Captain, never mind me."[43]

To avoid that happening again they returned to the road, and continued to move as quickly as they could toward the rear. For what seemed an interminable time, they remained under the federal fire, with shells bursting about them. It seemed to Benjamin Leigh like showers of falling stars.[44]

By then it had become generally known in this "pandemonium of death and confusion" that Jackson was wounded—despite all the effort to keep it hidden. Douglas saw that "a gloom that was worse than night and disaster seemed to settle upon the army."[45]

Many rebel soldiers that night would sleep on their muskets and question the value of a victory that had cost them Stonewall Jackson.

Death of the
Enthusiastic
Fanatic

D r. Hunter McGuire did not know that Jackson had been wounded until Sandie Pendleton found him and told him so. The doctor was in the rear organizing relief for wounded Confederate soldiers.

McGuire was another of those bright young men Jackson seemed to attract to his staff. But there was a limit to youth. When McGuire reported to Jackson at Harpers Ferry in the spring of 1861 as the newly-assigned medical director of the Army of the Shenandoah, he looked younger than a doctor ought to look. Jackson stared at him for a long time, and presently said: "You can go back to your quarters and wait there until you hear from me."

McGuire was puzzled, but he did as he was told and didn't hear from Jackson for a week. When he did, it was only indirectly, a simple announcement at dress parade that McGuire was the army's new medical director. Some months later McGuire, who often roomed with the general, asked him why there had been the long wait without a word that first week. Jackson told him he looked so young that he had sent to Richmond to see if there wasn't some mistake.[1]

Now, two years later at Chancellorsville, if Sandie Pendleton was

432

right, they might be dealing with one of the most tragic mistakes of the war. If Jackson was mortally wounded, by the hand of his own troops, it would be catastrophic. McGuire and Pendleton hurried together toward the Confederate front lines.

The first member of the Jackson party they met was Wilbourn, who had come looking for them. At that point McGuire received his first patient at the scene, and it wasn't Jackson; it was Pendleton. As Wilbourn was telling them what had happened, Pendleton dismounted. When his feet hit the ground, he fainted, weak from exhaustion. McGuire quickly administered a pull on a flask of whiskey, and when Pendleton was revived sufficiently, they rode on together to the Melzi Chancellor house, about two miles behind the Confederate front, to look for the main patient of the evening.[2]

There McGuire found Jackson, brought that far through the fire and the night by his four young staff officers. The doctor knelt beside the litter.[3]

"I hope you are not badly hurt, General," he said.

Jackson answered calmly, but feebly. "I am badly injured, Doctor; I fear I am dying."

After a pause, he added, "I am glad you have come. I think the wound in my shoulder is still bleeding."

McGuire saw that Jackson's clothes were saturated with blood, and that the wound was still hemorrhaging. He compressed the artery with his finger as lights were dragged from an ambulance. The handkerchief that had been wrapped around the wound had slipped; McGuire readjusted it.

Jackson's hands were cold, his skin was clammy, his face was pale, and his lips were compressed and bloodless. McGuire could see the impression of his teeth through the thin tightly drawn lips, but all else seemed under the stern control of that relentless iron will. There was no disposition to restlessness that McGuire so often saw attending a great loss of blood. The doctor administered more whiskey and morphine and Jackson was then lifted into the waiting ambulance, to be carried to the field infirmary at Wilderness Tavern. Torches were fired to light the way, and Leigh in his blood-soaked coat rode out ahead on a horse borrowed from one of Jackson's couriers.

Inside the ambulance, Jackson found he was not the only patient. Colonel Stapleton Crutchfield, his chief of artillery, was already there, wounded in the leg and suffering great pain. McGuire sat in the front of the ambulance with his finger resting on Jackson's artery above the wound, ready to arrest further bleeding.

Jackson placed his right hand on McGuire's head and pulled him closer.

"Is Crutchfield dangerously injured?" he asked.

"No, only painfully hurt," McGuire answered.

"I am glad it is no worse," Jackson said. The general was fond of his bookish chief of artillery; they had been on the faculty together at VMI.

A few moments later, Crutchfield pulled McGuire down and asked the same question about Jackson. McGuire told him the general appeared to be very seriously wounded.

Crutchfield groaned and cried out. "Oh, my God!"

When Jackson heard that, he ordered the ambulance halted and requested that McGuire do something to ease Crutchfield's suffering. It wasn't that simple, for Jackson's wound was now Crutchfield's greatest pain.[4]

In this halting and solicitous manner they finally reached the field infirmary and Jackson was put immediately in a bed, covered with blankets, and given another drink of whiskey and water. Jackson hadn't drunk this much liquor since that night at Brown's Hotel when he had danced the barefoot two-step with Dominie Wilson.

Two and a half hours passed before there was sufficient reaction to this to warrant McGuire making a detailed examination of Jackson's wounds. He did not like what he had already seen.

At 2:00 in the morning—it was now Sunday—and with three other surgeons present, McGuire told Jackson he would chloroform him now and examine his wounds. He advised him that amputation of the arm would probably be necessary. If so, should it be done at once?

"Yes, certainly," Jackson replied. "Doctor McGuire, do for me whatever you think best."

As the chloroform began to take hold, Jackson exclaimed, "What an infinite blessing," and continued to repeat the word, "blessing," until he lost sensibility.

With one doctor administering the blessed chloroform, another securing the arteries, another monitoring the pulse, and James Power Smith holding the lights, McGuire first extracted the round ball that had lodged under the skin on the back of Jackson's right hand. It was from a smooth-bore Springfield musket, the kind of weapon Confederate soldiers carried. The ball had entered the palm at about the middle of the hand and had fractured two of the bones. Very rapidly and with but slight loss of blood, McGuire amputated the left arm about two inches below the shoulder—by an ordinary circular operation. He dressed the lacerations on the general's face with isinglass plaster.

As soon as Jackson recovered consciousness, at about 3:00 in the morning, he called for Joseph Morrison.

"I want you to go to Richmond," he told his young brother-in-law, "and bring Anna up to stay with me."

Morrison found a horse and left immediately for Guiney's Station.[5]

At about 3:30, Sandie Pendleton arrived and asked to see the general. He told McGuire that Hill had been wounded and that the troops were in disorder. Stuart was now in command and had sent him to consult Jackson.

At first McGuire was reluctant to disturb his patient, but when Pendleton, now Jackson's chief of staff, argued that the success of the cause might depend on it, he relented.

"Well, major," Jackson greeted his young adjutant, "I am glad to see you. I thought you were killed."

Pendleton delivered Stuart's message, asking what Jackson thought ought to be done now. Jackson asked several questions in his quick, rapid way, and when they were answered, he fell silent for a moment, struggling to concentrate. For an instant his nostrils dilated and his eyes flashed their old fire. But it was only for a passing moment.

His face relaxed again. "I don't know, I can't tell," he said feebly. "Say to General Stuart he must do what he thinks best."[6]

When the ambulance left Melzi Chancellor's house for the field infirmary at Wilderness Tavern, Sandie Pendleton knew it was time Robert E. Lee was told what was happening. After consulting with General Rodes, he ordered Wilbourn, who had already had a long night, to ride to the general as quickly as possible. He was to explain their position, tell Lee that Jackson and Hill were wounded, and that Stuart was now in command of the corps.

Wilbourn galloped away at once, accompanied by that other survivor of the volley and the night, his signalman, W. T. Wynn. They reached Lee's headquarters before daybreak and announced themselves to Colonel Walter H. Taylor, Lee's chief of staff. Lee raised himself on one elbow as Wilbourn entered his improvised shelter, and invited the exhausted captain to sit beside him. Wilbourn recounted the battle and described the victory, and then related what had happened to Jackson.

Lee was visibly shaken. "Ah!" he said, "any victory is dearly bought which deprives us of the services of Jackson, even for a short time."

When Wilbourn told the general that it appeared Jackson had been shot by his own troops, Lee groaned. It seemed to Wilbourn that the general was about to burst into tears.

After a short silence, Lee said, "Ah! Captain, don't let us say anything more about it, it is too painful to talk about."

He seemed then to give way to grief. Wilbourn was not feeling so well himself. He was having the unhappiest night of his life as it was, and now the sight of this great man so much moved and looking as if he could weep, was more than the young captain could stand. He rose and left the shelter.[7]

Before the night was over Lee was to hear the bittersweet story of the victory at Chancellorsville and what it had cost him from two other messengers: Captain Taylor sent by Hill, and Jedediah Hotchkiss. It was too sad a story for one telling, let alone three.

Jackson slept through what was left of the night with Smith at his bedside. When he awoke, he was doing well; he was free of pain and it was Sunday morning. He believed he might live after all.

When Tucker Lacy, Jackson's corps chaplain, entered and saw the stump of an arm, he exclaimed, "Oh, General! what a calamity!"

That, however, wasn't the way Jackson was seeing it. Providence had once again been kind. "You see me severely wounded," Jackson replied, "but not depressed; not unhappy."

"I believe," he said, preaching to the preacher, "that it has been done according to God's holy will, and I acquiesce entirely in it. You may think it strange; but you never saw me more perfectly contented than I am to-day; for I am sure that my Heavenly Father designs this affliction for my good. I am perfectly satisfied, that either in this life, or in that which is to come, I shall discover that what is now regarded as a calamity, is a blessing."

Jackson's recalcitrant lieutenant, A. P. Hill, had once said that West Point was "that great panacea for impatience."[8] Jackson therefore had learned patience, as he had learned everything else thrown at him in the academy. It may have come hard, but once he had it he never let go of it. "I can wait, until God, in his own time, shall make known to me the object he has in thus afflicting me," he now told Lacy. Meanwhile why should he not rather rejoice in it as a blessing, and not look on it as a calamity at all? He would go even further than that. "If it were in my power to replace my arm," he told Lacy, "I would not dare to do it, unless I could know it was the will of my Heavenly Father."

Jackson confessed that when he fell from the litter he thought he would die on the field, and at that moment gave himself up into the hands of his Heavenly Father without a fear. But here he was still alive and it had all been a transforming experience: "I was brought face to face with death, and found all was well. I then learned an important lesson, that one who has been the subject of converting grace, and is the child of God, can, in the midst of the severest sufferings, fix the thoughts upon God and heavenly things, and derive great comfort and peace."[9]

At about 10:00 in the morning Jackson's side began to pain him. This was something new. He hadn't been hit in the side. But he had taken that tumble from the litter, and he believed he had struck it then against a stone or the stump of a sapling. McGuire examined him, but could find no sign of injury, no broken or bruised skin, and the lungs seemed to be performing normally. The doctor applied something simple; the pain soon disappeared.

The sound of cannon and musketry from the front boomed on through the morning. Jackson ordered all of his aides but Smith back to the battlefield to resume their duties, and wrote a dispatch to Lee telling of the victory and the wound.

Smith kept him abreast of the continuing battle and of the action of the troops engaged. He told him of the "magnificent onset" of the Stonewall Brigade, how Stuart had gone to them at the crisis of the battle and told them what must be done and commanded them to "charge and remember Jackson!" When Jackson then heard that his old brigade acted as it always had—with conspicuous courage—his eyes glowed and he fought back tears.

"It was just like them to do so," he said, "just like them. They are a noble body of men." He told Smith that someday the men in it would be proud to tell their children, "I was one of the Stonewall Brigade."

A message arrived from Lee. "I have just received your note, informing me that you were wounded," it said. "I cannot express my regret at the occurrence. Could I have directed events, I should have chosen, for the good of the country, to have been disabled in your stead.

"I congratulate you upon the victory which is due to your skill and energy."

"General Lee should give the praise to God," said Jackson.

Another message arrived from Lee directing McGuire to remove Jackson to Guiney's Station as soon as his condition justified it. There was some danger of capture yet by Union troops threatening to cross at Ely's Ford. For Jackson's safety he must be taken to the rear.

Jackson objected to being moved if in McGuire's opinion it would do him any injury. He said he didn't mind staying in a tent and would prefer it if Anna, when she arrived, could find lodging in a neighboring house.

"If the enemy does come," he said, "I am not afraid of them; I have always been kind to their wounded, and I am sure they will be kind to me."

Further word came from Lee, with orders for McGuire to turn his duties as the Second Corps medical director over to the surgeon next in rank and remain with Jackson. This was necessary to override Jackson, who had earlier declined to permit McGuire to accompany him to Guiney's, believing the doctor belonged with his command. Duty still came first with Jackson.

Told of Lee's countermanding order, Jackson of course acceded. "General Lee has always been very kind to me," he murmured, "and I thank him."[10]

Early Monday morning, May 4, Jackson was placed in an ambulance for the ride to Guiney's Station twenty-five miles away. Jed Hotchkiss and a party of engineers rode in front to clear the road. McGuire, Lacy, and Smith accompanied the general. There was traffic on the road and many of the campaign-tough teamsters at first refused to move their loaded wagons to make way for the ambulance. But when they were told who was inside—there was no longer reason to keep it secret—they hastily pulled off the road to let him pass, many of them standing with their hats off and tears in their eyes. Along the route men and women watched, and at Spotsylvania Court House they crowded about the ambulance with offerings, and to tell Jackson they were praying for his recovery.

The day was warm, and at one point Jackson felt a wave of nausea sweep over him. McGuire put a wet towel over his stomach, and it seemed to help. Most of the way the general bore up well and was cheerful—even talkative. He spoke of the battle. He told his fellow travelers that his intention, had he not been wounded, was to cut the Federals off from the United States Ford, to take a position between them and the river and oblige them to attack him if they wanted across.

"My men," he said, smiling, "sometimes fail to drive the enemy from a position, but they always fail to drive us away."[11]

Jackson thought Hooker's battle plan was sound. "It was, in the main, a good conception, sir; an excellent plan. But he should not have sent away his cavalry; that was his great blunder. It was that which enabled me to turn him, without his being aware of it, and to take him by his rear. Had he kept his cavalry with him, his plan would have been a very good one."[12]

On the porch at the Thomas Coleman Chandler house at Guiney's Station, Mrs. Chandler was taking a break from attending the several wounded Confederates she had been nursing in her living rooms and bedrooms. Her twelve-year-old daughter, Lucy, a serious child often in her mother's company, sat with her. As the two engaged in desultory conversation, a courier galloped into the yard and told them that the wounded Jackson was on his way.

Jackson was no stranger to the Chandlers. They had urged him to stay in their big home when he was camped on their plantation before the battle of Fredericksburg, but Jackson had preferred to sleep out with his soldiers. It was different this time. Mrs. Chandler called two of her servants and they hurriedly prepared a bed in the parlor with clean linens.

Chaplain Lacy was the first to arrive, riding ahead of the ambulance to make preliminary arrangements. He surveyed the quarters and decided they would be too public for Jackson's well-being. Mrs. Chandler assured him it would be very quiet, but he was unconvinced.

When McGuire arrived soon afterward and learned that a case or two of erysipelas had been reported in the house earlier, he also balked.

There was a little frame house at the edge of the yard that the Chandlers had used as an office. What about that? It was empty except for some old furniture and odds and ends. It had recently been whitewashed and Mrs. Chandler always kept it clean. It looked private and safe. Mrs. Chandler and her servants went to work again, moving the four-poster bed into one of the two rooms that comprised the cottage, turning the other into a waiting room and a place to prepare medicines and roll bandages. By now the day had turned stormy, and a chill hung in the rooms. They kindled a fire, and Mrs. Chandler and Lucy went upstairs in the big house to watch for the ambulance.

When it arrived, about 8:00 in the evening, Thomas Chandler met it at the gate as members of his family and the servants looked on. When Jackson was removed from the ambulance, Chandler deplored the occasion of the visit, but welcomed him warmly. Jackson nodded to his bandages and apologized for not shaking hands. They carried him into the room, now aglow with a blazing fire and overlooking the little terrace garden with its flowers and the railroad beyond. Jackson ate some bread and tea and was soon asleep.[13]

The next morning he appeared to be doing remarkably well. He ate heartily for one in his condition and was uniformly cheerful. His wounds looked good, the arm stump seemed to be healthy, the wound in his hand gave him little pain, the discharge was normal. He was beginning to heal. McGuire applied simple lime and water dressings to both wounds and attached a light short splint to the hand. Jackson wanted to know how long his wounds would keep him from the field, and talked theology with Smith, who was an aspiring minister.[14]

Wednesday, the sixth, came in cold, with a drenching rain. At McGuire's request Lacy went to fetch Dr. Samuel B. Morrison, another of Anna's kinsmen, who was the family doctor and a surgeon in Jubal Early's division. Lacy went to Lee to report what had been happening at Guiney's Station, brief him on Jackson's condition, and request Dr. Morrison's services. Lee cheerfully assented to the request and sent a message back to Jackson by Lacy.

"Give him my affectionate regards," Lee told Lacy, "and tell him to make haste and get well, and come back to me as soon as he can. He has lost his left arm; but I have lost my right arm."[15]

That night Hunter McGuire himself was about ready for a doctor.

He had not slept for three nights and was exhausted. Instructing Jim Lewis, Jackson's personal slave, to watch the general, he collapsed on the lounge in the sickroom. In the early morning hours as McGuire slept, Jackson became nauseous again and ordered Lewis to apply a wet towel to his stomach. The worried Lewis wanted to wake McGuire, but Jackson wouldn't hear of it.[16]

At about daylight on Thursday, the seventh, McGuire found Jackson in great pain. His pulse had quickened and his breathing was labored. McGuire quickly recognized the symptoms of pneumonia. It wasn't serious, yet, but it was there. The fall from the litter had probably done it, creating contusion of the lung, forcing blood into the chest. The nausea was probably the result of the inflammation that had already started. McGuire began applying heated glass cups to the chest, and mercury with antimony and opium, in an effort to beat back this new threat. Toward evening his condition had improved, and McGuire was hopefully optimistic.[17]

The Sunday that Joseph Morrison left the field infirmary to go to Richmond to bring his sister to Jackson's side, he ran into a problem. He caught the train at Guiney's Station early that morning, but at Ashland, about half way to Richmond, the cars were intercepted by Stoneman's troopers. As the train pulled into Ashland, it was hailed by pistol fire and met by a company of Union cavalry galloping up through the side streets. The engineer of the train quit his job and abandoned the cab as the troopers took possession. To his horror, Morrison found himself a prisoner.

He looked for every means to escape, and that evening succeeded, spending most of the rest of that night hurrying toward Richmond on foot. He was delayed throughout the next day, and it wasn't until early Tuesday evening that he finally reached the capital and Anna.[18]

In the last days of April and the first days of May, Anna had been in Richmond. She had not heard from her husband since the twenty-ninth, when he had sent her and Julia to the rear. Dispatches, however, had been coming in telling them that all was going well with the army and that a victory was confidently expected. On Sunday morning, the third, she had just risen from family worship at Reverend Moses D. Hoge's home, where she was staying, when her friend, Dr. William Brown, took her aside.

441

Sadly and with great feeling, he told her that Jackson had been wounded at Chancellorsville. The wound was apparently severe, but it was hoped not fatal.

Anna had never, since the war began, ceased to worry for his safety. He was not the most careful man on a battlefield. But God had so often before protected him and brought him through so many dangers, that she had held tightly to the thought that his precious life would always be spared. But now what she greatly dreaded had happened.

She ached to be at his side. But Stoneman was now raiding throughout the intervening country. All passenger trains were stopped. To go in a private conveyance was to court capture; she couldn't risk that. For three days she waited, hearing nothing more. On Tuesday night, the fifth, Joseph arrived. It had taken him three days to pick his way through Stoneman's raiding parties. He could tell her something. But not even he could get her to her husband's side. They still must wait for the rails to clear.

Not until Thursday morning was the blockade lifted. After five days of torturing suspense and distress of mind, the way was finally open. She, Joseph, Julia, and Julia's nurse, Hetty, were put on an armed train for Guiney's Station. A few hours later they arrived, and she was soon on the way to the Chandler house.

There she met still more frustration, more agonized waiting. She couldn't get in to see Jackson immediately; McGuire was dressing his wounds. One of the general's staff, answering her anxious questions, told her he was doing "pretty well." Pretty well? Her heart sank. She could tell from his tone and manner that something was wrong.

But still she had to wait. She felt she must do something to calm her distraught impatience, so she walked out into the piazza. But what she saw there was no more reassuring. Soldiers were exhuming a coffin. When they had placed it above ground she learned, to her horror, that it contained the body of Brigadier General Elisha F. Paxton.

Frank (Bull) Paxton! Anna was horrified. My god, she thought, the commander of the Stonewall Brigade, her husband's own dear neighbor and friend from Lexington! She was then told he had been killed at Chancellorsville in the fighting on May 3, and was being taken home for final interment. His poor young wife, Anna thought.

Paxton and Jackson had left Lexington for the Confederate service the same week in the spring of 1861. Paxton had served on

Jackson's staff for a time and just before the battle of Fredericksburg had been elevated to command of the Stonewall Brigade. He had been its fourth commander, and now he too was dead.

Anna remembered how bitterly Paxton's wife had wept as Paxton had marched away to the war. It had been so early in the conflict, and all their hearts were nearly bursting with foreboding and dread. Now, Anna thought, this cruel war had done its worst for Elizabeth Paxton, left a widow and her children fatherless. The coffin in the piazza was an unfitting preparation for her entrance into the presence of her own stricken husband.

The first sight of him sent a shudder through her. The change in him from only ten days before, when she had last seen him, was fearful. It took all of her effort to maintain self-control. He had been so happy, so handsome, so noble in those final joy-filled days in April. Now there were the wounds, the mutilated stump, the lacerated face, and now, she was told, the pneumonia, which was flushing his cheeks, oppressing his breathing, and numbing his senses.

When he saw her, Jackson's haggard face lit up with a joy and thankfulness that only further wrenched her heart. He instantly saw the anxiety and sadness in her face; she couldn't hide it.

"My darling," he told her, "you must cheer up, and not wear a long face. I love cheerfulness and brightness in a sick-room."

He asked her to speak distinctly. He was a little deaf in his right ear, as she knew, and he wanted to hear every word she said. But it was an effort for him to listen. He was heavily sedated with morphine and soon slipped back into a stupor and lost consciousness of her presence except when she spoke or ministered to him, which she began immediately to do.

As he drifted in and out of his stupor he spoke to her endearingly. "My darling, you are very much loved. . . ," he would wake and say and drift away again. Then he would return and say, "You are one of the most precious little wives in the world. . . ."

He told her he knew she would gladly take his place and suffer in his stead, but that God knew what was best for them. Knowing that the sight of his infant daughter would cheer him more than anything else, Anna proposed several times to bring the baby to his bedside.

"Not yet," he murmured, "wait till I feel better."

Through all his suffering, Anna saw resurgent glimpses of the old Stonewall. The grit that was such a part of him was still there. He was invariably patient, not uttering a cry or complaining in any way. Even in pain he was doing his duty.[19]

Thursday afternoon Dr. Morrison also arrived at Guiney's Station, and Jackson looked up and said, "That's an old, familiar face."

Jackson was now thoroughly examined, and his condition was found to be so critical that Smith was sent to Richmond to bring Mrs. Hoge. It was believed that with her bright, affectionate, and sympathetic nature she could comfort Anna and help Hetty care for Julia. Anna's whole time must now be concentrated on caring for her husband. Other doctors were sent for. While in Richmond Smith was ordered to find David Tucker, a pulmonary specialist, and bring him to Guiney's for consultation.

In the night Dr. Morrison roused Jackson from sleep to give him a drink.

"Will you take this, General?"

Jackson who had continued to slip in and out of delirium all through the evening, looked steadily into Morrison's face.

"Do your duty," he told him. Then again: "Do your duty."

On Friday morning, the eighth, McGuire dressed Jackson's wounds. The pain in his side had eased, but he still breathed with difficulty and complained of exhaustion. Dr. Morrison was worried. For the first time, he suggested to Jackson that the pneumonia might prove fatal.

Jackson was resigned, but he wasn't buying it. "I am not afraid to die; I am willing to abide by the will of my Heavenly Father. But I do not believe that I shall die at this time; I am persuaded the almighty has yet a work for me to perform."

On Saturday Julia was brought to his bedside and he played with her, caressing her and calling her his "little comforter."

Smith had returned with Mrs. Hoge and Dr. Tucker, and Jackson looked about the room and said to McGuire, "I see from the number of physicians that you think my condition dangerous, but I thank God, if it is His will, that I am ready to go."

Now as he faded in and out of his delirium, he was back on the battlefield issuing commands:

"Tell Major Hawkes to send forward provisions to the men. . . ."

And a final word for Hill: Order "A. P. Hill to prepare for action"—doubtless ready to put his old classmate under arrest again if necessary.

Anna asked if he would like her to read aloud from the Psalms. At first he told her no, he was suffering too much to pay proper attention. Then he relented.

"Yes, we must never refuse that," he said. "Get the Bible and read them."

In the afternoon he asked to see Chaplain Lacy. By now he was so ill and his breathing so difficult that the doctors thought all conversation would be hurtful, and tried to dissuade him. But he insisted and they yielded.

As Saturday afternoon wore on into evening, the pain increased. He asked Anna to sing to him, and she began, with her brother joining in. Jackson wished to hear the most spiritual pieces, and she sang several of his favorites, finishing with the Fifty-first Psalm.

She sang:

> Show pity, Lord; O Lord, forgive;
> Let a repenting rebel live;
> Are not thy mercies large and free?
> May not a sinner trust in thee?

All night Saturday he tossed with fever, and throughout the long weary hours they took turns sitting by his bedside sponging his brow with cool water.[20]

The next day was Sunday, the tenth, a beautiful clear day—the kind of day that had generally found Jackson out fighting. Dr. Morrison called Anna from the sickroom.[21]

They had done everything that human skill could do to save him, he told her, but it was hopeless. Not even Dr. Tucker, the pulmonary specialist from Richmond, could hold back this killer. Jackson was going to die. His life was very rapidly ebbing away; it was probably only a question of hours now. They wanted to prepare her for the worst.

They were words Anna knew were coming, but hoped she would never hear. When she had regained her composure she told them that Jackson must be informed. She had heard him say one time that although he was willing and ready to die at any moment that God might call him, still he would prefer a few hours' notice. He must be told. That wish must be honored. And that duty was hers. He heard and understood her better than he did any of the others. She must tell him herself.

Jackson was lying quietly as she approached and roused him. He recognized her immediately, but the progress of the illness had all but robbed him of speech.

She had to repeat it several times. "Do you know the Doctors say, you must very soon be in heaven?"

He did not at first seem to comprehend what she was saying. She repeated it, asking him if he was willing for God to do with him according to His will.

He now looked at her calmly, intelligently. *"I prefer it."* Then again: *"I prefer it."*

"Well," she said, every word a knife-thrust to her own heart, "before this day closes, you will be with the blessed Savior in His glory."

Distinctly, deliberately, he answered. "I will be an infinite gainer to be translated."

Anna asked him if it was his wish that she should return with Julia to her father's home in North Carolina.

"Yes," he said. "You have a kind, good father." This statement triggered another thought: "But no one is kind and good as your Heavenly Father."

He told her he had many things to say to her, but was too weak to say them.

She asked him where he wished to be buried.

"Charlotte," he said, his mind clouding again. Then, "Charlottesville."

Do you not wish it to be in Lexington? she asked him.

"Yes, Lexington," he said. "And in *my own plot.*"

Jackson had bought a burial plot for himself and his family when their first child had died in infancy.

Mrs. Hoge now entered with the baby. Jackson looked up and his face brightened.

"Little darling! Sweet one!" he exclaimed.

She was placed on the bed beside him and he watched her

intently, with a radiant smile. She returned smile for smile, until he drifted again into unconsciousness.

That morning Chaplain Lacy, knowing the end was near, wished to remain with Jackson. But the general insisted he too must do his duty, and preach to the soldiers as usual. When Sandie Pendleton came to his room at about midday, Jackson asked, "Who was preaching at headquarters to-day?"

Pendleton told him that Lacy was, and that the entire army was praying for him.

"Thank God," Jackson said. "They are very kind."

A moment passed, and he said, "It is the Lord's Day; my wish is fulfilled. I have always desired to die on Sunday."

At corps headquarters Lacy preached to nearly two thousand soldiers. Lee and several other generals listened as he took for his sermon one of Jackson's favorite texts, "We know all things work together for good to them that fear God."[22]

How is he? Lee asked Lacy.

It looks quite hopeless, the chaplain answered.

"Surely General Jackson must recover," Lee said. "God will not take him from us, now that we need him so much. Surely he will be spared to us, in answer to the many prayers which are offered for him."

Before Lacy left, Lee said to him, "When you return, I trust you will find him better." Then he said: "When a suitable occasion offers, give him my love, and tell him that I wrestled in prayer for him last night, as I never prayed, I believe, for myself."

At Guiney's Station Sandie Pendleton was so moved by what was happening inside the sickroom that he went out on the porch and wept.[23] At the big house, twelve-year-old Lucy Chandler said she wished she could die in the general's place, for then only her family would mourn, "but if General Jackson dies, everybody will be sorry."[24]

Even as Lacy preached and the men of Jackson's "foot cavalry" prayed, Jackson was dying. His mind continued to wander and to fail. He faded in and out, issuing orders as before. He was at the mess table with his staff, then at home with his wife and child, now at prayers with his men, and again in battle. In one brief interval when his mind was in the present, McGuire offered him some brandy and water.

He declined. "It will only delay my departure, and do no good; I want to preserve my mind, if possible, to the last."

He was still trying to be what he resolved to be.

At about 3:00 in the afternoon he issued another order for A. P. Hill to come up, for Major Hawks. . . .

Then he stopped, and smiled, one of those sweet smiles his West Point classmates remembered from so many years ago.

"Let us cross over the river," he said quietly, "and rest under the shade of the trees."

When Lacy arrived with Lee's message, he was dead.

How unspeakable and incalculable is his loss to me and that fatherless baby, Anna thought as she watched him die. All that night she struggled to stem the torrent of grief. The next day Sandie Pendleton, having suffered all night with his own sorrow, told her, "God knows I would have died for him."[25]

Anna went to see him once more in the crude casket they had improvised for him. It was covered with spring flowers and his face was wreathed in lily of the valley, the emblem of humility. Ah, thought Anna, his own predominating grace.

The South uttered a convulsive sob. "As one man," said Richard Taylor, "[it] wept for him."[26] There went up from every Southern heart a wail, "so long, so loud," one mourner wrote, "that in the sad sound was heard only the heart-breaking refrain, 'Jackson has fallen!' "[27]

This stiff, dogged, eccentric man from the western Virginia mountains had become the paladin of the Confederacy, the hero-idol of the South. This unlikely champion, who had demonstrated that in warfare intelligence, daring, courage, and celerity could win battles, had incredibly come to symbolize southern invincibility. Now, just as incredibly, he was dead. It seemed unreal. If Jackson could fall, perhaps they were not so invincible after all.

"The thunderbolt was too sudden," wrote Sallie Putnam in Richmond, "the blow too heavy. . . . the tower of strength upon which we had leaned had been overthrown."[28] It was, as Henry Douglas said, "the heart-break of the Southern Confederacy."[29]

Two of Jackson's staff, Sandie Pendleton and James Smith, numbly dressed him and put him in his crude coffin, and Pendleton went to tell Robert E. Lee. Lee, "with deep grief," told the army.

Writing from the anguish in his heart, Lee praised the daring, skill, and energy "of this great and good soldier," all now lost to them. "But while we mourn his death," he wrote, "we feel that his spirit still lives, and will inspire the whole army with his indomitable courage and unshaken confidence in God as our hope and our strength." He called on the grieving army to "let his name be a watchword to his corps, who have followed him to victory on so many fields. Let officers and soldiers emulate his invincible determination to do everything in the defense of our beloved country."[30]

Virginia Governor John Letcher, Jackson's neighbor from Lexington, told the Confederate government. Within hours the news nobody wanted to believe was everywhere that the telegraph could reach. President Jefferson Davis sent the first new Confederate flag, which was intended to fly from the roof of the capitol, to Guiney's Station as a winding sheet for the body and a gift from the mourning nation.

From everywhere the sorrow poured out. From Charleston, where two years ago he had started this whole unpleasant business, P.T.G. Beauregard ordered a gun to be fired every half hour from sunrise to sunset throughout his command, and flags lowered to half mast. Grieving for his lost friend, Beauregard evoked "the memory of his high worth, conspicuous virtues, and momentous services," which he predicted would "be treasured in the heart, and excite the pride of his country to all time."[31]

Nowhere was the outpouring of anguish so heartfelt as in the Shenandoah Valley, especially in Winchester, which had been the object of Jackson's special care and solicitude. The people there viewed Jackson as peculiarly their own. When Cornelia McDonald heard that he was dead she wrote in her diary, "The shadows are darkening around us in the devoted town. Jackson is certainly dead. There is no longer room to doubt it. . . . No loss could be felt as his will be." Who was there now to deliver them from the Yankees?[32]

In the army, the grief was to the point of despair. Few knew his worth so well as those who, as Lee said, had "followed him to victory on so many fields." Many of those who had followed him, and had no idea where they were going at the time, were predicting that their star of destiny would now fade. They feared that the cause would be lost without him, as there was no general who could execute a flank movement with so much secrecy and surprise.[33] "The supremest

449

flanker and rearer" the world has ever seen, admitted one Union officer.[34]

When Henry Douglas went to Lee representing the Stonewall Brigade and asked permission for the men to accompany their dead general to Richmond, Lee refused. No man felt the loss keener than he, Lee told Douglas, but "those people over the river" were again showing signs of movement and he needed them just now, as Jackson had always needed them. He said that even he could not now leave his headquarters long enough to ride to the depot and "pay my dear friend the poor tribute of seeing his body placed upon the cars."[35]

On Monday, May 11, Stonewall Jackson's body was placed on the cars, and Lee was not there to pay poor tribute, nor his brigade to march one more time with him.

Anna rode in the train in mourning clothes, with the baby. In the party were Joseph Morrison, Pendleton, McGuire, Douglas, Smith, Major Hawks, and Major Bridgeford—the bright young officers of Jackson's staff. There was an aide-de-camp from the governor's office, who had charge of the body, two doctors, and several others.[36]

On the outskirts of Richmond at a stop on the Fredericksburg line, the train paused to let off Anna and Julia. Meeting them with carriages was Mrs. Letcher, who carried them by an uncrowded route through the city to the governor's mansion. The train continued slowly on bearing the body into Richmond, along tracks lined for two miles with mourners. All business was shut down in the city, and people had been waiting for hours in the intense heat for the train to come. As it pulled into the station at about 4:00 in the afternoon bells pealed throughout the city, as they had all day and would until sundown, in token of the universal grief.

Commanding the military escort that met the train was another face Jackson would have recognized, Major General Arnold Elzey, who was to take the body of his old comrade-in-arms to the governor's mansion. As Pendleton, McGuire, Smith, and Douglas stepped down to flank the casket, minute guns boomed and a military dirge wailed over the melancholy procession.[37]

That night embalmers came to the governor's mansion to prepare the body. A more fitting metal casket arrived, a gift from the people of Fredericksburg, and Sandie Pendleton and Henry Douglas took up a vigil beside it. President and Mrs. Davis came to stand by the coffin and to gaze for a long while at the pallid face. Varina Davis saw a tear fall from her husband's eye and drop into the open casket. Perhaps he too sensed that something vital had gone from the Confederacy.[38]

Pendleton and Douglas were surprised to see Richard Garnett arrive at the mansion. Douglas had not seen him since that dismal day more than a year before when an angry Jackson had placed him in arrest for withdrawing the Stonewall Brigade prematurely from the fight at Kernstown. The two young staff officers met the general at the door and led him into the parlor where the body lay. Garnett raised the veil that covered Jackson's face and looked for a long while in silence. Tears began to well up in his eyes.

He took Pendleton and Douglas, one by each arm, and led them to the window. "You know of the unfortunate breach between General Jackson and myself," he began. "I can never forget it, nor cease to regret it. But I wish here to assure you that no one can lament his death more sincerely than I do. I believe he did me great injustice, but I believe also he acted from the purest motives. He is dead. Who can fill his place!"

Pendleton asked Garnett if he would be one of the pallbearers in the funeral procession the next day, and he willingly consented.[39]

Another who lamented his death more than most was also in Richmond to mourn. Richard Ewell—one-legged now—had come to pay his last respects. He had thought Jackson crazy in the days before the Valley campaign, and had called him "that enthusiastic fanatic." Now he admired him, respected him, grieved for him, and knew how much the South had lost. This hard-swearing, tenderhearted man would see his old commander through this national mourning the next day and follow the casket to its final resting place in Lexington.[40]

The next day, through the clear warm morning, the carriage bearing the body rolled slowly toward the capitol, the mourning plumes nodding dark and gloomy and casting long shadows over the flower-draped ensign. Following behind, led by a groom, came Little Sorrel, Jackson's empty boots thrown across his empty saddle. In front of the hearse marched two regimental bands—one playing a dirge. Behind them marched the public guard, and several regiments of Confederate infantry with reversed arms, a battalion of artillery, and a squadron of cavalry. At the head of this military escort rode another

451

mourner who long ago at West Point had, with his many demerits, taken Jackson's former place at the foot of the class: George Pickett, now a Confederate major general.[41]

Following the hearse drawn by four white horses toiled the cortege stretching for more than a mile, and led by the pallbearers— including Ewell, Garnett, and Longstreet. One mourner watched them pass and thought she had never seen human faces display such grief—almost despair.[42]

Behind the pallbearers came Jackson's desolate staff and more than a hundred veterans of the old Stonewall Brigade, many of them invalid and wounded, and all knowing they would never see his like again. Next came Jefferson Davis in a carriage and behind him Confederate officialdom on foot—cabinet members and others—and behind them and lining the streets thousands of mourners, bareheaded and mute, unreconciled to this calamity.[43]

Andrew Jackson Bowering, director of the Thirtieth Virginia regimental band, wasn't reconciled to it either. He and his musicians had been at Hamilton's Crossing when they were ordered to Richmond to play at the funeral, and nobody had told him what was expected. He knew they must play something historically appropriate. He had only one copy of the Dead March, and on the train he transcribed and arranged the dirge for twenty different instruments. That would have to do.

When George W. Randolph, master of ceremonies for the funeral, raised his sword to start the procession, Bowering waved his baton at the boys in the band and they broke into the "Psalm of David." Jackson would have liked that.

As they marched along to its unhappy strains, Bowering felt emotion sweeping him away. In his time he had played final music for men standing against walls waiting for the executioner's gun. He had played in hospitals to soothe the dying hours of shattered lives. But never had he been so overwhelmed as this. Tears rolled down the faces of his musicians, and they played as they had never played before. Bowering found that he too was weeping.[44]

At about noon the unhappy procession pulled up at the western entrance to the capitol and into a throng of weeping women and children. The thunder of artillery and the mournful wail of the music rolled over the scene. The pallbearers lifted the coffin from the hearse and carried it into the hall of the House of Representatives and placed it on a temporary altar before the speaker's chair. There the casket was draped in the Confederate flag and opened to view. Sorrowing Richmond began to file past—twenty thousand mourners by nightfall. Mary Chesnut came in the moonlight and looked at the body lying in state and wondered, "Shall I ever forget the pain and fear of it all?"[45]

As the last of them laid the last flower on the bier and the coffin was again closed, a mutilated veteran from Jackson's army appeared to see the general. Too late, they told him. But he pressed on as if he hadn't heard them; Jackson would have approved. When one of the marshals stepped in to force him back, the soldier lifted the stump of his right arm and with tears running down his bearded face said through gritted teeth, "By this arm, which I lost for my country, I demand the privilege of seeing my General once more."

The governor stopped the proceedings and the soldier was permitted to look on his general one last time.[46]

Sallie Putnam took comfort in another thought. "Though dead," she sighed, "he yet lives—shall ever live."[47]

Jackson's body started for home the next day, Wednesday, May 13. At every station along the tracks to Lynchburg, mourners brought flowers and silently watched. In Charlottesville all business was suspended and the church bells tolled as the train passed through the town. There were no speeches along the way, no ceremonies, just desolate grief. At Lynchburg the casket was put on the packet boat, the *Marshall*, to be borne the rest of the way to Lexington by the old James River and Kanawha Canal.[48]

As they floated along the canal through the spring afternoon, Henry Douglas perhaps remembered that this was the first time since Jackson left two springs before that he had returned to Lexington. The general had not taken a day of leave in two years. Once when Douglas, wanting leave himself and perhaps having a tryst with a young lady in mind, had suggested tentatively that he had not had a single day off either since entering the army, Jackson had missed the point entirely. "Very good," he had said, "I hope you will be able to say so after the war is over."[49]

It was the most beautiful time of the year in Lexington. The springtime flowers were abundant—lilacs, lilies of the valley, tuberoses, and calla lilies bloomed in profusion everywhere. At about 6:00 Thursday evening the corps of cadets met the packet, transferred the casket to an artillery caisson, and carried it to their old professor's bare lecture room, which was just as he had left it, but draped now in mourning. Many of these cadets had listened there to his dull lectures and sniggered at his eccentricities and called him "Old Blue Light." Now he was a fallen paladin, a military martyr, a saint, the first soldier of the Confederacy, the best of them all, and through the night they stood watches beside his bier and considered it the privilege of their lifetimes.[50]

The next day he was carried on the caisson to the church, where he had so often fallen asleep during the sermons, and Reverend White commended him to his final rest. The weeping congregation sang "How Blest the Righteous When He Dies," and his old minister read from First Corinthians 15, and preached the last sermon. The casket was then borne to the cemetery, to Jackson's own plot, and the corps of cadets fired the farewell salute over his grave. Anna Jackson looked out over the peaceful Valley that in his day he had rendered so unpeaceable, and thought, How "beautiful for situation." Her hero-husband was gone, and she must now go home alone.[51]

A decade before, Jackson had visited Canada with his young first bride, Ellie, and his sister-in-law, Margaret. On an August evening they had gone up on the Plains of Abraham, and as Jackson approached the foot of the monument to British General James Wolfe he removed his cap, as if in the presence of a sacred shrine. He rose to his tiptoes and his eye flashed with a fiery light his own soldiers would one day see on other battlefields. Overcome with emotion, with his arm he swept the plain and he quoted Wolfe's dying words.

" '*I die content*,' " he repeated. Then he said: "To die as *he* died, who would not die content."[52]

As so he had also died, "a death," a resolution by the officers and men of the old Stonewall Brigade said, "worthy of his life."[53]

Soon verse would begin to pour out from the verse-ridden times, and one of the more stirring stanzas would key on his own death-bed prediction:

> And men shall tell their children,
> Tho' all other memories fade,
> That they fought with Stonewall Jackson
> In the old "Stonewall Brigade!"[54]

Old Jack's classmates were amazed at what had become of him. William Montgomery Gardner, who had once considered him unprepossessing, admitted that his later career "was an astonishing revelation to me, and I doubt not it was the same to all of his classmates."[55]

Another fellow cadet of those West Point years shrugged and said he supposed he was "as Ephraim was, 'like unto a cake unturned' . . . a 'diamond in the rough.' . . ."[56]

The unflinching cadet from the mountains may not have resolved to be an American phenomenon; he was only doing his duty. But thanks to an all-kind Providence, that is what he had become—in life, and now in death.

The Dandy
at the Foot
of the Class

It was a stunning midsummer morning, clear and bright, and "all nature in her luxuriant garb seemed wooing peace."[1] Nature was smiling on this July 3 in 1863, even if James Longstreet wasn't. The time had come to take George Pickett to the crest of Seminary Ridge and show him the dirty job that he must do.

Longstreet dreaded it. He in fact deplored Lee's strategy entirely. He hadn't liked it from the start. He had opposed it as forcibly and vocally as a corps commander dared, nearly to the point of insubordination. But Lee's mind was made up. "The enemy is there," he had said, "and I am going to strike him."[2]

Pickett and Longstreet stared across at the Union line on Cemetery Hill. Striking it was a cheerless prospect. The enemy was massed there, across that empty little valley, at the clump of trees where the attack must be made. A skirmish line nearly as heavy as a single line of battle was thrown out all along the federal front. On the acclivity behind, two tiers of artillery frowned and two lines of infantry waited. Beyond, on the crest of the ridge, heavy reserves of infantry were massed in double column.

A low loose stone wall snaked along sections of the ridge, behind which the Union infantry crouched. In the bottomland between the two ridges, post and rail fences bordered the Emmitsburg road leading out of Gettysburg. It would have to be scaled on the way to the stone wall. From Seminary Ridge where the rebel army would emerge from the cover of the woods, to the Union position across the valley, lay half a mile of starkly open and exposed ground.

Over this empty, treeless space, within shell and shrapnel range of enemy guns the entire distance, Pickett's division must march. Even on this beautiful morning before a shot had been fired or a drop of blood spilled, it looked like "an open *quèt apens* for slaughter, a passage to the valley of death . . . like a truly 'forlorn hope' on an extensive scale."[3]

Longstreet knew that all the way across that valley Pickett's men would be swept by enfilade fire from a Union battery on Little Round Top, the little mountain on the right. Sharpshooters, artillery, and infantry would pound them from in front, and from God knows where else. Longstreet had little hope for it. His heart was heavy. These brave men were about to be sacrificed in a hopeless charge.[4]

It pained him that it had to be Pickett and his division. He and Pickett had served in the same infantry regiment in the old army. In Mexico they had groped together for the scaling ladders at Chapultepec, and when Longstreet was wounded, Pickett had snatched the falling colors and planted them on the castle heights for all to see and cheer. Longstreet was exceedingly fond of this elegant hell-for-leather officer who had graduated at the foot of the West Point class of 1846. In this war Pickett had commanded first a brigade and now a division in Longstreet's corps, and Longstreet had always favored him. He had ordered his staff to give him all he needed for his division, and sometimes directed them to stay with him "to make sure he did not get astray."[5] Now Longstreet was sending his division to certain destruction—against his own better judgment.

Pickett didn't see it that way, however. As he stared across at Cemetery Ridge, he saw that the job would cost lives. He saw the undeniable strength of the Union line. His division had seen little action at Fredericksburg and had not been at Chancellorsville. Although not at full strength, it was ready, and it was supported by the entire power of that great invincible Southern army led by Robert E. Lee. He was confident he could do it; he felt lucky to have the chance.[6]

* * *

Pickett had traveled far these seventeen years from the foot of the class to a major general's stars in the Confederate army. From Mexico he had gone to the Indian wars in the Pacific Northwest, where he had built on his reputation as a fighter. A fellow Confederate officer said of him, "Give George Pickett an order and he will storm the gates of hell."[7] Or he would hold those gates if necessary.

G. Moxley Sorrel, Longstreet's chief of staff, thought Pickett one of the most singular figures in the Confederate army. He was ordinary enough in size, of medium height and well-built, erect in bearing, always dandily dressed—in ruffles often as not—distinguished and striking with his elegant riding whip.

"But the head, the hair," marveled Sorrel, "were extraordinary. Long ringlets flowed loosely over his shoulders, trimmed and highly perfumed; his beard likewise was curling and giving out the scents of Araby."[8]

Looking this way, with his auburn hair cascading in corkscrew ringlets and his entire persona bathed in the headiest of aromas, it was all or nothing, elegance or disaster, with Pickett; for caught in the rain the hair went lank, and the scents of Araby went with the storm.[9]

Arthur Freemantle, an officer of the British Coldstream Guards observing the Confederate army about this time, thought him "altogether rather a desperate looking character."[10]

On this morning in early July 1863 when his division was to charge the Union position on Cemetery Hill, Pickett, a widower, was in love. He had fallen "with all the ardor of youth" for the young LaSalle Corbell of Suffolk, a breathtaking beauty half his own age. In their passionate courtship he had made long, often unauthorized night rides to woo her, with galloping returns to duty the next morning. "Carpet-knight doings," snuffed Sorrel, who didn't believe they much benefited his division. LaSalle, as much in love as he, called him her soldier and they were to marry in the fall.[11]

Socially, this aromatic dandy had always been the soul of courtesy, cheer, and gallantry. He believed that to fight like a gentleman, a man must eat and drink like a gentleman—and presumably love like one. He courted LaSalle with charm and grace, and must have sung her love songs as she had never heard them sung. One friend remembered him from an earlier time when Pickett led his enchanting sister to the piano, there "to flood the house with melody like that of the mocking-bird."[12]

Unlike his tone-deaf friend U. S. Grant, of the Union army, who knew only two tunes—"one was Yankee Doodle. The other wasn't"[13]— Pickett was a nightingale. His richly timbred voice soared and resonated. After helping subjugate the northwestern Indians, he learned their languages, translated hymns and national airs, including the Lord's Prayer, into their dialects and led them in soulful renditions. If LaSalle was to be believed, the Indians loved him, and called him "Hyas Tyee," "Hyas Kloshe Tyee," and "Nesika Tyee"—Great Chief, Great Good Chief, and Our Chief.[14] He had "married" an Indian woman while in the Pacific Northwest and fathered a son.

In this present war, so full of irregularities, Pickett was a partner to perhaps one of the choicest ironies of all. The man partly responsible for getting him into West Point, LaSalle would later claim, was Abraham Lincoln, the present president of the United States and commander in chief of the Union armies. Although a Virginian, Pickett was living in Illinois in 1842 with his uncle, Lincoln's friend and fellow lawyer, Andrew Johnston. It was from there that he had been appointed to the academy by Congressman John G. Stuart, largely, LaSalle insists, at Lincoln's urging.[15]

But now Pickett was on Seminary Ridge, about to lead an epic charge against his benefactor's army at the little Pennsylvania town of Gettysburg.

Pickett had left Virginia and LaSalle in June, his division comprising the rear guard of Lee's army as it invaded Pennsylvania. With him were the brigades of Lewis Armistead, Richard Garnett, and James Kemper. His two other brigades, under Montgomery Corse and Micah Jenkins, had been detained, over his ardent objections, for duty around Richmond and Petersburg. He arrived in Chambersburg on June 27 with 4,700 men, little more than half his full strength.

When Lee moved the Army of Northern Virginia's vanguard to Cashtown and then toward Gettysburg on the last day of June, Pickett's division was left in Chambersburg, with orders to destroy rail depots, workshops, and machinery. He was to follow the rest of the army when Brigadier General John Imboden came up from western Virginia to relieve him as the army's rear guard. The time in Chambersburg was uneventful, the work was routine, the streets of the city were deserted, and all the liquor was locked in the courthouse under guard. But it wasn't unpleasant duty. As Sergeant Levin Gayle said, it was summer, he was in a land of milk and honey, and he could "finde cherries a plenty."[16]

Imboden arrived on July 1, and in the late hours of the night Pickett got orders from Longstreet. The battle had been joined at Gettysburg and Lee needed him. So he put his division in motion in the early morning hours of the second, through slumbering Chambersburg and onto the Baltimore Pike. "And away we go againe," sighed Levin Gayle.[17] They marched that day under a vertical and broiling summer sun, over twenty-three long, hot, dusty miles "not conducive to enthusiasm in a pedestrian."[18] As they tramped down the eastern slope of South Mountain they heard ahead the thunder-roll of battle.

Pickett rode on in advance of his division to report to Longstreet. He sent Colonel Walter Harrison, his inspector general, to inform Lee that they had arrived, and that with two hours' rest his division would be at his service. Lee thanked Harrison and said, "Tell Gen. Pickett I shall not want him this evening, to let his men rest, and I will send him word when I want them."[19]

The division bivouacked that night four miles from Gettysburg, falling asleep, one soldier said, "to the lullaby of deep reverberations from the battle front"; "little dreaming," another said, "that upon such lovely eve, such awful morn should rise."[20]

As Pickett's men slept, Colonel Edward Porter Alexander, acting as Longstreet's chief of artillery, began rolling guns into line along Seminary Ridge under the light of a glorious moon. By daybreak, 140 cannon pointed from the heights toward the Union position on Cemetery Ridge across the way. A major piece of the awful day was in place.[21]

Early in the morning—it was now the third—"while the round red sun was yet balancing atop the mountains toward the east," Pickett brought his division to Seminary Ridge.[22] There, shielded from enemy view by the woods, two to three hundred yards behind Alexander's line of artillery, Pickett halted his men and waited. His own guns, commanded by James W. Dearing, of whom it was said that the whir of the bullet was the sweetest of all martial music, shouldered into Alexander's line of artillery opposite the Union left-center.[23]

As day broke, the sun lit Seminary Ridge, and the Union soldiers across the valley saw for the first time what the faint and distant rumbling of wagon wheels had signified in the night. One hundred forty pieces of artillery were in place and pointed at them. What did it mean? A cannonade certainly. But when? Followed by what? All they could do as the morning wore on was wait with a quickening sense of disquiet.[24]

That's all anybody on either side could do. On Seminary Ridge the Confederate soldiers knew as well as their Union counterparts that something terrible was about to happen. As Longstreet said, "strong battle was in the air."[25] Colonel Joseph May, Jr., of the Third Virginia, noticed that his troops, generally so merry and fun-loving, had become "as still and thoughtful as Quakers at a love feast."

"This news has brought about an awful seriousness with our fellows, Taz," he said to Colonel Tazwell Patton of the Seventh Virginia.

"Yes," Patton agreed, "and well they may be serious if they really know what is in store for them. I have been up yonder where Dearing is, and looked across at the Yankees."[26]

Some of the more carefree Confederates found diversion in pelting one another with green apples.[27] But Erasmus Williams of the Fourteenth Virginia looked at the long line of Alexander's massed artillery and took out his case knife and began digging a hole and piling the dirt in front of it. A lieutenant in his regiment leaned against a nearby sapling and watched him dig and laughed.

"Why Williams, you are a coward," he said.

"You may call me what you please," Williams said, "but when the time comes I will show up all right, and when the artillery begins the hole I am digging will be a good place for me to be in."

Williams settled into his makeshift fortification and the lieutenant said, "I am going to stand right up here and witness the whole proceeding."[28]

In places far more exalted than Williams's little dirt entrenchment, Lee and Longstreet were having a difference of opinion. Lee's intent was clear. He would hurl Pickett's division and eight brigades from A. P. Hill's corps—some twelve thousand men altogether—against the left-center of the Union army on Cemetery Hill, turn its position, and roll up its line. But first he would pound the Federals at the intended point of attack—a clump of trees beyond the stone wall—with his 140 guns. Under the thunder of this fire, he would send his infantry to Cemetery Hill.

Longstreet had argued instead for throwing the Confederate force between the Union army and Washington, selecting a strong defensive position, and forcing the enemy to attack them. Longstreet's distaste for assuming the offensive in this invasion had colored his late-starting attack on the Union left the day before—the second day at Gettysburg—which had ended with both armies battered and nothing decided. He entertained even less enthusiasm for the charge on the Union center that Lee contemplated for this third day.[29]

He said to Lee: "I have been a soldier, I may say, from the ranks up to the position I now hold. I have been in pretty much all kinds of skirmishes, from those of two or three soldiers up to those of an army corps, and I think I can safely say there never was a body of fifteen thousand men who could make that attack successfully."[30] But it was decided. The cannonade would begin after the firing of two signal guns by the Washington Artillery, and when the Union line was sufficiently softened, Pickett would charge.

The soldiers continued to wait. In midmorning there had been a struggle for possession of the Bliss barn between the lines, involving about a hundred guns. But that had died away. There had also been fighting all morning on the extreme Confederate left for possession of Culp's Hill, but that too had ended with the hill remaining in Union hands. At about eleven o'clock the whole field suddenly fell "as silent as a churchyard."[31]

It was the eerie kind of stillness that seeped to the marrow of men's bones, mysterious and oppressive, depressing the spirit like some "dreadful nightmare." It was a hush that foretold calamity, the terrifying silence which in nature portends the fury of a coming storm. "More trying on one's backbone and grit," as one soldier described such stillness, "than any charge on hill or breastworks," when a man's whole life "becomes a living panorama before him." As the silence stretched on through the late morning, through the noontime, and approached one o'clock, impatience to have the charge done with and over became almost unbearable. A line from Macbeth occurred to Walter Harrison: " ' 'Twere well it were done quickly,' " he thought, "holds quite as good in heroic action as in crime."[32]

33. Thomas J. (Stonewall) Jackson of the class of 1846—a Union officer called him "the supremest flanker and rearer" the world has ever seen.

34. Harpers Ferry, Jackson's first Confederate command in the Civil War.

35. (*Inset*) Engine 199, hijacked to the Confederacy in the spring of 1862—the biggest of the locomotives appropriated by Jackson's railroaders.

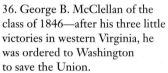

36. George B. McClellan of the class of 1846—after his three little victories in western Virginia, he was ordered to Washington to save the Union.

37. The battle of Rich Mountain—McClellan didn't know he had won it until the next day.

38. Samuel Davis Sturgis, hero of the Indian Wars who later had the bad luck to run into Nathan Bedford Forest, the Confederate Wizard of the Saddle, in Mississippi.

39. Jesse Lee Reno, killed at South Mountain and immortalized by the city of Reno, Nevada.

40. Darius Nash Couch, competent, acerbic Union major general.

41. Dabney Herndon Maury—he always preferred the middle of the class, but rose to excellence in the Confederate Army.

42. Birkett Davenport Fry—he flunked out of West Point, but became a Confederate general and "a man with a gunpowder reputation."

43. David Rumph (Neighbor) Jones—he and A. P. Hill threw back the Union attack at Antietam and then he died of a broken heart.

44. Stonewall Jackson and his staff of "your wide awake, smart young men."

45. Richard Stoddert Ewell, Jackson's right hand in the Shenandoah Valley—he thought his commander crazy, which was rather like the pot calling the kettle black.

46. George Henry Gordon of the class of 1846—he commanded the Union rear guard against his old classmate in the Valley, and acquitted himself well.

47. John C. Fremont's weary soldiers pursuing Jackson's foot cavalry up the Valley—one of the war's more thankless tasks.

48. George B. McClellan and his staff—it was said he was "the only man ever born who could strut while sitting down."

49. McClellan passing through Frederick, Maryland, on his way to Antietam.

50. Union soldiers attempt to carry the Burnside bridge "at all hazards."

51. A. P. Hill, erstwhile of the class of 1846—he drove his division from Harpers Ferry to Antietam at the tip of his sword and saved Lee's army.

52. President Lincoln confers with George McClellan in the general's tent at Antietam—a few days after the battle.

53. George Stoneman, Jackson's taciturn West Point roommate—victimized at Chancellorsville by the rain and the piles.

54. Lee and Jackson meet for the last time before Jackson's electrifying Saturday evening flank attack on Hooker's army at Chancellorsville.

55. Stonewall Jackson, as he looked in his last photograph taken only days before he fell at Chancellorsville.

56. Anna Jackson, the loving wife who watched her husband die at Guiney's Station.

57. Jackson's Mill in western Virginia, Stonewall Jackson's boyhood home.

58. The cottage at Guiney's Station, where Jackson died.

59. George Edward Pickett of the class of 1846—he finished last in the class and led the charge at Gettysburg that made his name immortal.

60. George Pickett, the soldier in love, and his young wife, LaSalle Corbell Pickett.

61. Pickett's charge, with General Lewis Armistead guiding the storm with his hat at the tip of his sword.

62. Cadmus Marcellus Wilcox of the class of 1846—the competent workaday Confederate general who turned up at Appomattox in his skivvies.

63. John Gibbon, erstwhile of the class of 1846—a fellow Union officer called him "steel-cold General Gibbon," but he commanded the Union divisions taking the Confederate surrender at Appomattox with sympathy and consideration.

64. Confederate soldiers sadly furl their flags for the final time at Appomattox.

* * *

As his corps waited in the silence under the beating sun, Union Brigadier General John Gibbon decided to have lunch. In another of those ironic matchups, Pickett would be hurling his division against the soldiers of this old friend and former classmate. Younger even than McClellan, Gibbon had joined the class late, with the September arrivals in 1842, three months behind the rest. He was soon "found," however, and put back into the class of 1847. He had proved an outstanding officer, and in this war he had matured into a valued, level-headed general. He was still young and ruggedly handsome, of slight build, with brown hair, and a reddish moustache. He seemed made of ice and born for battle. Nobody could remember ever seeing him either nervous or excited.[33] "Steel-cold General Gibbon," a fellow officer described him, "the most American of Americans, with his sharp nose and up-and-down manner of telling the truth, no matter whom it hurts."[34] He had been telling truth that hurt since the beginning of the war, when he decided to stay with the North and three of his brothers went with the South.

But now it was lunchtime at Gettysburg, and Gibbon had procured a chicken "in good *running* order." To share it, he invited Generals Winfield Hancock, John Newton, Alfred Pleasonton, and the army's new commanding general himself, George Meade. They all came and dined, and afterward leaned back, lit their cigars, rested under the shade of a small tree, and talked of yesterday's battle and of today's probabilities. So they passed the lunch hour in the silence in the rear of the Union line, a general now and then dispatching an orderly with a message. At about half past twelve, one by one, beginning with Meade, they rode off leaving Gibbon alone with his staff. There they continued to sit with half-shut eyes, nodding off in the heat and the quiet. At five minutes to one, Captain Frank Haskell looked at his watch and yawned.[35]

On Seminary Ridge, Brigadier General James J. Pettigrew paid a visit to one of his brigade commanders, Colonel Birkett Davenport Fry. Pettigrew was in temporary command of Major General Henry Heth's division of A. P. Hill's corps, which was to assault the Union line in partnership with Pickett's Virginians. Fry, erstwhile of the class of 1846, a second-year victim of mathematics, was commanding James Archer's brigade.

Pettigrew told Fry of Lee's plans. After a heavy cannonade they would assault the Union line. The Federals, of course, would return the fire with all the guns they had. "We must shelter the men as best we can," Pettigrew told Fry, "and make them lie down." He ordered him to go at once to Pickett and work out an understanding about dressing the lines in the coming assault, since Fry's brigade backed on Pickett's division.

Fry found his old classmate in good spirits. They had a lot in common, these two. They were both Virginians. Fry had flunked out of West Point and the demerit-laden Pickett had nearly done so. Both had gone on to win reputations as fearless fighters. They had charged the castle at Chapultepec together in the Mexican War, and they spoke now of those pleasant memories. Presently they were joined by Brigadier General Richard Garnett, who commanded the brigade abutting Fry's. It was decided among the three of them that the assaulting force would dress on Fry, who occupied the exact center of the Confederate line.[36]

About the time Fry was reporting this decision to Pettigrew, one of his soldiers, June Kimble, an orderly sergeant of the Fourteenth Tennessee, walked out alone to the edge of the open field and looked across at the Union position on Cemetery Ridge.

He stared at it a moment and then solemnly addressed a question to himself. "June Kimble," he demanded aloud, "are you going to do your duty to-day?"

"I'll do it, so help me God," he answered himself.

When he returned to his regiment, his lieutenant asked, "How does it look, June?"

"Boys, if we have to go," June said, "it will be hot for us, and we will have to do our best."[37]

As Frank Haskell was looking at his watch at five minutes to one, James Longstreet was passing an order to the Washington Artillery. "Let the batteries open," the message read. Major B. F. Eshleman received it, and at one o'clock the first signal shot shattered the hot sultry stillness. The fiction primer failed to fire on the second gun, but the delay was short. Seconds later it, too, bellowed out into the quiet afternoon.[38]

At John Gibbon's lunch site, the dozing officers lurched awake. The thunder of the two signal shots had hardly stopped echoing across the valley, and Seminary Ridge was belching fire from end to end.

Shells began exploding all around Gibbon and his staff as they sprang to their feet, shouting for their horses. When Gibbon's did not come at once—his groom had been ripped open by one of the first shells—he snatched up his saber and started forward on the run. It was as if Armageddon had arrived. The air was filled with screeching projectiles. Gibbon could see them plainly as they arched toward him and crashed into the Taneytown road. The long rifled shells careened in with a rush and a scream. He could see them above, upsetting and tumbling end over end through the air. Shots were bursting all about him now, throwing fragments everywhere, or plowing furrows in the earth and hurling shattered pieces of rock.[39]

Haskell found his own horse tethered to a nearby tree placidly munching oats as if nothing was happening. This is ridiculous, he thought. This horse, of the men and beasts in this hellhole, was the coolest of them all. He leaped on its back and galloped away after Gibbon.[40]

Cadmus Marcellus Wilcox of the class of 1846 had brought his Confederates to Seminary Ridge at about 7:00 that morning. His soldiers were tired and battle-worn, having been in the thick of yesterday's fighting. But they had been ordered to support the charge on the right of Pickett's division today, and Wilcox had the reputation of always being ready—fussily ready. They didn't call him "Old Billy Fixing" for nothing. Like his ex-classmate John Gibbon, Wilcox was a provider. He had procured a piece of cold mutton for lunch and was sharing it with Richard Garnett and Walter Harrison.

The water from the well in the yard where they lunched was so hard that Harrison decided they needed a chaser "to prevent [it] from freezing my whole internal economy, and petrifying my heart of hearts." As they ate, they took a pull on the Chambersburg whisky, then on the water. Then the signal guns went off, and Harrison and Garnett bolted for their horses, scarcely reaching them before the artillery on both ridges was in full cry.[41]

"*Lie down, men!* Lie down," the order echoed along Seminary Ridge. "Down! Down!" was the command everywhere on Cemetery Hill. These men, Union and Confederate, didn't need to be told that, and it hardly mattered. There was nowhere to hide. Along the Union line even the colors had to be furled and laid on the ground to keep from being shredded.[42]

The thunder of the cannonading rolled over the armies "like

doom."[43] "The air seethed with old iron," wrote a soldier from Maine. "Death and destruction were everywhere. Men and horses mangled and bleeding; trees, rocks, and fences ripped and torn. Shells, solid shot, and spherical case shot screamed, hissed, and rattled in every direction. Men hugged the ground and sought safety behind hillocks, boulders, ledges, stone walls, bags of grain—anything that could give or suggest shelter from this storm of death."[44]

It seemed to one Confederate that the solid fabric of the hills labored and shook. In Philadelphia over eighty miles away the roar of the thunder was heard and the jar of concussion felt. A federal soldier thought all the fiends of the unknown region had been turned loose. A Union chaplain believed it to be a "tempest of shot and shell such as never before, since the world began." Nothing, he thought, could have added to the noise. It was "like Heaven's thunder," said another. To James Longstreet it was as if the two armies were "mighty wild beasts growling at each other and preparing for a death struggle."[45]

Both ridges were soon ablaze with fire and covered with smoke, which eddied out into the valley between. The scene, thought Henry J. Hunt, the chief of the federal artillery, was "indescribably grand." The sun, so brilliant but a few moments before, was now eclipsed, and out of the gloom came the screaming shot and shell, plowing furrows among the men hugging the earth in the woods behind Seminary Ridge. The hailstorm of howling shot from the more than two hundred guns on the two ridges was worse even than that terrible silence that had preceded it. "No sound of roaring waters, nor wind, nor thunder, nor of these combined," one officer would write, "ever equaled the tremendous uproar, and no command, no order, no sound of voice, could be heard at all above the ceaseless din."[46]

Behind the line of massed cannon on Seminary Ridge the suffering was worst of all. The federal shells fell among the unprotected Confederate soldiers indiscriminately. "Some were stricken down with cigars in their mouths," a soldier wrote. One was killed clutching a picture of his sister in his hand.[47]

Within moments after the cannonade began Erasmus Williams, who lay in the makeshift fortification he had dug with his penknife, was covered with dirt kicked up by exploding shells. Almost instantly, the lieutenant who was standing to witness the whole proceeding was swept away by a shot, his blood splattering over Williams. A shell struck the ground nearby and stuck, its fuse still sputtering. Williams reached out and pulled the fuse before the shell exploded.[48]

A Confederate soldier in Joseph B. Kershaw's brigade rested his foot in the fork of a bush and a fragment tore into his ankle. He stared at the wound for a moment and said: "Boys, I'll be ——if that ain't a thirty-day days' furlough."[49] Brigadier General Lewis A. Armistead, who was known to be afraid of nothing, paced in the open in front of his line at an easy and unconcerned gait. One of his soldiers rose to his feet, and Armistead ordered him to lie down. When the soldier tried to justify himself by Armistead's own example, the general said, "Yes, but never mind me; we want men with guns in their hands."[50]

Cadmus Wilcox, another general who was up and about, approached Armistead and saluted.

"What do you think will follow this unusually heavy fire of artillery?" Wilcox shouted.

"To charge and carry the enemy's position in front of us, I suppose," Armistead answered.

Wilcox was dubious. It appeared to him that since the enemy had nearly twenty-four hours to strengthen their position, it was not a promising prospect. He rode away unconvinced, and as he did so a Union shell struck a small hickory tree nearby and glanced off, severely wounding a soldier and narrowly missing Armistead. A group of soldiers edged nervously away. "Lie still," Armistead ordered, "there is no safe place here."[51]

On Cemetery Ridge, John Gibbon had at last reached the brow of the hill behind the stone fence and found himself "in the most infernal pandemonium." His infantrymen were hugging the ground. Only the artillerymen were up and at work, busily serving their guns. Shells were bursting all about them, striking now a horse, now a limber box, and now a man. Low over the scene hung a heavy pall of smoke beneath which Gibbon could see only the rapidly moving legs of the men as they hurried back and forth between the guns and the limbers that held their ammunition.

He saw with wonder how perfectly still the horses stood. Even when a shell struck, bowling one of two of them over or throwing another to the ground, those not hit continued to stand fatalistically still. Although Gibbon was as unflappable as any man, he felt a wave of alarm rise within him. He thought only fools could remain unaffected in this situation.

However, he found Brigadier General Alexander Webb sitting placidly beside Lieutenant Alonzo H. Cushing's roaring battery, as though he had no interest in what was happening. It probably hadn't crossed Webb's mind that the intimate friend of his own West Point years, Edward Porter Alexander, was the Confederate hurling all this destruction down on them.[52]

"What does this mean?" Gibbon asked him. Webb shook his head; nobody knew.

Gibbon had lost track of time. He watched the chaos for what "might have been an age. . . . it might have been an hour or three or five," and grew weary of seeing men and horses torn to pieces. He noticed that while some shells were bursting among them, most were overshooting the Union line and exploding in the rear. He decided the safest place was closer to the front, so he rose and walked forward with Haskell. They had taken but a few steps when Cushing's limber boxes blew sky high.

They passed the clump of trees that was the main landmark on the ridge, and walked forward to the stone wall where his men were lying. Motioning to them to make room, he stepped over the wall to a clump of bushes in front of the line to see if he could detect any movement across the valley. There was nothing but smoke from the long line of batteries on the ridge, and the unending roar of the guns. As he stood there wondering what it would all bring and when, a staff aide arrived from Major General Winfield Scott Hancock, Gibbon's wing commander. Hancock wanted to know what Gibbon thought it all meant. Gibbon returned his compliments and his opinion: it was either the prelude to a retreat or the overture to an assault. Either way he was covered.[53]

There was no question in Edward Porter Alexander's mind what it all meant. Right then he had more responsibilities on his young shoulders than he wanted, more than a colonel of artillery ought to have. It had suited him that Longstreet had put him in charge of positioning the First Corps guns on Seminary Ridge the night before. That was his job. And it made sense that Alexander ought to be the one to decide when the cannonade had done its intended job and the assault ought to begin. To that end he had posted himself on the artillery line with one of Pickett's couriers at his elbow. As soon as the time seemed right he was to send the word to advance. But if he correctly read these messages he was now getting from Longstreet, he was also being asked to decide if the assault ought to go ahead at all.

Alexander knew that Longstreet did not favor the assault, but the message from the general just before the cannonade began seemed out of line. It said that if the artillery fire didn't drive off the enemy or greatly demoralize him and make success reasonably certain, he preferred that Pickett be advised not to make the charge. Longstreet said he would rely on Alexander's "good judgment" to make that decision, and Alexander had recoiled. That wasn't his job, for God's sake, it was General Lee's.

Alexander sent a message immediately to Longstreet that if there was to be any alternative to the attack it ought to be carefully considered now, before he opened fire, for "it will take all the artillery ammunition we have left to test this one thoroughly, and, if the result is unfavorable, we will have none left for another effort."[54]

Alexander walked over to Brigadier General Ambrose R. Wright and showed him Longstreet's messages.

"General," Alexander said, "tell me exactly what *you* think of this attack?"

"Well, Alexander," Wright said, "it is mostly a question of supports. It is not as hard to get there as it looks. I was there yesterday with my brigade. The real difficulty is to stay there after you get there—for the whole infernal Yankee army is up there in a bunch."[55]

Still troubled, Alexander rode over to Pickett to see what he thought. But Pickett was no help. He saw no objections; he was happy to be going.

So Alexander wrote Longstreet another note, committing himself to nothing beyond his original orders: "When our artillery fire is at its best, I shall order Pickett to charge."[56]

Now Alexander must decide when that ought to be. Before the guns opened, he had made up his mind to send Pickett the order fifteen or twenty minutes after the cannonade started. But now, looking at what was happening on Cemetery Ridge, he was uncertain. It looked like an erupting volcano all along the line. The enemy infantry seemed well shielded, and the Union counterfire hadn't slackened at all. It seemed madness to launch the Confederate infantry into the face of that fire now. He let the fifteen minutes pass, then twenty, then twenty-five, hoping vainly for something to turn up. And still nothing did, and the minutes continued to tick away. At last he wrote Pickett, "If you are coming at all you must come at once, or I cannot give you proper support; but the enemy's fire has not slackened at all; at least eighteen guns are still firing from the cemetery itself."[57]

Five minutes later the enemy fire suddenly began to slacken. The eighteen guns in the cemetery limbered up and left. If the enemy does not run fresh batteries in there in five minutes, Alexander thought, this is our fight. He stared anxiously through his glasses at the deserted position, still swept by Confederate fire and littered with dead men and horses and parts of disabled carriages. In five minutes nothing came.

He scribbled another urgent note to Pickett: "For God's sake, come quick. The eighteen guns are gone; come quick, or my ammunition won't let me support you properly."[58]

When Pickett received Alexander's second message, he rode with it to James Longstreet.

"General, shall I advance?" he asked.

Longstreet did not reply.

Pickett asked again. "General, shall I advance?"

Unable to bring himself to speak the word that he was convinced would send Pickett and his men to a needless slaughter, Longstreet simply bowed his head.

It was answer enough for Pickett. "Sir," he said, "I shall lead my division forward."

Longstreet watched his friend ride away, his perfumed hair, dark and glossy, falling nearly to his shoulders in their corkscrew ringlets. What wondrous pulchritude and magnetic presence, Longstreet thought. What a tragedy. He rose and mounted his own horse and rode toward Alexander, who waited anxiously for Pickett's men to begin their advance.[59]

On both sides, the firing, which had slackened, now stopped. All along the Union line men cautiously rose to their feet in the sudden silence, stretched, and pulled themselves together.[60] On Seminary Ridge Pickett shouted to his soldiers, "Up, men, and to your posts! Don't forget today that you are from old Virginia!"[61]

"Come on, boys," one of his soldiers said, "let's go and drive away those infernal Yankees."[62]

The order was passed to pile knapsacks, blankets—anything that would encumber the march—into company heaps. Then the brigades and divisions were quickly aligned. Pickett's division was on the right, Kemper in front, Garnett to his left, and Armistead immediately behind in support—three brigades, 4,500 men. To Garnett's left Birkett Fry's brigade, on which all would dress, stepped into line, and to his left the rest of Pettigrew's division—four brigades in all, 5,000 men. In support of Pettigrew were two brigades of Dorsey Pender's division, temporarily under the command of old Isaac Trimble, with 2,500 soldiers. On the extreme right behind Pickett, to cover his flank as needed, were the soldiers of Cadmus Wilcox—another 1,200 muskets.[63]

It seemed as if Lewis Armistead was created for this moment. He was the latest of a line of Armisteads who had been soldiers since the Revolutionary War. He had been the first man in the trench at Chapultepec, side by side with the two Confederates—Longstreet and Pickett—who were with him now on this field. Armistead was chafing because his brigade was not in the lead in this charge. Not even West Point had been able to harness his passions; he was "found," and ejected, it is said, in part for smashing a plate over Jubal Early's head in the mess hall. Considering the quality of the mess and Early's cantankerous personality, it may have been justified. Armistead was now in his forties, a widower in whom the passion for battle burned more fiercely than ever.[64]

"Rise men," he shouted, his voice, cavernous under ordinary conditions, blaring now like a bugle blast. "Men, remember what you are fighting for. Remember your homes, your firesides, your wives, mothers, sisters and your sweethearts." It was Armistead's set speech before every battle; it's what he always said.

"Sergeant," he demanded, addressing the color-bearer of his lead regiment, the Fifty-third Virginia, "are you going to put those colors on the enemy's works over yonder?"

"Yes, General," the sergeant replied, "if mortal man can do it."[65]

Richard Garnett had been ill. He shouldn't have been there at all. But there he was, ever courteous, kind, warm-hearted, and ready to fight. Before the war, he had been a strong Union man. The only public address he ever made was against secession. But when the war came he went with his state. He had never gotten over his rebuke and arrest by Stonewall Jackson after the battle of Kernstown in the Valley. Ever since, he had seemed anxious to expose himself, even unnecessarily, to wipe out by some distinctive action what he considered the unmerited slur on his courage and reputation. He had nothing to prove; nobody alive doubted his courage or questioned his reputation. But it seemed he must prove it anyhow.[66]

He was puffing quietly on his cigar as Pickett rode up.

"Have you any further instructions?" Garnett asked.

"No, Dick," Pickett answered, "I don't recollect anything else—unless it be to advise you to make the best kind of time in crossing the valley; *it's a h——l of an ugly looking place over yonder.*"[67]

Garnett privately agreed with Pickett. "This is a desperate thing to attempt," he confided to Armistead.

"It is," Armistead conceded, "but the issue is with the Almighty, and we must leave it in his hands."

Cadmus Wilcox rode up to Pickett and offered his flask. "Take a drink with me," he suggested, "in an hour you'll be in hell or glory."[68]

Pickett didn't need a pull; he was ready for either hell or glory without it. In a strong, clear voice, he commanded, "Forward! Guide Center! March!"[69]

James Pettigrew, the North Carolinian commanding the division in the center of the Confederate line, turned to Colonel J. K. Marshall, commanding his first brigade, and said, "Now Colonel, for the honor of the good Old North State. Forward."[70]

"Follow me!" roared Armistead as he unloosed his collar, threw off his cravat, placed his old black hat on the point of his sword, lifted it high over his head, and strode away at the front of his brigade of Virginians toward Cemetery Ridge.[71]

The Confederate line, more than half a mile long, moved up the slope, dressing on Birkett Fry in tight and perfect alignment. As they passed between the still smoking, but now silent row of cannon, the powder-grimed cannoneers watched from astride their pieces and cheered.[72]

James Longstreet stood beside Alexander on the artillery line, peering through his binoculars toward the stone wall across the valley. Alexander spoke. He told Longstreet that a battery of seven guns he had been counting on to support the advance were no longer available. He also told him that his ammunition supply was so low he could not properly support the charge now getting underway.

Longstreet was aghast. He ordered Alexander to stop Pickett's advance at once, until the supply could be replenished.

"There is no ammunition with which to replenish," Alexander said simply.

Longstreet sagged in despair. It had become one of the saddest days of his life. He would gladly at that moment have given up his rank, his position, everything, rather than let Pickett continue with this charge.[73]

But what could he do now to stop it? He lifted his binoculars to his eyes again, helpless to do anything. "I don't want to make this attack," he said grimly, pausing to search the Union position, perhaps seeking some sign of hope or reassurance and finding none. "I believe it will fail." He paused again. "I do not see how it can succeed." Another pause. "I would not make it even now, but that Gen. Lee has ordered & expects it."[74]

Alexander said nothing.

Now the army was passing. Pickett rode gracefully at the head of his division, his cap raked well over his right ear and his perfumed locks corkscrewing nearly to his shoulders. He seemed to Longstreet to look more the holiday soldier than a general about to lead one of the most desperate charges in military history. Longstreet felt another tug as he watched Brigadier James Kemper pass, leading the old brigade Longstreet himself had drilled and commanded at First Manassas.[75]

Alexander stared at the long line sweeping out of the woods and over the ridge, and it brought a lump to his throat. He thought it as grand a sight as ever a man looked upon: Who could see it without feeling pride in it? As Garnett passed and saluted Longstreet, Alexander galloped out and reined up next to him, and they rode on side by side for a few paces. The two men were old friends. They had crossed the plains together in 1858, along with Armistead. Alexander remembered how their favorite songs had been "Willie Brewed a Peck of Malt" and "Wife, Children & Friends," and how they had sung them together on the long trek across the frontier. After a moment, Alexander wished Garnett good luck, and returned to his guns.[76]

Pickett's and Pettigrew's divisions cleared the woods, and the sun glanced from the shining steel of their bayonets. Across the valley on Cemetery Ridge, the Union army saw the glistening line emerge and caught its collective breath. It was a sight such as they had never seen before and would never see again.

Where Is
My Division?

The officers on horseback appeared first over the brow of the ridge, rising gradually into view, their sabers glinting in the sun. Behind them followed the soldiers on foot, a solid gathering wall of butternut and gray, their bayonets flashing. Dust, "like the dash of spray at the prow of a vessel," rose gently from under the thousands of marching feet. Regimental flags fluttered and snapped. Along the line the low, muted commands of the officers rose almost inaudibly above the rustle of a great army in motion.[1]

Across the valley on the other ridge, the spellbound Union soldiers reacted according to the condition of their hopes and fears.

"Thank God! There comes the infantry!" one of them said, too glad to be rid of the oppressive cannonade to appreciate this new and ultimate terror marching toward them through the sultry afternoon.[2] But most of the men behind the stone wall understood all too well what was coming and what it meant. "We looked one another in the face," said one, "examined our muskets and said, 'Now we are in for it sure.' "[3]

A staff officer appeared leading a horse for John Gibbon. General, he told him, the rebels are coming in force. Gibbon mounted and galloped to the top of the hill. The sight was magnificent—spectacular enough, Gibbon thought, to excite the admiration of everyone. The first Confederate line was followed by a second, and yet a third, extending as far as he could see.[4]

Gibbon rode along his own line, cautioning his soldiers. "Do not hurry men, and fire too fast," he urged, "let them come up close before you fire, and then aim low and steadily." He turned to Frank Haskell, and ordered him to ride immediately to General Meade and tell him that the enemy was advancing.[5]

Behind the Union line Chaplain Winfield Scott walked with an old classmate from the University of Rochester. "Well, Scott," his friend said, "we have sat beside each other in the classroom many a day; but this is a new experience. This isn't much like digging out Greek roots."

Amen, thought Scott. He gazed at the Confederate army advancing toward them. To him the guns and the bayonets gleaming in the sunlight made the marching line look like a moving river of pure silver. A passage of scripture came to mind and he repeated it aloud: "Fair as the moon, bright as the sun, and terrible as an army with banners."[6]

The Confederates themselves were impressed by its grandeur. One of them, a veteran of other battles, believed it to be the most imposing sight he ever saw.[7] But the spectacle that lay ahead of them was just as imposing and far more frightening. Most of them were seeing it for the first time—the thicket of bristling Union muskets and bayonets, and the blackened mouths of the cannon waiting for them on the ridge behind the stone wall. Death and destruction hung in suspension, ready to drop on them at an instant.[8]

Suddenly it did, with the thunder-roll of a hundred guns. A storm of shot, shell, and shrapnel rained down, and seemed to take their breaths away, "causing whole regiments to stoop like men running in a violent sleet." Their only cover was the still-hovering smoke of the preceding cannonade. Shot and shell streamed in from the battery on Little Round Top, a single ball sweeping away half a dozen men at a time. Gaps opened, great jagged rents in the line. "Close up, men!" "Close up!"—an officer's head is blown off by a round shot and the men step over his body. "Not too fast on the left"—"Major, take command, the Colonel is down."[9]

"Always willing when Bob Lee wants me to fight for him," one Confederate said, "but I tell you that he puts me in some tight places sometimes. . . . They poured in the grape shot, canister and shells to us like hail, but on we went, now & then a man's hand or arm or leg would fly like feathers before the wind."[10] Another soldier compared crossing the tempest-swept field to a man pressing against a "a blinding storm."[11] But on they came, closing up, keeping the same steady forward movement even as their lines were being blown away and their numbers decimated. It seemed to an officer in the Sixty-ninth Pennsylvania watching them come "as if no power could hold them in check."[12] The Union brigadier, Alexander Hays, thought they came as if impelled by machinery.[13] The crash of shell and solid shot howling and whistling through their ranks seemed to make no impression. There was not a wavering in the line.[14]

The Union soldiers stared, appalled by the slaughter on the field in front of them. "Men went down like grain before the reaper," one soldier wrote. The gaps opened and closed, opened and closed. "Moments," said Chaplain Scott, "seemed ages. The shock to heart and nerve was awful." Admiration for the courage of this implacable advancing enemy was universal in the Union ranks. They advanced, said a major from the 116th Pennsylvania, "with a degree of ardor, coolness, and bravery worthy of a better cause."[15]

The marching line reached the fences that bordered the Emmitsburg road. As the soldiers scaled them, reformed, and began to push forward again, the Union infantry opened fire. Five thousand muskets poured bullets on top of the shot and shell. The Union line appeared suddenly to be "a sheet of fire, backed by a wall of steel." It seemed inconceivable that any man could march through that merciless storm and still live.[16] "The hiss of bullets was incessant," a Confederate officer wrote. "Men fell at every step; they fell, I thought, like grass before the scythe."[17] A soldier wrote, "You may judge of how severe the fire was between the contending armies when I say that the green grass burned."[18]

Armistead's booming voice roared above the tumult, "Steady, men! Steady."[19] A captain urged his command plaintively, "Don't crowd, boys; don't crowd." A colonel passing him said, "Pretty hot, Captain." "It's redicklous, Colonel; perfectly redicklous," and the colonel knew that coming from him that meant it was as bad as it could get.[20]

Robert W. Morgan of James Kemper's brigade was drilled in the instep of his right foot by a minie ball. As he stooped to see if he was hurt bad enough to go to the rear, a second ball struck his left foot at the back of his toes, tore through the full length of the foot, and lodged in his heel. That decided it. Picking up his own musket and another of a fallen comrade, he jammed the butt of each under an armpit, and using them for crutches hopped back toward Seminary Ridge.[21]

James Longstreet sat on a fence watching the fire-sheeted storm. It was all he feared it would be. He saw the withering musket fire erupt from behind the stone wall—the puff of smoke, the blinding, withering blast, and the long sheet of flame and lightning. When the smoke cleared, nearly two-thirds of Pickett's division no longer existed. But still the remnant moved on, closing up. Longstreet's practiced eye saw that the charge was failing. Pettigrew's left flank was beginning to crumble, and the disintegration was sweeping swiftly along the line toward Pickett's division.[22]

Arthur Freemantle, the observer from the British Coldstream Guards, rode up flush with excitement.

"General," he exclaimed, "I wouldn't have missed this for any thing."

"The devil you wouldn't!" Longstreet retorted. "I would like to have missed it very much; we've attacked and been repulsed: look there!"

Freemantle had not yet seen the crumbling of the line on the army's left and the beginning of the retreat: he had thought the charge was succeeding. But Longstreet knew better. They could not hold together ten minutes longer. What was left of Pickett's division would strike the Union position and be crushed. The attack was doomed.[23]

Pickett's men were marching now to the stone wall. Halfway across the valley they had executed a wheeling movement to the left, putting them on a direct line toward the clump of trees. The movement left the division's right flank utterly exposed to Union view. Wilcox would have covered it, but he had not yet been ordered to advance.

One of the first Union officers to see it was Brigadier General George Jerrison Stannard, commanding the nine-month Vermont brigade. Stannard was said to have been the first man in Vermont to volunteer when the war came.[24] In two years of fighting since then, he had never seen an opportunity such as this. Quickly he moved the

Thirteenth and Sixteenth regiments of his brigade out on the exposed Confederate flank.

"Change front forward on first company," he ordered, and the Thirteenth Vermont swung around squarely on Pickett's flank, rotating like a wheel around First Sergeant James B. Scully of Company A. Scully would be described later as the pivot of the pivotal movement of the pivotal battle of the war. The Sixteenth Vermont drew up on the left, and the two regiments opened fire point-blank, not a dozen rods from the Confederate flank. Every bullet hit something.[25]

H. T. Owen, of the Ninth Virginia, saw it coming: "Off to the right, there appeared in the open field a line of men at right angles with our own—a long, dark mass, dressed in blue and coming down at a 'double quick' upon the unprotected right flank of Pickett's men, with their muskets upon the 'right shoulder shift,' their battle flags dancing and fluttering in the breeze, created by their own rapid motion, and their burnished bayonets glistening above their heads like forest twigs covered with sheets of sparkling ice when shaken by a blast."[26]

Under this ruinous fire Pickett's men reeled and staggered and fell. The right of the line pressed against the center, crowding the companies into confusion. Garnett galloped along the line, shouting, "Faster, men! faster!" as his soldiers neared the stone wall and the clump of trees.[27]

One soldier, John Dooley, could have been speaking for them all when he said, "But who can stand such a storm of hissing lead and iron? What a relief if earth, which almost seems to hurl these implements of death in our faces, would open now and afford a secure retreat from threatening death."[28]

What happened in the First Virginia regiment in this murderous advance was typical. Its colonel was struck down almost immediately. A major took command and also was hit. A captain jumped to the front and was instantly bowled over. Such death-dealing descent down the chains of command ran through every regiment like a flame at the end of a fuse. By the time they neared the stone wall and were returning fire for fire, the regiments of every brigade were but skeletons of themselves, reduced to mere skirmish lines.[29]

None of this was in keeping with Confederate Brigadier James Kemper's general line of work. He had attended VMI, but he was not a professional soldier. He was a politician and a lawyer, a five-term member of the Virginia House of Delegates, the chairman of its Committee on Military Affairs, and but little more than a year ago—its speaker. But he was also a fighter, and had proved it on other fields. His men loved him for his fine bearing, fearlessness, dash, and politician's eloquence. Officers prized his good sense and high conception of duty.[30]

Rising in his stirrups, he shouted, "There are the guns, boys, go for them." Everything was now in a kaleidoscopic whirl.[31] But Kemper could see with crystal clarity—far clearer perhaps than he cared to. He was within yards of the Union troops, so near that he could make out the expressions on their faces—so near that he thought he could identify the individual soldier who shot him.[32]

Birkett Fry heard Richard Garnett give a command to his men, which in the din of the musketry he couldn't make out.

"I am dressing on you," Garnett shouted to him.

Those were perhaps the last words Garnett uttered. As Fry watched, a blast of canister caught him at the waist and wrenched him from his saddle. He probably never saw who shot him or knew what hit him. When the blast pulled him down, his horse, its shoulder ripped open by a shell, bolted and galloped away, leaving his rider free at last of Stonewall Jackson's curse.[33]

A moment later a bullet ripped into Fry's thigh, and he dropped instantly. Fry knew bullets. He had taken several of them on other fields. Earlier on this day, during the bombardment, he had been hit again in the shoulder by a shell fragment. But this last hit was a bad one. He was prostrate, couldn't move, couldn't get up, couldn't hope to continue.

Several of his soldiers leaped to his side, but he waved them off. "Go on," he shouted, "it will not last five minutes longer!" Fry believed if they could just reach the stone wall, the charge would succeed.[34]

Two-thirds of Pettigrew's division was now gone, blown away in the firestorm. It had absorbed the same punishment Pickett's had, and its collapse reached Fry's brigade just as its remnants hit the stone wall.

In Armistead's Virginia brigade, the colors tumbled to the ground and a sergeant named Robert Tyler Jones, a grandson of ex-President John Tyler, snatched them up and shook their folds in the air. Armistead said to him, "Run ahead, Bob, and cheer them up!" Jones ran past him, waving the colors over his head.

Armistead's men—all that was left of them—followed in a wild charge.[35]

Private William Monte, of the Portsmouth Rifle Company, took his watch from his pocket when the Confederate line was near enough to return fire and announced, "We have been just nineteen minutes coming." At that instant Monte had but two minutes left to live.[36]

Time, if not life, was also running out for John Gibbon. As he labored to swing one of his regiments out on the Confederate flank—for he saw the same opportunity Vermont's George Stannard had seen—he felt a stinging blow behind his left shoulder. Blood trickled down his sleeve over his left hand, and within minutes he felt himself beginning to lose consciousness. He ordered the command of his division turned over to Brigadier General William Harrow, and staggered from the field, the tumult of the battle ringing in his ears.[37]

Armistead's cap, which had been sliding down the shank of his saber to the hilt, was again at the tip, hoisted aloft, still guiding the storm.[38] At the stone wall, the fire was galling, and Armistead's position was untenable. He turned to Rawley Martin.

"Colonel," he said, "we cannot stay here."

"Forward with the colors," Martin shouted.

"Follow me, boys," Armistead roared, "give them the cold steel."[39]

What was left of his brigade—less than two hundred men—followed him over the wall, into what James Kemper called that "cul-de-sac of death"—into a "hell of fire," as another described it, where "nothing could live."[40]

President Tyler's grandson was already there, fallen with his colors now and bleeding from a shot in the head, but waving his pistol and threatening to shoot the first man who thought of surrender. Colonel Rawley Martin would fall beyond the wall at Armistead's side, hit in four places, his thigh shattered. Few officers in fact still stood. Colonel Joseph Mayo, Kemper's second in command, heard the dreaded hissing, "like the hooded cobra's whisper of death," followed by a deafening explosion, a sharp pang of pain somewhere in his body, and a momentary blank. When he regained his feet there were splinters of bone and lumps of flesh sticking to his clothing.[41]

For a moment, the Union line staggered under the impact of the Confederate charge. In and around the clump of trees there was pandemonium, all the fighting now hand to hand. "Every foot of ground," a Union officer said, "was occupied by men engaged in mortal combat." Every man in the copse of trees was either fighting, or lying wounded and dead under the feet of those who were.[42]

Armistead leaped to one of the Union guns. "The day is ours men," he cried, "come turn this artillery upon them." Erasmus Williams, who had dug his hole in the woods and survived the cannonade, was still surviving. He leaped to Armistead's side and caught his left forefinger in the gun, ripping the flesh as if sliced by a knife. They turned the guns, but a withering fire from federal reinforcements caught Armistead, and he slumped to the ground. The sword with the hat at its tip, which had led the storm for so long, fell beside him. Within moments he would be a prisoner. Within two days he would be dead.[43]

Also dead was the charge. The clump of trees was as far as the assault would go. The Confederacy had reached high tide. Union Colonel Norman J. Hall, commanding one of Gibbon's brigades, said later: "The decision of the rebel commander was upon that point; the concentration of artillery fire was upon that point; the din of battle developed in a column of attack upon that point; the greatest effort and the greatest carnage was at that point; and the victory was at that point." Brigadier Alexander Hays, commanding a federal division at the wall, said, "the angel of death alone can produce such a field as was presented." To Edward Porter Alexander, watching horrified from his line of guns on Seminary Ridge, "it seemed as if . . . human life was being poured out like water."[44]

Nobody on the field watched with greater horror than George Pickett. As his division marched on into the storm, he had peeled off to take a position that commanded a full view of the field. It was the job of the brigadiers and colonels to lead the charge; it was his job to stay alive and direct it.

He saw his line collapsing from the right to the left. He saw the remnants of his once proud division, Armistead with his hat on his sword, drive a narrow wedge into the federal line at the clump of trees. He saw his Virginians touch the vital point. He saw them stretch out a hand to grasp the victory. But suddenly there was only defeat.

Where was the rest of the army? Where was his support? Where then were Corse and Jenkins? With them, his two brigades left behind in Richmond and Petersburg, he might have kept his grip on this victory. But all he could see now was his line collapsing from end to end.[45]

Desperately he turned to a classmate for help. Cadmus Wilcox was his division's one remaining hope. Pickett sent one staff officer, and immediately afterward a second, with orders for Wilcox to begin his advance. Within moments after the first two messengers left, Pickett called up yet a third, Captain Robert A. Bright.

"Captain Bright," he said, "you go."

When Bright rode up, Wilcox was standing with both hands raised, shouting and waving him off. "I know, I know."

"But, General," Bright said, "I must deliver my message."[46]

When Bright had delivered it and returned, Pickett sent him galloping immediately to James Dearing's artillery battalion with orders to open fire on the column of federal troops now moving against his left flank. Bright returned to tell Pickett that the guns were virtually without ammunition. The meaning was clear. The enemy was closing around his command; nothing could be done to save his division. He could only watch it disintegrate. Even then, however, Pickett had not seen the worst. He had been so intent on watching the trouble on the left that he had not even seen Stannard's Vermont regiments pivoting into point-blank range of his exposed right.[47]

Wilcox, with his orders in triplicate from Pickett, put his twelve hundred men, including his own Alabama regiments and the Florida troops under Colonel David Lang, in motion. His eyes expectantly searched his front, but not a man of the division that he was ordered to support could he see. They simply didn't exist. But he had his orders, and he kept moving on toward the Union position, straight toward Stannard's Vermont brigade. If nobody else was going to call this off, neither was he—not yet anyhow. Stannard's men, preoccupied with taking prisoners, looked up with a start to see Wilcox "wandering across the field" toward them, not veering to the left as Pickett's division had done, but coming straight on. The Sixteenth Vermont swung about to confront this unexpected new arrival. The Union artillery opened fire.

Wilcox ordered his men to hold their ground as best they could, and galloped back for artillery support. But like Bright, he could find no guns that had ammunition. Having no hope of artillery support, still seeing none of the troops he had been summoned to help, and knowing his small force could do nothing but make a useless sacrifice of themselves, he ordered them back. The roar of artillery and small arms fire was so deafening that Colonel Lang could not make himself heard. His Floridians were badly scattered in the bushes and among the rocks, hemmed in front and flank by the federal artillery raking them with shell and canister. He knew they faced certain annihilation if they stayed there or attempted to advance farther, so he screamed for a retreat. Even that wasn't widely heard. Edward Alexander, seeing tragedy piling upon tragedy everywhere he looked, watched Wilcox and Lang hit this wall of fire, so senselessly late, and called it "at once both absurd and tragic."[48]

In the bloody maelstrom that was the clump of trees, the tattered remnants of Pickett's and Pettigrew's divisions looked up and saw Union reinforcements moving on them from in front. Looking behind they saw no help coming over the storm-raked field they had just crossed—no support at all from the rest of the Army of Northern Virginia. The entire Confederate line on the left had been swept away. Despite Bob Tyler Jones's threatening pistol, men with nowhere to go were falling prisoner wholesale.

Erasmus Williams, so skillful at seeing a need and taking measures, was still alive in the holocaust behind the wall. He now was seeing another urgent, very primitive need. If he had been consulted when Armistead had hesitated at the wall and Martin had shouted, "On with the colors," he would have proposed an alternative. But he was just an enlisted man. Moments later, before Martin fell riddled with four bullets, he offered his alternative anyhow.

"Look, Major," he said, "the Yankees are flanking us, we must get out from here."

"No, hold on men, rally, rally, right here!" Martin shouted. When Armistead fell, Williams began backing away, suggesting once again to Martin, "We must get away from here, Major."

But it was too late. Martin fell too, with his four bullets and his shattered hip. Williams moved swiftly now, striking out across the bloodied field on his own, back toward Seminary Ridge.[49]

George L. Christian, a Confederate cannoneer, watched from Seminary Ridge behind the disappearing line commanded by Isaac Trimble on the Union right. As he watched he became conscious that

Lieutenant General A. P. Hill was standing with him, not ten feet from his gun.

He watched Hill's face as Trimble's troops, men of his own corps, faltered, broke, and fell back. It seemed to Christian that Hill looked dazed and confounded by what was happening. It was a face he would not forget as long as he lived. Beyond the stone wall they could clearly see the federal reinforcements moving toward the Confederates in the clump of trees. Several of the artillery officers begged Hill to let them reopen on the Union reinforcements. They believed that with their guns they could turn the battle around. No, Hill said, the ammunition was too dear and too nearly exhausted. It must be saved for whatever was to come of this. A victory on that field was simply not to be.[50]

On the field itself Isaac Trimble was of the same mind. At sixty-one, Trimble was one of the oldest officers in the Confederate army, as old as the military academy from which he had graduated in 1822. With his fierce eyes and drooping moustache, he looked to be what he was—an aging but ferocious fighter. "There was fight enough in old man Trimble," Henry Kyd Douglas said, "to satisfy a herd of tigers."[51] He had fought under Jackson and Ewell in the Valley, and like Ewell had been desperately wounded at Second Manassas. He had returned to duty not ten days before Gettysburg, after nearly a year of convalescence. Only that afternoon, just before the cannonade, he had assumed command of the division of the wounded General Dorsey Pender. Now he was with it on that bloody field, commanding men he did not even know.

He had started his troops out across the open field two hundred yards behind Pettigrew's line, riding on horseback between his two brigades. They had marched steadily on, under a murderous artillery and infantry fire in front, a severe artillery fire on the right, and an enfilade of musketry on the left. Trimble had watched as Pettigrew's division seemed to sink into the earth and disappear.[52] About two-thirds of the way across, panicked troops from in front began tearing back through his ranks, causing some of his own men to bolt as well. But those who were left kept on until the right of the brigade touched the Union breastworks. By then Trimble's division had been reduced to no more than eight hundred muskets. His was now the only loosely cohesive Confederate command still on the field, and there was no support in view. His soldiers hesitated; there was also nobody now to tell them what to do or where to go. So they decided for themselves, and began retreating across a field that was as deadly in the going as it had been coming.[53]

Trimble was hit—yet again—and sat bleeding on his horse. His aide, Charley Grogan, helped him dismount and asked, "General, the men are falling back, shall I rally them?"

Trimble looked to the right toward Pickett's division and saw nothing but a few men in squads moving to the rear.

"No, Charley," he said quietly, "the best thing these brave fellows can do is to get out of this."

Remounting his horse, he rode back, slowly following them from the field.[54]

Major General Lafayette McLaws, watching from Seminary Ridge, saw the Confederate line hit the Union breastworks and rebound "like an Indian rubber ball."[55] The handful of soldiers who had survived getting there were now desperately trying to get back. They were dodging and weaving over a field littered with dead and dying men, pounded by shot and shell that tore the earth around them, and by hissing musket balls that filled the air.[56]

It was just one more "mighty unnatural storm." It was "as if all nature's power and strength were turned into one mighty upheaval; Vessuvius, Etna, and Popocatepetl . . . emptying their mighty torrents upon the heads of the unfortunate Confederates."[57]

Erasmus Williams had gone scarcely twenty-five yards when he was shot through the left wrist. June Kimble, who had kept his promise to himself and done his duty that day, sprinted from the stone wall, and for about one hundred yards "broke the lightning speed record." Then he remembered he had a horror of being shot in the back, so he faced about and back-pedaled the rest of the way out of range. General Pettigrew, with the bones of his left hand shattered by canister shot, was one of the last to leave.[58]

As the torn fragments of regiments, brigades, and divisions stumbled back into the Confederate line, the first thought on Robert E. Lee's mind—and James Longstreet's—was to brace for a Union counterattack. Already federal skirmishers were advancing in the train of the retreating Confederates. Longstreet immediately sent staff officers to begin collecting what was left of his command. Lee went out among the returning soldiers.[59]

As Randolph A. Shotwell dragged himself over the brow of Seminary Ridge, one of the first things he saw was Lee on horseback, his bridle rein lying carelessly across his horse's neck. Shotwell saw in the general's bearing an ineffable sadness, weariness, and regretfulness "such as I had never known in him before." Shotwell saluted and started to pass by when to his surprise Lee asked, "Are you wounded?"

"No, General—only a little fatigued," Shotwell answered, "but I am afraid there are but few so lucky as myself."

"Ah! Yes—I am very sorry—the task was too great for you—but we mustn't despond—another time we shall succeed. Are you one of Pickett's men?"

"Yes, sir," Shotwell said.

"Well, you had better go back and rest yourself," Lee said. "Captain Linthicum will tell you the rendezvous for your brigade."

In the rear Shotwell found C. F. Linthicum, Garnett's adjutant general, standing by Garnett's wounded horse with his head against the animal's bloody mane, silently weeping.[60]

Lee continued to ride among the returning soldiers, telling them as they passed, "It was all my fault; get together, and let us do the best we can toward saving that which is left us."[61]

"How are you off for ammunition, Major," he asked William T. Poague, commanding a battery of artillery.

Poague told him how much he had left—about one-fourth of a full supply. But he had ordered up six howitzers that had been sequestered in a protected part of the woods. They would have full chests.

"Ah! that's well," Lee said, "we may need them."[62]

George Pickett stared numbly at the bloodied battlefield, tears welling in his eyes.

"Great God," he said, "where, oh! where is my division?"[63]

A soldier watched the tears stream down his cheeks and heard him sob, "My brave men! My brave men!"[64]

William Poague had himself been staring at the field in disbelief, watching the small clumps of men stagger back toward Seminary Ridge, and wondering what he ought to do now. Suddenly Pickett was beside him on horseback.

"General," Poague said to him, "my orders are that as soon as our troops get the hill I am to move as rapidly as possible to their support. But I don't like the look of things up there."

Pickett neither replied nor turned his head to see who was speaking, but continued to gaze across the valley with eyes brimming with sadness and pain. At that moment a Virginia flag was borne rapidly aloft along the stone wall by a horseman.

"General," Poague exclaimed, "is that Virginia flag carried by one of our men or by the enemy?"

Pickett still did not reply.

"What do you think I ought to do under the circumstances?" Poague asked urgently. "Our men are leaving the hill."

At last Pickett spoke. "I think you had better save your guns."

He rode away leaving Poague wondering exactly what that meant. But now the gunner knew what he must do. He must prepare to meet the Union advance certain to follow.[65]

To Longstreet, Pickett said, "General, I am ruined; my division is gone—it is destroyed." He exclaimed, bitterly, that if he had had his two missing brigades left in Richmond and Petersburg he could have broken the Union line.[66]

Lee said to him, "General Pickett, place your division in rear of this hill, and be ready to repel the advance of the enemy should they follow up their advantage."

"General Lee," Pickett said, "I have no division now, Armistead is down, Garnett is down, and Kemper is mortally wounded."

"Come, General Pickett," Lee said, "this has been my fight and upon my shoulders rests the blame. The men and officers of your command have written the name of Virginia as high to-day as it has ever been written before."[67]

It was high praise from the great man, glory enough for one hundred years, thought Captain Robert Bright, who was standing with Pickett. But for Pickett it was empty consolation. His magnificent division had been hopelessly shattered in one brief hour in which "glory and disaster rode arm in arm."[68]

A litter bearing a wounded officer covered with a blanket was carried past by four soldiers, one of them the ubiquitous Erasmus Williams.

"Captain," Lee asked Robert Bright, "what officer is that they are bearing off?"

"General Kemper," Bright answered.

"I must speak to him," Lee said, reining his horse toward the litter.

The bearers halted and Kemper opened his eyes.

"General Kemper," Lee began, "I hope you are not very seriously wounded."

"I am struck in the groin, and the ball has ranged upwards," Kemper replied. "They tell me it is mortal."

Lee was distressed. "I hope it will not prove so bad as that," he said. "Is there anything I can do for you, General Kemper?"

Kemper raised himself painfully on one elbow. "Yes, General Lee," he said, "do full justice to this division for its work today."

"I will," Lee promised.[69]

Both glory and disaster were at an end for that day. Meade did not intend to follow up the repulse. He had thrown off the enemy attack and that was enough. Even as Lee and Longstreet braced for his counterassault, Meade was issuing orders to his army to reform and keep their places in the event of another Confederate attack.[70]

But Lee was reeling. This invasion of Pennsylvania had cost him a third of his army—and perhaps the war. He couldn't have attacked again if he wanted. The battle of Gettysburg, the invasion, was over.

At muster of Pickett's division the next morning the toll was evident. Not a thousand survivors answered the call. Four of every five of Pickett's men had been either killed, wounded, or captured. Two of his three brigadiers were gone, probably dead, the third perhaps mortally wounded. Every one of his regimental commanders had been killed, wounded, or captured.

"We gained nothing but glory," one surviving officer sighed, "and lost our bravest men."[71]

For some reason nobody could explain, the Confederates had pulled their punch. They had not thrown the full power of the Army of Northern Virginia at the Union army. Only eleven infantry brigades had carried the fight. Another twenty-seven had not been used; many had merely watched. It had been the grandest charge ever made by an army on this continent, and it had all been a forlorn hope.

At about 1:00 the next morning, Lee rode weary, dejected, and alone to his headquarters. Waiting for him there in the warm, moonlit night, on the grass under a tree, was John Imboden, commanding the army's rear guard. Lee spoke to him, reined in, and started to dismount. The effort betrayed such physical exhaustion that Imboden stepped forward to help. But before he could reach Lee's side, the general had alighted.

There he sagged with one arm across his saddle, leaning heavily against his horse, his eyes fixed on the ground. The moon shone full on his haggard face, illuminating an expression of sadness deeper than Imboden had ever seen. After a few moments of uncomfortable silence, Imboden spoke.

"General, this has been a hard day on you."

Lee looked up and said, "Yes, it has been a sad, sad day to us." He fell silent again.

Imboden waited, but said no more.

After a moment or two, Lee suddenly straightened to his full height, as Imboden would recall a generation later, and said: "I never saw troops behave more magnificently than Pickett's division of Virginians did to-day in that grand charge upon the enemy. And if they had been supported as they were to have been,—but, for some reason not yet fully explained to me, were not,—we would have held the position and the day would have been ours."

He paused. Then in a loud and sorrowing voice he cried, "Too bad! *Too bad!* OH! TOO BAD!"[72]

PART 6

CLOSING OUT THE WAR

The Meeting
on the
Court House Steps

It was worse than Lee imagined. It was the beginning of the end. There would be no more stunning victories for him such as Chancellorsville. There would be instead dramatic Union victories in the West—the surrender of Vicksburg the day after the defeat at Gettysburg, the fall of Atlanta, and Major General William T. Sherman's march to the sea. For Lee in the East it would just be more fighting: the grim scorching, man-killing defensive battles in the Wilderness, the bloody encounter at Spotsylvania Court House, the senseless Union charge at Cold Harbor—all leading to the tedious standoff in the trenches at Petersburg.

In March 1864, Abraham Lincoln made a lieutenant general of Sam Grant. Grant had come far since that early summer twenty-three years before when as a first-classman he had watched the plebes of the class of 1846 struggle up from the steamboat landing. On April Fools' Day in 1865, Grant finally succeeded in doing something to Lee's Army of Northern Virginia that Lee had done so often to Union armies in the past—when Tom Jackson was still alive. He turned his right flank.

After months of denying Grant victory in the trenches before Petersburg, Lee's army was suddenly in peril. His right had been smashed at Five Forks, Petersburg and Richmond were lost, and time was running out for the Confederacy. There was nothing he could do now but retreat west along the line of the Appomattox River. The one hope was to slip the noose Grant was tightening about him and make for Danville. From there he might yet unite with Joseph E. Johnston's remnant of an army in the Carolinas.

Lee lit out in that direction on the run. Instantly the Union cavalry under Major General Philip H. Sheridan leaped to the pursuit, paralleling his retreat, striking at him as he ran. Grant's armies of the Potomac and the James followed in full cry. It became a running fight toward a little town in the middle of Virginia called Appomattox Court House.

From that moment on Lee's ragged, hungry army knew no rest. "Not only was my command in almost incessant battle as we covered the retreat," said Lee's combatative little corps commander, John Gordon, "but every portion of our marching column was being assailed by Grant's cavalry and infantry. The roads and fields and woods swarmed with eager pursuers."[1]

Like a fox chased by hounds, a tattered Confederate division would turn to snap at the pursuers, checking them momentarily to let some other Confederate command move on. Lee was everywhere, watching everything. But it was a grim, depressing business. His once proud army was but a battle-weary remnant of what it had been, reduced to two consolidated corps under Longstreet and Gordon. Jackson was nearly two years dead. A. P. Hill had been gunned down and killed on April 2 attempting to rally his corps at Petersburg. Ewell, back fighting again on his wooden right leg, had been taken prisoner during the retreat, at a fight in the bottomlands of Sayler's Creek on April 6. The Confederates called the Sayler's Creek disaster Black Thursday. Eight thousand rebels, including six generals—a quarter of Lee's rebel army—were captured.

For those who were left it continued to be "march, march, march night and day," as one Confederate officer described it, "no sleeping, no cooking, save a piece of cornbread and a slice of bacon, stuck on a stick and held to the fire." Yankees were everywhere, before and behind, on both flanks, forcing them from a line of railroad over which they might get supplies, to another on which they could get nothing. The ration was two ears of parched corn a day, and a day's supply of raw bacon for an entire week.[2] Not only were feet and body weary and sore, but so were gums and teeth.[3]

Sheridan's cavalry, supported by the Army of the Potomac's Fifth Corps commanded by Major General Charles Griffin, raced to get around in front of the retreating Confederates. The way was shrouded in constant smoke and dust. Firearms rattled and artillery roared in an unending counterpoint, threatening at any moment to break out in yet one more general engagement. A pace behind Sheridan and Griffin marched Major General John Gibbon's Twenty-fourth Corps of the Army of the James. The rest of Major General George Meade's Army of the Potomac pressed hard on Lee's rear. There was no letup, no relief, nowhere to go but ahead. And how long would even that be possible?

Pattie Guild was caught in the path of the Union juggernaut. She had been traveling with her husband, Dr. Lafayette Guild, the chief surgeon of Lee's Army of Northern Virginia. In the chaos of the flight, her husband had left her in a house on the way that seemed safe at the time. But suddenly it, too, was besieged, like everything else Confederate, and filled with marauding Union troops. As she wondered what was to become of her, she heard a soldier mention John Gibbon's name. Gibbon was near—a ray of hope. She asked the Union soldiers if she could send him a note.

As she hastily wrote, the memory of Gibbon, such a dear friend of her and her husband in the Old Army, came flooding back. Could he help her now? Would he help her?

The reply came almost instantly from Gibbon, saying he would come to her immediately. Even as she was reading his note, he appeared at her door, "the same kind old friend" he had always been. He ordered a guard thrown around the house to protect her, and then pushed on in pursuit of her fleeing husband.[4]

On the night of April 8, Sheridan's cavalry got around in front of Lee's army at about sundown and captured four railway trains of supplies and twenty-six pieces of artillery that had been sent to Lee from Lynchburg. There, just beyond Appomattox Station, Sheridan threw his cavalry across Lee's front, blocking his one way of escape.

It was late when George A. Forsyth, one of Sheridan's young colonels, swung wearily down from his saddle. It had been a hard day.

But it was now a mild spring night under a cloudy sky, and the soft mellow smell of earthiness was in the air, the kind of feel to it that so often foreshadows a coming rain. Sheridan had urgently sent for the infantry to come up, to put the seal on things, for he could not contain Lee's army without help.

As one of Forsyth's men started to lead the colonel's horse away to be fed, groomed, and saddled before daylight, he asked, "Do you think, Colonel, that we'll get General Lee's army tomorrow?"

It was not a question Forsyth could answer. But he did feel certain about one thing. One way or the other, tomorrow's sun would rise big with the fate of the Southern Confederacy.[5]

Lee must have shared this feeling of grim inevitability. Suddenly there was nowhere for him to go. Sheridan was across the road in front of him. Union infantry were on his flanks and rear. His army was at bay. That night he met with his generals and talked about what they should do next. He had been in touch with Grant; surrender had been suggested. Would it be that, or would they try to break through? It was decided they would attempt to break through. It would be done in the morning, and it must be done quickly while only Sheridan's cavalry still stood in their way. If the Union infantry got up it would be too late.

At dawn on April 9, Gordon moved forward with his footsore, starving, but willing remnant, supported by Fitzhugh Lee's cavalry, as Longstreet turned to hold off the Union Second and Sixth corps. Gordon rammed his way through the front line of Sheridan's cavalry. But beyond this outer layer, he hit bedrock; a powerful column of John Gibbon's infantry had already arrived. "Large bodies of the enemy were visible, crowding the hill tops like a blue or black cloud," a rebel soldier wrote.[6]

The Confederate line hit Gibbon's corps and shuddered to a stop. They "staggered back," a Union officer said, "as Don Giovanni does before the ghost." Palsied by surprise, they "rolled back like a receding wave which has spent the force of its assault against the earth-works of the shore." Longstreet's corps was hit at the same time.[7]

From a short distance in the rear, Lee sent his aide-de-camp, Colonel Charles S. Venable, ahead with a question for Gordon: Could he break through?

Venable found Gordon at the front in the dim light of the early morning. "Tell General Lee I have fought my corps to a frazzle,"

Gordon said, "and I fear I can do nothing unless I am heavily supported by Longstreet's corps."

"Then there is nothing left me but to go and see General Grant," Lee said sadly, "and I would rather die a thousand deaths."[8]

For John Gibbon it had looked to be another day of fighting. He had gotten his divisions up and was going at it as usual when suddenly all firing along the line ceased. Since this was highly irregular, he galloped rapidly to the front to see what was happening. He found his line of battle emerging from the wood into the cleared ground beyond. Not an enemy was in sight and no bullets were flying. He rode forward to within sight of the little village of Appomattox Court House. In the valley beyond he saw troops, Confederates apparently. To his right a party of horsemen appeared, riding past on the way to the town. Gibbon immediately recognized Major General E.O.C. Ord, commander of the Army of the James, and his staff and escort. Gibbon rode up to Ord, his boss, and was told that Lee was surrendering. They continued on together into Appomattox, which Gibbon saw was but "a little straggling place of a dozen or two houses."[9]

It was late morning and the contending armies were now ranged on either side of the town, with their picket lines out, but their guns silent. The Union soldiers stared at Lee's ragged little army. "It was a sad sight," one of Gibbon's officers said, his sympathy overriding all the memories of desperate past killing and fighting, "—cavalry, artillery, horses, mules and half-starved soldiers in a confused mass. It was a scene to melt the bravest heart."[10]

In the town, in the square between the two armies, Gibbon dismounted in front of the courthouse steps and suddenly found himself in a cluster of other generals who had been drifting in from both sides of the line. Among them were the familiar faces of men he had not met, but in battle, for four long years. They smiled and greeted one another, grasping hands as they had so often before when they were at peace. As their respective armies waited, suspended between peace and war, the old friends—fellow West Pointers mostly—stood together on the courthouse steps and wondered which way the scales would now tip. Were they grasping hands now only to part and fight again?

Gibbon greeted Henry Heth, his old friend from the class of 1847, whom he had last seen as they were leaving Camp Floyd in

Utah Territory. Longstreet was there, and John Gordon, a non–West Pointer, whom he was meeting for the first time. The group on the courthouse steps continued to grow as officers drifted in from both camps. From the Union army came Ord and Sheridan, and Generals Wesley Merritt, Rom Ayres, Charles Griffin, Joshua Chamberlain, William Bartlett, and George Crook. Sheridan introduced Ord to Longstreet and the two ranking generals stepped aside to talk. The other officers mingled in small groups.

Someone said, "There is Cadmus."

Gibbon looked up to see Wilcox, the classmate of so long ago, riding into the square on a sorry-looking nag, its ribs showing through its gray hide. Of Wilcox little could be seen, for he wore a long thick overcoat. Together the rider and his horse appeared the perfect embodiment of the present pitiful plight of the Confederate cause.[11]

It is doubtful that any of the men on the courthouse steps saw this specter from the class of 1846 without a smile—both for what he looked like and for who he was. Henry Heth would one day say, "I know of no man of rank who participated in our unfortunate struggle on the Southern side, who had more warm and sincere friends, *North* and *South*."[12]

Wilcox seemed born to be liked by both sides. His mother was a North Carolina beauty, his father a Connecticut Yankee. Born in Carolina, he grew up in Tennessee. U. S. Grant, now commanding the Union armies, liked him so much that he had asked him to be the best man at his wedding. Even inanimate objects appeared to favor Wilcox— bullets, for instance. Just as his onetime classmate Birkett Fry could not seem to dodge a bullet, Wilcox seemed unable to attract one. After the battle at Frayser's Farm on the Peninsula, Wilcox counted six bullet holes in his clothing, but his body was untouched. He had fought in nearly every important battle the Army of Northern Virginia had waged, and never been scratched. However, despite this, he appeared to know bullets very well; he was an expert on rifles and rifle practice, having written the prevailing standard text on the subject in 1859.[13]

By disposition Wilcox was nervous and fussy, so his soldiers called him "Old Billy Fixing." On duty he was precise and exacting. In easy company he was kindly, generous, friendly, and informal. For a photograph he would dress to the teeth in his best uniform and glare viciously into the camera. On the battlefield, however, he wore a short round jacket and a broad-brimmed straw hat and prodded his mount, an old white pony, with a long hickory switch.[14]

Wilcox had proved himself not just indestructible over the years, but reliable—he reported to battle with the day-in-day-out regularity of a bureaucrat punching a time clock. He was one of the most able brigadiers and then division commanders in Lee's army. Lee could always count on his battlefield savvy, tactical instinct, and powers of observation to do what needed to be done. His talents belied his class standing at West Point—fifty-fourth—only four files removed from George Pickett at the bottom. It was generally thought that his finest hour had been at Chancellorsville in early May 1863, when alone with his brigade at Salem Church, he had held the Union army off Lee's flank and helped turn the battle in the Confederate favor.[15]

Now here he was at Appomattox, having seen better days. He dismounted and shook hands all around. Was he so cold he had to wear that overcoat? Gibbon asked.

"It's all I have," said Wilcox glumly.

He opened his coat. Underneath he was wearing only his underclothes. He pointed to a pair of saddlebags on his nag. "That's all the baggage I have left," he said.

Then turning to Sheridan, he entered a formal complaint: "You have captured all of the balance, and you can't have that until you capture me!"

Henry Heth, in spiffy contrast, was clad in his best gray uniform and able to explain to Wilcox how he had managed it. When he found that the Federals were capturing baggage, Heth had put on his newest outfit to keep it out of enemy hands.[16]

The conversation on the courthouse steps drifted quickly from fashion considerations to other more important matters—war and peace among them, and the contents of the various flasks being passed around. Mutual healths were toasted, and the little group began spreading out from the steps into the square and onto the nearby fence. Gordon entertained the group with details about how he thought the Confederacy was about played out. The last hope had been riding on his attempt to break through on the Lynchburg road that morning.

It was decided that pending Lee's anticipated meeting with Grant, which was expected momentarily, hostilities should not be resumed or troops moved from their present positions on either side without due and timely notice. Gibbon proposed that if Grant and Lee couldn't come to terms and stop the fighting, they should order their soldiers to fire only blank cartridges to prevent further bloodshed.

The generals continued this rump negotiating session and reunion for nearly an hour and a half. Uncountable pairs of field glasses were trained on them from both armies. It was "a singular spectacle," a reporter wrote.[17]

For the West Pointers among them it was a particularly poignant reunion. It had never been in their hearts to hate the classmates they were fighting. Their lives and affections for one another had been indelibly framed and inextricably intertwined in their academy days. No adversity, war, killing, or political estrangement could undo that. Now, meeting together when the guns were quiet, they yearned to know that they would never hear their thunder or be ordered to take up arms against one another again.

But this reunion at the courthouse square was but a meeting awaiting a more important meeting, which would decide if it was to be peace or war. After an hour and a half it broke up. The officers scattered, all hoping there would be no further bloodshed, all regretting that they had not the power among them to end the fighting at once.[18]

Early in the afternoon Lee rode into Appomattox and entered the ample living room of the Wilbur McLean house, a spacious home on the square. Soon after, Grant entered the town, rode through the square, dismounted, strode up the wide steps, across the porch, and into the house to meet his old adversary. Two and a half hours later Lee's army surrendered.

In the ragged Confederate lines, hearts began to break. The shock of the news that Lee had surrendered was "terrible," a South Carolina soldier wrote, "appalling, numbing, crushing. It is as if a mighty concord of instruments were instantaneously smitten with silence—as if a star were struck from the firmament of glory and hurled into abysmal depths of darkness."[19]

"Such scenes as followed were never before witnessed in the old Army of Northern Virginia," mourned Stonewall Jackson's ex-gunner, William Poague. "Men expressed in various ways the agonizing emotions that shook their souls and broke their hearts. Some cried like children. Others sat on the ground with faces buried in hands, quietly sobbing. Others embraced friends, their bodies trembling and shaking. Others, struck dumb and with blanched faces, seemed to strain their eyes to catch the form of some awful horror that suddenly loomed before them."[20]

Frederick M. Colston, a Confederate ordnance officer, saw tears "in many eyes and on many cheeks where they had never been brought by fear."[21] "Ragged and dirty, gaunt with hunger, and physically exhausted," a soldier said, "men went into paroxysms of grief or rage, tears running down grizzly old faces of some, while others broke up their guns, swords, or drums. We knew not what was to become of us."[22]

"I would rather have embraced the tabernacle of death," said white-haired Brigadier General Henry A. Wise.[23]

For the rank and file in the Union army, the first week in April had been days of fierce enthusiasm and fiery excitement, "red hot days," one of them said. For four years many of them had followed the basic philosophy of their kind, going "where we were told, if we could conveniently get there," and staying "where we were put till it evidently was time to leave." But when the news came out of the McLean House at about three in the afternoon, the air on the Union side was in the next minute "black with hats and boots, coats, knapsacks, shirts and cartridge-boxes, blankets and shelter tents, canteens and haversacks"—anything that could be hurled skyward. Soldiers fell without embarrassment on one another's necks, laughing and crying. Brawny, lumbering, bearded men embraced and kissed like schoolgirls and danced and sang and shouted, stood on their heads, and played leapfrog with one another. The war, the cruel, ghastly, unending war was over and they had won.[24]

John Gibbon threw nothing in the air and hugged nobody. But a powerful feeling of triumph and relief swept over him. He didn't let it show, would never let it show, out of respect for his Confederate friends and classmates, whose anguish he understood. That afternoon General Grant informed Gibbon that he was to head the three-general delegation to work out the details of the formal surrender with three Confederate counterparts. Gibbon with his corps and Charles Griffin's Fifth Corps was to remain at Appomattox to oversee the surrender, and to collect the public property and arms. Gibbon spent that night in a tent between the lines, and slept more soundly in front of his pickets than he had behind them only the night before.[25]

Another general got orders from Grant later that night. Brigadier General Joshua Chamberlain, of Maine, one of the most heroic and sensitive of Grant's officers, was told he was to handle the formal surrender of the Confederate infantry. Grant had demanded that there be a formal surrender, and he wanted the ceremonies to be as simple as possible. He wanted nothing done to humiliate the manhood of the southern soldiers, who had fought the Union army so bravely and so desperately all these months, all those years. He could trust Chamberlain to see that it was done right.[26]

The next morning in a drizzling rain, Lee and Grant met one more time at the edge of town and talked on their horses. After they had conversed for a short while, Grant motioned to Gibbon, who waited at a discreet distance with other generals and staff. Gibbon rode forward.

Lee received him courteously, but gravely and without indicating that he had ever seen him before, although they had known one another in the old army.

"Gen. Lee is desirous that his officers and men should have on their persons some evidence that they are paroled prisoners, so that they will not be disturbed," Grant told Gibbon.

Lee explained that he desired to do simply what was in his power to protect his men from anything disagreeable.

Gibbon said he thought that could be arranged. He carried in his corps a small printing press. He could have blank forms struck off to be filled in and issued to each Confederate soldier, signed by their own officers and distributed as required.

Lee assented, then said to Grant, "You have excepted private horses from the Surrender. Now most of my couriers and many of the artillery and cavalry own their own horses. How will it be about them?"

Grant at once turned to Gibbon. "They will be allowed to retain them." He then turned back to Lee. "They will need them in putting in their spring crops!"[27] Grant had tried to kill these men for four bloody years, and now he was concerned that they get their spring crops in the ground so that they might live. The time had come for peace.

When the meeting broke up, Gibbon, Griffin, and Major General Wesley Merritt, the three Union negotiators, accompanied by a number of other officers and escorted by a member of James Longstreet's staff, rode through the Confederate picket line. Longstreet, Gordon, and Brigadier General William Pendleton, Lee's chief of artillery and the gospel-preaching father of young Sandie Pendleton, now dead like Jackson, were to represent the Confederate army.

Longstreet was absent from his headquarters, but Gordon and Pendleton were immediately sent for. Pendleton looked to Gibbon very much like Lee and nearly as old. Gordon, whom Gibbon had met for the first time the day before, was a man of about his own make and height, and Gibbon was struck with him. Gordon's pleasant face and remarkably polished manners had impressed them all. Like Birkett Fry, Gordon had been riddled with bullets—five times at Antietam alone—and a deep scar ran across his left cheek. When his wife had hurried to his side after Antietam, she looked at his black and shapeless face and bandaged limbs and blanched. Hoping to reassure her, he had said, "Here's your handsome husband; been to an Irish wedding." Her answer was a stifled scream.[28]

The two delegations arranged to meet immediately in a room somewhere on the Appomattox Court House square. They rode back through the Union lines accompanied by Rooney Lee and Gibbon's former classmate, Cadmus Wilcox, who presumably was better dressed than he had been the day before. On the way they overtook two more of Gibbon's ex-classmates, Henry Heth and George Pickett, who were riding together into the Union lines. On the road they also met Lee and Longstreet, and Longstreet turned back to ride with them to the town.

The six peacemakers began their meeting in a room at the hotel, but it was so bare and cheerless that Gibbon suggested they adjourn to the McLean house where Lee and Grant had met the day before. At the suggestion of the others, Gibbon began writing out several clauses to govern the surrender. The first four were quickly adopted. But at the fifth, they all hesitated. It was more thorny than the rest: Who should be included in the surrender, and who not? Longstreet suggested that the list embrace all Confederate troops belonging to the Army of Northern Virginia, except such cavalry as had escaped and any artillery that had been beyond twenty miles of Appomattox Court House at the time Grant and Lee were meeting at the McLean house. This was unanimously adopted, the terms were drawn up in final form, and signed.

It was agreed that the Confederate infantry was to march by brigades and detachments to a designated point to stack arms and deposit their flags, sabers, and pistols; and then to march to their homes under the charge of their officers. That afternoon the cavalry and artillery began surrendering, and Gibbon's printing press began turning out parole passes. Since thirty thousand would be required, it promised to take all night and probably all the next day. So Gibbon ordered a detail of qualified printers recruited from the army to work in relays until the job was finished. There seemed to be more than enough men in the ranks with this specialized talent. Gibbon reasoned that if they had needed fifty watchmakers or blacksmiths, they would have just as readily found them. After four years of organized war, it was an army prepared for anything.[29]

Grant came up and sat on the porch of the McLean house as he waited for his officers to prepare his army to leave Appomattox. As he sat there, his generals began arriving with many of Grant's old comrades from the Confederate army, who had been his friends far longer than they had been his enemies, and who were now his friends again. Sheridan, Gibbon, and Rufus Ingalls brought Cadmus Wilcox, the best man from Grant's wedding day. As Longstreet passed—another old and dear friend who had been present at his marriage vows— Grant called out and rose to greet him affectionately and offer him a cigar. Heth, who had been a subaltern with Grant in Mexico, came up on the porch, and Gordon and Pickett and a number of others. Grant received them all cordially and talked with them until it was time to leave. About noon he rode out of Appomattox for the last time, without entering Confederate lines.[30]

The next day, the eleventh, Confederate cavalrymen and artillerymen finished surrendering their guns, ammunition, and flags. It was a foggy, gloomy day. "The very heavens seem to sympathize with my humour and my country's agony," a Confederate soldier said.[31]

The next day was no better, chill and gray and depressing. It was April 12, four years to the day that the Confederate guns had opened fire on the little Union garrison at Fort Sumter and started the war. Joshua Chamberlain had been ordered to have his lines formed to accept the surrender of the Confederate infantry at sunrise. He positioned his soldiers along the principal street of the town, from the bank of the Appomattox to the courthouse, facing the last line of battle. His troops, a representative portion of the Union army, were as much remnants as the soldiers whose surrender they were about to receive—tattered veterans themselves from Massachusetts, Maine, Michigan, Maryland, Pennsylvania, and New York.

At about nine in the morning the Confederate infantry began to come, for the last time, "with the old swinging route step and swaying battle-flags," the Stonewall Brigade in the lead.[32] At their head rode John Gordon, with a grief "which almost stifled utterance."[33] Chamberlain watched them come with compassion welling in his heart. He would not let this once proud army surrender to him without a salute from his own. He passed the order, and as the head of the rebel columns drew opposite the Union line, a single bugle blared and the entire Union column from right to left, regiment by regiment in succession, passed from "order arms" to "carry."[34] It was the marching salute, "a soldierly salute to those vanquished heroes—a token of respect from Americans to Americans, a final and fitting tribute from Northern to Southern chivalry."[35]

Gordon caught the sound of the shifting arms and looked up. Instantly taking its meaning, he wheeled, making of himself and his horse one uplifted figure and dropping the point of his sword to his boot toe in a returning salute. He then ordered his own successive brigades to pass at carry arms—"honor answering honor." On the Union side there was no further sound of trumpet, no roll of drum, not a cheer nor a word or whisper of vainglorying, but "an awed stillness rather, and breath-holding, as if it were the passing of the dead."[36]

The Confederates fixed bayonets, stacked arms, then hesitating, removed their cartridge boxes and laid them down.

"Good-bye, gun," one Confederate soldier said to his musket, "I am darned glad to get rid of you. I have been trying to for two years."[37]

In agony, they folded their flags, "battle-worn and torn, blood-stained, heart-holding colors," and laid them down. Some Confederate soldiers rushed from the ranks, bent over the flags and pressed them to their lips "with burning tears."[38] Gordon watched sadly. The tattered and faded banners his men were laying on the stacked guns appeared to him like "trappings on the coffin of their dead hopes."[39]

"What visions thronged as we looked into each other's eyes!" Chamberlain later wrote. Recollections of past battles flooded his own memory as he sat on his horse and took the surrender, regiment after regiment and division after division, throughout the morning and afternoon. It was by miracles, he thought, that any of them standing there had lived to see this day. When the day ended, in the dusk of the evening, the long lines of scattered cartridge boxes were set on fire and "the lurid flames wreathing the blackness of earthly shadows [gave] an unearthly border to our parting."[40]

Paroled in those three wrenching days at Appomattox were 28,231 Confederates—all that was left of Lee's army: 22,349 infantry; 1,559 cavalry; 1,747 general headquarters and miscellaneous troops; and 2,576 artillerymen with 63 cannon.[41]

To Edward Porter Alexander, Longstreet's artillery commander, the next day seemed to usher in a new life in a new world. "We had lived through the war," he marveled. "There was nobody trying to shoot us, and nobody for us to shoot at. Our guns were gone, our country was gone, our very entity seemed to be destroyed. We were no longer soldiers, and had no orders to obey, nothing to do, and nowhere to go."[42]

Now the "instinctive love of home" called them all. To some the thought was bittersweet. "Home to many, when they reached it," a soldier said, "was graves and ashes." At any rate, he thought, "there must be somewhere on earth, a better place than a muddy, smoky camp in a piece of scrubby pines—better company than gloomy, hungry comrades and inquisitive enemies, and something in the future more exciting, if not more hopeful, than nothing to eat, nowhere to sleep, nothing to do and nowhere to go."[43]

So they left for home, many of them passing through Union lines. But there was not heard a taunting cry or rude remark as the two armies turned their backs upon each other for the first time in four long bloody years. "The truth was," Gibbon said, "that these men had won our admiration and consideration by their conduct in battle and we could well afford now that we were the victors, to treat them with respect."[44]

When Lee left Appomattox on the twelfth, as the last of his army was surrendering, Gibbon sent his own escort to accompany him for twelve miles on the road to Richmond.[45] Gibbon himself left when his work was done, carrying with him the surrendered flags from Lee's army. With two staff officers and a number of enlisted men who had especially distinguished themselves in the closing campaign, he traveled to the war department in Washington and turned the colors over to Secretary of War Edwin Stanton.[46]

The war for him was over.

The Wind That
Shook the Corn

O n their honeymoon trip in the summer of 1857, Tom and
Anna Jackson visited West Point.

Anna watched as her new husband reveled in his return
to the past. "His delight was unbounded," she remembered. He met
old professors and brother officers, and they talked and laughed and
relived the days on the blackboards and on the plain. With the dawn
he was off to climb to Fort Putnam, and once more to watch the river
wind past the Highlands and to remember old joys and agonies. There
was scarcely a spot, Anna said, that he didn't visit.[1]

It would be the last time Jackson would ever see West Point, the
last time he would shake the hand of many of these brother officers.
It would be the last they would see of him. How could they know
then how large Old Jack would write his name in the military pan-
theon? How could he himself know?

George McClellan returned to West Point seven years later in
the summer of 1864. By then he knew. He had seen it all happen;
he had been at the center of much of it. Now he was returning to
deliver the principal oration at the dedication of the site of a battle
monument to all the Union officers and enlisted men of the regular
army who had fallen in the war. He had never been recalled to duty

507

after Lincoln sacked him in those days of disillusionment after Antietam. But neither had he dropped out of sight. He was this summer the leading candidate for the Democratic nomination to oppose the president who had fired him. Since it was a summer of more discontent and disillusionment—the Union armies seemed stalled everywhere and war weariness had seized the nation—thousands had turned up at West Point to see and hear him. It seemed probable that this member of the class of 1846 would be the next president of the United States.

Spectators lined the route to the monument site at Trophy Point on the northern brow of the plain. The speaker's stand was festooned with flags and flowers. At about half past noon, thirty-five guns thundered a salute, and the procession of dignitaries, moving to the music of more than half a dozen military bands and led by the battalion of cadets, started the slow march to the site. With McClellan were the academic board, the board of visitors, the academic staff—all honoring him who little more than twenty years before had been but a homesick plebe. At about one o'clock he stepped from the carriage with a man nearly as celebrated as himself—Robert Anderson of Fort Sumter, now a brigadier general. They marched together down an avenue lined with people saluting them with cheers on both sides. McClellan replied with a military salute, and to the continuing acclaim, took his seat on the decorated dais.

The academy band played "Hail Columbia," and at the end of the benedictions Anderson rose to introduce his fellow officer.

"Fellow-citizens, members of the corps of cadets, and brother soldiers," he said, "I have the pleasure of going through the form of introducing to you one who is better known to you than I who introduce him."[2]

McClellan stood by the speaker's table and was saluted with three loud and prolonged cheers. When he began to speak, it was in a clear, calm voice, audible across the plain and echoing down the years.

"God knows," he said, among many other things, "that David's love for Jonathan was no more deep than mine for the tried friends of many long and eventful years, whose names are to be recorded upon the structure that is to rise upon this spot. . . . Such an occasion as this should call forth the deepest and noblest emotions of our nature— pride, sorrow, and prayer; pride that our country has possessed such sons; sorrow that she has lost them; prayer that she may have others like them." He spoke of West Point, "with her large heart," who "adopts us all—graduates and those appointed from civil life, officers and privates. In her eyes we are all her children. . . . Such are the ties which unite us, the most endearing which exist among men; such the relations which bind us together, the closest of the sacred brotherhood of arms. . . ."[3]

What McClellan was saying then, his classmate Tom Jackson must have also felt seven years before when he had returned to this plain with his young bride. His name would not appear on the battle monument, because he was in rebellion against the country he had forsworn. Even so, these two classmates were both mystically bound by that "sacred brotherhood of arms" of which McClellan spoke, and by the mother institution that had made them brothers.

Like them, West Point had been tried in the crucible of the Civil War, and like them it had been both exalted and diminished. Only one of these two classmates was still alive to ask whether in any way the academy had failed them, or if they had failed it. The answer to both questions—and McClellan must have known it—was yes and no.

John Calhoun was secretary of war in early 1818, when the academy had just fallen under the guiding hand of Sylvanus Thayer, the man who was to shape its direction for decades to come. In a message to Thayer, Calhoun wrote: "In future wars the Nation must look to the Academy for the skill to conduct valor to victory."[4]

In the time between then and the Civil War, West Pointers had gradually taken over command of the army. It had been a slow process, for officers moved up through the echelons in the years between the wars as molasses pours from a bottle. But gradually they had replaced the older generation that had risen to prominence in the War of 1812 and to high command in the Mexican War. By as early as 1833, over half of the officers in the regular army were West Pointers. A monopoly was building, and as it grew, outsiders found it harder and harder to break in and move up.

Hand in hand with this creeping academization came a new professionalization of the army that American arms had never known, and it was disturbing to many. Citizen-soldiers had always fought the wars of the young nation, and commanded its armies. Now the educated military professional, trained at West Point, was taking over. It was a quiet revolution, but by the beginning of the Civil War it was a fixed fact of life. By 1860, nearly eight of every ten officers in the army were West Pointers. Until then not a one of them was a general. But when the Civil War came, the floodgate to higher command simply broke; West Pointers became generals wholesale, in both the Union and Confederate armies.[5]

It could be argued that this revolutionary transformation didn't necessarily make for a better army—indeed it was argued violently during the Civil War. In some cases West Point training turned out to be a liability. To the small extent that West Point taught them to wage war on a large scale at all, it was as Napoleon had waged it. But when the war came, those tactics and strategies had either gone out of date or required drastic amendment in the face of more powerful weaponry and the peculiar requirements of the geography and the times.

It was a war that could not be fought from textbooks. Tactics had to be changed on the spot. The war had to be improvised and victory had to be learned on the job. Some learned it and some didn't.

U. S. Grant, one of those who did, would one day say:

Some of our generals failed because they worked out everything by rule. They knew what Frederick did at one place, and Napoleon at another. They were always thinking about what Napoleon would do. Unfortunately for their plans, the rebels would be thinking about something else. I don't underrate the value of military knowledge, but if men make war in slavish observances of rules, they will fail. . . . Consequently, while our generals were working out problems of an ideal character, problems that would have looked well on a blackboard, practical facts were neglected. To that extent I consider remembrances of old campaigns a disadvantage. Even Napoleon showed that, for my impression is that his first success came because he made war in his own way, and not in imitation of others. . . . The only eyes a general can trust are his own. He must be able to see and know the country, the streams, the passes, the hills. . . . The conditions of war in Europe and America are so unlike that there can be no comparison.[6]

Richard Taylor, who became a Confederate lieutenant general without benefit of a West Point education, wouldn't have had one had it been offered.

"Take a boy sixteen from his mother's apron-strings," he told Dabney Maury, "shut him up under constant surveillance for four years at West Point, send him out to a two-company post upon the frontier where he does little but play seven-up and drink whiskey at the sutler's, and by the time he is forty-five years old he will furnish the most complete illustration of suppressed mental development of which human nature is capable, and many such specimens were made generals on both sides when the war began."[7]

Attacks on West Point and West Pointers were as old as the institution. In 1821, when it was well on its way to becoming the country's preeminent school of engineering, a motion was made in the House of Representatives to discontinue pay and rations for the cadets and discharge them—in short, abolish the institution. The motion was voted down.

During the democratic revolution of the Jacksonian era—the 1830s and 1840s—West Point had to fight repeatedly for its life. The Tennessee Legislature in 1833 urged that it be abolished. The Ohio Legislature followed a year later with a similar resolution. A House committee issued a virulent attack on the academy in 1837.

West Point was undemocratic, the Jacksonians argued. Worse, it was aristocratic. In the egalitarian America of the times it was considered inconsistent with republican institutions, with its free education for the favored few at the public expense. It was freezing out the common man, the citizen-soldier who was equally deserving but less favored. It was a seedbed of special privilege and political favoritism. Moreover, it was turning out too many officers, far more than were needed. Part of the problem was the basic American distrust of a standing army of any kind, and alarm over the creeping professionalism of arms. Wars were things that ought to be dealt with when they came, and by patriot-soldiers from civil life who were apt to have more common sense than these coddled products of West Point.

In 1844, about the time the class of 1846 was anticipating its furlough, another House committee investigated charges that it was aristocratic, anti-republican, extravagant, expensive, unnecessary, and different from what it was intended to be. The committee found the charges were unsupported by the facts, and the academy lived on. Then the Mexican War came and West Pointers played such a visible role in winning it that the criticism faded.

But in the Civil War it rose again, more virulent than ever. The old Jacksonian criticisms resurfaced, fueled in the North by early defeats on the battlefield of Union armies commanded by West Pointers. Its critics not only believed that West Point was elitist and undemocratic, but that it cranked out incompetents.

Horace Greeley of the *New York Tribune*, who got into the middle of nearly every disagreement that came along on any subject, got into this one. "The atmosphere, the fume of the bivouac," he argued, not an academy education, is what produces military genius. Hannibal, Alexander, Caesar, and Napoleon never went to West Point.[8]

"War being an art, not a science," *Harper's Weekly* editorialized, "a man can no more be made a first-class general than a first-class painter, or a great poet, by professors and text-books; he must be born with the genius of war in his breast. Very few such men are born in a century, and the chances are rather that they will be found among the millions of the outside people than in the select circle who are educated at West Point."[9]

One critic wrote his senator in early 1862 that academy graduates were "invariably men of all theory and no execution of results," capable of conducting defensive works, "but for active offensive and successful results—never."[10] He perhaps had been watching McClellan in Washington and had not noticed that the Confederate generals who had beaten the Union generals at Bull Run were also academy graduates. Nor had he yet seen Jackson in the Valley or Lee at Chancellorsville or Grant at Vicksburg or Sherman at Atlanta—graduates all.

But there was something else—a new argument against West Pointers, more serious even than the question of competence.

Senator Ben Wade of Ohio raised the issue on the Senate floor in 1861. "I cannot help thinking," he growled, "that there is something wrong about this whole institution. I do not believe that in the history of the world you can find as many men who have proved themselves utterly faithless to their oaths, ungrateful to the Government that supported them, guilty of treason and a deliberate intention to overthrow that Government which has educated them and given them its support, as have emanated from this institution. . . . I believe that from the idleness of these military-educated gentlemen this great treason was hatched."[11]

It wasn't just that many West Pointers had defected to the Confederacy that irked Wade and the other Republican Radicals. But many of them who hadn't defected had done something almost as reprehensible: they had become Democrats who were soft on slavery and loath to fight—McClellan came to mind. Wade figured that political apostasy must have been taught at West Point as well, and he didn't know which sin was worse—it or treason.[12]

So now West Point was not only a breeding ground for incompetents and aristocrats, but for Democrats and traitors. Certainly many West Pointers had defected to the Confederacy—304 of them, one of every five of its graduates, including ten members of the class of 1846. And many of the generals holding high command in the North were West Pointers with pro-slavery sympathies. However, many West Pointers from the southern states—162 of them—had withstood the pull of birth and kin to remain with the Union. Wade didn't mention them.[13]

Secretary of War Simon Cameron labeled the defection of West Pointers to the Confederacy as "extraordinary treachery," and called on Congress to find out what caused it and try to fix it.[14]

Senator Zachariah Chandler of Michigan, Wade's fellow Radical and ally, called it worse than that. Like Wade he wanted Congress to fix the institution by getting rid of it. He insisted that but for West Point there would never have been a rebellion. The academy, he said, "has produced more traitors within the last fifty years than all the institutions of learning and education that have existed since Judas Iscariot's time."[15]

Most senators, of course, didn't agree with these Wade-Chandler theories of treason and incompetence. Maine Senator William Pitt Fessenden, although a fellow Radical, thought Wade had "his peculiar views about this institution. He thinks commanders are born, not made."[16] New Hampshire Senator Daniel Clark said: "Treason has resulted from a political education, obtained elsewhere. The Government itself, the Senate of these United States, has been more the school of treason than the academy at West Point."[17] Senator James Nesmith of Oregon said: "Treason was hatched and incubated at these very desks around me."[18]

West Pointers themselves weighed in on the argument. Dennis

Hart Mahan, their stern professor of engineering and tactics, struck back at every opportunity in one letter to the *New York Times* after another. Mahan took any assault on the academy as if it were an attack on his own reputation. Well he might, for the two armies that had gone to war against one another were both in large measure his creation. He had taught virtually every one of the West Point generals, Confederate and Union, their military engineering and their science of war.[19]

The news from the battlefields was sometimes hard on Mahan. A stern Unionist and patriot, he disliked seeing any Confederate general succeed, even those he had taught. And Union generals who were once his prized cadets were disappointing him. Too often the wrong protégés were winning the battles. One of his former cadets said that Mahan had "a sovereign contempt for all knowledge that did not come through regular school channels." That meant to a large degree through his own works. He graded the value of every officer by his class ranking, regarding such middle-of-the-pack former students as Grant, Sheridan, and Jackson as freaks of chance. When those of inferior academic standing rose to distinguished leadership, "the world was turned topsy-turvy." In Mahan's mind, it logically should be the McClellans who succeeded, not these others. But that was not the way it was working out.[20]

The class of 1846's own Truman Seymour, the hero of Sumter, lashed out publicly at West Point's critics in a letter published in the *Army and Navy Journal* in 1864 and reprinted in a pamphlet. Every sensible American ought to be proud of the academy, Seymour argued. In his days at West Point, politics "were never even referred to. The discussion of slavery was unknown." If any sentiments had been inculcated they would certainly have been "of Northern stamp." He said, "the only 'peculiarity' they ever sought to impress was that devotion to duty and to country that has ever been considered, through all ages, the chief glory of a soldier's life." Seymour put the blame for the poor showing of northern generals on Union policymakers. "The South," he said bluntly, "owes whatever of successful resistance it has made to her proper employment of her military education, and the North has failed in using its overpowering strength to insure quick success, because of its entire inappreciation of its military duties and its abusive or wilful perversion of its military skill. The best possible vindication of the Military Academy is to be found in the history of

The Wind That Shook the Corn

the Confederacy." In short, the South had used its West Point–trained talent properly; the North hadn't.[21]

The venomous debates over West Point in the Senate in 1861 and 1863 ultimately came to nothing. The academy was sustained and refunded. As northern armies commanded by West Pointers began to win battles, the assault on the academy collapsed, as it had in the Mexican War.[22]

Ironically, in the end West Point's finest hour came not on a battlefield, but at a peace table.

Morris Schaff, class of 1862, saw this irony clearly when after the war he wrote that "West Point friendships did more at the close of the war than any other agency to heal the scars." And it began with Grant and Lee at Appomattox.

Schaff wrote:

. . . on that day two West Point men met, with more at stake than has ever fallen to the lot of two Americans to decide. On the manner in which they should meet, on the temper with which they should approach the mighty issue, depended the future peace of the country and the standards of honor and glory for the days to come. There was the choice between magnanimity to a gallant foe and a spirit of revenge; there was the choice between official murders for treason, and leaving the page of our country's history aglow with mercy; there was the choice between the conduct of a conqueror, and the conduct of a soldier and a gentleman; finally, there was the choice for these two men, who for over a year had fronted each other on so many fields, to garland the occasion by the display of what is greater than victory—terms that the Christian and the lover of peace in all ages of the world will honor. Those two West Point men knew the ideals of their old Alma Mater, they knew each other as only graduates of that institution know each other, and they met on the plane of that common knowledge. . . . And then what happened? The graduates of both armies met as brothers and planted then and there the tree that has grown, blooming for the Confederate and blooming for the Federal, and under whose shade we now gather in peace. . . . Her [West Point's] greatest service was in inspiring and revealing the ideals of the soldier and the gentleman, and in

515

knitting friendships which, when called on by the world's love of gentleness, responded at Appomattox by bringing back enduring peace. . . .

Grant and Lee, Schaff believed, had honored both their Alma Mater and their country, and in the end saved their country endless torment, division, and misery. That moment at Appomattox, and not all the battles they had fought and for which they had been schooled, was their crowning achievement.[23]

Even that fierce debunker of West Pointers, Richard Taylor, was to admit that peace came "under the tender ministrations of the hands that fought the battles!"[24]

But what of those hands? What is to be said of George McClellan, from whom so much was expected; and of his classmate, Tom Jackson, of whom so little was expected? One did indeed become great, one of the half-dozen greatest generals in American history, perhaps in world history. But it had been the wrong one.

What makes a general great? Most people know it when they see it. One Confederate officer once said the rules of war are simple enough, it all "consists in two words—luck and pluck."[25] But it is more complicated than that and more difficult than it looks.

A great general must have the will to win whatever the mission. He must have an absolute, unbreakable, unbending passion to succeed no matter what the obstacles, no matter who the enemy or the frustrations. He must have cool judgment, immune to panic and unshakable by emergencies of any kind or by unexpected twists of fortune. He must have accurate knowledge of everything around him—of terrain, resources, and the enemy's position and strength. He must be able to anticipate events; have a plan, certainly, but then be willing to abandon it instantly if it isn't working and the circumstances require. He must know his enemy—intuitively or by any other means—and what he is likely to do. He must have character; some call it moral courage, some call it temperament, some call it plain nerve. He must have magnetism or charisma, whatever that means and from wherever it comes. He must be able to stir the enthusiasm and devotion of his men by his own example. He must be able to take the best of Mahan's advice: move fast and use common sense. He must be whatever it takes—skeptical, critical, flexible, or obstinate.

And he must win.

With all that in mind, we will now compare the two most famous members of the class of 1846. At West Point they heard the same lectures, read the same books, recited at the same blackboards, lived the same life, shared the same hopes and fears. But when push came to shove in a war of brothers, they joined different armies and they were not the same at all.

As a battlefield commander, McClellan violated virtually all of the requirements of a great general. Nobody could concoct a sounder strategy. Nobody could organize a great army better or faster than he could. Nobody could then do less with it.

David Strother said of him, "He created an army which he failed to handle, and conceived plans which he failed to carry out."[26] Lincoln is said to have compared him and his army to "an admirable engineer" and a "stationary engine."[27]

As early as October 1861, one stern critic said of him that he had "more men and equipments now here [in Washington] than Napoleon moved when he prostrated Prussia in a three weeks campaign. . . . more men here on the Potomac than he moved when he marched to the heart of Austria, occupied Vienna, and dictated laws to the sovereigns of Europe from the Palace of Schoenbrunn"; more men than he knew what to do with.[28]

McClellan puzzled and mystified not only his friends, but his enemies. However it was not in the way that Jackson puzzled and mystified them—with speed of unexpected movement and hard lightning blows.

"Are you acquainted with General McClellan?" Lee asked one of his lieutenants before Antietam. "He is an able general but a very cautious one. His enemies among his own people think him too much so. His army is in a very demoralized and chaotic condition, and will not be prepared for offensive operations—or he will not think it so—for three or four weeks. Before that time I hope to be on the Susquehanna."[29]

"No one but McClellan could have hesitated to attack," his friend Confederate General Joseph E. Johnston said of him at Yorktown.[30]

Edward Porter Alexander, the Confederate artilleryman, said of him at Antietam: "Common Sense was just shouting, 'Your adversary is backed against a river, with no bridge & only one ford, & that the worst on the whole river. If you whip him now, you destroy him utterly, root & branch & bag & baggage. Not twice in a life time does such a chance come to any general. Lee for once has made a mistake, & given you a chance to ruin him if you can break his lines, & such a game is worth great risk. Every man must fight & keep on fighting for all he is worth.' " But instead McClellan hurled his army piecemeal at Lee, a corps and a division at a time, and kept one corps and most of another out of the battle altogether, even as the Confederate center was collapsing.[31]

No general in the war had greater charisma, or failed so utterly to use it to stir his soldiers to win battles. One of his officers said of him that he "could so move upon the hearts of a great army, as the wind sways long rows of standing corn."[32]

But having moved his army so, he could not translate that hypnotic sway he held over it into victory in the hour of battle. "He made absolutely no use of the magnificent enthusiasm which the army then [at Antietam] felt for him," a Union officer said.[33]

It is doubtful that Professor Mahan ever had a more brilliant pupil than McClellan. When the war came he had mastered the military literature as thoroughly as any American of his time. He translated that mastery into magnificent strategic plans. But on the field of battle all of the instincts of a great general failed him. War is an imperfect chaotic world, where plans often come to grief or must be changed. Commanders must be able to seize the hour and move with the changes. McClellan couldn't. When his knowledge had to be applied, his imagination failed him.

"He was assuredly not a great general," a northern reporter wrote, "for he had the pedantry of war rather than the inspiration of war. . . . his power as a tactician was much inferior to his talent as a strategist, and he executed less boldly than he conceived: not appearing to know well those counters with which a commander must work—time, place, and circumstance."[34] McClellan seemed unable to "pluck the passing day."[35]

He could always see how he could improve his army, make it better, given time. And he took the time, at the expense of lost opportunities. He had an imperfect awareness of place. That became apparent in the mountains of western Virginia, on the Peninsula, and at Antietam. And from western Virginia to the Peninsula to Antietam he misunderstood the circumstances, wildly overestimated enemy numbers, and misdivined enemy intentions. Those are not things a great general does.

U. S. Grant would one day say, with mitigating kindness, that "McClellan is to me one of the mysteries of the war. As a young man he was always a mystery. He had the way of inspiring you with the idea of immense capacity, if he would only have a chance. . . . I have never studied his campaigns enough to make up my mind as to his military skill, but all my impressions are in his favor. . . . the test which was applied to him would be terrible to any man, being made a major-general at the beginning of the war. It has always seemed to me that the critics of McClellan do not consider this vast and cruel responsibility—the war, a new thing to all of us, the army new, everything to do from the outset, with a restless people and Congress. McClellan was a young man when this devolved upon him, and if he did not succeed, it was because the conditions of success were so trying. If McClellan had gone into the war as Sherman, Thomas, or Meade, had fought his way along and up, I have no reason to suppose that he would not have won as high a distinction as any of us."[36]

The usually clamp-mouthed Tom Jackson occasionally spoke of tactics. He told John Imboden of two rules that a general must never fail to follow:

Always mystify, mislead, and surprise the enemy, if possible; and when you strike and overcome him, never let up in the pursuit so long as your men have strength to follow; for an army routed, if hotly pursued, becomes panic-stricken, and can then be destroyed by half their number. The other rule is, never fight against heavy odds, if by any possible manoeuvring you can hurl your own force on only a part, and that weakest part, of your enemy and crush it. Such tactics will win every time, and a small army may thus destroy a large one in detail, and repeated victory will make it invincible.[37]

Dr. Hunter McGuire in his days and months close to Jackson heard him say at various times:

War means fighting; to fight is the duty of a soldier; march swiftly, strike the foe with all your strength and take away from him everything you can. Injure him in every possible way, and do it quickly. . . . Don't wait for the adversary to become fully prepared, but strike him the first blow. . . . We must do more than defeat their armies; we must destroy them.[38]

What Jackson didn't say of his own genius, a host of others since have.

Even his enemies spoke of his "peculiar strategic ability."[39] One Northerner wrote, "The pomp and glitter of war were not for him. His banners grew old and faded and shot-torn. His legions grew ragged and foot-sore and weary. No matter who hesitated, Jackson advanced. Fierce in the heat of battle, because it was his duty to kill."[40]

John Tidball, another Northerner and former neighbor in West Point's old south barracks, said: "His chief characteristics as a military leader were his quick perception of the weak points of his enemy, his ever readiness, the astounding rapidity of his movements, his sudden and unexpected onslaughts and the persistency with which he followed them up. . . . Naturally taciturn and by habit the keeper of his own designs, it was as difficult for his friends to penetrate them, as it was easy for him to deceive his enemy. . . . In any other person this would have been taken as cunning and deceit; but with him it was the voice of the Lord piloting him to the tents of the Midianites."[41]

Henry Kyd Douglas, who rode with him, called him a bold leader, "probably the boldest the war produced. . . . But he mingled with his boldness great prudence and judgment. . . . If he played war as poker, he knew exactly when to bluff, and against whom; consequently he was never beaten." Douglas believed Jackson's opinion of opposing generals was always "wonderfully correct." But perhaps most important of all, in Douglas's mind, "he dared and won."[42]

One of his cavalrymen said, quoting Abraham Lincoln, " 'He always ploughed around the log.' "[43] A reporter, who had perhaps tried at one time or another to find him, said he was "everywhere when unexpected, and nowhere when sought."[44] Another of his soldiers said that if the enemy had a rear he would find it.[45] As he approached that rear he was invariably "as still as the breeze," and when he found it he was "as dreadful as the storm."[46]

Douglas said of Jackson, "He had no moments of deplorable indecision and no occasion to lament the loss of golden opportunities."[47] After McClellan found Lee's special orders before Antietam, he began to move faster than he ordinarily did. But even then he did not move boldly. Instead of seizing the South Mountain passes immediately, he rested that night and attacked the next day. Would Jackson have waited? Not likely.

When McClellan had Lee at bay before Sharpsburg, with much of his army still at Harpers Ferry, instead of attacking at once he waited for the mass of his own army to arrive. Then he spent all the next day reconnoitering, giving Lee precious time to regroup. Would Jackson have done that? Would Jackson have hesitated to throw in all of his reserves if he had seen the enemy's center collapsing? Not likely.

At Antietam, McClellan's classmate Darius Couch waited near Harpers Ferry with an unused and rested division. McClellan might have ordered it up in a forced march, as Lee had ordered up A. P. Hill, flanked the Confederates at the river crossing and cut off their only avenue of escape. Would Jackson have thought to do that? Very likely.

But who knows for certain? McClellan, one of West Point's best and brightest, fails in nearly every measure of what a general ought to be. Jackson, the rube from the hills back in the pack at West Point, turned out to be one of the best generals the world has ever produced.

In the end Jackson even eclipsed his classmate in McClellan's own speciality, the love of the soldiers. Before he was killed at Chancellorsville, Jackson was almost as popular with Union troops as he was with his own, not because he was more charismatic but because winning is the father to charisma. McClellan could never claim such bipartisan support. In the presidential election in 1864, he would even lose the soldier vote to Abraham Lincoln, the man he thought his inferior in every way.

Perhaps Jackson was never fully tested. U. S. Grant thought not. It is widely believed that Jackson's Valley campaign was one of the most remarkable displays of strategic science, based on accurate reasoning, correct anticipation of the enemy's plans, rapid marches, and judicious disposition of an inferior force in American military history.[48]

But Grant said:

I question whether his campaigns in Virginia justify his reputation as a great commander. He was killed too soon, and before his rank allowed him a great command. It would have been a test of generalship if Jackson had met Sheridan in the Valley, instead of some of the men he did meet. . . . If Jackson had attempted on Sheridan the tactics he attempted so successfully upon others he would not only have been beaten but destroyed. Sudden, daring raids, under a fine general like Jackson, might do against raw troops and inexperienced commanders, such as we had in the beginning of the war, but not against drilled troops and a commander like Sheridan. The tactics for which Jackson is famous, and which achieved such remarkable results, belonged entirely to the beginning of the war and to the peculiar conditions under which the earlier battles were fought. They would have insured destruction to any commander who tried them upon Sherman, Thomas, Sheridan, Meade, or, in fact, any of our great generals.[49]

Grant was right, Jackson died at Chancellorsville before his generalship could be tested against a truly great commander. "He went to the grave with the richness of the mine unexplored," Douglas admitted, but until the moment of his death, he had proved equal to each new occasion as it arose. "He was better as brigadier than as colonel; better still as major-general; and as lieutenant-general was best of all," the writer-biographer John Esten Cooke said of him. Cooke believed that "the brain which conceived and executed the campaign of the Valley, must have been equal to any position." Even Richard Taylor, that critic of West Pointers, said, "What limit to set to his ability, I know not, for he was ever superior to occasion." And Grant even said, "No doubt so able and patient a man as Jackson, who worked so hard at anything he attempted, would have adapted himself to new conditions and risen with them. He died before his opportunity."[50]

Jackson himself said, a man could be whatever he resolved to be. He would have resolved to succeed no matter what the circumstances. His sister-in-law, who had been allowed unguarded insight into "the very pulse of the machine," said: "Under any circumstances he was a man *sui generis*; and none who came into close enough contact with him to see into his inner nature were willing to own that they had ever known just such another man."[51]

* * *

Decoration Day, May 30, 1885, was different from most such celebrations at Antietam. It was special. For the first time that Henry Kyd Douglas could remember, a large delegation of the "men who wore the grey" crossed the river for the occasion. They had come to see George McClellan, who had been asked to deliver the annual address. Like many of the men who wore the gray, it was the first time since the battle that McClellan had revisited this scene of exultation and sorrow.

Douglas invited McClellan to be his guest at his home in nearby Hagerstown, and the two men walked the battlefield together. In a sense it was the two old classmates walking it—George McClellan and Tom Jackson, by proxy. They perhaps bantered back and forth more than they would had Jackson been there, for both McClellan and Douglas were men of wit and charm.

On the rostrum later, before the veterans of both armies, McClellan delivered his address. Nearly twenty-three years had passed since the battle of Antietam. McClellan had run against Abraham Lincoln in the presidential election of 1864 and lost. He had since been the governor of New Jersey and had led a distinguished career in civil life. He and Nelly now had grown children of their own—like many of these veterans now waiting to hear what he would say on this field where they had fought in the bloodiest single day of the war.

McClellan looked about him a moment and remembered when he had last stood there. "The smoke of battle still wreathed these hills and filled these valleys," he reminded the soldiers, "these rocks still re-echoed the harsh sounds of strife, and the ground was all too thickly strewn with the forms of the quiet dead, and of those still writhing in agony."

He gazed on the veterans of both armies now sitting beside one another in peace, and spoke to them as one: "Those who fought on either side; men who, clad in grey, followed the noble Lee. . . ." There was a stir among the Confederates as they uncovered in memory of the name of their old commander. McClellan continued, ". . . and we who wore the blue." They were all there now, he told them, with a common purpose—"to testify our reverence for the valiant dead."

"Let us bury all animosity, all bitter recollections of the past . . . ." McClellan urged. "I am glad, inexpressibly glad, that I have been permitted to live until the fame and exploits of these magnanimous rivals have become the common property of our people; when the ability and virtues of Robert Lee, and the achievements of the magnificent Army of Northern Virginia, as well as the heroism and renown of the proud Army of the Potomac, have already become a part of the common heritage of glory of all the people of America."

He wished, he confessed to those soldiers of both armies, that just once more he could take Lee by the hand, "that splendid man and soldier," as he had "in those long past days when we served together in the land of the Montezumas...." But that could never be. It was too late. Lee was gone.

When McClellan finished speaking, the veterans of both armies rose and marched together, and he watched them pass in review and took their salutes. As his own soldiers passed the dais they perhaps remembered how he had once so moved on their hearts as the wind sways the rows of standing corn; the men in gray perhaps remembered how they had marched and fought so hard for Old Jack and stormed so willingly into the cannon's mouth for Marse Robert.[52]

Five months later McClellan was also gone. In early October he suffered a severe attack of angina pectoris. On the evening of October 28 he complained again of recurring chest pains. His condition rapidly worsened in the night and at about three the next morning he turned and looked with deepest affection at his beloved Nelly. "Tell her I am better now," he whispered weakly to his physician, and peacefully passed away. He was 58 years old.[53]

On a dark rainy day as mournful as the occasion, they buried him in the McClellan and Marcy family plot in the Riverview Cemetery in Trenton, overlooking the Delaware River. Henry Douglas stood by the graveside and looked across at the sorrowing faces of two of McClellan's own generals, Winfield Scott Hancock and William B. Franklin. Standing between them, uncovered and as heartbroken as either of them, was McClellan's old Confederate enemy and friend, Joseph E. Johnston.[54]

McClellan had failed to fulfill the shining promise of greatness, but he had not failed these friends. It didn't matter any more that many of those who loved him the most had been his Confederate enemies. Johnston called him "a dear friend whom I have so long loved and admired." Dabney Maury would say that "a brighter, kindlier, more genial gentlemen did not live than he." William Gardner, a Confederate classmate whom the war had made a cripple for life, would remember: "I was one of his intimates at the academy, and I still cherish a tender memory of him."[55]

Memories were all that were left now. The days of war and glory were over—for all of them.

Epilogue

For A. P. Hill there would be no life after the Civil War. He was riding to reach the shattered lines of his corps at Petersburg on April 2, 1865, when he was shot and killed by a federal infantryman.

He fell, it was said, "where his gallant spirit was ever found, in the path of duty." When told he was dead, Robert E. Lee said: "He is at rest now, and we who are left are the ones to suffer." Pattie Guild, Lee's doctor's wife, awoke that night to sounds of sobbing in an adjoining ambulance and was told it was Dolly Hill weeping for her lost husband.[1]

David Rumph (Neighbor) Jones did not survive either. Within a month after Antietam where he and Hill had met in the embattled outskirts of Sharpsburg to drive back the Union line together, he was stricken by a heart attack. Three months later he was dead. Some said he died not of an ailing, but of a broken heart. For his brother-in-law, Colonel Henry W. Kingsbury of the Eleventh Connecticut, whom he loved, had been killed at Antietam near the Burnside Bridge—by Jones's own troops.[2]

Neither did another classmate, Confederate Brigadier John Adams, live. He died leading the bloody Confederate charge of the

Union works at Franklin, Tennessee, on November 30, 1864. Union soldiers found him under his horse, shot nine times. As he died in their arms he said, "It is the fate of a soldier to die for his country."[3]

Of the two Union classmates whom Neighbor Jones had last seen in the smoking ruins of Fort Sumter, John G. Foster died first. When he was carried to his grave in 1874, all business in Nashua, New Hampshire, was suspended. Mourning badges floated from public and private buildings throughout the city, and the air was filled with the peel of tolling bells, the roar of minute guns, and the beat of muffled drums.[4]

Truman Seymour became, like Foster, a Union major general and fought through the war all the way to Appomattox. He retired after thirty years in the army, then he and Louisa moved to Europe, where he became an artist. His drawings, like those he sketched for Robert Anderson at Fort Sumter, had a way of capturing a mood and recording a particular moment in time. He died in Florence, Italy, in 1891.[5]

Birkett Davenport Fry, who survived Gettysburg and lived for twenty-six more years after the war, despite all the bullets he had taken, became a cotton manufacturer in Richmond. He was "a most useful and valued citizen," whose nature, despite his reputation as "a man with a gunpowder reputation," continued to be "as gentle, his bearing as modest as his life was momentous."[6]

William Montgomery Gardner, who took nearly as many bullets in his body as Fry did, also lived long after the war. His leg was shattered at First Manassas. Despite that, he became a Confederate brigadier general, and in one of the very last small engagements of the war, he met, fought, and was defeated by his Union classmate George Stoneman, who was on another raid. Gardner died peacefully in Tennessee in 1901.

George Stoneman became a politician after the war. He moved to California, bought a beautiful estate, and became governor. His administration was as stormy as the weather at Chancellorsville had been in April 1863, when he could not get his cavalry across the swollen Rappahannock. He died in his native New York in 1894.

John Gibbon remained in the army after the war, and in 1876 commanded the column that rescued the living and buried the dead of George Armstrong Custer's bloody last stand at Little Big Horn. A year later he marched 250 miles to attack the Nez Perce under Chief

Joseph. It was typical of Gibbon that afterward Joseph became his dearest friend. Gibbon died in Baltimore in 1896 and was buried in Arlington National Cemetary.

George Henry Gordon, the classmate who had so courageously parried Tom Jackson's swift and heavy blows down the Valley in 1862, became a Union major general. After Appomattox, he practiced law in Boston and wrote about the war. He was at John Foster's bedside when he died in 1874, and died himself twelve years later.

George Horatio Derby, the class prankster, became one of the army's best topographical engineers in the American West, where he became nationally famous not as a soldier, but as a humorist. His published writings, collected into two books, foreshadowed the works of a more famous admirer, Mark Twain. But Derby fell ill and died just as the Civil War began and took to the grave with him his two most famous noms de plume—Squibob and John Phoenix. It is probably just as well. The war that was just beginning would have been too serious for the three of them.

Edmund Lafayette Hardcastle, who manned the cannon at Vera Cruz and saw more of death than he ever cared to in Mexico, left the army before the Civil War and never returned. He became a delegate to the two Democratic national conventions in 1860, and after the war a railroad president and a member of the Maryland House of Delegates. He died in Maryland in the last year of the nineteenth century.

William Dutton, who wrote such descriptive letters to his sweetheart and did so well at West Point, fell ill after graduation and was forced to resign, never realizing his military potential. He died in New York City on the Fourth of July in 1862.

Sam Bell Maxey, who had graduated only one file removed from George Pickett at the bottom of the class, ably commanded the Indian Territory for the Confederacy in the last year of the war. Afterward he became a two-term U.S. Senator from Texas and a member of West Point's board of visitors. He died honored and distinguished in 1895.

Samuel Davis Sturgis, who had saved his cavalry regiment from the buffalo stampede in the Indian wars, became a Union brigadier, and was spectacularly defeated by the fierce-fighting Confederate cavalryman Nathan Bedford Forrest, at Brice's Cross Roads in Mississippi in 1864. After Appomattox he went back to doing what he did best, fighting Indians. He died in St. Paul, Minnesota, in 1889.

Dabney Herndon Maury became a Confederate major general and commanded at Mobile in the last year of the war. One of his men said of him that he was " 'every inch a soldier,' but then there were not many inches of him. The soldiers called him 'puss in boots,' because half of his diminutive person seemed lost in a pair of immense cavalry boots of the day."[7] After the war he continued to serve the memory of the Confederacy with his heart and his pen as a founder of the Southern Historical Society and as an editor of its Papers. Before he died in the first year of the twentieth century in Peoria, Illinois, he said that there must be no pomp at his funeral: "Let the services be simple. Let the coffin be hauled to the railroad station on a caisson, followed by a few of my old comrades. I want my body to be sent to the old family burying ground, at Fredericksburg, that I may sleep with my people." And it was done.[8]

George Pickett married his beautiful LaSalle in old St. Paul's Church in Petersburg on September 15, 1863, to the salute of a hundred guns, chimes, cheers, bells, and bugles. But he never recovered from the trauma of the charge at Gettysburg. An excellent brigade commander, he never proved he could handle a division. Lee would blame him for the army's defeat at Five Forks and ostracize him, and Pickett would later say bitterly of Lee, "that old man . . . had my division massacred at Gettysburg." George McClellan said of Pickett that "perhaps there is no doubt that he was the best infantry soldier developed on either side during the Civil War." He became an insurance agent in Richmond and died in Norfolk in 1875, but a single tragic charge had made his name immortal.[9]

Jesse Reno, who died on South Mountain in 1862, was immortalized in a very different way when Reno, Nevada, was named for him. He said before he died, "Tell my command that if not in body, I will be with them in spirit."[10]

And Cadmus Wilcox, who fought from the day the war opened until the day it closed in such a workmanlike manner—always punctual, always present, always popular—never did meet a bullet. The four Confederate and four Union generals who carried him to his grave in Washington, after a natural death in December 1890, never did anything they hated to do more than that—except fight against one another in the war of brothers.

Darius Couch, the competent and acerbic New Yorker, rose to the highest echelons of the Union army, but had the misfortune to serve under incompetent generals in chief. He lived to write the obituaries of many of his classmates before dying himself in 1897.

James Oakes, who also became a general in the Union army, though never a star, saw his greatest days of military glory in the Mexican and Indian wars, where he was a star. Although desperately wounded in Texas fighting Indians in the 1850s, he lived until 1910.

Charles Seaforth Stewart, finishing first in this class of such enormous talent, also never became a star, rising only to the rank of colonel of engineers—and that not until after the war. He died on Nantucket Island in 1904.

In 1917, when yet another war was just beginning, Francis Theodore Bryan, sixth ranked in the class of 1846 and the last living, died in St. Louis.

They were all gone then, those who were touched by the fire of fame and immortality, and those who were not. But of them all it might be said, as James Longstreet said of George Pickett:

> Green be the turf above thee,
> Friend of my better days!
> None knew thee but to love thee,
> Nor named thee but to praise.[11]

In Appreciation

It takes a number of things to write a book. Aside from time and solitude, these things tend to become people, primarily librarians, a sensitive editor, a good agent, and numerous friends, cohorts, and relatives.

The librarian most important in the life of this book has been Charley Hively, the research specialist at the Harrison County Public Library in Clarksburg, West Virginia, my hometown. It would also have been young Stonewall Jackson's library had he not been born 175 years too soon, for Clarksburg was also his hometown. Gifted with an industry and inventiveness that Jackson would have admired, Charley was able to find any book anywhere and get it on loan. He repeatedly did this throughout the research and writing phase. I am likewise indebted to Charley's predecessor, Cathy Culp, who suffered me for a shorter time, but was also of great help.

The archivists and librarians at the U.S. Military Academy at West Point opened their manuscript treasures most graciously. I am particularly indebted to Suzanne Christoff at the academy archives, and her assistants at the time, Dorothy Rapp and Kathy Boyd. Judith Sibley in the academy's special collections division was most helpful, together with her director, Alan Aimone, and another of his staff, Dawn Crumpler.

Kathleen E. Beldsoe, of the special collections department at the James E. Morrow Library at Marshall University in Huntington, West Virginia, which often contained materials available nowhere else in the state, accommodated more than one of my irregular trips to see her. I am also indebted to the book and archival collections and librarians at the University of Maryland, West Virginia University, the Library of Congress, the National Archives, the United States Army Military History Institute at the Carlisle Barracks, the library at the Gettysburg Military Park, and the Museum of the Confederacy and the Virginia Historical Society in Richmond.

Mauro DiPreta, my editor at Warner Books, was the soul of sensitivity, attacking my manuscript when it grew long and diarrhetic not with a machete, but a scalpel. My agent, Michael J. Hamilburg, a gentle and loving man whose nature shatters all of the stereotypes about agents, matched Mauro in sensitivity and consideration.

Edwin C. Bearss, chief historian emeritus of the National Park Service and a walking encyclopedia of the Civil War, caught errors in the manuscript that a lesser mind, such as mine, might never have caught. James M. McPherson, the much esteemed Civil War scholar, was more than generous in his comments. To both I am heavily indebted.

Linda C. Durkee, a friend and fellow-writer in Washington, reviewed early parts of the manuscript for stylistic, literary, and organization faults before they got too far out of hand.

And my family has been the model of patience and longsuffering while their husband, father, and in-law was off all those months in the nineteenth century. They always did suspect that he lived in the past. Now they are certain of it.

Notes

PART 1 WEST POINT

From Every Degree of Provincialism

1. Details in the opening paragraphs are from Roy Bird Cook, *The Family and Early Life of Stonewall Jackson*, 5th ed. (Charleston, WV: Education Foundation, 1967), pp. 83–86.

2. Andrew Jackson to Andrew Jackson Donelson, 5 March 1823, *Correspondence of Andrew Jackson*, ed. John Spencer Bassett, 7 vols. (Washington: Carnegie Institution, 1926–1935), vol. 3, p. 191.

3. For a discussion of West Point's standing as an engineering school in the antebellum years, see Sidney Forman, *West Point: A History of the United States Military Academy* (New York: Columbia University Press, 1950), pp. 88–89.

4. Cook, *Family and Early Life*, pp. 84–85. A slightly different version of how Jackson answered this question is in Mary Anna Jackson, *Memoirs of Stonewall Jackson* (1895; reprint, Dayton: Press of Morningside Bookshop, 1985), p. 31; and R. L. Dabney, *Life and Campaigns of Lieut.-Gen. Thomas J. Jackson (Stonewall Jackson)* (1865; reprint, Harrisonburg, VA: Sprinkle Publications, 1983), p. 31.

5. Jackson's trip to Washington is mainly from Cook, *Family and Early Life*, p. 85. For years afterward, a widely accepted version of the journey—retold with poetic embellishment by the "old citizens" of Clarksburg—had him walking the entire three hundred miles and arriving road-weary and travel-stained. For this romantic version see John G. Gittings, *Personal Recollections of Stonewall Jackson, Also Sketches and Stories* (Cincinnati: Editor Publishing Co., 1899), pp. 11–12.

6. Cook, *Family and Early Life*, p. 84. For a thumbnail sketch of Hays see James Morton Callahan, *History of West Virginia Old and New and West Virginia Biography*, 3 vols. (Chicago and New York: American Historical Society, 1923), vol. 3, p. 203.

7. Gibson Butcher to Samuel L. Hays, 14 June 1842, Cook, *Family and Early Life*, pp. 85–86.

8. Smith Gibson to Samuel L. Hays, and Evan Carmack to Samuel L. Hays, 14 June 1842, Cook, *Family and Early Life*, pp. 86–87.

9. Cook, *Family and Early Life*, pp. 87–89.

10. Samuel L. Hays to John C. Spencer, 17 June 1842, U.S. Military Academy, Cadet Application Papers, 1805–1866, U.S. Military Academy Archives, No. 162, 1842. The letter is also reprinted in Cook, *Family and Early Life*, p. 89, although under a different date, 19 June 1842.

11. John Tyler, Jr.'s recollection is in Cook, *Family and Early Life*, p. 91. Some versions of Jackson's appointment have Hays taking him personally to the secretary of war's office, where Spencer gave the cadet-to-be some fatherly advice about how to conduct himself at West Point. For that version see Jackson, *Memoirs of Stonewall Jackson*, p. 32; and Dabney, *Life and Campaigns of Lieut.-Gen. Thomas J. Jackson*, pp. 31–32.

12. The price of the steamboat fare in 1842 is in Samuel H. Raymond to Joshua Raymond, 31 July 1842, Samuel H. Raymond Papers, U.S. Military Academy Library.

13. Timothy Dwight, *Travels in New England and New York*, ed. Barbara Miller Solomon with the assistance of Patricia M. King, 4 vols. (1822; reprint, Cambridge: Harvard University Press, Belknap Press, 1969), vol. 3, pp. 303–4, p. 313.

14. Harriet Martineau, *Retrospect of Western Travel*, 3 vols. (1838; reprint, New York: Greenwood Press, 1969), vol. 1, pp. 57–59.

15. Charles Dickens, *American Notes* (1892; reprint, New York: St. Martin's Press, 1985), p. 199.

16. George McClellan to his sister, Frederica English, 28 June 1842, George B. McClellan Papers, Manuscript Division, Library of Congress. All of McClellan's letters cited throughout the book, unless otherwise noted, are to be found in series A, container 1, reel 1 (A1:1).

17. Peter S. Michie, *General McClellan* (New York: D. Appleton, 1915), p. 7; Stephen W. Sears, *George B. McClellan: The Young Napoleon* (New York: Ticknor & Fields, 1988), pp. 1–3.

18. Dabney Herndon Maury, "General T. J. ('Stonewall') Jackson: Incidents in the Remarkable Career of the Great Soldier," *Southern Historical Society Papers* 25 (1897), p. 311. In future citations, the title of these Papers will be shortened to *SHSP*.

19. Dabney Herndon Maury, *Recollections of a Virginian in the Mexican, Indian, and Civil Wars*, 3d ed. (New York: Charles Scribner's Sons, 1894), p. 22.

20. William Dutton to C. Dutton, 19 June 1842, William Dutton Papers, U.S. Military Academy Library.

21. John C. Tidball, "Getting through West Point by One Who Did," typescript, John C. Tidball Papers, U.S. Military Academy Library. For an edited, published version of this sprightly account of life at West Point in the mid 1840s, see James L. Morrison, Jr., ed., "Getting through West Point: The Cadet Memoirs of John C. Tidball, Class of 1848," *Civil War History* 26 (December 1980). The remark on provincialism is in Morrison, p. 308.

22. Synonyms for the lowly are from Henry Heth, *The Memoirs of Henry Heth*, ed. James L. Morrison, Jr. (Westport, CT: Greenwood Press, 1974), p. xvii. Heth answered to all of these epithets as a plebe with the class of 1847. Also see Oliver E. Wood, *The West Point Scrap Book: A Collection of Stories, Songs, and Legends of the United States Military Academy* (New York: D. Van Nostrand, 1871), p. 338.

23. The number of appointees to the class varies from 133 to 164, depending on whom you read. The 122 figure is Cadet George Horatio Derby's count of the actual number who had arrived by early July. See Derby to Mary Townsend Derby, 2 July 1842, George Horatio Derby Papers, U.S. Military Academy Library, box 7.

24. Maury's account of Jackson's arrival is in "General T. J. ('Stonewall') Jackson," pp. 309–10; and *Recollections of a Virginian*, pp. 22–23.

25. Erasmus D. Keyes, *Fifty Years' Observation of Men and Events Civil and Military* (New York: Charles Scribner's Sons, 1884), p. 190.

Sighing for What We Left Behind

1. Derby to his mother, Mary Townsend Derby, 2 July 1842, Derby Papers. All of his letters to her from West Point are in box 7.

Notes

2. See correspondence between John Quincy Adams and Mary Townsend Derby, Derby Papers, box 6; and U.S. Military Academy, Cadet Application Papers, No. 91, 1841.

3. Derby to Walter Janes, 12 June 1842, Derby Papers, box 6. For a description of Kinsley's Classical and Mathematical School see *A Guide Book to West Point and Vicinity; containing descriptive, historical, and statistical sketches of the United States Military Academy, and other objects of interest* (New York: J. H. Colton, 1844), pp. 42–47.

4. The cadet physical examination is described in Morrison, "Getting through West Point," p. 312; Derby to Mary Townsend Derby, 2 July 1842, Derby Papers; and William Montgomery Gardner, "The Memoirs of Brigadier-General William Montgomery Gardner," ed. Elizabeth McKinne Gardner, typescript of a series of articles appearing in the *Memphis Commercial Appeal* in 1912, U.S. Military Academy Library, p. 5.

5. Morrison, "Getting through West Point," p. 312.

6. Derby to Mary Townsend Derby, 2 July 1842, Derby Papers.

7. Ibid.

8. Stephen E. Ambrose, *Duty, Honor, Country: A History of West Point* (Baltimore: Johns Hopkins University Press, 1966), p. 103.

9. Lloyd Lewis, *Captain Sam Grant* (Boston: Little, Brown and Company, 1950), p. 89.

10. A list of successful candidates, with Jackson's name at the very end, is in U.S. Military Academy, Staff Records, No. 3, 1842 to 1845, U.S. Military Academy Archives, pp. 51–53. William Montgomery Gardner, his classmate, says Jackson actually failed to pass, but was not sent home as many others were. "There must have been something about him which impressed the authorities. . . ." Gardner says. "For some reason he was permitted to occupy a room in the barracks during the summer while the cadet corps was in camp. In September he was again examined and passed." The academic board's records, however, list Jackson as qualifying in June. Gardner's version is in his typescript "Memoirs," p. 9.

11. Derby to Mary Townsend Derby, 2 July 1842, Derby Papers.

12. McClellan to Frederica English, 28 June 1842, McClellan Papers.

13. Raymond to Mrs. Joshua Raymond, 12 June 1842, Raymond Papers.

14. Morrison, "Getting through West Point," p. 307. Also see Morrison's *"The Best School in the World": West Point, the Pre-Civil War Years, 1833–1866* (Kent, OH: Kent State University Press, 1986), p. 65.

15. Gardner, "Memoirs," pp. 5–6.

16. Dutton to C. Dutton, 19 June 1842, Dutton Papers.

17. Raymond to David Raymond, 16 October 1842, Raymond Papers.

18. "Rabid beast" is defined in Wood, *The West Point Scrap Book*, p. 338, as an impertinent plebe.

19. Lowe's brassy behavior is described in Gardner, "Memoirs," p. 6.

20. Raymond to David Raymond, 16 October 1842, Raymond Papers.

21. Ibid.

22. Raymond to Joshua Raymond, 30 September 1842, Raymond Papers.

23. Dutton to John W. Matthews, 31 July 1842, Dutton Papers.

24. Ibid.

25. Derby to Mary Townsend Derby, 8 August 1842, Derby Papers.

26. Hill to Frances Russell Hill, 3 April 1843. Hill Family Papers, Virginia Historical Society, Richmond.

27. Dutton to John W. Matthews, 20 September 1842, Dutton Papers.

28. Morrison, "Getting through West Point," p. 310.

29. Ibid.

30. Maury, *Recollections of a Virginian*, p. 25.

31. Dutton to C. Dutton, 19 June 1842, Dutton Papers.

32. Derby to Mary Townsend Derby, 2 July 1842, Derby Papers.

33. Raymond to Mrs. Joshua Raymond, 12 June 1842, and to Joshua Raymond, 31 July 1842, Raymond Papers.

34. William Whitman Bailey, "My Boyhood at West Point," *Personal Narratives of Events in the War of the Rebellion*, 4th ser, no. 12 (Providence: Rhode Island Soldiers and Sailors Historical Society, 1891), pp. 10–13.

35. The Pompeii image is a direct steal from the O. Henry short story "Schools and Schools," in *The Complete Works of O. Henry*, 2 vols. (Garden City, NY: Doubleday, 1953), vol. 1, p. 712.

36. Derby recounts these nighttime shenanigans in a newsy letter to Mary Townsend Derby, 2 July 1842, Derby Papers.

37. Ibid.; Dutton to John W. Matthews, 12 July 1842, Dutton Papers.

38. Dutton to John W. Matthews, 12 and 31 July 1842, Dutton Papers.

39. George W. Cullum to Alfred Huidekoper, 30 July 1832, Sidney Forman, *Cadet Life before the Mexican War*, Bulletin No. 1 (West Point: U.S. Military Academy Library, 1945), p. 11.

40. Derby to Mary Townsend Derby, 2 July 1842, Derby Papers. There is a brief description of the nightly summertime "stag dances" in *A Guide to West Point and Vicinity*, pp. 17–18.

41. Dutton to John W. Matthews, 12 July 1842, Dutton Papers.

42. Jackson, *Memoirs of Stonewall Jackson*, p. 35.

43. Maury's second frustrated overture to Jackson is in "General T. J. ('Stonewall') Jackson," p. 310. For a word about the police detail see Morrison, "Getting through West Point," p. 313.

44. A few representative euphemisms for the examinations are to be found in Forman, *Cadet Life before the Mexican War*, p. 17.

45. Jackson, *Memoirs of Stonewall Jackson*, pp. 33–34.

46. Fort Putnam and the view it commanded are described in *A Guide Book to West Point and Vicinity*, pp. 35–40. The note on the foundry is from Thomas J. Fleming, *West Point: The Men and Times of the United States Military Academy* (New York: William Morrow & Co., 1969), p. 66. Jackson's love for Old·Put is in Jackson, *Memoirs of Stonewall Jackson*, p. 39.

47. Jackson's maxims, which would have made a saint—or a monk—of anybody, are listed in full in *Memoirs of Stonewall Jackson*, pp. 35–38.

As Intelligible as Sanskrit

1. McClellan to Frederica English, 10 September 1842, McClellan Papers.

2. Ibid.

3. Raymond to Joshua Raymond, 2 September 1842, Raymond Papers.

4. Ulysses S. Grant, *Personal Memoirs of U. S. Grant*, 2 vols. (1894; reprint [2 vols. in 1], New York: AMS Press, 1972), p. 27.

5. Morris Schaff, *The Spirit of Old West Point, 1858–1862* (Boston: Houghton Mifflin, 1907), pp. 60–61.

6. McClellan to Frederica English, 10 September 1842, McClellan Papers; Morrison, "Getting through West Point," p. 315.

7. McClellan recreates Thomas's pep talk in the letter to Frederica English, 10 September 1842, McClellan Papers.

8. Derby to Mary Townsend Derby, 8 August 1842, Derby Papers.

9. Wood, *The West Point Scrap Book*, p. 338.

10. Raymond to Joshua Raymond, 2 September 1842, Raymond Papers.

11. Dutton copied off the posted order of things, not precisely in that language, in a letter to his cousin and sweetheart, Lucy J. Matthews, 18 February 1843, Dutton Papers.

12. Morrison, "Getting through West Point," p. 307.

13. The Academy building is described in *A Guide Book to West Point and Vicinity*, pp. 12–13, pp. 26–29.

14. Maury, "General T. J. ('Stonewall') Jackson," p. 311.

15. Morrison, "Getting through West Point," p. 322, p. 308.

16. Maury, *Recollections of a Virginian*, p. 60.

17. Morrison, *"The Best School in the World,"* p. 87. Derby uses the phrase "perfect rag" in letters to Mary Townsend Derby. For example, the letter of 5 January 1844, Derby Papers. There were several ways to describe a perfect recitation, all of them rolling fondly off the tongue. For instance: "to max it," "to make a cold max," and "to rag out"—the last also

meaning to dress well, which was also important to Derby, who was something of a dandy. See Wood, *The West Point Scrap Book*, p. 339.

18. Morrison, "Getting through West Point," p. 320.

19. Derby to Mary Townsend Derby, 3 October 1842, Derby Papers.

20. Morrison, *"The Best School in the World,"* p. 91, p. 101.

21. Schaff, *The Spirit of Old West Point*, p. 68.

22. George W. Cullum, *Biographical Register of the Officers and Graduates of the U.S. Military Academy ... from its Establishment, in 1802, to 1890*, 3 vols. with Supplements, 3d ed. (Boston and New York: Houghton Mifflin, 1891), vol. 1, pp. 404–5.

23. Richard Henry Savage, "Literature and Art at West Point," *Army and Navy Journal*, 39 (14 June 1902), p. 1025.

24. Schaff, *The Spirit of Old West Point*, p. 68.

25. Morrison, "Getting through West Point," p. 316.

26. Keyes, *Fifty Years' Observation of Men and Events*, pp. 195–96.

27. Morrison, *"The Best School in the World,"* p. 52.

28. Sylvanus Thayer to George Graham, 28 August 1817, Sylvanus Thayer Papers, U.S. Military Academy Library.

29. Cullum, *Biographical Register*, vol. 1, pp. 36–37.

30. Morrison, "Getting through West Point," p. 317.

31. Raymond describes the recitation procedure in a letter to his brother, Josiah Raymond, 1 October 1842, Raymond Papers.

32. Wood, *The West Point Scrap Book*, p. 337.

33. Morrison, "Getting through West Point," pp. 316–17.

34. Dabney, *Life and Campaigns of Lieut.-Gen. Thomas J. Jackson*, pp. 33–34.

35. Important orders, messages, disciplinary actions and sometimes philosophical discourses, were communicated to the cadets in the daily Post Orders, a handwritten ledger containing a running account of the main events of the day. For the order to change uniforms see U.S. Military Academy, Post Orders, No. 2, 1 June 1842 to 22 June 1846, U.S. Military Academy Archives, p. 34. Hereafter this source will be cited simply as Post Orders.

36. Raymond to Josiah Raymond, 16 October 1842, Raymond Papers.

37. Raymond to Josiah Raymond, 1 October 1842, Raymond Papers; Dutton to John W. Matthews, 20 September and 19 October 1842, Dutton Papers.

38. John Tidball describes the drums in Morrison, "Getting through West Point," p. 307, p. 310.

39. Ibid., p. 318.

40. The complete list of disciplinary rules is in U.S. Military Academy, *Regulations Established for the Organization and Government of the Military Academy* (New York: Wiley & Putnam, 1839), pp. 31–36, pp. 40–43.

41. Dutton to John W. Matthews, 20 September 1842, Dutton Papers.

42. Morrison, "Getting through West Point," p. 318.

43. John Adams to Cave Couts, 19 January 1845, John Adams Letters, 1844–1845, Henry E. Huntington Library and Art Gallery, San Marino, CA.

44. Post Orders, p. 48, p. 54, p. 60.

45. Hashmaking is vividly described in Morrison, "Getting through West Point," pp. 317–18; and in Raymond to Josiah Raymond, 1 October 1842, Raymond Papers.

46. Lewis, *Captain Sam Grant*, p. 70.

47. Mahan to Joel Poinsett, 20 September 1838, in Morrison, *"The Best School in the World,"* p. 42.

48. Schaff, *The Spirit of Old West Point*, p. 37.

49. Percy Gatling Hamlin, ed., *The Making of a Soldier: Letters of General R. S. Ewell* (1935; reprint, Gaithersburg, MD: Ron R. Van Sickle Military Books, 1988), p. 32.

50. Keyes, *Fifty Years' Observation of Men and Events*, p. 193.

51. Post Orders, p. 17; U.S. Military Academy, *Regulations*, p. 62.

52. Delafield is described in Morrison, *"The Best School in the World,"* p. 38, pp. 40–43; Ambrose, *Duty, Honor, Country*, p. 126; and Cullum, *Biographical Register*, vol. 1, pp. 180–86.

53. McClellan to Frederica English, 18 January 1843, McClellan Papers.

54. Post Orders, p. 52.

Oh, for the Sight of Our Native Land

1. The description of Jackson in 1843 is a composite drawn from Morrison, "Getting through West Point," pp. 315–16; Gardner, "Memoirs," p. 9; and Thomas Jackson Arnold, *Early Life and Letters of General Thomas J. Jackson* (1916; reprint, Richmond, VA: Dietz Press, 1957), p. 76.

2. Dabney, *Life and Campaigns of Lieut.-Gen. Thomas J. Jackson*, p. 20, p. 37.

3. Tidball, "Getting through West Point by One Who Did," typescript, Tidball Papers.

4. G.F.R. Henderson, *Stonewall Jackson and the American Civil War*, 2 vols. (1936; reprint, Secaucus, NJ: Blue and Grey Press, n.d.), vol. 1, p. 20.

5. Maury, *Recollections of a Virginian*, p. 23; George B. McClellan, Jr. "Reminiscences of Geo. B. McClellan and 'Stonewall' Jackson," *Blue and Gray* 1 (1893), p. 29.

6. John Russell Young, *Around the World with General Grant: A Narrative of the Visit of General U. S. Grant, Ex-President of the United States, to Various Countries in Europe, Asia, and Africa, in 1877, 1878, 1879*, 2 vols. (New York: American News Company, 1879), vol. 2, p. 210.

7. Tidball and Gardner shared this assessment of Jackson. See Morrison, "Getting through West Point," p. 315; and Gardner, "Memoirs," pp. 8–9.

8. Raymond to Mrs. Joshua Raymond, 12 January 1843, Raymond Papers.

9. U.S. Military Academy, Staff Records, pp. 121–22.

10. McClellan to Frederica English, 18 January 1843, McClellan Papers.

11. McClellan to John McClellan, 21 January 1843, McClellan Papers.

12. Dutton to Lucy J. Matthews, 18 February 1843, Dutton Papers.

13. Post Orders, p. 66.

14. McClellan to Frederica English, 18 January, and to John McClellan, 21 January 1843, McClellan Papers.

15. Raymond to Mary Raymond, 22 February 1843, Raymond Papers.

16. Quoted in Kenneth W. Rapp, *West Point: Whistler in Cadet Gray, and Other Stories about the United States Military Academy* (Croton-on-Hudson, NY: North River Press, 1978), p. 101.

17. Albert E. Church, *Personal Reminiscences of the Military Academy, from 1824 to 1831* (West Point: U.S.M.A. Press, 1879), p. 19.

18. Gardner, "Memoirs," p. 8.

19. Reprinted in Forman, *Cadet Life before the Mexican War*, 1. Except as otherwise cited, the material on Benny Havens and his tavern is from Robert J. Wood, "Early Days of Benny Havens," *The Pointer* 14 (26 February 1937), pp. 6–13, p. 29.

20. Hill to Frances Russell Hill, 3 April 1843, Hill Family Papers.

21. Raymond to Mrs. Joshua Raymond, 19 May 1843, Raymond Papers.

22. U.S. Military Academy, *Regulations*, p. 7.

23. Morrison, "Getting through West Point," p. 311.

24. Schaff, *The Spirit of Old West Point*, p. 51.

25. Dutton to Lucy J. Matthews, 23 June 1843, Dutton Papers.

26. Ibid.

27. The post-examination rankings are in U.S. Military Academy, *Official Register of the Officers and Cadets of the U.S. Military Academy* (West Point, June 1843), pp. 12–14.

28. A complete list of the new corporals is in Post Orders, p. 102, p. 113.

29. Raymond to Joshua Raymond, 6 May 1843, Raymond Papers.

30. McClellan to John McClellan, 21 January 1843, McClellan Papers.

31. Raymond to Mrs. Joshua Raymond, 11 August 1843, Raymond Papers.

32. Morrison, "Getting through West Point," p. 320.

33. George W. Cullum to Catherine Cullum, 24 April 1831; Forman, *Cadet Life before the Mexican War*, p. 14.

34. The background on Weir is from Cullum, *Biographical Register*, vol. 1, pp. 38–40.

35. Morrison, "Getting through West Point," p. 321.

36. Michael E. Moss, "Robert W. Weir as Teacher," in *Robert W. Weir of West Point: Illustrator, Teacher and Poet*, ed. Michael E. Moss (West Point, NY: U.S. Military Academy, 1976), p. 48.

37. The various holiday celebrations, glad tidings, and strictures from the superintendent, although by no means couched in precisely those terms, are from the Post Orders, p. 136, p. 138.

38. U.S. Military Academy, Staff Records, pp. 225–27.

39. Jackson's euphoria is reflected in a letter to Laura Jackson, 28 January 1844; Arnold, *Early Life and Letters of General Thomas J. Jackson*, pp. 62–64.

40. These cadet infractions were publicized and commented on by the superintendent in the Post Orders, pp. 139–40, p. 149, p. 158.

41. Derby to Mary Townsend Derby, 25 December 1843, Derby Papers.

42. Derby to Mary Townsend Derby, 12 May 1844, Derby Papers.

43. Derby to Mary Townsend Derby, 17 June 1844, Derby Papers.

44. U.S. Military Academy, *Official Register*, June 1844, pp. 10–12, pp. 17–19.

45. Post Orders, p. 170.

46. Ibid., p. 169.

Death in the Family

1. Morrison, "Getting through West Point," p. 315.

2. Darius N. Couch, "George Stoneman," *Twenty-sixth Annual Reunion of the Association of the Graduates of the United States Military Academy . . . June 10th, 1895* (Saginaw, MI: Seemann & Peters, 1895), p. 26.

3. Morrison, *"The Best School in the World,"* pp. 50–51.

4. Oliver Otis Howard, *Autobiography of Oliver Otis Howard*, 2 vols. (New York: Baker & Taylor Company, 1907), vol. 1, p. 56.

5. Morrison, *"The Best School in the World,"* p. 51.

6. Edward S. Holden, "Biographical Memoir of William H. C. Bartlett, 1804–1893," *National Academy of Sciences Biographical Memoirs* 7 (June 1911), p. 186.

7. Morrison, "Getting through West Point," p. 320.

8. The low-down on optics is from Maury, *Recollections of a Virginian*, pp. 25–26.

9. Derby to Mary Townsend Derby, 8 October and 24 December 1844, Derby Papers.

10. Post Orders, p. 209.

11. Adams to Cave Couts, 30 September 1844, Adams Letters.

12. Derby to Mary Townsend Derby, 24 December 1844, Derby Papers.

13. Adams to Cave Couts, 19 January 1845, Adams Letters.

14. Derby to Mary Townsend Derby, 24 December 1844, Derby Papers.

15. Hill to Frances Russell Hill, 3 April 1843, Hill Family Papers.

16. Raymond to Mary Raymond, 28 December 1844, Raymond Papers.

17. Jackson to Laura Arnold, 10 February 1845, Arnold, *Early Life and Letters of Thomas J. Jackson*, p. 69.

18. Wood, *The West Point Scrap Book*, p. 337.

19. Ibid., p. 339.

20. McClellan to Elizabeth McClellan, 1 February 1845, McClellan Papers. Also see Derby to Mary Townsend Derby, 4 February 1845, Derby Papers.

21. Richard Delafield to Josiah Raymond, 20 January 1845, Raymond Papers.

22. Arnold, *Early Life and Letters of Thomas J. Jackson*, p. 76.

23. Gardner, "Memoirs," p. 9.

24. Delafield to Josiah Raymond, 20 January 1845, Raymond Papers.

25. Derby to Mary Townsend Derby, 4 February 1845, Derby Papers; William Dutton, Truman Seymour, and Charles Stewart to Mr. and Mrs. Joshua Raymond, 30 January 1845, Raymond Papers.

26. Irene Weir, *Robert W. Weir* (New York: House of Field-Doubleday, 1947), p. 112.

27. Post Orders, pp. 214–15.

28. Derby to Mary Townsend Derby, 4 February 1845, Derby Papers; McClellan to Elizabeth McClellan, 1 February 1845, McClellan Papers; Jackson to Laura Arnold, 10 February 1845; Arnold, *Early Life and Letters of Thomas J. Jackson*, p. 69.

29. Derby describes the funeral in his letter to Mary Townsend Derby, 4 February 1845, Derby Papers.

30. Dutton, Seymour, and Stewart to Mr. and Mrs. Joshua Raymond, 30 January 1845, Raymond Papers.

31. McClellan to Elizabeth McClellan, 1 February 1845, McClellan Papers.

32. Dutton to Lucy J. Matthews, 13 February 1845, Dutton Papers.

33. Washington's birthday celebration is described in Dutton to Lucy J. Matthews, 22 and 23 February 1845, Dutton Papers; and Derby to Mary Townsend Derby, 26 February 1845, Derby Papers.

34. Derby to Mary Townsend Derby, 9 May 1845, Derby Papers.

35. A. A. Gould, "An Address in Commemoration of Professor J. W. Bailey," *American Association for the Advancement of Science* (19 August 1857), p. 7.

36. Ibid, pp. 3–5.

37. Morrison, *"The Best School in the World,"* p. 54.

38. Dutton to Lucy J. Matthews, 19 March 1845, Dutton Papers.

39. Cullum, *Biographical Register*, vol. 1, p. 505.

40. Shakespeare, *As You Like It*, act 2, scene 1, lines 16–17.

41. Cullum, *Biographical Register*, vol. 1, pp. 505–6. For descriptions of Bailey see Cullum, vol. 1, pp. 501–8, and Morrison, *"The Best School in the World,"* pp. 52–53.

42. Dutton to Lucy J. Matthews, 19 March 1845, Dutton Papers.

43. Derby to Mary Townsend Derby, 26 February 1845, Derby Papers.

44. McClellan to Frederica English, 6 January 1845, McClellan Papers.

45. McClellan to Elizabeth McClellan, 1 February 1845, McClellan Papers.

46. Jackson to Laura Arnold, 10 February 1845, Arnold, *Early Life and Letters of Thomas J. Jackson*, p. 69.

47. Gardner, "Memoirs," p. 9.

48. Derby to Mary Townsend Derby, 21 November 1844, Derby Papers.

49. The Derby-Oremieulx story is told in Rapp, *West Point*, pp. 71–72.

50. George R. Stewart, *John Phoenix, Esq., the Veritable Squibob: A Life of Captain George H. Derby*, *U.S.A.* (1937; reprint, New York: De Capo Press, 1969), p. 38.

51. Keyes, *Fifty Years' Observation of Men and Events*, p. 198. Keyes paraphases the conversation; the quotation marks are mine.

52. Mark Twain, *Autobiography*, 2 vols. (New York: Harper & Brothers, 1924), vol. 1, pp. 25–26.

53. Morrison, "Getting through West Point," p. 315, p. 315n.

54. Derby's encounter with Crittenden and its aftermath are described in letters from Derby to Mary Townsend Derby, 21 November, 4 December, and 24 December 1844, Derby Papers. Crittenden managed to remain at the academy his final year and graduate last in the class of 1845. He fought in the Mexican War, then resigned from the army in 1849 to become a filibusterer. He was captured in the filibustering venture in Cuba in 1851 at the age of twenty-eight and lined up to be shot. It is said that when all the prisoners were ordered to kneel before the firing squad, all did so but Crittenden, who cried defiantly, "I never kneel except to my God." He was then shot dead. (See Parmenas Taylor Turnley, *Reminiscences of Parmenas Taylor Turnley: From the Cradle to Three-Score and Ten* [Chicago; Donohue & Henneberry, 1892], pp. 114–15.)

55. Wood, *The West Point Scrap Book*, p. 338.

56. Derby to Mary Townsend Derby, 2 July and 8 August 1842, Derby Papers. Derby apparently believed one didn't have to observe all of the niceties when addressing an Irishman.

57. Derby to Mary Townsend Derby, 26 February 1845, Derby Papers.

58. Derby to Mary Townsend Derby, 12 May 1844, Derby Papers.

59. Derby to Mary Townsend Derby, 3 October 1845, Derby Papers.

60. Jackson to Laura Arnold, 10 February 1845; Arnold, *Early Life and Letters of General Thomas J. Jackson*, p. 68.

61. Dutton to Lucy J. Matthews, 27 February 1845, Dutton Papers.
62. Derby to Mary Townsend Derby, 26 February 1845, Derby Papers.
63. Dutton to Lucy J. Matthews, 3 March 1845, Dutton Papers.
64. Dutton to Lucy J. Matthews, 17 March 1845, Dutton Papers.
65. Derby to Mary Townsend Derby, 26 December 1845, Derby Papers.
66. Maury, "General T. J. ('Stonewall') Jackson," p. 315; and *Recollections of a Virginian*, p. 23.
67. U.S. Military Academy, *Official Register*, June 1845, pp. 9–10.
68. This is a puzzling fact. There is nothing in the records to explain why Jackson was not promoted with many of the others, after having been a cadet sergeant his second-class year. He had continued to race upward through the pack in class rankings and his conduct all that year had been faultless, without a single demerit. He led the entire corps in conduct. It seemed that if anybody deserved promoting, it was Jackson. Since only third-classmen could be corporals and only second-classmen sergeants, all non-officered first-classmen were therefore high privates. Many were their number, and no stigma was attached. Nor is there anything in the records to indicate that Jackson was disappointed. The list of new officers is in the Post Orders, p. 240, p. 262.
69. Dutton to Lucy J. Matthews, 29 March 1845, Dutton Papers.
70. Derby to Mary Townsend Derby, 26 February 1845, Derby Papers.
71. Ibid.

Gone Are the Days of Our Youth

1. Dutton to Lucy J. Matthews, 16 May 1845, Dutton Papers.
2. Impressions of the artillery laboratory are in Dutton to Lucy J. Matthews, 1 April 1845, Dutton Papers; and Morrison, "Getting through West Point," p. 321.
3. Joseph Stewart, "The Class of 1842," *Army and Navy Journal* 39 (14 June 1902), p. 1028.
4. Derby to Mary Townsend Derby, 1 November 1845, Derby Papers.
5. Derby to Mary Townsend Derby, 28 November 1845, Derby Papers.
6. Ibid.
7. *A Guide Book to West Point and Vicinity*, p. 26.
8. Morrison, *"The Best School in the World,"* p. 43, pp. 59–60.
9. *A Guide Book to West Point and Vicinity*, pp. 26–28.
10. Cullum, *Biographical Register*, vol. 1, p. 323, p. 325.
11. Ibid., p. 323.
12. William D. Puleston, *Mahan: the Life and Work of Captain Alfred Thayer Mahan, U.S.N.* (New Haven, CT: Yale University Press, 1939), p. 9.
13. Morrison, "Getting through West Point," p. 322.
14. Dennis Hart Mahan, *Advanced-Guard, Out-Post, and Detachment Service of Troops, with the Essential Principles of Strategy, and Grand Tactics for the Use of Officers of the Militia and Volunteers*, new ed. (New York: John Wiley, 1863), p. 30.
15. For Mahan's opinions on celerity see Ibid., p. 200.
16. Morrison, *"The Best School in the World,"* p. 95.
17. Maury, *Recollections of a Virginian*, pp. 51–52.
18. Cullum, *Biographical Register*, vol. 1, p. 320; Puleston, *Mahan*, p. 6. For brief sketches of Mahan see Cullum, vol. 1, pp. 319–25; Ambrose, *Duty, Honor, Country*, pp. 99–102; Morrison, *"The Best School in the World,"* pp. 47–49.
19. Derby to Mary Townsend Derby, 18 September 1845, Derby Papers.
20. Derby to Mary Townsend Derby, 18 January and 14 February 1846, Derby Papers.
21. James L. Morrison, Jr., "Educating the Civil War Generals: West Point, 1833–1861," *Military Affairs* 38 (October 1974), p. 109.
22. McClellan to Elizabeth McClellan, 18 March 1846, McClellan Papers.
23. McClellan to Frederica English, 13 May 1846, McClellan Papers.
24. Derby to Mary Townsend Derby, 14 and 24 May 1846, Derby Papers.

25. Complete, final class rankings are in U.S. Military Academy, *Official Register*, June 1846, pp. 7–8.

26. Gardner, "Memoirs," p. 8.

27. William B. Franklin, "George Brinton McClellan," *Seventeenth Annual Reunion of the Graduates of the United States Military Academy . . . June 10th, 1886* (East Saginaw, MI: Evening News, Printers and Binders, 1886), p. 56.

28. Gardner, "Memoirs," p. 8.

29. Maury, *Recollections of a Virginian*, p. 59.

30. Keyes, *Fifty Years' Observation of Men and Events*, p. 197.

31. Gardner was among those who thought Jackson unprepossessing. See "Memoirs," p. 9.

32. Maury, *Recollections of a Virginian*, p. 23.

33. Maury, "General T. J. ('Stonewall') Jackson," p. 311.

34. Turnley is quoted in Henderson, *Stonewall Jackson* vol. 1, p. 20.

35. Jackson to Laura Arnold, 1 January 1846; Cook, *The Family and Early Life of Stonewall Jackson*, p. 96.

36. Jackson to Laura Arnold, 2 August 1845; Arnold, *Early Life and Letters of General Thomas J. Jackson*, p. 71.

37. The matching of ranking with assignments is in the U.S. Military Academy, Register of Merit, 1836 to 1852, No. 2, U.S. Military Academy Archives. The descriptive sidequotes are from the whimsical pen of John C. Tidball, in Morrison, "Getting through West Point," pp. 323–24.

38. Darius N. Couch, "Cadmus M. Wilcox," in *Twenty-second Annual Reunion of the Graduates of the United States Military Academy . . . June 12th, 1891* (Saginaw, MI: Seemann & Peters, 1891), p. 28.

39. Maury, "General T. J. ('Stonewall') Jackson," pp. 311–12. Maury closes the account with the comment that "this was 'Old Jack's' first and last frolic, to which in years long after his fame had filled the world he dimly alluded, when he said he was too fond of liquor to trust himself to drink it."

40. Maury, "General T. J. ('Stonewall') Jackson," p. 309, p. 311; and *Recollections of a Virginian*, p. 22.

41. Maury, *Recollections of a Virginian*, pp. 14–15. For brief biographical sketches of Maury's famous uncle see *Dictionary of American Biography*, s.v. "Maury, Matthew Fontaine"; "Matthew Fontaine Maury," *Confederate Veteran* 26 (February 1918), pp. 54–56; and Charles Lee Lewis, "Matthew Fontaine Maury," *Confederate Veteran* 33 (August 1925), pp. 296–301.

42. Maury, *Recollections of a Virginian*, pp. 16–17.

43. Seymour to William Dutton, 31 August 1846, Dutton Papers.

44. Post Orders, pp. 323–24.

PART 2   GONE FOR A SOLDIER

War at Last

1. McClellan to Frederica English, 13 May 1846, McClellan Papers.

2. Derby to Mary Townsend Derby, 14 May 1846, Derby Papers.

3. Background on the war is available in several good histories. One of the earliest general accounts was written by a member of the class of 1846: Cadmus Marcellus Wilcox, *History of the Mexican War*, ed. Mary Rachel Wilcox (Washington: Church News Publishing Company, 1892). A somewhat later history, and still one of the best, is the two-volume work by Justin H. Smith, *The War with Mexico*, 2 vols. (1919; reprint, Gloucester, MA: Peter Smith, 1963). The most recent history is by John S. D. Eisenhower, *So Far from God: The U.S. War with Mexico, 1846–1848* (New York: Random House, 1989). One of the most interesting and useful books, a combined narrative and compilation of original accounts, is George Winston Smith and Charles Judah, eds., *Chronicles of the Gringos: The U.S. Army in the Mexican War, 1846–1848. Accounts of Eye-witnesses & Combatants* (Albuquerque: University of New Mexico Press, 1968). An excellent

bibliography of works on the war is in Seymour V. Connor and Odie B. Faulk, *North America Divided: The Mexican War, 1846–1848* (New York: Oxford University Press, 1971).

4. Smith and Judah, *Chronicles of the Gringos*, p. 1.

5. McClellan to Frederica English, 13 May 1846, McClellan Papers.

6. The genesis of the engineer company is mainly from Gustavus W. Smith, *Company "A," Corps of Engineers, U.S.A., 1846–'48, in the Mexican War* (Battalion Press, 1896), pp. 7–10. Also see William M. Robinson, Jr., "The Engineer Soldiers in the Mexican War," *The Military Engineer* 24 (January–February, 1932), pp. 2–3; Sears, *George B. McClellan*, 13; William Addleman Ganoe, *The History of the United States Army*, rev. ed. (New York: D. Appleton-Century Company, 1942), p. 206; and Morrison, *"The Best School in the World,"* p. 8.

7. McClellan to Frederica English, 16 August 1846, and to Elizabeth McClellan, 23 August 1846, McClellan Papers.

8. George Brinton McClellan, *The Mexican War Diary of George B. McClellan*, ed. William Starr Myers (Princeton, NJ: Princeton University Press, 1917), pp. 7–9; McClellan to Frederica English, 8 October 1846, McClellan Papers.

9. Jackson to Laura Arnold, 25 September 1846, Arnold, *Early Life and Letters of General Thomas J. Jackson*, pp. 80–81; Cook, *The Family and Early Life of Stonewall Jackson*, pp. 98–99.

10. Maury, *Recollections of a Virginian*, pp. 27–28. For background on the Mounted Rifles: Robert M. Utley, *Frontiersmen in Blue: The United States Army and the Indian, 1848–1865* (Lincoln, NE: University of Nebraska Press, 1967), p. 65; and Theo F. Rodenbough and William L. Haskin, eds., *The Army of the United States: Historical Sketches of Staff and Line with Portraits of Generals-in-Chief*, (New York: Maynard, Merrill, 1896), pp. 193–210.

11. McClellan to Frederica English, 8 October 1846, McClellan Papers.

12. Gardner, "Memoirs," p. 10.

13. Ephraim Kirby Smith, *To Mexico with Scott: Letters of Captain E. Kirby Smith to His Wife*, ed. Emma Jerome Blackwood (Cambridge: Harvard University Press, 1917), p. 91.

14. Gardner "Memoirs," pp. 10–11.

15. Maury, *Recollections of a Virginian*, pp. 28–29.

16. McClellan to Frederica English, 8 October 1846, McClellan Papers.

17. McClellan to Elizabeth McClellan, 14 November 1846, McClellan Papers; Sears, *George B. McClellan*, p. 15.

18. Smith, *Company "A"*, p. 10.

19. McClellan to Elizabeth McClellan, 14 November 1846, and to Frederica English, 20 December 1846, McClellan Papers.

20. McClellan, *The Mexican War Diary*, p. 12.

21. Ibid., p. 16.

22. Thomas Williams, quoted in Smith and Judah, *Chronicles of the Gringos*, pp. 39–40.

23. Hill to Frances Russell Hill and Thomas Hill, 16 March 1847, Hill Family Papers.

24. Wilcox, *The Mexican War*, pp. 113–14; Charles Winslow Elliott, *Winfield Scott: The Soldier and the Man* (New York: Macmillan, 1937), p. 454.

25. Smith, *Company "A"*, p. 10, p. 13.

26. Ibid., p. 13, pp. 15–16.

27. McClellan to Elizabeth McClellan, 4 February 1847, McClellan Papers.

28. Daniel Harvey Hill, "The Real Stonewall Jackson," *Century Magazine* 47 (February 1894), p. 624.

29. T. Harry Williams, *The History of American Wars from 1745 to 1918* (New York: Alfred A. Knopf, 1981), pp. 173–74.

30. William A. Keleher, *Turmoil in New Mexico, 1846–1868* (Santa Fe: Rydal Press, 1952), p. 21.

31. Smith and Judah, *Chronicles of the Gringos*, p. 126.

32. The reporter is quoted in Smith and Judah, *Chronicles of the Gringos*, pp. 127–28.

33. From an account by Abert in Keleher, *Turmoil in New Mexico*, p. 117n. For detail on the aborted plans of insurrection also see Jacob P. Dunn, *Massacres of the Mountains: A History of the Indian Wars of the Far West, 1815–1875* (New York: Archer House, 1958), p. 65; and E. Bennett Burton, "The Taos Rebellion," *Old Santa Fe: A Magazine of History, Archaeology, Genealogy and Biography* 1 (October 1913), p. 179.

34. Lawrence R. Murphy, "The United States Army in Taos, 1847–1852," *New Mexico Historical Review* 47 (January 1972), p. 33; Burton, "The Taos Rebellion," pp. 180–83.

35. The engagement at Taos is described in Price's official report of 15 February 1847, in Senate Exec. Doc. No. 1, 30 Cong., 1 sess., pp. 520–25. Added detail is in a letter from Oliver Hazard Perry Taylor to George W. Cullum, 20 July 1855, Cullum File, Class of 1846, U.S. Military Academy Library; and from Dunn, *Massacres of the Mountains*, p. 72.

That City Shall Soon Be Ours

1. Maury, *Recollections of a Virginian*, p. 34.
2. Ibid.
3. A lively and colorful account of the voyage to Vera Cruz and the landing in the bay is in Smith, *The War with Mexico*, vol. 2, pp. 17–26.
4. Arnold, *Early Life and Letters of General Thomas J. Jackson*, p. 82.
5. Smith describes the activity of the engineers at Vera Cruz in *Company "A"*, p. 21, p. 24.
6. Ethan Allen Hitchcock, *Fifty Years in Camp and Field: Diary of Major-General Ethan Allen Hitchcock, U.S.A.*, ed. W. A. Croffut (New York: G. P. Putnam's Sons, Knickerbocker Press, 1909), p. 241.
7. Pierre Gustave Toutant Beauregard, *With Beauregard in Mexico: The Mexican War Reminiscences of P. G. T. Beauregard*, ed. T. Harry Williams (Baton Rouge: Louisiana State University Press, 1956), p. 27.
8. Smith, *Company "A"*, pp. 17–20.
9. Edmund Hardcastle to his uncle, 27 March 1847, Edmund Lafayette Hardcastle, Journal and Letters, U.S. Military Academy Library.
10. Hitchcock, *Fifty Years in Camp and Field*, p. 244.
11. The quotes are from Smith, *The War with Mexico*, vol. 2, p. 29.
12. Hardcastle to his uncle, 27 March 1847, Hardcastle Letters.
13. Turnley, *Reminiscences*, p. 85.
14. Hardcastle's account of his twenty-four hours on the guns at Vera Cruz is in the letter to his uncle, 27 March 1847, Hardcastle Letters. Also see Derby, "Diary of Military Activities, 1846–1859," a report to Col. J. J. Abert, Chief of Topographical Engineers, Derby Papers, box 6.
15. Gardner, "Memoirs," pp. 13–14.
16. Jackson to Laura Arnold, 30 March 1847, Arnold, *Early Life and Letters of General Thomas J. Jackson*, p. 85.
17. The statistics are from Turnley, *Reminiscences*, p. 87.
18. Hardcastle to his aunt, 10 April 1847, Hardcastle Letters.
19. A. P. Hill describes the buzzards of Vera Cruz in a letter to his parents, Frances Russell Hill and Thomas Hill, 23 October 1847, Hill Family Papers.
20. Smith, *Company "A,"* pp. 28–29; McClellan, *The Mexican War Diary*, p. 74.
21. Smith, *Company "A,"* p. 29.
22. McClellan, *The Mexican War Diary*, pp. 74–75.
23. Gardner, "Memoirs," pp. 15–16.
24. Jackson to Laura Arnold, 22 April 1847, Arnold, *Early Life and Letters of General Thomas J. Jackson*, p. 88.
25. Maury describes Twiggs in *Recollections of a Virginian*, pp. 29–30.
26. Hitchcock, *Fifty Years in Camp and Field*, p. 250.
27. Derby, "Diary of Military Activities," Derby Papers.
28. Winfield Scott, *Memoirs of Lieut.-General Scott, LL.d, Written by Himself*, 2 vols. (New York: Sheldon & Company, 1864), vol. 2, p. 433.
29. Smith, *The War with Mexico* vol. 2, pp. 51–52.
30. Maury at Cerro Gordo is from his *Recollections of a Virginian*, pp. 35–38. Reno's role is mentioned in Robert Selph Henry, *The Story of the Mexican War* (Indianapolis and New York: Bobbs-Merrill, 1950), pp. 284–85. Also see Smith, *The War with Mexico*, vol. 2, p. 520.
31. Smith, *The War with Mexico*, vol. 2, p. 52.

32. Smith and Judah, *Chronicles of the Gringos*, p. 207.
33. The long grueling night on Atalaya Hill is described in "The Hardships of War," correspondence of the *New York Commercial Advertiser* cited in the *Cambridge* (MA) *Chronicle*, 3 June 1847, in Smith and Judah, *Chronicles of the Gringos*, p. 208.
34. Smith, *Company "A"*, p. 30.
35. "The Hardships of War," in Smith and Judah, *Chronicles of the Gringos*, p. 208.
36. Ibid., pp. 208–9.
37. Smith and Judah, *Chronicles of the Gringos*, p. 209.
38. Derby to Mary Townsend Derby, 25 April 1847, Stewart, *John Phoenix, Esq.*, pp. 50–52.
39. Stewart, *John Phoenix, Esq.*, p. 52.
40. Ibid., pp. 3–4.
41. Derby to Mary Townsend Derby, 25 April 1847, Stewart, *John Phoenix, Esq.*, pp. 53–54.
42. Scott, *Memoirs* vol. 2, p. 438, p. 446, p. 450.
43. Maury tells of Derby in *Recollections of a Virginian*, pp. 36–39.
44. Raphael Semmes, *The Campaign of General Scott in the Valley of Mexico* (Cincinnati: Moore & Anderson, 1852), pp. 73–74.
45. John B. Weld to Mary Townsend Derby, 19 May 1847, Derby Papers, box 8.
46. Gardner, "Memoirs," pp. 16–17.
47. Jackson to Laura Arnold, 25 May 1847, Arnold, *Early Life and Letters of General Thomas J. Jackson*, p. 91.
48. Arnold, *Early Life and Letters of General Thomas J. Jackson*, pp. 93–95, pp. 129–30.
49. The descriptive passages are by a Carolina soldier, H. Judge Moore, quoted in Smith and Judah, *Chronicles of the Gringos*, p. 227.
50. Gardner, "Memoirs," pp. 17–18.
51. Smith, *To Mexico with Scott*, p. 189.
52. Jackson to Jonathan Arnold, 21, March 1848, Arnold, *Early Life and Letters of General Thomas J. Jackson*, p. 134.
53. Scott, *Memoirs* vol. 2, p. 467.

The Seventeen-Minute Victory

1. Gardner, "Memoirs," p. 22.
2. Gardner to his brother, 24 October 1847, Smith and Judah, *Chronicles of the Gringos*, p. 243.
3. The Pedregal is described in detail in Smith, *The War with Mexico*, vol. 2, p. 101.
4. George H. Gordon, "The Battles of Contreras and Churubusco," in *Papers of the Military Historical Society of Massachusetts*, vol. 13, *Civil and Mexican Wars, 1861, 1846* (1913; reprint, Wilmington, NC: Broadfoot Publishing Company, 1990), p. 577. Hereafter these Papers will be cited as *MHSM*. Gordon, a member of the class, writes from firsthand experience. Also see Lenoir Chambers, *Stonewall Jackson*, 2 vols. (1958; reprint, Wilmington, NC: Broadfoot Publishing Company, 1988), vol. 1, pp. 103–4.
5. Jackson to Laura Arnold, 25 May 1847, Arnold, *Early Life and Letters of General Thomas J. Jackson*, p. 92.
6. Jackson's preference to be where honor beckoned and distinction waited is well known. See Arnold, *Early LIfe and Letters of General Thomas J. Jackson*, p. 95; Gardner, "Memoirs," p. 18.
7. McClellan's activity is described in Smith, *Company "A"*, pp. 36–37.
8. Sears, *George B. McClellan*, p. 22.
9. Hamlin, *The Making of a Soldier*, p. 71.
10. Gordon, "The Battles of Contreras and Churubusco," pp. 579–83.
11. Hamlin, *The Making of a Soldier*, p. 71.
12. Smith, *Company "A"*, p. 38.
13. The events of the night of August 19 and the approach of the storming party in the early morning hours of the twentieth are in Gardner to his brother, 24 October 1847, Smith and Judah, *Chronicles of the Gringos*, pp. 243–44; and Gardner, "Memoirs," pp. 25–27.

14. Gardner, "Memoirs," pp. 27–28.
15. Maury, *Recollections of a Virginian*, p. 85.
16. Hamlin, *The Making of a Soldier*, pp. 71–72.
17. Entry of 20 August 1847, Hardcastle Journal.
18. Ibid.
19. Gardner's account is in his "Memoirs," pp. 29–31.
20. The image is borrowed from Ephraim Kirby Smith, *To Mexico with Scott*, pp. 200–1.
21. Hardcastle to his uncle, 24 August 1847, Hardcastle Letters; Robinson, "The Engineer Soldiers in the Mexican War," p. 7.
22. Hardcastle to his uncle, 24 August 1847, Hardcastle Letters.
23. Gardner, "Memoirs," p. 22. See opening paragraphs of this chapter.
24. Scott, *Memoirs* vol. 2, p. 492, p. 494, p. 501.
25. Gardner, "Memoirs," pp. 31–33.
26. Hardcastle to his uncle, 24 August 1847, Hardcastle Letters.

To the Halls of the Montezumas

1. The description of the castle is a mosaic drawn from Arnold, *The Early Life and Letters of General Thomas J. Jackson*, p. 105; Elise Trigg Shields, "The Storming of Chapultepec," *Confederate Veteran* 26 (September 1918), p. 399; and Scott, *Memoirs* vol. 2, p. 511.
2. Semmes, *The Campaign of General Scott in the Valley of Mexico*, p. 326.
3. Foster's classmate, George Gordon, wrote a detailed account of the storming of the Molino in his "Battles of Molino del Rey and Chapultepec," *MHSM*, vol. 13, *Civil and Mexican Wars 1861, 1846*. pp. 603–14.
4. Gordon was also to write Foster's obituary many years later. The quote is from that work: "John G. Foster," in *Sixth Annual Reunion of the Association of the Graduates of the United States Military Academy . . . June 17th, 1875* (New York: A.S. Barnes & Co., 1875), p. 36.
5. Ibid.
6. Hardcastle to his aunt, 2 September 1847, Hardcastle Letters.
7. Gordon, "Battles of Molino del Rey and Chapultepec," pp. 613–14.
8. Foster to William Dutton, 12 May 1848, Dutton Papers.
9. Gordon, "John G. Foster," p. 36.
10. McClellan to Foster, 5 May 1848, Frank G. Noyes, "Biographical Sketch of Maj.-Gen. John G. Foster, Son of New Hampshire, Soldier of the Republic," *The Granite Monthly* 26 (June 1899), p. 335.
11. Noche Triste, "Night of Sorrows," the battle in 1520 in which Cortez was driven with heavy losses from the Aztec capital of Tenochtitlan by the rebelling Indians. He would return the next year, lay siege to the city, and seize the Aztec empire.
12. Gordon, "Battles of Molino del Rey and Chapultepec," pp. 622–23.
13. Strategy for the assault is from Shields, "The Storming of Chapultepec," pp. 399–400.
14. Jackson's heroic stand at Chapultepec is mainly from Henderson, *Stonewall Jackson*, vol. 1, pp. 41–42. Also see Jackson, *Memoirs of "Stonewall" Jackson*, p. 43; Frank E. Vandiver, *Mighty Stonewall* (1957; reprint, College Station, TX: Texas A&M University Press, 1989), pp. 37–38; and Lester R. Dillon, Jr., "American Artillery in the Mexican War, 1846–1847," *Military History of Texas and the Southwest* 11 (1973), p. 165.
15. Scott, *Memoirs* vol. 2, p. 515.
16. Gordon, "Battles of Molino del Rey and Chapultepec," p. 628.
17. Scott, *Memoirs* vol. 2, p. 515. The description of the battle is a mosaic drawn from his *Memoirs*, vol. 2, pp. 513–15; Shields, "The Storming of Chapultepec," pp. 399–400; Henry, *The Story of the Mexican War*, p. 361; and Rodenbough and Haskin, *The Army of the United States*, p. 518.
18. Gordon, "Battles of Molino del Rey and Chapultepec," p. 632.
19. Henderson, *Stonewall Jackson and the American Civil War* vol. 1, p. 43.
20. Arnold, *Early Life and Letters of General Thomas J. Jackson*, p. 110.
21. Smith, *Company "A"*, pp. 49–50.

22. Beauregard, *With Beauregard in Mexico*, p. 98; Wilcox, *History of the Mexican War*, p. 472.

23. Scott, *Memoirs* vol. 2, p. 538, p. 535.

24. Rodenbough and Haskin, *The Army of the United States*, p. 197.

25. Smith, *Company "A"*, p. 56.

26. Hardcastle to his aunt, 2 [?] September 1847, Hardcastle Letters. The date on the typescript version of this letter is incorrect. It was written instead sometime after the army entered the city.

27. Obituary of Alexander Perry Rodgers, undated, Cullum Files.

28. Gardner, "Memoirs," pp. 31–34.

29. Childs is described in Smith, *The War with Mexico* vol. 2, p. 174.

30. Scott, *Memoirs* vol. 2, p. 550. Also see Morrison, *"The Best School in the World,"* pp. 53–54.

31. S. G. Merck, "Class of 1843," *Army and Navy Journal* 39 (14 June 1902), p. 1028.

32. Hill to Frances Russell Hill and Thomas Hill, 23 October 1847, Hill Family Papers.

33. Smith, *The War with Mexico* vol. 2, p. 176.

34. Hill to Frances Russell Hill and Thomas Hill, 23 October 1847, Hill Family Papers.

35. Detail on the march to Puebla and the lifted siege is from Smith, *The War with Mexico* vol. 2, pp. 174–78.

36. Gardner, "Memoirs," p. 33.

37. Maury, *Recollections of a Virginian*, p. 45.

38. Quoted in *The Centennial of the United States Military Academy at West Point, New York, 1802–1902*, 2 vols. (Washington: Government Printing Office, 1904), vol. 1, p. 602.

39. Hitchcock, *Fifty Years in Camp and Field*, p. 310.

40. Beauregard, *With Beauregard in Mexico*, p. 56.

41. *The Centennial of the United States Military Academy*, vol. 1, p. 601, p. 604, p. 629.

42. On Stuart, see Benjamin R. Stuart, *Magnolia Cemetery: An Interpretation of Some of Its Monuments and Inscriptions, with a Reminiscence of Captain James Stuart. . . .* (Charleston, SC: Kahrs & Welch, 1896), pp. 24–25.

43. See Arnold, *Early Life and Letters of General Thomas J. Jackson*, p. 115.

44. Ibid., pp. 116–17.

45. Gibbon relates this incident in Henderson, *Stonewall Jackson and the American Civil War* vol. 1, pp. 46–47.

46. Jackson to Laura Arnold, 26 October 1847; Arnold, *Early Life and Letters of General Thomas J. Jackson*, pp. 128–29.

47. Company A's return to West Point is remembered by Bailey in "My Boyhood at West Point," p. 9. Derby's quote is from Derby to Mary Townsend Derby, 1 November 1845, Derby Papers.

Indian Country

1. Wilson's encounter with the Indian chief is described by his classmate, Oliver O. P. Taylor, in a letter to George W. Cullum, 20 July 1855, Cullum File.

2. Keyes, *Fifty Years' Observation of Men and Events*, p. 253.

3. Augustus Meyers, *Ten Years in the Ranks, U.S. Army* (New York: Stirling Press, 1914), p. 49.

4. Williams, *The History of American Wars*, p. 188.

5. Utley, *Frontiersmen in Blue*, p. 12.

6. Ibid.

7. Ganoe, *The History of the United States Army*, p. 230.

8. *The Centennial of the United States Military Academy*, vol. 1, p. 526.

9. Utley, *Frontiersmen in Blue*, pp. 6–7.

10. The musketoon is described in Zenus R. Bliss, "Extracts from the Unpublished Memoirs of Maj. Gen. Z. R. Bliss," *Journal of the Military Service Institution of the United States* 38 (January–February 1906), p. 128.

11. Utley, *Frontiersmen in Blue*, pp. 26–27.

12. Williams, *The History of American Wars*, pp. 189–90.

13. Russell F. Weigley, *History of the United States Army*, enlarged edition (Bloomington: Indiana University Press, 1984), p. 240.

14. The quotes are all from Averam B. Bender, "The Soldier in the Far West, 1848–1860," *Pacific Historical Review* 8 (June 1939), pp. 161–62.

15. Smith to his mother, 17 June 1856, Joseph Howard Parks, *General Edmund Kirby Smith, C. S. A.* (Baton Rouge: Louisiana State University Press, 1954), pp. 90–91.

16. *The Centennial of the United States Military Academy*, 1, p. 488.

17. Teresa Griffen Viele, *Following the Drum: A Glimpse of Frontier Life* (1858; reprint, Lincoln, NE: University of Nebraska Press, 1984), pp. 174–75.

18. Stuart, *Magnolia Cemetery*, pp. 25–27.

19. Ibid., p. 24.

20. Maury, *Recollections of a Virginian*, p. 57.

21. Stuart's premonitions and death are described in Stuart, *Magnolia Cemetery*, pp. 26–27; and Maury, *Recollections of a Virginian*, pp. 57–59.

22. Quoted in Gerhard Spieler, "Captain Stuart—a Soldier's Life, a Soldier's Death," *Beaufort (SC) Gazette* (12 December 1974), copy in the Cullum File.

23. McClellan, *The Mexican War Diary*, p. 14n.

24. Stuart, *Magnolia Cemetery*, p. 29.

25. Hamlin, *The Making of a Soldier*, p. 76.

26. Maury, "General T. J. ('Stonewall') Jackson," p. 312.

27. Taylor to George W. Cullum, 20 July 1855, Cullum File.

India-Rubber Women and Buffalo Men

1. Charles P. Roland and Richard C. Robbins, eds., "The Diary of Eliza (Mrs. Albert Sidney) Johnston: The Second Cavalry Comes to Texas," *Southwestern Historical Quarterly* 60 (April 1957), p. 467.

2. Viele, *Following the Drum*, p. 17.

3. The fantasy portrait of the soldiering wife is also from Teresa Viele's delightful memoir, *Following the Drum*, pp. 13–15.

4. Quoted in Edward M. Coffman, *The Old Army: A Portrait of the American Army in Peacetime, 1784–1898* (New York: Oxford University Press, 1986), p. 104.

5. Eliza describes the typical marching day in Roland and Robbins, "The Diary of Eliza Johnston," pp. 468–69. Also see George F. Price, *Across the Continent with the Fifth Cavalry* (1883; reprint, New York: Antiquarian Press, 1959), p. 32.

6. Harold B. Simpson, "The Second U.S. Cavalry in Texas, 1855–1861," *Texas Military History* 8 (1970), p. 57.

7. Price, *Across the Continent with the Fifth Cavalry*, pp. 26–29, pp. 30–31.

8. Jay A. Matthews, Jr., "The Second U.S. Cavalry in Texas, 1855–1861," *Military History of Texas and the Southwest* 11 (1973), p. 230; Price, *Across the Continent with the Fifth Cavalry*, pp. 29–30.

9. The Indian problems in Texas are discussed at length in George D. Harmon, "The United States Indian Policy in Texas, 1845–1860," *Mississippi Valley Historical Review* 17 (December 1930), pp. 377–403.

10. The numbers are from Simpson, "The Second Cavalry in Texas," p. 59. The line of march is from Price, *Across the Continent with the Fifth Cavalry*, p. 32.

11. Roland and Robbins, "The Diary of Eliza Johnston," pp. 467–68.

12. Quoted in T. E. Ballenger, "Colonel Albert Sidney Johnston's March through Indian Territory in 1855," *Chronicles of Oklahoma* 47 (Summer 1969), p. 133.

13. Ibid., p. 136.

14. Eliza Johnston's description of these terrible five days is in Roland and Robbins, "The Diary of Eliza Johnston," pp. 483–85.

15. Albert Sidney Johnston to William Preston Johnston, 17 January 1856, in William Preston

Johnston, *The Life of Gen. Albert Sidney Johnston* (New York; D. Appleton and Company, 1878), p. 188.

16. Roland and Robbins, "The Diary of Eliza Johnston," pp. 483–85; Johnston, *The Life of Gen. Albert Sidney Johnston*, p. 188.

17. Price, *Across the Continent with the Fifth Cavalry*, p. 41, pp. 280–81, pp. 44–45.

18. Simpson, "The Second Cavalry in Texas," pp. 61–62, p. 70.

19. Charles P. Roland, *Albert Sidney Johnston: Soldier of Three Republics* (Austin: University of Texas Press, 1964), pp. 182–83. For an account of the Second Cavalry's early activity in Texas see Price, *Across the Continent with the Fifth Cavalry*, pp. 41–50. In August 1861 all of the mounted regiments of the army were reshuffled, reorganized, and redesignated to fight the Civil War. At that time the Second Cavalry became the Fifth Cavalry.

20. U.S. Military Academy, Cadet Application Papers, No. 321, 1842.

21. Jerusha Wilcox Sturgis, "Life of Mrs. S. D. Sturgis," typescript copy, Sturgis Family Papers, U.S. Military Academy Library, p. 6, p. 7.

22. The circumstances that made Sturgis a prisoner of war in Mexico are described in Samuel E. Chamberlain, *My Confession* (New York: Harper & Brothers, 1956), pp. 106–7.

23. Quoted in Robert W. Frazer, ed., *Mansfield on the Condition of Western Forts, 1853–54* (Norman: University of Oklahoma Press, 1963), p. xvi.

24. Sturgis's pursuit of the Apaches is recounted in Utley, *Frontiersmen in Blue*, pp. 150–51.

25. Maury, *Recollections of a Virginian*, p. 113.

26. Eugene Bandel, *Frontier Life in the Army, 1854–1861*, ed. Ralph P. Bieber (Glendale, CA: Arthur H. Clark Company, 1932), p. 79.

27. Percy Gatling Hamlin, *"Old Bald Head" (General R. S. Ewell): The Portrait of a Soldier* (1940; reprint, Gaithersburg, MD: Ron R. Van Sickle Military Books, 1988), p. 19.

28. The biographical information on Sedgwick is from Patricia L. Faust, ed., *Historical Times Illustrated Encyclopedia of the Civil War* (New York: Harper & Row, 1986), p. 665.

29. Sturgis, "Life of Mrs. S. D. Sturgis," p. 12.

30. The account of the buffalo stampede is from R. M. Peck's journal in LeRoy R. Hafen and Ann W. Hafen, eds., *Relations with the Indians of the Plains, 1857–1861: A Documentary Account of the Military Campaigns, and Negotiations of Indian Agents—with Reports and Journals of P. G. Lowe, R. M. Peck, J. E. B. Stuart, S. D. Sturgis, and Other Official Papers* (Glendale, CA: Arthur H. Clark Company, 1959), pp. 100–3. Peck was a soldier in Sturgis's company.

The Bloody Saddle

1. Benjamin Franklin Manring, *The Conquest of the Coeur d'Alenes, Spokanes and Palouses: The Expeditions of Colonels E. J. Steptoe and George Wright against the "Northern Indians" in 1858* (Spokane, WA: John W. Graham & Co., 1912), p. 123, p. 277.

2. Ibid., pp. 67–73. Also see Dunn, *Massacres of the Mountains*, p. 284.

3. Steptoe's report to the Department of the Pacific in San Francisco, 23 May 1858, in Manring, *The Conquest of the Coeur d'Alenes, Spokanes and Palouses*, p. 127. In the narrative of the Steptoe expedition and the fight that follows I have relied, but for the exceptions specifically cited, on Manring's detailed account, pp. 67–157.

4. Quoted in Manring, p. 91.

5. Ibid., p. 103.

6. Utley, *Frontiersmen in Blue*, p. 205.

7. George Wright to W. W. Mackall (Assistant Adjutant General in San Francisco), 30 September 1858, in Manring, *The Conquest of the Coeur d'Alenes, Spokanes and Palouses*, pp. 255–56.

8. Lawrence Kip, *Army Life on the Pacific: A Journal of the Expedition against the Northern Indians . . .* (New York: Redfield, 1859), pp. 111–12.

9. Ibid., p. 110, pp. 116–17.

10. Wright to Mackall, 30 September 1858, in Manring, *The Conquest of the Coeur d'Alenes, Spokanes and Palouses*, p. 254.

11. Kip, *Army Life on the Pacific*, pp. 122–24.

12. Bailey, "My Boyhood at West Point," p. 19.

13. The reburial of Taylor and Gaston at West Point is described by Schaff, who was present, in *The Spirit of Old West Point*, pp. 117–19.

14. Taylor to George C. Cullum, 20 July 1855, Cullum File.

The Courtship of Miss Nelly

1. Several books describe Ellen Marcy, none in great detail: W. Eugene Hollon, *Beyond the Cross Timbers: The Travels of Randolph B. Marcy, 1812–1887* (Norman: University of Oklahoma Press, 1955), p. 190; James I. Robertson, Jr., *General A. P. Hill: The Story of a Confederate Warrior* (New York: Random House, 1987), p. 27; Sears, *George B. McClellan*, p. 60; William Woods Hassler, *A. P. Hill: Lee's Forgotten General* (1957; reprint, Chapel Hill: University of North Carolina Press, 1962), pp. 17–18; William Starr Myers, *George Brinton McClellan: A Study in Personality* (New York: D. Appleton-Century Company, 1934), p. 130. The few existing photographs don't do her justice. But it was generally conceded she was compellingly attractive, bright, and highly gifted in the social graces.

2. Randolph B. Marcy to Ellen Marcy, 20 May 1846, McClellan Papers, B1:44.

3. Myers, *George Brinton McClellan*, pp. 125–26.

4. Marcy to Ellen Marcy, 20 May 1846, McClellan Papers, B1:44.

5. For a good example of Marcy's nonstop advice to his daughter see Marcy to Ellen Marcy, 4 February 1849, McClellan Papers, B1:44.

6. McClellan to Mary Marcy, 14 May 1854, McClellan Papers, B2:44.

7. Elizabeth B. McClellan to George McClellan, 15 April 1854; Sears, *George B. McClellan*, p. 41.

8. McClellan to Mary Marcy, 14 May 1854, McClellan Papers, B2:44.

9. Quoted in Hollon, *Beyond the Cross Timbers*, p. 172.

10. McClellan to Mary Marcy, 27 August 1854, McClellan Papers, B3:44; Shakespeare, *The Two Gentlemen of Verona*, act 3, scene 1, line 246.

11. McClellan to Mary Marcy, 10 September 1854, McClellan Papers, B3:44.

12. McClellan to Mary Marcy, 22 March 1855, McClellan Papers, B3:44.

13. Quoted in William J. Robertson, " 'Up Came Hill'—Soldier of the South," *Richmond Times-Dispatch*, Sunday Magazine Section, part 4 (4 November 1934), p. 8.

14. Ibid., part 2 (21 October 1934), p. 8.

15. Hill to Frances Russell Hill and Thomas Hill, 8 November 1847, Hill Family Papers.

16. Robertson, *General A. P. Hill*, pp. 11–12.

17. Hassler, *A. P. Hill: Lee's Forgotten General*, p. 17; Robertson, *General A. P. Hill*, p. 19.

18. Hollon, *Beyond the Cross Timbers*, pp. 191–92.

19. U.S. Military Academy, Cadet Application Papers, No. 131, 1842.

20. Marcy to Ellen Marcy, 22 May 1856, McClellan Papers, B3:44.

21. Marcy's scorcher was written to Ellen on 28 May 1856, McClellan Papers, B3:44.

22. Marcy to Ellen Marcy, 3 June 1856, McClellan Papers, B3:44.

23. Marcy to Ellen Marcy, 12 June 1856, McClellan Papers, B3:44. This narrative has the effect of appearing one sided, because none of Ellen's letters to her father are extant. We catch only a fleeting glimpse of her arguments between the lines of his letters.

24. Robertson, *General A. P. Hill*, p. 28.

25. McClellan to Mary Marcy, 14 January 1856, McClellan Papers, B3:45.

26. McClellan to Mary Marcy, 22 July 1856, McClellan Papers, A8:4.

27. Ibid.

28. Marcy to Ellen Marcy, 31 July 1856, McClellan Papers, B3:44.

29. Quoted in Hollon, *Beyond the Cross Timbers*, pp. 193–94.

30. Hill to Randolph Marcy, 29 May 1857, McClellan Papers, B4:45.

31. Quoted in Hassler, *A. P. Hill: Lee's Forgotten General*, p. 21.

32. Background on Kitty is mainly from Robertson, *General A. P. Hill*, pp. 30–31.

33. Hill to McClellan, 18 June 1859, McClellan Papers, A11:5.

34. Hassler, *A. P. Hill: Lee's Forgotten General*, p. 24; Robertson, *General A. P. Hill*, p. 32.

35. The Marcy expedition is described in detail in Hollon, *Beyond the Cross Timbers*, pp. 215–24.

36. McClellan to Ellen Marcy, 17 March 1858, McClellan Papers, B5:45.

37. McClellan to Ellen Marcy, 11 September 1859, McClellan Papers, B5:45.

38. Marcy to Ellen Marcy, 4 February 1857, McClellan Papers, B3:45.

39. Marcy to McClellan, 16 September 1859, McClellan Papers, B5:45.

40. Hollon, *Beyond the Cross Timbers*, pp. 236–37.

41. W. H. Lewis to Ellen Marcy, 13 October 1859, McClellan Papers, B6:46.

42. George Granger to Ellen Marcy, 25 October 1859, McClellan Papers, B6:46.

43. From extracts of letters from McClellan to Ellen Marcy before their marriage, 1859–60, McClellan Papers, A11:5.

44. Ibid.

45. Elizabeth McClellan to Ellen Marcy, 5 January 1860, McClellan Papers, B6:26.

46. *New York Herald*, 23 May 1860; William W. Chamberlaine, *Memoirs of the Civil War between the Northern and Southern Sections of the United States of America, 1861 to 1865* (Washington, DC: Press of Byro S. Adams, 1912), p. 109. We are not absolutely certain the Major Hill listed in the newspaper account was A. P. Hill. Chamberlaine in his memoirs says Hill was there as one of McClellan's groomsmen, but Chamberlaine had this second or third hand. I like to think, for the sake of romance, that it was indeed our Hill. This is, after all, a love story.

47. Diary entry, 22 May 1860, McClellan Papers, D4:67.

PART 3   AND THE WAR CAME

Our Men at Sumter

1. The record of Seymour's army career is in Cullum, *Biographical Register* vol. 2, pp. 270–72.

2. Kent Ahrens, "The Drawings and Watercolors by Truman Seymour," in *Water Color and Drawings by Brevet Major General Truman Seymour, USMA 1846* (Published on the occasion of an exhibit of Seymour's work at West Point, NY, 1974), p. 3.

3. U.S. Military Academy, Cadet Application Papers, No. 284, 1840.

4. Abner Doubleday, *Reminiscences of Forts Sumter and Moultrie in 1860–61* (1876; reprint, Spartanburg, SC: The Reprint Company, 1976), p. 22.

5. Detail of this incident is from Truman Seymour, "Memo of a Circumstance of 1860, Fort Moultrie, S.C., Recorded November 2, 1874," handwritten copy, U.S. Military Academy Library. Also see Doubleday, *Reminiscences of Forts Sumter and Moultrie*, pp. 30–31.

6. Doubleday, *Reminiscences of Forts Sumter and Moultrie*, p. 22. For details on Foster's army career and a biographical sketch, see Cullum, *Biographical Register*, vol. 2, pp. 256–60. Also: W. A. Swanberg, *First Blood: The Story of Fort Sumter* (New York: Charles Scribner's Sons, 1957), p. 5.

7. John G. Nicolay and John Hay, *Abraham Lincoln: A History*, 10 vols. (New York: Century Co., 1886), vol. 2, p. 439.

8. Abner Doubleday, "From Moultrie to Sumter," in Robert Underwood Johnson and Clarence Clough Buel, eds., *Battles and Leaders of the Civil War*, 4 vols. (1887; reprint, Secaucus, NY: Castle, n.d.), vol. 1, p. 43. Also see James Chester, "Inside Sumter in '61," in *Battles and Leaders*, vol. 1, p. 50; and Samuel Wylie Crawford, *The Genesis of the Civil War: The Story of Sumter, 1860–1861* (New York: Charles L. Webster & Company, 1887), p. 4.

9. U.S. War Department, *The War of the Rebellion: A Compilation of the Official Records of the Union and Confederate Armies*, 70 vols. in 128 parts (1880–1901; reprint, Harrisonburg, PA: Historical Times, 1985), ser. 1, vol. 1, p. 77. (Hereafter, this indispensable multivolume work will be cited as *O.R.*)

10. Quoted in Crawford, *Genesis of the Civil War*, p. 6.

11. Moultrie at that time is described in Doubleday, "From Moultrie to Sumter," p. 40; and in Crawford, *The Genesis of the Civil War*, p. 6.

12. *O.R.*, ser. 1, vol. 1, p. 5; Nicolay and Hay, *Abraham Lincoln*, vol. 2, p. 440.

13. Crawford, *The Genesis of the Civil War*, pp. 21–23.

14. George Templeton Strong, *The Diary of George Templeton Strong*, ed. Allan Nevins and Milton Halsey Thomas, 4 vols. (New York: Macmillan, 1952), vol. 3, p. 95.

15. Crawford, *The Genesis of the Civil War*, p. 23, pp. 213–14; Doubleday, *Reminiscences of Forts Sumter and Moultrie*, p. 18.

16. Doubleday, *Reminiscences of Forts Sumter and Moultrie*, pp. 18–19, p. 22.

17. O.R., ser. 1, vol. 1, pp. 72–73.

18. Doubleday, *Reminiscences of Forts Sumter and Moultrie*, pp. 41–42.

19. Keyes, *Fifty Years' Observation of Men and Events*, pp. 367–68.

20. Paul M. Angle and Earl Schenck Miers, *Tragic Years, 1860–1865: A Documentary History of the American Civil War*, 2 vols. (New York: Simon and Schuster, 1960), vol. 1, p. 10.

21. Doubleday, *Reminiscences of Forts Sumter and Moultrie*, 41.

22. Anderson's portrait is sketched from Keyes, *Fifty Years' Observation of Men and Events*, p. 368; *The Battle of Fort Sumter and the First Victory of the Southern Troops* (Charleston, SC: Evans & Cogswell, 1861), pp. 29–30; and Theodore Talbot to his mother, 26 November 1860, Theodore Talbot Papers, Documents Division, Library of Congress. Also see Clarence E. E. Stout, "John Gray Foster," *The Granite Monthly* 5 (May 1882), p. 260.

23. O.R., ser. 1, vol. 1, pp. 74–76.

24. Ibid., pp. 89–90.

25. Ibid., p. 103. Also see Eba Anderson Lawton, *Major Anderson and Fort Sumter, 1861* (New York: Knickerbocker Press, 1911), pp. 3–5.

26. O.R., ser. 1, vol. 1, p. 79.

27. Ibid., p. 78.

28. Doubleday, "From Moultrie to Sumter," pp. 41–42.

29. O.R. ser. 1, vol. 1, p. 88, p. 93.

30. Ibid., p. 95.

31. Ibid., p. 82.

32. Ibid., pp. 91–92.

33. Doubleday, *Reminiscences of Forts Sumter and Moultrie*, p. 31, p. 33; Doubleday, "From Moultrie to Sumter," p. 43.

34. Foster's gun incident is described in O.R., ser. 1, vol. 1, pp. 95–101.

35. Quoted in Crawford, *The Genesis of the Civil War*, p. 100.

36. Doubleday, "From Moultrie to Sumter," p. 43.

37. O.R., ser. 1, vol. 1, p. 105.

38. Anderson's account of the move is in Nicolay and Hay, *Abraham Lincoln*, vol. 3, p. 47n. Also see John G. Nicolay, *The Outbreak of Rebellion* (1881; reprint, Wilmington, NC: Broadfoot Publishing Company, 1989), p. 28.

39. Crawford, *The Genesis of the Civil War*, pp. 102–3.

40. Nicolay and Hay, *Abraham Lincoln*, vol. 3, p. 45.

41. Doubleday, *Reminiscences of Forts Sumter and Moultrie*, p. 61.

42. Truman Seymour, "An Episode of Fort Sumter: 1860," handwritten chiefly from the dictation of his wife, Louisa Seymour, 20 October 1874, U.S. Military Academy Library, p. 1.

43. Doubleday, "From Moultrie to Sumter," p. 44.

44. Ibid., p. 45.

45. "Report of Major General J. G. Foster," in U.S. Congress, Joint Committee on the Conduct of the War, *Supplemental Report*, 2 vols. (Washington: Government Printing Office, 1866), vol. 2, p. 6.

46. Details of the transfer from Moultrie to Sumter are distilled from accounts in Doubleday, "From Moultrie to Sumter," p. 45; and Nicolay and Hay, *Abraham Lincoln*, vol. 3, pp. 52–53.

47. Doubleday, "From Moultrie to Sumter," p. 46n.

48. O.R., ser. 1, vol. 1, p. 2. Mary Doubleday's activity is described in Doubleday, "From Moultrie to Sumter," pp. 45–46.

49. Foster's Report to the Committee on the Conduct of the War, pp. 6–7; Nicolay and Hay, *Abraham Lincoln*, vol. 3, p. 55.

50. O.R., ser. 1, vol. 1, p. 124.

51. Seymour, "An Episode of Fort Sumter," pp. 1–2.

52. O.R., ser. 1, vol. 1, p. 3.

53. Ibid.

54. Ibid., p. 90.

55. Ibid., p. 3.

56. Talbot to his mother, 31 December 1860, Talbot Papers.

57. Seymour, "An Episode of Fort Sumter," unnumbered page.

58. Ibid., p. 2.

59. Seymour's wanderings in Charleston are recounted in a second unnumbered page in "An Episode of Fort Sumter."

60. The account of these conjugal visits is also taken largely from Seymour, "An Episode of Fort Sumter," pp. 2–4. But also see Doubleday, *Reminiscences of Forts Sumter and Moultrie*, pp. 95–96, and "From Moultrie to Sumter," p. 46. The Seymour and Doubleday accounts are remarkably dissimilar. Doubleday's version has his wife coming over with the boatload of workmen and returning with Mrs. Seymour in the sutler's boat. Seymour's account has Mrs. Doubleday coming over in the rowboat with Louisa as well as leaving with her. I have used Doubleday's version for his wife's visit and the Seymour version for Louisa's.

61. Mrs. Anderson's recruitment of Peter Hart is from Benson J. Lossing, *Mathew Brady's Illustrated History of the Civil War* (1912; reprint, New York: Fairfax Press, n.d.), pp. 82–84.

Waiting for the Ball to Begin

1. The scene is set from detail in Doubleday's two works, *Reminiscences of Forts Sumter and Moultrie*, p. 100; and "From Moultrie to Sumter," p. 46.

2. Captain McGowan's troubles are recorded in an account in *Harper's Weekly: A Journal of Civilization*, 26 January 1861.

3. H. M. Clarkson, "Story of the Star of the West," *Confederate Veteran* 21 (May 1913), pp. 235–36.

4. *Harper's Weekly*, 26 January 1861.

5. Doubleday, "From Moultrie to Sumter," pp. 46–47.

6. Chester, "Inside Sumter in '61," p. 61.

7. *Within Fort Sumter; or, a View of Major Anderson's Garrison Family for One Hundred and Ten Days, by One of the Company* (New York: N. Tibbals & Company, 1861), pp. 14–15.

8. O.R., ser. 1, vol. 1, p. 134, p. 136.

9. Doubleday, *Reminiscences of Forts Sumter and Moultrie*, pp. 100–1.

10. O.R., ser. 1, vol. 1, p. 136, p. 138.

11. Strong, *The Diary of George Templeton Strong*, vol. 3, pp. 89–90.

12. O.R., ser. 1, vol. 1, p. 140.

13. *Harper's Weekly*, 26 January 1861.

14. *Within Fort Sumter*, p. 11.

15. Ibid., p. 24.

16. Ibid., p. 25.

17. *Harper's Weekly*, 23 February 1861; Crawford, *Genesis of the Civil War*, p. 207; O.R., ser. 1, vol. 1, pp. 161–63.

18. O.R., ser. 1, vol. 1, p. 5.

19. Chester, "Inside Sumter in '61," pp. 54–56.

20. Ibid., p. 60.

21. *Within Fort Sumter*, p. 22.

22. Chester, "Inside Sumter in '61," p. 56.

23. Doubleday describes his fellow officers in *Reminiscences of Forts Sumter and Moultrie*, pp. 22–24.

24. O.R. ser. 1, vol. 1, p. 163, p. 191.

25. Samuel Millens, " 'When Once the Ball is Commenced . . .': A Pennsylvania Irishman at Fort Sumter," ed. Rowland T. Berthoff, *Pennsylvania History* 24 (July 1957), p. 221.

26. O.R., ser. 1, vol. 1, p. 171, p. 173. Six of these elegant sketches are in George B. Davis, Leslie J. Perry, and Joseph W. Kirkley, *The Official Military Atlas of the Civil War*, compiled

by Calvin D. Cowles (1891; reprint, New York: Arno Press and Crown Publishers, 1978), Plates I and II.

27. O.R., ser. 1, vol. 1, p. 173.

28. Lawton, *Major Robert Anderson and Fort Sumter*, p. 9.

29. O.R., ser. 1, vol. 1, p. 182.

30. Crawford, *The Genesis of the Civil War*, p. 69, p. 290.

31. O.R., ser. 1, vol. 1, p. 158.

32. Ibid., p. 212.

33. Talbot to his mother, 15 March 1861, Talbot Papers.

34. The English journalist, William Howard Russell, describes Beauregard in *My Diary North and South*, ed. Fletcher Pratt (New York: Harper & Brothers, 1954), p. 56.

35. *Within Fort Sumter*, pp. 32–33; O.R. ser. 1, vol. 1, p. 26.

36. For Jones see G. Moxley Sorrel, *Recollections of a Confederate Staff Officer* (1905; reprint, Dayton: Press of Morningside Bookshop, 1978), p. 56; and *Dictionary of American Biography*, s.v., "Jones, David Rumph."

37. O.R., ser. 1, vol. 1, pp. 190–91.

38. Crawford, *The Genesis of the Civil War*, pp. 278–79.

39. Russell, *My Diary North and South*, p. 65.

40. O.R., ser. 1, vol. 1, p. 272, p. 275.

41. Abraham Lincoln, *The Collected Works of Abraham Lincoln*, ed Roy P. Basler, 8 vols. (New Brunswick, NJ: Rutgers University Press, 1953), vol. 4, p. 266.

42. O.R., ser. 1, vol. 1, p. 202.

43. Ibid., p. 197.

44. Ibid., pp. 196–97.

45. Nicolay, *The Outbreak of the Rebellion*, p. 57; Samuel Wylie Crawford, "The First Shot against the Flag," in *The Annals of the War Written by Leading Participants North and South* (1879; reprint, Dayton: Morningside, 1988), p. 324.

46. O.R. ser. 1, vol. 1, p. 245.

47. Ibid., p. 235.

48. Ibid., p. 294.

49. Ibid., p. 251.

50. Nicolay, *The Outbreak of the Rebellion*, p. 57.

51. O.R., ser. 1, vol. 1, p. 289, p. 297.

52. Crawford, *The Genesis of the Civil War*, pp. 398–99.

53. O.R., ser. 1, vol. 1, pp. 250–51.

54. Ibid., pp. 16–17.

55. Ibid., p. 249, p. 294, p. 251.

56. Nicolay and Hay, *Abraham Lincoln*, vol. 4, pp. 41–42; O.R., ser. 1, vol. 1, pp. 17–18.

57. O.R., ser. 1, vol. 1, p. 297.

58. Mary Boykin Chesnut, *Mary Chesnut's Civil War*, ed. C. Vann Woodward (New Haven, CT: Yale University Press, 1981), p. 45.

59. Horace Greeley, *The American Conflict: A History of the Great Rebellion in the United States of America, 1860–'65*, 2 vols. (Hartford, CT: O.D. Case & Company, 1866), vol. 1, p. 448.

60. Chesnut, *Mary Chesnut's Civil War*, p. 44.

61. Quoted in Crawford, *The Genesis of the Civil War*, p. 305.

The First Shot

1. The guns and their positions are pinpointed in O.R., ser. 1, vol. 1, p. 18.

2. Ibid., pp. 18–19.

3. Ibid., p. 59.

4. Ibid., p. 13.

5. Crawford, "The First Shot against the Flag," p. 326.

6. O.R., ser. 1, vol. 1, p. 13.

7. Ibid., p. 59; Crawford, *The Genesis of the Civil War*, p. 424.

8. *The Battle of Fort Sumter*, p. 3.

9. This train of events is distilled from Stephen D. Lee, "The First Step in the War," *Battles and Leaders*, vol. 1, pp. 75–76. Also see A. R. Chisolm, "Notes on the Surrender of Fort Sumter," *Battles and Leaders*, vol. 1, p. 82; O.R., ser. 1, vol. 1, p. 14, p. 60; Crawford, *The Genesis of the Civil War*, pp. 424–26; and "Fort Sumter—Who Fired the First Gun on the Fort?" *SHSP* 20 (December 1892), pp. 62–63.

10. Chesnut, *Mary Chesnut's Civil War*, p. 55.

11. "Fort Sumter—Who Fired the First Gun on the Fort?" p. 63.

12. Lee, "The First Step in the War," p. 76.

13. Chisolm, "Notes on the Surrender of Fort Sumter," p. 82.

14. Stephen D. Lee, "Who Fired the First Gun at Sumter?" Letter From S. D. Lee with Reply from Julian M. Ruffin, *SHSP* 11 (1883), p. 502.

15. Beauregard describes the signal shot in Otto Eisenschiml and Ralph Newman, *The Civil War: The American Iliad as Told by Those Who Lived It* (1947; reprint, Secaucus, NJ: Blue and Grey Press, 1985), p. 20. Also see Lee, "The First Step in the War," p. 76.

16. Edmund Ruffin, *The Diary of Edmund Ruffin*, ed. William Kauffman Scarborough, 3 vols. (Baton Rouge: Louisiana State University Press, 1972–1989), vol. 1, p. 482, p. 588, p. 602.

17. Doubleday, "From Moultrie to Sumter," p. 47; Doubleday, *Reminiscences of Forts Sumter and Moultrie*, pp. 142–44.

18. Lee, "The First Step in the War," p. 77.

19. Susie Pennal Beaty, "The Battle of Fort Sumter," *Confederate Veteran* 18 (September 1910), p. 419.

20. Chesnut, *Mary Chesnut's Civil War*, p. 46.

21. O.R., ser. 1, vol. 1, p. 11.

22. Parker describes the early hours of the bombardment in "The Battle of Fort Sumter as Seen from Morris Island," *South Carolina Historical Magazine* 62 (April 1961), p. 66.

23. Chester, "Inside Sumter in '61," pp. 66–67.

24. *Within Fort Sumter*, p. 44.

25. Ibid., pp. 44–45.

26. Doubleday, *Reminiscences of Forts Sumter and Moultrie*, p. 146; Parker, "The Battle of Fort Sumter as Seen from Morris Island," p. 66.

27. *Charleston Courier*, 13 April 1861, quoted in *SHSP* 26 (1898), p. 106.

28. *Within Fort Sumter*, pp. 47–48.

29. Doubleday, *Reminiscences of Forts Sumter and Moultrie*, p. 151.

30. Ibid., pp. 148–49.

31. Foster describes the situation in O.R., ser. 1, vol. 1, pp. 19–20.

32. Ibid., p. 21; Beaty, "The Battle of Fort Sumter," p. 419.

33. Chester, "Inside Sumter in '61," p. 54.

34. Parker, "The Battle of Fort Sumter as Seen from Morris Island," p. 67.

35. Ibid., p. 69.

36. *Within Fort Sumter*, pp. 52–54.

37. Parker, "The Battle of Fort Sumter as Seen from Morris Island," p. 69.

38. O.R., ser. 1, vol. 1, p. 22.

39. *Within Fort Sumter*, pp. 54–56; Crawford, *The Genesis of the Civil War*, pp. 437–38.

40. Chesnut, *Mary Chesnut's Civil War*, p. 517.

41. Wigfall's description is a composite drawn from Chester, "Inside Sumter in '61," p. 72; Russell, *My Diary North and South*, pp. 62–64; Greeley, *The American Conflict* vol. 1, p. 448; and Chesnut, *Mary Chesnut's Civil War*, p. 12.

42. Wigfall's visit is an amalgam combining accounts by three different firsthand sources, all differing in detail: *Within Fort Sumter*, pp. 56–59; Chester, "Inside Sumter in '61," pp. 72–73; and O.R., ser. 1, vol. 1, p. 23.

43. O.R., ser. 1, vol. 1, p. 32.

44. Anderson's confrontation with Beauregard's three official representatives is from O.R., ser. 1, vol. 1, pp. 63–64.

45. Ibid., pp. 64–65.

46. Ibid., p. 65.
47. Ibid., p. 25; Foster's Report to the Committee on the Conduct of the War, p. 9.
48. O.R., ser. 1, vol. 1, p. 24.
49. *The Battle of Fort Sumter*, p. 10.
50. *Within Fort Sumter*, pp. 64–68.
51. O.R., ser. 1, vol. 1, p. 314.
52. Ibid., 28; *Within Fort Sumter*, pp. 68–69; Parker, "The Battle of Fort Sumter as Seen from Morris Island," p. 69.
53. *London Times*, April 27, 1861, in Frank Moore, *The Rebellion Record: A Diary of American Events*, 12 vols. (1868; reprint, New York: Arno Press, 1977), vol. 1: doc., p. 228; George Ticknor, *Life, Letters, and Journals of George Ticknor*, eds. Anna Ticknor and George S. Hilliard, 2 vols. (Boston: James R. Osgood and Company, 1876), vol. 2, p. 433; Lee, "The First Step in the War," p. 77; Theodore F. Upson, *With Sherman to the Sea: The Civil War Letters, Diaries & Reminiscences of Theodore F. Upson*, ed. Oscar Osburn Winther (Bloomington: Indiana University Press, 1958), p. 10.
54. Schaff, *The Spirit of Old West Point*, pp. 246–47.
55. John Gibbon, *Personal Recollections of the Civil War* (1928; reprint, Dayton: Press of Morningside Bookshop, 1988), pp. 4–6.
56. Maury, *Recollections of a Virginian*, pp. 128–30.
57. Gibbon, *Personal Recollections of the Civil War*, p. 6, p. 9.
58. Maury, *Recollections of a Virginian*, pp. 131–32.

Stonewall's Great Locomotive Heist

1. James H. Lane, "Stonewall Jackson: Reminiscences of Him as a Professor in the Virginia Military Institute," *SHSP* 20 (1892), p. 3.
2. Jackson, *Memoirs of Stonewall Jackson*, p. 141.
3. William A. Obenchain, "Stonewall Jackson's Scabbard Speech," *SHSP* 16 (1888), p. 46.
4. Jackson, *Memoirs of Stonewall Jackson*, p. 150. Other accounts differ in detail. See for example Cook, *Family and Early Life*, pp. 156–57; and John Esten Cooke, *Stonewall Jackson: A Military Biography*, (New York: D. Appleton, 1876), pp. 35–36.
5. Jackson, *Memoirs of Stonewall Jackson*, p. 151.
6. The traffic on the B&O main line is described in Festus P. Summers, *The Baltimore and Ohio in the Civil War* (New York: G. P. Putnam's Sons, 1939), pp. 63–66; and in George Edgar Turner, *Victory Rode the Rails* (Indianapolis: Bobbs Merrill, 1953), p. 73.
7. Edward Hungerford, *The Story of the Baltimore & Ohio Railroad, 1827–1927*, 2 vols. (New York: G. P. Putnam's Sons, 1928), vol. 2, p. 7.
8. *Dictionary of American Biography*, s.v. "Garrett, John Work."
9. Hungerford, *The Story of the Baltimore & Ohio Railroad*, pp. 6–7. For additional detail: Summers, *Baltimore and Ohio in the Civil War*, p. 66; Chambers, *Stonewall Jackson* vol. 1, pp. 338–39.
10. John D. Imboden, "Jackson at Harper's Ferry in 1861," *Battles and Leaders* vol. 1, p. 123.
11. Ibid., pp. 122–23. Jackson's high-handed diversion of B&O property is also described in Chambers, *Stonewall Jackson* vol. 1, p. 339; Turner, *Victory Rode the Rails*, pp. 74–75; Summers, *Baltimore and Ohio in the Civil War*, pp. 65–67; and Angus James Johnston, *Virginia Railroads in the Civil War* (Chapel Hill: Published for the Virginia Historical Society by the University of North Carolina Press, 1961), pp. 22–23.
12. Brief descriptions of this initial operation are in Chambers, *Stonewall Jackson* vol. 1, p. 339; and Hungerford, *The Story of the Baltimore & Ohio Railroad*, vol. 2, p. 7.
13. Jackson, *Memoirs of Stonewall Jackson*, p. 167.
14. The background on Sharp and the account of the hijacking procedures in the paragraphs that follow are mainly from Hungerford, *The Story of the Baltimore & Ohio Railroad*, vol. 2, p. 135n, pp. 8–14. Bits of detail are added from Johnston, *Virginia Railroads in the Civil War*, p.

24; Chambers, *Stonewall Jackson* vol. 1, pp. 349–50; and George B. Abdill, *Civil War Railroads* (Seattle: Superior Publishing Co., 1961), p. 61.

15. Quoted in Hungerford, *The Story of the Baltimore & Ohio Railroad*, vol. 2, p. 10.

16. Hungerford, *The Story of the Baltimore & Ohio Railroad*, vol. 2, p. 12.

17. Engine 199's passage from Mount Jackson to Staunton is described by Hungerford in *The Story of the Baltimore & Ohio Railroad* vol. 2, pp. 12–14, although he does not tell us where he got it. Also see Turner, *Victory Rode the Rails*, pp. 89–90.

18. Baltimore and Ohio Railroad, *Thirty-fifth Annual Report of the President and Directors to the Stockholders . . . for the Year Ending September 30, 1861* (Baltimore: William M. Innes, 1863), p. 25.

19. Hungerford, *The Story of the Baltimore & Ohio Railroad*, vol. 2, p. 135n.

The Shirttail Skedaddle

1. Russell, *My Diary North and South*, pp. 230–31.

2. O.R., ser. 1, vol. 2, p. 753.

3. *Dictionary of American Biography*, s.v. "McDowell, Irvin"; Whitelaw Reid, *Ohio in the War: Her Statesmen, Her Generals, and Soldiers*, 2 vols. (Cincinnati: Moore, Wilstach & Baldwin, 1868), vol. 1, p. 693.

4. Russell, *My Diary North and South*, p. 193, p. 196.

5. McClellan's biographer, Stephen W. Sears, has compiled the general's important wartime writings and messages into a published volume, *The Civil War Papers of George B. McClellan: Selected Correspondence, 1860–1865* (New York: Ticknor & Fields, 1989). The letter to Fitz John Porter is on pages 4–5 of that work, which will be cited hereafter as McClellan, *Civil War Papers*. The sentiment addressed to Ellen is from a short note to her in the George B. McClellan, Jr. Papers, Manuscript Division, Library of Congress, container 5.

6. For more on Dennison, see Reid, *Ohio in the War*, vol. 1, p. 26, pp. 1017–19.

7. How McClellan looked fifteen years out of West Point is a mosaic weaved from Jacob D. Cox, "War Preparations in the North," *Battles and Leaders*, vol. 1, pp. 89–90; *Washington Evening Star*, 5 August 1861; and Russell, *My Diary North and South*, 240.

8. Cox, "War Preparations in the North," pp. 89–90. McClellan, *Civil War Papers*, p. 82.

9. Sears, *George B. McClellan*, pp. 68–69.

10. Cox, "War Preparations in the North," p. 90.

11. McClellan, *Civil War Papers*, p. 11.

12. O.R., ser. 1, vol. 2, p. 802.

13. Theodore F. Lang, *Loyal West Virginia from 1861–1865* (Baltimore: Deutsch Publishing Co., 1895), p. 320.

14. For the living room scene: George Brinton McClellan, *McClellan's Own Story*, ed. William C. Prime (New York: Charles L. Webster & Company, 1887), p. 50. The texts of McClellan's various telegrams are in O.R., ser. 1, vol. 2, pp. 44–49.

15. Philippi in 1861 is described by Ruth Woods Dayton in "The Beginning—Philippi, 1861," *West Virginia History* 13 (July 1952), pp. 254–56.

16. Lang, *Loyal West Virginia*, p. 320.

17. Dayton, *The Beginning—Philippi, 1861*, p. 261.

18. Catharine Merrill, *The Soldier of Indiana in the War for the Union*, 2 vols. (Indianapolis: Merrill and Company, 1866), vol. 1, p. 28. Also see *Dictionary of American Biography*, s.v. "Morris, Thomas Armstrong."

19. Merrill, *The Soldier of Indiana*, vol. 1, p. 25.

20. Activity in the Confederate camp is reported in John A. McNeil, "Famous Retreat from Philippi," *SHSP* 34 (1906), p. 290.

21. Merrill, *The Soldier of Indiana*, vol. 1, p. 31.

22. E. Douglas Branch, "Frederick West Lander, Road-Builder," *Mississippi Valley Historical Review* 16 (September 1929), p. 172n, p. 184. Also see *Dictionary of American Biography*, s.v. "Lander, Frederick West," and "Lander, Jean Margaret Davenport."

23. Mrs. Humphreys's contribution to the battle is described in Hu Maxwell, *The History*

of Barbour County, West Virginia (1899; reprint, Parsons, WV: McClain Printing Company, 1968), pp. 255– 56; and in Fritz Haselberger, *Yanks From the South! The First Land Campaign of the Civil War: Rich Mountain, West Virginia* (Baltimore: Past Glories, 1987), pp. 68–69.

24. Merrill, *The Soldier of Indiana,* vol. 1, p. 33.

25. *New York Express,* 10 June 1861, in Moore, *The Rebellion Record,* vol. 2: doc., p. 82; Merrill, *The Soldier of Indiana* vol. 1, p. 33.

26. Lander, his horse, and his gallop through the town are described in Merrill, *The Soldier of Indiana,* vol. 1, p. 33; and in the *New York Express* account cited above.

27. *Wheeling (VA) Intelligencer,* 6 June 1861, in Moore, *Rebellion Record,* vol. 1: doc., p. 336.

28. McNeil, "Famous Retreat from Philippi," p. 289.

29. *Wheeling (VA) Intelligencer,* in Moore, *Rebellion Record,* vol. 1: doc., p. 336.

30. Lang, *Loyal West Virginia,* p. 321.

31. Thomas J. Arnold, "Battle of Rich Mountain," *Randolph County Historical Society Magazine of History and Biography* 2 (1925), p. 46.

32. *New York Express,* in Moore, *Rebellion Record,* vol. 2: doc., p. 82.

33. Rosecrans to McClellan, 5 June 1861, McClellan Papers, A13: 6.

34. *Dictionary of American Biography,* s.v. "Garnett, Robert Selden."

35. These depressing adjectives, plus "dreary-hearted man" in the next paragraph are from Chesnut, *Mary Chesnut's Civil War,* p. 176.

36. Edward Porter Alexander, *Military Memoirs of a Confederate: A Critical Narrative* (New York: Charles Scribner's Sons, 1907), p. 14.

37. O.R., ser. 1, vol. 2, p. 237.

38. Elizabeth Cometti and Festus P. Summers, eds., *The Thirty-Fifth State: A Documentary History of West Virginia* (Morgantown: West Virginia University Library, 1966), p. 8.

39. Merrill, *The Soldier of Indiana,* vol. 1, p. 20.

40. William Swinton, *Campaigns of the Army of the Potomac* (1866; reprint, Secaucus, NJ: Blue & Grey Press, 1988), p. 36.

41. The aroma at Laurel Hill is evoked by Whitelaw Reid in the *Cincinnati Gazette,* reprinted in Moore, *Rebellion Record,* vol. 2: doc., p. 288. Garnett's doomsday prophecy is from Chesnut, *Mary Chesnut's Civil War,* p. 176.

42. Most of McClellan's observations and remarks from western Virginia are in his letters to his wife. This description of the adulation along the road is from one of those, reprinted in McClellan, *Civil War Papers,* p. 32.

43. O.R., ser. 1, vol. 2, p. 197.

44. The two quotes are from letters to Nelly in McClellan, *Civil War Papers,* p. 40; and in the McClellan Papers, C7:63.

45. McClellan, *Civil War Papers,* p. 33, p. 34.

46. Ibid., p. 41.

47. Ibid., p. 46, p. 40.

48. Betty Hornbeck, *Upshur Brothers of the Blue and the Gray* (Parsons, WV: McClain Printing Company, 1976), p. 45.

49. McClellan, *Civil War Papers,* p. 46.

50. The estimate of enemy numbers is from Jacob D. Cox, "McClellan in West Virginia," in *Battles and Leaders,* vol. 1, p. 131.

51. Maury, *Recollections of a Virginian,* p. 129.

52. McClellan, *Civil War Papers,* p. 44.

53. Reid, *Ohio in the War,* vol. 1, pp. 311–14, p. 349.

54. O.R., ser. 1, vol. 2, p. 215.

55. Alec Hart's running cannon count is from Arnold, "Battle of Rich Mountain," p. 48.

56. McClellan's indecision: John Beatty, *Memoirs of a Volunteer, 1861–1863,* ed. Harvey S. Ford (New York: W. W. Norton, 1946), p. 27. McClellan's account of the Confederate officer's oration and his interpretation of what it meant: George Brinton McClellan, *Report on the Organization and Campaigns of the Army of the Potomac, to Which Is Added an Account of the Campaign in Western Virginia . . .* (New York: Sheldon & Company, 1864), p. 30.

57. Rosecrans later reported this heavily ballooned estimate of enemy strength at Rich Mountain—lapping reality by four to seven times—in testimony before the Committee on the

Conduct of the War. He said it came from McClellan and others. See U.S. Congress, "Rose-crans's Campaigns," *Report of the Joint Committee on the Conduct of the War*, Report 142, 3 vols., 38th Cong., 2d sess. 1865, vol. 3, p. 5.

58. *Cincinnati Commercial*, in Moore, *Rebellion Record*, vol. 2. doc., pp. 291–92.

59. *Cincinnati Gazette*, in Moore, *Rebellion Record* 2: doc., p. 291.

60. Reid's account of the action at Corricks Ford and Garnett's death is in Ibid., pp. 288–91.

61. Merrill, *The Soldier of Indiana*, vol. 1, p. 21.

62. W. G. Fuller, "The Corps of Telegraphers under General Anson Stager during the War of the Rebellion," in *Sketches of War History, 1861–1865: Papers Read before the Ohio Commandery of the Military Order of the Loyal Legion of the United States, 1886–1888*, vol. 2 (Cincinnati: Robert Clarke & Co., 1888), p. 396.

63. William R. Plum, *The Military Telegraph during the Civil War in the United States*, 2 vols. (Chicago: Jansen, McClurg & Co., 1882), vol. 1, p. 94.

64. Stager's line-laying: Plum, *The Military Telegraph during the Civil War*, vol. 1, pp. 92–99. McClellan's introduction to the telegraph in the Crimean War: Robert Luther Thompson, *Wiring a Continent: The History of the Telegraph Industry in the United States, 1832–1866* (Princeton, NJ: Princeton University Press, 1947), p. 385n. McClellan's use of it at Rich Mountain and his alias, Mecca: Donald L. Rice, "The Military Telegraph in Western Virginia," *Randolph County Historical Society Magazine of History and Biography* 12 (April 1961), pp. 26–27.

65. O.R., ser. 1, vol. 2, p. 204.

66. Ibid., p. 236.

67. Ibid., p. 204, for "charmed;" Scott's follow-up comment is in Scott to McClellan, 14 July 1861, McClellan Papers, A19: 9.

68. *Congressional Globe*, 37th Cong., 1st sess., p. 148.

69. Quoted in Sears, *George B. McClellan*, p. 85.

70. *New York Times*, 20 July 1861; *Louisville Journal*, 20 July 1861.

71. Ellen McClellan to McClellan, 12 July 1861, McClellan Papers, A19: 9.

72. McClellan, *Civil War Papers*, p. 71.

73. O.R., Ser. 1, vol. 2, p. 239.

PART 4 DOWN IN THE VALLEY

The Valley Man

1. O.R., ser. 1, vol. 5, p. 909.

2. Richard Taylor, *Destruction and Reconstruction: Personal Experiences of the Late War*, ed. Richard B. Harwell (New York: Longmans, Green and Co., 1955), p. 47.

3. Cooke, *Stonewall Jackson*, p. 102.

4. Ibid., p. 84.

5. O.R., ser. 1, vol. 5, p. 921.

6. Henry Kyd Douglas, *I Rode with Stonewall* (Chapel Hill: University of North Carolina Press, 1968). pp. 16–17.

7. Ibid., p. 15.

8. Maury, *Recollections of a Virginian*, p. 29.

9. John B. Jones, *A Rebel War Clerk's Diary*, ed. Earl Schenck Miers (New York: Sagamore Press, 1958), p. 61.

10. O.R., ser. 1, vol. 5, p. 1033, p. 1043.

11. Cooke, *Stonewall Jackson*, pp. 101–2.

12. Taylor describes the Valley in *Destruction and Reconstruction*, pp. 45–46. Also see Robert G. Tanner, "Jackson in the Shenandoah," in *The Guns of '62*, vol. 2 of William C. Davis, ed., *The Image of War: 1861–1865*, a project of the National Historical Society (Garden City, NY: Doubleday & Company, 1982), p. 327.

13. English Combatant, *Battle-Fields of the South, from Bull Run to Fredericksburgh; with Sketches of Confederate Commanders, and Gossip of the Camps* (New York: John Bradburn, 1864), p. 142.

14. Jedediah Hotchkiss, *Make Me a Map of the Valley: The Civil War Journal of Stonewall Jackson's Topographer*, ed. Archie P. McDonald (Dallas: Southern Methodist University Press, 1989), p. 10. For biographical background on Hotchkiss see the Introduction to that work, pp. xv–xx.

15. McClellan, *Civil War Papers*, p. 162.

16. Joseph E. Johnston, *Narrative of Military Operations Directed, during the Late War Between the States* (1874; reprint, Bloomington: Indiana University Press, 1959), p. 106.

17. Jedediah Hotchkiss, *Virginia*, vol. 4 of Clement A. Evans, ed., *Confederate Military History*, *Extended Edition* (1899; reprint, Wilmington, NC: Broadfoot Publishing Company, 1987), p. 215.

18. William G. Bean, ed., "The Valley Campaign of 1862 as Revealed in Letters of Sandie Pendleton," *Virginia Magazine of History and Biography* 78 (July 1970), p. 337.

19. George M. Neese, *Three Years in the Confederate Horse Artillery* (1911; reprint, Dayton: Morningside, 1988), p. 27.

20. There is an excellent summary of all of these preliminaries in Hotchkiss, *Virginia*, pp. 214–17.

21. The thinking in the federal camp: David Hunter Strother in *A Virginia Yankee in the Civil War: The Diaries of David Hunter Strother*, ed. Cecil D. Eby, Jr. (Chapel Hill: The University of North Carolina Press, 1961), p. 3; and in O.R., ser. 1, vol. 12, pt. 1, p. 340.

22. O.R. ser. 1, vol. 12, pt. 1, p. 340.

23. Hotchkiss is also a good source for the preliminaries leading up to the battle of Kernstown. See *Virginia*, pp. 217–20.

24. Bean, "The Valley Campaign of 1862 As Revealed in the Letters of Sandie Pendleton," p. 342.

25. "The Valley after Kernstown," *SHSP* 19 (1891), p. 318.

26. Neese, *Three Years in the Confederate Horse Artillery*, p. 10, p. 36.

27. O.R., ser. 1, vol. 12, pt. 1, pp. 383–84.

28. Ashby's rear guard action is described in James F. Huntington, "Operations in the Shenandoah Valley, from Winchester to Port Republic, March 10–June 9, 1862," *MHSM*, vol. 1, *Campaigns in Virginia, 1861–1862* (1895; reprint, Wilmington, NC: Broadfoot Publishing Company, 1989), p. 305.

29. Neese, *Three Years in the Confederate Horse Artillery*, pp. 43–44.

30. James B. Avirett, *The Memoirs of General Turner Ashby and His Compeers* (Baltimore: Selby & Dulany, 1867), p. 171.

31. George Henry Gordon, *Brook Farm to Cedar Mountain in the War of the Great Rebellion, 1861–62* (Boston: James R. Osgood and Company, 1883), pp. 136–37.

32. Douglas, *I Rode with Stonewall*, p. vii.

33. Hotchkiss, *Make Me a Map of the Valley*, p. 22. For background on Douglas see *I Rode with Stonewall* and *Dictionary of American Biography*, s.v. "Douglas, Henry Kyd."

34. Douglas vividly recounts his midnight ride in *I Rode with Stonewall*, pp. 42–47.

35. Bean, "The Valley Campaign of 1862 as Revealed in Letters of Sandie Pendleton," p. 350.

36. Jackson's thoughts and motivations are reflected in O.R., ser. 1, vol. 12, pt. 3, p. 838, pp. 843–44. The quote is on p. 863.

37. Ibid., p. 872.

The Odd Couple

1. Kate Sperry, "Kate Sperry's Diary, 1861–1866," ed. Christine Andreae, *Virginia Country's Civil War* 1 (1983), p. 47.

2. John S. Robson, *How a One-Legged Rebel Lives: Reminiscences of the Civil War* (1898; reprint, Gaithersburg, MD: Butternut Press, 1984), p. 32.

3. English Combatant, *Battle-Fields of the South*, p. 141.

4. Cooke, *Stonewall Jackson*, p. 196.

5. Charles Hallock, *A Complete Biographical Sketch of "Stonewall" Jackson, Giving a Full and*

Notes

Accurate Account of the Leading Events of His Military Career, His Dying Moments, and the Obsequies at Richmond and Lexington (Augusta, GA: Steam Power-Press Chronicle and Sentinel, 1863), p. 11.

6. The description of Jackson is a composite from many sources, principally: Cooke, *Stonewall Jackson*, pp. 196–97; Douglas, *I Rode with Stonewall*, p. 234; McHenry Howard, *Recollections of a Maryland Confederate Soldier and Staff Officer under Johnston, Jackson and Lee* (1914; reprint, Dayton: Press of Morningside Bookshop, 1975), pp. 79–80; John Cheves Haskell, *The Haskell Memoirs*, ed. Gilbert E. Govan and James W. Livingood (New York: G.P. Putnam's Sons, 1960), p. 20; Margaret Junkin Preston, "Personal Reminiscences of Stonewall Jackson," *Century Magazine* 32, new ser. 10 (October 1886), p. 927; and John S. Wise, "Stonewall Jackson as I Knew Him," *The Circle* (March 1908), p. 143. (A copy is in the Virginia Historical Society Library.)

7. Douglas, *I Rode With Stonewall*, p. 234.
8. Jackson, *Memoirs of Stonewall Jackson*, p. 171.
9. Cooke, *Stonewall Jackson*, p. 469.
10. Jackson, *Memoirs of Stonewall Jackson*, p. 171.
11. The portrait of Jackson and Little Sorrel uses Hallock, *A Complete Biographical Sketch of "Stonewall" Jackson*, p. 11; James Power Smith, *With Stonewall Jackson in the Army of Northern Virginia* (1920; reprint, Gaithersburg, MD: Zullo and Van Sickle Books, 1982), pp. 96–97; Taylor, *Destruction and Reconstruction*, p. 53; and Louise K. Dooley, "Little Sorrel: A War-Horse for Stonewall," *Army* 25 (April 1975), pp. 34–39.
12. Cooke, *Stonewall Jackson*, pp. 83–84.
13. Hallock, *A Complete Biographical Sketch of "Stonewall" Jackson*, pp. 11–12.
14. George Cary Eggleston, *A Rebel's Recollections* (1959; reprint, New York: Kraus Reprint Co., 1969), p. 132.
15. Robert Garlick Hill Kean, *Inside the Confederate Government: The Diary of Robert Garlick Hill Kean*, ed. Edward Younger (New York: Oxford University Press, 1957), p. 60.
16. Quoted in Shelby Foote, *The Civil War: A Narrative*, 3 vols. (New York: Random House, 1958–1974), vol. 1, p. 429.
17. John Esten Cooke, *Stonewall Jackson and the Old Stonewall Brigade*, ed. Richard Barksdale Harwell (Charlottesville: University of Virginia Press for the Tracy W. McGregor Library, 1954), p. 27, p. 14.
18. Jackson, *Memoirs of Stonewall Jackson*, p. 61.
19. O.R., ser. 1, vol. 12, pt. 3, p. 842.
20. Jackson, *Memoirs of Stonewall Jackson*, p. 75; Preston, "Personal Reminiscences of Stonewall Jackson," p. 931.
21. Preston, "Personal Reminiscences of Stonewall Jackson," p. 930, p. 933.
22. Hill, "The Real Stonewall Jackson," p. 626.
23. Jackson, *Memoirs of Stonewall Jackson*, p. 72.
24. Thomas J. Jackson, Order Book, Harpers Ferry 1861, Eleanor S. Brockenbrough Library, Museum of the Confederacy.
25. John N. Opie, *A Rebel Cavalryman with Lee, Stuart, and Jackson* (1899; reprint, Dayton: Press of Morningside Bookshop, 1972), pp. 19–20.
26. Charles W. Squires, "The Last of Lee's Battle Line," typescript autobiography, ed. W.H.T. Squires, Manuscript Division, Library of Congress, p. 9.
27. Hill, "The Real Stonewall Jackson," p. 627; Douglas, *I Rode with Stonewall*, p. 149.
28. Preston, "Personal Reminiscences of Stonewall Jackson," p. 927.
29. Hill, "The Real Stonewall Jackson," p. 625.
30. See Jackson, *Memoirs of Stonewall Jackson*, for numerous examples.
31. Ibid., pp. 46–47.
32. Maury, "General T. J. ("Stonewall") Jackson," p. 315, pp. 311–12.
33. Jackson, *Memoirs of Stonewall Jackson*, p. 71.
34. Maury, *Recollections of a Virginian*, p. 71.
35. Vandiver, *Mighty Stonewall*, p. 119.
36. Preston, "Personal Reminiscences of Stonewall Jackson," p. 936; Hill, "The Real Stonewall Jackson," p. 625.

37. Douglas, *I Rode with Stonewall*, p. 234.

38. Cooke, *Stonewall Jackson*, p. 152.

39. Hill, "The Real Stonewall Jackson," p. 626.

40. William Allan, *History of the Campaign of Gen. T. J. (Stonewall) Jackson in the Valley of Virginia from November 4, 1861 to June 17, 1862* (1880; reprint, Dayton: Morningside, 1987), p. 123n; Hotchkiss, *Virginia*, pp. 247–48.

41. J. William Jones, " 'Stonewall' Jackson: Anecdotes," *Confederate Veteran* 12 (April 1904), p. 174.

42. Cooke, *Stonewall Jackson and the Old Stonewall Brigade*, pp. 42–43.

43. Chesnut, *Mary Chesnut's Civil War*, p. 499.

44. Taylor, *Destruction and Reconstruction*, p. 37, p. 89. Also see Thomas T. Munford, "Reminiscences of Jackson's Valley Campaign," *SHSP* 7 (1879), p. 523.

45. Quoted in Percy Garland Hamlin, "Richard S. Ewell: His Humanity and Humor," *Virginia Cavalcade* 21 (Autumn 1971), p. 10.

46. Taylor, *Destruction and Reconstruction*, p. 36; Sorrel, *Recollections of a Confederate Staff Officer*, p. 53.

47. Eggleston, *A Rebel's Recollections*, p. 136.

48. Wise, "Stonewall Jackson as I Knew Him," p. 144.

49. *Dictionary of American Biography*, s.v. "Ewell, Benjamin Stoddert" and "Ewell, Richard Stoddert."

50. Quoted in T. Harry Williams, ed., "General Ewell to the High Private in the Rear," *Virginia Magazine of History and Biography* 54 (April 1946), p. 159.

51. Robert Walter Frazer, *Forts of the West: Military Forts and Presidios and Posts Commonly Called Forts West of the Mississippi River to 1898* (Norman: University of Oklahoma Press, 1972), p. 150; Hamlin, *The Making of a Soldier*, p. 95.

52. Taylor, *Destruction and Reconstruction*, p. 38.

53. O.R., ser. 1, vol. 12, pt. 3, p. 890.

54. Taylor, *Destruction and Reconstruction*, pp. 36–37. A caoutchouc man is a man made of rubber.

55. Ewell Family Papers, handwritten notes on Richard Ewell, The Earl Gregg Swem Library, College of William and Mary, folder 21.

56. Taylor, *Destruction and Reconstruction*, p. 37.

57. The Ewell anecdotes are from John B. Gordon, *Reminiscences of the Civil War* (New York: Charles Scribner's Sons, 1903), pp. 38–42.

58. Ibid., p. 158.

59. Campbell Brown, "Notes on Ewell's Division in the Campaign of 1862," *SHSP* 10 (1882), pp. 255–56; "Strength of Ewell's Division in the Campaign of 1862—Field Returns," *SHSP* 8 (1880), pp. 301–3.

60. Hotchkiss, *Make Me a Map of the Valley*, pp. 34–35.

61. Douglas, *I Rode with Stonewall*, p. 235.

62. John D. Imboden, "Stonewall Jackson in the Shenandoah," *Battles and Leaders*, vol. 2, p. 297, p. 293.

63. Douglas, *I Rode with Stonewall*, p. 155.

64. Squires, "The Last of Lee's Battle Line," p. 8.

65. Jones, " 'Stonewall' Jackson: Anecdotes," p. 175.

66. J. William Jones, "The Old Virginia Town, Lexington: Where Lee and Stonewall Jackson Are Buried—Reminiscences of Stonewall Jackson," *Confederate Veteran* 1 (January 1893), p. 19.

67. Hamlin, *"Old Bald Head,"* p. 84.

From under the Little Faded Cap

1. Neese, *Three Years in the Confederate Horse Artillery*, p. 50.

2. Hotchkiss, *Make Me a Map of the Valley*, p. 36.

3. Edward A. Moore, *The Story of a Cannoneer under Stonewall Jackson* (Lynchburg, VA: J. P. Bell Company, 1910), p. 45.

4. Ibid., pp. 47–48.

5. The muddy roundabout march to Staunton is described in Allan, *History of the Campaign in the Valley of Virginia*, pp. 69–71; Hotchkiss, *Virginia*, pp. 227–28; and Douglas, *I Rode with Stonewall*, pp. 47–48.

6. Bean, "The Valley Campaign of 1862, as Revealed in the Letters of Sandie Pendleton," p. 355.

7. Dabney tells his story in "Stonewall Jackson," *SHSP* 11 (1883), pp. 127–29.

8. Hotchkiss, *Make Me a Map of the Valley*, pp. 36–37.

9. Robson, *How a One-Legged Rebel Lives*, p. 28.

10. Chesnut, *Mary Chesnut's Civil War*, p. 444.

11. Bean, "The Valley Campaign of 1862 as Revealed in Letters of Sandie Pendleton," p. 356.

12. O.R., ser. 1, vol. 12, pt. 3, p. 884.

13. Hotchkiss, *Make Me a Map of the Valley*, p. 39.

14. Robson, *How a One-Legged Rebel Lives*, p. 29.

15. O.R., ser. 1, vol. 12, pt. 1, p. 470; also see Imboden, "Stonewall Jackson in the Shenandoah," pp. 287–88.

16. Robson, *How a One-Legged Rebel Lives*, p. 30.

17. Neese, *Three Years in the Confederate Horse Artillery*, p. 54.

18. Quoted in Munford, "Reminiscences of Jackson's Valley Campaign," p. 527.

19. This story is from Ibid., pp. 526–27.

20. Hamlin, *The Making of a Soldier*, p. 108.

21. Strother, *A Virginia Yankee in the Civil War*, p. 32, p. 58.

22. Ibid., pp. 34–35; Hotchkiss, *Virginia*, pp. 234–35.

23. Moore, *The Story of a Cannoneer*, p. 51.

24. O.R., ser. 1, vol. 12, pt. 3, pp. 892–93.

25. Bean, "The Valley Campaign of 1862 as Revealed in Letters of Sandie Pendleton," p. 359.

26. Ewell's visit to Jackson is from Douglas, *I Rode with Stonewall*, p. 93; and Dabney, *Life and Campaigns of Lieut.-Gen. Thomas J. Jackson*, pp. 359–60.

27. Strother, *A Virginia Yankee in the Civil War*, p. 36.

28. Taylor, *Destruction and Reconstruction*, pp. 50–51.

29. Robson, *How a One-Legged Rebel Lives*, p. 39.

30. Dabney Herndon Maury, "Sketch of General Richard Taylor," *SHSP* 7 (1879), pp. 343–45.

31. Taylor, *Destruction and Reconstruction*, p. 52.

32. The impression of Jackson is from the viewpoint of one of the Louisiana soldiers, in Hamlin, *"Old Bald Head,"* p. 89.

33. O.R., ser. 1, vol. 12, pt. 1, p. 524.

34. Strother, *A Virginia Yankee in the Civil War*, pp. 37–38.

35. Bradley T. Johnson, "Memoir of the First Maryland Regiment," Paper No. 3, *SHSP* 10 (1882), pp. 53–54.

36. Gordon, *Brook Farm to Cedar Mountain*, p. 186.

37. Johnson, "Memoir of the First Maryland Regiment," p. 54.

38. For the most part I have used Douglas's version of this bizarre encounter with the famous Confederate female spy in *I Rode with Stonewall*, pp. 51–52. I have embellished it with Belle Boyd's own account in her memoirs, *Belle Boyd in Camp and Prison, Written by Herself*, ed. Curtis Carroll Davis (1865; reprint, South Brunswick, NJ: Thomas Yoseloff, 1968), pp. 161–64. The two accounts differ in some details, but what can you do? Douglas's version is the more romantic.

39. Sperry, "Kate Sperry's Diary," p. 46.

40. Johnson, "Memoir of the First Maryland Regiment," p. 54.

41. Robson, *How a One-Legged Rebel Lives*, p. 39.

42. Ibid.

43. Dabney, *Life and Campaigns of Lieut.-Gen. Thomas J. Jackson*, pp. 365–66.
44. Robson, *How a One-Legged Rebel Lives*, p. 39.
45. Johnson, "Memoir of the First Maryland Regiment," p. 55.

My Friend, My Enemy

1. Gordon, *Brook Farm to Cedar Mountain*, p. 190.
2. Ibid., p. 119.
3. Gordon's account is in Ibid., pp. 191–94, p. 172n; Also see Strother, *A Virginia Yankee in the Civil War*, p. 40.
4. O.R., ser. 1, vol. 12, pt. 1, p. 703.
5. Dabney, *Life and Campaigns of Lieut.-Gen. Thomas J. Jackson*, p. 371.
6. Strother, *A Virginia Yankee in the Civil War*, p. 40.
7. Gordon's descriptions of the retreat and the stand at Newtown are in *Brook Farm to Cedar Mountain*, pp. 194–217. Jackson's is in O.R., ser. 1, vol. 12, pt. 1, pp. 703–4.
8. O.R., ser. 1, vol. 12, pt. 1, p. 704.
9. Boyd, *Belle Boyd in Camp and Prison*, p. 167.
10. Douglas, *I Rode with Stonewall*, p. 55.
11. Ibid., pp. 56–57.
12. Dabney, *Life and Campaigns of Lieut.-Gen. Thomas J. Jackson*, pp. 374–75; Shelby Foote artfully describes the scene in *The Civil War*, vol. 1, p. 433.
13. Katherine M. Jones, ed., *Heroines of Dixie: Confederate Women Tell Their Story of the War* (Indianapolis: Bobbs Merrill, 1955), p. 141.
14. Moore, *The Story of a Cannoneer*, p. 56.
15. O.R., ser. 1, vol. 12, pt. 1, pp. 704–5, p. 779.
16. Gordon, *Brook Farm to Cedar Mountain*, pp. 225–27.
17. Taylor, *Destruction and Reconstruction*, p. 62.
18. Douglas, *I Rode with Stonewall*, p. 58.
19. Taylor, *Destruction and Reconstruction*, p. 70, pp. 62–63.
20. Gordon, *Brook Farm to Cedar Mountain*, p. 241.
21. Taylor, *Destruction and Reconstruction*, p. 64.
22. Douglas, *I Rode with Stonewall*, p. 59.
23. Taylor, *Destruction and Reconstruction*, p. 64.
24. Strother, *A Virginia Yankee in the Civil War*, pp. 41–42, pp. 49–50.
25. Johnson, "Memoir of the First Maryland Regiment," Paper No. 4, *SHSP* 10 (1882), p. 99; Dabney, *Life and Campaigns of Lieut.-Gen. Thomas J. Jackson*, p. 380; and John H. Worsham, *One of Jackson's Foot Cavalry*, ed. James I. Robertson, Jr. (1912; reprint, Jackson, TN: McCowat-Mercer Press, 1964), pp. 46–47.
26. Cornelia McDonald, *A Diary with Reminiscences of the War and Refugee Life in the Shenandoah Valley, 1860–1865*, ed. Hunter McDonald (Nashville: Cullom & Ghertner Co., 1934), p. 163.
27. Robson, *How a One-Legged Rebel Lives*, p. 43.
28. O.R., ser. 1, vol. 12, pt. 1, p. 617.
29. Gordon, *Brook Farm to Cedar Mountain*, p. 243n.
30. Douglas, *I Rode with Stonewall*, p. 60.
31. Imboden, "Stonewall Jackson in the Shenandoah," p. 297.
32. Dabney, *Life and Campaigns of Lieut.-Gen. Thomas J. Jackson*, pp. 381–82.
33. Bean, "The Valley Campaign of 1862 as Revealed in Letters of Sandie Pendleton," p. 330.
34. Opie, *A Rebel Cavalryman with Lee, Stuart, and Jackson*, pp. 21–22.
35. The background on Pendleton is largely from Bean, "The Valley Campaign of 1862 as Revealed in Letters of Sandie Pendleton," p. 327. Bean has also written an excellent biography of Pendleton: *Stonewall's Man: Sandie Pendleton* (1959; reprint, Wilmington, NC: Broadfoot Publishing Company, 1987).
36. Pendleton's account is in O.R., ser. 1, vol. 12, pt. 1, pp. 709–10.
37. Dabney, *Life and Campaigns of Lieut.-Gen. Thomas J. Jackson*, p. 383.

38. Neese, *Three Years in the Confederate Horse Artillery*, p. 20.
39. O.R., ser. 1, vol. 12, pt. 1, p. 551.
40. Ibid., p. 701, p. 707.

Delightful Excitement

1. Lincoln, *Collected Works*, vol. 5, p. 232.
2. O.R., ser. 1, vol. 12, pt. 1, p. 643.
3. Ibid., p. 644.
4. Frémont's thinking is in O.R., ser. 1, vol. 12, pt. 1, pp. 10–14.
5. Boteler's account is in "Stonewall Jackson in Campaign of 1862," *SHSP* 40 (1915), pp. 163–66.
6. Hotchkiss, *Make Me a Map of the Valley*, p. 50.
7. For Jackson's possessive attitudes toward plunder see Hamlin, *"Old Bald Head,"* p. 96; Munford, "Reminiscences of Jackson's Valley Campaign," p. 528; Worsham, *One of Jackson's Foot Cavalry*, p. 31.
8. Johnson, "Memoir of the First Maryland Regiment," p. 101.
9. William Dorsey Pender, *The General to His Lady: The Civil War Letters of William Dorsey Pender to Fanny Pender*, ed. William W. Hassler (1962; reprint, Gaithersburg, MD: Ron R. Van Sickle Military Books, 1988), p. 171, p. 173, p. 197.
10. Cooke, *Stonewall Jackson*, p. 123.
11. Quoted in Bell Irvin Wiley, *The Life of Johnny Reb: The Common Soldier of the Confederacy* (Baton Rouge: Louisiana State University Press, 1978), p. 366.
12. Douglas, *I Rode with Stonewall*, p. 21.
13. Avirett, *The Memoirs of General Turner Ashby*, pp. 196–97.
14. Imboden, "Stonewall Jackson in the Shenandoah," pp. 297–98.
15. Robson, *How a One-Legged Rebel Lives*, pp. 40–41.
16. Howard, *Recollections of a Maryland Confederate Soldier and Staff Officer*, p. 116; Johnson, "Memoir of the First Maryland Regiment," pp. 101–2; Hotchkiss, *Virginia*, pp. 250–51.
17. O.R., ser. 1, vol. 12, pt. 1, p. 648.
18. Howard, *Recollections of a Maryland Confederate Soldier and Staff Officer*, pp. 116–17.
19. Neese, *Three Years in the Confederate Horse Artillery*, p. 64.
20. O.R., ser. 1, vol. 12, pt. 1, pp. 711–12.
21. Jackson, *"Memoirs of Stonewall Jackson*, pp. 268–69.
22. William Augustus McClendon, *Recollections of War Times by an Old Veteran while under Stonewall Jackson and Lieutenant General James Longstreet: How I Got in and How I Got out* (1909; reprint, San Bernardino, CA: California Church Press, 1973), p. 62.
23. Hotchkiss, *Virginia*, p. 253; Hotchkiss, *Make Me a Map of the Valley*, p. 51.
24. Howard, *Recollections of a Maryland Confederate Soldier and Staff Officer*, p. 78.
25. Neese, *Three Years in the Confederate Horse Artillery*, p. 28; Avirett, *The Memoirs of General Turner Ashby*, p. 47.
26. Dabney, *Life and Campaigns of Lieut.-Gen. Thomas J. Jackson*, pp. 401–2.
27. Cooke, *Stonewall Jackson*, pp. 174–75.
28. Munford, "Reminiscences of Jackson's Valley Campaign," pp. 528–29.
29. O.R., ser. 1, vol. 19, pt. 1, p. 821.
30. Dabney, *Life and Campaigns of Lieut.-Gen. Thomas J. Jackson*, pp. 399–400.
31. Ibid., p. 401.
32. O.R., ser. 1, vol. 12, pt. 1, p. 712.
33. Neese, *Four Years in the Confederate Horse Artillery*, pp. 70–71.
34. Cooke, *Stonewall Jackson*, pp. 175–76.
35. Shields's situation is distilled from his reports and messages in O.R., ser. 1, vol. 12, pt. 1, pp. 685–86, p. 22.
36. Howard, *Recollections of a Maryland Confederate Soldier and Staff Officer*, p. 122, p. 122n, p. 124.
37. Robson, *How a One-Legged Rebel Lives*, p. 53.

38. O.R., ser. 1, vol. 12, pt. 1 pp. 712–13.

39. John W. Fravel, "Jackson's Valley Campaign," *Confederate Veteran* 6 (September 1898), p. 419.

40. Johnson, "Memoir of the First Maryland Regiment," p. 109.

41. O.R., ser. 1, vol. 12, pt. 1, pp. 21–22.

42. Taylor, *Destruction and Reconstruction*, p. 84.

43. Douglas, *I Rode with Stonewall*, p. 91.

44. O.R., ser. 1, vol. 12, pt. 1, p. 685, p. 689.

45. Jed Hotchkiss, who was with Jackson throughout the campaign in the Valley, has written an excellent concise account in *Virginia*, pp. 214–68. His accounts of the battles of Cross Keys and Port Republic are on pages pp. 255–64.

46. Robson, *How a One-Legged Rebel Lives*, p. 60.

47. Jones, *A Rebel War Clerk's Diary*, p. 78, p. 10.

48. Chesnut, *Mary Chesnut's Civil War*, p. 361.

49. Robson, *How a One-Legged Rebel Lives*, p. 36.

50. The quotes on Jackson are all from O.R., ser. 1, vol. 12, pt. 3, pp. 905–8.

51. Strother, *A Virginia Yankee in the Civil War*, p. 55.

52. Taylor, *Destruction and Reconstruction*, p. 37; Gordon, *Reminiscences of the Civil War*, pp. 128–29.

53. Benjamin S. Ewell, "Jackson and Ewell: The Latter's Opinion of His Chief," *SHSP* 20 (1892), p. 32.

54. Taylor, *Destruction and Reconstruction*, p. 37.

55. Jones, *A Rebel War Clerk's Diary*, pp. 78–79.

56. Munford, "Reminiscences of Jackson's Valley Campaign," p. 530.

57. Jackson, *Memoirs of Stonewall Jackson*, p. 287.

58. Boteler, "Stonewall Jackson in Campaign of 1862," pp. 172–73.

59. O.R., ser. 1, vol. 12, pt. 3, p. 908. Also see p. 913.

PART 5 BROTHER AGAINST BROTHER

High Hopes and Paranoia

1. Nicolay and Hay, *Abraham Lincoln* vol. 4, pp. 443–44.

2. The idea that these two generals resented him is in a letter from McClellan to his wife in McClellan, *Civil War Papers*, p. 70. McClellan's letters to Ellen are in the McClellan Papers in the Library of Congress. But they are far more accessible in Sears's comprehensive, well-edited, and recently published collection. I have dipped into it repeatedly in putting together the next four stories.

3. Russell, *My Diary North and South*, p. 240.

4. André Maurois, "A Princely Service," *American Heritage* 17 (April 1966), p. 58.

5. McClellan, *Civil War Papers*, p. 70.

6. Ibid., p. 71.

7. O.R., ser. 1, vol. 5, pp. 6–8.

8. McClellan, *Civil War Papers*, p. 75.

9. Nicolay and Hay, *Abraham Lincoln*, vol. 4, p. 446.

10. McClellan, *Civil War Papers*, p. 70, p. 70n.

11. O.R., ser. 1, vol. 11, pt. 3, p. 3.

12. McClellan, *Civil War Papers*, p. 106.

13. Ibid., p. 87, p. 84.

14. O.R., ser. 1, vol. 11, pt. 3, p. 4.

15. McClellan, *Civil War Papers*, p. 85.

16. Ibid., p. 75, p. 79.

17. Ibid., p. 81.

18. Ibid., p. 84.

19. Ibid., p. 75.

20. Ibid., p. 86.

21. Ibid., pp. 85–86.
22. Ibid., pp. 106–7, p. 114.
23. Ibid., p. 89, p. 91.
24. Ibid., p. 89.
25. Ibid., p. 98, p. 112.
26. Ibid., pp. 123–24.
27. John Hay, *Lincoln and the Civil War in the Diaries and Letters of John Hay*, ed. Tyler Dennett (New York: Dodd, Mead & Company, 1939), pp. 32–33.
28. McClellan, *Civil War Papers*, p. 107, p. 136.
29. Ibid., p. 135.
30. Ibid., pp. 135–36, p. 113.
31. Ibid., p. 113.
32. Nicolay and Hay, *Abraham Lincoln*, vol. 4, p. 469n.
33. Hay, *Lincoln and the Civil War*, pp. 34–35.
34. McClellan, *Civil War Papers*, p. 114.
35. Ibid., p. 128.
36. Hay, *Lincoln and the Civil War*, p. 27.
37. Ibid., p. 31.
38. Nicolay and Hay, *Abraham Lincoln*, vol. 4, p. 470.
39. Lincoln, *Collected Works*, vol. 5, p. 94, p. 94n.
40. O.R., ser. 1, vol. 7, p. 535, p. 533.
41. Montgomery C. Meigs, "General M. C. Meigs on the Conduct of the Civil War," *American Historical Review* 26 (January 1921), p. 292.
42. Ibid., pp. 292–93.
43. McClellan, *Civil War Papers*, p. 155.
44. Ibid., p. 187.
45. Henry J. Raymond, *The Life and Public Services of Abraham Lincoln* . . . (New York: Derby and Miller, 1865), p. 773.
46. Nicolay and Hay, *Abraham Lincoln*, vol. 5, pp. 171–72.
47. For this general order see Lincoln, *Collected Works*, vol. 5, pp. 111–12.
48. Nicolay and Hay, *Abraham Lincoln*, vol. 5, pp. 168–69.
49. McClellan, *Civil War Papers*, p. 143, p. 154.
50. O.R., ser. 1, vol. 5, pp. 42–45; McClellan, *Civil War Papers*, pp. 162–70.
51. O.R., ser. 1, vol. 5, p. 42.
52. McClellan, *Civil War Papers*, p. 223.
53. Ibid., p. 196.
54. Ibid., p. 211.

Maryland, My Maryland

1. Lincoln, *Collected Works*, vol. 5, p. 182.
2. McClellan, *Civil War Papers*, p. 234.
3. Lincoln, *Collected Works*, vol. 5, p. 185.
4. O.R., ser. 1, vol. 11, pt. 1, p. 406.
5. O.R., ser. 1, vol. 5, p. 1101.
6. O.R., ser. 1, vol. 11, pt. 3, p. 71.
7. McClellan, *Civil War Papers*, p. 230.
8. Ibid., p. 235.
9. Ibid., p. 269.
10. Nicolay and Hay, *Abraham Lincoln*, vol. 5, p. 366.
11. Lincoln, *Collected Works*, vol. 5, p. 203.
12. O.R., ser. 1, vol. 51, pt. 1, p. 589.
13. McClellan, *Civil War Papers*, p. 252.
14. O.R., ser. 1, vol. 11, pt. 3, p. 135.
15. O.R., ser. 1, vol. 11, pt. 1, p. 26.

16. McClellan, *Civil War Papers*, pp. 262–63.

17. Ibid., pp. 244–45.

18. Nicolay and Hay, *Abraham Lincoln*, vol. 5, pp. 414–15.

19. McClellan, *Civil War Papers*, pp. 305–6.

20. O.R., ser. 1, vol. 11, pt. 1, p. 51.

21. O.R., ser. 1, vol. 11, pt. 3, p. 259.

22. McClellan, *Civil War Papers*, p. 330.

23. Ibid., p. 361.

24. O.R., ser. 1, vol. 11, pt. 1, p. 61.

25. David Homer Bates, *Lincoln in the Telegraph Office: Recollections of the United States Military Telegraph Corps during the Civil War* (New York: Century Co., 1907), pp. 109–10.

26. Lincoln, *Collected Works*, vol. 5, p. 322.

27. Ibid., vol. 5, p. 301.

28. McClellan, *Civil War Papers*, p. 348.

29. Ibid., p. 362.

30. Oliver Willcox Norton, " "Little Mac's A-Coming," in Henry Steele Commager, ed., *The Blue and the Gray: The Story of the Civil War as Told by Participants* (1950; reprint [2 vols. in 1], New York: Fairfax Press, 1982), p. 195.

31. McClellan, *Civil War Papers*, pp. 354–55.

32. Ibid., p. 383.

33. Ibid., p. 368.

34. O.R., ser. 1, vol. 11, pt. 1, p. 89.

35. McClellan, *Civil War Papers*, p. 417.

36. Ibid., p. 419.

37. O.R., ser. 1, vol. 11, pt. 1., p. 98.

38. See Sears's discussion in McClellan, *Civil War Papers*, p. 403.

39. Salmon Portland Chase, *Inside Lincoln's Cabinet: The Civil War Diaries of Salmon P. Chase*, ed. David Donald (New York: Longmans, Green and Co., 1954), p. 119.

40. Hay, *Lincoln and the Civil War*, p. 47.

41. Helen Nicolay, *Lincoln's Secretary: A Biography of John G. Nicolay* (New York: Longmans, Green and Co., 1949), p. 149.

42. McClellan, *Civil War Papers*, p. 406.

43. Ibid., p. 435.

44. Moore, *The Story of a Cannoneer*, p. 132; Hotchkiss, *Make Me a Map of the Valley*, p. 78.

45. Clement Anselm Evans, *Intrepid Warrior: Clement Anselm Evans, Confederate General from Georgia; Life, Letters, and Diaries of the War Years*, comp. and ed. Robert Grier Stephens, Jr. (Dayton: Morningside, 1992), p. 169.

46. Henry Kyd Douglas describes the crossing in "Stonewall Jackson in Maryland," *Battles and Leaders*, vol. 2, p. 620, p. 621n.

47. Alexander Hunter, "A High Private's Account of the Battle of Sharpsburg," Paper No. 1, *SHSP* 10 (1882), p. 509.

48. Hotchkiss, *Make Me a Map of the Valley*, p. 82.

49. Hunter, "A High Private's Account of the Battle of Sharpsburg," Paper No. 1, pp. 510–11.

50. John Greenleaf Whittier, "Barbara Frietchie," quoted in Sorrel, *Recollections of a Confederate Staff Officer*, p. 108.

51. O.R., ser. 1, vol. 19, pt. 1, pp. 25–26.

52. McClellan, *Civil War Papers*, p. 445.

53. Ibid., p. 449.

54. Gibbon, *Personal Recollections of the Civil War*, p. 73.

55. Lincoln, *Collected Works*, vol. 5, p. 426.

56. Edward Porter Alexander, *Fighting for the Confederacy: The Personal Recollections of General Edward Porter Alexander*, ed. Gary W. Gallagher (Chapel Hill: University of North Carolina Press, 1989), p. 141. The text of the lost orders are in O.R., ser. 1, vol. 19, pt. 2, pp. 603–4. D. H. Hill argued after the war that the lost orders actually misled McClellan and in the end

did Lee more good than harm. See Daniel Harvey Hill, "The Lost Dispatch," *The Land We Love* 4 (February 1868), pp. 276–78.

57. David H. Strother describes Reno's death in "Personal Recollections of the War. By a Virginian," *Harper's New Monthly Magazine* 36 (February 1868), p. 278; and in *A Virginia Yankee in the Civil War*, p. 107.

58. McClellan's thinking is in O.R., ser. vol. 19, pt. 1, pp. 29–30.

59. Douglas, *I Rode with Stonewall*, p. 155.

60. Compte de Paris, *History of the Civil War in America*, ed. Henry Coppée, rev. ed., 3 vols. (Philadelphia: Porter & Coates, 1876, 1883), vol. 2, pp. 325–26.

61. Douglas, "Stonewall Jackson in Maryland," p. 627; Hill's report of this action is in O.R., ser. 1, vol. 19, pt. 1, p. 980.

62. See Lee's summary of the capture of Harpers Ferry, O.R., ser. 1, vol. 19, pt. 1, pp. 144–48.

63. Lee's dispositions at Sharpsburg are in O.R., ser. 1, vol. 19, pt. 1, p. 148. Also see Alexander, *Military Memoirs of a Confederate*, pp. 245–46.

64. McClellan's plans and dispositions are in O.R., ser. 1, vol. 19, pt. 1, p. 30.

65. The description of Jackson's arrival is from English Combatant, *Battle-Fields of the South*, pp. 482–83.

66. David L. Thompson, "With Burnside at Antietam," *Battles and Leaders*, vol. 2, p. 660.

67. Charles Carleton Coffin, "Antietam Scenes," *Battles and Leaders*, vol. 2, p. 682–83.

68. Mary Bedinger Mitchell, "A Woman's Recollections of Antietam," *Battles and Leaders*, vol. 2, pp. 690–91.

69. John Gordon describes the terrain at Antietam in *Reminiscences of the Civil War*, p. 82. Also see Hunter H. McGuire and George L. Christian, *The Confederate Cause and Conduct in the War between the States . . .* (Richmond: L.H. Jenkins, 1907), p. 203.

70. John G. Walker, "Sharpsburg," *Battles and Leaders*, vol. 2, p. 677.

71. Douglas, *I Rode with Stonewall*, p. 169.

72. Alexander, *Military Memoirs of a Confederate*, p. 247.

73. O. R., ser. 1, vol. 19, pt. 1, pp. 496–97.

74. The description of McClellan's headquarters during the battle draws from Strother, "Personal Recollections of the War," pp. 282–83.

75. McClellan, *Civil War Papers*, p. 468.

The Man in the Red Battle Shirt

1. Detailed firsthand accounts of Hill's dramatic march are hard to come by. But see J.F.J. Caldwell, *The History of a Brigade of South Carolinians, Known First as "Gregg's,' and Subsequently as 'McGowan's' Brigade* (1866; reprint, Marietta, GA: Continental Book Company, 1951) pp. 44–45; and Alexander, *Fighting for the Confederacy*, p. 152.

2. B. F. Brown, "A. P. Hill's Light Division," *Confederate Veteran* 30 (July 1922), p. 246. The description of Hill is a mosaic drawn for the most part from W. J. Robertson, " 'Up Came Hill'—Soldier of the South," part 1 (October 14, 1934), p. 10, and part 3 (October 28, 1934), p. 8; and John Wheeler-Bennett, "A. P. Hill: A Study in Confederate Leadership," *Virginia Quarterly Review* 37 (Spring 1961), pp. 200–01. The two Hill biographies cited earlier are also excellent sources: Hassler, *A. P. Hill: Lee's Forgotten General*; and Robertson's more recent *General A. P. Hill: The Story of a Confederate Warrior*.

3. Douglas, *I Rode with Stonewall*, pp. 177–78.

4. James C. Birdsong, comp., *Brief Sketches of North Carolina Troops in the War between the States* (Raleigh, NC: Josephus Daniels, 1894), p. 54; Also see Robertson, *General A. P. Hill*, p. 12, p. 148.

5. Alexander, *Fighting for the Confederacy*, p. 141.

6. Jedediah Hotchkiss writes a strictly pro-Jackson account of this incident in a typescript document, "Lieut. General A. P. Hill," Hotchkiss Papers, Manuscript Division, Library of Congress, cont. 56, reel 49. Most of the dialogue comes from that, p. 3. Also see Robertson, *General A. P. Hill*, pp. 130–32.

7. Walter Clark, ed., *Histories of the Several Regiments and Battalions from North Carolina in the Great War, 1861–65*, 5 vols. (1901; reprint, Wilmington, NC: Broadfoot Publishing Company, 1991), vol. 4, p. 165. (Henceforth this work will be cited as *NC Regiments*.)

8. Douglas, *I Rode with Stonewall*, p. 158. Hotchkiss vigorously disputes Douglas's story, contending that Hill would never have asked such a favor of Jackson, even for a fight. See Hotchkiss, "Lieut. General A. P. Hill," Hotchkiss Papers, p. 4.

9. Clark, *NC Regiments*, vol. 4, p. 165.

10. Jacob D. Cox, "The Battle of Antietam," *Battles and Leaders*, vol. 2, pp. 648–49.

11. Strother, "Personal Recollections of the War," p. 283.

12. O.R., ser. 1, vol. 19, pt. 1, p. 419.

13. William Allan, *The Army of Northern Virginia in 1862* (Boston: Houghton Mifflin, 1892), pp. 430–32.

14. Strother, "Personal Recollections of the War," p. 284.

15. Douglas, "Stonewall Jackson in Maryland," p. 629.

16. Thompson, "With Burnside at Antietam," pp. 661–62.

17. David E. Johnston, "Concerning the Battle of Sharpsburg," *Confederate Veteran* 6 (January 1898), p. 28.

18. Ibid.

19. Alexander Hunter, "A High Private's Sketch of Sharpsburg," Paper No. 2, *SHSP* 11 (1883), p. 18. The key official reports describing the action on the Confederate right up to this point—by Burnside, Cox, Willcox, Sturgis, and Toombs—are in O.R., ser. 1, vol. 19, pt. 1, pp. 419–20, pp. 424–26, pp. 429–31, pp. 444–45, and pp. 890–91. For a lucid summary see Francis Winthrop Palfrey, *The Antietam and Fredericksburg* (1882; reprint, Wilmington, NC: Broadfoot Publishing Company, 1989), pp. 107–13.

20. Caldwell, *The History of a Brigade of South Carolinians*, pp. 44–45.

21. Douglas Southall Freeman, *Lee's Lieutenants: A Study in Command*, 3 vols. (New York: Charles Scribner's Sons, 1942–1944), vol. 2, p. 222.

22. O. R., ser. 1, vol. 19, pt. 1, p. 981.

23. Moore, *The Story of a Cannoneer*, p. 158.

24. For an account of Lee's accident see Sorrel, *Recollections of a Confederate Staff Officer*, pp. 102–3.

25. This first sighting of Hill's troops is from Ramsay's account in Clark, *NC Regiments*, vol. 1, p. 575.

26. O.R., ser. 1, vol. 19, pt. 1, pp. 137–38.

27. Cox, "The Battle of Antietam," p. 655.

28. William E. Cameron, "The Career of General A. P. Hill," in *The Annals of the War Written by Leading Participants North and South*, p. 701.

29. James Longstreet, *From Manassas to Appomattox: Memoirs of the Civil War in America*, 2d ed. rev. (Philadelphia: J. B. Lippincott, 1903), p. 261.

30. Johnston, "Concerning the Battle of Sharpsburg," p. 28.

31. Caldwell, *A History of a Brigade of South Carolinians*, pp. 46–47.

32. Douglas, *I Rode with Stonewall*, p. 173; Douglas, "Stonewall Jackson in Maryland," p. 629.

33. Brown, "A. P. Hill's Light Division," p. 246.

34. Hunter, "A High Private's Sketch of Sharpsburg," Paper No. 2, pp. 19–20.

35. Francis W. Palfrey, "The Battle of Antietam," *Papers of the Military Historical Society of Massachusetts*, vol. 3, *Campaigns in Virginia, Maryland and Pennsylvania, 1862–1863* (1903; reprint, Wilmington, NC: Broadfoot Publishing Company, 1989), p. 23.

36. Clark, *NC Regiments*, vol. 2, p. 33.

37. Ibid.

38. Walker, "Sharpsburg," p. 681.

39. Clark, *NC Regiments*, vol. 2, p. 437.

40. O.R., ser. 1, vol. 19, pt. 1, p. 887.

41. Quoted in Richard Wheeler, *Voices of the Civil War* (New York: Thomas Y. Crowell Company, 1976), p. 194.

42. Strother, "Personal Recollections of the War," pp. 284–85, p. 287.

43. Cox, "The Battle of Antietam," p. 658.
44. McClellan, *Civil War Papers*, p. 469.
45. O. R., ser. 1, vol. 19, pt. 1, p. 68.
46. McClellan, *Civil War Papers*, p. 473.

The Night the General Was Fired

1. Hay, *Lincoln and the Civil War*, p. 67.
2. Strother, "Personal Recollections of the War," p. 289.
3. McClellan, *Civil War Papers*, p. 481, p. 426.
4. O.R., ser. 1, vol. 19, pt. 1, pp. 70–71.
5. McClellan, *Civil War Papers*, p. 488.
6. Nicolay and Hay, *Abraham Lincoln*, vol. 6, p. 175.
7. Hay, *Lincoln and the Civil War*, p. 218.
8. O.R., ser. 1, vol. 19, pt. 1, p. 10.
9. Lincoln, *Collected Works*, vol. 5, p. 474.
10. McClellan, *Civil War Papers*, p. 511.
11. O.R., ser. 1, vol. 19, pt. 1, pp. 13–14.
12. Darius N. Couch, "Sumner's 'Right Grand Division,' " *Battles and Leaders*, vol. 3, pp. 105–6.
13. McClellan, *Civil War Papers*, p. 515.
14. Ibid., p. 516.
15. Hay, *Lincoln and the Civil War*, p. 219.
16. McClellan, *Civil War Papers*, p. 518.
17. George Ticknor Curtis, *McClellan's Last Service to the Republic, Together with a Tribute to His Memory* (New York: D. Appleton and Company, 1886), p. 96.
18. William Ernest Smith, *The Francis Preston Blair Family in Politics*, 2 vols. (New York: Macmillan, 1933), vol. 2, p. 144.
19. Boatner, Mark Mayo III, *The Civil War Dictionary* (New York: David McKay Company, 1959), p. 95; Ezra J. Warner, *Generals in Blue: Lives of the Union Commanders* (Baton Rouge: Louisiana State University Press, 1964), pp. 49–50.
20. The account that follows of the firing of George McClellan, unless otherwise cited, is from a letter by Buckingham to the *Chicago Tribune*, 4 September 1875, in Paris, *History of the Civil War in America*, pp. 555–57n.
21. Burnside is described in Francis A. Walker, *History of the Second Army Corps in the Army of the Potomac* (New York: Charles Scribner's Sons, 1886), p. 137. While he was well-liked, simply nobody thought Burnside commander-of-the-army material. Parmenas Taylor Turnley, an acid-tongued member of the class of 1846, wrote: "All there ever was of him [was], to-wit, *his whiskers!*" (Turnley, *Reminiscences*, p. 409.)
22. McClellan's thoughts, actions, and reactions are from *McClellan's Own Story*, pp. 651–52; and *Civil War Papers*, p. 520.
23. U.S. Congress, *Report of the Joint Committee on the Conduct of the War*, Rep. Com. 108, 3 vols. 37th Cong., 3d sess., 1863, vol. 1, p. 650.
24. McClellan, *Civil War Papers*, p. 520.
25. Couch, "Sumner's 'Right Grand Division,' " p. 106.
26. O.R., ser. 1, vol. 19, pt. 2, p. 551.
27. Marsena R. Patrick, *Inside Lincoln's Army: The Diary of Marsena Rudolph Patrick, Provost Marshal General, Army of the Potomac*, ed. David S. Sparks (New York: Thomas Yoseloff, 1964), pp. 173–74.
28. O.R., ser. 1, vol. 19, pt. 2, p. 551; McClellan, *McClellan's Own Story*, p. 652–53.
29. *New York World*, 12 November 1862.
30. Patrick, *Inside Lincoln's Army*, p. 174.
31. Charles S. Wainwright, *A Diary of Battle: The Personal Journals of Colonel Charles S. Wainwright, 1861–1865*, ed. Allan Nevins (New York: Harcourt, Brace & World, 1962), p. 125.
32. McClellan, *Civil War Papers*, p. 522. It should be said that not every soldier in the army

was shattered by McClellan's departure. Some were overjoyed, thinking little of him as a general and believing his firing a good thing. For that point of view see *New York Times*, 12 November 1862; and Henry Morford, *Red-Tape and Pigeon-Hole Generals: As Seen from the Ranks during a Campaign in the Army of the Potomac* (New York: Carleton, 1864), pp. 178–92.

33. Wainwright, *A Diary of Battle*, p. 125; Walker, *History of the Second Army Corps*, p. 138.

34. McClellan, *McClellan's Own Story*, p. 150.

35. Gibbon, *Personal Recollections of the Civil War*, p. 97.

36. Douglas, *I Rode with Stonewall*, p. 202.

37. James Cooper Nisbet, *Four Years on the Firing Line*, ed. Bell Irvin Wiley (1963; reprint, Wilmington, NC: Broadfoot Publishing Company, 1987), p. 116.

38. James Longstreet, "The Battle of Fredericksburg," *Battles and Leaders* vol. 3, p. 70.

39. A. K. McClure, *Abraham Lincoln and Men of War Times: Some Personal Recollections of War and Politics during the Lincoln Administration*, 3d ed. (Philadelphia: Times Publishing Company, 1892), pp. 192–93.

Caught in the Rain

1. Samuel L. Gracey, *Annals of the Sixth Pennsylvania Cavalry* (Philadelphia: E. H. Butler & Co., 1868), pp. 133–34; O.R., ser. 1, vol. 25, pt. 1, p. 1088.

2. O.R., ser. 1, vol. 25, pt. 1, p. 1088, p. 1090.

3. Willard Glazier, *Three years in the Federal Cavalry* (New York: R. H. Ferguson & Co., 1972), pp. 171–72.

4. O.R., ser. 1, vol. 25, pt. 2, pp. 220–21.

5. Couch, "George Stoneman," p. 27.

6. O.R., ser. 1, vol. 25, pt. 2, p. 51, p. 59, p. 111.

7. Worthington Chauncey Ford, ed., *A Cycle of Adams Letters, 1861–1865*, 2 vols. (Boston: Houghton Mifflin, 1920), vol. 2, p. 8.

8. George Alfred Townsend, *Rustics in Rebellion: A Yankee Reporter on the Road to Richmond, 1861–1865* (Chapel Hill: University of North Carolina Press, 1950), p. 77.

9. Couch, "George Stoneman," p. 33.

10. Alexander K. McClure, *Colonel Alexander K. McClure's Recollections of Half a Century* (Salem, MA: Salem Press Company, 1902), p. 347. Hooker outlined his plan of campaign for Lincoln on April 11th. It is in O.R., ser. 1, vol. 25, pt. 2, p. 199.

11. O.R., ser. 1, vol. 25, pt. 1, p. 1066.

12. Glazier, *Three Years in the Federal Cavalry*, p. 166.

13. O.R., ser. 1, vol. 25, pt. 2, pp. 204–5.

14. O.R., ser. 1, vol. 25, pt. 1, pp. 1067–68.

15. O.R., ser. 1, vol. 25, pt. 2, p. 213.

16. Bliss Perry, *Life and Letters of Henry Lee Higginson* (1921; reprint, Freeport, NY: Books for Libraries Press, 1972), pp. 184–86.

17. Wainwright, *A Diary of Battle*, p. 182.

18. O.R., ser. 1, vol. 25, pt. 2, p. 213.

19. Ibid., p. 214.

20. Ibid., p. 220.

21. Wainwright, *A Diary of Battle*, pp. 180–81.

22. O.R., ser. 1, vol. 25, pt. 2, pp. 243–44.

23. Gracey, *Annals of the Sixth Pennsylvania Cavalry*, pp. 134–35.

24. Ford, *A Cycle of Adams Letters*, vol. 1, p. 286.

25. Wainwright, *A Diary of Battle*, pp. 184–85.

26. O.R., ser. 1, vol. 25, pt. 1, p. 1060.

27. Frederick W. Mitchell, "A Personal Episode of the First Stoneman Raid," *War Papers* No. 85, Military Order of the Loyal Legion of the United States, Commandery of the District of Columbia (6 December 1911), p. 3.

28. The logistical arrangements are described in O. R., ser. 1, vol. 25, pt. 1, p. 1058, pp. 1068–69.

29. Ibid., p. 1083.

30. Perry, *Life and Letters of Henry Lee Higginson*, p. 187.

31. Ford, *A Cycle of Adams Letters*, vol. 1, pp. 287–88.

32. O.R., ser. 1, vol. 25, pt. 1, p. 1072.

33. Edward P. Tobie, *History of the First Maine Cavalry, 1861–1865*, published by the First Maine Cavalry Association (Boston: Press of Emery & Hughes, 1887), p. 138, pp. 143–44.

34. Paul, E. A., "Account by a Participant," *New York Times*, in Moore, *Rebellion Record*, vol. 6, doc., p. 606.

35. O.R., ser. 1, vol. 25, pt. 1, p. 1096.

36. Ford, *A Cycle of Adams Letters*, vol. 2, p. 4.

37. O.R., ser. 1, vol. 25, pt. 1, p. 1097.

38. Ford, *A Cycle of Adams Letters*, vol. 2, p. 5.

39. Jones, *A Rebel War Clerk's Diary*, p. 200.

40. Ford, *A Cycle of Adams Letters*, vol. 1, p. 295, vol. 2, p. 3.

41. O.R., ser. 1, vol. 25, pt. 2, p. 438.

42. Paul, "Account by a Participant," p. 609.

43. O.R., ser. 1, vol. 25, pt. 2, p. 463.

44. Frederick Whittaker, *A Complete Life of Gen. George A. Custer* (New York: Sheldon & Company, 1876), pp. 144–45.

45. Frederick C. Newhall, *With General Sheridan in Lee's Last Campaign* (Philadelphia: J. B. Lippincott, 1866), p. 43.

46. John Algernon Owens, *Sword and Pen; or, Ventures and Adventures of Willard Glazier* (Philadelphia: P. W. Ziegler & Company, 1881), p. 144.

47. O.R., ser. 1, vol. 25, pt. 2, p. 543.

48. Owens, *Sword and Pen*, p. 146.

49. Palfrey, *The Antietam and Fredericksburg*, p. 55.

50. Hay, *Lincoln and the Civil War*, pp. 84–85.

51. Henry R. Pyne, *The History of the First New Jersey Cavalry* (Trenton, NJ: J. A. Beecher, 1871), pp. 146–47.

52. Tobie, *History of the First Maine Cavalry*, pp. 143–44.

53. James Rodney Wood, "Miscellaneous Writings: Civil War Memoirs," typescript, Maud Wood Park Papers, Manuscript Division, Library of Congress, container 4.

Shots in the Night

1. Douglas, *I Rode with Stonewall*, pp. 217–18.

2. Ibid., p. 218.

3. The description of the prebattle maneuvering and planning is borrowed mainly from Dabney, *Life and Campaigns of Lieut.-Gen. Thomas J. Jackson*, pp. 661–75.

4. James Power Smith, "Stonewall Jackson's Last Battle," *Battles and Leaders*, vol. 3, p. 205; Hotchkiss, *Make Me a Map of the Valley*, p. 137.

5. Alexander, *Military Memoirs of a Confederate*, p. 329.

6. John O. Casler, *Four Years in the Stonewall Brigade* (1906; reprint, Dayton: Press of Morningside Bookshop, 1982), p. 142.

7. Detail on the first phase of the march is from Dabney, *Life and Campaigns of Lieut.-Gen. Thomas J. Jackson*, p. 677.

8. See a facsimile of this henscratched note in Smith, "Stonewall Jackson's Last Battle," p. 206.

9. Murray F. Taylor, "Stonewall Jackson's Death," *Confederate Veteran* 12 (October 1904), p. 492.

10. Smith, "Stonewall Jackson's Last Battle," p. 208.

11. Benjamin Watkins Leigh to his wife, 13 May 1863, typescript, Hotchkiss Papers, Manuscript Division, Library of Congress, cont. 39, reel 39. A shorter, edited version of Leigh's account, titled "The Wounding of Stonewall Jackson—Extracts from a Letter of Major Benjamin

Watkins Leigh," is in *SHSP* 6 (1878), pp. 230–34. This quote is on page 231 of that work. I will cite the more accessible *SHSP* version hereafter whenever possible.

12. Casler, *Four Years in the Stonewall Brigade*, p. 143.

13. William F. Randolph, "Chancellorsville: The Flank Movement that Routed the Yankees; General Jackson's Mortal Wound," *SHSP* 29 (1901), P. 332.

14. O.R., ser. 1, vol. 25, pt. 1, p. 787.

15. James F. Huntington, "The Battle of Chancellorsville," *MHSM*, vol. 3, *Campaigns in Virginia, Maryland and Pennsylvania, 1862–1863* (1903; reprint, Wilmington, NC: Broadfoot Publishing Company, 1989), pp. 171–73.

16. Charles I. Wickersham, "Personal Recollections of the Cavalry at Chancellorsville," *War Papers Read before the Commandery of the State of Wisconsin, Military Order of the Loyal Legion of the United States*, vol. 3. (Milwaukee: Burdick & Allen, 1903), p. 460.

17. Theodore A. Dodge, "The Romances of Chancellorsville," *MHSM*, vol. 3, *Campaigns in Virginia, Maryland and Pennsylvania, 1862–1863*, p. 212.

18. Dabney, *Life and Campaigns of Lieut.-Gen. Thomas J. Jackson*, p. 682.

19. Ibid., p. 683.

20. Casler, *Four Years in the Stonewall Brigade*, p. 145.

21. Robert E. Wilbourn to Jubal A. Early, 19 February 1873, in Jubal A. Early, "Stonewall Jackson—the Story of His Being an Astrologer Refuted—An Eyewitness Describes How He Was Wounded," *SHSP* 6 (1878), p. 266.

22. I. C. Haas, "Stonewall Jackson's Death," *SHSP* 32 (1904), pp. 94–95; Bean, *Stonewall's Man: Sandie Pendleton*, p. 115.

23. The scene-setting is from Dabney, *Life and Campaigns of Lieut.-Gen. Thomas J. Jackson*, pp. 685–86.

24. The account of Jackson's wounding and what immediately transpired is largely from Wilbourn, who was at his side. It is in Early, "Stonewall Jackson—the Story of His Being an Astrologer Refuted," pp. 266–69, p. 271. Other sources are cited as they are used.

25. Hunter McGuire describes Jackson's wounds in some detail in "Death of Stonewall Jackson," *SHSP* 14 (1886), p. 157. This article, originally published in the *Richmond Medical Journal* in May 1866, has been reprinted many times and in many other places under the title, "Account of the Wounding and Death of Stonewall Jackson." When citing it in this story and the next, I will use *SHSP*, perhaps the most readily accessible of the reprinted versions.

26. Joseph Graham Morrison, "Stonewall Jackson at Chancellorsville," *Confederate Veteran* 13 (May 1905), pp. 230–31.

27. Although this mystery rider was never seen again, he has caused great controversy ever since. Joseph W. Revere, a Union officer, claimed it was he. Revere's story is fantastic. He wrote that he met Jackson on a Mississippi River boat trip in 1852 and that after consulting the stars, something nobody had ever known him to do, Jackson predicted that in the first days of May 1863 his life would be in mortal danger. The stars, presumably, had not lied. They had also put Revere in the thicket at the very moment Jackson fell, to witness the culmination of this startling prediction. After the war Jubal Early went to great pains to prove that the entire astrological story was claptrap. He produced letters from those who should know, that Jackson had not been anywhere near the Mississippi River in 1852. Early also refuted the whole idea that the mystery rider could have been Revere. For Revere's account see his book, *Keel and Saddle: A Retrospect of Forty Years of Military and Naval Service* (Boston; J. R. Osgood, 1872), pp. 254–57; pp. 275–78. For Early's refutation see "Stonewall Jackson—The Story of His Being an Astrologer Refuted," pp. 261–82.

28. The Hill-Jackson-Lee correspondence is in O.R., ser. 1, vol. 19, pt. 2, pp. 729–33. Hill's letter to Stuart is in William W. Hassler, "A. P. Hill Rings Down the Curtain on Act III, Scene 3, at Antietam," *Virginia Country* 10 (Summer 1987), p. 99.

29. Leigh, "The Wounding of Stonewall Jackson," p. 232. For the series of events that follows, to the moment Dr. McGuire finds Jackson at the Chancellor house, I have drawn primarily from the first-person accounts of the four staff officers attending him: Leigh's letter to his wife and the *SHSP* version cited above, pp. 232–34; Wilbourn to Early, in "Stonewall Jackson—The Story of His Being an Astrologer Refuted," pp. 269–73; Smith, "Stonewall

Jackson's Last Battle," pp. 209–13; and Morrison, "Stonewall Jackson at Chancellorsville," pp. 229–32. All bits of dialogue will be specifically attributed, and the use of any other sources than these four will be appropriately cited.

30. Taylor, "Stonewall Jackson's Death," p. 493.

31. Leigh to his wife, 12 May 1863, Hotchkiss Papers.

32. Wilbourn to Early, "Stonewall Jackson—the Story of His Being an Astrologer Refuted," p. 269.

33. Morrison, "Stonewall Jackson at Chancellorsville," p. 230; Wilbourn to Early, "Stonewall Jackson—the Story of His Being an Astrologer Refuted," p. 270.

34. Smith, "Stonewall Jackson's Last Battle," pp. 209–10.

35. Bean, *Stonewall's Man: Sandie Pendleton*, p. 116.

36. Wilbourn to Early, "Stonewall Jackson—The Story of His Being an Astrologer Refuted, p. 270.

37. Douglas, *I Rode with Stonewall*, p. 219, p. 223, pp. 225–26.

38. Taylor, "Stonewall Jackson's Death," p. 493.

39. Leigh to his wife, 12 May 1863, Hotchkiss Papers.

40. Dabney, *Life and Campaigns of Lieut.-Gen. Thomas J. Jackson*, pp. 689–90.

41. Wilbourn to Early, "Stonewall Jackson—the Story of His Being an Astrologer Refuted," p. 270.

42. The Pender incident is an amalgam from Smith, "Stonewall Jackson's Last Battle," p. 212; and McGuire, "Death of Stonewall Jackson," p. 155.

43. Smith, "Stonewall Jackson's Last Battle," p. 212; Dabney, *Life and Campaigns of Lieut.-Gen. Thomas J. Jackson*, p. 691; McGuire, "Death of Stonewall Jackson," p. 155. The details and timing of many of the events of that night differ from account to account. It often becomes a matter of reconciling them or picking the most logical sequence.

44. Leigh, "The Wounding of Stonewall Jackson," p. 234.

45. Douglas, *I Rode with Stonewall*, pp. 223–24.

Death of the Enthusiastic Fanatic

1. Hunter McGuire, "General Thomas J. Jackson," *SHSP* 19 (1891), p. 301.

2. Wilbourn to Early, "Stonewall Jackson—the Story of His Being an Astrologer Refuted," pp. 272–73.

3. McGuire's initial measures to treat Jackson's wounds, the trip to the field infirmary, and the amputation of his arm are from McGuire, "Death of Stonewall Jackson," pp. 155–57; with complementing material from Leigh to his wife, 12 May 1863, Hotchkiss Papers; and Dabney, *Life and Campaigns of Lieut.-Gen. Thomas J. Jackson*, p. 695.

4. For a profile of Crutchfield see Charles D. Walker, *Memorial, Virginia Military Institute: Biographical Sketches of the Graduates and Eleves of the Virginia Military Institute Who Fell during the War Between the States* (Philadelphia: J. B. Lippincott, 1875), pp. 143–59.

5. Morrison, "Stonewall Jackson at Chancellorsville," p. 232.

6. McGuire, "Death of Stonewall Jackson," pp. 157–58.

7. Wilbourn's account of his interview with Lee is in Early, "Stonewall Jackson—the Story of His Being an Astrologer Refuted," p. 273. Also see Dabney, *Life and Campaigns of Lieut.-Gen. Thomas J. Jackson*, pp. 701–2.

8. Hill to his parents, 23 October 1847, Hill Family Papers.

9. Jackson's theological musings to Lacy are from Dabney, *Life and Campaigns of Lieut.-Gen. Thomas J. Jackson*, pp. 707–8.

10. The events of Jackson's post-operational Sunday are from McGuire, "Death of Stonewall Jackson," pp. 158–59; and Dabney, *Life and Campaigns of Lieut.-Gen. Thomas J. Jackson*, pp. 708–10. The text of Lee's message is in Dabney, p. 702.

11. The description of the trip and the conversation to this point are from McGuire, "Death of Stonewall Jackson," pp. 159–60.

12. Dabney, *Life and Campaigns of Lieut.-Gen. Thomas J. Jackson*, p. 713.

13. The description of the Chandlers, the frame house, and Jackson's arrival at Guiney's Station owes much to Ralph Happel's excellent pamphlet, *Jackson: Let Us Cross Over the River . . .*

(Richmond: Eastern National Park and Monument, in cooperation with Fredericksburg and Spotsylvania National Military Park Association, 1971), pp. 33–37. For added first-hand detail see " 'Stonewall' Jackson: Reminiscences of the Great Confederate Soldier as Related by Mrs. Lucy Chandler Pendleton to Edward T. Stuart at the Jackson Shrine at Guiney Station, Virginia, 'Memorial Day' May 30, 1930," typescript copy, Fredericksburg and Spotsylvania National Military Park.

14. McGuire, "Death of Stonewall Jackson," p. 160. McGuire appeared to have his days confused. He placed the trip to Guiney's Station on Tuesday and the sequence of events in the graph cited above on Wednesday. They occurred on Monday and Tuesday respectively.

15. Dabney, *Life and Campaigns of Lieut.-Gen. Thomas J. Jackson*, p. 716.

16. Happel, *Jackson*, pp. 39–40; McGuire, "Death of Stonewall Jackson," p. 160.

17. McGuire, "Death of Stonewall Jackson," pp. 160–61; Dabney, *Life and Campaigns of Lieut.-Gen. Thomas J. Jackson*, p. 716.

18. Morrison, "Stonewall Jackson at Chancellorsville," p. 232.

19. Anna's thoughts and her experiences getting to Jackson's bedside are from *Memoirs of Stonewall Jackson*, pp. 447–52. The background on Paxton is from the preface and introduction to Elisha Franklin Paxton, *The Civil War Letters of General Frank "Bull" Paxton, CSA, a Lieutenant of Lee & Jackson*, ed. John Gallatin Paxton (Hillsboro, TX: Hill Junior College Press, 1978), pp. vi–viii.

20. Thursday afternoon, Friday, and Saturday in the sickroom are re-created from McGuire, "Death of Stonewall Jackson," p. 161; Dabney, *Life and Campaigns of Lieut.-Gen. Thomas J. Jackson*, pp. 717–22; and Jackson, *Memoirs of Stonewall Jackson*, pp. 452–53. For the text of the psalm Anna sang, see Happel, *Jackson*, p. 42.

21. In the account that follows of Jackson's last day on earth, I have mainly used Anna Jackson's *Memoirs of Stonewall Jackson*, pp. 453–59. But there is considerable mortar added from McGuire, "Death of Stonewall Jackson," pp. 161–63; and Dabney, *Life and Campaigns of Lieut.-Gen. Thomas J. Jackson*, pp. 722–25. Anna and McGuire were present in the room, and Dabney was presumably well-informed. All of them differ in detail. Where something is added from elsewhere, it is specifically cited.

22. Douglas, *I Rode with Stonewall*, p. 227.

23. Bean, *Stonewall's Man: Sandie Pendleton*, p. 118.

24. Happel, *Jackson*, p. 44.

25. Bean, *Stonewall's Man: Sandie Pendleton*, p. 118.

26. Taylor, *Destruction and Reconstruction*, p. 91.

27. Sallie A. Putnam, *Richmond during the War: Four years of Personal Observation* (New York: G. W. Carleton, 1867), p. 218.

28. Putnam, *Richmond during the War*, p. 219.

29. Douglas, *I Rode with Stonewall*, p. 228.

30. O. R., ser. 1, vol. 25, pt. 2, p. 793.

31. Cooke, *Stonewall Jackson*, pp. 445–46.

32. McDonald, *A Diary with Reminiscences of the War*, pp. 161–63.

33. Casler, *Four Years in the Stonewall Brigade*, p. 153.

34. Douglas, *I Rode with Stonewall*, p. 220.

35. Ibid., p. 228.

36. Ibid., p. 229.

37. The account of the arrival of Jackson's body in Richmond draws from the *Richmond Daily Sentinel*, 12 May 1863; Dabney, *Life and Campaigns of Lieut.-Gen. Thomas J. Jackson*, p. 729; Jackson, *Memoirs of Stonewall Jackson*, p. 459; Cooke, *Stonewall Jackson*, p. 446; and Bean, *Stonewall's Man: Sandie Pendleton*, pp. 120–21.

38. Bean, *Stonewall's Man: Sandie Pendleton*, pp. 119–20; Cooke, *Stonewall Jackson*, p. 447; Varina H. Davis, *Jefferson Davis, Ex-President of the Confederate States of America: A Memoir by His Wife*, 2 vols. (New York: Belford Company, 1890), vol. 2, pp. 382–83.

39. Douglas, *I Rode with Stonewall*, p. 38.

40. Hamlin, *"Old Bald Head,"* p. 135. Hamlin, *The Making of a Soldier*, p. 108.

41. Putnam, *Richmond during the War*, p. 223; *Richmond Daily Sentinel*, 13 May 1863; Cooke, *Stonewall Jackson*, p. 447.

42. Cooke, *Stonewall Jackson*, p. 447; Marietta Minnigerode Andrews, *Scraps of Paper* (New York: E. P. Dutton., 1929), p. 109.

43. *Richmond Daily Sentinel*, 13 May 1863; Putnam, *In Richmond during the Confederacy*, p. 223; Jones, *A Rebel War Clerk's Diary*, p. 207; Thomas Cooper DeLeon, *Four Years in Rebel Capitals: An Inside View of Life in the Southern Confederacy from Birth to Death* (Mobile, AL: Gossip Printing Company, 1890), pp. 251–52.

44. From an article by Bowering in the *Baltimore Sun*, resurrected by Bean in *Stonewall's Man: Sandie Pendleton*, p. 122.

45. Description from the *Richmond Daily Sentinel*, 13 May 1863; Dabney, *Life and Campaigns of Lieut.-Gen. Thomas J. Jackson*, p. 730; Cooke, *Stonewall Jackson*, p. 448; and Chesnut, *Mary Chesnut's Civil War*, p. 498.

46. Dabney, *Life and Campaigns of Lieut.-Gen. Thomas J. Jackson*, pp. 730–31.

47. Putnam, *Richmond during the War*, p. 224.

48. Dabney, *Life and Campaigns of Lieut.-Gen. Thomas J. Jackson*, p. 731; "Stonewall Jackson's Body Passes through Charlottesville," *The Magazine of Albemarle County History* 22 (1963–1964), p. 22; Bean, *Stonewall's Man: Sandie Pendleton*, p. 124.

49. Douglas, *I Rode with Stonewall*, p. 217.

50. John S. Wise, *The End of an Era* (Boston: Houghton, Mifflin, 1899), p. 270; Wise, "Stonewall Jackson as I knew Him," p. 145; Cooke, *Stonewall Jackson*, p. 449.

51. Jackson, *Memoirs of Stonewall Jackson*, pp. 463–64.

52. Preston, "Personal Reminiscences of Stonewall Jackson," p. 932.

53. Casler, *Four Years in the Stonewall Brigade*, p. 161.

54. Cooke, *Stonewall Jackson and the Old Stonewall Brigade*, p. 3.

55. Gardner, "Memoirs," pp. 8–9.

56. Morrison, "Getting through West Point," p. 316.

The Dandy at the Foot of the Class

1. B. L. Farinholt, "Battle of Gettysburg—Johnson's Island," *Confederate Veteran* 5 (September 1897), p. 468.

2. James Longstreet, "Lee in Pennsylvania," in *The Annals of the War Written by Leading Participants North and South*, p. 429.

3. Walter Harrison, *Pickett's Men: A Fragment of War History* (1870; reprint, Gaithersburg, MD: Butternut Press, 1984), pp. 91–93.

4. James Longstreet, "Lee's Right Wing at Gettysburg," in *Battles and Leaders*, vol. 3, p. 343; Longstreet, "Lee in Pennsylvania," p. 430.

5. Sorrel, *Recollections of a Confederate Staff Officer*, p. 54.

6. Longstreet, "Lee's Right Wing at Gettysburg," p. 343; Edward Porter Alexander, "The Great Charge and Artillery Fighting at Gettysburg," *Battles and Leaders*, vol. 3, p. 363.

7. *A Soldier of the Civil War*, by a member of the Virginia Historical Society (Cleveland: Burrows Brothers Company, 1900), p. 33.

8. Sorrel, *Recollections of a Confederate Staff Officer*, p. 54.

9. Francis W. Dawson, *Reminiscences of Confederate Service, 1861–1865*, ed. Bell Irvin Wiley (Baton Rouge: Louisiana State University Press, 1980), p. 91.

10. Arthur James Lyon Freemantle, *Three Months in the Southern States: April–June, 1863* (1864; reprint, Lincoln: University of Nebraska Press, 1991), p. 247.

11. Sorrel, *Recollections of a Confederate Staff Officer*, pp. 155–56.

12. Wise, *The End of an Era*, p. 69, p. 338. Also see Jesse Bowman Young, *The Battle of Gettysburg: A Comprehensive Narrative* (1913; reprint, Dayton: Press of Morningside Bookshop, 1976), p. 315.

13. Quoted in Foote, *The Civil War*, vol. 3, p. 9.

14. LaSalle Corbell Pickett, *Pickett and His Men* (Atlanta: Foote & Davis Company, 1899), pp. 97–98; LaSalle Corbell Pickett, ed., *The Heart of a Soldier as Revealed in the Intimate Letters of Genl. George E. Pickett, C. S. A.* (New York: Seth Moyle, 1913), pp. 4–5. It is not considered safe to believe Pickett's wife, who wrote or edited the two works here cited. After Pickett's

death in 1875, LaSalle wrote extensively about her husband, his career, and their love. She wrote eloquently, and apparently with great poetic license. Her collection of lyric letters from her soldier is particularly suspect. Did Pickett write the letters, or did she? Most Civil War scholars believe she did, and are therefore loath to use them, as wonderful as they are. And so am I. It is a pity, for few letters from the Civil War are more quotable. If he didn't write such eloquent letters, he should have. See Gary W. Gallagher, "A Widow and Her Soldier: LaSalle Corbell Pickett as Author of the George E. Pickett Letters," *The Virginia Magazine of History and Biography* 94 (July 1986), pp. 329–44.

15. Pickett, *Pickett and His Men*, p. 126, p. 128.

16. Levin Christopher Gayle, Diary, typescript portion, Gettysburg National Park Library. Also see Charles T. Loehr, *War History of the Old First Virginia Regiment, Army of Northern Virginia* (Richmond: Wm. Ellis Jones, 1884), p. 35. For an account of the division's diluted strength and activity around Chambersburg see Harrison, *Pickett's Men*, pp. 78–79; pp. 86–87.

17. Gayle, Diary, typescript portion.

18. Randolph A. Shotwell, "Virginia and North Carolina in the Battle of Gettysburg," *Our Living and Dead* 4 (March 1876), p. 87.

19. Harrison, *Pickett's Men*, pp. 87–88.

20. Shotwell, "Virginia and North Carolina in the Battle of Gettysburg," p. 87; David E. Johnston, *The Story of a Confederate Boy in the Civil War* (Portland, OR: Glass & Prudhomme Company, 1914), p. 198.

21. Alexander, *Fighting for the Confederacy*, p. 244.

22. Shotwell, "Virginia and North Carolina in the Battle of Gettysburg," p. 87.

23. Sketch on Dearing in the John W. Daniel Papers, University of Virginia Library, copy in the Gettysburg National Park Library. Also see O.R., ser. 1, vol. 27, pt. 2, p. 388.

24. S. A. Ashe, *The Charge at Gettysburg*, North Carolina Booklet, vol. 1, no. 11 (Raleigh, NC: Capital Printing Company, 1902), p. 5; Henry J. Hunt, "The Third Day at Gettysburg," *Battles and Leaders*, vol. 3, p. 372.

25. Longstreet, *From Manassas to Appomattox*, p. 390.

26. Joseph Mayo, Jr., "Pickett's Charge at Gettysburg," *SHSP* 34 (1906), p. 328.

27. John Dooley, *John Dooley, Confederate Soldier: His War Journal*, ed. Joseph T. Durkin (South Bend, IN: University of Notre Dame Press, 1963), p. 102.

28. Account by Erasmus Williams, Daniel Papers.

29. Longstreet describes his preferred strategy in "Lee in Pennsylvania," p. 414, p. 429.

30. Longstreet, "Lee's Right Wing at Gettysburg," p. 343.

31. Alexander, "The Great Charge and Artillery Fighting at Gettysburg," p. 362.

32. The descriptions of the silence and its affect are from H. T. Owen, in Jacob Hoke, *The Great Invasion of 1863; or General Lee in Pennsylvania* (Dayton: W. J. Shuey, 1887), p. 367; M. Jacobs, *Notes on the Invasion of Maryland and Pennsylvania and the Battle of Gettysburg. . . .* (Philadelphia: J. B. Lippincott, 1863), pp. 40–41; Richard S. Thompson, "A Scrap of Gettysburg," in *Military Essays and Recollections: Papers Read before the Commandery of the State of Illinois, Military Order of the Loyal Legion of the United States*, vol. 3 (Chicago: Dial Press, 1899), p. 101; William Witherspoon, in *As They Saw Forrest: Some Recollections and Comments of Contemporaries*, ed. Robert Selph Henry (1956; reprint, Wilmington, NC: Broadfoot Publishing Company, 1987), p. 115; and Harrison, *Pickett's Men*, pp. 94–95.

33. John Day Smith describes Gibbon in *The History of the Nineteenth Regiment of Maine Volunteer Infantry, 1862–1865* (Minneapolis: Nineteenth Maine Regimental Association, 1909), pp. 77–78.

34. Theodore Lyman, *Meade's Headquarters, 1863–65: Letters of Colonel Theodore Lyman from the Wilderness to Appomattox*, ed. George R. Agassiz (Boston: Atlantic Monthly Press, 1922), p. 107.

35. Frank A. Haskell, *The Battle of Gettysburg*, ed. Bruce Catton (Boston: Houghton Mifflin, 1958), pp. 78–81.

36. Birkett Davenport Fry, "Pettigrew's Charge at Gettysburg," *SHSP* 7 (1879), p. 92.

37. June Kimble, "Tennesseeans at Gettysburg—the Retreat," *Confederate Veteran* 18 (October 1910), p. 460.

38. Alexander, "The Great Charge and Artillery Fighting at Gettysburg," p. 362n.

39. Gibbon, *Personal Recollections of the Civil War*, pp. 146–47.

40. Haskell, *The Battle of Gettysburg*, pp. 82–83.

41. Harrison, *Pickett's Men*, pp. 95–96.

42. Shotwell, "Virginia and North Carolina in the Battle of Gettysburg," p. 88; Thompson, "A Scrap of Gettysburg," p. 101.

43. Whitelaw Reid, *A Radical View: The "Agate" Dispatches of Whitelaw Reid, 1861–1865*, ed. James G. Smart, 2 vols. (Memphis: Memphis State University Press, 1976), vol. 2, p. 57.

44. John West Haley, *The Rebel Yell & the Yankee Hurrah: The Civil War Journal of a Maine Volunteer*, ed. Ruth L. Silliker (Camden, ME: Down East Books, 1985), p. 103.

45. Ashe, *The Charge at Gettysburg*, p. 7; Robert Goldthwaite Carter, *Four Brothers in Blue, or Sunshine and Shadows of the War of the Rebellion: A Story of the Great Civil War from Bull Run to Appomattox* (Austin: University of Texas Press, 1978), p. 317; Winfield Scott, "Pickett's Charge as Seen from the Front Line," *War Papers*, no. 1, California Commandery, Military Order of the Loyal Legion of the United States (8 February 1888), p. 8; Shotwell, "Virginia and North Carolina in the Battle of Gettysburg," p. 89; Longstreet, "Lee's Right Wing at Gettysburg," p. 343.

46. Hunt, "The Third Day at Gettysburg," p. 372; Johnston, *The Story of a Confederate Boy*, pp. 205–6; H. T. Owen in Hoke, *The Great Invasion*, p. 368.

47. Clark, *North Carolina Regiments*, vol. 2, p. 363.

48. Account of Erasmus Williams, Daniel Papers.

49. Augustus D. Dickert, *History of Kershaw's Brigade, with Complete Roll of Companies, Biographical Sketches, Incidents, Anecdotes, etc.* (Newberry, SC: Elbert H. Aull, 1899), pp. 200–1.

50. Robert Tyler Jones, "Gen. L. A. Armistead and R. Tyler Jones," *Confederate Veteran* 2 (September 1894), p. 271.

51. B. L. Farinholt to John W. Daniel, 15 April 1905, Daniel Papers.

52. Alexander, *Fighting for the Confederacy*, p. 547.

53. Gibbon describes his walk through the tempest in *Personal Recollections of the Civil War*, pp. 147–49.

54. Alexander, "The Great Charge and Artillery Fighting at Gettysburg," p. 362.

55. Alexander, *Fighting for the Confederacy*, p. 255.

56. Alexander, "The Great Charge and Artillery Fighting at Gettysburg," p. 363.

57. Ibid., p. 364.

58. Ibid.

59. The moment is described by Longstreet, in "Lee's Right Wing at Gettysburg," pp. 344–45; *From Manassas to Appomattox*, p. 392; and in his introduction to Pickett, *Pickett and His Men*, p. xi.

60. L. A. Smith, "Recollections of Gettysburg," *War Papers Read before the Michigan Commandery of the Military Order of the Loyal Legion of the United States* (Detroit: James H. Stone, 1898), vol. 2, p. 304.

61. Johnston, *The Story of a Confederate Boy*, p. 207.

62. William H. Morgan, *Personal Reminiscences of the War of 1861–5* (Lynchburg, VA: J. P. Bell Company, 1911), p. 166.

63. The order of march is nicely laid out in Douglas Southall Freeman, *R. E. Lee: A Biography*, 4 vols. (New York: Charles Scribner's Sons, 1962), vol. 3, p. 112. Also see Harrison, *Pickett's Men*, 90–91; Hoke, *The Great Invasion*, p. 393; and B. L. Farinholt to John W. Daniel, 15 April 1905, Daniel Papers.

64. Harrison, *Pickett's Men*, pp. 33–34.

65. Rawley W. Martin, "Armistead at the Battle of Gettysburg," *SHSP* 39 (1914), p. 186. Also see Rawley W. Martin and John Holmes Smith, "The Battle of Gettysburg, and the Charge of Pickett's Division," *SHSP* 32 (1904), p. 188.

66. Harrison, *Pickett's Men*, pp. 20–21.

67. Shotwell, "Virginia and North Carolina in the Battle of Gettysburg," p. 90.

68. Gerard A. Patterson, "George E. Pickett—A Personality Profile," *Civil War Times Illustrated* 5 (May 1966), p. 22.

69. Hoke, *The Great Invasion*, p. 385.

70. Clark, *North Carolina Regiments*, vol. 2, p. 365.

71. Jones, "Gen. L. A. Armistead and R. Tyler Jones," p. 271; John H. Lewis, *Recollections from 1860 to 1865* (Washington: Peake & Company, 1895), p. 79.

72. H. T. Owen in Hoke, *The Great Invasion*, p. 385; Shotwell, "Virginia and North Carolina in the Battle of Gettysburg," p. 90.

73. Longstreet, "Lee's Right Wing at Gettysburg," p. 345.

74. Alexander, *Fighting for the Confederacy*, p. 261.

75. Longstreet, "Lee's Right Wing at Gettysburg," p. 345.

76. Alexander, "The Great Charge and Artillery Fighting at Gettysburg," p. 365; Alexander, *Fighting for the Confederacy*, p. 261.

Where Is My Division?

1. Shotwell, "Virginia and North Carolina in the Battle of Gettysburg," p. 91.

2. Thompson, "A Scrap of Gettysburg," p. 102.

3. Smith, "Recollections of Gettysburg," p. 304.

4. Gibbon, *Personal Recollections of the Civil War*, p. 150; O. R., ser. 1, vol. 27, pt. 1, p. 417.

5. Haskell, *The Battle of Gettysburg*, p. 98, p. 101.

6. Scott, "Pickett's Charge as Seen from the Front Line," pp. 10–11.

7. B. L. Farinholt to John W. Daniel, 15 April 1905, Daniel Papers.

8. Lewis, *Recollections from 1860 to 1865*, p. 81.

9. Shotwell, "Virginia and North Carolina in the Battle of Gettysburg," pp. 92–93.

10. W. B. Robertson to his niece Mattie, 28 July 1863, Daniel Papers.

11. Ashe, *The Charge at Gettysburg*, pp. 10–11.

12. O.R., ser. 1, vol. 27, pt. 1, p. 431.

13. Ibid., p. 454.

14. Lewis, *Recollections from 1860 to 1865*, p. 81.

15. Smith, "Recollections of Gettysburg," p. 304; Scott, "Pickett's Charge as Seen from the Front Line," pp. 11–12; O.R., ser. 1, vol. 27, pt. 1, pp. 392–93.

16. Haley, *The Rebel Yell & the Yankee Hurrah*, p. 106.

17. James E. Poindexter, "General Armistead's Portrait Presented," *SHSP* 37 (1909), p. 147.

18. W. B. Robertson to his niece Mattie, 28 July 1863, Daniel Papers.

19. Jones, "Gen. L. A. Armistead and R. Tyler Jones," p. 271.

20. Mayo, "Pickett's Charge at Gettysburg," p. 332.

21. Morgan, *Personal Reminiscences of the War of 1861–5*, p. 167.

22. Longstreet, "Lee's Right Wing at Gettysburg," p. 346; Shotwell, "Virginia and North Carolina in the Battle of Gettysburg," p. 93; Longstreet, "Lee in Pennsylvania," p. 431; Alexander, *Military Memoirs of a Confederate*, p. 431.

23. Freemantle, *Three Months in the Southern States*, pp. 265–66.

24. Ralph Orson Sturtevant, *Pictorial History Thirteenth Regiment Vermont Volunteers, War of 1861–1865* (Burlington, VT: Regimental Association, 1910), p. 19.

25. G. G. Benedict, *Vermont in the Civil War: A History of the Part Taken by the Vermont Soldiers and Sailors in the War for the Union, 1861–5*, 2 vols. (Burlington, VT: Free Press Association, 1886–1888), vol. 2, pp. 468–69, p. 469n.

26. H. T. Owen in the *Philadelphia Weekly Times*, 26 March 1881, quoted in Benedict, *Vermont in the Civil War*, p. 471.

27. Ibid.

28. Dooley, *John Dooley, Confederate Soldier*, p. 106.

29. Charles T. Loehr, "The 'Old First' Virginia at Gettysburg," *SHSP* 32 (1904), p. 35; Clark, *North Carolina Regiments*, vol. 2, p. 366.

30. *Dictionary of American Biography*, s.v. "Kemper, James Lawson."

31. Mayo, "Pickett's Charge at Gettysburg," p. 333.

32. James Kemper to John B. Bachelder, 4 February 1880, John B. Bachelder Papers, Gettysburg National Military Park Library.

33. Fry, "Pettigrew's Charge at Gettysburg," p. 93; O.R., ser. 1, vol. 27, pt. 2, p. 387; Winfield Peters, "The Lost Sword of Gen. Richard B. Garnett, Who Fell at Gettysburg," *SHSP* 33 (1905), p. 29.

34. Fry, "Pettigrew's Charge at Gettysburg," p. 93.

35. Jones, "Gen. L. A. Armistead and R. Tyler Jones," p. 271.

36. John W. H. Porter, "The Confederate Soldier," *Confederate Veteran* 24 (October 1916), p. 460.

37. Gibbon, *Personal Reminiscences of the Civil War*, pp. 152–53.

38. Longstreet, *From Manassas to Appomattox*, p. 394.

39. Poindexter, "General Armistead's Portrait Presented," p. 149.

40. James Kemper to John B. Bachelder, 4 February 1880, Bachelder Papers; Poindexter, "General Armistead's Portrait Presented," p. 149.

41. Jones, "Gen. L. A. Armistead and R. Tyler Jones," p. 271; Farinholt, "Battle of Gettysburg—Johnson's Island," p. 469; "Col. and Dr. R. W. Martin, of Virginia," *Confederate Veteran* 5 (February 1897), p. 70; Mayo, "Pickett's Charge at Gettysburg," pp. 333–34.

42. Edmund Rice, "Repelling Lee's Last Blow at Gettysburg," *Battles and Leaders*, vol. 3, p. 389.

43. B. L. Farinholt to John W. Daniel, 15 April 1905, and Erasmus Williams's account, Daniel Papers.

44. O.R., ser. 1, vol. 27, pt. 1, p. 441, p. 454; Alexander, "The Great Charge and Artillery Fighting at Gettysburg," p. 366.

45. That is how Pickett's inspector general, Walter Harrison, saw it in *Pickett's Men*, p. 98. Without question it is the way Pickett also saw it.

46. Robert A. Bright, "Pickett's Charge," *SHSP* 31 (1903), p. 232.

47. Ibid., pp. 233–35.

48. The Wilcox and Lang accounts are in O.R., ser. 1, vol. 27, pt. 2, p. 620, p. 632; the Vermont point of view is from Benedict, *Vermont in the Civil War*, vol. 2, p. 473; Alexander's comment is in *Military Memoirs of a Confederate*, p. 425.

49. Account by Erasmus Williams, Daniel Papers.

50. George L. Christian to John W. Daniel, 4 January 1898, Daniel Papers.

51. Douglas, *I Rode with Stonewall*, p. 212.

52. O.R., ser. 1, vol. 27, pt. 2, p. 659; Clark, *North Carolina Regiments*, vol. 5, p. 146.

53. O.R., ser. 1, vol. 27, pt. 2, p. 672.

54. Isaac R. Trimble, "North Carolinians at Gettysburg," *Our Living and Our Dead* 4 (March 1876), p. 60.

55. Clark, *North Carolina Regiments*, vol. 5, p. 128.

56. H. T. Owen in Hoke, *The Great Invasion*, p. 390.

57. Dickert, *History of Kershaw's Brigade*, p. 246.

58. Account by Erasmus Williams, Daniel Papers; Kimble, "Tennesseeans at Gettysburg—the Retreat," p. 461; Clark, *North Carolina Regiments*, vol. 2, p. 366.

59. Longstreet, "Lee's Right Wing at Gettysburg," p. 347.

60. Shotwell, "Virginia and North Carolina in the Battle of Gettysburg," pp. 95–96.

61. Longstreet, "Lee's Right Wing at Gettysburg," p. 347.

62. William Thomas Poague, *Gunner with Stonewall: Reminiscences of William Thomas Poague*, ed. Monroe F. Cockrell (1957; reprint, Wilmington, NC: Broadfoot Publishing Company, 1898), pp. 75–76.

63. Dawson, *Reminiscences of Confederate Service*, p. 97.

64. William Nathaniel Wood, *Reminiscences of Big I*, ed. Bell Irvin Wiley (Jackson, TN: McCowat-Mercer Press, 1956), p. 47.

65. Poague, *Gunner with Stonewall*, p. 75.

66. William Youngblood, "Unwritten History of the Gettysburg Campaign," *SHSP* 38 (1910), p. 317; Longstreet, "Lee's Right Wing at Gettysburg," p. 349.

67. Bright, "Pickett's Charge," p. 234. No two accounts agree on Lee's exact words. I have used Bright's version since he was standing beside Pickett when they were spoken. But see, for instance, Loehr, *War History of the Old First Virginia*, p. 38; and Armistead L. Long, *Memoirs of Robert E. Lee* (New York: J. M. Stoddart & Co., 1886), p. 296.

68. Bright, "Pickett's Charge," p. 234; *A Soldier of the Civil War*, p. 42.
69. Bright, "Pickett's Charge," p. 234. Alexander describes this incident with a slightly different dialogue in *Fighting for the Confederacy*, p. 266. Williams's role as one of Kemper's stretcher bearers is mentioned in his account in the Daniel Papers.
70. Gibbon, *Personal Recollections of the Civil War*, p. 166.
71. Thomas D. Houston, "Storming Cemetery Hill," with a letter by John T. James, *Philadelphia Weekly Times*, 21 October 1882.
72. John D. Imboden, "The Confederate Retreat from Gettysburg," *Battles and Leaders*, vol. 3, pp. 420–21.

PART 6   CLOSING OUT THE WAR

The Meeting on the Court House Steps

1. Gordon, *Reminiscences of the Civil War*, p. 430.
2. Frank Potts, *The Death of the Confederacy: The Last Week of the Army of Northern Virginia as Set Forth in a Letter of April, 1865*, ed. Douglas Southall Freeman (Richmond: Private printing, 1928), p. 9.
3. Carlton McCarthy, "Detailed Minutiae of Soldier Life," Paper No. 5, *SHSP* 6 (1878), p. 209.
4. Pattie Guild, "Journey to and from Appomattox," *Confederate Veteran* 6 (January 1898), p. 11.
5. George A. Forsyth, "The Closing Scene at Appomattox Court House," *Harper's New Monthly Magazine* 96 (1897–1898), pp. 700–1.
6. McCarthy, "Detailed Minutiae of Soldier Life, Paper No. 5, p. 210.
7. Newhall, *With General Sheridan in Lee's Last Campaign*, p. 211.
8. Venable's account is in Long, *Memoirs of Robert E. Lee*, p. 421.
9. Gibbon, *Personal Recollections of the Civil War*, pp. 316–17.
10. Samuel C. Lovell, "With Lee after Appomattox," ed. Stuart H. Buck, *Civil War Times Illustrated* 17 (November 1978), pp. 40–41.
11. Gibbon describes this gathering on the courthouse steps in *Personal Recollections of the Civil War*, pp. 317–20. Also see his "Personal Recollections of Appomattox," *Century Magazine*, new jer. 41 (April 1902), p. 939.
12. Henry Heth to Darius N. Couch, 25 March 1891, Couch, "Cadmus M. Wilcox," pp. 34–35.
13. Wilcox's book is *Rifles and Rifle Practice: An Elementary Treatise upon the Theory of Rifle Firing* (New York: D. Van Nostrand, 1859).
14. William C. Davis and Julie Hoffman, eds., *The Confederate General*, 6 vols. (Harrisburg, PA: National Historical Society, 1991), vol. 6, p. 141; Gerard A. Patterson, *Rebels from West Point* (New York: Doubleday, 1987), pp. 15–16.
15. The sketch of Wilcox borrows also from *Dictionary of American Biography*, s.v. "Wilcox, Cadmus Marcellus"; *Washington Post*, 3 December 1890; Freeman, *Lee's Lieutenants* vol. 2, pp. 619–26 and vol. 3, pp. 202–3; and James D. Porter, *Tennessee*, vol. 10 of Evans, *Confederate Military History*, pp. 342–43.
16. Gibbon, *Personal Recollections of the Civil War*, pp. 320–21.
17. The meeting on the courthouse steps was described in the *New York Freeman's Journal and Catholic Register*, 22 April 1865. A good modern summary is in Frank P. Cauble, *The Surrender Proceedings: April 9, 1865 Appomattox Court House*, 3d ed. (Lynchburg, VA: H. E. Howard, 1987), pp. 38–44. Wilcox tells of Gibbon's blank cartridge proposal in his typescript report on the Petersburg campaign, Lee Headquarters Papers, Virginia Historical Society, p. 21.
18. Wesley Merritt, "Note on the Surrender of Lee," *The Century Magazine*, new ser. 41 (April 1902), p. 944.
19. Caldwell, *The History of a Brigade of South Carolinians*, p. 237.
20. Poague, *Gunner with Stonewall*, p. 125.
21. Frederick M. Colston, "Recollections of the Last Months in the Army of Northern Virginia," *SHSP* 38 (1910), p. 12.

22. Julius L. Schwab, "Some Closing Events at Appomattox," *Confederate Veteran* 8 (February 1900), p. 71.

23. McCarthy, "Detailed Minutiae of Soldier Life," Paper No. p. 5, p. 212.

24. Henry T. Lee, "The Blue, Rank and File, at Appomattox," *Confederate Veteran* 3 (February 1895), pp. 44–45.

25. Gibbon, *Personal Recollections of the Civil War*, pp. 321–22, pp. 324–25.

26. Joshua Lawrence Chamberlain, *The Passing of the Armies: An Account of the Final Campaign of the Army of the Potomac*. . . . (1915; reprint, Dayton: Press of Morningside Bookshop, 1989), pp. 248–49.

27. Gibbon, *Personal Recollections of the Civil War*, pp. 326–28.

28. Gordon, *Reminiscences of the Civil War*, p. 91.

29. Gibbon, *Personal Recollections of the Civil War*, pp. 328–32, is the source for the meeting of the negotiators, the only exception being the Irish wedding quote from Gordon.

30. Horace Porter, "The Surrender at Appomattox Court House," *Battles and Leaders*, vol. 4, p. 746; Grant, *Personal Memoirs*, p. 634; *Dictionary of American Biography*, s.v. "Wilcox, Cadmus Marcellus."

31. Quoted in Cauble, *The Surrender Proceedings*, p. 93.

32. Chamberlain, *The Passing of the Armies*, p. 259.

33. Gordon, *Reminiscences of the Civil War*, p. 449.

34. Chamberlain, *The Passing of the Armies*, pp. 260–61.

35. Gordon, *Reminiscences of the Civil War*, p. 444.

36. Chamberlain, *The Passing of the Armies*, p. 261.

37. Quoted in Chris M. Calkins, *The Final Bivouac: The Surrender Parade at Appomattox and the Disbanding of the Armies, April 10–May 20, 1865,* (Lynchburg, VA: H. E. Howard, 1988), p. 37.

38. Chamberlain, *The Passing of the Armies*, pp. 261–62.

39. Gordon, *Reminiscences of the Civil War*, pp. 448–49.

40. Chamberlain, *The Passing of the Armies*, pp. 262–65, p. 269.

41. "The Opposing Forces in the Appomattox Campaign," *Battles and Leaders*, vol. 4, p. 753.

42. Edward Porter Alexander, "Lee at Appomattox: Personal Recollections of the Break-up of the Confederacy," *Century Magazine*, new ser. 41 (April 1902), p. 931.

43. Carlton McCarthy, "Detailed Minutia of Soldier Life," Paper No. 6 *SHSP* 7 (1879), pp. 176–77.

44. Gibbon, *Personal Recollections of the Civil War*, p. 332. Also see Porter, "The Surrender at Appomattox Court House," p. 746.

45. Lovell, "With Lee after Appomattox," p. 42.

46. Gibbon, *Personal Reminiscences of the Civil War*, p. 348.

The Wind That Shook the Corn

1. Jackson, *Memoirs of Stonewall Jackson*, p. 39.

2. George B. McClellan, *Oration by Maj.-Gen. McClellan* (New York: Sheldon & Co., 1864), p. 14.

3. Ibid., pp. 16–19. The scene is described in an unidentified news report of 16 June 1864, in the Richard Delafield Papers, U.S. Military Academy Library.

4. Quoted in Edward Carlisle Boynton, *History of West Point, and Its Military Importance during the American Revolution; and the Origin and Progress of the United States Military Academy* (New York: D. Van Nostrand, 1863), p. 219. Boynton was a member of the class of 1846. He graduated twelfth and served as adjutant and quartermaster at West Point through the Civil War years and beyond.

5. Morrison, *"The Best School in the World,"* p. 15.

6. Young, *Around the World with General Grant*, vol. 2, pp. 352–53.

7. Maury, *Recollections of a Virginian*, p. 229.

8. *New York Tribune*, 14 December 1861.

Notes

9. *Harper's Weekly*, 17 January 1863.

10. W. G. Wheaton to Lyman Trumbull, 9 January 1862, T. Harry Williams, "The Attack upon West Point during the Civil War," *Mississippi Valley Historical Review* 25 (March 1939), pp. 498–99.

11. *Congressional Globe*, 37th Cong., 1st sess., p. 89.

12. For a further discussion of the political aspect, see Williams, "The Attack on West Point during the Civil War," pp. 495–96.

13. The figures are from Ellsworth Eliot, Jr., *West Point in the Confederacy* (New York: G. A. Baker & Co., 1941), p. xii; and U.S. Military Academy, *Centennial of the United States Military Academy* vol. 1, p. 488.

14. U.S. Senate, Report of the Secretary of War, 37th Cong., 1st sess., 1 July 1861, S. Doc. 1, pp. 27–28.

15. *Congressional Globe*, 37th Cong., 2d sess., pp. 164–65.

16. Ibid., 1st sess., p. 180.

17. Ibid., 2d sess., p. 200.

18. Ibid., 1st sess., p. 111.

19. Cullum, *Biographical Register*, vol. 1, p. 322, p. 324.

20. John Tidball said these things about Mahan in Morrison, "Getting through West Point," p. 322.

21. Truman Seymour, *Military Education: A Vindication of West Point and the Regular Army*, republication of a letter in the *Army and Navy Journal*, 24 September 1864, pp. 3–4, p. 7.

22. Besides Williams's "The Attack on West Point during the Civil War," see another excellent, more recent discussion by Lori A. Lisowski, "The Future of West Point: Senate Debates on the Military Academy during the Civil War," *Civil War History* 34 (March 1988), pp. 5–21.

23. Schaff, *The Spirit of Old West Point*, p. 140, pp. 251–53.

24. Richard Taylor, "The Last Confederate Surrender," *SHSP* 3 (1877), p. 158.

25. James R. Chalmers, "Forrest and His Campaigns," *SHSP* 7 (1879), p. 454.

26. Strother, "Personal Recollections of the War," p. 581.

27. Isaac Newton Arnold, *The Life of Abraham Lincoln*, 6th ed. (Chicago: Jansen, McClurg & Company, 1893), p. 300.

28. Charles Ellet, Jr., *The Army of the Potomac and its Mismanagement* (Washington: L. Towers & Co., 1861), p. 13.

29. John G. Walker, "Jackson's Capture of Harper's Ferry," *Battles and Leaders*, vol. 2, pp. 605–6.

30. O.R., ser. 1, vol. 11, pt. 3, p. 456.

31. Alexander, *Fighting for the Confederacy*, p. 146.

32. Walker, *History of the Second Army Corps*, p. 138.

33. Palfrey, *The Antietam and Fredericksburg*, p. 119.

34. Swinton, *Campaigns of the Army of the Potomac*, p. 228.

35. Ellet, *The Army of the Potomac and Its Mismanagement*, p. 16.

36. Young, *Around the World with General Grant*, vol. 2, pp. 216–17.

37. Imboden, "Stonewall Jackson in the Shenandoah," p. 297.

38. McGuire and Christian, *The Confederate Cause*, pp. 212–13.

39. Nathan Kimball, "Fighting Jackson at Kernstown," *Battles and Leaders*, vol. 2, p. 310.

40. M. Quad [pseud] in "Notes and Queries," *SHSP* 10 (1882), p. 334.

41. Tidball, "Getting through West Point," typescript, Tidball Papers.

42. Douglas, *I Rode with Stonewall*, pp. 62–93.

43. Opie, *A Rebel Cavalryman with Lee, Stuart, and Jackson*, p. 139.

44. Townsend, *Rustics in Rebellion*, p. 216.

45. Casler, *Four Years in the Stonewall Brigade*, p. 154.

46. Hill, "The Real Stonewall Jackson," p. 628.

47. Douglas, *I Rode with Stonewall*, p. 235.

48. *Dictionary of American Biography*, s.v. "Jackson, Thomas Jonathan."

49. Young, *Around the World with General Grant*, vol. 2, pp. 210–11.

50. Douglas, *I Rode with Stonewall*, p. 236; Cooke, *Stonewall Jackson*, p. 454; Taylor,

584

Destruction and Reconstruction, p. 91; Young, *Around the World with General Grant*, vol. 2, pp. 211–12.

51. Preston, "Personal Reminiscences of Stonewall Jackson," p. 927.

52. Douglas's account of the day is in *I Rode with Stonewall*, pp. 176–77. McClellan's speech is reported in the *Hagerstown* (MD) *Mail*, 5 June 1885.

53. Michie, *General McClellan*, p. 458.

54. Douglas, *I Rode with Stonewall*, p. 178.

55. Sears, *George B. McClellan*, p. 401; Maury, *Recollections of a Virginian*, p. 60; Gardner, "Memoirs," p. 8.

Epilogue

1. G. W. Tucker, "Death of General A. P. Hill," *SHSP* 11 (1883), p. 565; "Further Details of the Death of General A. P. Hill," *SHSP* 12 (1884), p. 184; Guild, "Journey to and from Appomattox," p. 11.

2. Longstreet, *From Manassas to Appomattox*, p. 262.

3. Davis and Hoffman, *The Confederate General* vol. 1, p. 5.

4. Noyes, "Biographical Sketch of Maj.-Gen. John G. Foster," p. 343.

5. Earl Whitmore, "Introduction," *Water Color and Drawings by Brevet Major General Truman Seymour, USMA 1846*, published on the occasion of an exhibit of Seymour's work, West Point, NY, p. 1974.

6. R. A. Brock, "General Burkitt Davenport Fry," *SHSP* 18 (1890), p. 286–87; Thomas McAdory Owen, *History of Alabama and Dictionary of Alabama Biography*, 4 vols. (Chicago: The S. J. Clarke Publishing Company, 1921), vol. 3, p. 619.

7. P. D. Stephenson, "Defence of Spanish Fort: On Mobile Bay—Last Great Battle of the War," *SHSP* 39 (1914), p. 119.

8. *Richmond Dispatch*, 12 January 1900.

9. Pickett, *Heart of a Soldier*, pp. 10–11; John S. Mosby, *The Memoirs of Colonel John S. Mosby*, ed. Charles Wells Russell (1917; reprint, Bloomington: Indiana University Press, 1959), p. 381; Pickett, *Pickett and His Men*, p. 425.

10. Cullum, *Biographical Register*, vol. 2, p. 264.

11. Pickett, *Pickett and His Men*, p. xiii.

Bibliography

Key to Abbreviated Citations

Annals of the War

Philadelphia Weekly Times. *The Annals of the War Written by Leading Participants North and South*. 1878. Reprint. Dayton: Morningside, 1988.

Annual Reunion

U.S. Military Academy. *Annual Reunion of the Association of the Graduates of the United States Military Academy at West Point, New York.* . . . New York: Cocker and Company/A. S. Barnes & Co., East Saginaw, MI: Evening News, Printers and Binders; Saginaw, MI: Seemann & Peters, Printers and Binders. Published annually by these various publishers, 1872–1918. These citations will be preceded in Works Cited by the number of the reunion and the short title, followed by the date.

Battles and Leaders

Johnson, Robert U., and Clarence C. Buel, eds. *Battles and Leaders of the Civil War*. 4 vols. 1887. Reprint. Secaucus, NJ: Castle, n.d.

586

Confederate Military History   Evans, Clement A., ed. *Confederate Military History, Extended Edition.* 1899. Reprint. Wilmington, NC: Broadfoot Publishing Company, 1987.

MHSM   *Papers of the Military Historical Society of Massachusetts.* 15 vols. 1895–1918. Reprint. Wilmington, NC: Broadfoot Publishing Company, 1989.

Rebellion Record   Moore, Frank, ed. *The Rebellion Record: A Diary of American Events.* 12 vols. 1861–1868. Reprint. New York: Arno Press, 1977.

SHSP   *Southern Historical Society Papers.* 52 vols. 1876–1959. Reprint. Millwood, NY: Kraus Reprint Co., 1977.

Works Cited

Abdill, George B. *Civil War Railroads.* Seattle: Superior Publishing Co., 1961.

Adams, John. Letters, 1844–1845. Henry E. Huntington Library and Art Gallery, San Marino, CA.

Ahrens, Kent. "The Drawings and Watercolors by Truman Seymour." In *Water Color and Drawings by Brevet Major General Truman Seymour, USMA 1846.* Published on the occasion of an exhibit of Seymour's work at West Point, NY, 1974.

Alexander, Edward Porter. *Fighting for the Confederacy: The Personal Recollections of General Edward Porter Alexander.* Edited by Gary W. Gallagher. Chapel Hill: University of North Carolina Press, 1989.

———. *Military Memoirs of a Confederate: A Critical Narrative.* New York: Charles Scribner's Sons, 1907.

———. "The Great Charge and Artillery Fighting at Gettysburg." Vol. 3 of *Battles and Leaders.*

———. "Lee at Appomattox: Personal Recollections of the Break-up of the Confederacy." *Century Magazine* New ser. 41 (April 1902): 921–31.

Allan, William. *The Army of Northern Virginia in 1862.* Boston: Houghton Mifflin, 1892.

———. *History of the Campaign of Gen. T. J. (Stonewall) Jackson in the Valley of Virginia from November 4, 1861 to June 17, 1862.* 1880. Reprint. Dayton: Morningside, 1987.

Ambrose, Stephen E. *Duty, Honor, Country: A History of West Point.* Baltimore: Johns Hopkins University Press, 1966.

Andrews, Marietta Minnigerode. *Scraps of Paper.* New York: E. P. Dutton, 1929.

Angle, Paul M., and Earl Schenck Miers. *Tragic Years 1860–1865: A Documentary History of the American Civil War.* 2 vols. New York: Simon and Schuster, 1960.

Arnold, Isaac Newton. *The Life of Abraham Lincoln.* 6th ed. Chicago: Jansen, McClurg & Company, 1893.

Arnold, Thomas Jackson. *Early Life and Letters of General Thomas J. Jackson ("Stonewall" Jackson)*. 1916. Reprint. Richmond, VA: Dietz Press, 1957.

————. "Battle of Rich Mountain." *Randolph County Historical Society Magazine of History and Biography* 2 (1925): 46–52.

Ashe, S. A. *The Charge at Gettysburg*. North Carolina Booklet, vol. 1, no. 11. Raleigh, NC: Capital Printing Company, 1902.

Avirett, James B. *The Memoirs of General Turner Ashby and His Compeers*. Baltimore: Selby & Dulany, 1867.

Bachelder, John B. Papers. Gettysburg National Military Park Library, Gettysburg, PA.

Bailey, William Whitman. "My Boyhood at West Point," *Personal Narratives of Events in the War of the Rebellion*. 4th ser., no. 12. Providence: Rhode Island Soldiers and Sailors Historical Society, 1891.

Ballenger, T. L. "Colonel Albert Sidney Johnston's March through Indian Territory in 1855." *Chronicles of Oklahoma* 47 (Summer 1969): 132–37.

Baltimore and Ohio Railroad. *Thirty-fifth Annual Report of the President and Directors to the Stockholders . . . for the Year Ending September 30, 1861*. Baltimore: William M. Innes, 1863.

Baltimore Sun.

Bandel, Eugene. *Frontier Life in the Army, 1854–1861*. Edited by Ralph P. Bieber. Glendale, CA: Arthur H. Clark Company, 1932.

Bates, David Homer. *Lincoln in the Telegraph Office: Recollections of the United States Military Telegraph Corps during the Civil War*. New York: Century Co., 1907.

The Battle of Fort Sumter and the First Victory of the Southern Troops. Charleston, SC: Evans & Cogswell, 1861.

Bean, William G. *Stonewall's Man: Sandie Pendleton*. 1959. Reprint. Wilmington, NC; Broadfoot Publishing Company, 1987.

————, ed. "The Valley Campaign of 1862 as Revealed in Letters of Sandie Pendleton." *Virginia Magazine of History and Biography* 78 (July 1970): 326–64.

Beatty, John. *Memoirs of a Volunteer, 1861–1863*. Edited by Harvey S. Ford. New York: W. W. Norton, 1946.

Beaty, Susie Pennal. "The Battle of Fort Sumter." *Confederate Veteran* 18 (September 1910): 419–20.

Beaufort (SC) *Gazette.*

Beauregard, Pierre Gustave Toutant. *With Beauregard in Mexico: The Mexican War Reminiscences of P. G. T. Beauregard*. Edited by T. Harry Williams. Baton Rouge: Louisiana State University Press, 1956.

Bender, Averam B. "The Soldier in the Far West, 1848–1860." *Pacific Historical Review* 8 (June 1939): 159–78.

Benedict, G. G. *Vermont in the Civil War: A History of the Part Taken by the Vermont Soldiers and Sailors in the War for the Union, 1861–5*. 2 vols. Burlington, VT: Free Press Association, 1886–1888.

Birdsong, James C., comp. *Brief Sketches of North Carolina Troops in the War between the States*. Raleigh, NC: Josephus Daniels, 1894.

Bliss, Zenas R. "Extracts from the Unpublished Memoirs of Maj. Gen. Z. R. Bliss." *Journal of the Military Service Institution of the United States* 38 (January–February 1906): 120–34, 303–13, 517–29.

Boatner, Mark Mayo III. *The Civil War Dictionary*. New York: David McKay Company, 1959.

Bibliography

Boteler, Alexander R. "Stonewall Jackson in Campaign of 1862." *SHSP* 40 (1915): 162–82.

Boyd, Belle. *Belle Boyd in Camp and Prison, Written by Herself.* Edited by Curtis Carroll Davis. 1865. Reprint. South Brunswick, NJ: Thomas Yoseloff, 1968.

Boynton, Edward Carlisle. *History of West Point, and Its Military Importance during the American Revolution; and the Origin and Progress of the United States Military Academy.* New York: D. Van Nostrand, 1863.

Branch, E. Douglas. "Frederick West Lander, Road-Builder," *Mississippi Valley Historical Review* 16 (September 1929): 172–87.

Bright, Robert A. "Pickett's Charge." *SHSP* 31 (1903): 228–36.

Brock, R. A. "General Burkett Davenport Fry." *SHSP* 18 (1890): 286–88.

Brown, B. F. "A. P. Hill's Light Division." *Confederate Veteran* 30 (July 1922): 246–47.

Brown, Campbell. "Notes on Ewell's Division in the Campaign of 1862." *SHSP* 10 (1882): 255–61.

Burton, E. Bennett. "The Taos Rebellion." *Old Santa Fe: A Magazine of History, Archaeology, Genealogy and Biography* 1 (October 1913): 176–209.

Caldwell, J.F.J. *The History of a Brigade of South Carolinians, Known First as "Gregg's," and Subsequently as "McGowan's Brigade."* 1866. Reprint. Marietta, GA: Continental Book Company, 1951.

Calkins, Chris M. *The Final Bivouac: The Surrender Parade at Appomattox and the Disbanding of the Armies, April 10–May 20, 1865.* Lynchburg, VA: H. E. Howard, 1988.

Callahan, James Morton. *History of West Virginia Old and New and West Virginia Biography.* 3 vols. Chicago and New York: American Historical Society, 1923.

Cameron, William E. "The Career of General A. P. Hill." *Annals of the War.*

Carter, Robert Goldthwaite. *Four Brothers in Blue, or Sunshine and Shadows of the War of the Rebellion: A Story of the Great Civil War from Bull Run to Appomattox.* Austin: University of Texas Press, 1978.

Casler, John O. *Four Years in the Stonewall Brigade.* 1906. Reprint. Dayton: Press of Morningside Bookshop, 1982.

Cauble, Frank P. *The Surrender Proceedings: April 9, 1865 Appomattox Court House.* 3d ed. Lynchburg, VA: H. E. Howard, 1987.

Chalmers, James R. "Forrest and His Campaigns." *SHSP* 7 (1879): 451–86.

Chamberlain, Joshua Lawrence. *The Passing of the Armies: An Account of the Final Campaign of the Army of the Potomac. . . .* 1915. Reprint. Dayton: Press of Morningside Bookshop, 1989.

Chamberlain, Samuel E. *My Confession.* New York: Harper & Brothers, 1956.

Chamberlaine, William W. *Memoirs of the Civil War between the Northern and Southern Sections of the United States of America, 1861 to 1865.* Washington, DC: Press of Byron S. Adams, 1912.

Chambers, Lenoir. *Stonewall Jackson.* 2 vols. 1959. Reprint. Wilmington, NC: Broadfoot Publishing Company, 1988.

"Charles Seaforth Stewart." *Thirty-Sixth Annual Reunion . . . June 13th, 1905. Charleston* (SC) *Courier.*

Chase, Salmon Portland. *Inside Lincoln's Cabinet: The Civil War Diaries of Salmon P. Chase.* Edited by David Donald. New York: Longmans, Green and Co., 1954.

Chesnut, Mary Boykin. *Mary Chesnut's Civil War.* Edited by C. Vann Woodward. New Haven, CT: Yale University Press, 1981.

Chester, James. "Inside Sumter in '61." Vol. 1 of *Battles and Leaders.*

Chicago Tribune.

Chisolm, A. R. "Notes on the Surrender of Fort Sumter." Vol. 1 of *Battles and Leaders.*

Church, Albert E. *Personal Reminiscences of the Military Academy, from 1824 to 1831.* West Point: U.S.M.A. Press, 1879.

Cincinnati Commercial.

Cincinnati Gazette.

Clark, Walter, ed. *Histories of the Several Regiments and Battalions from North Carolina in the Great War, 1861–65.* 5 vols. 1901. Reprint. Wilmington, NC: Broadfoot Publishing Company, 1991.

Clarkson, H. M. "Story of the Star of the West." *Confederate Veteran* 21 (May 1913): 234–36.

Coffin, Charles Carleton. "Antietam Scenes." Vol. 2 of *Battles and Leaders.*

Coffman, Edward M. *The Old Army: A Portrait of the American Army in Peacetime, 1784–1898.* New York: Oxford University Press, 1986.

"Col. and Dr. R. W. Martin, of Virginia." *Confederate Veteran* 5 (February 1897): 70.

Colston, Frederick M. "Recollections of the Last Months in the Army of Northern Virginia." *SHSP* 38 (1910): 1–15.

Cometti, Elizabeth, and Festus P. Summers, eds. *The Thirty-Fifth State: A Documentary History of West Virginia.* Morgantown: West Virginia University Library, 1966.

Congressional Globe. 46 vols. Washington, DC, 1834–73.

Connor, Seymour V., and Odie B. Faulk. *North America Divided: The Mexican War, 1846–1848.* New York: Oxford University Press, 1971.

Cook, Roy Bird. *The Family and Early Life of Stonewall Jackson.* 5th ed. Charleston, WV: Education Foundation, 1967.

Cooke, John Esten. *Stonewall Jackson: A Military Biography.* New York: D. Appleton and Company, 1876.

———. *Stonewall Jackson and the Old Stonewall Brigade.* Edited by Richard Barksdale Harwell. Charlottesville: University of Virginia Press for the Tracy W. McGregor Library, 1954.

Couch, Darius N. "Cadmus M. Wilcox." *Twenty-Second Annual Reunion . . . June 12th, 1891.*

———. "George Stoneman." *Twenty-Sixth Annual Reunion . . . June 10th, 1895.*

———. "Sumner's 'Right Grand Division.' " Vol. 3 of *Battles and Leaders.*

Cox, Jacob D. "The Battle of Antietam." Vol. 2 of *Battles and Leaders.*

———. "McClellan in West Virginia." Vol. 1 of *Battles and Leaders.*

———. "War Preparations in the North." Vol. 1 of *Battles and Leaders.*

Crawford, Samuel Wylie. *The Genesis of the Civil War: The Story of Sumter, 1860–1861.* New York: Charles L. Webster & Company, 1887.

———. "The First Shot against the Flag." *Annals of the War.*

Cullum, George W. *Biographical Register of the Officers and Graduates of the U.S. Military Academy . . . from Its Establishment, in 1802, to 1890.* 3 vols. with supplements. 3d ed. Boston and New York: Houghton Mifflin, 1891.

———. Cullum File, Class of 1846. U.S. Military Academy Library, West Point, NY.

Curtis, George Ticknor. *McClellan's Last Service to the Republic, Together with a Tribute to His Memory.* New York: D. Appleton and Company, 1886.

Dabney, R. L. *Life and Campaigns of Lieut.-Gen. Thomas J. Jackson, (Stonewall Jackson).* 1865. Reprint. Harrisonburg, VA: Sprinkle Publications, 1983.

———. "Stonewall Jackson." *SHSP* 11 (1883): 125–35, 145–58.

Daniel, John W. Papers. University of Virginia Library, Charlottesville, VA. Copy in the Gettysburg National Park Library, Gettysburg, PA.

Davis, George B., Leslie J. Perry, and Joseph W. Kirkley. *The Official Military Atlas of the Civil War.* Compiled by Calvin D. Cowles. 1891. Reprint. New York: Arno Press and Crown Publishers, 1978.

Davis, Varina H. *Jefferson Davis, Ex-President of the Confederate States of America: A Memoir by His Wife.* 2 vols. New York: Belford Company, 1890.

Davis, William C., ed. *The Image of War: 1861–1865.* 6 vols. A project of the National Historical Society. New York: Doubleday & Company, 1981–1984.

————, and Julie Hoffman, eds. *The Confederate General.* 6 vols. Harrisburg, PA: National Historical Society, 1991.

Dawson, Francis W. *Reminiscences of Confederate Service, 1861–1865.* Edited by Bell Irvin Wiley. Baton Rouge: Louisiana State University Press, 1980.

Dayton, Ruth Woods. "The Beginning—Philippi, 1861." *West Virginia History* 13 (July 1952): 254–66.

Delafield, Richard. Papers. U.S. Military Academy Library, West Point, NY.

DeLeon, Thomas Cooper. *Four Years in Rebel Capitals: An Inside View of Life in the Southern Confederacy from Birth to Death.* Mobile, AL: Gossip Printing Company, 1890.

Derby, George Horatio. Papers. U.S. Military Academy Library, West Point, NY.

Dickens, Charles. *American Notes.* 1892. Reprint. New York: St. Martin's Press, 1985.

Dictionary of American Biography. Edited by Allen Johnson and Dumas Malone. 20 vols. New York: Charles Scribner's Sons, 1964.

Dickert, D. Augustus. *History of Kershaw's Brigade, with Complete Roll of Companies, Biographical Sketches, Incidents, Anecdotes, etc.* Newberry, SC: Elbert H. Aull Company, 1899.

Dillon, Lester R., Jr. "American Artillery in the Mexican War, 1846–1847." *Military History of Texas and the Southwest* 11 (1973): 7–27, 109–30, 149–70, 233–40.

Dodge, Theodore A. "The Romances of Chancellorsville." *Campaigns in Virginia, Maryland and Pennsylvania, 1862–1863.* Vol. 3 of *MHSM.*

Dooley, John. *John Dooley, Confederate Soldier: His War Journal.* Edited by Joseph T. Durkin. South Bend, IN: University of Notre Dame Press, 1963.

Dooley, Louise K. "Little Sorrel: A War-Horse for Stonewall." *Army* 25 (April 1975): 34–39.

Doubleday, Abner. *Reminiscences of Forts Sumter and Moultrie in 1860–'61.* 1876. Reprint. Spartanburg, SC: Reprint Company, 1976.

————. "From Moultrie to Sumter." Vol. 1 of *Battles and Leaders.*

Douglas, Henry Kyd. *I Rode with Stonewall.* Chapel Hill: University of North Carolina Press, 1968.

————. "Stonewall Jackson in Maryland." Vol. 2 of *Battles and Leaders.*

Dunn, Jacob P. *Massacres of the Mountains: A History of the Indian Wars of the Far West, 1815–1875.* New York: Archer House, 1958.

Dutton, William. Papers. U.S. Military Academy Library, West Point, NY.

Dwight, Timothy. *Travels in New England and New York.* Edited by Barbara Miller Solomon, with the assistance of Patricia M. King. 4 vols. 1822. Reprint. Cambridge: Harvard University Press, Belknap Press, 1969.

Early, Jubal A. "Stonewall Jackson—the Story of His Being an Astrologer Refuted—An Eyewitness Describes How He Was Wounded." *SHSP* 6 (1878): 261–82.

Eggleston, George Cary. *A Rebel's Recollections.* 1959. Reprint. New York: Kraus Reprint Co., 1969.

Eisenhower, John S. D. *So Far from God: The U.S. War with Mexico, 1846–1848*. New York: Random House, 1989.

Eisenschiml, Otto, and Ralph Newman. *The Civil War: The American Iliad as Told by Those Who Lived It*. 1947. Reprint. Secaucus, NJ: Blue and Grey Press, 1985.

Eliot, Ellsworth, Jr. *West Point in the Confederacy*. New York: G. A. Baker & Co., 1941.

Ellet, Charles, Jr. *The Army of the Potomac and Its Mismanagement*. Washington, DC: L. Towers & Co., 1861.

Elliott, Charles Winslow. *Winfield Scott: The Soldier and the Man*. New York: Macmillan, 1937.

[English Combatant.] *Battle-Fields of the South, from Bull Run to Fredericksburgh; with Sketches of Confederate Commanders, and Gossip of the Camps*. New York: John Bradburn, 1864.

Evans, Clement Anselm. *Intrepid Warrior: Clement Anselm Evans, Confederate General from Georgia: Life, Letters, and Diaries of the War Years*. Compiled and edited by Robert Grier Stephens, Jr. Dayton, OH: Morningside, 1992.

Ewell, Benjamin S. "Jackson and Ewell: The Latter's Opinion of His Chief." *SHSP* 20 (1892): 26–33.

Ewell Family Papers. The Earl Gregg Swem Library, College of William and Mary, Williamsburg, VA.

Farinholt, B. L. "Battle of Gettysburg—Johnson's Island." *Confederate Veteran* 5 (September 1897): 467–70.

Faust, Patricia L., ed. *Historical Times Illustrated Encyclopedia of the Civil War*. New York: Harper & Row, 1986.

Fleming, Thomas J. *West Point: The Men and Times of the United States Military Academy*. New York: William Morrow & Co., 1969.

Foote, Shelby. *The Civil War: A Narrative*. 3 vols. New York: Random House, 1958, 1963, 1974.

Ford, Worthington Chauncey, ed. *A Cycle of Adams Letters, 1861–1865*. 2 vols. Boston: Houghton Mifflin, 1920.

Forman, Sidney. *Cadet Life before the Mexican War*. Bulletin no. 1. West Point: U.S. Military Academy Library, 1945.

———. *West Point: A History of the United States Military Academy*. New York: Columbia University Press, 1950.

Forsyth, George A. "The Closing Scene at Appomattox Court House." *Harper's New Monthly Magazine* 96 (1897–1898): 700–11.

"Fort Sumter—Who Fired the First Gun on the Fort?" *SHSP* 20 (1892): 61–63.

Franklin, William B. "George Brinton McClellan." *Seventeenth Annual Reunion . . . June 10th, 1886*.

Fravel, John W. "Jackson's Valley Campaign." *Confederate Veteran* 6 (September 1898): 418–20.

Frazer, Robert Walter. *Forts of the West: Military Forts and Presidios and Posts Commonly Called Forts West of the Mississippi River to 1898*. Norman: University of Oklahoma Press, 1972.

———, ed. *Mansfield on the Condition of Western Forts, 1853–54*. Norman: University of Oklahoma Press, 1963.

Freeman, Douglas Southall. *Lee's Lieutenants: A Study in Command*. 3 vols. New York: Charles Scribner's Sons, 1942–1944.

———. *R. E. Lee: A Biography*. 4 vols. New York: Charles Scribner's Sons, 1962.

Freemantle, Arthur James Lyon. *Three Months in the Southern States: April–June, 1863.* 1864. Reprint. Lincoln: University of Nebraska Press, 1991.

Fry, Birkett Davenport. "Pettigrew's Charge at Gettysburg." *SHSP* 7 (1879): 91–93.

Fuller, W. G. "The Corps of Telegraphers under General Anson Stager during the War of the Rebellion." In *Sketches of War History, 1861–1865: Papers Read before the Ohio Commandery of the Military Order of the Loyal Legion of the United States, 1886–1888.* Vol. 2. Cincinnati: Robert Clarke & Co., 1888.

"Further Details of the Death of General A. P. Hill." *SHSP* 12 (1884): 183–87.

Gallagher, Gary W. "A Widow and Her Soldier: LaSalle Corbell Pickett as Author of the George E. Pickett Letters." *The Virginia Magazine of History and Biography* 94 (July 1986): 329–44.

Ganoe, William Addleman. *The History of the United States Army.* Rev. ed. New York: D. Appleton-Century Company, 1942.

Gardner, William Montgomery. "The Memoirs of Brigadier-General William Montgomery Gardner." Edited by Elizabeth McKinne Gardner. Typescript copy of a series of articles in the *Memphis Commercial Appeal,* 1912. U.S. Military Academy Library, West Point, NY.

Gayle, Levin C. Diary. Typescript portion. Gettysburg National Military Park Library, Gettysburg, PA.

Gibbon, John. *Personal Recollections of the Civil War.* 1928. Reprint. Dayton: Press of Morningside Bookshop, 1988.

———. "Personal Recollections of Appomattox." *The Century Magazine* New ser. 41 (April 1902): 936–43.

Gittings, John G. *Personal Recollections of Stonewall Jackson, also Sketches and Stories.* Cincinnati: Editor Publishing Co., 1899.

Glazier, Willard. *Three Years in the Federal Cavalry.* New York: R. H. Ferguson & Co., 1872.

Gordon, George Henry. *Brook Farm to Cedar Mountain in the War of the Great Rebellion, 1861–62.* Boston: James R. Osgood and Company, 1883.

———. "The Battles of Contreras and Churubusco." In *Civil and Mexican Wars 1861, 1846.* Vol. 13 of *MHSM.*

———. "Battles of Molino del Rey and Chapultepec." In *Civil and Mexican Wars 1861, 1846.* Vol. 13 of *MHSM.*

———. "John G. Foster." *Sixth Annual Reunion . . . June 17th, 1875.*

Gordon, John B. *Reminiscences of the Civil War.* New York: Charles Scribner's Sons, 1903.

Gould, A. A. "An Address in Commemoration of Professor J. W. Bailey." *American Association for the Advancement of Science* (19 August 1857): 1–8.

Gracey, Samuel L. *Annals of the Sixth Pennsylvania Cavalry.* Philadelphia: E. H. Butler & Co. 1868.

Grant, Ulysses S. *Personal Memoirs of U. S. Grant.* 2 vols. 1894. Reprint. (2 vols. in 1). New York: AMS Press, 1972.

Greeley, Horace. *The American Conflict: A History of the Great Rebellion in the United States of America, 1860–'65. . . .* 2 vols. Hartford, CT: O. D. Case & Company, 1866.

A Guide Book to West Point and Vicinity; Containing Descriptive, Historical, and Statistical Sketches of the United States Military Academy, and of other Objects of Interest. New York: J. H. Colton, 1844.

Guild, Pattie. "Journey to and from Appomattox." *Confederate Veteran* 6 (January 1898): 11–12.

Haas, I. C. " 'Stonewall' Jackson's Death." *SHSP* 32 (1904): 94–98.

Hafen, LeRoy R., and Ann W. Hafen, eds. *Relations with the Indians of the Plains, 1857–1861: A Documentary Account of the Military Campaigns, and Negotiations of Indian Agents—with Reports and Journals of P. G. Lowe, R. M. Peck, J. E. B. Stuart, S. D. Sturgis, and Other Official Papers.* Glendale, CA: Arthur H. Clark Company, 1959.

Hagerstown (MD) *Mail.*

Haley, John West. *The Rebel Yell & the Yankee Hurrah: The Civil War Journal of a Maine Volunteer.* Edited by Ruth L. Silliker. Camden, ME: Down East Books, 1985.

Hallock, Charles. *A Complete Biographical Sketch of "Stonewall" Jackson, Giving a Full and Accurate Account of the Leading Events of His Military Career, His Dying Moments, and the Obsequies at Richmond and Lexington.* Augusta, GA: Steam Power-Press Chronicle and Sentinel, 1863.

Hamlin, Percy Gatling. *"Old Bald Head" (General R. S. Ewell): The Portrait of a Soldier* and *The Making of a Soldier: Letters of General R. S. Ewell.* 1940 and 1935. Reprint (2 vols. in 1). Gaithersburg, MD: Ron R. Van Sickle Military Books, 1988.

———. "Richard S. Ewell: His Humanity and Humor." *Virginia Cavalcade* 21 (Autumn 1971): 5–11.

Happel, Ralph. *Jackson: Let Us Cross Over the River.* . . . Richmond: Eastern National Park and Monument Association in cooperation with Fredericksburg and Spotsylvania National Military Park, 1971.

Hardcastle, Edmund Lafayette. Journal and Letters. U.S. Military Academy Library, West Point, NY.

Harmon, George D. "The United States Indian Policy in Texas, 1845–1860." *Mississippi Valley Historical Review* 17 (December 1930): 377–403.

Harper's Weekly: A Journal of Civilization.

Harrison, Walter. *Pickett's Men: A Fragment of War History.* 1870. Reprint. Gaithersburg, MD: Butternut Press, 1984.

Haselburger, Fritz. *Yanks from the South! The First Land Campaign of the Civil War—Rich Mountain, West Virginia.* Baltimore: Past Glories, 1987.

Haskell, Frank A. *The Battle of Gettysburg.* Edited by Bruce Catton. Boston: Houghton Mifflin, 1958.

Haskell, John Cheves. *The Haskell Memoirs.* Edited by Gilbert E. Govan and James W. Livingood. New York: G. P. Putnam's Sons, 1960.

Hassler, William Woods. *A. P. Hill: Lee's Forgotten General.* 1957. Revised reprint. Chapel Hill: University of North Carolina Press, 1962.

———. "A. P. Hill Rings down the Curtain on Act III, Scene 3, at Antietam." *Virginia Country* 10 (Summer 1987): 95–100.

Hay, John. *Lincoln and the Civil War in the Diaries and Letters of John Hay.* Edited by Tyler Dennett. New York: Dodd, Mead & Company, 1939.

Henderson, G.F.R. *Stonewall Jackson and the American Civil War.* 2 vols. 1936. Reprint. Secaucus, NJ: Blue and Grey Press, n.d.

Henry, O. [William Sidney Porter]. *The Complete Works of O. Henry.* 2 vols. Garden City, NY: Doubleday & Company, 1953.

Henry, Robert Selph. *The Story of the Mexican War.* Indianapolis and New York: Bobbs-Merrill, 1950.

———, ed. *As They Saw Forrest: Some Recollections and Comments of Contemporaries.* 1956. Reprint. Wilmington, NC: Broadfoot Publishing Company, 1987.

Heth, Henry. *The Memoirs of Henry Heth.* Edited by James L. Morrison, Jr., Westport, CT: Greenwood Press, 1974.

Hill, Ambrose Powell. Hill Family Papers. Virginia Historical Society, Richmond, VA.

Hill, Daniel Harvey. "The Lost Dispatch." *The Land We Love* 4 (February 1868): 270–84.

———. "The Real Stonewall Jackson." *Century Magazine* 47 (February 1894): 623–28.

Hitchcock, Ethan Allen. *Fifty Years in Camp and Field: Diary of Major-General Ethan Allen Hitchcock, U.S.A.* Edited by W. A. Croffut. New York: G. P. Putnam's Sons, The Knickerbocker Press, 1909.

Hoke, Jacob. *The Great Invasion of 1863; or, General Lee in Pennsylvania.* Dayton: W. J. Shuey, 1887.

Holden, Edward S. "Biographical Memoir of William H. C. Bartlett, 1804–1893." *National Academy of Sciences Biographical Memoirs* 7 (June 1911): 173–93.

Hollon, W. Eugene. *Beyond the Cross Timbers: The Travels of Randolph B. Marcy, 1812–1887.* Norman: University of Oklahoma Press, 1955.

Hornbeck, Betty. *Upshur Brothers of the Blue and the Gray.* Parsons, WV: McClain Printing Company, 1967.

Hotchkiss, Jedediah. *Make Me a Map of the Valley: The Civil War Journal of Stonewall Jackson's Topographer.* Edited by Archie P. McDonald. Dallas: Southern Methodist University Press, 1989.

———. *Virginia.* Vol. 4 of *Confederate Military History.*

———. Papers. Manuscript Division, Library of Congress, Washington, DC.

Houston, Thomas D. "Storming Cemetery Hill." With John T. James letter. *Philadelphia Weekly Times*, 21 October 1882.

Howard, McHenry. *Recollections of a Maryland Confederate Soldier and Staff Officer under Johnston, Jackson and Lee.* 1914. Reprint. Dayton: Press of Morningside Bookshop, 1975.

Howard, Oliver Otis. *Autobiography of Oliver Otis Howard.* 2 vols. New York: Baker & Taylor Company, 1907.

Hungerford, Edward. *The Story of the Baltimore & Ohio Railroad, 1827–1927.* 2 vols. New York: G. P. Putnam's Sons, 1928.

Hunt, Henry J. "The Third Day at Gettysburg." Vol. 3 of *Battles and Leaders.*

Hunter, Alexander. "A High Private's Account of the Battle of Sharpsburg." Papers no. 1 and 2. *SHSP* 10 (1882): 503–12; 11 (1883): 10–21.

Huntington, James F. "The Battle of Chancellorsville." In *Campaigns in Virginia, Maryland and Pennsylvania, 1862–1863.* Vol. 3 of *MHSM.*

———. "Operations in the Shenandoah Valley, from Winchester to Port Republic, March 10–June 9, 1862." In *Campaigns in Virginia, 1861–1862.* Vol. 1 of *MHSM.*

Imboden, John D. "The Confederate Retreat from Gettysburg." Vol. 3 of *Battles and Leaders.*

———. "Jackson at Harper's Ferry in 1861." Vol. 1 of *Battles and Leaders.*

———. "Stonewall Jackson in the Shenandoah." Vol. 2 of *Battles and Leaders.*

Jackson, Andrew. *Correspondence of Andrew Jackson.* Edited by John Spencer Bassett. 7 vols. Washington, DC: Carnegie Institution, 1926–1935.

Jackson, Mary Anna. *Memoirs of Stonewall Jackson.* 1895. Reprint. Dayton: Press of Morningside Bookshop, 1985.

Jackson, Thomas J. Order Book, Harpers Ferry, 1861. Eleanor S. Brockenbrough Library, Museum of the Confederacy, Richmond, VA.

Jacobs, M. *Notes on the Invasion of Maryland and Pennsylvania, and the Battle of Gettysburg . . . .* Philadelphia: J. B. Lippincott, 1863.

Johnson, Bradley T. "Memoir of the First Maryland Regiment." Papers no. 3 and 4 *SHSP* 10 (1882): 46–56; 97–109.

Johnston, Angus James. *Virginia Railroads in the Civil War*. Chapel Hill: Published for the Virginia Historical Society by the University of North Carolina Press, 1961.

Johnston, David E. *The Story of a Confederate Boy in the Civil War*. Portland, OR: Glass & Prudhomme Company, 1914.

———. "Concerning the Battle of Sharpsburg." *Confederate Veteran* 6 (January 1898): 27–29.

Johnston, Joseph E. *Narrative of Military Operations Directed, during the Late War between the States*. 1874. Reprint. Bloomington: Indiana University Press, 1959.

Johnston, William Preston. *The Life of Gen. Albert Sidney Johnston*. New York: D. Appleton and Company, 1878.

Jones, J. William. "The Old Virginia Town, Lexington: Where Lee and Stonewall Jackson are buried—Reminiscences of Stonewall Jackson." *Confederate Veteran* 1 (January 1893): 18–20.

———. " 'Stonewall' Jackson: Anecdotes." *Confederate Veteran* 12 (April 1904) 174–75.

Jones, John B. *A Rebel War Clerk's Diary*. Edited by Earl Schenck Miers. New York: Sagamore Press, 1958.

Jones, Katherine M., ed. *Heroines of Dixie: Confederate Women Tell Their Story of the War*. Indianapolis and New York: Bobbs-Merrill Company, 1955.

Jones, Robert Tyler. "Gen. L. A. Armistead and R. Tyler Jones." *Confederate Veteran* 2 (September 1894): 271.

Kean, Robert Garlick Hill. *Inside the Confederate Government: The Diary of Robert Garlick Hill Kean*. Edited by Edward Younger. New York: Oxford University Press, 1957.

Keleher, William A. *Turmoil in New Mexico, 1846–1868*. Santa Fe: Rydal Press, 1952.

Keyes, Erasmus D. *Fifty Years' Observation of Men and Events Civil and Military*. New York: Charles Scribner's Sons, 1884.

Kimball, Nathan. "Fighting Jackson at Kernstown." Vol. 2 of *Battles and Leaders*.

Kimble, June. "Tennesseans at Gettysburg—the Retreat." *Confederate Veteran* 18 (October 1910): 460–63.

Kip, Lawrence. *Army Life on the Pacific: A Journal of the Expedition against the Northern Indians*. New York: Redfield, 1859.

Lane, James H. "Stonewall Jackson: Reminiscences of Him as a Professor in the Virginia Military Institute." *SHSP* 20 (1892): 307–11.

Lang, Theodore F. *Loyal West Virginia from 1861–1865*. Baltimore: Deutsch Publishing Co., 1895.

Lawton, Eba Anderson. *Major Robert Anderson and Fort Sumter, 1861*. New York: Knickerbacker Press, 1911.

Lee, Henry T. "The Blue, Rank and File, at Appomattox." *Confederate Veteran* 3 (February 1895): 44–45.

Lee, Stephen D. "The First Step in the War." Vol. 1 of *Battles and Leaders*.

———. "Who Fired the First Gun at Sumter?: Letter from S. D. Lee with Reply from Julian M. Ruffin." *SHSP* 11 (1883): 501–4.

Leigh, Benjamin Watkins. "The Wounding of Stonewall Jackson—Extracts from a Letter of Major Benjamin Watkins Leigh." *SHSP* 6 (1878): 230–34.

Lewis, Charles Lee. "Matthew Fontaine Maury." *Confederate Veteran* 33 (August 1925): 296–301.

Lewis, John H. *Recollections from 1860 to 1865*. Washington, DC: Peake & Company, 1895.

Lewis, Lloyd. *Captain Sam Grant*. Boston: Little, Brown and Company, 1950.

Lincoln, Abraham. *The Collected Works of Abraham Lincoln*. Edited by Roy P. Basler. 8 vols. New Brunswick, NJ: Rutgers University Press, 1953.

Lisowski, Lori A. "The Future of West Point: Senate Debates on the Military Academy during the Civil War." *Civil War History* 34 (March 1988): 5–21.

Loehr, Charles T. *War History of the Old First Virginia Regiment, Army of Northern Virginia*. Richmond: Wm. Ellis Jones, 1884.

———. "The 'Old First' Virginia at Gettysburg." *SHSP* 32 (1904): 33–40.

London Times.

Long, Armistead L. *Memoirs of Robert E. Lee*. New York: J. M. Stoddart & Co., 1886.

Longstreet, James. *From Manassas to Appomattox: Memoirs of the Civil War in America*. 2d ed. rev. Philadelphia: J. B. Lippincott, 1903.

———. "The Battle of Fredericksburg." Vol. 3 of *Battles and Leaders*.

———. "Lee in Pennsylvania." *Annals of the War*.

———. "Lee's Right Wing at Gettysburg." Vol. 3 of *Battles and Leaders*.

Lossing, Benson J. *Matthew Brady's Illustrated History of the Civil War*. 1912. Reprint. New York: Fairfax Press, n.d.

Louisville Journal.

Lovell, Samuel C. "With Lee after Appomattox." Edited by Stuart H. Buck. *Civil War Times Illustrated* 17 (November 1978): 38–43.

Lyman, Theodore. *Meade's Headquarters, 1863–65: Letters of Colonel Theodore Lyman from the Wilderness to Appomattox*. Edited by George R. Agassiz. Boston: Atlantic Monthly Press, 1922.

McCarthy, Carlton. "Detailed Minutiae of Soldier Life." Papers no. 5 and 6. *SHSP* 6 (1878): 193–214; 7 (1879): 176–85.

McClellan, George Brinton. *The Civil War Papers of George B. McClellan: Selected Correspondence, 1860–1865*. Edited by Stephen W. Sears. New York: Ticknor & Fields, 1989.

———. *McClellan's Own Story: The War for the Union, the Soldiers Who Fought It, the Civilians Who Directed It, and His Relations to It and to Them*. Edited by William C. Prime. New York: Charles L. Webster & Company, 1887.

———. *The Mexican War Diary of George B. McClellan*. Edited by William Starr Myers. Princeton, NJ: Princeton University Press, 1917.

———. *Oration by Maj.-Gen. McClellan*. New York: Sheldon & Co., 1864.

———. *Report on the Organization and Campaigns of the Army of the Potomac, to Which Is Added an Account of the Campaign in Western Virginia. . . .* New York: Sheldon & Co., 1864.

———. Papers. Manuscript Division, Library of Congress, Washington, DC.

McClellan, George B., Jr. Papers. Manuscript Division, Library of Congress, Washington, DC.

———. "Reminiscences of Geo. B. McClellan and 'Stonewall' Jackson." *Blue and Gray* 1 (1893): 29–31.

McClendon, William Augustus. *Recollections of War Times by an Old Veteran while under Stonewall Jackson and Lieutenant General James Longstreet: How I Got in, and How I Got out*. 1909. Reprint. San Bernardino, CA: California Church Press, 1973.

McClure, Alexander K. *Abraham Lincoln and Men of War Times: Some Personal Recollections of War and Politics during the Lincoln Administration*. 3d ed. Philadelphia: Times Publishing Company, 1892.

———. *Colonel Alexander K. McClure's Recollections of Half a Century*. Salem, MA: Salem Press Company, 1902.

McDonald, Cornelia. *A Diary with Reminiscences of the War and Refugee Life in the Shenandoah Valley, 1860–1865.* Edited by Hunter McDonald. Nashville: Cullom & Ghertner Co., 1934.

McGuire, Hunter. "Death of Stonewall Jackson." *SHSP* 14 (1886): 154–63.

———. "General Thomas J. Jackson." *SHSP* 19 (1891): 298–318.

———, and George L. Christian. *The Confederate Cause and Conduct in the War between the States . . . and Other Confederate Papers.* Richmond: L. H. Jenkins, 1907.

McNeil, John A. "Famous Retreat from Philippi." *SHSP* 34 (1906): 280–93.

Mahan, Dennis Hart. *Advanced-Guard, Out-Post, and Detachment Service of Troops, with the Essential Principles of Strategy, and Grand Tactics for the Use of Officers of the Militia and Volunteers.* New Edition. New York: John Wiley, 1863.

Manring, Benjamin Franklin. *The Conquest of the Coeur d'Alenes, Spokanes and Palouses: The Expeditions of Colonels E. J. Steptoe and George Wright against the "Northern Indians" in 1858.* Spokane, WA: John W. Graham & Co., 1912.

Martin, Rawley W. "Armistead at the Battle of Gettysburg," *SHSP* 39 (1914): 186–87.

———, and John Holmes Smith. "The Battle of Gettysburg, and the Charge of Pickett's Division." *SHSP* 32 (1904): 183–95.

Martineau, Harriet. *Retrospect of Western Travel.* 3 vols. 1838. Reprint. New York: Greenwood Press, 1969.

"Matthew Fontaine Maury." *Confederate Veteran* 26 (February 1918): 54–56.

Matthews, Jay A., Jr. "The Second U.S. Cavalry in Texas, 1855–1861." *Military History of Texas and the Southwest* 11 (1973): 229–31.

Maurois, André. "A Princely Service." *American Heritage* 17 (April 1966): 52–63; 80–81.

Maury, Dabney Herndon. *Recollections of a Virginian in the Mexican, Indian, and Civil Wars.* 3d ed. New York: Charles Scribner's Sons, 1894.

———. "General T. J. ('Stonewall') Jackson: Incidents in the Remarkable Career of the Great Soldier." *SHSP* 25 (1897): 309–16.

———. "Sketch of General Richard Taylor." *SHSP* 7 (1879): 343–45.

Maxwell, Hu. *The History of Barbour County, West Virginia.* 1899. Reprint. Parsons, WV: McClain Printing Company, 1968.

Mayo, Joseph, Jr. "Pickett's Charge at Gettysburg." *SHSP* 34 (1906): 327–35.

Meigs, Montgomery C. "General M. C. Meigs on the Conduct of the Civil War." *American Historical Review* 26 (January 1921): 285–303.

Merck, S. G. "Class of 1843." *Army and Navy Journal* 39 (14 June 1902): 1028.

Merrill, Catharine. *The Soldier of Indiana in the War for the Union.* 2 vols. Indianapolis: Merrill and Company, 1866.

Merritt, Wesley. "Note on the Surrender of Lee." *Century Magazine.* New ser. 41 (April 1902): 944.

Meyers, Augustus. *Ten Years in the Ranks, U.S. Army.* New York: Stirling Press, 1914.

Michie, Peter S. *General McClellan.* New York: D. Appleton and Company, 1915.

Millens, Samuel. " 'When Once the Ball Is Commenced . . .': A Pennsylvania Irishman at Fort Sumter." Edited by Rowland T. Berthoff. *Pennsylvania History* 24 (July 1957): 219–22.

Mitchell, Frederick W. "A Personal Episode of the First Stoneman Raid." *War Papers* 85. Military Order of the Loyal Legion of the United States, Commandery of the District Columbia. Read 6 December 1911.

Mitchell, Mary Bedinger. "A Woman's Recollections of Antietam." Vol. 2 of *Battles and Leaders.*

Moore, Edward A. *The Story of a Cannoneer under Stonewall Jackson.* Lynchburg, VA: J. P. Bell Company, 1910.

Morford, Henry. *Red-Tape and Pigeon-Hole Generals: As Seen from the Ranks during a Campaign in the Army of the Potomac.* New York: Carleton, 1864.

Morgan, William H. *Personal Reminiscences of the War of 1861–5.* Lynchburg, VA: J. P. Bell Company, 1911.

Morrison, James L., Jr. *"The Best School in the World": West Point, the Pre-Civil War Years, 1833–1866.* Kent, OH: Kent State University Press, 1986.

———. "Educating the Civil War Generals: West Point, 1833–1861." *Military Affairs* 38 (October 1974): 108–11.

———, ed. "Getting through West Point: The Cadet Memoirs of John C. Tidball, Class of 1848." *Civil War History* 26 (December 1980): 304–25.

Morrison, Joseph Graham. "Stonewall Jackson at Chancellorsville." *Confederate Veteran* 13 (May 1905): 229–33.

Mosby, John S. *The Memoirs of Colonel John S. Mosby.* Edited by Charles Wells Russell. 1917. Reprint. Bloomington: Indiana University Press, 1959.

Moss, Michael E., ed. *Robert W. Weir of West Point: Illustrator, Teacher and Poet.* West Point, NY: U.S. Military Academy, 1976.

Munford, Thomas T. "Reminiscences of Jackson's Valley Campaign." *SHSP* 7 (1879): 523–34.

Murphy, Lawrence R. "The United States Army in Taos, 1847–1852." *New Mexico Historical Review* 47 (January 1972): 33–48.

Myers, William Starr. *General George Brinton McClellan: A Study in Personality.* New York: D. Appleton-Century Company, 1934.

Neese, George M. *Three Years in the Confederate Horse Artillery.* 1911. Reprint. Dayton: Morningside, 1988.

Newhall, Frederick C. *With General Sheridan in Lee's Last Campaign.* Philadelphia: J. B. Lippincott, 1866.

New York Express.

New York Freeman's Journal and Catholic Register.

New York Herald.

New York Times.

New York Tribune.

New York World.

Nicolay, Helen. *Lincoln's Secretary: A Biography of John G. Nicolay.* New York: Longmans, Green and Co., 1949.

Nicolay, John G. *The Outbreak of Rebellion.* 1881. Reprint. Wilmington, NC: Broadfoot Publishing Company, 1989.

———, and John Hay. *Abraham Lincoln: A History.* 10 vols. New York: Century Co., 1886.

Nisbet, James Cooper. *Four Years on the Firing Line.* Edited by Bell Irvin Wiley. 1963. Reprint. Wilmington, NC: Broadfoot Publishing Company, 1987.

Norton, Oliver Willcox. "Little Mac's A-Coming." In *The Blue and the Gray: The Story of the Civil War as Told by Participants.* Edited by Henry Steele Commager. 1950. Reprint (2 vols. in 1). New York: Fairfax Press, 1982.

Noyes, Frank G. "Biographical Sketch of Maj.-Gen. John G. Foster, Son of New Hampshire, Soldier of the Republic." *Granite Monthly* 26 (June 1899): 331–44.

Obenchain, William A. "Stonewall Jackson's Scabbard Speech." *SHSP* 16 (1888): 36–47.

Opie, John N. *A Rebel Cavalryman with Lee, Stuart, and Jackson.* 1899. Reprint. Dayton: Press of Morningside Bookshop, 1972.

"The Opposing Forces in the Appomattox Campaign." Vol. 4 of *Battles and Leaders.*

Owen, Thomas McAdory. *History of Alabama and Dictionary of Alabama Biography.* 4 vols. Chicago: S. J. Clarke Publishing Company, 1921.

Owens, John Algernon. *Sword and Pen; or, Ventures and Adventures of Willard Glazier.* Philadelphia: P. W. Ziegler & Company, 1881.

Palfrey, Francis Winthrop. *The Antietam and Fredericksburg.* 1882. Reprint. Wilmington, NC: Broadfoot Publishing Company, 1989.

———. "The Battle of Antietam." In *Campaigns in Virginia, Maryland and Pennsylvania, 1862–1863.* Vol. 3 of *MHSM.*

Paris, Compte de. *History of the Civil War in America.* Edited by Henry Coppee. Rev. ed. 3 vols. Philadelphia: Porter & Coates, 1876, 1883.

Parker, Francis Lejau. "The Battle of Fort Sumter as Seen from Morris Island." *South Carolina Historical Magazine* 62 (April 1961): 65–71.

Parks, Joseph Howard. *General Edmund Kirby Smith, C. S. A.* Baton Rouge: Louisiana State University Press, 1954.

Patrick, Marsena R. *Inside Lincoln's Army: The Diary of Marsena Rudolph Patrick, Provost Marshal General, Army of the Potomac.* Edited by David S. Sparks. New York: Thomas Yoseloff, 1964.

Patterson, Gerard A. *Rebels from West Point.* New York: Doubleday & Company, 1987.

———. "George E. Pickett—A Personality Profile." *Civil War Times Illustrated* 5 (May 1966): 19–24.

Paul, E. A. "Account by a Participant." In Vol. 6 of *Rebellion Record.*

Paxton, Elisha Franklin. *The Civil War Letters of General Frank "Bull" Paxton, CSA, a Lieutenant of Lee & Jackson.* Edited by John Gallatin Paxton. Hillsboro, TX: Hill Junior College Press, 1978.

Pender, William Dorsey. *The General to His Lady: The Civil War Letters of William Dorsey Pender to Fanny Pender.* Edited by William W. Hassler. 1962. Reprint. Gaithersburg, MD: Ron R. Van Sickle Military Books, 1988.

Perry, Bliss. *Life and Letters of Henry Lee Higginson.* 1921. Reprint. Freeport, NY: Books for Libraries Press, 1972.

Peters, Winfield. "The Lost Sword of Gen. Richard B. Garnett, Who Fell at Gettysburg." *SHSP* 33 (1905): 26–31.

Philadelphia Weekly Times.

Pickett, LaSalle Corbell. *Pickett and His Men.* Atlanta: Foote & Davis Company, 1899.

———, ed. *The Heart of a Soldier as Revealed in the Intimate Letters of Genl. George E. Pickett, C. S. A..* New York: Seth Moyle, 1913.

Plum, William R. *The Military Telegraph during the Civil War in the United States.* 2 vols. Chicago: Jansen, McClurg & Co., 1882.

Poague, William Thomas. *Gunner with Stonewall: Reminiscences of William Thomas Poague.* Edited by Monroe F. Cockrell. 1957. Reprint. Wilmington, NC: Broadfoot Publishing Company, 1989.

Poindexter, James E. "General Armistead's Portrait Presented." *SHSP* 37 (1909): 144–51.

Porter, Horace. "The Surrender at Appomattox Court House." Vol. 4 of *Battles and Leaders.*

Porter, James D. *Tennessee.* Vol. 10 of *Confederate Military History.*

Porter, John W. H. "The Confederate Soldier." *Confederate Veteran* 24 (October 1916): 460–61.

Potts, Frank. *The Death of the Confederacy: The Last Week of the Army of Northern Virginia as Set Forth in a Letter of April, 1865.* Edited by Douglas Southall Freeman. Richmond: private printing, 1928.

Preston, Margaret Junkin. "Personal Reminiscences of Stonewall Jackson." *Century Magazine* New ser. 10 (October 1886): 927–36.

Price, George F. *Across the Continent with the Fifth Cavalry.* 1883. Reprint. New York: Antiquarian Press, 1959.

Puleston, William D. *Mahan: The Life and Work of Captain Alfred Thayer Mahan, U.S.N.*. New Haven, CT: Yale University Press, 1939.

Putnam, Sallie A. *Richmond during the War: Four Years of Personal Observation.* New York: G. W. Carleton, 1867.

Pyne, Henry R. *The History of the First New Jersey Cavalry.* Trenton, NJ: J. A. Beecher, 1871.

Quad, M. [pseud]. In "Notes and Queries." *SHSP* 10 (1882): 332–35.

Randolph, William F. "Chancellorsville: The Flank Movement that Routed the Yankees; General Jackson's Mortal Wound." *SHSP* 29 (1901): 329–37.

Rapp, Kenneth W. *West Point: Whistler in Cadet Gray, and Other Stories about the United States Military Academy.* Croton-on-Hudson, NY: North River Press, 1978.

Raymond, Henry J. *The Life and Public Services of Abraham Lincoln. . . .* New York: Derby and Miller, 1865.

Raymond, Samuel H. Papers. U.S. Military Academy Library, West Point, NY.

Reid, Whitelaw. *Ohio in the War: Her Statesmen, Her Generals, and Soldiers.* 2 vols. Cincinnati: Moore, Wilstach & Baldwin, 1868.

———. *A Radical View: The "Agate" Dispatches of Whitelaw Reid, 1861–1865.* Edited by James G. Smart. 2 vols. Memphis: Memphis State University Press, 1976.

Revere, Joseph W. *Keel and Saddle: A Retrospect of Forty Years of Military and Naval Service.* Boston: J. R. Osgood and Company, 1872.

Rice, Donald L. "The Military Telegraph in Western Virginia." *Randolph County Historical Society Magazine of History and Biography* 12 (April 1961): 25–28.

Rice, Edmund. "Repelling Lee's Last Blow at Gettysburg." Vol. 3 of *Battles and Leaders.*

Richmond Daily Sentinel.

Richmond Dispatch.

Robertson, James I., Jr. *General A. P. Hill: The Story of a Confederate Warrior.* New York: Random House, 1987.

Robertson, William J. " 'Up Came Hill'—Soldier of the South." *Richmond Times-Dispatch*, series of 5 articles in Sunday magazine, 14 October to 11 November 1934.

Robinson, William M., Jr. "The Engineer Soldiers in the Mexican War." *The Military Engineer* 24 (January–February 1932): 1–8.

Robson, John S. *How a One-Legged Rebel Lives: Reminiscences of the Civil War.* 1898. Reprint. Gaithersburg, MD: Butternut Press, 1984.

Rodenbough, Theo F., and William L. Haskin. eds. *The Army of the United States: Historical Sketches of Staff and Line with Portraits of Generals-in-Chief.* New York: Maynard, Merrill, 1896.

Roland, Charles P. *Albert Sidney Johnston: Soldier of Three Republics.* Austin: University of Texas Press, 1964.

———, and Richard C. Robbins, eds. "The Diary of Eliza (Mrs. Albert Sidney)

Johnston: The Second Cavalry Comes to Texas." *Southwestern Historical Quarterly* 60 (April 1957): 463–500.

Ruffin, Edmund. *The Diary of Edmund Ruffin*. Edited by William Kauffman Scarborough. 3 vols. Baton Rouge: Louisiana State University Press, 1972–1989.

Russell, William Howard. *My Diary North and South*. Edited by Fletcher Pratt. New York: Harper & Brothers, 1954.

Savage, Richard Henry. "Literature and Art at West Point." *Army and Navy Journal* 39 (14 June 1902): 1025.

Schaff, Morris. *The Spirit of Old West Point, 1858–1862*. Boston: Houghton Mifflin, 1907.

Schwab, Julius L. "Some Closing Events at Appomattox." *Confederate Veteran* 8 (February 1900): 71.

Scott, Winfield. *Memoirs of Lieut.-General Scott, LL.D, Written by Himself*. 2 vols. New York: Sheldon & Company, 1864.

Scott, Winfield. "Pickett's Charge as Seen from the Front Line." *War Papers*. No. 1. California Commandery, Military Order of the Loyal Legion of the United States, 8 February 1888.

Sears, Stephen W. *George B. McClellan: The Young Napoleon*. New York: Ticknor & Fields, 1988.

Semmes, Raphael. *The Campaign of General Scott in the Valley of Mexico*. Cincinnati: Moore & Anderson, 1852.

Seymour, Truman. *Military Education: A Vindication of West Point and the Regular Army*. Re-publication of a letter in the *Army and Navy Journal*, 24 September 1864.

———. "An Episode of Fort Sumter: 1860." Hand-written chiefly from the dictation of his wife, Louisa Seymour. 20 October 1874. U.S. Military Academy Library, West Point, NY.

———. "Memo of a Circumstance of 1860, Fort Moultrie, S.C. Recorded November 2, 1874." U.S. Military Academy Library, West Point, NY.

Shakespeare, William. *As You Like It*, and *The Two Gentlemen of Verona*. *The Complete Works of William Shakespeare*. 6 vols. New York: Bantam Books, 1988.

Shields, Elise Trigg. "The Storming of Chapultepec." *Confederate Veteran* 26 (September 1918): 399–401.

Shotwell, Randolph A. "Virginia and North Carolina in the Battle of Gettysburg." *Our Living and Dead* 4 (March 1876): 80–97.

Simpson, Harold B. "The Second U.S. Cavalry in Texas, 1855–1861." *Texas Military History* 8 (1970): 55–75.

Smith, Ephraim Kirby. *To Mexico with Scott: Letters of Captain E. Kirby Smith to His Wife*. Edited by Emma Jerome Blackwood. Cambridge: Harvard University Press, 1917.

Smith, George Winston, and Charles Judah, eds. *Chronicles of the Gringos: The U.S. Army in the Mexican War, 1846–1848. Accounts of Eye-Witnesses & Combatants*. Albuquerque: University of New Mexico Press, 1968.

Smith, Gustavus W. *Company "A," Corps of Engineers, U.S.A., 1846–'48, in the Mexican War*. Battalion Press, 1896.

Smith, James Power. *With Stonewall Jackson in the Army of Northern Virginia*. 1920. Reprint. Gaithersburg, MD: Zullo and Van Sickle Books, 1982.

———. "Stonewall Jackson's Last Battle." Vol. 3 of *Battles and Leaders*.

Smith, John Day. *The History of the Nineteenth Regiment of Maine Volunteer Infantry, 1862–1865*. Minneapolis: Nineteenth Maine Regimental Association, 1909.

Smith, Justin H. *The War with Mexico*. 2 vols. 1919. Reprint. Gloucester, MA: Peter Smith, 1963.

Smith, L. A. "Recollections of Gettysburg." In *War Papers Read before the Michigan Commandery of the Military Order of the Loyal Legion of the United States*. Vol. 2. Detroit: James H. Stone & Co., 1898.

Smith, William Ernest. *The Francis Preston Blair Family in Politics*. 2 vols. New York: Macmillan, 1933.

A Soldier of the Civil War. By a Member of the Virginia Historical Society. Cleveland: Burrows Brothers Company, 1900.

Sorrel, G. Moxley. *Recollections of a Confederate Staff Officer*. 1905. Reprint. Dayton: Press of Morningside Bookshop, 1978.

Sperry, Kate. "Kate Sperry's Diary, 1861–1866." Edited by Christine Andreae. *Virginia Country's Civil War* 1 (1983): 43–75.

Spieler, Gerhard. "Captain Stuart—a Soldier's Life, a Soldier's Death." *Beaufort* (SC) *Gazette*. (12 December 1974). Copy in Cullum File, Class of 1846, U.S. Military Academy Library, West Point, NY.

Squires, Charles W. "The Last of Lee's Battle Line." Typescript autobiography. Edited by W.H.T. Squires. Manuscript Division, Library of Congress, Washington, DC.

Stephenson, P. D. "Defence of Spanish Fort: On Mobile Bay—Last Great Battle of the War." *SHSP* 39 (1914): 118–36.

Stewart, George R. *John Phoenix, Esq., The Veritable Squibob: A Life of Captain George H. Derby, U.S.A.* 1937. Reprint. New York: De Capo Press, 1969.

Stewart, Joseph. "The Class of 1842." *Army and Navy Journal* 39 (14 June 1902): 1028.

" 'Stonewall' Jackson: Reminiscences of the Great Confederate Soldier as Related by Mrs. Lucy Chandler Pendleton to Edward T. Stuart at the Jackson Shrine at Guiney Station, Virginia, 'Memorial Day' May 30, 1930." Typescript copy. Fredericksburg and Spotsylvania National Military Park.

"Stonewall Jackson's Body Passes through Charlottesville." *The Magazine of Albemarle County History* 22 (1963–1964): 21–22.

Stout, Clarence E. E. "John Gray Foster." *Granite Monthly* 5 (May 1882): 260–61.

"Strength of Ewell's Division in the Campaign of 1862—Field Returns." *SHSP* 8 (1880): 301–5.

Strong, George Templeton. *The Diary of George Templeton Strong*. Edited by Allan Nevins and Milton Halsey Thomas. 4 vols. New York: Macmillan, 1952.

Strother, David Hunter. *A Virginia Yankee in the Civil War: The Diaries of David Hunter Strother*. Edited by Cecil D. Eby, Jr. Chapel Hill: University of North Carolina Press, 1961.

———. "Personal Recollections of the War. By a Virginian." *Harper's New Monthly Magazine* 36 (February 1868): 273–91 (April 1868): 567–82.

Stuart, Benjamin R. *Magnolia Cemetery: An Interpretation of Some of Its Monuments and Inscriptions, with a Reminiscence of Captain James Stuart. . . .* Charleston, SC: Kahrs & Welch, 1896.

Sturgis, Jerusha Wilcox. "Life of Mrs. S. D. Sturgis." Typescript. Sturgis Family Papers, U.S. Military Academy Library, West Point, NY.

Sturtevant, Ralph Orson. *Pictorial History Thirteenth Regiment Vermont Volunteers, War of 1861–1865*. Burlington, VT: Regimental Association, 1910.

Summers, Festus P. *The Baltimore and Ohio in the Civil War*. New York: G. P. Putnam's Sons, 1939.

Swanberg, W. A. *First Blood: The Story of Fort Sumter*. New York: Charles Scribner's Sons, 1957.

Swinton, William. *Campaigns of the Army of the Potomac.* 1866. Reprint. Secaucus, NJ: Blue & Grey Press, 1988.

Talbot, Theodore. Papers. Manuscript Division, Library of Congress, Washington, DC.

Tanner, Robert G. "Jackson in the Shenandoah." In *The Guns of '62.* Vol. 2 of *The Image of War: 1861–1865.* Edited by William C. Davis. A project of the National Historical Society. Garden City, NY: Doubleday & Company, 1982.

Taylor, Murray F. "Stonewall Jackson's Death." *Confederate Veteran* 12 (October 1904): 492–94.

Taylor, Richard. *Destruction and Reconstruction: Personal Experiences of the Late War.* Edited by Richard B. Harwell. New York: Longmans, Green and Co., 1955.

———. "The Last Confederate Surrender." *SHSP* 3 (1877): 155–58.

Thayer, Sylvanus. Papers. U.S. Military Academy Library, West Point, NY.

Thompson, David L. "With Burnside at Antietam." Vol. 2 of *Battles and Leaders.*

Thompson, Richard S. "A Scrap of Gettysburg." In *Military Essays and Recollections: Papers Read before the Commandery of the State of Illinois, Military Order of the Loyal Legion of the United States.* Vol. 3. Chicago: Dial Press, 1899.

Thompson, Robert Luther. *Wiring a Continent: The History of the Telegraph Industry in the United States, 1832–1866.* Princeton, NJ: Princeton University Press, 1947.

Ticknor, George. *Life, Letters, and Journals of George Ticknor.* Edited by Anna Ticknor and George S. Hillard. 2 vols. Boston: James R. Osgood and Company, 1876.

Tidball, John C. "Getting through West Point by One Who Did." Typed manuscript. John C. Tidball Papers. U.S. Military Academy Library, West Point, NY.

Tobie, Edward P. *History of the First Maine Cavalry, 1861–1865.* Published by the First Maine Cavalry Association. Boston: Press of Emery & Hughes, 1887.

Townsend, George Alfred. *Rustics in Rebellion: A Yankee Reporter on the Road to Richmond, 1861–65.* Chapel Hill: University of North Carolina Press, 1950.

Trimble, Isaac R. "North Carolinians at Gettysburg." *Our Living and Our Dead* 4 (March 1876): 53–60.

Tucker, G. W. "Death of General A. P. Hill." *SHSP* 11 (1883): 564–69.

Turner, George Edgar. *Victory Rode the Rails.* Indianapolis: Bobbs-Merrill Company, 1953.

Turnley, Parmenas Taylor. *Reminiscences of Parmenas Taylor Turnley: From the Cradle to Three-Score and Ten.* Chicago: Donahue & Henneberry, 1892.

Twain, Mark. *Autobiography.* With an introduction by Albert Bigelow Paine. 2 vols. New York: Harper & Brothers, 1924.

Upson, Theodore F. *With Sherman to the Sea: The Civil War Letters, Diaries & Reminiscences of Theodore F. Upson.* Edited by Oscar Osburn Winther. Bloomington: Indiana University Press, 1958.

U.S. Congress. *Report of the Joint Committee on the Conduct of the War.* 6 vols. Washington: Government Printing Office, 1863, 1863–65.

———. *Supplemental Report of the Joint Committee on the Conduct of the War.* 2 vols. Washington: Government Printing Office, 1866.

———. Senate. Report of the Secretary of War. 37th Cong., 1st sess. 1 July 1861. S. Doc. 1.

———. Report of Sterling Price on the Taos Rebellion, 30th Cong., 1st sess. S. Exec. doc. 1.

U.S. Military Academy. Cadet Application Papers, 1805 to 1866. U.S. Military Academy Archives, West Point, NY.

————. *The Centennial of the United States Military Academy at West Point, New York, 1802–1902.* 2 vols. Washington: Government Printing Office, 1904.

————. *Official Register of the Officers and Cadets of the U.S. Military Academy.* West Point, NY: pub. annually, 1818–1850.

————. Post Orders, No. 2, 1 June 1842 to 22 June 1846. U.S. Military Academy Archives, West Point, NY.

————. Register of Merit, 1836 to 1852. No. 2. U.S. Military Academy, Archives, West Point, NY.

————. *Regulations Established for the Organization and Government of the Military Academy.* New York: Wiley & Putnam, 1839.

————. Staff Records, No. 3, 1842 to 1845. U.S. Military Academy Archives, West Point, NY.

U.S. War Department. *The War of the Rebellion: A Compilation of the Official Records of the Union and Confederate Armies.* 70 vols. in 128 parts. 1880–1901. Reprint. Harrisburg, PA: Historical Times, 1985.

Utley, Robert M. *Frontiersmen in Blue: The United States Army and the Indian, 1848–1865.* Lincoln, NE: University of Nebraska Press, 1967.

"The Valley after Kernstown." *SHSP* 19 (1891): 318–23.

Vandiver, Frank E. *Mighty Stonewall.* 1957. Reprint. College Station, TX: Texas A&M University Press, 1989.

Viele, Teresa Griffin. *Following the Drum: A Glimpse of Frontier Life.* 1958. Reprint. Lincoln, NE: University of Nebraska Press, 1984.

Wainwright, Charles S. *A Diary of Battle: The Personal Journals of Colonel Charles S. Wainwright, 1861–1865.* Edited by Allan Nevins. New York: Harcourt, Brace & World, 1962.

Walker, Charles D. *Memorial, Virginia Military Institute: Biographical Sketches of the Graduates and Élèves of the Virginia Military Institute Who Fell during the War between the States.* Philadelphia: J. B. Lippincott, 1875.

Walker, Francis A. *History of the Second Army Corps in the Army of the Potomac.* New York: Charles Scribner's Sons, 1886.

Walker, John G. "Jackson's Capture of Harper's Ferry." Vol. 2 of *Battles and Leaders.*

————. "Sharpsburg." Vol. 2 of *Battles and Leaders.*

Warner, Ezra J. *Generals in Blue: Lives of the Union Commanders.* Baton Rouge: Louisiana State University Press, 1964.

Washington Evening Star.

Washington Post.

Weigley, Russell F. *History of the United States Army.* Enlarged ed. Bloomington: Indiana University Press, 1984.

Weir, Irene. *Robert W. Weir.* New York: House of Field-Doubleday, 1947.

Wheeler, Richard. *Voices of the Civil War.* New York: Thomas Y. Crowell, 1976.

Wheeler-Bennett, John. "A. P. Hill: A Study in Confederate Leadership." *Virginia Quarterly Review* 37 (Spring 1961): 198–209.

Wheeling (VA) *Intelligencer.*

Whitmore, Earl. "Introduction" *Water Color and Drawings by Brevet Major General Truman Seymour, USMA 1846.* Published on the occasion of an exhibit of Seymour's work, West Point, NY, 1974.

Whittaker, Frederick. *A Complete Life of Gen. George A. Custer.* New York: Sheldon & Company, 1876.

Wickersham, Charles I. "Personal Recollections of the Cavalry at Chancellorsville."

War Papers Read before the Commandery of the State of Wisconsin, Military Order of the Loyal Legion of the United States. Vol. 3. Milwaukee: Burdick & Allen, 1903.

Wilcox, Cadmus Marcellus. *History of the Mexican War.* Edited by Mary Rachel Wilcox. Washington, DC: Church News Publishing Company, 1892.

———. *Rifles and Rifle Practice: An Elementary Treatise upon the Theory of Rifle Firing.* New York: D. Van Nostrand, 1859.

———. Petersburg Campaign Report. Typescript. Lee Headquarters Papers. Virginia Historical Society, Richmond, VA.

Wiley, Bell Irvin. *The Life of Johnny Reb: The Common Soldier of the Confederacy.* Baton Rouge: Louisiana State University Press, 1978.

Williams, T. Harry. *The History of American Wars from 1745 to 1918.* New York: Alfred A. Knopf, 1981.

———. "The Attack upon West Point during the Civil War." *Mississippi Valley Historical Review* 25 (March 1939): 491–504.

———. "General Ewell to the High Private in the Rear." *Virginia Magazine of History and Biography* 54 (April 1946): 157–60.

Wise, John S. *The End of an Era.* Boston: Houghton Mifflin, 1899.

———. "Stonewall Jackson as I Knew Him." *The Circle* (March 1908): 143–45. Copy in the Virginia Historical Society Library, Richmond, VA.

Within Fort Sumter; or, a View of Major Anderson's Garrison Family for One Hundred and Ten Days, by One of the Company. New York: N. Tibbals & Company, 1861.

Wood, James Rodney. "Miscellaneous Writings: Civil War Memoirs." Typescript. Maud Wood Park Papers, Manuscript Division, Library of Congress, Washington, DC.

Wood, Oliver E. *The West Point Scrap Book: A Collection of Stories, Songs, and Legends of the United States Military Academy.* New York: D. Van Nostrand, 1871.

Wood, Robert J. "Early Days of Benny Havens." *The Pointer* 14 (26 February 1937): 6–13, 29.

Wood, William Nathaniel. *Reminiscences of Big I.* Edited by Bell Irvin Wiley. Jackson, TN: McCowat-Mercer Press, 1956.

Worsham, John H. *One of Jackson's Foot Cavalry.* Edited by James I. Robertson, Jr. 1912. Reprint. Jackson, TN: McCowat-Mercer Press, 1964.

Young, Jesse Bowman. *The Battle of Gettysburg: A Comprehensive Narrative.* 1913. Reprint. Dayton: Press of Morningside Bookshop, 1976.

Young, John Russell. *Around the World with General Grant: A Narrative of the Visit of General U. S. Grant, Ex-President of the United States, to Various Countries in Europe, Asia, and Africa, in 1877, 1878, 1879.* 2 vols. New York: American News Company, 1879.

Youngblood, William. "Unwritten History of the Gettysburg Campaign." *SHSP* 38 (1910): 312–18.

Index

607

Illustration Credits

JOHN C. WAUGH is a veteran former newspaper correspondent and bureau chief of *The Christian Science Monitor*, who has since turned historical reporter. His writing has appeared in *The New York Times*, *The Washington Post*, *Civil War Times Illustrated*, *The New Republic*, *The Nation*, and numerous other national publications. He has served on the senior staffs of a Republican vice president and a Democratic U.S. senator. A lifelong student of the Civil War, he is also the author of *Reelecting Lincoln*, published in 1998. He and his wife, Kathleen Lively, live in Arlington, Texas.